Neglected Powers

by the same author

*

on Shakespeare
THE WHEEL OF FIRE (Tragedies)
THE IMPERIAL THEME (Tragedies and Roman Plays)
THE CROWN OF LIFE (Final Plays)
THE SHAKESPEARIAN TEMPEST (Symbolism)
THE SOVEREIGN FLOWER (Royalism; General Index)
THE MUTUAL FLAME (Sonnets)
SHAKESPEARE AND RELIGION
SHAKESPEARIAN PRODUCTION

*

on other writers
POETS OF ACTION (Spenser, Milton, Swift, Byron)
THE STARLIT DOME (Wordsworth, Coleridge, Shelley, Keats)
LAUREATE OF PEACE; reissued as THE POETRY OF POPE
LORD BYRON: CHRISTIAN VIRTUES
LORD BYRON'S MARRIAGE
BYRON AND SHAKESPEARE
IBSEN
THE SATURNIAN QUEST (John Cowper Powys)
THE CHRISTIAN RENAISSANCE
CHRIST AND NIETZSCHE
THE GOLDEN LABYRINTH (British Drama)

*

General
ATLANTIC CROSSING
THE DYNASTY OF STOWE
HIROSHIMA

*

Drama
THE LAST OF THE INCAS

*

Poetry
GOLD-DUST

Tape-recordings: Shakespeare; Byron (McGraw-Hill)

NEGLECTED POWERS

Essays on Nineteenth and Twentieth Century Literature

G. WILSON KNIGHT

BARNES & NOBLE BOOKS
(a division of Harper & Row Publishers, Inc.)
49 East 33rd Street
New York, N.Y. 10016

First published in the United States of America in 1971
by Barnes & Noble Books
(a division of Harper & Row Publishers, Inc.)
49 East 33rd Street
New York, N.Y. 10016
Reprinted 1972

ISBN 0-389-01790-6

Printed in Great Britain

for
ENID M. HANDS

Down to the gutter
Up to the glitter
Into the city where the truth lies
Hair

Contents

5

Contents

PART FOUR

Totalities

PART FIVE

Epilogue

Acknowledgments

I WISH to extend my thanks to the following: Mr. Michael Ayrton and Methuen & Co. Ltd. for permission to quote from *The Testament of Daedalus*; Professor Francis Berry, Methuen & Co. Ltd. and Routledge & Kegan Paul Ltd. for permission to quote from the works of Francis Berry; Mr. C. Day-Lewis, Chatto & Windus Ltd. and the Hogarth Press Ltd. for permission to quote from the *Collected Poems* of C. Day-Lewis; Mrs. Valerie Eliot and Faber & Faber Ltd. for permission to quote from the works of T. S. Eliot; Professor G. S. Fraser for permission to quote from his poem 'Instead of an Elegy'; Robert Graves, A. P. Watt & Son and Cassell & Co. Ltd. for permission to quote from Robert Graves's *Poetic Craft and Principle*; Miss Gillian Grimwood for permission to quote her sonnet 'Trident'; Miss Dallas Kenmare for permission to quote her poem 'The Altar-Flower'; Laurence Pollinger Ltd., the Estate of the late Mrs. Frieda Lawrence and William Heinemann Ltd. for permission to quote from D. H. Lawrence's essay 'Pornography and Obscenity', reissued in *Phoenix*; the Executors of the T. E. Lawrence Estate for permission to quote from T. E. Lawrence's *The Mint* and *Seven Pillars of Wisdom* and from Professor A. W. Lawrence's collection *T. E. Lawrence by his Friends*; Mrs. Mary Middleton Murry for permission to quote from the works of John Middleton Murry; Mr. Francis Powys and Laurence Pollinger Ltd. for permission to quote from John Cowper Powys's poems and letters; Mrs. Adelaide Ross for permission to quote from a letter by Nicholas Ross; the Society of Authors for permission to quote from the Preface to Bernard Shaw's *On the Rocks*, from A. E. Housman's 'Inaugural Lecture' which was first published in *The Times Literary Supplement*, and from the works of John Masefield; *Twentieth Century* Magazine Ltd. for permission to quote from Alfred Lord Tennyson's poem 'The Christ of Ammergau'; United Artists Music Ltd. for permission to quote from the musical *Hair*.

A*   7

Preface

IT IS a little unfortunate that in presenting this, which is likely to be my last, volume of poetic interpretation I find it necessary to offer an apology.

My introductory chapter opens with a statement on the importance of my literary viewpoint and attendant labours. I hope that this statement may be forgiven. I have for long incurred severe criticism; opposition is still strong; and I cannot expect it to be softened by the essays here collected. Forthright speaking is nowadays, in such matters, respected; it even appears to lead to an increase in public estimation. Others are not backward in their claims. I wish only to make some, I hope not unreasonable, claims of my own.

There is much misunderstanding. Not only do many scholars regard some of my most precise analyses as mysterious or inept, but this very misunderstanding is reflected into stories about myself which are false. I hope that any regarding my having arrived in Canada in 1931 to occupy a Chair in English at Toronto University in a state of blissful ignorance in regard to the elements of Shakespearian scholarship will be set against my 1931 review (reprinted in *Shakespeare and Religion*, 1967) of E. K. Chambers' *William Shakespeare* and my footnotes in *The Imperial Theme*, all written before I left for Canada (armed, as I recall, with a number of Folio facsimiles of single plays which I had bought from Middleton Murry). To Toronto I owe much; it, and its University, have for me a romantic aura. But I had qualified well enough at Oxford, where I had taken a reasonably good degree; and I had, since my boyhood, been immersed in Shakespearian commentary, reading Gervinus as a hobby.

Such misconceptions arise from an unconscious projection of confused literary response into fictions of a misleading kind; and since these may lead to problems after my death, I wish to state

9

that no reminiscences should be regarded as authoritative without close scrutiny. Meanwhile, as a personal touchstone, I would point to D. W. Jefferson's sensitive memoir in the recent collection of essays so kindly offered to me under his editorship, entitled *The Morality of Art* (Routledge & Kegan Paul, 1969); and to the generous comments by Alan Over and by Michael Millgate in *The University of Leeds Review* (VIII. 2, December 1962; XII. 2, October 1969).[1] I am grateful to Mr. John E. Van Domelen and Miss Esther Irene Nelson for composing theses on my work (Michigan State University, 1964, and The University of Calgary, 1968); and to Mr. Van Domelen, again, for compiling a provisional bibliography and also for an article, to be added to those listed below (p. 19, note to p. 18), on my 'spatial' theories, soon to appear in *Approach Magazine*, Oxford (IV. 1, Summer 1970).

My references on p. 18 below to writers whose work may be grouped with my own as what I call 'interpretation' may appear arbitrary. No doubt there are many others I might have included; but here again a personal element intrudes. The list is one mainly of personal contact and association. All were, or became, friends of mine. D. G. James and C. S. Lewis were warmly sympathetic to my early writings: the sensitive references to my *Myth and Miracle* in James's *Scepticism and Poetry* were an early assurance that was subsequently, as is witnessed by his preface to *The Dream of Prospero*, confirmed; and on my first meeting with him, C. S. Lewis told me that in reading *The Christian Renaissance* his interest had been such that he had made notes on nearly every page. Charles Williams was my main, and always friendly, editorial contact at the Oxford University Press when the Press was publishing my books in the 1930s. During my early years at Trinity College, Toronto, Northrop Frye, then a postgraduate student at the University, had many discussions with me; he visited us at Cheltenham, where I returned every summer, and at one time, according to a letter of my brother's to me of 30 December 1937, was expecting to work with me on Shakespeare. Roy Walker has been a valued associate, to whose comments on my acting I owe a

---

[1] I am especially anxious that my stage record should be assessed by my tape recordings and by such contemporary reviews and letters as are stored, or will be stored, in my 'Dramatic Papers' at the City Library of Birmingham, and not by reminiscences after a lapse of years. Dramatic art exists in the immediate, the 'now', and that is where we should look for an authentic response.

lasting gratitude (*Shakespearian Production*, 1964; 288, note, and 313-16); as indeed to others, including Kenneth Young, Richard Courtney, Robin Skelton. Francis Berry has been a life-long friend and, even as a schoolboy, an influence. To these I might add another friend, Una Ellis-Fermor, whose *Christopher Marlowe* as early as 1927 struck an interpretative note of primary importance.

Nor should I forget Colin Still who, after reviewing my *Myth and Miracle* in 1929, drew my attention to his *Shakespeare's Mystery Play*, on *The Tempest*. This I had not read, though, as I have recorded in *Shakespeare and Religion* (201), I subsequently found among my papers some early notes on its thesis, based on a review. When I told Still that T. S. Eliot was writing an introduction to *The Wheel of Fire*, Still called to see him to tell him, too, of his book. Of this visit Eliot wrote to me on 17 May 1930: 'I was glad to meet Mr. Still, and hope to see him again to discuss matters more fully. I read his book with great interest and some speed, as I felt that I ought to see it before sending in my introduction. It did not, as a matter of fact, make any difference to what I wrote; but I am glad to have read it.' Eliot did however refer to the book, and was right to do so.[1]

I never forget what I owe to Bonamy Dobrée, whose essay on Eliot in *The Lamp and the Lute* was for me a seminal influence, and without whose general support so much of my work since the last War could never have matured.

In preparing my present volume I have received favours which call for acknowledgment. To the Exeter City Library I am again, as so often in the past, indebted. I would thank Mrs. Gordon Lothian for secretarial help, and Mr. John Brebner for bringing exact insight to a problem of Powysian interpretation. Dr. Michael Phillips has spent two sessions at Exeter for the checking of references. Both he and Dr. Patricia Ball have offered comments, for which I am grateful. Mr. Iain Stewart has been a strong support, devoting many hours to my proofs and to the composition of indexes. Finally, Mr. John D. Christie, without whose survey I now realize that no text can be called safe, has, with his

---

[1] On p. 398 below I notice important variants in one of Eliot's poems. Another instance may be noted. The first, 'Ariel', text of 'Triumphal March' (p. 386 below) reads 'those eyes', whereas the *Collected Poems* (1963 ed.) reads, more weakly, 'his eyes'. For Eliot's poetry I have, in general, followed the early editions. I have to thank Mrs. Valerie Eliot for her courtesy in providing and allowing me to use Xerox copies of two of Eliot's letters and an unpublished lecture.

usual generosity, given time to the detection of inexactitudes and errors; and has also, in a more general way, brought his wide knowledge and acute judgment to the improvement of my pages.

Many of the following essays were composed for journals or collections. To these they owe their existence, and I would record my obligation to each of the various Editors who so kindly asked me for a contribution. In reprinting them I have made occasional adjustments.

My book is dedicated to Mrs. Enid M. Hands. A dedication can seldom have been more appropriate. Mrs. Hands has typed all my own, and much of my brother's, work, now for over forty years. She has patiently endured my untidy scripts, and encouraged me when encouragement was most needed. My gratitude is deep.

Page references to my present volume have the prefix 'p'; page references to other books have numerals only. With some exceptions 'Spiritualism' is capitalised only when referring to the modern movement.

G. W. K.

ADDITIONAL NOTE, 1969

I draw attention to an inaccuracy in my recent volume of poetry, *Gold-Dust*. There, as noted in my preface, I attributed to myself a sonnet to which I gave the title 'Contentment'. I had found it copied out in my own writing, sent to my brother about 1923; though, as stated in my preface (xiv), I could not recall ever having composed it; nor did it seem to tone with the other lyrics in the volume. I have since discovered that it was written by my Oxford friend, J. F. Bleasdale, the 'younger contemporary' referred to in my preface (xxiii), who had originally enclosed it in a letter to me, noting that it was 'faulted' by a repeated rhyme. Faulty or not, at least one of my most discerning correspondents singled it out from the rest for an especial praise. I should add that in revising it for publication I had made some small adjustments. The original has in line 3 'life' instead of 'hope'; in line 4 'things' instead of 'life'; in line 11, 'blind' instead of 'dumb'.

If *Gold-Dust* is reprinted after my death I have three other corrections. On xxii, '*Doctor Faustus*' should be '*Tamburlaine*'; on xxiii, last line but 7, after 'teacher' insert '; as well as a younger colleague'; and on 27 ('Gold-Dust', XIV), stanza 3, change 'quiet friendliness' to 'still friendliness'.

In 1916 three lyrics were published over my initials in *The Hampshire Chronicle*. They are 'To a Mother', 22 January; 'To the New Moon, Venus and Jupiter, seen together in the West', 12 February; and 'Our Idol', on the death of Lord Kitchener, on 10 June. The first two appeared in my 1916 *Light and Shade* (referred to in *Gold-Dust*, ix); both are derivative in manner and weak in content. The third, of which I have no recollection, appears to me much stronger. It has—apart from one obtruding archaism—a maturity not evident in any other of my 1916 poems. Though I had no strong patriotic feelings at the time, being inclined to a Tolstoyan pacifism, I remember that I could assume them for a purpose in a sonnet I wrote on Rumania's entry into the war. The Kitchener lines must, I suppose, have been mine.

PART ONE

Introduction

CHAPTER I

Poetry and Magic

Then, as I watched, lo, suddenly, the truth
Enlightened him, as it enlightened me:
I was received into the Land of Youth
All understanding, utter ecstasy,
All music, colour, form,
Niamh and I were spirits linked together
With Sun and Stars, the Seasons and the Weather
All moods and modes of life, earth, air and sea.

(John Masefield, 'Ossian', III, *The Bluebells and other Verse*, 1961)

I

IN PUTTING FORWARD what is probably the last of my books of
literary interpretation it is natural to review yet again the difficulties which they have encountered. I have already, in *Essays in
Criticism* ('The New Interpretation', III. 4, October 1953; see also
IV. 2, April 1954; and IV. 4, October 1954, 430-1), firmly stated
their claims. These I repeat: again and again my new approach has
revealed the key symbol or theme in poem, drama, life-work, or
personal life which, once recognized, throws the rest into focus.
This has been done for British poets and dramatists and for whole
periods of our drama, for Goethe's *Faust*, Ibsen, and Nietzsche's
Thus Spake Zarathustra, and for the New Testament. What is
revealed is of enduring use for subsequent investigators. Future
students of the life-work of John Cowper Powys will not fail to be
guided by his 'Saturnian' and Cerne Giant recurrences. Large
areas, including the true significance of Lord Byron as both man
and writer, have been illuminated. And yet, while workers in each

field in turn use these discoveries, a general and admitted response does not appear.[1]

When, as sometimes happens, authoritative articles are composed on the literary theories today active, well-known and justly honoured names are listed and their contributions reviewed: T. S. Eliot, I. A. Richards, F. R. Leavis, William Empson, L. C. Knights. These have their differences, but are all recognized and placed. Meanwhile my own labours on such occasions are not; nor, for that matter, are Middleton Murry's.

Interpretative writing of a high order, such as C. S. Lewis's on Spenser in *The Allegory of Love*, Charles Williams's on Dante in *The Figure of Beatrice*, Northrop Frye's on Blake in *Fearful Symmetry*, and, on Shakespeare, D. G. James's *Scepticism and Poetry*, Roy Walker's *The Time is Out of Joint* and *The Time is Free*, and Francis Berry's *The Shakespeare Inset*, exist in our 'literary situation' as isolated units without mutual reinforcement. There is no open recognition of what started over forty years ago and has continued, exerting a submerged yet vigorous influence, ever since. It was new and of great importance. In 1864, in an essay 'Wordsworth, Tennyson and Browning', Walter Bagehot wrote:

All about and around us a *faith* in poetry struggles to be extricated, but it is not extricated. Some day, at the touch of the true word, the whole confusion will by magic cease; the broken and shapeless notions cohere and crystallize into a bright and true theory. But this cannot be yet.

He looked, rightly, to the time of 'our children's children' for the new advance. It has come, but remains veiled. Veiled, that is, despite the many instances of support and encouragement which I have received and for which my gratitude is warm, from an open and creative understanding.[2]

---

[1] For an expanded polemic see my letter in *Scrutiny*, XVI. 4; Winter 1949; also *The Times Literary Supplement*, 'Shakespeare's Problem Plays', 21 April 1950.

[2] I only refrain from more explicit acknowledgments because the list of my many supporters might involve me in an invidious selection. The honour of the recent volume of essays collected at Leeds by D. W. Jefferson and offered to me under the title *The Morality of Art* may appear to show my complaints as peevish and unwarranted; but it is to be noticed that response has come best from those who know me, while my writing, alone and as such, arouses opposition.
Impersonal assessments, when unfavourable, tend, at their worst, to regard my efforts as variously presumptuous, chaotic or mad. An interesting example is Roger Sale's article in the *Modern Language Quarterly* (University of Washington, Seattle),

Poetry and Magic

I shall attempt once again to clarify the issue: I call these labours 'interpretation'.

Interpretation submits the intellect to the imagination. The 'imagination' I regard as the sovereign faculty, following Coleridge and Shelley. In the *Biographia Literaria* (XIII) Coleridge divided imagination into two categories, 'primary' and 'secondary'; the one standing for ordinary perception, the other, of the same kind and differing only in 'degree' and 'mode', for poetic creation. The latter contains an element of 'conscious will', intellect and judgement being included:

The poet, described in ideal perfection, brings the whole soul of man into activity, with the subordination of its faculties to each other according to their relative worth and dignity. He diffuses a tone and spirit of unity that blends, and (as it were) *fuses*, each into each, by that synthetic and magical power to which I would exclusively appropriate the name of Imagination.

(XIV)

'Magical': 'will' and 'understanding' put this 'power' which he calls magical into 'action'; and they still, he says, *unobtrusively*, 'control' it. The result is a blending of opposites, including the 'general' and the 'concrete'. 'Judgement' remains awake, joined to 'profound' feelings. Though the 'natural' and the 'artificial' are both present, 'art' is nevertheless subordinated to 'nature', and 'manner' to 'matter'; that is, *there is a reality being apprehended as surely as in ordinary sense-perception.*

Coleridge adduces some lines by Sir John Davies on the soul,

XXIX. 1; March 1968. For much of the 'stuff and nonsense' he finds, I am myself responsible, but not for my 'fatuous titles' where the blame (if blame there be) lies rather with the Oxford University Press, who in 1930 wanted a pictorial title for my first book instead of the heavily academic one I had chosen. The rest followed. Mr. Sale wrongly attributes (79n.) a passage, which belongs elsewhere, to *The Crown of Life*, and ruins by misquotation (82) my phrase on Cranmer's prophecy, 'a life's wisdom'. I am nevertheless grateful for so extended a notice.

More helpful, and on a different level, are Anthony Mortimer's 'Wilson Knight and Shakespearean Interpretation' in *Studi e ricerche di Letteratura Inglese e Americana* (Istituto Editoriale Cisalpino, Milan 1967); and George A. Panichas's 'G. Wilson Knight: Interpreter of Genius', in *English Miscellany*, ed. Mario Praz (Rome, 1969). See also Philip L. Marcus, 'T. S. Eliot and Shakespeare', *Criticism* (U.S.A.), IX. 1, Winter 1967, 63-79, especially 68-72; also my Preface, above.

I am deeply honoured by the place accorded my commentaries in Professor Clifford Leech's authoritative introduction to his volume *Shakespeare; the Tragedies* (Chicago 1965); and I would record my gratitude for the valued support, over a number of years, of Professor Sadhan Kumar Ghosh.

which, he says, may be roughly, and 'even more appropriately', applied to 'the poetic Imagination':

> Doubtless this could not be, but that she turns
> Bodies to *spirit* by sublimation strange,
> As fire converts to fire the things it burns,
> As we our food into our nature change.
>
> From their gross matter she abstracts *their* forms
> And draws a kind of quintessence from things;
> Which to her proper nature she transforms
> To bear them light on her celestial wings.
>
> *Thus* does she, when from *individual states*
> She doth abstract the universal kinds;
> *Which then re-clothed in divers names and fates*
> *Steal access through the senses to our minds.*

'Sublimation' is a term from alchemy (for alchemy, see pp. 43-4 below). Piercing through 'matter' to essential 'forms', imagination grips what is 'universal', which is then 're-clothed'. The result is addressed to a new sense-perception, resembling yet transcending ordinary sense-perception. Coleridge continues:

Finally, Good Sense is the Body of poetic genius, Fancy its Drapery, Motion its Life, and Imagination the Soul that is everywhere, and in each; and forms all into one graceful and intelligent whole.

(XIV)

'Intelligent' suggests that the result holds meaning. 'Fancy' Coleridge defines as a use of 'fixities and definites' (i.e. objective entities) without any necessary relation to 'time and space'; that is, to normal experience (XIII). By itself it may have little value; all depends on how, and for what purpose, it is used.

John Heath-Stubbs, in his admirable poem *Ars Poetica*, makes a neat, Coleridgean, statement:

> But poetry is not 'emotional truth'.
> The emotions have much less to do with the business
> Than is commonly supposed. No more than the intellect.
> The intellect shapes, the emotions feed the poem,
> Whose roots are in the senses, whose flower is imagination.

The senses flower into the beyond-sensory or extra-sensory, intellect and emotions being no more than aids to the process.

Interpretation uses the same faculty that made, and constitutes, the poem. Intellect and judgement, though active, are nevertheless used in submission to the imaginative whole being inspected. This will not be a proper approach unless we regard the poem as authentic: if our imaginative response, which will already contain, as does all true imagination, elements of reason and judgement, has ratified the poem, then our duty will be submission; but there is no obligation to submit intelligence to writing which has not been so ratified. It is we ourselves who have put the greater writers on their pedestals, and I ask only that we remain true to our own recognition. What so often happens, however, is that after a genuine imaginative experience – and that means an experience of the whole self – the abstracting and memorizing intelligence proceeds to shrivel it, becomes 'critical', unaware that the critical faculty has already been active within the imaginative response, and that there is no call for it to do more, usurping a sovereignty to which it has no right. There is a barrier between imaginative response and critical judgement that must be broken: that is my main contention.

Where matters of deepest import are concerned, I would deny that the philosophic or scientific intelligence is equipped to cope directly with life. Rather, its business is, as Heath-Stubbs said of emotion, to feed the imagination, in which, as Sir John Davies suggests, it is transmuted, like food. A scientific thought may have to wait many generations before it can be imaginatively assimilated. Occult science is in this position today. The greater poets and dramatists from the ancients onwards have tended to leave it to the mystery religions or other secret societies – 'occult' means 'hidden' – while themselves favouring mythology, superstition and magic, which arouse a more traditional and earthly response; though the life-work of John Masefield indicates what may be the more direct approach of future poets. Meanwhile, the philosophic or scientific intelligence, so often at a loss with life, and still more with death, is well enough equipped – and this discovery is my main contribution – to approach the symbolisms of established literature, provided that this intelligence is used in correct imaginative subjection. It will then find the mysteries not so intransigent after all.

Such a use of the intelligence does not *reduce* the poem to philosophy. If interpretation tells us that the dome of 'Kubla Khan' corresponds to the 'eternal dimension', this is not to turn a specific symbol into an abstract concept. Rather, a link has been made with discursive thought, with the abstracting intellect which rules so much of our waking existence, so that we can henceforth read the poem with a richer awareness of its content and a full intellectual collaboration; and intelligence is, as Coleridge tells us, a contained part of the poetic imagination, which is not less than intellectual, but more. Often such a collaboration is needed to perceive the poem's unity, or the unity of a great writer's life-work, such as Ibsen's. In 'Kubla Khan', interpretation alone makes sense of the conclusion, and never since the interpretation was first offered (in *Programme*, Oxford, October 1935; *The Starlit Dome*, 1941) has it been safe for commentators to regard it as a meaningless fragment. It is sometimes objected that interpretation takes poems 'to pieces'; but it is doing precisely the opposite. After reading a poem the sieve of memory leaves one with only certain favoured, because congenial, bits. It is already now 'in pieces'. The aim of interpretation is to put it together again. When it is all put together, the instinctively rejected bits are seen in place, and the result may be embarrassing. That is why interpretation is feared. It may be embarrassing to some admirers of Eliot's poetry to discover that its final key is less theological than spiritualistic; but such is the fact.

Within limits interpretations may differ; but the limits are there, and errors may be dangerous. In Eliot's *The Waste Land*, to regard 'death by water' as a step in spiritual progress rather than the one impediment to spiritual progress – and it has been done – is a blunder. Or, if I am wrong, then I myself am blundering; there is no case here for an 'ambiguity'. I have heard a renowned literary expert expound a difficult modern poem in abstract, 'critical', terms in order to inculcate an 'appreciation'. Questioned by a student on one, factual, point concerning a precise meaning, he was, so far as I could judge, wrong. It is generally assumed that such errors do not matter, and much modern poetry is composed on this assumption; but they do matter. We cannot say that definable meanings are irrelevant. If someone who did not know the play arrived a little late for the first scene of *Hamlet* and did not realize that the Ghost was a ghost, would not his response to Horatio's address be affected? Failure to understand the references in many a modern lyric is just like that: one has no introduction,

no context, and allusions are missed. To ask a poet for his meanings is, in the best literary circles, bad form. All one can do is to
read the unique creation, and remain silent. But no one really
wants this, least of all the poet. Silence is an admission that poetry
lacks communal relevance, that its proper home is the Ivory
Tower. If, however, we admit a relation, we must think and talk
of meanings: interpretation is a statement of relevance.

We have made a transition from critical theory to poetic
practice. The two may be closely related, especially today when
the critical consciousness tends to usurp the place of imagination;
which itself, as already noted, contains, or should contain, all the
intellectual categories and critical judgements which concern the
creative act. The trouble is that we are today more conscious than
ever of complexities in both literature and life. Great poets of
the past may be difficult but their difficulty derives not from an
absence of meaning but from a plethora of meanings; and yet this
is not to assert chaos. On one level they are, or should be, reasonably simple; other levels are assimilated by close reading and study.
But today, under the stresses of modern sophistication and modern
complications, with scientific theory becoming more and more
intangible and no generally accepted religious faith to assist us,
literature, faced as never before by a chaos of meaningless and
unco-ordinated facts and fancies, is turned in on itself and becomes
too often more aware of the need for complexity than of the
subject in hand. Trying to remain true at all costs to the modern
sense of complexity, it renounces lucidity and logic; obscurity
becomes a fetish and simplicity a vice. Critics will often, and
naturally – since the critical consciousness is itself in large part
responsible for the trouble – approve. But meanwhile the writer
has had his eye not on the ball but on his swing; his course through
woods and streams and bunkers may indeed be fascinating; but
there are things, for our purpose, more important. My aim is to
redirect attention to the ball and the flag.

I have for long been troubled by our reception of two great
works, perhaps the two greatest prose works, in English, of our
time; John Cowper Powys's *A Glastonbury Romance* and James
Joyce's *Ulysses*. The one has been no more than half-heartedly
received and spasmodically praised, whereas the other rapidly
won world renown and has spawned numerous commentaries.
A Glastonbury Romance is organically rooted in its legendary soil

23

and handles with exact selection themes of the greatest importance to mankind. *Ulysses* is arbitrarily patterned on a scarcely relevant Homeric scheme, and, though some important psychological issues are treated, the over-ruling impression is one of confusion, if not chaos, rising to a climax towards the end (when Bloom returns to his home), where irrelevancies are listed as with a perverted pleasure in their irrelevance. As a *tour de force* of language and styles of composition, and a breaking of new ground in the exact treatment of obscenities, *Ulysses* arouses not only admiration, but awe. It has strokes of profound insight and a vivid artistry (see pp. 50-1 below). In its amplitude and cumbrous movement, it has, to quote from Flecker's *Hassan*, 'a monstrous beauty like the hind-quarters of an elephant'; but it remains ruinously overloaded and its best purposes are too often fogged. Why, then, do we so honour Joyce and neglect Powys? Why, with our cross-word mentality – and much modern literature demands of us a cross-word technique – must we prefer puzzles to profundities? Is it not perhaps a way of avoiding embarrassing simplicities? Of using intellectual complexity to shield us from obvious truth? Much of our best poetry is puzzle-poetry; but when a poet knows exactly what he wants to say, and is not afraid to say it, his poetry will be, at least if we are at home with his symbols, lucid enough, as we shall find when discussing Powys's *The Ship*.

Complexities and obscurities may be forced; they may be, and often are, a sign of merit; but they are always a second-best. I do not question the main trend of William Empson's famous analyses of poetic ambiguities, except to insist that in the best poetry a general meaning will be clear enough, and the rest subsidiary. Empson himself states the matter perfectly:

An ambiguity, then, is not satisfying in itself, nor is it, considered as a device on its own, a thing to be attempted; it must in each case arise from, and be justified by, the peculiar requirements of the situation. On the other hand, it is a thing which the more interesting and valuable situations are more likely to justify. Thus the practice of 'trying not to be ambiguous' has a great deal to be said for it, and I suppose was followed by most of the poets I have considered. It is likely to lead to results more direct, more communicable, and hence more durable; it is a necessary safeguard against being ambiguous without proper occasion, and it leads to more serious ambiguities when such occasions arise. (*Seven Types of Ambiguity*, 1930, VIII. 297)

Empson knows, however, that a poet cannot always choose his course, since there are activating factors beyond his conscious will.

T. E. Lawrence once said that modern poets 'did not let them-selves go, for fear of giving themselves away; that for fear of being laughed at, they tried to laugh at themselves first' (*T. E. Lawrence by his Friends*, 295; p. 309 below). T. S. Eliot repeated the thought. Writing of poetic 'inspiration' he once noted that, though to the poet his lines may seem 'only a means of talking about himself without giving himself away', they may yet corres-pond to the 'secret feelings' of his readers, and express 'the exulta-tion' or 'despair' of a generation ('Vergil and the Christian World', *The Listener*, 13 September 1951).

For myself, I am at least consistent. My own tendency has always been to honour lucidity; all my interpretations derive from *the will to clarify*; my own creative writing has always aimed, as my preface to my early poems in *Gold-Dust* recently made clear, at simplicity. Meanwhile I see our various cultural industries – I say 'cultural' because far more than literature is involved – lacking purpose and direction; and the more violently they assert them-selves, the more deeply are they mazed and bogged.

It may be argued that the school of *Scrutiny* has given a direction that remains valid.[1] It arose after my own interpretations started, and some of its members followed them: L. C. Knights's *How Many Children had Lady Macbeth?*, recently related in a Penguin anthology (*Shakespeare's Tragedies*, 1963) to the school of *Scrutiny*, derived directly, as the author freely stated, from my own published interpretations of *Macbeth*.[2] I am grateful for the notice my books received in *Scrutiny*, however critical; but I would deny that *Scrutiny*, unless through notices of my own writings and their followers, was, as F. R. Leavis has recently claimed in his intro-duction to the reissued volumes, itself the main agent in the reorientation of Shakespearian studies.

[1] My remarks here are necessarily brief. I have written at greater length on *Scrutiny* in *Essays in Criticism*, XIV. 1; January 1964.

[2] 'Since writing my essay I have been embarrassed to find how much of my criticism of *Macbeth* is directly indebted to the admirable essay on the Life Themes in *Macbeth* in *The Imperial Theme*' (*How Many Children had Lady Macbeth?*, Cambridge 1933; Notes, B, 69-70). I realize that the Penguin editor's error was readily excusable as the kind of imprecision that may be expected to occur in complicated anthologies. I merely wish to get the record straight. Professor Knights has recently himself been, generously, at pains to keep it straight in his Preface to *Further Explorations*, 1965; 186-7.

Scrutiny had purpose and direction, certainly; but its direction was only maintained through a severe and often suicidal limitation: it showed little awareness of the imponderables, of the mysteries, of the magical, of what Wordsworth called, in his 'Elegiac Stanzas suggested by a picture of Peele Castle', 'the light that never was, on sea or land'. This is why it was so predominantly 'critical', and was to many best known for its rejections. Important modern works, to say nothing of the classics, were summarily dismissed: neither John Cowper Powys nor Francis Berry was accorded status, or even notice. *Scrutiny* had many virtues, including exactitude of response and integrity on the verbal or linguistic level, and a recognition that poetic language should be a correlative of psychological poise, or being, and in its chosen line it was fearless. But, despite its apparent boldness, its judgements arose from and appealed to the prisoned mentality of twentieth-century scepticism. It was more at home with the novel, an art-form of recent development adapted to this mentality, than with the great traditions of poetic drama that explode it. Its approach tended towards the moral, the sociological or, in the modern sense, the 'psychological'. The great literatures of the past, bursting such limits, demand a response best defined as 'metaphysical', often involving the 'magical', and sometimes the 'spiritualistic'. To such categories *Scrutiny* was not attuned.

2

The root cause of our confusion may be readily defined. Our normal ways of thought reject the supernatural; literature is full of supernatural, or some would prefer 'supernormal', happenings of central importance; reason jibs, throws intelligence into place and power, and criticism comes into play, rejecting what it cannot assimilate and commenting adversely on the rest. This is not new. It has been going on, with an increasing threat, for centuries. No doubt the *Epic of Gilgamish* was coldly received by the Sumerian intelligentsia. Criticism tears at the throat of literature.

Since I am here concerned with the literary product rather than the process of its composition, we need not say anything much of 'inspiration'. That most, if not all, great writers have been aware of an inspiratory power needs no argument. The ancients talked of the Muse, or Muses; the word 'genius' itself indicates, according to the dictionary, a 'tutelary spirit'. The nature of artistic inspiration has been helpfully studied by N. K. Chadwick in *Poetry and Prophecy* (1942) and also by Rosamond E. M. Harding in *An Anatomy of Inspiration* (1948), a work rich in recorded example. The records are indeed abundant, drawn not only from writers of mystical or metaphysical tendencies but also from novelists. All high-quality creation is involved. In *Rudyard Kipling, Realist and Fabulist* (1967) Bonamy Dobrée writes (11-13) of Kipling as 'a Maker, possessed by a Personal Daemon'. To this 'Daemon' Kipling was loyal, saying: 'When your Daemon is in charge, do not try to think consciously. Drift, wait and obey' (*Something of Myself*, VIII). Again, in his prefatory essay to *A Choice of Kipling's Verse* (19-20, 20nn.), T. S. Eliot draws attention to the part played by 'second sight' in Kipling himself and in his fictions, with an adverse criticism, at one point, of a 'psychological explanation' in one of the narratives. Eliot also draws attention to the chapter 'Art and Magic' in 'that very remarkable book, *The Principles of Art*, by Professor R. G. Collingwood', while agreeing with the author's suggestion that Kipling is a good example of 'the artist as magician'.

Perhaps all thought is best regarded as originating from outside us. Such is the teaching of the famous spirit-guide Silver Birch:

You do not make thoughts. You receive thoughts and send them on their way. The thoughts you receive are determined by the kind of apparatus that you are. Just like your radio and television, the apparatus determines the quantity and quality of the reception. Similarly your attunement qualifies the kind of thought you can receive.

The passage appears in 'Man's Spiritual Nature cannot be Isolated' (in *Two Worlds*, No. 3899, December 1968). We may note an interesting correspondence with Eliot's famous definition of the poet as 'catalyst'. The poet is, however, a creator in fusing thought with expression. Silver Birch continues:

But unlike these material appliances, once thought has lodged with you, you add or detract from its nature before sending it winging away to lodge somewhere else.

We have a perfect description of the poetic process. Thoughts, some dangerous, come unbidden to all of us. The poet, or any artist, is one who successfully transmutes them and sends them winging on their new course. The process, there driven to an extreme, is described in Powys's poem *The Ship*.

There is accordingly a distinction to be made between what we call 'literary composition' and what is known as 'automatic writing'. The artist has to do his share of the work. In *Homer and the Aether* (1959; see p. 408 below) John Cowper Powys is at pains to analyse the respective parts played by *inspiration* and *technique* in the poetry of Homer (in the chapter 'The Aether Speaks', 23-9).[1] With this reservation we can say that works of literary genius are both powerfully inspired from, and themselves likely to be engaged with, planes of reality beyond normal perception.[2]

Apart from comedy, poetry is largely concerned with death; and with death as a positive. Ibsen's 'in death I see not overthrow' (*Brand*, V) is a key statement. Tragedy might be said to celebrate a union with death, as comedy a union with life; and to discuss tragedy with no sense of the greater mysteries, which involve spirit-powers, is like discussing Restoration Comedy with no sense of sexual intercourse. But this is regularly done: to sprinkle a literary essay with occult terminology is the surest way to arouse hostility in an examiner or critic.

What can I say to reassert the age-old saturation of human records with the mysteries? I can point to my own books, and to the recent publication of my brother W. F. Jackson Knight's *Elysion* (1970). My first published article, 'Poetry and Immortality', in *The Adelphi* (IV. 3, September 1926; 169-72), stated my position, which has not varied. I had been discussing the necessity of paradox in the handling of immortality, and continued:

But it must be granted that we cannot use paradox as the currency of everyday thought. It would be like consulting the Space-Time Continuum in measuring a cricket pitch. It is possible that our nearest approach to the truth of immortality would have to be stated in a paradoxical form; and possibly those who positively support and those who deny the theory of personal survival after death are both wide of

[1] In three lectures, 'Vergil's Conscious Art', given at King's College, Newcastle-upon-Tyne in 1960, my brother W. F. Jackson Knight investigated the interplay of conscious and unconscious factors in Vergil's poetry. These lectures will be published.

[2] In a review of Ernest Newman's *The Unconscious Beethoven* in *The Observer* (review section, 29 December 1968), Philip Toynbee, considering the sharp dichotomy of life and art in Beethoven, and unsatisfied with Newman's phrase 'the Spirit of Music', concludes that the works are simply 'messages from God to man'.

the mark, since the spiritual is not only extra-material but by nature probably unfettered in time and space. But though it may not be a clear definition of the fact to say that we go to another place after death (a statement involving both space and time), it is, I feel, a nearer approximation to the truth than the statement that the spirit is killed.

I also adduced (169) 'supernatural appearances', while adding that the assertions of Spiritualists 'add something more positive'; as indeed they do, and with abundant evidence. My subsequent books have been largely concerned with playing variations on this first statement. My comprehensive account of British Drama, *The Golden Labyrinth*, established the close relation in all periods between drama and the occult, and showed how, since the Spiritualistic movement started in the last century, the emphasis has become more emphatic than ever.

If I were asked to name two brief works which we, as literary students, should read and ponder in order to clarify our metaphysics, I might choose Walter de la Mare's poem 'The Listeners' and E. M. Forster's short story *The Celestial Omnibus*.

My present collection of essays drives at all this once again, though with a new balancing of 'spiritualities' and 'obscenities' – the latter term covering a wide range of sexual perversions in fantasy or practice. The relation of these to the spiritualities is obscure, but that there is a relationship seems clear. In *The Price of an Eye* (1961) Thomas Blackburn has written powerfully on the need for descent into the dark underworld of the mind as a prerequisite to poetic vision:

The poet has the double vision of the god Odin; with his blinded eye he beholds what goes on in the night of himself; his other eye watches the outer scene.   (II.25)

Poetic creation blends the two worlds and 'interprets them to each other'. In *The Unquiet Grave* (Penguin, 1967) Cyril Connolly groups descent and vision *together* against normal day-to-day rationality:

A life based on reason will always require to be balanced by an occasional bout of violent and irrational emotion, for the instinctual drives must be satisfied. In the past this gratification was provided by the mystery religions, somewhat grossly by the cults of the Great Mother, more spiritually by the Eleusinian and Orphic mysteries.

(*The Unquiet Grave*, by 'Palinurus', 1. 28)

29

We may recall the medieval Church's celebration of the Feast of Fools and the ritual of the Boy Bishop (*The Golden Labyrinth*, 29-30).

The more orgiastic indulgences are most likely to occur in private fantasy. One of my present essays follows Powys's doctrine on the acceptance of such dangerous, sex-impelled, instincts. These, since the ethical judgement is relaxed, and probably with a vital pleasure in its very relaxation, must be distinguished from the higher 'imagination' which, as Coleridge tells us, includes elements of judgement and therefore ethic; but they are more than meaningless fancies. Being sexually impelled or accompanied they go to, or rather come from, the roots of the psyche. They are as the raw, but no more than 'raw', material of art; and I suggest that their acceptance on this, seemingly crude, level, may be a prerequisite to any rich poetic understanding. In my own life I recall first a period of sexual frustration, with frantic and futile thoughts and lonely actions related to *normal* sexuality; but this was followed by a more successful release through indulgence in thoroughly *abnormal* fantasies; and it was about then, according to my recollection, that the literary patterns of my Shakespearian interpretations began suddenly to unfurl. My conclusion is that, because of some moral censorship and 'barrier' (p. 21 above) at the lower level, so many minds find it all but impossible to focus in full consciousness the patterns poetically revealed on the higher level. Those higher levels will inevitably involve us in spiritual categories. In my own experience, a relation seems to have been active. My friend Derek Langridge once imputed to me, with approval, the association of a close relationship between obscenity and great music. I doubt if the passage in question, though it grouped the two together (*Christ and Nietzsche*, IV. 136), stated a relationship; but he found the association important. Certainly both seem to belong to planes outside our normal thinking.

Remembering the definition of poetic creation offered by John Heath-Stubbs (p. 20 above), we can suggest that the obscenities are its *roots* and the spiritualities its *flowering*. Both these, as in Cyril Connolly's passage, counter, and seem to threaten, the rational mind-structure of our society. They are both aspects of Dionysus, god of drama, comedic or tragic. In more conventionalized forms they have given us the Don Juan myth and the Faust myth. When worked up into imaginative and, to that extent, conventionalized structures – for the artistic imagination, we remember, contains an element of judgement – we accept them, provided that we are not faced with a close-up which shows us their roots and their flowering. Both these, and especially – strange though it be – the 'flowering', strike fear. We are at ease only with the half-way substances of generally accepted viewpoints and values: these we abstract and attend to. We discuss the psychology of Leontes while ignoring the resurrection of Hermione.

Obscenities are usually thought of as 'physical'; but we must remember that there is no final distinction between body and spirit. In my 1926 *Adelphi* article I observed that the physical envelope changes every seven years. What we mean by the 'body' is the enduring form infused and shaped by some unifying principle which exists in the spiritual order. Sex-functioning is quite as much spiritual as physical (p. 186 below); and sex-prompted fantasies are accordingly spirit-prompted. Our real opposition is of body and spirit on the one side and the abstracting 'intellect', the conventional mind-structure, on the other. 'Imagination' covers both. Literary interpretation assists in resolving this opposition, helping us to *think* what we have imaginatively experienced.

Our fear appears on many fronts, and it has been going on for centuries, ever since the Christian Church rejected the Gospel simplicities and the practice of spirit-communication for the complexities of scholasticism and dogma.[1] Modern science, starting from a praiseworthy attempt to face facts, soon itself became an orthodoxy rejecting anything that disturbed its system and disregarding such esoteric thinking as that of Goethe, Blake, and Rudolf Steiner. The chaos foreseen by Alexander Pope at the conclusion of *The Dunciad* is now abundantly evident. Physics has dissolved objects to abstractions, philosophy replaces concepts by linguistics, theology fights a rearguard action while attempting to embrace its pursuers. On every side we have disparate and autonomous subjectivities, none of which understands the others. It is easier to communicate with spirits than for one university department to communicate with another.[2] Each, in its own field, may be efficient: theology may be wise to make what terms it can with Mammon; science has its wonder-works; and as for

[1] For an account of the process, written from an anti-ecclesiastical viewpoint, see Arthur Findlay, *The Psychic Stream*, 1939; also, for a discussion without bias, W. F. Jackson Knight, *Elysion*, 1970.

[2] For the difficulties of verbal communication with modern science, see George Steiner, 'The Retreat from the Word' in *Language and Silence*, 1967.

philosophy, the linguistic approach can at least show up the self-deception inherent in any reliance on such words as 'genius', 'spirit' and 'spiritual' by thinkers who repudiate spirits.

Our minds are undisciplined. There is no co-ordination nor any apparent desire for it. The following passage from Chapter II of Mrs. Radcliffe's *The Italian* makes a neat comment on the culture of our supposedly 'Christian' era:

The elder brothers of the convent said that he had talents, but denied him learning; they applauded him for the profound subtlety which he occasionally discovered in argument, but observed that he seldom perceived truth when it lay on the surface; he could follow it through all the labyrinths of disquisition, but overlooked it when it was undisguised before him. In fact he cared not for truth, nor sought it by bold and broad argument, but loved to exert the wily cunning of his nature in hunting it through artificial perplexities. At length, from a habit of intricacy and suspicion, his vitiated mind could receive nothing for truth which was simple and easily comprehended.

It is my contention that this critique may be applied to our culture at the present time.

In a speech (printed in *The University of Leeds Review*, VIII. 2; December 1962) on the occasion of my retirement at the University of Leeds, I asserted that there lies, ready to hand, the *resolving factor*. Spiritualism touches each of our academic disciplines: theology, physics, medicine, psychology, philosophy, literature. A brief glance at the monthly syllabus of the Spiritualist Association of Great Britain (published as *Service*) indicates the range of its activities, all far beyond the competence of our universities. There is here a barrier which must, and eventually will, be broken. There are, as I see it, only two promising ways open: one is the Churches' Fellowship for Psychical and Spiritual Studies; the other is literature. My present concern is with the latter.

In an essay 'Of Heroic Plays', prefixed to *The Conquest of Granada*, John Dryden defended his use of supernatural phenomena by drawing attention to the part played by magic and spiritual beings in the poetry of the ancients. He continues:

It is enough that, in all ages and religions, the greatest part of mankind have believed the power of magic, and that there are spirits or spectres which have appeared. This, I say, is foundation enough for poetry; and I dare further affirm, that the whole doctrine of separated beings, whether those spirits are incorporeal substances (which Mr.

Poetry and Magic

Hobbes, with some reason, thinks to imply a contradiction), or that they are a thinner or more aerial sort of bodies (as some of the fathers have conjectured), may better be explicated by poets than by philosophers or divines. For their speculations on this subject are wholly poetical; they have only their fancy for their guide; and that, being sharper in an excellent poet than it is likely it should in a phlegmatic, heavy gownman, will see further in its own empire, and produce more satisfactory notions on those dark and doubtful problems.

Some men think they have raised a great argument against the use of spectres and magic in heroic poetry by saying they are unnatural; but whether they or I believe there are such things, is not material; it is enough that, for aught we know, they may be in nature; and whatever is, or may be, is not properly unnatural.

Dryden's 'philosophers' will include what we call 'scientists'; his 'fancy' corresponds to Coleridge's 'imagination'.

Spiritualism offers a lucid philosophy of life and death, with evidence. It is rooted in man's nature and has been known and practised, as my brother's *Elysion* demonstrates, throughout the ages. Those who accept it write simply; and I would take this opportunity of pointing to the lucid handling of metaphysical discussion, week by week, in *Psychic News*. It is no chance that of all the writers studied in my book the most lucid is the one whose human survey concentrates most consistently on spirits: John Masefield.

3

Literature is not all about spirits and perversions. My whole argument for interpretation is that it serves to relate poetic imponderables to discursive reason; and in doing that it develops further what the imaginative work in question did in relating the mysteries to daylight normality. It is precisely this admixture, this impingement, that makes what we call 'literature'. Literature aims either to raise sense-perception beyond itself or to realize the extrasensory through the senses. Both processes may be evident.[1]

[1] Compare Joseph Rykwert, writing in 'The Dark Side of the Bauhaus' (*The Listener*, 3 October 1968): 'The fundamental doctrine which Steiner claimed to have found through – or rather in – Goethe was that the artist does not (as Hegel thought) make a sensory phenomenon *out of* an idea, but shapes the sensory phenomenon *into* an idea. The artist's work does not open the doors for the spirit to enter everyday life: he raises the everyday to the spiritual plane, he releases the spiritual content of physical reality.' It is not a matter for dogmatism, and any definition in terms of *process* remains provisional.

Poetry and Magic

I shall now concentrate more on the spiritualities than the obscenities, the flowerings rather than the roots. The latter are more easily placed and understood. The former, leading to realms of mystery and magic, are more difficult.

Thinking of William Empson's study of poetic 'ambiguities', I suggest that the archetypal ambiguity behind and justifying the rest is the one great ambiguity of earthly perception and spiritual significance. That this ambiguity reflects the theological dogma of the two natures inhering in Christ will be obvious; which suggests – the argument is deployed in *The Christian Renaissance* – that Christianity is a supreme poetry. Some such recognition of a basic duality lies behind our modern poets' habit of interspersing 'poetic' language with colloquial idiom. So much is simple. But complications arise when we turn to another modern tendency: the tendency to favour a packed poetic language, often condensing, of set purpose, ambiguities. If, as Empson warned us, this may become dangerous, I should define the danger as follows. First, meanings are better not clamped arbitrarily together; instead, one should flower easily from the other; there should be on one level at least a simplicity, on the other (or others), flowering from it, the richer intimations. Also there should be not merely diversities, but *levels* of meaning. To join two meanings from one level of normal thinking, of 'realism', is unlikely to help anyone; at the best it makes an intriguing puzzle-poetry; it is not creative. But when the two levels of realism and spiritual perception coincide, we may have gems of poetry.

I offer examples where the quintessentially poetic appears to me to be evident in miniature. Geoffrey Hill, whose poetry is sometimes, to my mind, over-packed, can also use compression to fine purpose. In 'Assisi Fragments' (*King Log*, 1968) some lines concentrating on nature before the Fall tell how there the serpent 'innocently shone its head'. 'Shone' holds manifold suggestions: the lift and curve of the snake's head, normally a threat, radiates sweetness and calm; the purified eye sees a snake's primal beauty without secondary reactions, as in the pivot-incident of *The Ancient Mariner*. Nature as Nature has become supernal, beyond our good-and-evil; being utterly simple, it is transfigured. All this holds true on the level, too, of sexual symbolism. Light is a constituent. The word 'shone' qualifies as a 'burning atom of inextinguishable thought', the

34

phrase applied by Shelley to Dante in his *Defence of Poetry*.

To explain the poetry of a single word is difficult. Let us try a larger example. During the penultimate part of *Ulysses*,[1] Joyce writes of the night sky as

The heaventree of stars hung with humid nightblue fruit.

The infinite becomes near, the cosmos earthy, the cold warm, the inhuman nourishing. Nature is magical, like the 'other lands and other seas' of Andrew Marvell's 'The Garden'; or Wordsworth's 'light that never was, on sea or land' (p. 26 above). Those are only descriptions: Joyce's words *realize* the wonder, as indeed does Marvell's poem later on, in its silver soul-bird.

All 'poetic diction' is aiming towards such effects. They have what may be called 'lustre'. Light is present in both our examples, but there is also solidity. They are as gems, like the many Biblical descriptions of the supernal in terms of rich metals (e.g. Daniel, X. 6: 'his body gleaming like a topaz'; discussed in *The Christian Renaissance*, 1962 edn., 'The Seraphic Intuition', 289). The phrase 'diamond body', sometimes used for the soul-body, has a solidity which terms such as 'astral' or 'etheric' have not. Rich gems have been, throughout the centuries, correlatives to the spiritual or divine; as pre-eminently, in the writings of Oscar Wilde (*The Christian Renaissance*, 287-95; and see *Christ and Nietzsche*, V. 194). We are reminded of Aldous Huxley's experience under mescalin in *The Doors of Perception* and his extension of it in *Heaven and Hell* (App. III) into discussion of our delight in sparkling jewels and fireworks; and in stage illumination, under which nature's forms become magical. In poetry such gem-like creations may depart too far from nature, lacking sap; Milton is over-greedy for them (*Poets of Action*, 47n.); they may very easily 'smell of the lamp'. Joyce's image does, just a little; but 'magic' is not quite nature; the word's primary meaning is for something done, presupposing a human agent. Light is present, as in Shelley's 'burning atoms'; and even in our own derogatory phrase 'smell of the lamp'. In the poetry light is radiated or reflected or transfused to give a more-than-normal dimension of rich colouring, as suggested by the old term 'magic lantern' (for projecting colour plates or films), or as in stained glass windows. There are risks in concentration on such

---

[1] Among the failings of *Ulysses* is its lack of chapter numerals. If ever a book needed them, this is it, and their absence is unfortunate.

condensed miracles, but nowhere else can we see so clearly what is meant by calling an isolated effect 'magical'.

There must be the two main constituents of (i) 'realism' in the normal sense and (ii) the supernal. When they are fused we have a magical activity. A more extended example will help us. Here is Francis Berry's sonnet 'For John Cowper Powys on his Ninetieth Birthday' (composed for a B.B.C. programme in 1962 and published in Derek Langridge's *John Cowper Powys: a Record of Achievement*, 1966; 218). The poem's references are to thoughts, incidents and people in *A Glastonbury Romance*:

> Sir, what you give, we have and hold.
>
> Magus, you kiss life into the dead stone;
> The plain woman and the crazed man in the dull town
> Make quick and green with loving, and make the moon
> React to the stretcht dog's pain, and the plant's groan.
>
> J. C. Powys has felt the thuds of the sun
> Startle the wild block of wood; he has shown
> Us the Arthurian sword as down it shone
> Yesterday afternoon; and he has seen
>
> Unshudderingly the livid spear; caught the sheen
> Of that hovering oval, roseate Urn
> Repolished till it throbs; has made the mean
> Insect thrilling and ghostly, and the dead return.
>
> Sir, what you give, we have and hold:
> John Cowper Powys, ninety years old.

Various opposites become unities; we grow aware of a single, living universe. The lines describe what is going on in our other poetic miniatures, and they contain one of their own which repays attention. The Grail, seen by Sam (*A Glastonbury Romance*, XXVIII. 981-2 or 938-9), is in Berry's lines first felt as a vague luminance in 'sheen', and next as an ethereal entity, 'hovering'. Its circularity suggests a universal harmony; 'roseate' suggests both nature and the rose as a sacred emblem. But it comes quickly nearer and more solid within a rapidly developing human experience, indicated by the domesticity of 'repolished', which in the most practical terms possible adds both solidity and lustre. Finally it has become warmly animate, a biological fact, like our own bodies, which 'throbs'. Surely nowhere else is what we call the 'spiritual' more effectively realized as warm life. There is lustre, but no even distant suggestion of the 'lamp', of an artifact, though it is superb artistry. Here 'airy nothing' (for the Shakespearian 'nothing' see *The Sovereign Flower*, General Index B, VI, 'Nothing') has been given 'a local habitation and a name' (*A Midsummer Night's Dream*, V. i, 17).

It is seldom easy to say why words or phrases or short poems are in themselves poetic. In the interpretation of small effects it is so easy to begin reading into them our own subjective, and perhaps irrelevant, meanings. To take us further I now assert this principle: since what we designate 'imaginative literature' must be supposed to possess a common quality, we may assume that what is true of a large work generally recognized as 'literature' will, even though it does not contain any gems of compacted verbal excellence, be subtly at work within anything, large or small, that deserves the name of poetry. We shall accordingly seek guidance from some larger imaginative works which, though they may not engage in separate miracles of expression, will nevertheless show on a grand, and therefore clear, scale what is the purpose of literature.

In the larger works there will be found mysterious powers, either angelic or satanic; but there is also a 'realistic' concern. Consider how the technicalities of whaling in Melville's *Moby Dick* are jostled by higher flights of metaphysical speculation; or how Hardy's exactly located rusticity is impinged on by atmospheric powers. Where one finds the fanciful alone, as in Barrie's *Peter Pan*, or the normalities alone, as in Galsworthy's *Forsyte Saga*,[1] there is creation, however fine, of a lower order. The novel, growing as it has from recent social conditions and speaking primarily in such terms, will clearly remain in general constricted to the one, obvious, level, as poetry and drama are not.[2] The 'Gothic' novels of Mrs. Radcliffe, M. G. Lewis and others stand out as an interesting if transient reaction, or protest, emphasizing what was being

[1] The remarkable B.B.C. television dramatization of Galsworthy's *Forsyte Saga* shows how dangerous a final critique of a 'novel' as a 'novel' on the level of 'literature' may be. There is always an appeal from words to that which lies behind the words. Dramatization and a new medium may reveal powers unguessed by the literary critic. It brings out strongly the importance of Jo's hearing of his dead father's voice advising him on the crucial decision that leads to his own death.

[2] In 'Ishmael's Trip' (*The Listener*, 3 August 1967), a fascinating talk on *Moby Dick* as an amalgam of novel, epic and drama, Leslie Fiedler refers to the 'novel form' as 'invented precisely (as Samuel Richardson himself once boasted) to drive the "marvellous" and "wonderful" from the realm of prose fiction'.

omitted. It is true that Tolstoy's *War and Peace* is both evidently great literature and yet speaks almost wholly along the surfaces of life. Here we must suppose that the spiritualities are nevertheless present, but easier to feel than to demonstrate. This problem I have discussed elsewhere (*The Christian Renaissance*, III; and see p. 468 below), concluding that so perfected an incarnation may be, however wonderful, of less use to us in our distracted state than works which throw the spirit-powers into relief; until we know that they are there we must be shown them. Certainly where a novel such as *Wuthering Heights* wins general acceptance as a work of similar power to that of a Shakespearian tragedy, the numinous, and indeed actual spirits of the dead, are present. In political writing Burke's speeches were, as speeches, not very successful. But they alone, from all the possible choices, have become 'literature', put on examination syllabuses for 'English'. Why? Surely, just because Burke projects a sense of eternal verities and power over-watching the ephemeral event.

It does not always matter if the realism is at fault, as in Shakespeare's *Richard III* and *Macbeth*, both historically inaccurate, or if the supernatural element is crude and superstitious; for it is from experience of the blend, the interweaving, the impingement, that the importance matures.

As I have before observed, many Jacobean or Restoration dramatists, Chapman and Lee pre-eminently, show an occult knowledge that might seem to shame the impossible Ghost of *Hamlet*[1] and the witch-lore and Apparitions of *Macbeth*. Shakespeare relies variously on traditional beliefs and his own artistry to make us, at whatever cost to truth, experience the needed impact.[2] The power of the Ghost scenes in *Hamlet*, like that of Cassandra's

---

[1] On the paradoxes of Shakespeare's Ghost see H. A. Mason, *The Cambridge Quarterly*, III. 2; Spring 1968.

[2] To what extent Shakespeare himself believed in traditional lore need not concern us; but he used it as a needed and relevant constituent. Probably he accepted it in the main. Here is Edward Dowden, writing of *Macbeth*:

> We slighter and smaller natures can deprive ourselves altogether of the sense for such phenomena; we can elevate ourselves into a rare atmosphere of intellectuality and incredulity. The wider and richer natures of creative artists have received too large an inheritance from the race, and have too fully absorbed all the influences of their environment for this to be possible in their case.

(*Shakespeare: his Mind and Art*, 1879 edn., 249)

The greater Shakespearian authorities – R. G. Moulton was another – have shown a responsiveness to the powers in question. To these powers lesser commentators remain cold.

clairvoyance in Aeschylus' *Agamemnon*, serves to show how closely what we feel to be the specifically 'dramatic' depends on supernormal categories. Drama is not, however, philosophy; in the theatre we do not think so much as experience; and for experience the greater writers know that traditional lore, carrying with it centuries of human belief, may be more useful than spiritualistic exactitudes. If false, it nevertheless transfixes. Information, even information directly expounded by spirit-personalities, of whose doctrines there are today numerous books, though highly important nevertheless remains no more than information. To be told that the etheric plane is one of colour and form does not prevent it from seeming tenuous and abstract. It is so difficult to live the information. We need to experience it in our own terms, as Berry's lines make us experience the Grail. This is why the New Testament account of the empty tomb became the originating impulse of British, perhaps European, drama. In this matter a Spiritualist may well be sceptical;[1] the tomb may not have been empty; but the story has attuned millions to a truth.

There have, it is true, been many recent examples of straight spiritualistic drama, such as Masefield's *Melloney Holtspur*, and we may expect more. J. B. Priestley has used his time-philosophy to present survival of death in convincing terms (*The Golden Labyrinth*, 386-8); and his recent television drama *Anyone for Tennis?* had great force. British drama since the 1870s shows a wide range of Spiritualistic works of varying quality. Eliot in *The Cocktail Party*, in the manner of Shakespearian poetry, dramatizes his mysteries so far as may be in terms of accepted or traditional beliefs, psychiatry, priest-craft, ancient ritual, with comparatively little emphasis – though there is some – on clairvoyance (see p. 397 below). If, as I believe, the result is less cogent than Priestley's plays or Masefield's *Melloney Holtspur*, it looks as though the more direct expression will in due course dominate the dramas of the world.

Whether we call the more imponderable elements of the New Testament and literature 'spiritualistic', 'magical', or 'superstitious', the danger remains that we abstract from our review what is 'realistic' and reject what is supernormal. My own

---

[1] A spiritualistic interpretation of the empty tomb in terms of 'dematerialization' has, however, been advanced by Geraldine Cummins in a lecture to the Spiritualist Association of Great Britain: see the report in *Psychic News*, 17 April 1965.

Shakespearian interpretations developed from the readiness to see supernormal events or atmospheric powers as keys or pointers. Such were Death in *Hamlet*, evil presences in *Macbeth*, Jupiter in *Cymbeline*, and the statue-resurrection of *The Winter's Tale*, and much else.

This recognition was all part of what I have called the 'spatial' approach, or understanding. In literary studies this approach was, in effect, new, though it had been used in Biblical exegesis by Milton in his *De Doctrina Christiana*. Patterns were unfurled that had never previously been suspected. They must always have been within our imaginative response, but since they had not been intellectually focussed it was natural now to abstract them and study them as though they were extras. The stories and obvious sequences were already well known, but these patterns, which reflected over-brooding, or in-brooding, powers that qualified and in part interpreted the sequence, had eluded attention. Though they were themselves dynamic, their dynamism may be called vertical rather than horizontal, containing significances from a dimension beyond the story (*The Sovereign Flower*, 253-6); or again, they could short-circuit time, allowing one to group widely-spaced recurrences so that they could be seen in a flash, as with a panoramic view. For these reasons they were best regarded as 'spatial' in contrast to the story. The two elements, temporal and spatial, were linked by symbolism (*Shakespeare and Religion*, 311-12).

I once (in *Laureate of Peace*, reissued as *The Poetry of Pope*, 'Symbolic Eternities', 81) argued that interpretation of the temporal arts, literature and music, should naturally emphasize spatial form, pattern, unifying theme or *motif* and other recurrences; and that interpretation of the spatial arts will as inevitably be engaged with the temporal, noting our gradual assimilation of a cathedral's effects (Byron, *Childe Harold*, IV. 157-8); the action-pose, hinting a before and after, of sculpture (*Childe Harold*, IV. 161); whatever narrative elements there may be in a picture, or, if there are none, the leading of the eye to some significant point in the composition; and so on. Of especial interest is Sigmund Freud's extended interpretation of the 'Moses' of Michelangelo, relating detail on detail to the narrative situation (*Collected Papers*, London 1934; IV. xvi). Interpretation tries to help each art to say what it is trying to say but cannot quite say because of its own spatial or temporal limitations.

Poetry and Magic

In Pope's *Temple of Fame* the Temple is felt as dynamic, as creating itself moment by moment. The spatial sequences of temporal arts are no more than metaphorically 'spatial', and the life of spatial art may seem to pulsate within some vertical rather than horizontal time-dimension. Confusion is inevitable since, and this is the main fact to be remembered, all art equally represents a fusion of space and time. 'Space' and 'time' may be unreal abstractions; and so may the spatial and temporal elements of art; but they remain necessary intellectual counters, and the way to get beyond them is not by denying them, but by reintegrating them; whence further insights may mature.

My literary analyses have led me to conclude that 'space-time' may be equated with 'eternity'. Art is its language. My theories have grown from the thought-atmosphere of our time, and may be used to illuminate some of the more disturbing tendencies of modern poetry: Eliot's disregard for temporal links in *The Waste Land* is symptomatic of an over-reliance on the spatial with a corresponding neglect of the temporal. Much modern writing incurs a similar danger. Another thought: it is always dangerous to regard 'eternity' as static; it has its own dynamism (*Atlantic Crossing*, VII. 215, quoted in *Laureate of Peace*, as above, 89-90; see also T. S. Eliot, *Four Quartets*, 'Burnt Norton', II; also V). In the New Testament the 'eternal' of 'eternal life' is a translation of the Greek *aionios* meaning 'through the ages'; and whatever that may indicate, it is not static. Our equation of 'eternity' with 'space-time' comes naturally.

All of these are abstractions, but what they define are not. Poetry is rich; indeed it is the most comprehensive of all the arts. Its intellectual content acts in combination with sensuous appeal, and, as Francis Berry says in *Poetry and the Physical Voice* (1962; 110), there may be danger when 'the meaning is weighed by the intellect in disengagement from the act of hearing'. We possess sense-inlets of sound, sight, smell and touch; poetry can use all, entwisting them with thought. In poetry, sound and sight may be all but identified, an image appealing to one reader as sound and to another as sight. In Edmund Blunden's sonnet *Bells*, on church bells ringing over the countryside, we hear that

> when the bells begin
> Song colours, colour sings.

Edith Sitwell aroused criticism in the 1920s by such phrases as 'the morning light creaks down again', in 'Aubade', and 'The light is braying like an ass', in 'Trio for Two Cats and a Trombone'.

Joseph Conrad said that literature should aspire 'strenuously' to the qualities of painting and sculpture, and to the 'magic' of music (p. 243 below). Because it so aspires we have the rich deployments of drama, opera and ballet. Performance of any literary work always strives to embody its more spatial and colourful elements. These are the elements on which interpretation, too, will have concentrated. With a play interpretation is a prerequisite to production, and even for non-dramatic works it should be, in its way, always as a mental *staging*, bringing to solidity what was previously flat, and releasing a magic which had been missed. It attunes us to spatial symbolisms containing yet transcending thought.

Poetry is made of words; and yet, paradoxically, the discussion of it in terms of language holds danger. For the words only exist to conjure into being that which is behind, or beyond, transcending the words themselves. It awakes the various senses for its purpose; and this may be done in various ways, sometimes through words that appear weak. Remembering our definition of poetry as rooted in the senses before flowering (p. 20 above), we may suppose that we do well to use all our earth-senses as a preparation, not so much for an *extra-sensory* as for a *super-sensory* experience. This will resemble the true nature of higher planes beyond death, where the breaking of the body makes possible a total response to reality at present limited by the separate inlets. In his 'Epilogue' to *The Triumph of Mammon* (1907; 156-62) John Davidson wrote fervently of the metaphysical interdependence of light, or colour, and sound. Spirit communicators tell us that on higher planes music is, or creates, colour; as also in Walt Disney's *Fantasia*. Thoughts take on form, as with the coloured thought-angels sent out by Powys for healing (*Autobiography*, VIII. 373, XII. 630-2, 638-41).

The third section of my present volume is headed 'Totalities'. This handles work that has no primary or obtrusive emphasis but contains much, perhaps all, that we discuss elsewhere, in harmonious balance. Of its three subjects the first, Tennyson, is included for the vast reach of his poetic survey; the next, Powys's *Owen Glendower*, for its blend of colourful artistry and historic exactitude; the third, Berry, for his application of sensory power to human destiny. All three are concerned with great communal issues. All literary art is magical, and magic is a way of transmutation. World affairs today are in need of it.

4

We have equated poetry with magic. Eliot admired Collingwood's *The Principles of Art* with its chapter 'The Artist as Magician', and agreed that Kipling was a good example (p. 27 above). Kipling was an eminently practical writer; but then magic is, as surely as science, practical. It aims at control and transmutations; it is active, as wisdom and mysticism, by themselves, are not.

Christianity is a grand-scale magic. All the peak persons of our literature are associated with magic. Oedipus in the *Oedipus Coloneus* housed magical powers. In the Middle Ages, Vergil had the reputation of a magician and his works were thought to hold a magical potency: the story is told and the implications discussed in Domenico Comparetti's *Vergil in the Middle Ages*.[1] Shakespeare's furthest human delineation, Prospero in *The Tempest*, is not a philosopher nor a mystic, but a magician; so is Byron's superman, Manfred, who compares himself with 'the Magi' and is called a 'Magian' (II. ii. 91, III. iv. 105; for *Manfred*, see *Byron and Shakespeare*, 175-7, 298-301). The central myth of Renaissance Europe is the Faust myth, handled by Marlowe, Goethe and others. John Cowper Powys's early ambition was to be a magician (*Autobiography*, I. 7, 29; VIII. 352, 357), and this ambition he came near to realizing in his life as well as writing. Berry chose well in addressing him as 'Magus'. Note that our sequence develops from old-style magic to the *mental*, or psychological, magic of Byron and Powys, corresponding to the mind-control of *The Scholar Gipsy* (p. 235 below).

Modern science has affinities with 'magic'. Science has taken over the magician's responsibilities so far as external nature is concerned, but where the human mind and personality are concerned we remain baffled; here science may be of less use than magic.

In *The Integration of the Personality* (translated by Stanley M. Dell, London 1940), Carl G. Jung draws heavily on medieval alchemy. It was more than superstition or fraud: in it 'we are called upon to

---

[1] Translated into English in 1895; revised 1908; reprinted 1966.

deal, not with chemical experimentations as such, but with something resembling psychic processes expressed in pseudo-chemical language' (210); the experimenter had 'psychic experiences' which he thought of as 'chemical process' (213).[1] He searched not only, or even mainly, for ordinary gold, but for a 'golden understanding' which required a spiritual awakening (217). For the alchemists there was no sharp distinction between the 'physical' and the 'psychic'; rather they were working in an 'intermediate realm' of 'subtle bodies' relating to both; and this realm, in which 'physical' and 'psychic' are fused, is likely, says Jung, soon to re-assume importance (222-3); its expression will be symbolic (226). Byron is thinking in such terms when he shows his Manfred as feeling that 'the golden secret, the sought "Kalon"', is all but 'found' and 'seated' in his 'soul' (*Manfred*, III. i. 13).

Poetry exists to enlarge and transmute our existence. Its magic works on the mind. Byron writes of 'the power of Thought, the magic of the Mind' in *The Corsair* (I. 8). In his 'Recluse' fragment (Preface to *The Excursion*, 1814) Wordsworth writes with awe of 'the Mind of Man', which he calls the 'haunt' and 'main region' of his poetry, as being so interfused with the objective universe that it creates a new humanity (*The Starlit Dome*, 1-2; *Christ and Nietzsche*, IV. 133). Nietzsche's Zarathustra is a magician of the mind, willing the transformation of man to superman; and Powys, concentrating on the magic of the inanimate and the art of soul-projection, announces a new evolutionary advance, 'a new self-created self' (*In Spite Of*, V. 130, IV. 106 etc.; see *The Saturnian Quest*, 88). Ibsen's *Emperor and Galilean* sees the creation of a new type of man, one who 'wills himself' (i.e. uses his total being) as a prerequisite to the establishment of his 'Third Empire' (*The Emperor Julian*, III. iv).

No discussion of poetry can get far without the use of the word 'magic'; quotations from Dryden and Coleridge have already shown that. Edith Sitwell's poetry is crammed with magical thoughts and themes, blending childlike acceptance with a sophisticated technique. In his comprehensive survey of the nature

---

[1] Jung's life-work was spiritualistically based. He had a spirit-guide, whom he called 'Philemon'. He describes an experience of a ghostly assembly which impelled him, in 1916, to the writing of his *Septem Sermones ad Mortuos*. From then on, he says, the dead became ever more distinct for him: 'These conversations with the dead formed a kind of prelude to what I had to communicate to the world about the unconscious' (C. G. Jung, *Memories, Dreams, Reflections*, 1963; VI. 175-8, 182-4).

and meaning of poetry, *The Poetic Pattern* (1956), Robin Skelton devotes a chapter to 'Poetry and Magic'; and references recur throughout; 'magic' is a key-concept in his book.

The word's suggestions outspace all easily understood categories; they may be as mysteriously fearful as Keats's

> magic casements, opening on the foam
> Of perilous seas, in faery lands forlorn

in his *Ode to a Nightingale*. In his *Apology for Bad Dreams* Robinson Jeffers, pondering the horrors in man and beyond, decides as poet to 'imagine victims' instead and by his art to 'magic horror away from the house'. Poetic magic transmutes evil, builds it into the personality, diffuses it into good.

In *Poetic Craft and Principle* (1967) Robert Graves writes powerfully on magic. For him 'poetic principle' involves 'a simple, obstinate belief in miracle' (30). Magic, he says, was born from the love of man and girl; it encouraged arts and inventions, and also the more 'supernatural faculties' of prophecy, healing, telepathy and 'disembodied travel'; that is, astral travel (99). Love, magic and poetry are interrelated: love is the main theme and origin of true poems (116). For Graves this love is heterosexual, but distinguished from marriage. Though 'to marry the woman in whom the Muse is resident negates poetic principle', the pursuit is creative: '*For me, poetry implies a courtship of the Muse prolonged into a magical principle of living*' (118; my italics).

Our Western society is far removed from such concerns. The Bantus of Africa find our civilization hostile to their *muntu*, or vital force. For them magic, involving trances and spiritual powers able 'to dominate the material' (i.e. matter), is active (132). Though our civilization would destroy them, 'these are the very same principles that provide the *muntu* for Western poets who look hopefully beyond the universal mechanistic catastrophe to their restoration' (132).

Graves himself is, as was Byron, superstitious: he will only take an important decision under a 'new moon' (133). The Moon is important to him. He accepts Theseus' lines in *A Midsummer Night's Dream* (V. i. 7) comparing lunatic, lover and poet; for 'lunatic' derives from 'moon'; and the poet's Muse, he says, is traditionally a 'Moon Goddess' (133). The problem of writing poems is 'like that of reconciling the solar with the lunar calendar'.

At present the poet's 'soul' enjoys only 'rare and hidden correspondences' with his 'Muse woman'; but there is a certitude that
'true lovers will one day reconcile lunar with solar time, imagination with reason, intuition with planning, honour with freedom;
the male with the female mind' (134-5). The thought corresponds
to the awakening of the Hermaphrodite in Shelley's *The Witch of
Atlas* (XLIII-XLV; discussed in *The Starlit Dome*, 229); and also
to Byron's development from moon-poetry to sun-poetry in treatment of love (*Byron and Shakespeare*, 231, 244, 254). Such a consummation happens – he may mean 'as things are at present,
happens' – in what he calls 'a timeless *now*', which must not be
subsequently dismissed as 'a fanciful *then*': we must remain loyal to
the experience (135). Graves's thinking is often fascinatingly correlative to that of Powys's lyrics, and never more so than when
he works on the mutual interrelations and interchangings of Sun
and Moon (see below, pp. 223-5).

Much of the argument recalls Plato. In Plato, and often later, it
occurs in homosexual terms; and often too, in drama especially,
with an emphasis on bisexuality, integrating the male and female
elements in the psyche. This Graves finds 'physiologically confusing' (148); but he has already, as we have seen, looked for a
reconciliation of 'the male with the female mind'; and he proceeds
to investigate poetic transversals whereby Sun as male and Moon
as female change places.[1] 'In extreme cases of poetic love' an
interchange may be observed, each borrowing from the other:

When the Unicorn (who began as a metaphor of the Sun's course
through the five 72-day Egyptian seasons) lays his horned head on the
lap of the pure Moon-Virgin, their spirits are united.   (149)

The Unicorn may, like the Phoenix, symbolize a Platonic, perfected, soul-state, beyond or outside normal sexual intercourse
(for the Phoenix, see *The Mutual Flame* Part 2, II. III, on *Love's
Martyr*; for the Unicorn, see *The Golden Labyrinth*, 326-7). Graves is
clearly thinking along such lines, and also on the lines of Rupert
Brooke's poem 'On the Shape of the Human Body' (p. 296 below).

Graves claims, again like Rupert Brooke (p. 295 below), to have
had experience of 'celestial illumination', as a boy, in which he
'knew everything'; he had a key 'to open any lock of any door';

---

[1] Compare the sexual ambivalences of *Love's Martyr*, discussed in *The Mutual
Flame*, 156-92; especially 184-5, on Chapman's 'Male Turtle'.

46

he was just 'looking sideways at disorderly facts so as to make perfect sense of them'. It was a state of 'supra-logic that cuts out all routine processes of thought and leaps straight from problem to answer' (137-8). Afterwards the experience dissolved.

What, now, of death? Graves claims to be, as it were, beyond, or outside, it. He is instinctively impelled, as stated by the poem 'In Her Praise' (*New Poems*, 1962), 'to parley with the pure, oracular dead', and in his *Poetic Craft and Principle* says that a poet is 'one who has, as it were, already died and conversed with the oracular dead, thus being gifted with the spirit of prophecy' (135). He had himself 'officially died of wounds' in the war, though he later recovered (135). Relying, it seems, on this experience, he offers us a poem, 'The Second-Fated', describing himself as one who has visited 'the Pit' of shades and afterwards 'the silver-bright Hyperborean Queendom' where 'pure souls' are 'shot through by merciful lunar shafts' and become poets scorning the 'factitious universe', believing in 'wind' as the original power and living in a 'moon-warmed world of discontinuance' (135-6). The impressions of silver, wind, and moon correspond closely to those in Powys (pp. 200-2, 206, below).

He does not accept traditional descriptions of a heavenly after-life, but prefers 'Paradise' as glimpsed in Genesis. He has visited Paradise twice: once when he was supposed dead in the war when, according to a poem he wrote at the time, he saw 'new stars in the subterrene sky'; but Proserpina returned him 'breathless, with leaping heart', to 'the track' (170-1).

The other visit was made under the influence of a Mexican mushroom drug,[1] when he met the Mexican equivalents of Dionysus and his mother Semele (whom Graves equates with Proserpina, or Persephone). Both Dionysus and his Mexican equivalent Tlalóc were 'born from a flash of lightning'. We have a poem of his experience. He follows Dionysus and Semele through a 'rainbow-limbo, webbed in white'; through cold and under water, through jungles and terrors; then more happily past treasure-chambers and naked statued maidens:

> Then mount at last on wings into pure air,
> Peering down with regal eye upon
> Five-fruited orchards of Elysium,
> In perfect knowledge of all knowledges. (172)

---

[1] See *The Sacred Mushroom*, Andrija Puharich, 1959.

That is as firm an Elysian statement as one could wish for. The experience is described more expansively in Graves's *Oxford Addresses on Poetry*, 1962 ('The Poet's Paradise', 122-6).

As to what normally happens to us after death, he is as enigmatic as Powys. He states firmly his beliefs in timeless love-ecstasies and other ecstatic visions: 'if I die in a state of grace, my timeless paradise will be the secret garden of the woman I love best' (176-7). The conception of timelessness, as always, makes any simple statement – which must itself be a grammatical time-sequence – difficult. If, as science tells us, 'time is no more than a useful terrestrial convention' and we are to accept 'a time-space continuum in which the moment of miracle not only has its place but can be endlessly observed from endless points of vantage', then to demand an 'after-life' in the temporal sequence as normally understood would be to expect to occupy 'two places at once in the time-space continuum' (177). The statement leaves us still baffled: we merely have a non-terrestrial infinitude ('endlessly') instead of temporal continuation. The mystery is expressed in terms of space instead of time; but it is the same mystery. As I suggested in my article in *The Adelphi* (p. 28 above) we cannot drive any such thinking *towards a negative*. The matter was fully discussed in the chapter 'Immortality' in my book *The Christian Renaissance* (1933 and 1962).

From Graves I select these thoughts. Poetry is magical, with the purpose of inducing 'a magical principle of living'. It is related to a highly esoteric love, such as I have so often designated as 'seraphic'. Though Graves's teaching appears in heterosexual terms, the result is, as we have seen, not so very different: at a choice moment sexes change places. More: at a key-moment in his own lines on his Elysian visit he writes on Dionysus as

> Little slender lad, lightning-engendered,
> Grand master of magicians.

> (172)

This was Graves's *objective experience under the drug*; and to this extent it may be supposed to hold an authenticity over his own more personal, heterosexual, inspirations.

Man, in quest of purification and enlargement, is clogged and hampered with all the fears which Graves observed as preliminaries to Elysium. He is like an over-loaded donkey on a difficult road. Like a donkey he has to be lured on by a carrot. His carrot is the 'seraphic'.

5

Greek culture appears to have flowered from two main sources of inspiration: the Delphic Oracle and the cult of *paederastia*, which means the 'love of boys'. In Plato's *Phaedrus* this love, or love-vision, is regarded by Socrates as the key to supernal insight and spiritual ascent. In *The Symposium* it is the basis of noble actions and true virtue (*The Mutual Flame* 216-19).

This I call the 'seraphic' intuition: ages may vary from boys to young men, but that this intuition has a wide authority will scarcely be questioned. Superlative men of literature and legend are so attuned: Achilles has his Patroclus and David his Jonathan.

In the New Testament and Christian tradition Christ's two closest personal loves are his mother and the beloved disciple of St. John's Gospel, traditionally accepted as John himself, who lay 'on Jesus' breast' at the Last Supper (John, XIII. 23); the phrase was remembered by the early Fathers, and also by Dante, in whose *Paradiso* John comes, signifying Love, like a young 'virgin', gay, innocent, and of blinding power (*Paradiso*, XXV. 100-39, XXVI. 9-12); his function is really the same as that of Beatrice, the girl Dante knew in pre-sexual perfection and now his guide through Paradise. In the Apocryphal *Acts of John* he and Jesus are regarded as personal lovers. All this I have discussed at length in 'The Seraphic Intuition', appended to the 1962 reissue of *The Christian Renaissance*. The grouping of Mother and Beloved was usual in medieval art. Angels were regularly depicted, and in pageantry performed, by boys, and there was the deeply purposeful ritual of the Boy Bishop (discussed in *The Golden Labyrinth*, 30).

The theme is widespread: in Vergil, as noted in a peculiarly valuable passage in my brother W. F. Jackson Knight's *Roman Vergil* (enlarged edn., Penguin, 1966, IV. 146); in the sonnets of Michelangelo and Shakespeare; in the life and work, especially the 'Thyrza' poems and those to Loukas, of Byron (*Lord Byron's Marriage*, 30-5, 217-19); in Tennyson, Wilde, T. E. Lawrence. The list could be expanded, at home and abroad. Drama in all periods shows a succession of boys, youths, or girls in boy-disguise, to enact perfection.

49

What do such figures signify? I call them 'seraphic', drawing the term from the 'naked Seraph' of the Fragments appended to Shelley's *Epipsychidion* (145), Byron's *Childe Harold* (IV. 121) and *Don Juan* (IX. 47), Tennyson's reference to Hallam's 'seraphic intellect' in *In Memoriam* (CIX); and elsewhere. They blend male and female, as in Shakespeare's 'master-mistress' of Sonnet 20 and Tennyson's 'manhood fused with female grace', again Hallam, in *In Memorian* (CIX). They witness to the infusing of body with spirit; they are delicate yet strong; boys are called 'delicate strong' in Francis Berry's 'Salvo for Spring' (*Mediterranean Year*, I). In them love and strength, grace and power, church and state, blend. Poetry and drama must return, again and again, and in all periods, to such perceptions. In Day-Lewis's 'Singing Children: Luca Della Robbia' (*An Italian Visit*, Part V), 'angels with choir-boy faces' of 'jaunty, angelic pose' contrast with doubts as to the enigma of the 'Primal Sapience' and the poet's recognition of his own fall to maturity. Francis Berry's 'Malta Elegy' has a vivid quatrain, on a pupil who had died:

> Child, Musician, Genius, Quest,
> Whom I looked for, found, now lost;
> In you sublime, my youth, my past;
> That better self is now a ghost.

Often enough the theme is stated elegiacally, in terms of death: in *Lycidas*, in the 'Thyrza' poems, in *In Memoriam*. Supernal categories are involved. 'Quest' is a, or *the*, poetic 'quest'. Lines attributed to Plato on the youth 'Aster' sets the mode:

> Thou wert the morning star among the living,
> Ere thy fair light had fled—
> Now, having died, thou art as Hesperus, giving
> New splendour to the dead.

The translation is Shelley's.

A fascinating example occurs at a key moment in Joyce's *Ulysses*. The long brothel section, a sequence of ludicrous and obscene material from the subconscious, concludes happily with the appearance of Bloom's long-dead child, Rudy, appearing at the age he would be, had he lived, having presumably grown, in accordance with spiritualistic doctrine, on the next plane:

Against the dark wall a figure appears slowly, a fairy boy of eleven, a changeling, kidnapped, dressed in an Eton suit with glass shoes and a little bronze helmet, holding a book in his hand. He reads from right to left inaudibly, smiling, kissing the page. . . . He has a delicate mauve face. On his suit he has diamond and ruby buttons. In his free left hand he holds a slim ivory cane with a violet bowknot. A white lambkin peeps out of his waistcoat pocket.

Bloom calls, 'inaudibly', to him, 'wonderstruck', but he only 'gazes unseeing into Bloom's eyes', and goes on reading and smiling. It is typical of Joyce that he should drive the normal poetic method of concrete realization to the limit. Sense-suggestion is vivid. Spirit-life, suggested by 'inaudibly', is given colour in 'mauve' and 'violet'.[1] 'Mauve' recalls his face as it looked in the coffin (Stuart Gilbert, *James Joyce's Ulysses*, 2nd edn., 1932; 337), but leads on to 'violet'. Rich stones come in, being traditional symbols of the supernal. 'Fairy' and 'changeling' are from folklore. 'Right to left' suggests a looking-glass world, as in *Alice through the Looking-glass*; the lambkin, referring back to the jacket of lamb's wool he was buried in, might also suggest a conjurer at a children's party. It is a child with a toy helmet, in a child's world, the world of magic lanterns. The art-symbol for this whole section of *Ulysses* is, according to Stuart Gilbert, 'Magic'. The total result is a peculiarly vivid concretization all made of known substances a little off-centre, as in a dream, and yet wonderfully solid. The figure is removed, and unaware. This is presumably part of the meaning, enigmatic as Beckett's boy-messengers in *Waiting for Godot*. The fabrication is of the same order as the night-sky passage already discussed. One last suggestion: we find the fairy boy arising from the nightmare of absurd perversions and obscenities as the Child Apparitions rise from the equally absurd hell-broth of the cauldron in *Macbeth*. The seraphic is shown as conditioned by, and flowering from, the obscenities. The relation we have been suggesting (p. 30) is, if not explained, quite wonderfully dramatized.

Joyce's deployment conforms to a usual dramatic opposition of troubled protagonist, trammelled in evils, confronted by some seraphic appearance that brings light. A fine example comes in Philip Massinger and Thomas Dekker's *The Virgin Martyr*, when

---

[1] These are natural 'spirit' colours. Compare Nietzsche's supreme vision in *Thus Spake Zarathustra* (III. 14) of the 'Golden Wonder' with around it 'whatsoever hath light miraculous feet that can run on violet-blue paths'.

the persecutor Theophilus is shown Paradise by the 'delicate' page-boy Angelo, who is really an angel in disguise:

> It is, it is, some angel! Vanished again!
> Oh, come back, ravishing boy! Bright messenger!
> Thou hast, by these mine eyes fixed on thy beauty,
> Illumined all my soul.
>
> (V. i)

Such contrasts occur continually in British drama from Shakespeare's day to our own.

The basic contrast goes back to Plato. The protagonist may be a seer, ugly like Socrates, and the setting educational, as so much of the Greek *paederastia* was; as, indeed, was the relation of Christ to John as disciple. Or we may have a troubled, part-evil dramatic hero, reflecting the author, and his perversions, as in *Ulysses*. Either way, life-worn maturity is nourished by the seraphic presence which, as Plato tells us, reflects the inward soul, or soul-quest, of the protagonist.

The balance is peculiarly clear today in the writings of John Cowper Powys. His many seers are ugly, often repellent, sometimes death-impregnated, as Uryen in *Maiden Castle*, the most impressive being Myrddin Wyllt (Merlin) in *Porius*; all these are reflections of Powys's sadistically tormented yet magian personality as described in the *Autobiography*. But there we have also strong homosexual and bisexual idealisms (*Autobiography*, VI. 206-7, IX. 406-10). Elsewhere we have the many youths noted in my study *The Saturnian Quest*: sometimes as simple boys, in *Wolf Solent* and *Weymouth Sands* (*Jobber Skald*); sometimes idealized, as in *Owen Glendower*; as seraphic visions, in *Rodmoor* and *Ducdame*; or as the young heroes of the final period (see pp. 164, 406 below). In *Rodmoor* and *Ducdame* the boy is the hero's son, like Joyce's Rudy; and it was so too, in Powys's own life, for his friendship with his son was unusually strong. Of his 'beautiful beloved son' Littleton, who became a Roman Catholic priest, Powys wrote to me, on 6 January 1957:[1]

There was never the faintest filial or paternal relation between us: we were simply devoted friends who *knew everything*, just *everything*, about each other's sexual peculiarities. We were like an elderly orator of the

---

[1] Powys's only son, Littleton Alfred, was born in 1902, and died at the age of 51. Llewelyn Powys admired him greatly: see Kenneth Hopkins, *The Powys Brothers*, 1967; 218. For Powys's letters to myself, see p. 161 below.

heathen days with some youth between whom there was not the faintest homosexual love but just deep and understanding comradeship.

Terms should not be too rigid; there probably was a 'parental' element in play, and we do well to admit a sexual element as normally constituent to the seraphic. Parental or educational feeling may often be present without any dilution of the magic.

The opposition of troubled maturity and idealized youth is a simulacrum, with a difference, of the normal sexual opposition, which it often replaces, with or without physical contact; at an extreme of idealism we have seer and youth as unities without contact and the 'complete bosom' untouched by Cupid's dart of the Duke in *Measure for Measure* (I. iii. 3; see *Byron and Shakespeare*, 58; also *The Mutual Flame*, 22-57, 'The Integration Pattern'). The seraphic ideal so fulfils the being that it attains integrity: this is the 'perfection' of the Phoenix poems in *Love's Martyr* (*The Mutual Flame*, 183-4).

We may sometimes find, either in literature or in life, the opposites of spiritual depth and physical charm coalescing to give us protagonist and youth, hero and seraph, in one magical person. This we find in Rupert Brooke and T. E. Lawrence, and again in Charles Lindbergh, whose solo Atlantic flight in 1927 won him an unprecedented acclaim.

Kenneth S. Davis, to whose biography *The Hero* (U.S.A. 1959; London 1960) my page references will refer, writes that Lindbergh 'was worshipped by his fellow countrymen as no other private individual, while yet contemporary with his worshippers, had ever been' (227). Unattracted by sex and society and given neither to tobacco nor drink he was obsessed, like T. E. Lawrence, with dangerous speeding on motor-cycles, which was 'wine to his spirit' (72), and with flying. At an early age he became an experienced airman, expert at public displays and dangerous stunts.

The challenge of the Atlantic gripped him. Danger always sharpened 'his every sensation and mental process' and the appeal was 'irresistible' (147). If death came, says his biographer, presumably reporting Lindbergh's own thoughts, he would know both it and life intensely; if it did not, he would be aware of life's meaning as only those can who risk its loss (148; cp. p. 322 below). His aeroplane, which he regarded nearly as a live being, he called the 'Spirit of St. Louis'.

He succeeded famously; but, as he himself recorded (p. 271 below), *only with the help of Spirits*, whose presences and voices when he was at the limit of exhaustion directed his navigation; and from then on he was aware of a spirit-world and of human survival.[1]

On his return 'the reception given him in Washington was probably greater than any given to a private citizen in all history until then' (231). Both for the flight and for his charm, his 'smile', 'slenderly boyish' appearance, 'voice' and 'modesty' (236), he became a public idol. Above all, his *youth* was emphasized:

Spirit was now firmly established as the key word of every public discussion of the flier and his flight. The *Spirit of St. Louis* had become the Spirit of Youth . . .   (217)

Popular songs and poems in vast numbers were composed in which he featured as angel, eagle, and sky-lover, one of them proclaiming: 'You are the answer . . . the riddle has ended' (238-240).

His was a peculiarly lonely and near-integrated personality, but he found a wife who had for long been fascinated by 'flight as a spiritual or aesthetic experience', had written of aeroplanes as 'silver birds', and had felt herself riding a unicorn with brightly polished hoofs (274). She became a co-pilot with him on flights of geographical research in which 'this cold-eyed young man' treated her as a 'masculine partner' (282). She wrote a book *Listen! the Wind*, called by a reviewer 'this story of two mortals bound by the whim of the uncontrollable wind' (330).

His fame he accepted mainly as a means to the advancement of aeronautics, but after a while he reacted strongly against it, and was disgusted with the attendant vulgarities (247). He grew to despise the masses. When his son was kidnapped and subsequently

---

[1] The passage on the Spirits in Lindbergh's hour-by-hour diary-account of the flight in *The Spirit of St. Louis* (1953) is most important and highly dramatic: 'There's no longer weight to my body, no longer hardness to the stick. The feeling of flesh is gone. I become independent of physical laws – of food, of shelter, of life. I'm almost one with these vaporlike forms behind me, less tangible than air, universal as aether. I'm still attached to life; they, not at all; but at any moment some thin band may snap and there'll be no difference between us.' He experiences past, present and future, 'here and in different places, all at once' (VI. 389-90). His biographer unfortunately omits all mention of what appears to have been the key-incident of Lindbergh's life.

found murdered, this nightmare, together with the new wave of cheap publicity, increased his scorn.

He had scientific interests and, being interested in the possibility of a 'mechanical heart' (339), was a close associate and partner of Alexis Carrel, a French doctor and sage whose mind (said Lindbergh) flashed 'between the logical world of science and the mystical world of God'. Together they envisaged the 'liberation' of men from the 'cosmos' of matter into a world 'beyond the frontiers of the body' (368). This new, vitalistic mystique, together with his experiences of mass vulgarity, attuned Lindbergh to sympathy with the rise of Nazi Germany. Roosevelt he had already had occasion to oppose, and when the Second World War started he was strong in his insistence that America should not become involved. He had for some time been suspected of using people's 'emotions' for his own purposes; his supposed dislike of publicity was, as was T. E. Lawrence's, disbelieved (266-70). More and more he was now regarded as dangerous, and his unpopularity increased (409). When America was drawn into the war he offered his services, which were rejected (416). But he worked indirectly and strenuously as a civilian in the testing and design of aircraft; and was sometimes even engaged actively against the Japanese (418-22). His contribution was, in fact, considerable. After the war he worked in various capacities for his country in so far as they would not involve any 'high and conspicuous public office', preferring quietude and anonymity (430), like T. E. Lawrence.

His home life was by the sea; in the early 1940s he spent much time in 'water and sun', and was a bold long-distance swimmer (406); and later engaged in skin-diving, whatever the cold, to which he seemed impervious (431). As he grew older he still looked young as though 'immune to the ravages of time' (431).

In its will to virility and vitalism the challenge of Nazi Germany has always deserved respect, and Lindbergh's support, at the time, was understandable; later he concluded that Germany had failed through a lack of Christianity (425-6). With Dr. Carrel he had been working for a fusion of science and Christianity; and also for the 'development of a superior type of human being' (423). Lindbergh believed simultaneously in higher and lower types of man, and in Christ: it was, says his biographer, 'as if the New Testament and *Thus Spake Zarathustra* presented to his mind the same ethical message' (426). My own *Christ and Nietzsche* took a similar course.

As for Hitler's Germany, my essay on Francis Berry (pp. 452-7 below) shows how subtle was the interplay of good and bad in the Nazi assertion. Lindbergh's reaction to the Hiroshima bomb and forecast of future dangers and alignments were sound (427). What he finally wanted was a world organization of overwhelming military might guided by Christian principles (425).

He was by nature, from youth, a lover of machines more than of people, again like T. E. Lawrence; but his flying was also impelled by his love of the expanses of earth, sea and sky (255). He had himself a 'machine-like efficiency' (251) and a 'granite-hard mind and will' (407). His only humour seems to have been in the exercise of practical jokes which, like Byron and T. E. Lawrence, he enjoyed (255, 270, 282); like these, and Wilde too, he was at ease with children (406). He planned everything, cautiously guarding against every contingency (412). With all this he was religious. His converse with the Spirits during his great flight proved fertile. He came to regard his life as a pilgrimage from 'scientific materialism' toward God. Man he saw as fragmented between emotion and intellect, externalism and inwardness, and only through religion could he be made whole. Relation to the natural world must be re-established. In our civilization, materialism has gone too far; scientific truths are partial and should be properly subordinate to those glimpses of the whole which the mystic experiences (428). If, as John Davidson once said, 'all convincing imagery is scientific truth' (*The Triumph of Mammon*, 1907; Epilogue, 160), Lindbergh's gospel is poetic. His story conforms to type: fame, severance, reversal, and a return to simplicities and the elements. This course we find, with variations, in Shakespeare's *Timon*, and in the lives of Byron, Wilde and T. E. Lawrence (for Wilde and the elements, see *Shakespeare and Religion*, 220). Lindbergh had the magic of those, and paid the price.

There is a natural tendency to find, or to imagine, a coalescence of hero and seraph, of strength and delicacy. Powys does it in his *Porius*, where the Emperor Arthur's strength is countered by a chin of 'almost feminine sensitivity' and a mouth with 'perfect curves' like that of the 'god Eros'. This lively 'master in the art of war' is said to have a *boy's* gaiety and 'smile' above the *feminine* chin. Danger merely arouses his good spirits, but in a military crisis he becomes wholly concentrated and acts with a seemingly 'infallible' and 'automatic' instinct (XVII. 356-8). What Powys is doing is this. Elsewhere, his men of power and seraphic youths are clearly differentiated; his protagonists are not themselves seraphic; but here in a book crammed with his *own* very different favourite powers, including Myrddin Wyllt as magus, he has to show us – once at least – the well-known Arthur, and gives us this thumb-nail sketch showing him, by a brilliant stroke of historical intuition, as *just the kind of man who would have become legendary*. He accordingly delineates him on the analogy of a Byron, or, more exactly, a T. E. Lawrence.

Another fascinating example appears in Randolph Stow's *Tourmaline* (1963). A mysterious young water-diviner, Michael, arrives at a remote Australian town and functions simultaneously as a diviner and as a prophet awaking religious perceptions. He is associated variously with Christ, Lucifer and a possible criminal record (174, 219, 206; for good and evil, 185). He is angelic, dressed in blue shirt and trousers (162, 191, 214; and see 167); his hair gleams (167, 215), making a 'halo' or 'aureole' (162, 196); he is 'blue and golden' (157, 173). He has 'dreadful eyes' of a unique colour (191, 213; see also 219, 221). Through his divining rod works a spirit-power (166) and he has a 'shaman's voice' (166). In him youth and power are blended:

He was simpler, more innocent than ever; a solemn boy, indeed. But with this went such fierceness, such coldness of conviction, that the diviner we had first known looked pale by comparison, a faint shadow thrown in advance of the man who had now arrived. (162-3)

That might have been written of T. E. Lawrence.

By the Church's altar we are aware of 'the flame of him' and 'the blaze of his yearning' (187). But though he is dazzling and brings love and faith to the little community, he can seem also 'a great hater', with a 'ferocious pride' (192-3), though the pride is one with his 'yearning' (214). Like T. E. Lawrence, he can be suspected of being a fraud till suddenly his 'brightness' and 'force' are 'beyond resisting' (205). If he had indeed been a criminal he had been one 'of quite extraordinary distinction' (206). Like Lawrence, his contact with others can be suddenly 'turned off', as an electric current (215; cp. p. 338 below). Like Lawrence, he bears a scar on his body (191). He knows that others are not his 'equal' (216).

At the crucial test his divining fails; he is, as it were, deflated.

But all the points have been made. Shaw's Joan first succeeds and then fails; in Masefield's *Multitude and Solitude* and *Lost Endeavour* the spirit-guided quest proves ineffectual. Such failures merely reflect the human situation, the disparity, in a world at present out of alignment with the greater powers. The 'common-sense' or 'moral' framework of such artistic excursions must never be allowed to blunt their central impact. One who had not believed all Michael's claims, on being asked why he had followed him replies: 'He was there. That's all' (211).

That a craving for superlative and sometimes beautiful persons of magical power exists is clear: it beats within all epic, drama, legend and religion; it is as central to Christianity as to Nietzsche. Today our heroes or supermen-approximations will not be saints: they will have religious or other spiritual elements but also, as poetic incarnations – for they and poetry are interdependent – they will have worldly attributes and powers. Michael in *Tourmaline* is a practical water-diviner before appearing as a prophet; mechanic skills, airmanship and spiritual force were combined to make Lindbergh. Powys's Arthur is a famous warrior and king. By such personalities we are being drawn towards the fusion of body and soul, state and church, to Nietzsche's Arthurian dream of 'Roman Caesars with the soul of Christ' (*The Will to Power*, 983).

Since our twentieth century finds the spiritual categories hard to accept, it has chosen for a dominating superman-dream one who claims to rely entirely on intellect and logic: Sherlock Holmes, in the stories by Sir Arthur Conan Doyle. These appeared from 1887 to 1927.

Holmes seems to exercise uncanny forms of thought-reading. He can follow Dr. Watson's thoughts and suddenly spring a question that amazes; then he proceeds to show how it was all simple deduction (*The Resident Patient*; *The Dancing Men*). Again, he can deduce from a simple object both its own past and the character of its owner (e.g., at the opening of *The Hound of the Baskervilles*; also *The Sign of Four*, I). These two practices correspond respectively to (i) telepathy and (ii) psychometry, though they turn out to have normal explanations. They are constructed along the lines of what a sceptic might suggest in order to show that a telepathic or psychometrical success was rationally explainable. Sometimes Watson, after hearing Holmes's explanation, agrees that it was all simple; or else he may still be deeply impressed. In reading we derive pleasure from a dual sense of uncanny power and rational explanation.

Holmes regularly insists that his methods are logical; yet the faculty used is not all simple. It is discussed in two chapters, both called 'The Science of Deduction', in *A Study in Scarlet* and *The Sign of Four*. Though he is always drawing on vast stores of knowledge for his purpose, he can only do this by having for long deliberately rejected from his mind all knowledge which is certain to be irrelevant; so that on some obvious questions he seems childishly ignorant. He admits to using 'a kind of intuition'; or steps of reasoning pass so quickly that he is immediately aware, like a computer, of the result; it may be easier for him to 'know' than to 'explain' (*A Study in Scarlet*, I, II). The powers are of the same order as those I once discussed in relation to chess-mastery (*The Christian Renaissance*, I). Holmes's speeding mentality abhors 'the dull routine of existence', and he takes cocaine, which he finds 'transcendently stimulating and clarifying to the mind' when it has no task to engage it (*The Sign of Four*, I). Speed is a key-concept: Watson's mental 'slowness' contrasts with the speed of Holmes's 'flame-like intuitions and impressions' (*The Adventure of the Creeping Man*). We may recall Shakespeare's regular use of 'swift' thought to designate intuitions and emotions (*The Sovereign Flower*, General Index, B, VI, 'Swift Thought'; *Shakespeare and Religion*, 324-7, 'Shakespeare and Bergson'). On one occasion Holmes is aware of something deep in his mind which he needs; thought of a certain book arises 'like a flash'; though all is still 'vague', he turns up the book, which points to a possible, though as yet uncertain, solution, which eventually proves correct (*The Lion's Mane*). This is not all logic: it is nearer what we call a 'hunch', or inspiration. When at work on a difficult problem Holmes smokes heavily all night, searching in his mind for the solution (*The Man with the Twisted Lip*). In action his eyes gleam as a 'bird's'; in motion he is 'swift, silent and furtive' like a bloodhound on the scent (*The Sign of Four*, VI).

Mediums have often been called in to help the police, and Holmes can on occasion act like a medium, as in *The Valley of Fear* (VI):

I shall sit in that room and see if its atmosphere brings me inspiration. I'm a believer in the *genius loci*. You smile, friend Watson. Well, we shall see.

He reads up the history of the house to bring him 'in conscious sympathy' with the place's 'historical atmosphere' (7). Holmes is, in fact, a composite of many skills both rational and super-rational.

He has limitations. He is so unresponsive to feminine charm that Watson calls him inhuman, an 'automaton' (*The Sign of Four*, II); but he can also show an unsuspected feeling (*The Veiled Lodger*). He is happier with Watson, or with his following of street-boys, the 'Baker Street Irregulars' (*The Sign of Four*, VIII). He likes best being with inferiors who recognize his mastery. He has vanity, and his 'proud, self-contained nature' can be un-generous in acknowledgment (*The Sussex Vampire*). These are the natural failings of his kind. His powers are frightening and one wonders 'what a terrible criminal he would have made', had he so chosen (*The Sign of Four*, VI). However, he is on the side of the angels, and all blemishes are slight compared with the beneficent powers radiated. One respects his unswerving devotion: like a mystic he sometimes fasts 'because the faculties become refined when you starve them'; he is a 'brain', and the rest a mere appendix (*The Mazarin Stone*). But there is really more than that. He has physical prowess, being 'an expert singlestick player, boxer, and swordsman', and, though he neglects literature and philosophy, he is an accomplished violinist, playing improvised tunes, grave or gay, to aid his thoughts (*A Study in Scarlet*, II; *The Sign of Four*, VIII). This is a pointer:

I left Holmes seated in front of the smouldering fire, and long into the watches of the night I heard the low, melancholy wailings of his violin, and knew that he was still pondering over the strange problem which he had set himself to unravel.

(*A Study in Scarlet*, V)

Even when he plays a well-known piece, it is 'that most haunting of tunes' (*The Mazarin Stone*). Visits to concerts are among his main interests. He believes Darwin's theory that music antedated speech and now awakes 'vague memories in our souls of those misty centuries when the world was in its childhood' (*A Study in Scarlet*, V).

Though he has no specifically 'seraphic' attributes in appearance or emotion – for the Seraphs were love-powers – he has strong spiritual and artistic qualities.

He is to be ranked among the 'great artists' (*The Problem of Thor*

Bridge). His powers came not only, we are told, from self-training; 'art' is in his 'blood', descending from an artistic ancestry (*The Greek Interpreter*). He is called a 'genius':

His pale, eager face had suddenly assumed that tense, far-away expression which I had learned to associate with the supreme manifestations of his genius.

(The Problem of Thor Bridge)

His eyes seem to see beyond normal horizons (*A Study in Scarlet*, II, III). 'You seem to have powers that are hardly human' comes naturally (*The Priory School*); he is called a 'wizard' (*The Adventure of the Blanched Soldier*); and these two thoughts occur together (*The Abbey Grange*). He 'seems to have powers of magic' (*The Sussex Vampire*). When his absence over a number of years has to be accounted for, we hear that his visits have included Tibet and Mecca (*The Empty House* in the collection *The Return of Sherlock Holmes*).

We are clearly being given more than a series of lessons in observation and logic. Dr. Watson and Inspector Lestrade represent professional norms which Holmes transcends. He can be simultaneously stern and merciful: in compounding a felony, he may be 'saving a soul' (*The Blue Carbuncle*). Holmes is conceived as a superman, in act and wisdom. That is why these stories so tower over other detective novels, which may have as good or better plots, but are not aiming at anything of the kind. Why then does Conan Doyle go to such pains to make Holmes insist so often on the rationality of his methods? This is certainly as germane to our enjoyment as his aura of wizardry.

Heroes and supermen are often disturbing. Holmes, however, functions in a moral society as the defender of the state and of morality and good sense; though, when circumstances demand it, he makes his own judgements and is ready to act, for good, against the law. For the most part an atmosphere of cosiness and settled life in the London of his time soothes us; and as part of this general presentation Holmes's powers are shown as rational, and to that extent safe. Nevertheless, the two categories, rational and magical, must both be present, for without both there would be no poetic radiations. *The Hound of the Baskervilles* is probably the most famed and successful of the stories because (i) we have a strong element of the supernatural which (ii) Holmes traces to a human cause. The dark hinterland of our existence becomes, with Holmes as guide, safe.

We can now return to our start. When Holmes explains his apparent clairvoyance and psychometry, his explanations are not wholly convincing; each link of the chain is too hazardous for that, and we have to make a goodly allowance for fictional licence. We are not, in effect, so very far from Shaw's Joan: 'Well, I have to find reasons for you, because you do not believe in my voices. But the voices come first; and I find the reasons after: whatever you may choose to believe' (*Saint Joan*, V). As we have seen, Holmes's own thinking is often intuitive and may be difficult to explain. To go a little farther: I am arguing throughout this essay that literary art aims to bring the mysteries near to us. Conan Doyle devoted the later years of his life to Spiritualism, and was a fervent propagandist. But we cannot at all easily *understand* the powers of mediums and miracle workers, the claims of religious mystics, nor our own future survival (of which there is nevertheless abundant evidence) of death. What if, following the Duke's words in *Measure for Measure* (which itself follows Matthew, X. 26),

Put not yourself into amazement how these things should be: all difficulties are but easy when they are known

(IV. ii. 219)

it should turn out that the answers, when known, will be as rationally simple as Holmes's explanations? Perhaps a distant recognition of this is part of our pleasure; and this is why Holmes exerts so enduring an appeal.

6

The themes we are discussing do not apply only to great individuals; these are rather to be felt as peaks rising from a general tendency. Poetry and poetic personalities serve to link earth to higher spheres.

Ours is an age of science and mechanization. Space-travel was adumbrated by Shelley's *Queen Mab* and Byron's *Cain*; much was forecast by Mary Shelley's *Frankenstein*; and we watch a steady actualization of the various possibilities heralded by Jules Verne and H. G. Wells. Science, as Robin Skelton in *The Poetic Pattern* (59) reminds us, itself grew, like poetry, from magic and ritual. But a divergence is obvious. Day-Lewis in *A Hope for Poetry* (1944 edn., 30) wrote well of this divergence:

Poetry was born from magic, and science is the great enemy of magic: for magic is the personal interpretation of the universe; science, the impersonal rationalization. So it would seem that in a 'scientific' age the flower of poetry must wither. Yet it need not be so. As a magician can prevail against a rival witch-doctor by getting possession of some hair from his head or a few of his toe-nails, vehicles by which the rival influence may pass into the control of his own spirit, so it is possible for poetry to steal the thunder of science, to absorb these trivial business incantations and turn them to its own uses.

Commenting (62) on this passage Robin Skelton considers how far it has been possible for Auden, Day-Lewis, Spender and MacNeice to succeed in this endeavour.

The opposition may be stark. 'Can the poet', writes Bonamy Dobrée in *The Broken Cistern* (1954; 87), 'by making a public theme of science, foster the imagination which alone can make our knowledge something by which we essentially live?' That, he says, is 'the fundamental question'.[1]

Science and imagination, so often at enmity, may come together in terms of speed and aerial adventure.

In *The Short Stories of H. G. Wells* (in one volume, 1927 etc.), those on aeronautics are well-known; and so is 'The Time Machine', on time-travel. Others more precisely 'psychic' have been neglected. 'Under the Knife' blends an anaesthetic, out-of-the-body experience with space-travel through the stellar cosmos:

My perceptions were sharper and swifter than they had ever been in life; my thoughts rushed through my mind with incredible swiftness, but with perfect definition. I can only compare their crowded clarity to the effects of a reasonable dose of opium.

Wells uses semi-scientific fantasy to investigate spiritualistic fact. 'The Truth about Pyecraft' amusingly handles levitation; 'The Remarkable Case of Davidson's Eyes' describes a case of – if I may coin the word – 'tele-clairvoyance'; 'The Door in the Wall' is on

[1] Both in *The Broken Cistern* and *English Literature in the Early Eighteenth Century* (1959) Bonamy Dobrée has shown how effectively poetry at first responded to the findings of Newtonian science. The stimulus gradually failed.

the insights of childhood and university-age youth in relation to death; in 'The Plattner Story' an explosion opens out a new dimension wherein the dead are seen watching and worrying about our lives on earth; and 'The Last Trump' satirizes our imperviousness to vision.

Speed corresponds to psychic speed and that to the swifter vibrations of higher spheres (see p. 59 above, Shakespeare's 'swift thought'; also on T. E. Lawrence pp. 336-7). Of air-adventures there is much to say. Many examples suggest that, following H. G. Wells, we should make no final distinction between the aerial and the spiritual: Lindbergh conversed with spirits over the Atlantic. Birds and spirits are often correlative: Aristophanes' birds in *The Birds* may be understood as spirit-beings (*The Golden Labyrinth*, 16); and birds in Shakespeare are continually so used (*The Shakespearian Tempest*, Appendix A, 'The Shakespearian Aviary'). The name 'Ariel' is a pointer. The great imaginative precursors, or prophets, of our speed-intoxicated, air-minded and space-minded, age were T. E. Lawrence and Charles Lindbergh.

In W. H. Auden's *The Orators* (II) the Airman, brilliantly snap-shotted in the phrase 'Laughter in leather', is a personification of enlightened activity. Our present poet laureate, C. Day-Lewis, has written of heroic flight in his narrative *A Time to Dance*, 'In Memory of L. P. Hedges' (1935); and 'Flight to Italy' in *An Italian Visit* (1953) has extended passages on clouds, mountains and earth of vivid aerial description; together with relevant associations of 'clairvoyance', 'crystal', 'ghosts' and a contrast of aero-plane-as-'angel' with the danger of mountains-as-'Calibans'. Else-where mountains are themselves natural spirit-powers, as in *The Magnetic Mountain* (1933):

> Somewhere beyond the railheads
> Of reason, south or north,
> Lies a magnetic mountain
> Riveting sky to earth.

(Part 1, iii)

The move from Masefield's idealization of ships to the concentration on aeronautics in T. E. Lawrence, Lindbergh, Auden and Day-Lewis, registers a necessary shift in consciousness, and space-travel will do still more. These adventures have not only psychological effects; they are metaphysically meaningful too. They are shaping our future, impelled from within:

> A hungry soul
> Urged them to try new air-routes, and their skill
> Raftered the sky with steel. . . . .
>
> (Epilogue, *A Time to Dance*)

Aeroplanes today fuse the spirit-attributes traditionally held by (i) birds and (ii) ships. Gillian Grimwood has a fine sonnet entitled 'Trident'.[1]

> From London lift to windward delta-winged
> Through corridors of cloud to open blue;
> On climb from cumulus and out of view,
> A silhouette in silence silver-ringed,
> She heads for France, relentlessly to hold
> High path for Paris and the Alpes afar,
> By Moulins, Vichy and Montélimar,
> And south to sun beyond the Isles of Gold.
>
> And where the blue-green glide, the azure stream,
> Slow sweeps the Esterel from Saint-Tropez,
> Low to the water's edge across the bay
> She thunders down the sky, her journey done,
> Where white and gold the airport buildings gleam,
> And runway ribbons silver in the sun.

Another, 'Comet', compares its subject to (i) a swan and (ii) an archangel. The associations come naturally. Such men as T. E. Lawrence and Lindbergh and such poets as Auden and Day-Lewis accept the machine-age; they are its prophets; they feel it as not only air-borne but as spirit-born. Once again we do well – T. E. Lawrence's well-known lines (p. 336 below) were a pointer – to make no final distinction between such categories as air, ether, space, spirit (for ether see p. 409 below). As Jung has suggested, the Flying Saucers, whatever they may be, function as a necessary filling of a vacuum in our earth-bound existence; they link aerial science to the spiritualistic.

As for modern Spiritualism itself, this great movement crowns

---

[1] This sonnet, which has not been published, is quoted by kind permission of the author.

centuries of human experience and literature in full consciousness, considered deployment, and careful organization. Despite inertia in church and universities, Spiritualism, being based on experiences known from the ancients onwards,[1] and active today, must prevail. It already prevails: in its myriad churches and other centres throughout the world, its authoritative trance-addresses,[2] its accumulation of books and vigorous periodicals. For public evidence – since today nothing either secular or religious is safe without publicity, the day of suffering Christs being past – I would point to the annual autumn ceremonial at the Albert Hall; and when that is regularly televised, as it soon may be, new powers will be injected into our directionless and paralysed society.

It is no chance that the list of Honorary Vice-Presidents of the Spiritualist Association of Great Britain should include names of distinction from the Services; response is far easier there, from men of action who face death, than from the intelligentsia. Nor is it by chance that one of Spiritualism's finest propagandists has been the great Lord Dowding, Master of the Battle of Britain.[3]

Following T. E. Lawrence and Charles Lindbergh, we are obsessed with speed on the roads and adventures in air and space. We are also volatile in act and thought. Our minds, like that of Sherlock Holmes, are ever-active, and often over-active. We are being forced to live among the higher vibrations, and finding this hard, become neurotic, take drugs, make war. However high our aims, we remain earth-bound and clogged. Day-Lewis puts it well at the opening of *The Magnetic Mountain*:

> Now to be with you, elate, unshared,
> My kestrel joy, O hoverer in wind,
> Over the quarry furiously at rest
> Chaired on shoulders of shouting wind.

[1] See, on the death-beliefs of the ancient world, W. F. Jackson Knight, *Elysion*, 1970.

[2] By 'trance-addresses' I mean sermons from spirit-personalities spoken by mediums in trance. These are frequent in Spiritualist churches and may be deeply impressive. Many such addresses have been published: e.g., *Guidance from Silver Birch*, ed. Anne Dooley, Psychic Press. But the full power and authenticity of the greater Spirit Guides cannot always be received from the written word; one needs to hear them, and see the gestures.

[3] See Basil Collier, *Leader of the Few*, 1957; the authorized biography of Air Chief Marshal the Lord Dowding of Bentley Priory, G.C.B., G.C.V.O., C.M.G. Also, now, Robert Wright, *Dowding and The Battle of Britain*, 1969.

> Where's that unique one, wind and wing married,
> Aloft in contact of earth and ether;
> Feathery my comet, Oh too often
> From heav'n harried by carrion cares.

The kestrel preserves stillness within the wind's motion (compare Eliot's 'Teach us to sit still' in *Ash-Wednesday*, I). 'Carrion cares' is exact, for this is exactly what trammels us: our ailing bodies and our sense of death.

Never was man more distraught by fears. His main fear is now not fear of externals, but, as I wrote in *Hiroshima*, directly after the dropping of the atomic bomb, fear of himself. When in the 1930s I was writing on the importance of Powys's investigations of the sadistic instinct, some of my friends thought that I was wasting time on irrelevant perversions. The word 'sadistic' was little used then, and sounded unrespectable, if not phoney. Today sadism is on everyone's lips as a conscious obsession; and in drama, television and journalism. Recent poetry concentrates on a murderous centrality:

> By blood we live, the hot, the cold,
> To ravage and redeem the world:
> There is no bloodless myth will hold.

That is from Geoffrey Hill's 'Genesis' (*For the Unfallen*, 1959). George MacBeth's poetry is tormented by blood-horrors ranging throughout creation and fixed in man. Nor do we know what to do about it, for the excellent reason that we are, in the depths, as much, or almost as much, in favour of it as against it. It seems to be rooted, for many, in sexual instinct, and so all but ineradicable. With sadism we may group the many less dangerous obscenities that have gushed within our permissive society, from Henry Miller to Genet.

Sexual functioning, though physical, is also psychic: it acts at the meeting-point of the two, where body and spirit touch. Here something goes wrong; perhaps because we make too sharp a distinction between body and spirit. We reject sexually located enjoyments on moral grounds while being driven on by them; perhaps only from some new recognition and acceptance, even of the worst, including the sadisms, shall we break free. To such problems I shall apply an extended analysis in writing of Powys (pp. 156-227 below).

Sometimes we pretend to believe only in materiality – whatever that may be, for scientists are today dematerializing it before our eyes. Nevertheless for practical purposes we can still say that we are in a belief-world of what is called 'materialism', and simultaneously ill-at-ease with our 'bodies'. Modern sculpture is an interesting symptom: apart from certain nightmarish forms which may be related to the horrors of vivisectional experiments, such as the Monster in Powys's *Up and Out*, or even to future growths conditioned by hydrogen bombs, we can clearly detect, in this most material of the arts, an excessive emphasis on bodily mass and physical process. Epstein's 'Genesis' is a typifying example.

Henry Moore's recent sculptures relate human forms to tunnelled stone-formations, and perhaps roots. The smooth surfaces please; stone, as stone, is honoured and vitalized while transmitting a mystique of the inanimate such as that favoured by Wordsworth, Hugh MacDiarmid, Robinson Jeffers and Powys; a mystique which may be supposed symbolized by the Christian doctrine of the 'real presence' housed within the material elements at Mass or Communion; for we often do well to *expand* Church dogma into universal meaning.

Jung, writing of alchemy in *The Integration of the Personality*, discusses the spiritual element believed to be dormant in stone or metal, awaiting release (228):

It is not man who is in need of redemption, but matter, in which the divine soul is imprisoned in a sleeping and confined condition. Matter, which contains the divine mystery, is everywhere, and also in the human body. It is easily had, and is found everywhere – even in the most horrible filth.
(237)

The earth is not dead, but has 'life and soul' (245). The sculptor often feels, we may suppose, or anyway expresses, some such truths as these; as Browning recognizes in *Pippa Passes* (p. 248 below).

Our writers assert a new interdependence and reciprocity between man and the 'inanimate'; sculpture today attempts to realize that relation. We might however reasonably complain that modern sculpture shows a predominance of mass and materiality with a correspondent slighting of mental and spiritual categories.[1]

---

[1] I write from little knowledge of modern sculpture, but what impressions I have received are so germane to my present purpose that I may be forgiven for recording them.

Henry Moore's small and uninteresting heads contrast with his vast reclining bodies. Is this saying that man is *primarily* mass and inertia? If so, this is surely false: he is at the lowest a complex of obscene lusts and sadistic excess, a living nightmare; all these are energetic, electric, sex-activated and impelled either by spirits or by demons. Man is simultaneously earth-bound and air-borne. The visual arts are necessarily involved in materiality, but they should not be clogged by it. Their highest achievement will be to identify body with soul, solidity with grace, nature with rondure; a result perfectly achieved in Valentine Dobrée's painting 'Virgin and Child'. Such a balance is rarely struck.

Our visual arts show little or no use of seraphic grace and mobility to counter our sense of mass. Ariel-figures, Eros-figures, have for long been out of fashion: Epstein's 'Rima' was a significantly disturbing interpretation of W. H. Hudson's girl-spirit in *Green Mansions*. When thinness is attempted, we are as likely as not to have sickeningly elongated statuettes. Our plastic and visual arts appear to be quite un-at-home with seraphic grace. The symptom is interesting. We cannot say that we have no sense of it, since it may be vivid on the stage, in photography, cinema, and television, as well as in literature. We have noticed how the obscenities of the Nighttown episode in Joyce's *Ulysses* lead to, and perhaps themselves create, the vision of the fairy boy, Rudy; and how Powys's sequence of massively cumbrous and ugly seers is balanced against his equally insistent intuition of seraphic youth.

Another sculptor, Michael Ayrton, can help our enquiry. Ayrton has for long been obsessed by the Cretan myth of Daedalus and Icarus. He has treated it in sculpture, drawings, and writing. His sculptured figures concentrate on the heavily material, with weighty bodies and weak legs, variously in labour or under stress, as with his Minotaur, or Bull-Man, labouring to attain humanity, and a prophetess seeming to labour for speech; whether through the subhuman or the superhuman, there is labour for ascent. Ayrton also has drawings of the body distorted by stress in flight, as in an aeroplane or space-travel.

He has written two books on the Daedalus myth: *The Testament of Daedalus* (1962) and its expansion into *The Maze Maker* (1967). I shall quote from the first, and shorter, work, which is more relevant to my present purpose. The myth interests Ayrton because it illustrates so well the contrast of mass and flight, or body and spirit.

Daedalus, the narrator, is an able technician, a master with stones and metals, his arts being meticulously described; but he is no visionary. To escape from King Minos' maze he constructs wings for himself and his son Icarus. Daedalus personifies *our technological age*, making engines for flight; Icarus, again with modern implications, aspires too high, like Goethe's Euphorion (=Byron) in *Faust*, challenges the Sun, and burns himself.

Daedalus' skills have been indirectly responsible for the birth, from an unnatural union of King Minos' wife with a Sacred Bull, of the Minotaur, which has been shut up 'in the centre of night, within a maze, divorced even from moonlight' (33); like all such obscenities, or obscene imaginings, it must be hidden. It represents the pervertedly bestial within man.

Icarus is conceived as a 'hero'. He aspires to union with the Sun-god at the cost of death. 'Mazed in the dark', he rejects his stone prison and the Minotaur's 'maze of sleep', feels himself 'growing' beyond the 'monstrous', and is instead being 'hatched' into a 'griffon'. Clever though his father be, he could not, says Icarus, 'make a kestrel's egg'. He thinks Daedalus a murderer and believes him to be the father of the Minotaur (21-3). Icarus signifies the youth revolt of a new generation, despising the old. He is proud: though formerly 'reptile-wrought', he is no longer a 'lizard', but has now a 'high-born state in feathered fury' (26).

Such heroic aspirations and speculations are to Daedalus all rather pointless. He is 'baffled by heroes'. They are disorderly, he himself orderly; but he admits that he is 'insensitive' and knows that 'there is a kind of stupidity buried' in such 'intelligence' as his own (34). Nevertheless the Sun-challenge of Icarus, 'a boy dressed as a bird' (37), seems to him very silly. 'Poets and prophets being madmen are all unmanageable forces'. He himself is no 'hero' but prefers to make what is useful without being 'beset by my own personality' (41). He cannot see that there is any 'philosophy', any metaphysical or spiritual achievement, 'to be whittled out of flight' (46). Even so he realizes that Icarus was, when aspiring to Sun-union, able somehow to draw on 'death' to infuse the fabricated wings with more life drawn *from himself* than any mechanic skill had given them, and so ascend higher than his father intended (47). Daedalus could make 'magic' from the

inanimate, by his art; but Icarus somehow 'touched himself alive
with death and this was his creation'. He reverses all normal
science, technology and art; some new personal and spiritual
'factor' comes in (48).

At the climax, Icarus 'joined the god'. 'His moving mass
changed its form'; his body was expanded and its disordered and
fractured limbs 'became the vectors of an energy beyond mortal
strength'; the prisoning body-cage infuses the wings, 'descent'
being suddenly equated with 'ascent'; negatives and positives join.
Meanwhile the wings make a 'bowl' in which 'the duration of his
flight was contained like a liquid'. Speed in time becomes spatial;
the changes are instantaneous. Icarus is simultaneously 'compact'
yet 'spread across the sky'. At this instant he caps the evolutionary
process of embryo, fish, lizard, and bird, while 'disintegration' is
one with 'the impulse towards birth' (48-9).

This striking passage may be compared with passages of Masefield and T. E. Lawrence in which new life springs from bodily
disruption (pp. 287, 326 below). Ayrton strives to define the birth
of some higher state from physical death in terms of flight, speed,
and the crushing together of time and space. Without use of
words such as 'soul' or 'spirit', analysis can go no further. The
main emphasis is on the timeless and the spatial. It is brilliantly
done. Somehow a super-being is made. This Daedalus recognizes:

The shape of flight itself embraced him and his humanity took on
another shape. It was not of the order of my own.   (49)

The relation of speed and flight to some higher state of being
follows T. E. Lawrence (p. 336 below).

Though Icarus is not too happy, at least at first, plunged in
darkness, and crying that his god is lost to him, Daedalus'
comments are more reassuring: 'He was a hero and these people
I distrust and avoid, but to be a hero one must conquer death.
That is the sole function of heroes. I think that Icarus conquered
death'. His fame anyway survived (53-4). Daedalus also had
spiritualistic experience of his son's survival: 'I could not think
him dead. I felt too that in some way, falling out of the sky, he
had returned to me and come to love me and I could find no
sensible reason why this should be' (54).[1]

[1] Such experiences are fairly normal. A beautiful record exists in Jon Silkin's
poem 'The Child' (in *Nature with Man*, 1965).

Icarus' voice, sometimes telepathically, interpenetrates, in poetry, Daedalus' prose narrative. The whole is to this extent spiritualistically planned. In death the voice is a spirit-voice. 'He speaks', says Daedalus, 'either in fragments or through me'. Icarus speaks in verse, but there are 'ambiguities', coming like 'this unreal sea-sound in the shell' (11). It is a sea-voice (11, 56). Daedalus can refer to his death, 'if death it was' (14), but the voice itself is in no doubt:

> I who was fish and lizard yet can prize
> The kestrel flying future loose from death,
> For Icarus there is no death to die.
>
> (58)

The darkness he defies, aspiring still:

> What death is there for me who died in flight?
>
> (59)

The spirit-voice is uncompromising in its statement of survival.

As in Graves's thoughts, the question is complicated by a pervading intuition of timelessness, which beats through the whole book. Daedalus is from the first insistent that it is not an *old* story, but an eternal one. 'If you must see this story in time', he says, we may think of Icarus fighting our two great wars from the air and 'spilling death on whole cities' (12); and there may be more inventions to come of remote control without the use of airmen (38).

This sense of timelessness relates to the problem of death. As we have seen, Icarus' tragic climax fused space and time. Later Daedalus, writing of the gods' powers of ubiquity, says:

To do this requires a simultaneity which is no problem to gods. It is a matter of time which is a circle and space which, like life, curls to bite its own tail. Death, it seems, follows the same pattern.

> (60)

As Icarus puts it:

> Time curves across the arch and where it ties
> The slender strands of seasons, there is death
> Who knots them into mesh and makes them one.
>
> (58)

We may compare Nietzsche's 'The thirst of the Ring is within you: for every ring striveth and turneth about that it may reach itself again' (*Thus Spake Zarathustra*, II. 5); and Eliot in *Four Quartets* (p. 174 below).

As I suggested when discussing Graves, we may respond, though with this reservation: the timeless dimension, though it may be felt, cannot for long be thought; and within our day-to-day thinking the concept of survival in time, as I noticed in my *Adelphi* article (p. 28 above), may be a necessity. Either that, or some empowered spatial symbolism.

Ayrton adds a postscript underlining his book's contemporary relevance and relating it to his 'passion for early aeronautics' and 'recurring dreams of flight'; like Graves and Rupert Brooke he looks back to boyhood (65). He refers to his service in the Air Force, and to recent cosmonauts. His 'vital problem', he says, was 'the time-stopped climax' of Icarus' flight. He points to his designs, but admits that no artistry can match 'what I *know* Daedalus saw happen' (68). That is likely enough, but one might complain that the earlier drawings of Icarus, following the prevailing manner of contemporary art, do not adequately express his youth ('a boy dressed as a bird', 37); after all, he is pre-eminently a *young* hero, and an opportunity appears to have been missed. Ayrton sees himself as in the main an artist-workman, like Daedalus: he says that he would like to be free of Icarus, and concentrate on his craft. The artist is a 'maker' trying to understand man: 'Perhaps he also hopes to extend man's experience of himself – by strapping some kind of wings on him – but this would be a fortunate chance and is not the crux of the matter' (70).

The Daedalus myth is obviously appropriate to our time of astronauts and aspiration. Horatio Colony's 'The Flight and Fall of Icaros' in *The Flying Ones* (poems of flight, Boston, 1964) blends mythical fancy with sharp detail. Aerial views of earth and sea are exact. Air-flight is at one point compared with astral travel in dream. Especially gripping is the boy's craving for the Sun-world:

> And Icaros loves these gauds
> And figures and flames
> And golden games
> And tricks and frauds.

He loves the smithy, unlike his father's, of 'bright sky-stuff', he responds to the Sun's 'hot coquetry'. But his supports are melted and he falls, 'his wings turned trash', in flames. The boy's youth is emphatic; he is a very real boy; and the end is tragic.

Graves and Ayrton emphasize both youth and the timeless dimension; and so, in his own fashion, does Eugène Ionesco. In my article on recent drama 'The Kitchen Sink' (*Encounter* XXI. 6; December 1963; 51, 54) I drew attention to the spiritualistic elements in the structures of Jean-Paul Sartre's *Huis Clos* and Arthur Miller's *Death of a Salesman*, where so much depends on the spirit-return of Uncle Ben. Of Samuel Beckett's *Waiting for Godot* I wrote:

At one point there are extended thoughts on the spirit-voices of the dead. Now the Boy who comes from Godot is clearly conceived in the age-old dramatic tradition, descending from Plato, in which some boy or youth represents, as I have shown throughout *The Golden Labyrinth*, some angel or spirit-link. That he, who looks after the goats, should not be beaten by Godot whereas his brother, who looks after the sheep, is, constitutes a neat comment on the ethical transvaluations for which the occult and Dionysian, or Faustian, powers of our dramatic tradition have for centuries been labouring.

The two boys' enigmatic quality reminds one of the inconclusive nature, on occasion, of certain spiritualistic communications.

That these three renowned dramas should be making spiritualistic contacts suggests that such contacts are related, perhaps intrinsic, to their eminence.

Ionesco is yet more interesting.[1] What is called 'the drama of the absurd', of which Ionesco is the foremost exponent, is a critique of our over-rationalist society. Its true function is provisional; from its topsy-turvydom new vision, like Rudy from the obscene phantasmagoria of *Ulysses*, may be born. In Ionesco's prefatory 'The Starting Point' (*Plays*, translated by Donald Watson, Vol. I, 1958) he says that his dramas are made from 'two fundamental states of consciousness', the one of solidities, in a 'stifling dungeon' of 'heavy forces'; the other of 'a spaceless universe made up of pure light and colour'. To Ionesco material objects in their myriad obtrusions become nightmare, and physical being a torment. The higher vision makes normality and all its ways absurd; and our

---

[1] For a general introduction, see Richard N. Coe, *Ionesco*, Writers and Critics Series, 1961.

sense of this absurdity is evidence that we have already 'gone a stage further'. To quote again from my *Encounter* essay (52):

In *Victims of Duty* we move from a kind of psycho-analysis, through converse with the dead by means of a good imitation of the 'direct voice' (since according to the author's first intention the Father's words are bodiless), to a mystical experience which includes levitation, and finally back to a mad torment of food-stuffing.

Exit the King, concentrating wholly on death, is as 'a composite of *Everyman*, *King Lear* and W. Y. Evan-Wentz's *The Tibetan Book of the Dead*' (*Encounter*, 54).

In his *Fragments of a Journal* (translated by Jean Stewart, 1968) Ionesco is obsessed on page after page with Death; the journal reads as a monologue on Death. His probing metaphysics leave nothing in human reason basically reliable, and death is the one great question.

Many dreams are recounted, and also moments of supreme vision regarded as outside time. Time oppresses him (11, 21-2), and space is baffling (32). In childhood he knew 'a golden age' with no sense of time and death (20-1, 40). Sometimes since then the world has been suddenly 'transformed', everything, indoors and out-of-doors, flooded with 'golden light' (39). He had a dream, too, similar in quality, of 'earth and heaven interpenetrating one another, feeding one another and feeding me myself with vital sap', so that he knew 'I belong elsewhere' (63). As a youth of eighteen he had felt his surroundings transfigured, 'unreality' and 'reality' were 'indissolubly interconnected', white houses grew 'whiter', all so amazingly *clean*, 'dissolved and yet reconstituted' by 'light'. Like Graves (p. 46 above) he 'knew everything' and 'learnt that man does not die' (68). Again, another such experience assures him that 'ignorance is the cause of our suffering, perhaps indeed the very substance of it'. He feels the marvel of the world, all 'rejuvenated' by his own sudden rejuvenation (96-7). Youth is an insistent concept.

The contrast of mass and materiality as against a buoyant translucency is in Ionesco driven to extremes. But somehow, he says, we need to see, or feel, the earthly and heavenly interpenetrating and interconnected (63, 70, 73, 104). We should learn to 'imagine things spatially, not temporally' (113). Both Graves and Ayrton were forced to a similar conclusion (pp. 48 and 71 above). So was

Powys, in whose later writing space assumes more and more importance in contrast to time: he even personifies it in the Space Monster of *All or Nothing* (see *The Saturnian Quest*, VIII, especially 111, on Kant). But perhaps, suggests Ionesco, we should break free from both conceptions (113), the thought corresponding to Powys's remark in *Mortal Strife* (VII. 113) that the meaning of death must remain hidden 'simply because Time and Space *get in the way*'. Ionesco is sure that so long as 'our immortality is not guaranteed' we shall continue to hate each other; for himself, he is inclined to believe in survival (104, 107; and see 70-1, 109). Once he fascinatingly argues that 'the ultimate *why*', though unanswerable, is as a 'blinding light', utterly, and beyond everything, fundamental (26-7). The 'Why?' is *itself the light*: as in Nietzsche's sense of power as 'the shining interrogative set against premature answers' (*Thus Spake Zarathustra*, III. 10). We must conclude that the central purpose of human existence is *to strive for the ultimate answer*, as in St. Paul's thought, awakened by the 'unknown god' of the Greeks, that men have been put on earth precisely in order to seek for God 'on the chance of finding him in their groping for him' (Acts, XVII. 27; James Moffatt's translation). Perhaps here we are close to the perennial appeal of detective stories: Holmes's mind has to be fed with either problems or drugs (*The Sign of Four*, I).[1] Instead of wondering disconsolately 'What is the purpose?' we should realize that that very question *is* our purpose. 'To have understood', says Ionesco, 'is to be fixed, immobilized' (27); Holmes is always craving a *new* problem. If all this is so, it seems that education, in the word's proper, which is the Socratic, meaning, is the key to human destiny.

Though he recognizes a 'magical element' in the art of a dramatist (17) and can write well on the complex meanings of literary creation (130), Ionesco puts no final trust in literary statements. He reacts coldly to Socrates' description of survival as *reported* in

---

[1] That detective fiction may house deep meanings has been suggested by John Wren-Lewis in his article 'The Cosmic Enemy' in *The Listener* of 18 May 1967. In Genesis the Fall was caused by the knowledge of good-and-evil; the true 'Cosmic Enemy' is the moral judgement; and this is taken to explain the unprecedented appeal of Agatha Christie's *The Mousetrap*, in which the detective turns out to be the criminal. The author's plea is for a new morality, in line with both the New Testament and psycho-analysis, by which humanity may learn to respect 'creativity and love' and repudiate the attempt 'to be as gods themselves, judging good and evil'.

Plato's *Phaedo* (25) and also to Rimbaud: 'I don't believe in his visions nor in any other literary visions'. Art brings only 'a tiny hint of illumination, swamped in garrulousness' (72). His attitude is not surprising, since visionaries regularly tend to discount all visions but their own. But he is really only rejecting second-hand *reports*. Talk of St. John of the Cross, Plotinus and the Neo-Platonists, and Moses' burning bush, is, he says, of little use: 'If one has not experienced this light, it remains a wretched, futile literary flicker' (70). That may be, but my own contribution is to assert, despite what I once wrote in *Atlantic Crossing* (IX. 301-2), that literary art can so act though the imagination that we experience, in terms reasonably close to ordinary existence, that very *interrelation* of the earthly and the heavenly for which, as we have seen, Ionesco craves. More: a mystical experience is transitory and might be distrusted, but what is experienced through the creative imagination exists for us independent of external evidence; for the imaginative act is itself a recognition and a ratification fuelled from the spark within to fuse divinity with fact. It is always saying, in the words of Shakespeare's Antony, 'I tell you that which you yourselves do know'.

Ionesco recounts an interesting psychic experience whereby through a nightmare of his own he was made to take on himself the recurrent suffering of what seems to have been an earth-bound ghost, or spirit, so that it was heard no more (109-10).

Perhaps his most important conclusion is: 'We should attain the state of mind of the Mexicans of old, for whom death was an occasion for rejoicing. The whole of humanity should be re-organized in this direction. . . . It's because we have staked everything on life that we are incapable of living' (143).

7

We need to listen in to the positive powers impinging on our present society from beyond. There are two primary powers: (i) spiritualistic and (ii) seraphic. The spiritualistic, together with air and space travel, we have discussed. We turn to the 'seraphic', which means the expression of spirit in human form; the link, through youth and youth-beauty, for a world, to use Ionesco's word, 'rejuvenated'.

Poetry and Magic

Our notes may be introduced by thought of John F. Kennedy. Rarely, if ever, has the seraphic hero also held high office. There is usually a divergence, and had Kennedy lived on, there might have been one. It is indeed usual, perhaps best, for seraphic figures, as such, to die young, and be celebrated in elegies. But it was Kennedy's lot to be honoured in a fine poem by G. S. Fraser entitled 'Instead of an Elegy', printed in *The Times Literary Supplement* of 5 December 1963:

> Bullets blot out the Life-Time smile,
> Apollo of the picture-page,
> Blunt-faced young lion. . . .

'Lion': for he had met a test demanding more than a Churchillian tenacity, the test of an appalling choice. We cannot expect that man's endurance of strife slowly up-building throughout the centuries to world order may be summarily and suddenly at this late hour transformed into a facile pacifism; and yet wholesale warring is now impossible. Instead we have a more sickening gamble with imponderables: instead of spears and bullets and bombs, now bluff and risk are the final counters of world-exchange, of world-warring, abstract as finance itself; making 'mouths', as Hamlet says of Fortinbras, 'at the invisible event'.

'It's because', wrote Ionesco (p. 77 above), 'we have staked everything on life that we are incapable of living'. In 1962 it fell to Kennedy to balance millions of lives, perhaps earth itself, on a decision. At the limit, he did not stake *everything* on *life*; and we lived on. Remembering the close of *Hamlet*, our poem concludes:

> But not your heart, America,
> Beating so slow and sure and strong,
> Stricken in his
> > Triumphal car,
> Guard Caesar's bitter laurels long
>
> With soldiers' music, rites of war:
> He had proved bravely when put on!
> The soldiers shoot.
> > Waste echoes far
> Above the grave at Arlington.

'Put on'. It is strange how the unique and all but inexpressible occasion is exactly covered by those two, tiny, Shakespearian, words.

Poetry and Magic

War has today become psychological; and also, in the main, defensive. T. E. Lawrence's campaign in Arabia was a forecast of it; and Cassius Clay's technique as a boxer is a symptom.[1] We have recently watched the meteoric career of this young heavyweight boxer, Cassius Marcellus Clay, now Muhammad Ali; for he was, like T. E. Lawrence, and under a not dissimilar compulsion, moved to change his name. I shall, with apologies, use his old name, which has lustre. He is a negro, though with some white in his ancestry. Two studies have appeared: John Cottrell's *Man of Destiny* (1967) and Jack Olsen's *Cassius Clay* (1967). I quote from the first.

Cassius Clay's amazing self-confidence put, in reversal of expectations, into swift action; his unbroken record of championship successes; his exact forecasting of results – he clearly predicted, with the help of a recurring dream, the nature of his second extraordinary fight with Sonny Liston (222-4); his use of psychological propaganda, as though softening down his opponent before a fight; his mesmeric powers when in action, 'mesmeric' being a term he or Cottrell applies to what Clay calls the 'Ali Shuffle', meaning his elusive footwork (301); his method of non-engagement joined with speed, which I compare (on p. 315n.) to T. E. Lawrence's campaigning; his sense of himself as a man of destiny and reliance on prayer and divine help (158, and see 174), together with a calm submission, whatever the event, to Allah's will (195-6) – all this is fascinating enough. He is far from a normal boxer. After denying that he has 'no punch' (350) he says that if people complain that he lacks 'the killer instinct', he answers that he does not wish to do his opponent any 'physical harm'; nor to be hurt himself, for his appearance means much to him. His style protects him, and 'it wins' (349-50). He tends to leave himself off guard, with hands dropped: 'my speed enables me to do certain things which you may call faults' (351-2).

He has, it is true, been insulting to his opponents; but much of it was, as he says, done for publicity, and the worst recent example,

---

[1] So perhaps, though less certainly, is the chess-technique of the brilliant young chess-player, Ray Keene: 'His strategy is to set up an impregnable position which he will cheerfully maintain until his opponent is goaded into self-destructive action.' His method is intuitive: 'I trust in my own intuition. Quite often I do the right thing, knowing I'm doing the right thing but not knowing why' (Adam Hopkins, 'Taking on the Masters', *Sunday Times*, 12 January 1969). Compare my remarks on chess in *The Christian Renaissance*, I.

during his fight with Ernie Terrell, was motivated entirely by his anger at Terrell's deliberate use of what he now calls his 'slave' name, Cassius Clay (317-18).

Paradoxes certainly abound. Like others of his kind, Byron, T. E. Lawrence, Lindbergh, he arouses a sharp hostility. Cottrell refers to 'the peculiar way in which he generates extreme feelings and divides boxing followers into two distinctly opposed camps' (317). We find here a compact fusion of power and pacifism. Clay's refusal to join the U.S. army falls naturally into place. He is by instinct as much a pacifist as a fighter, and in this instance motivated too by allegiance to the 'Black Muslim' community: 'We don't bear weapons. We don't fight wars unless it's a war declared by Allah himself' (252). His devotion to his religion and his race has cost him severely: he has deliberately thrown away popularity and wealth (7, 321-5).

In years to come it will probably seem that his treatment by his contemporaries has lacked grace and gratitude. For has he not been vastly invigorating, at the least a superb entertainer, with a grand humour, conscious and unconscious, in his gorgeous rant and doggerel rhymes? 'I may', he says, 'be the last heavyweight champion. If there's fightin' after I'm gone, it'll just be a dull old thing. No more poems, no predictions, no more hollering' (354). But there has been more in it than fun. Cottrell calls him a 'great and highly original creative artist', 'the Picasso of pugilism' (352). He is humble before the mystery of his peculiar powers. He finds all nature mysterious and proceeds to wonder what makes him know how to move his head, on the instant, 'just enough', and let a blow whistle past (352).

Cassius Clay may be grouped among our seraphic heroes. He is young, and radiates youth. He is also wonderful to look at. Once he characteristically remarked: 'I'm so beautiful I should be chiselled in gold' (198).

Cottrell regards boxing as an art. Both Byron and Sherlock Holmes were boxers. Art and athletics are close, but there is this difference: athletics function on the level of earth-plane results, whereas it is the function of art to push beyond. That Clay has such further instincts may be felt in his indulgence in doggerel rhymes, as our first versifying professional pugilist on record; and also in his religious devotions. Apart from such considerations we today watch athletics serving the great purpose of international collaboration through friendly rivalry, bringing the war-energies under control (cp. p. 261 below).

At the recent Olympic games in Mexico the successes of negro contestants resounded. Negroes are beautifully made, and they are strong. Today Black Power holds both threat and fascination.

For many years now the European imagination has been haunted by a jungle fascination, whose aural symbol is the tom-tom. Sean O'Casey's *The Silver Tassie* defines it:

Mrs. Foran: I do love the ukelele, especially when it goes tinkle, tinkle, tinkle in the night-time.
Sylvester: Bringin' before you glistenin' bodies of blacks, coilin' themselves an' shufflin' an' prancin' in a great jungle dance; shakin' assegais an' spears to the rattle, rattle, rattle an' thud, thud, thud of the tom-toms.
Mrs. Foran: There's only one possible musical trimmin' to the air of a Negro Spiritual, an' that's the tinkle, tinkle, tinkle of a ukelele.   (IV)

The fecundity of negro savagery is here placed in contrast to the maimed war-heroes, no longer able to feel 'the rising sap in trees' or see 'the hues of branch or leaf'. They are symbols of white Europe, maimed, and with only 'the half of life' left. As Robert Graves tells us (p. 45 above), the African has contacts for want of which Europe is starving.

Eugene O'Neill's *The Emperor Jones* may be best read as a drama not only of a Europeanized negro, but also, by analogy, of European man himself. Summoned by the insistent tom-toms, he sinks back to the jungle origins that lie within him. As I wrote in *The Golden Labyrinth* (375), 'Jones is Western civilization, trying to escape itself, going in circles, brought to judgement; he is a would-be superman reduced to a savage'. In Edith Sitwell's *Gold Coast Customs* (1929) a negative satire is conveyed in rhythms of verbal dance and tom-tom thud that awake in us a fascinated sense of that very kinship which the satire drives home; and the fascination is one with a recognition and an enjoyment that joins with the poem's glittering title to create a more than satiric response. As Graves reminded us, Africa has powers which we have lost, and need. They may seem, or be, a threat. Long ago Charles Williams in his *Shadows of Ecstasy* (1933) saw Africa awaking to challenge Europe. In Francis Berry's *Morant Bay* (pp. 462-7 below) the issues attending black revolt are poetically analysed and deployed.

Africa can create in English. In our youth many of us responded to the epic strength of Rider Haggard's Zulu narratives, but today we have a more authentic treatment. Modern English can show no finer writing in the epic mode than Vusamazulu Credo Mutwa's *Indaba, my Children* and *Africa is my Witness*;[1] works on Bantu history as handed down by generations of witch-doctors, and themselves rich in occult lore, and belief in ancestral spirits, with some incisive chapters added to the second work on European irreligion and insincerity in contrast to the negro's more full-blooded and body-percolating religious feelings. These feelings may be naïve, but they are real, as in that moving drama Marc Connelly's *Green Pastures*, in which negro simplicity brought reality to the Old Testament. I am not supposing that African history is all sweet; all the horrors of Europe are found there too, and Mutwa's account included (*Africa is My Witness*, 128) perhaps *the* most fearful description of pure sadism that I have ever read.

In drama Wole Soyinka's *A Dance of the Forests* and *The Road*[2] fuse the occult traditions of the Yorubas with a European technique. The first turns on a ceremonial for which the dead return. *The Road* is primarily on Death. I quote the author's prefatory note on 'Agemo', called 'a religious cult of flesh-dissolution':

The dance is the movement of transition; it is used in the play as a visual suspension of death – in much the same way as Murano, the mute, is a dramatic embodiment of this suspension. He functions as an arrest of time, or death, since it was in his 'agemo' phase that the lorry knocked him down. Agemo, the mere phase, includes the passage of transition from the human to the divine essence (as in the festival of Ogun in this play), as much as the part psychic, part intellectual grope of Professor towards the essence of death.

'Arrest of time' recalls Ayrton (p. 71 above). As will be evident, Soyinka's dramas are not all easy. 'Professor' is a central authority,

[1] Published by Blue Crane Books, Johannesburg, and Stanmore Press, London; 1964, 1966. See also *My People*, Anthony Blond, London, 1969 (based on the earlier volumes).

[2] Published by the Oxford University Press, the first in *Five Plays*, 1963, and the other by itself in 1965. Wole Soyinka contributed an important essay on the Yoruba Mysteries to *The Morality of Art*, ed. D. W. Jefferson, 1969. See Rex Collings in the *New Statesman*, 20 December 1968, 'Wole Soyinka: A Personal View'.

searching for 'the Word'. This 'Word', he says, 'may be found companion not to life but death' (I). His final command is: 'Power your hands with the knowledge of death' (II).

Somehow we have got 'life' and 'death' all wrong. Fear of death through the hydrogen bomb has distorted life; but fear by itself is no guide. Hitherto war-heroism has been foremost among our valuations; now it is, perhaps too uncompromisingly, repudiated. Instincts for centuries war-pointed, whether in act or imagination, are now adrift. Energies are prisoned and nervous disorders increase; man is a whirling dynamism ungeared to purpose. Especially does this thwarting bear heavily on youth: John Osborne's Jimmy Porter was a true symptom; the 'angry young men' of the fifties have developed into the youth-revolts of the sixties. Our youth grow up without the great traditions of either religion or heroism to point their aspirations. There is no generally accepted ritual to match the transition from youth to maturity, nor any valid guidance. The energies cannot be stifled, and the results are before us.

Youth Power is as great a threat as Black Power. They are part really of one movement: the awakening African states and the negroes of America are politically young, and Youth Power is largely an awakening to the rights of primitive instinct.[1] The modern Pop songs and music, like the old jazz 'Blues' from which they descend, may be related to African rhythms, which have now, since Rock and Roll, become more emphatic. The slave-population of America has, as I noticed in *Atlantic Crossing* (VII. 228), provided, by a happy paradox, the popular and redeeming art of its former masters.

I say 'happy paradox' because the movement is, to my mind, good. Youth has always been an ideal to the imagination. For many years I have written of the seraphic, bisexual and homosexual idealisms in literature; and today they are coming into even clearer focus and fulfilment. The looming threat of over-population itself throws many of the old taboos, based on natural preservation, into a new relief. Removals of censorship leave books and stage newly free. Above all, there is our witness on every side to this new assertiveness in youth. It could be called 'bisexual'.

[1] My remarks on instinct in this introductory chapter should be read in association with my chapters 'Mysticism and Masturbation' and 'The Ship of Cruelty', below; where certain solutions are offered to what may appear an insoluble problem.

Each sex so assumes the appearance of the other that you often cannot tell boy from girl. But the main emphasis is male. D. H. Lawrence once said that if our men were to wear red trousers the rest would follow. In this he was wrong – he tends to be just off-centre in such matters – and T. F. Powys was on firmer ground when in *Mr. Weston's Good Wine* he gave his Angel on the inn's sign *blue* trousers. For many years now our boys and young men have been wearing trousers of the Air Force colour, the spirit-colour.

Francis Berry has a poem, 'Outbreak' (published in *Ghosts of Greenland*, 1966), about young people out on a sex-spree, in a keen, semi-spiritualized, setting:

> And O the air was shrill in this late May
> And the ice-capped mountains sprang O in this light blue day
> And O the high slim cloudlets jazzed in the jive-gold sky
> And O the young volcanoes spirt up
> > Fly up
> > Cry up
> > Titillatingly.

The action is grouped by the poet among such great and pivotal 'happenings' as the origin of man, Christ's birth and second coming, and the Russian revolution of 1917. What can this mean? Sex-action by itself is not regarded as a final solution but the young ones are congratulated for 'giving it a try'; and so onwards, with a 'new electric guitar', to some new and true 'kingdom'. This is among our most remarkable contemporary poems.

Youth today shows many excitements and many excesses. Its love of motor-cycle speeding follows T. E. Lawrence and Charles Lindbergh; its indulgence in drugs has at least some authority in Sherlock Holmes and the paradisal experiments of Aldous Huxley and Robert Graves.[1] Youth is searching, adventuring,

---

[1] We are all, naturally, aware of the fearful dangers attending resort to drugs. Ecstatic experiences may be bought at a cost. But drugs have been used for religious purposes by some races, and a careful study, without prejudice, is required. Aldous Huxley's *The Doors of Perception, Heaven and Hell* and *Island* make good introductions: Hell as well as Heaven may be involved. See also Graves in *Poetic Craft and Principle*, 161-5 and Colin Wilson's discussion 'The Mescalin Experience' in *Beyond the Outsider* (1965).

In *Man's Concern with Death*, essays, ed. R. Denniston (1968), Rosalind Heywood quotes the Pop singer Marianne Faithfull: 'Drugs are the doors . . . you just see a crack. I think LSD was important'; people were opened up and made the better by

asserting, as never before. Despite its excesses, there is an over-ruling instinct for artistry, for self-dramatization, seen in their self-chosen costuming and their Shakespearian, and even Miltonic, hair-styles; as though the male sex were, Samson-like, reasserting itself after centuries of aesthetic abnegation. The costumes started with the extraordinary and quite un-tutored impulse of the Teddy Boys whose Edwardian styles symbolized a nostalgia, like John Osborne's, for life before the 1914 war. Since then we have on both sides of the Atlantic the decorated shirts and other costuming, tasteful or tasteless, and yet always with the intention of artistry, of the Pop Groups and Flower Children.

The Teddy Boys were a threat, and the threat has continued. Never has Youth as Youth so challenged maturity with a culture of its own. On the one side there have been crimes, riots and destructions; on the other, new assertions for peace and love, and a new art-cult, from individual singers, and from groups.

The 'Top of the Pops' television programme might be called the B.B.C.'s most vital weekly event. It can be raucous, items may repel, some performers appear to be in physical agony; but it is never dull. Much is interesting and some of it entrancing. For better or worse it throbs from the heart of youth.[1]

The songs are often thoughtful. Many, but not all, are on love. The variations are original. The famous 'Puppet on a String', sung by Sandie Shaw, is a brilliant condensation of *Antony and Cleopatra*.

---

it, and most of them then gave it up. What was experienced was: 'Something I think we've forgotten about completely, something like God; something calming. You realize that the state we should be in is perfection, that we're not in it; and that the reason we're here is to find it'.

An expedition (May 1968) to the primitive Guaica Indians, shown on B.B.C. television on 19 January 1969 (*Radio Times*, 16 January), was planned to investigate a drug used there, made from tree-bark. Questioned on its effect one of them replied that it made them see spirits, like themselves but in wonderful robes. On the world-wide use of vegetation-drugs by savage tribes, see 'Palinurus' (Cyril Connolly), *The Unquiet Grave*, Penguin 1967; I. 59.

In a recent address the famous spirit-guide Silver Birch rules against such prac-tices: 'I am completely and utterly opposed to the idea of the use of drugs to try to heighten psychic faculty. I am opposed to anything which tries to achieve right results by the wrong way.... You cannot short-cut spiritual growth' ('Spirit purpose behind difficulty', *Two Worlds*, No. 3900, January 1969).

[1] It is, of course, true that much may be owed variously to promoters, directors, composers, orchestral help, and script-writers, who are not young. But the youthful performers are the heart of it, without whom the cult would not exist. George Melly refers to 'the incoherent frustration and the child-like yearning of the best of the music' ('A personal Pop credo', *The Observer*, Review section, 10 November 1968).

In 'No Milk Today' Herman's Hermits bring to love-disaster a mischievously fascinating understatement; in 'Those were the days' Mary Hopkin recalls youth's timeless (cp. p. 75 above) romance in a voice of transfixing timbre.[1] Suggestion may be exotically spiritual, as in the title 'Blue Birds over the Mountain' (The Beach Boys). Themes are many: we may be on earth among the Eskimos with Manfred Mann to honour the 'Mighty Quinn', or caught up in the most fearful of the elements by Arthur Brown in 'Fire'; or with Amen Corner to 'fly high in the sky' ('High in the Sky'); or with The Scaffold, to honour as 'Saviour of the human race' Lily the Pink and her 'medicinal compound', ending on thoughts of heaven and angels. The Beatles have a song teaching us, with a depth of possible meaning, to change 'Good-bye' into 'Hallo'. In Simon and Garfunkel's 'The Sound of Silence' metaphysic takes on wings and charm. The exquisite 'Morningtown Ride' of The Seekers makes of its children's melody and travelling children a microcosm of human destiny. The metaphysical trend is well shown in Peter Sarstedt's

> Where do you go to, my lovely,
>   When you're alone in your bed?
> Tell me the thoughts that surround you,
>   I want to look inside your head.

'Surround': thoughts are felt as part of the aura; or perhaps as objective visitors, swarming around before entry.

Some of the music is known as 'soul music'; sometimes there are organ accompaniments. If a new religion is striving for expression, it is natural that it should come first through a popular music. Music and Spiritualism are close. 'Ever since I was a child', writes Beverley Nichols, 'it has given me a total and quite unshakable conviction that we have living contact with the dead' (Service of Reunion and Remembrance, Royal Albert Hall, November 1968; printed in *The Spiritualist*, Spiritualist Association of Great Britain, VII. 1). According to Masefield (p. 287 below) music is the language of the spirit-world.

Most interesting of all is the design of Philip Travers for The

---

[1] To Mary Hopkin herself the song means 'remembering my childhood', since 'you never enjoy anything in quite that way again'. See Sheila More, 'The Restless Generation. 2', the second of three valuable weekly articles, *The Times*, 11 December 1968.

Moody Blues' record jacket 'In Search of the Lost Chord', which shows low down in shadow a grey-black embryo one side and a skull on the other; and between them a seer, and above his head a second head, from which flowers up a silvery gold stem splaying out into a region of interblending gold, pink, mauve and white, with many opening hands to right and left; and in the centre, dominating, a powerful Golden Face. The glory does not come from pursuing the horizontal time-stream beyond death, but towers vertically from it, mid-way. The plan follows that of my interpretation of Coleridge's 'Kubla Khan' (*The Starlit Dome*, 90-7; and see *The Christian Renaissance*, X, 'Immortality').

The more urgent compositions are related to elements in the old negro Blues. The strong beat of the music usually kills the words, so it is hard to comment on meanings; but I should say that the thoughts differ from the jazz tradition in being, if not less 'sexual', certainly less 'sexy'. So is the music. The rock-beat of drum and rolls of rhythm curve and crash with a controlled abandon, never afraid, as Keats put it, to 'surprise by a fine excess' (to John Taylor, 27 February 1818). There is a strength and rhetoric of sound such as once was made for Dionysus; and a use of rising volume and impact that our Shakespearian actors and producers would do well to emulate. Or we may have one level of beat and pound, reminiscent of Indian music, as when The Cream (Eric Clapton, Jack Bruce, and Ginger Baker) prolong their resource of guitar and percussion to an overpowering and hypnotic effect.

The new art is challenging. Thom Gunn's poem 'Elvis Presley' sees the singer's 'stance' as a 'posture for combat', perhaps because the guitar is held as a tommy-gun; certainly many of the performances could be called 'aggressive'; such as those of The Rolling Stones, whose 'barbaric hedonism' has been acutely characterized by Tony Palmer in *The Observer* (Review section, 19 May and 1 December 1968). Others of lighter tone, especially when accompanied, as with the leader of Herman's Hermits, by close-up effects of smile and eye,[1] touch the seraphic. The deity of the old, pre-eminently female, jazz cult was Aphrodite, whereas

---

[1] The 'Sandie Shaw Supplement', now (October 1968) running on B.B.C. television, is remarkable for its amazing resource of phantasmagoric innovation all centred on close-ups of facial play of striking quality. The close-ups of films were embarrassing; in television Pop programmes their beauty and vitality often transfix.

the new art-culture, in which, though it has strong individual female performers, the male element of the groups in general dominates, may be said to vary between Dionysus and Eros – 'Eros' being regarded as deity of the erotic essence, often taking other than normal forms, homosexual, bisexual, celibate, ascetic, and so forth (see *The Starlit Dome*, 302-4; *Christ and Nietzsche*, IV. 136-7; also p. 221 below). Effects may be astringent and keen, as with the weird and cutting vocal flights of Cilla Black. The extraordinary magnetic power exerted by The Beatles must be supposed one with their peculiarly non-sensuous and spiritualized vocalization, suffusing and clouding, and over-clouding, the words.

In watching the informal dancing during and after Top of the Pops, I find the dancers' instinctive body-action interesting; and also their *separateness*. Couples face each other, without contact, their body-movements mutually imitative, as in Plato's thought of love as a self-reflection, and those passages in Shakespeare on lovers' eyes in mutual exchange and self-mirroring (e.g. Sonnet 24; *The Phoenix and the Turtle*, 33-6; *The Merchant of Venice*, V. i. 242-4; *Troilus and Cressida*, III. iii. 107-8; also John Donne, *The Ecstasy*). Important figures of near-integration, Nietzsche's Zarathustra, Rupert Brooke, T. E. Lawrence, Powys, are solitary, and in this solitariness they are extreme exemplars of that aloneness and integrity which D. H. Lawrence regarded as a necessary basis for all sexual health. In that drugs induce a solitary mysticism, they are nearer to religion than to sexuality and art; and may indeed be criticized, as Mr. Quintin Hogg once (so I am told) criticized them in contrast to the more social affinities of alcohol, for this very reason.

I am not suggesting that our popular art stands for any sexual rejections; that physical partnerships are being repudiated; or that there is no sexual reaction among Pop audiences. Many of the songs are on normal love-themes; but many of these are newly pointed, and many range wider. It is a pity that the words are so often killed. In Pop songs emphasis falls less on the words than on personalities and vocal tone; and, if seen, on dress, body-action, and facial expression; and on the powerful music. Very much is included and the general implications of the cult are more subtle and more interesting than those of the jazz age.

Youth Power has now become an educational challenge. The widespread 1968 student revolts across the globe have added a new and unexpected dimension to our cultural evolution: unexpected, but scarcely unheralded, since all our literature, with its recurring emphasis on the seraphic as a source of light, has been its herald. There is more here than instinct: there is also vision.

In Plato the seer sees his own soul imaged in a youth's beauty; or even if the youth be not beautiful, he may still be seeing, as in Berry's 'Malta Elegy', what was once his own youthfulness and 'better self', the self of Thomas Hood's *I remember, I remember*, recalling how

> My spirit flew in feathers then,
> That is so heavy now

and concluding

> It was a childish ignorance,
> But now 'tis little joy
> To know I'm farther off from heav'n
> Than when I was a boy.

Such poems recognize a state still, as Wordsworth says in his *Immortality* ode, 'trailing clouds of glory'. H. G. Wells, Rupert Brooke, Robert Graves and Eugène Ionesco (see pp. 46, 63-4, 75 and 295) tell us of supernal insights experienced in youth and rarely recovered in maturity. Though university-age is not quite boyhood or girlhood, it is nearer to it and has qualities of its own of mental and sexual unfurling and all the attendant excitements and magical insights. I used to think, years ago, that youth was no longer having such insights, had become hard and cynical; but not today. Whatever else they are, they are not that; it is their elders who are cynical.

In all true education, as I explained in *The Dynasty of Stowe* (III. 36-43), the teacher should be as humble as Socrates; should be both preceptor and learner. Youth is a time of unfurling, and therefore wisdom; the wisdom is in the very unfurling, the eagerness, the expectance. This wisdom we should listen in to, and tap.

The young both need, and can give, wisdom. That there are dangers is obvious. The crimes of young people have been disturbing and their politics and sociology are, naturally, unshaped. William Golding's *Lord of the Flies* is a warning; youth touches, and yet can no better than ourselves live out, the vision. Besides, they will soon be no longer young. As Ionesco tells us, youth thinks in timeless terms; its wisdom is simultaneously authentic and ephemeral, based on what Eliot in *Ash-Wednesday* (I) called 'the one veritable transitory power'.

Meanwhile such terms as 'Flower Children' are pointers; within all the turmoil, the crude and the senseless, is a love, a hope, an expectance challenging the horrors of maturity. Our ethics of moral absolutes and theological damnation have given youth neither sexual health nor religious wisdom. It is our fault, the fault of our churches and our universities, if excessive taboos have forced an over-violent revolt; and if our young people have been trained to regard the spirit-powers asking for entry as fraudulent or phoney. Every time we do, or hint, this, we are distorting vision, as when the Troll King tries to twist the vision of Ibsen's Peer Gynt. When religious counsel is barren and education distorts, the drugs which Sherlock Holmes found so mentally 'clarifying' (p. 59 above) – or to use the new term 'psychedelic'[1] – are signs of grace; for man is a religious being, made for vision. Youth has taken its own way. All the things that used to be called 'sissy' are now aggressive. Young men, on their own impulse, have taken to pictorial dress, and to a rhythmic art; an art which serves not only to ravish the souls of teen-agers, but also to crowd the broadcast programmes for their elders. Song and music are fierce with a new pacifism, as though Christianity had somehow got out of the Churches into life; while tommy-guns are turned, not into ploughshares, but guitars.

Student revolt is instinctive but directionless. Its aims should not be limited to, nor primarily concerned with, politics and sociology; such revolutions are no better than oscillations, or undulations, from age to age, whereas this is, or should be, far more than that. Besides, in those fields the young have nothing new to offer, no peculiar insight. Youth has, however, visions which are subsequently lost; and therefore its revolt, to be creative, should be metaphysical and spiritual. Socially our young revolutionaries are crying for a celestial city; that is their instinct; but socially that cannot be yet. Their basic claim, we are told, is that within the soul-killing mechanizations of our twentieth century, recognition should be accorded to everyone's *full humanity*;

---

[1] I assume that the term derives from the Greek word *dēloō*, to 'make clear', and therefore means 'soul-clarifying'; see L. A. Huxley, *This Timeless Moment*, 1969; 134. Compare Wells's definition of the opium experience as a consciousness of 'crowded clarity' (p. 63 above).

and that *involves a recognition of spirit-reality*.[1] To this recognition we are being driven. For long it has been obvious that any true religious revival must come *first* from outside the Churches, based less on doctrine than on impulse; as in the recent insistence, even among Catholics, on the rights of conscience as against command. In his 'Four Sketches for Herbert Read' (*The Listener*, 19 December 1968) Stephen Spender has well related the 1968 student-rising in France to Read's individualistic philosophy:

> Their mouths sang the chant
> Of a poet's final hour:
> *Imagination seizes power*.

Politically that may hold danger; more deeply, it gives hope. Today, religious 'faith' is only for the few, and even 'imagination' divorced from direct evidence is no longer, in a 'scientific' age, able to bear *all* the stresses of an enduring religion. But evidence is available for those who want it; and there are powers waiting to guide in the great Spirit-Guides whose doctrines now fill many books, as well as in men, and works, of genius. An important youth-movement is now active within Spiritualism (see the extended account 'Young Mediums etc.' in *Psychic News*, 7 December 1968. The movement has its periodical '*Psicon*').

Youth and genius are close.[2] In *The Dynasty of Stowe* (III. 42) I wrote:

Boyhood, girlhood, and genius – all drink from the same refreshing springs, living in the Renaissance world of ever-new discovery and perpetual romance. Each is integrated because each is eternally, and gladly, immature; and their bond of recognition is Truth, spelt not with a small, but with a capital T; love not for the thing learned, but for the essence of the learning, joy in the never-finished unfurling, the fleeting excellence dynamic and unformulated, for ever youthful and for ever virgin, adored and symbolized, but never mastered, never possessed.

---

[1] Compare, from a review of Blake's *Europe, a Prophecy* in *The Times Literary Supplement*, 22 January 1970: 'What is certain and explicit in Blake is his perception that false ideologies are the root of social evils. From a materialist philosophy and a mechanistic view of nature had arisen those social institutions and injustices which come from regarding human beings as things and not as immortal spirits; wars and revolutions will inevitably follow . . .'

[2] See Theodore Roszak, 'The Visionary Sociology of Paul Goodman', *The Listener*, 5 December 1968: 'It is one of the controversial glories of Gestalt that it has – against the entire psychiatric tradition since Freud, with its grim demand for conformity to a joyless conception of adulthood – asserted the nobility and healthiness of the child and the artist'.

Youth has vision: 'Your old men', wrote the prophet Joel (II. 28), 'shall dream dreams' and 'your young men shall see visions'. These visions are one with a quest, living in the light and radiance of Ionesco's 'Why?' (p. 76 above).

This 'Why?' involves religion. Religious tendencies are evident: in Cassius Clay's Moslem allegiance, Cliff Richard's Christianity, The Beatles' adventures in Indian mysticism and spiritualistic communication, David Bowie's Buddhism (see Sheila More in *The Times*, p. 86n. above). Free sex and drugs are, as Berry's *Outbreak* suggests of sex, no final answer. Cliff Richard's collaboration with The Settlers in a Manchester church for the B.B.C. 'Songs of Praise' (29 December 1968) heralds a necessary fusion. Our full-length study of youth-revolt, Francis Berry's *Fall of a Tower*, is a study of religious revolt, on the destruction and re-making of religion and the inauguration of a new, sun-flooded, 'Christ-ness'. The 'Hippie' movement in America is closely entangled with religion, mainly oriental.

Among our younger philosophers, Colin Wilson has, in a succession of incisive studies, fought vigorously for a new metaphysical and religious apprehension. His approach is throughout positive, optimistic and health-giving; in his fiction he shows sympathy with the occult; and we may accordingly expect from him an ever-increasing access of strength.

Of essential youth, too, is Murray Hickey Ley's *A is All*, a brilliantly fresh wording of positive response to the totality of today's experience.[1] Introducing it, my brother wrote:

The Myth is a daring enough attempt to express the never expressed and perhaps inexpressible. It is an attack on the barricade of words by means of a battering ram of words.

A is All, built on the letters of the alphabet, is a quest, searching out new thought-ways on old themes. In my own 'Comment', appended as an epilogue, I wrote:

One medium is life, and another is art, and another is thought. Or we may find a thinker for whom thought is itself art, whose language is broken down and remade in the very act of thinking. Mr. Ley is such a

[1] Murray Hickey Ley, *A is All, a Myth for a Time*. Preface by W. F. Jackson Knight and a concluding comment by G. Wilson Knight; cover design drawn by Henry Moore and an illustration from his 'Reclining Figure'; frontispiece a reproduction from the work of Richard Diebenkorn. The Grabhorn Press, San Francisco, 1953.

thinker. At his best moments, his thought is shaped into a new-winged style darting free from all the constrictions of the past; a style of to-morrow rather than of yesterday, making of this old and wrinkled world and its problems something new, and young. And in that youth lies its authority.

The Myth envisages creation's drive from lacerating evils toward 'distant, shriekless harmonies' (P, 47) and the 'final assault on Death' (D, 30). Modern science is throughout contained; solid and fluid are aspects of a single 'occurrence', and 'Spaciness' and 'Minute-Maker' intermingle ('A Word at the End', 73-4). Spirit, though as my brother notes it comes late, comes as an urgent 'Now' to confront the 'yestershapen' constructs of mind with sense of 'present Spirit crowding present fact' (W, 59, Y, 61; see also D, 29-30). A dynamic immediacy – the 'presentational im-mediacy' of Whitehead's philosophy – is unveiled.

Religion can only now be reborn in direct contact with nature and natural instinct; and with the elements. It must also today be based on evidence and experience; which means a return to the sources of all religion in spiritualistic communion, both in re-ceiving messages from loved ones and, probably yet more im-portant, the hearing of trance-addresses from powerful Guides.[1] Before trying to reform society, young Hamlet conversed with a ghost. In his confrontation of Western learning with gipsy lore and the 'spark from Heaven', Arnold's Scholar, in what is surely the greatest educational document in our language, has made of his ever-youthful truant an archetypal figure for what is valid in student revolt.

There is no more significant work of the new movement than the 'American Tribal Love-Rock Musical', *Hair*, put on at the Shaftesbury Theatre, London in September 1968.[2] The Lord Chamberlain's censorship has now been abrogated, and *Hair* was the first British production to take advantage of the new dispensa-tion. In word and action it breaks taboos freely and contains abundant satire on Politics, War, Society, Religion and Education. The cast contains performers of various nations, including negro

---

[1] Of the greater Guides it has been written: 'They and their message will some day prove to be the rock upon which Spiritualism will stand, while the sands of phenomena (which have possibly served their purpose) drain away' (Ivan and Grace Cooke in *Psychic News*, 1 May 1965; 5).

[2] The book and lyrics are by Gerome Ragni and James Rado; music by Galt MacDermot; dances by Julie Arenel. The whole directed by Tom O'Horgan.

performers. The dominant cultural tone is Red Indian. Other races are dramatized; the general effect is multi-racial. Costumes vary and flowers are used, some handed to the audience, and incense is burned. High on the setting is a weeping Christ. 'The stage', wrote Harold Hobson in *The Sunday Times* (29 September 1968), 'is littered with the symbols of our possibly fading civilization', while on it the young company performs 'the singing and dancing rites of a new religion, tribal, totemistic, Indian and Red Indian'. 'Nothing else remotely like it', wrote Irving Wardle in *The Times* (30 September 1968), 'has yet struck the West End'. Its purpose, he says, is 'to send up a great hymn to freedom and love'.[1]

The performance is dominated by sound and movement. The Company's resource of stage-action seems unlimited: ritual devotion, primitive African dance, reptilian crawls as of Red Indian scouts, mock-battles with arrows, guns and explosions, and much else. Throughout, the throb and pound of the music reaches crescendos of almost frightening Dionysian sound.

Most powerful are the African dances in which self-generated ecstasy is expressed through physical quiverings and gyrations, as though each individual is acting out his energies to no obviously practical end but yet to some creative purpose. All such dance holds an analogy to masturbation (discussed in Chapters V, VI), though with a more evident sense conveyed of some katharsis and accomplishment, grinding from biological energy some magical power.[2]

There is less story than there was in the American production, but what there is is important, and the surrounding philosophy of considerable interest.[3]

[1] A review of Peter Brook's *The Empty Space* in *The Times Literary Supplement* of 28 November 1968 suggests that Brook's dual demands for 'The Holy Theatre' and 'The Rough Theatre' are together realised in *Hair*. The American movement from which *Hair* originated is discussed by Henry Popkin in *The Times* of 4 December 1968, 'U.S. Theatre of Rites'.

[2] I am thinking along the lines of Panthea's speech in Shelley's *Prometheus Unbound*, IV. iv. 236-68, discussed in *The Starlit Dome*, 220-2.

[3] It seems that the London version is superior to the original New York version, which had narrative and local elements now cut; this leaves the general implications more emphatic. See Irving Wardle's article 'A not to be forgotten experience', subsequent to his first notice, in *The Times* of 5 October 1968.
The play's thought cannot all be expected to get across in performance. I received enough to make me want to know more, and through the kind collaboration of the Company's Manager, Mr. Frank K. McKay, and Messrs. James Verner Ltd. I was privileged to see a typed script. I give page references to this script.

The hero, Claude, is being called up with his companions for military service. The main satiric target is the Vietnam war for which 'white people' send 'black people to make war on yellow people to defend the land they stole from the red people' (II. 4). In opposition, we have talk of love on all its levels, sexual and social. Normal sexuality is covered but is not emphatic and is at one point repudiated: 'New York is fun city – Blah!'; 'Physical contact with any of these animals would repulse me'; 'Sex isn't love, it isn't even pleasure any more' (I. 42). The most vivid instance shown of sex-impulse is homosexual, and that is for a picture. Erotically and imaginatively the males get most attention, as in the three Negresses' song on boys:

> White boys are so lovely
> Beautiful as girls
>
> (II. 7)

and the statement made elsewhere that long hair – which gives the piece its title – and flamboyant dress signify a healthy and entirely natural 'emergence' of the male from past drabness; we are reminded that Jesus himself wore long hair (I. 29). Such general considerations are more important here than personal romance. Instead of love-pairs, the action prefers group-clusters of four or more entwining or clustering, like bees in a swarm. And more important than any personal or group contacts are drugs, regarded as a means to a *solitary* mysticism.

The positive thought-directions are less social or moral – certainly not 'moral' as usually understood – than metaphysical and spiritual. We open with an invocation to the 'Aquarian Age' of which we have heard so much of late from the esoteric cults (cp. p. 224 below):

> When the moon is in the seventh house
> And Jupiter aligns with Mars
> Then peace will guide the planets
> And love will steer the stars
>
> (I. 2)

The Aquarian Age will bring mutual understanding (I. 2). This sets the direction. Aquarius, the Water-Bearer of the constellation, was identified with Ganymede, the beautiful youth taken to Olympus by Zeus to be his cup-bearer (*Oxford Classical Dictionary*, 'Ganymedes'). Richard Cavendish relates Aquarius as Ganymede

D   95

to the water-pouring girl of the Tarot pack, symbol of intuition, new life, 'potentiality', 'the shining possibilities of the future' (Richard Cavendish, *The Black Arts*, p. 225 below, III. ii. 124). We may accordingly relate the 'Aquarian Age' to what I call the 'seraphic' (p. 50 above).[1]

Hair has references to names or words of oriental religion: Krishna (I. 41), Buddha (II. 15), 'Shantih' (I. 37), 'the yogi light' (I. 4). To oriental music the Tribe dances the 'Kama Sutra' (I. 14). The general thought-atmosphere may be called 'spiritualistic'. 'Reality' is regarded as variable: it may be 'astral' (I. 16); one of the people has a book *The Art and Practice of Astral Projection* (I. 38). There is no explicit doctrine, and all constraints are opposed: parents should tell their children to be *themselves*, and without sense of guilt, provided only that they hurt no one (I. 29). The new powers are regarded as powers of good sense levelled, by a neat transversal, against the demoniac powers of state and society: what is needed is an 'exorcism of the Khaki'; so 'Let's go down to the induction centre and we'll yip out the bad vibrations and yip up the sun' (II. 5).

Sun, Moon and the Stars are our pantheon. We are in a pantheistic world of 'flowah powah' (II. 25). It is a poetic, sometimes Shakespearian, world. Lines of Horatio's address to the Ghost in *Hamlet* are used (I. 37) and Hamlet's 'What a piece of work is a man' speech is sung (II. 17-18). *Hamlet* is a natural god-father to any drama of youthful idealism, just as Red Indians, whose culture gives the production its prevailing tone, are a natural medium for a spiritualistic gospel.

The narrative action pivots on the taking of drugs. With drugs we are 'evolving', and we are given a list: hashish, cocaine, heroin, and others, including alcohol, tobacco and cough-syrup (I. 4-5). We are in 'the Psychedelic Stone Age', called 'the most exciting time this weary square globe has seen for generations' (I. 14). Drug-invocation leads naturally on to a bold use of Christian phraseology in the words 'This is the body and blood of Jesus Christ'. Human love is also involved in 'I'm going to eat you'; and after this comes 'In the name of the Father, the Son and the Holy Ghost', and then a song to sodomy, fellatio, cunnilingus and pederasty. Why, we are asked, do such words, and 'mastur-

[1] For a seraphic youth as 'archetypal symbol of man's spiritual rebirth', see Idwal Jones, 'Stefan George: Poet and Hierophant', *Edda* (Oslo), LXIX. 2, 1969; 101.

bation' too, sound 'nasty'? We are invited to 'join the holy orgy';
for 'we are all one' (I. 5-6).

Air-flights and spiritual adventure are identified. Drugs are
'like a jet to Miami' (II. 7); you 'bail out' for a 'sky-dive' (II. 10).
Or they give us a journey to 'outer space' (I. 6; and see II. 3) into
the 'ionosphere' (I. 43):

> My body
> Is walking in space
> My soul is in orbit
> With God, face to face

(II. 9)

It is a 'floating' to 'the fourth dimension' in 'total self-awareness',
the mind 'as clear as country air' and all colours blending, the
clarity and the colours recalling Ionesco (p. 74 above). So 'we
rediscover sensation' and find 'the purpose of peace' (II. 9). We are
reminded of Blake's 'If the doors of perception were cleansed
every thing would appear to man as it is, infinite' (*The Marriage of
Heaven and Hell*); of Keats's plea for 'a life of Sensations rather than
of Thoughts', leading to a 'Vision in the form of Youth' as 'a
shadow of reality to come . . .' (to Benjamin Bailey, 22 November
1817); of Oscar Wilde's aim to make of the senses elements of a
new spirituality, curing the 'soul' by the 'senses' and the 'senses'
by the 'soul' (*The Picture of Dorian Gray*, II; and see XI); and of
Edith Sitwell's

> Then with angels he'll go a-dancing hence
> From sensuality into sense!

(*The Higher Sensualism*)

Man's eye, 'that most pure spirit of sense' (*Troilus and Cressida*,
III. iii. 106), is as a soiled 'lamp' which must be 'purified'
(Matthew, VI. 22-3; *Thus Spake Zarathustra*, I. 8). Sensuous-
mystical experiences may occur without the use of drugs: John
Cowper Powys knew them (e.g. *Autobiography*, VII. 276; IX. 409);
one of his works of mystical philosophy is entitled *In Defence of
Sensuality*.

Claude, the central person in the story of *Hair*, makes high
claims. He introduces himself as a 'genius' who believes in
'Gawd' and believes that 'Gawd' believes in him (I. 7). He is
'Aquarius – destined for greatness or madness' (I. 8). He is
physically beautiful, with blue eyes, fair hair, smooth skin, indeed

97

a 'living hunk of gold' (I. 13); also his is 'the purest mind on Avenue C' (I. 31). On him the drama's conflicts and values converge. He is not only seraphic; he is also a Hamlet-figure, searching.

The first of the two parts concludes with his moving song, in accord with Ionesco's 'Why?' (p. 76 above):

> Where do I go
> Follow the river
> Where do I go
> Follow the gulls
>
> Where is the something
> Where is the someone
> That tells me why
> I live and die
>
> Where do I go
> Follow the children
> Where do I go
> Follow their smiles
>
> Is there an answer
> In their sweet faces
> That tells me why
> I live and die
>
> Follow the wind song
> Follow the thunder
> Follow the neon in young lovers' eyes
>
> Down to the gutter
> Up to the glitter
> Into the city where the truth lies
>
> (I. 44)

Directly after this some of the company appear completely naked, in subdued light. Their figures are simultaneously question and answer. The effect is as much spiritual as physical.

In Part II Claude, after taking a drug, experiences no happy dream, but a nightmare of American history. Red Indians fight and kill General Washington's men who have come to steal their land; then the Civil War, General Grant and Lincoln; whites are attacked by African witch-doctors, and killed; then to emancipation of the slaves. After that Buddhist monks – with a reference to incidents in Vietnam – set one of their number on fire. Catholic nuns come to strangle the monks with rosaries, and the nuns are in turn killed by astronauts with ray-guns. Chinese kill the astronauts; Red Indians kill the Chinese; American commandos with machine-guns kill first the Indians, and then each other. The piled-up dead bodies revive as children, whose games grow frantic till they too turn into 'monsters', and kill each other. Then a grim song brings the Vietnam war to us in all its horror and misery. All this is followed by the singing of Hamlet's passage 'What a piece of work is a man . . .', comparing him to 'angel' and 'god'. Claude wakes up (II. 10-18).

He feels lonely. All normal ambitions are gone:

I'll tell you the thing I'd really like to be . . . invisible. I don't need drugs. An invisible man, and I could float and see into people's minds and know what they're thinking. (II. 19)

'Tonight', he says, is 'the last night of the world' (II. 21). The Tribe says 'Look at the moon', and follows with a song to the stars, 'Good-morning Starshine' (II. 22). There is a symbolic action, indicating love in bed, procreation, children, new birth (II. 23).

Claude, saluted as 'Aquarius', is left alone. The others had burned their enlistment cards, but he has surrendered to the State; perhaps because his nightmare has shown him the apparent inevitability of human slaughter. He stands central, seraphic, in blue trousers only, white light on body and bronze-gold hair: 'I'm human being number 1005963297' (II. 24).

The others return. Claude is in military uniform: 'Like it or not, they got me' (II. 26). He is invisible to the rest. He is not in despair:

Somewhere inside something there is a rush of greatness
Who knows what stands in front of our lives

I fashion my future on films in space
Silence tells me secretly . . . everything.

(II. 26)

He says to a friend, 'I feel like I died'. The others cannot see, or perhaps hear, him. He continues: 'If I am unseen, I can perform miracles'. Is he dead, killed in action, or just dead to the others?

There may be an intended ambiguity, but the action is certainly constructed in conformance with reports from those who have died. Claude repeats his introductory

> I believe in Gawd
> I believe that Gawd
> Believes in Claude   (II. 26)

The others sing

> Eyes look your last
> Arms take your last embrace
> And lips O you the doors of breath
> Seal with a righteous kiss   (II. 26)

from *Romeo and Juliet*, and 'The rest is silence' (II. 26) from *Hamlet*. Then they sing the final, rising, song 'Let the sunshine, let the sunshine in' (II. 27). This concluding song corresponds with that of Berry's *Fall of a Tower* (p. 456 below).

Hair dramatizes an interplay of obscenity and spirituality, as though the one conditions the other. Both are part of man's freedom. We have a free use of taboo-words such as 'fuck' and 'shit'. But there is no irreverence, except towards the conventional values. There is a deep reverence: before the magic of physical existence; before heightened sensation; and before a mysterious destiny. Neither sex nor drugs are put forward as final solutions: Claude passes beyond drugs. The concluding actions of each of the two parts emphasize both (i) the spiritualistic and (ii) in my use of the term, which may involve bodily presence (Shelley's 'naked seraph'), the 'seraphic'. The general theme is Ionesco's 'Why?'. But a 'why' more happy than Hamlet's, and one with Ionesco's 'light' (p. 76 above).

8

What holds us back is fear. Fear not only of our obscene and sadistic instincts but still more, fear of what is bright and beautiful; especially of Spiritualism and its poetic projection and earthly counterpart, the 'seraphic'.

Our best insights remain transitory. At high moments we may be, as was Ionesco, aware of earth-life magically irradiated; or of people, when we are in love. Such experiences are our key, or entry, to wisdom. Women, perhaps, find it easier than men to live within this consciousness: or one like it. A woman poet will, if powerful, write as a prophetess, or sibyl. Two in our time have written like that: Edith Sitwell and Dallas Kenmare. The one has had, despite a considerable public advantage, a cool reception from the literary intelligentsia; the other has been neglected. The male mind does not respond to such uncompromising and reiterated, spiritualized, assertions as theirs: the total output of each appears too fluid, perhaps too 'Aquarian', without structure, with too little respect to the details of worldly commitment, too uncompromising in assertion.[1]

Edith Sitwell's poetry has vivid light, often coloured or in association with colour; amazing sense-transversals; intricate rhythms and gambollings with verbal sound. These can tire, perhaps irritate; and the long lines of her later poetry, with their reiterations of favourite symbols, may lack, or seem to lack, control. But all are surface ebulliences rising from her sense of a magical creation. From the child-lore and witchery of her early poems, through the packed rhythms and social incisiveness of *Gold Coast Customs*, to the prophetic fluencies of her final period, her utterances come from awareness of a great power thundering within creation, as well in a tree's sap as a heart's blood. And of Death, too, in 'Eurydice':

> Love is not changed by Death,
> And nothing is lost and all in the end is harvest.

In a poem of more tragic contemplation, 'The Road to Thebes', winter yet holds the waiting fires of spring; and human death, at its most wraithly, has direction:

> The Dead Man, thin as water,
> Or as a vine-tendril, and shod with gold
> As for a journey – (but upon what road?) . . .   (1)

Somehow within the great economy of nature, Birth and Death are 'the same' ('The Road to Thebes', I). Even if beyond nature there lies 'the Cold', 'the Nothing', from which all Being arose,

---

[1] Compare Middleton Murry's fine essay on Indian Culture, 'Patriotism *is* enough' in *The Adelphi* of November 1926 (IV. 5). Though seeming 'backboneless' to the Westerner, it is nevertheless 'pure and valid in its own right'. Murry's leader essays in *The Adelphi* in the issues for 1926 and 1927 (which I have in two bound volumes) are among the best general reading of my experience.

there is hope: 'It is the sound too high for our hearing' ('The Shadow of Cain'). (See p. 88 above, on Cilla Black.)

In a period of parched thought and international disruption, of social agony and the atom bomb, Edith Sitwell has poured out in her poetry a glittering lava of suffering and sympathy. Deep and dark penetrations are housed within a jewelled magnificence that denies their horror, while singing lines and battering symbols of sun and gold and lion and harvest assert, despite every anguish, an assurance.

Her considered aim, stated in her prefatory notes to her *Collected Poems* (1957, xlvi), is: 'To produce a poetry that is the light of the Great Morning, wherein all beings whom we see passing in the common street are transformed into the epitome of all beauty, or of all joy, or of all sorrow'.[1]

Dallas Kenmare's poetry is like silver, a favourite impression, to Edith Sitwell's gold. Her free exploitation of the long line is developed with a remarkable control, probably more assured than Sitwell's; her words are unassertive yet strong; her statement is simple and single. For her, nature is a power of enduring beauty made to collaborate with love. She writes much of love. She speaks through the voices of famous women who have loved or been loved: Sappho, Héloïse, Isoud (Isolt), Beatrice, Laura, Ophelia. And of music. But all these are being desecrated. In 'The Altar-Flower' she writes;[2]

There is too much talk of invasion,
too much talk of a decaying world,
too much speculation,
too little knowledge,
no wisdom.

Too many guns thunder across the sky,
too many searchlights eclipse the stars,
too many death-gorged 'planes slink heavily among the clouds,
the heavens declare the infamy of man,
no glory.

[1] Edith Sitwell's poetry has been well studied and assessed by Sir Maurice Bowra in *Edith Sitwell*, The Lyrebird Press (J. B. Hanson), The Ramparts, Monaco, 1947.

[2] I quote from *Collected Poems* (1929-1950), Burrows Press, Cheltenham, which includes the main poems from eleven earlier volumes. Subsequent volumes have appeared from the same Press.

Dallas Kenmare died on 15 February 1970. An obituary statement appeared in *The Times*, 3 March 1970.

Yet myself, I fear other invaders,
quite other forms of decay.
I dread the subtle legions that can occupy the mind, and undermine
  its stability,
I watch closely for the plague-rats that can infect the soul,
and against them I build my fortress, and, within, my crystal shrine:
there I will stay alone, silver-armoured against assault,
deaf at last to the thunder-roll of the guns,
blind to the sky-invaders that have robbed the birds of their age-long
  heritage;
this fortress and this delicate-strong shrine I am compelled to build,
nowhere is there refuge in the chaotic world
neither in the world of action, nor the unbalanced world of thought –
I am driven to my fortress and my shrine, where in solitude I can
  worship the altar-flower, the glistening rose.

This may be called a 'retreat-poetry'; but, if so, it is a retreat to the
citadel to which all of us, sooner or later, must return. The language
has a fine purity. One might suggest that in no poet of our time
has T. S. Eliot's demand of poetic style in 'Little Gidding' (V)

> The common word exact without vulgarity,
> The formal word precise but not pedantic,
> The complete consort dancing together

been more admirably met.

The male intellect may find the romantic vision hard to hold
within the mind; but we all know it exists; and for practical purposes in a busy life the literary imagination should be our contact.
In our literary heritage, and in what is going on around us in
fulfilment of that heritage, are imaginative powers, one would
have thought, of compelling authority. To these our official seats
of devotion and learning remain unresponsive.

We pay lip-service to 'genius' without recognizing that all
genius is spiritualistically impelled and attuned: the word means
'tutelary spirit'; and all true poetry has this basis, and true poets
know it.[1] In drama, Gordon Craig is obviously one, however we
rate his contribution, to be accounted a 'genius'; and his creative
activity might be defined as an attempt to realize a spirit-world

---

[1] Victor Hugo was actively engaged in Spiritualism: see the account given in the
review-article in *The Times Literary Supplement*, 22 April 1965. This article is discussed
and amplified in *Psychic News*, 8 May 1965.

in the theatre. In his early productions he favoured spirit-colours (p. 51n. above) such as rich mauves and greys, and throughout his life was driving for a drama less of speech than of silence, beyond normal existence; the silence of Eliot's 'Burnt Norton' (p. 377 below). He was himself clairvoyant and conversed with the spirit of Irving.[1]

To return to 'interpretation'. When all in our introductory survey, to say nothing of the essays that follow, is so richly loaded with marvels and mysteries tugging us up to insights and experiences beyond normal comprehension, it should be clear, at least where the greater works and main issues are in question, that the pronouncing of *judgements* is an unprofitable, indeed scarcely a sane, pursuit: the only responsible activity will be interpretative. Our powers of judgement are better employed in the more difficult task of weighing and assessing spiritualistic evidences than in worrying over works of literature already ratified by the imagination to which alone they are addressed (p. 19 above). My present volume has no, or very few, critical asides. Nor are my choices of writers to be read as a 'critical' selection; it would be very wrong to suppose that any names omitted are to that extent being adversely 'judged'. I write primarily of certain themes, works, or men that have been either unduly neglected, or their true nature not hitherto recognized and mapped.

Nor must it be supposed that in my hands 'interpretation' is a facile extraction of spirit meanings from complex wholes. What I always aim to interpret is not a readily paraphrasable thought-content, but, so far as may be, each whole in turn; and that whole is, as we have seen (p. 33 above), made from the admixture of matter-of-fact and mystery; it is from that *admixture* that the magical effect comes; and it is this magic that I aim, and always have aimed, to interpret.

Magic is a very practical matter. If one reviews what have been in the past my own major poetic concerns, they are found not to be Donne, the seventeenth-century religious poets, nor Christopher Smart, nor Blake, nor Hopkins, nor Francis Thompson, but those with a more human, and so more practical, reference: Shakespeare, Pope, Byron and the Romantics,

---

[1] See my account of Gordon Craig in *Shakespearian Production*, enlarged 1964. In calling his stage colourings 'soft' (219) I may there have given a slightly false impression: they were that, but rich also, and deep.

Nietzsche, Ibsen, Wilde, Powys, Berry. The New Testament and Dante have been treated to emphasize their *human* reference. Nor, if my more creative activities are adduced, do we find anything different. My *Atlantic Crossing* and *The Dynasty of Stowe* are sharply autobiographical though artistically pointed and controlled: in my own mind their peculiar blend of fact and fancy has always been felt to derive from Joyce's patterning in *Ulysses*. My drama *The Last of the Incas* exactly follows its sources, driving to the limit Byron's tenet that 'pure invention is but the talent of a liar' (to John Murray, 12 April 1817; *LJ*, IV. 93).[1] My recently published poems in *Gold-Dust* are, as its introduction explains, based on personal experiences of the humanly seraphic.[2] Of my unpublished works there are the three early novels which, though certainly fiction, were experientially impelled. *Road to Kasvin*, on my years in the army, attains artistic form and climax within confinement to what Othello calls 'a plain, unvarnished tale'. *Soldier's Daughter*, on my mother, on my visit in 1951 to the scenes of her childhood in Jamaica, and on spiritualistic communications with her, is an art-form made from the interrelation of factual sections.

Symbol of Man, my esoteric work on the dramatic and spiritual significances of body-action illustrated by nude poses, remains, I suspect, unpublished by reason of the *physical* impact of its illustrations. My emphasis on nudity as a stage power in *Shakespearian Production* has been abundantly justified in recent years; not only in the advanced American musicals, but in Shakespeare, at Stratford-on-Avon.

Whether this absence of supernatural emphasis – though *Atlantic Crossing* has its speculations and *The Dynasty of Stowe* its ghosts – reduces the stature of the works concerned, it is not for me to say. Perhaps I am so used to handling the marvellous in other writers that I am the less anxious to work in that vein myself. There is, however, a unifying principle to be observed: in my commentaries I have laboured to establish a human and realistic reference in the apparent extravagances of great literature, whereas in creative writing I have given imaginative form to actualities. Both

[1] The various productions of my play are listed in *Shakespeare and Religion*, 'Shakespeare and the Incas', 139. It is well devised for broadcasting.

[2] My poem 'The Gift' might almost be regarded as a forecast of what is today happening as youth takes suicidally to drugs in reaction to a murderous and vision-thwarting society.

types of composition derive equally from an awareness of the impingement of mystery on fact. But I am myself no mystic nor clairvoyant, and have made no visionary claims. If I had such gifts I would not have spent my life searching for truth elsewhere.

If I were to praise myself, it would be for very different qualities, among them a strong sense of evidence. To this my support of formerly disputed but now accepted Shakespearian plays or passages has, over the years, borne witness; and so surely has my handling of Byronic controversy, as summarized in the Appendix to *Byron and Shakespeare*. It is indeed precisely because I feel at home with evidence that in religion I turn to Spiritualism; for, whatever our views as to its evidence, it unquestionably has a massive amount of it, much of a high order; whereas all other religious philosophies, including atheism, make far greater claims on no real evidence at all, relying on 'faith'. Religious faith is close to the poetic imagination, and I am obviously not out to denigrate either (p. 34 above). Christianity with its Fall and Cross faces horrors which Spiritualist doctrine, following Christ himself, and Nietzsche's *Zarathustra*, appears to transcend (pp. 183-7 below). But the horrors exist; and Dostoievsky's Grand Inquisitor had a case. Moreover, my trust in human survival derived first from my study of great poetry, not from Spiritualism, which served simply as a ratification. But after many years of meditating the metaphysics of poetry and thinking, or trying to think, in terms of the timeless, or space-time, dimension, I have decided that, for the more immediate and practical purposes of earthly life and death, Spiritualism, in tune with the teaching of Christ rather than Christianity, will be, at least if complemented by the doctrine of Powys (pp. 162-5 below), our best guide. Spiritualism, in close alignment with Pope's *Essay on Man* – Pope is sometimes quoted by the famous spirit-guide Moontrail – has the makings of a world-religion. To our moods of scepticism, Spiritualism brings evidence, and to our mental complexities, simplicity. It has what I regard as the most convincing of all philosophies, without which our various university departments cannot become mutually communicative; for it touches them all (see pp. 31-2, 393).

World affairs have been handled in many of my books; we are too ready to neglect the relevance of our literature to what is happening today. Others have laboured too, and I would point to Bonamy Dobrée's survey of public themes in *The Broken Cistern* (1954), and his *Rudyard Kipling* (1967); and to the devotion of James B. Fell, in both lectures and poetry (*Song of Noel and other poems*, 1961), to awake a national consciousness from great figures of the past, especially Cromwell and Milton. My own interpretations have been politically neither 'right' nor 'left', but have relied rather, in accord with the Shakespearian magic, on the Crown. The Crown still exerts magic, if nothing else; it is precisely for its magic that it has been preserved. Today we see two widespread impulses: (i) natural and libertarian assertions and (ii) a forced drive towards world-order. When that world-order is established, it would be well if the royal principle were active; for its function is to link earthly existence to higher spheres. All that I have written of empire, royalism, and liberty – my essay on Tennyson points my meaning – would then find its place. But what of Britain? For her, much has changed, but General Smuts' prophecy that after the last war Britain's role would, despite imperial weakening, become culturally central, has been fulfilled. Her language is fast becoming a natural esperanto, and Shakespeare binds the world. Of Britain's new, multi-racial, vocation, Francis Berry is the poetic voice (p. 473 below). Even with our Pop groups we have been leaders: The Beatles have peregrinated and permeated the globe.

My concern with national affairs was evident in my *Hiroshima*, written within a fortnight of the dropping of the bomb; its forecasts and alignments were sound, and I would alter nothing. I tried, during the recent (1967) Arab and Israel troubles, to put forward my views on them, and on the Suez crisis; but without success. Perhaps more important for my present argument, I have twice attempted to put forward a solution to the Rhodesian *impasse* in terms of royalty; believing that its magic, to which Rhodesia responds, might yet make a unique contribution.

All this I write to insist that my writings are closely involved in the earthly drama; but I see that drama as part of a greater drama. I wish that more people today would take to heart Pope's *Essay on Man* (I. 57):

> So Man, who here seems principal alone,
> Perhaps acts second to some sphere unknown,
> Touches some wheel, or verges to some goal;
> 'Tis but a part we see, and not a whole.

Or Blake, in *The Marriage of Heaven and Hell*:

Man has no Body distinct from his Soul; for that call'd Body is a portion of Soul discern'd by the five Senses, the chief inlets of Soul in this age.

That is one of those ultimate simplicities so hard to hold in the mind; but it must be done.

For our last word we turn to A. E. Housman. His elegiac poetry in *A Shropshire Lad* sounded in the early years of this century a note of tragic youth prophetic of what was to follow. He was poetically within death, and its meaning. One of the few longer lyrics, 'The Merry Guide' (XLII), describes a beyond-death flight, guided by a Hermes-spirit, within a spirit company refined from earthly existence:

> With the great gale we journey
>   That breathes from gardens thinned,
> Borne in the drift of blossoms
>   Whose petals throng the wind;
>
> Buoyed on the heaven-heard whisper
>   Of dancing leaflets whirled
> From all the woods that autumn
>   Bereaves in all the world.
>
> (XLII)

With the legion of 'all that ever died' he journeys on, beside him the silent guide

> With lips that brim with laughter
>   But never once respond,
> And feet that fly on feathers,
>   And serpent-circled wand.

In this seraphic being Housman's concentration on tragic youth re-appears transfigured. More, it illuminates the rest; for within his survey of life's transience and love's brittleness his invocations to death are not wholly sad. He can salute 'the lads that will die in their glory and never be old' (XXIII), and in 'The Immortal Part' can endue *bones* with the eternality usually accorded spirit:

> Bring the eternal seed to light
> And morn is all the same as night.
>
> (XLIII)

He is often found reaching out to, or at least towards, the statement of 'The Merry Guide'.

What, we may ask, was the relation of his poetic intuition to his astringent classical scholarship? He specialized in Manilius, author of the *Astronomica*, a poem on astrology. The Oxford Classical Dictionary records: 'Manilius writes as an enthusiast for his subject, anxious to make converts and to provide practical instruction for their use'. Here is, at least, a possible link; perhaps Housman found in astrology intimations of a cosmic harmony beyond earthly science. He enjoyed using his own ruthless intellect in attacking the tendencies of contemporary scholarship, which he thought over-ready to reverse the emendations of the past and so reduce harmony to chaos. The excessive venom of these attacks may perhaps be regarded as a compensation for Housman's inability or reluctance to write openly of his more visionary instincts. Some of his phrases read well if expanded into a general critique of our over-confident seats of learning.

We live in an age of scepticism, unlike any that has preceded. We would do well to remember this, and be diffident of claiming a unique enlightenment. In his inaugural lecture at Cambridge in 1911, recently published in *The Times Literary Supplement* (9 May 1968) and now published as *The Confines of Criticism* (Cambridge 1969), Housman, who made a practice of dealing with matters of classical scholarship as though the destiny of man was at stake – and who can be sure that he was wrong? – said:

This is the felicity of the house of bondage, and of the soul which is so fast in prison that it cannot get forth; which commands no outlook upon the past or the future, but believes that the fashion of the present, unlike all fashions heretofore, will endure perpetually, and that its own flimsy tabernacle of second-hand opinions is a habitation for everlasting. And not content with believing these improbable things it despises those who do not believe them, and . . .

– but it is safer to close here. In controversy Housman had a manner all his own.

The final wisdom of John Cowper Powys was given in stories of space-travel. On Christmas morning 1968 three astronauts read, from Moon to Earth, the account in Genesis of God's Spirit within Creation.

PART TWO

Obscenities

CHAPTER II

Who Wrote *Don Leon?*

The Twentieth Century, CLVI. 929; July 1954.

IN 1866 THERE WAS published in London, under the publisher's title 'Printed for the Booksellers', a work apparently printed in Alençon and bearing on the title-page:

> *Don Leon:* a poem by the late Lord Byron, and forming part of the Private Journal of his lordship, supposed to have been entirely destroyed by Thos. Moore. To which is added *Leon to Annabella*, an epistle from Lord Byron to Lady Byron.

To the second poem is prefixed a statement describing how the lines were discovered in a cottage near Pisa. The poems are in rhymed couplets and extend to 1465 and 330 lines respectively. To the first are added 63 pages of notes ranging from obvious pornography to research among the poets of the ancient world (though these headings are not mutually exclusive). No editor is named, nor is the author, or authors (since there are probably more than one) of the notes. In his *Index Librorum Prohibitorum* (London, privately printed, 1877), 'Pisanus Fraxi' (i.e. H. S. Ashbee) says that W. Dugdale, whom he names as the publisher, showed him the MS., which appeared to have been 'written some years previously', but 'was evidently not the original written by the author', having been copied by some 'illiterate person' with many errors among the Greek and Latin quotations. He also records that he pointed out to Mr. Dugdale that *Don Leon* refers to events which happened after Byron's death.

The 1866 volume appears, apart from a single letter in *Notes and Queries* asking for information regarding it, to have attracted little notice. In his bibliography of Byron, T. J. Wise describes it as 'of course, spurious'. There was a reissue, unedited, in 1934, but it was regarded as spurious. Sales were prohibited, and since then no critical attention seems to have been focused on it.

The first poem, *Don Leon*, contains: (i) a powerful attack on the prevailing laws, which included the death-penalty, in force against homosexual practices, with attacks on statesmen such as Mackintosh, Sidmouth and Peel; (ii) a supposedly autobiographical account of Byron's youthful anxieties regarding his own instincts and the passionate friendships to which they led him, together with some vivid descriptions of the East; (iii) a large number of references to men of public note in connection variously with statesmanship, literature, Byron's own affairs, and homosexuality; and (iv) an intimate description, supposedly by Byron, of an irregular relation with his wife during her pregnancy, leading on to the second poem, *Leon to Annabella*, which tells the story of the marriage-break and Byron's gradually formed conviction that knowledge of irregular intercourse must have been drawn from Lady Byron by the opposing party, who is regarded as responsible for poisoning her mind with respect to it, and so ruining the marriage. These themes we shall notice in turn.

(i) The attack lies in the great tradition of English satire. Here is part of the opening movement:

> And shall the Muse, whilst pen and paper lie
> Upon the table, hear the victim's cry,
> Nor boldly lay her cauterizing hand
> Upon a wound that cankers half the land?
> No! were the bays that flourish round my head
> Destined to wither when these lines are read;
> Could all the scourges canting priests invent
> To prop their legendary lies, torment
> My soul in death or rack my body here,
> My voice I'd raise insensible to fear.
> When greedy placemen drain a sinking state,
> When virtue starves and villains dine off plate;
> When lords and senators, untouched by shame,
> For schemes of basest fraud can lend their name;
> When elders, charged to guard the pauper's trust,
> Feast on the funds, and leave the poor a crust;
> When knaves like these escape the hangman's noose,
> Who e'en to Clogher a pardon would refuse?

Who Wrote Don Leon?

Who would not up and lend a hand to save
A venial culprit from a felon's grave?
Sheer indignation quickens into rhyme,
And silence now were tantamount to crime.
I know not in what friendly breast to pour
My swelling rage, save into thine, dear Moore,
For thou, methinks, some sympathy will own,
Since love, no matter in what guise 'tis shown,
Must ever find an echo from that lyre
Which erst hath glowed with old Anacreon's fire.

(Don Leon, 19)

That sets the stage for a lengthy apologia, with many references to great men of ancient, medieval and Renaissance times, including Shakespeare, who possessed homosexual tendencies.

(ii) In my *Lord Byron: Christian Virtues*, I set down the story of Byron's romantic friendships with Robert Rushton, John Edleston, Nicolo Giraud, William Harness, and others (67-74). This had not, as far as I know, been done before. Separate instances had been noted by biographers from Moore to Quennell, but they had not been allowed to take the stage-centre, and there had been no apparent consciousness of the sequence as an important and cohering unit; nor perhaps could there have been without use of the new biographical technique which I was using. My account was composed before ever I read *Don Leon*, which tells the same story with all the attendant detail and vivid extensions that might be supposed to characterize an autobiographical treatment; and that would have been an amazing *tour de force* for a mid-nineteenth century biographer, working on the published sources at that time available. Here are some lines introducing John Edleston, the Cambridge chorister:

Oft, when the evening bell to vespers rung,
When the full choir the solemn anthem sung,
And lips, o'er which no youthful down had grown,
Hymned their soft praises to Jehovah's throne,
The pathos of the strain would soothe my soul,
And call me willing from the drunkard's bowl.
Who that has heard the chapel's evening song,
When peals divine the lengthened note prolong,
But must have felt religious thoughts arise,
And speed their way melodious to the skies?

(Don Leon, 201)

Byron's relations with Edleston and Nicolo Giraud are exactly handled. Of this strain in Byron's emotional life there is more evidence than has yet been pointed out, including his alteration of a title and the veiling of a designation in *Childe Harold* (see *Works, Poetry*, ed. E. Hartley Coleridge, I. 18-19, and II. 162-3, notes); and also Augusta's anxiety on one occasion (Byron to Augusta, 14 September 1816; Lord Lovelace, *Astarte*, 1921; XI. 268) as to his actions on the Continent. All this is scarcely surprising. Had Byron not shown such a tendency we might, having regard to others of comparable powers, have nevertheless suspected it.

(iii) The references to contemporaries of Byron are numerous. They are names which occur elsewhere in his writings. I have checked them with his own authenticated comments, in prose or poetry, and the correspondences in judgement and tone are correct.

(iv) The mystery of Byron's marriage-disaster has never been satisfactorily explained. Whether or not incest had occurred earlier, it is known not to have been the immediate cause of the separation. Richard Edgcumbe long ago argued from internal evidence that Byron's letter from Venice of 17 May 1819, was not addressed to Augusta at all (*Byron: The Last Phase*, 1909; III. 368-73); Samuel Chew accepts his conclusion (*Byron in England*, 1924; XV. 338-9); but the argument does not appear to have been faced, and in *Byron: a Self-Portrait* Peter Quennell's annotation merely states that it 'has been assumed' to be addressed to Augusta (II. 451). More than incest is involved, since, if Edgcumbe was right, why did Augusta pretend to be the addressee? Either way, the behaviour of Lady Byron and Augusta after the separation has hitherto remained inexplicable. But from the start dark hints were thrown out of something worse than incest (J. C. Hobhouse, Lord Broughton, *Recollections of a Long Life*, II. xv. 301, 349-352; and see Lovelace, *Astarte*, VIII. 182); and to this Moore might have been referring when he wrote of the uselessness of judging by 'ordinary standards' the 'passions untamed' of such a man as Byron (*Life*, I. 656, or XXV. 298). Beside Walter Scott's reported remark on the destruction of the *Memoirs*, 'It was a pity, but there *was* a reason – *premat nox alta*' (*Astarte*, VI. 122), we may place certain of the Maniac's lines in *Julian and Maddalo*, read according to my recently argued and firmly substantiated interpretation (*Lord Byron: Christian Virtues*, 251-3), with the Maniac as an aspect of Byron. From this interpretation *Julian and Maddalo* becomes, for the first time, evidence regarding the separation. The Maniac speaks, addressing the lady who has rejected him:

> That you had never seen me – never heard
> My voice, and more than all had ne'er endured
> The deep pollution of my loathed embrace –
> That your eyes ne'er had lied love in my face –
> That, like some maniac monk, I had torn out
> The nerves of manhood by their bleeding root
> With mine own quivering fingers, so that ne'er
> Our hearts had for a moment mingled there
> To disunite in horror . . .
>
> (*Julian and Maddalo*, 420)

That is addressed by the Maniac to his lady, and may be supposed to correspond to 'that one slip of my poor silly tongue' in *Leon to Annabella* (264). There has been a 'deadly change in love' from 'one vowed deeply' (527-8), and the lady is said to rain 'plagues of blistering agony' (453) on him. The secret is divulged by Maddalo's daughter at the poem's conclusion, which reads:

> I urged and questioned still; she told me how
> All happened – but the cold world shall not know.
>
> (616)

The operative word is 'cold'. Col. Stanhope's reference to Hobhouse's destroying 'from motives of high honour' one of Byron's last and finest works of which he himself refuses ever to divulge the nature (*Lord Byron: Christian Virtues*, 32) may be apposite. In one of the best discussions yet advanced on the subject John Drinkwater suggested that the elusive nature of the riddle behind the correspondence of Lady Byron and Augusta 'so plausibly taken to be incest' might turn out to be 'a yet more obscure secret than is commonly allowed'; he suspects that 'the circumstances, themselves', may be 'out of our reckoning'; and says that his own view is 'that the conclusive last word of the story has yet to be revealed' (*The Pilgrim of Eternity*, 1925; I. 70-1, 75-6, 77).

Neither Byron's break with London nor the weight of his invectives against British 'cant' can be explained in terms of ordinary sexual freedom, since he does not appear to have been a peculiarly licentious man (*Lord Byron: Christian Virtues*, 42-3), and his record in Regency society was, according to Hobhouse, merely that of 'a man of the world' (*Recollections*, II. xv. 196). Nevertheless, in a less accessible passage listing his great qualities, Hobhouse made a reservation regarding his 'many failings' (*Lord Byron: Christian Virtues*, 94). That is typical; Moore and others have said the same; but *no one tells us what they were.*

Was the cause of all this mystery-mongering less a matter of good and evil than one of *embarrassment*? Even if Byron did not write *Don Leon*, its facts may bear some relation to the truth. Do *Julian and Maddalo* and *Don Leon* together answer to the 'x' of our equation, throwing everything into significant pattern? Was incest played up by Lady Byron's party *as a mask*?

The instinct in question appears to have been a constituent in a number of men of poetic genius, from the ancients down. That *Don Leon* should speak out on the general matter of homosexuality more boldly than its predecessors or successors, is only what we should expect from Byron or anyone deliberately aiming at a Byronic effect. But the poem offers no simple thesis. The defence is strongly countered by words or phrases of traditional condemnation, such as 'weakness' (276), 'infirmities' (376), 'infamy' (392), 'morbid lust' (17), 'depravity of mind' (381), 'these inclinations rank and strong' (243). This address to Peel is typical:

> A single scratch of thy reforming pen,
> Had from our code erased a peccant lust,
> And left its punishment to men's disgust.
>
> *Don Leon*, 1344)[1]

Such phraseology appears beside the idealism. We have both, presented in sharp contrapuntal, or dramatic, opposition:

> Look, how infected with this rank disease
> Were those who held St. Peter's holy keys,
> And pious men to whom the people bowed,
> And kings, who churches to the saints endowed;
> All these were Christians of the highest stamp –
> How many scholars, wasting o'er their lamp,
> How many jurists, versed in legal rules,
> How many poets, honoured in the schools,
> How many captains, famed for deeds of arms,
> Have found their solace in a minion's arms!

---

[1] For the line-references of *Don Leon* from 1210 onwards see p. 127n. 1, below.

Who Wrote Don Leon?

> Nay, e'en our bard, Dame Nature's darling child,
> Felt the strange impulse, and his hours beguiled
> In penning sonnets to a stripling's praise,
> Such as would damn a poet now-a-days.
>
> *(Don Leon, 305)*

'Rank disease' holds irony. But it is not all irony. Such phrases are variously used. The defence is fully aware of, has taken into account, lived through, and surmounted, moral condemnation and abhorrence. This extraordinary balance and control of emotionally charged opposites might well seem in itself to constitute evidence for Byron's authorship.

But there are difficulties. Though the emotional impulse and accent is Byronic, the poetic surface is not exactly his. Indeed, I know nothing in rhymed couplets quite like it. Pope's influence is present, and the strong central caesura of his earlier manner is occasionally found, as in the fourth of these lines:

> Then tell me not of sex, if to one key
> The chords, when struck, vibrate in harmony.
> No virgin I deflower, nor, lurking, creep,
> With steps adult'rous, on a husband's sleep.
> I plough no field in other men's domain;
> And where I delve no seed shall spring again.
>
> *(Don Leon, 247)*

The general movement at times recalls the swing and impetus of the later Pope, but is perhaps nearer Byron's *English Bards and Scotch Reviewers* or *The Age of Bronze*, though the poetry shows a more rounded solidity of phrase, or rather of *word*, and in general a weightier impact, than those. There is, too, a dark anger beyond anything in Byron's poetry elsewhere, except, significantly, for his *Sketch*; but this would be understandable, since his deepest personal instincts would have been engaged, as in the terrible letter on Sir Samuel Romilly discussed in my Byron Foundation Lecture *Byron's Dramatic Prose* (reprinted in *Poets of Action*, 1967). Such are the emotions which give us this couplet on, presumably, since he is mentioned elsewhere, Lady Byron's other legal adviser, Dr. Lushington:

> Behold yon reptile with his squinting eyes:
> Him shall my curses follow till he dies . . .
>
> *(Don Leon, 1042)*

If such lines are not Byron's, who in the nineteenth century could have written them? It is as though they combined the fire of Byron's poetry with the verbal weight of his prose; certainly the impact of a total personality is behind them.

Yet, again, there are qualities that are not Byronic. In Byron's couplets, words do not so assert themselves as integral, weighted, units. Besides, words are used, and repeated, that do not belong to Byron's work as we know it, and there is no Byronic parallel to the masterly punning of the obscene passages. Moreover, as 'Pisanus Fraxi' observed, incidents appear to be mentioned which occurred after Byron's death. Analysis suggests that the date-limit lies somewhere about the year 1833. The incidents are of three sorts: (i) certain references to Peel regarding matters of legislation; (ii) correct forecasts of trouble to come in respect of homosexuality to people of note living in Byron's day; and (iii) a warning to Moore, as from Byron, not to *burn* these confessions, which appears to presuppose a knowledge of what actually happened to the *Memoirs* after Byron's death. That these are additions is theoretically possible, but there is no variation whatsoever in style.

That some charlatan later in the century could have shown so brilliant an insight into Byron's story and steered his course among a number of themes and persons without a slip in reference, opinion, and emotion, is, as we have already suggested, most unlikely. Nor can Byron be the author of, at least, the first poem, as it stands, though *Leon to Annabella* contains no late references. We are left with only one possibility: a contemporary and intimate of Byron, who lived beyond the year 1833, and whose mastery of language and general outlook were of a kind that could have written the poems.

Such a candidate, however, is not so easy to hit on. Scott, Moore, and Crabbe must, for obvious reasons, be rejected. It was not until George Colman the dramatist, who died in 1836, was suggested as a possible candidate, that light began to dawn. Colman was one of those whom Byron urged in *English Bards and Scotch Reviewers* to 'awake' and chastise the age as it deserved. Afterwards, the two became friendly. Byron spent convivial evenings with him and Sheridan. In his *Detached Thoughts* (107; *LJ*, V. 461) he wrote that 'Sheridan was a Grenadier Company of Life Guards, but Colman a whole regiment – of *light Infantry*, to be sure, but still a *regiment'*. Knowing Byron's admiration of Sheridan, we can call that high praise. It would seem that *Don Juan* owes something to Colman's light verse. Here is the opening of *The Knight and the Friar* (in *Broad Grins*, 1802):

> In our Fifth Harry's reign, when 'twas the fashion
>   To thump the French, poor creatures! to excess –
> Though Britons, now-a-days, show more compassion,
>   And thump them, certainly, a great deal less –
> In Harry's reign, when flush'd Lancastrian roses
>   Of York's pale blossoms had usurp'd the right;
> As wine drives nature out of drunkards' noses,
>   Till red, triumphantly, eclipses white;
> In Harry's reign – but let me to my song,
> Or good King Harry's reign may seem too long.

Colman's verbal resource is remarkable, and his more bitter satiric thrusts, levelled against pomposity and pride, draw close to *Don Leon*. He is, after all, best known for his study of pedantic pomposity in Dr. Pangloss in *The Heir-at-Law*. In his *Two Parsons, or the Tale of a Shirt* (*Poetical Vagaries*, 1812) he writes of Bow Street officers and

> Those infinitely grander drudges,
> The big-wigg'd circuiteering Judges

and

> The vice-suppressing, starch'd Society –
> That tribe of self-erected prigs – whose leaven
> Consists in *buckramizing* souls for Heaven;
> Those stiff-rump'd buzzards, who evince the vigour
> Of Christian virtue by unchristian rigour;
> Those quacks and Quixotes, who in coalition
> Compose the canters' secret Inquisition;
> Dolts, in our tolerating constitution,
> Who turn morality to persecution,
> And, through their precious pates' fanatick twists,
> Are part informers, spies, and Methodists.

Though this is earlier work and comes from a light poem, there is nevertheless something of the same punch and pungency, the same easy use of well-loaded single words, the same bitterness, the same moral valuation, as in *Don Leon*.

A cursory glance through his pages shows a number of parallels in vocabulary and thought. With 'the Key-keeper of Chandos

Street' occurring in *Two Parsons*, compare the references to 'the Key' at *Don Leon*, 877, and the note on it as a brothel in Chandos Street. The word 'urchin' is used in relation to 'Hymen' and amorous 'play' in *The Knight and the Friar* (Part I); and we have 'Hymen' and 'the playful urchin' (i.e. sexual organ) together in *Leon to Annabella* (281, 285). With 'He bit him in the part where honour's placed' in *Low Ambition* (*Poetical Vagaries*), compare the similar connotations in *Don Leon* of 'Where honour, sensitive, a shelter seeks' (1449) and 'Health, ease, and honour centre in that spot' (1455). In 'A Reckoning with Time' in *Low Ambition* we have:

> Grains of the grammar, which the flails
> Of Pedants thresh upon our tails,

corresponding to 'Boys, tickled by the tail, in wisdom grow' in *Don Leon* (1425). We have an association of Bashaws and tails in 'The Lady of the Wreck', II. 21 (*Poetical Vagaries*), the play *Blue-Beard* (I. i; II. v), and *Don Leon* (1426; for Bashaws and tails see pp. 131-2 below). In both *Don Leon* (844-5) and the play *John Bull* (II. ii), we find a carriage in St. James's Street associated with a woman's love-life. Some of the notes to Colman's poetry recall the notes to *Don Leon*.

The plays themselves, superficially so different from *Don Leon*, are nevertheless basically akin. *Don Leon* contains passages of remarkable punning, and Colman and his plays were noted for puns: Jeremy F. Bagster-Collins in *George Colman the Younger* (New York, 1946; I. 34) says that they were for him 'a life-long devotion, both on and off the stage'. The oriental settings and ceremonies of such plays as *Blue-Beard*, *The Mountaineers*, *The Africans* and *The Law of Java* would have given Colman the equipment for the oriental descriptions of *Don Leon*. As for his serious themes, these show a general satire against selfish nobility, the heartless rich, a moneyed society where every one tries to ruin every one else (*John Bull*, II. i), tyranny of any kind, brutal justice, humbug of all sorts, with an especial horror of executions, the slave-trade, and imperialism in general. All this suits the author of *Don Leon*:

> Now turn your eyes athwart the Speaker's chair:
> A pious orator is seated there.
> In vain the negro's cause he nightly pleads;
> Tells how the gangrened back with lashes bleeds ...
> (*Don Leon*, 978)

Who Wrote Don Leon?

The plays show regularly a firm support of the lowly, simple country-folk, and savages, and all in whom the vices of civilization and sophistication are not present. Love is central, suffering or succeeding in relation to these themes and values; though it is, of course, love of a conventional kind. We can say that a central emphasis falls on emotional integrity, expanding to generosity and gratitude as natural powers; and on the other side, there is horror at false friends, money-greed, ingratitude, and time-servers. Colman's serious work is to this extent Byronic, and also on the exact wave-length of *Timon of Athens*, his embittered recluse Orzinga in *The Law of Java* being a far from unsatisfying replica of Shakespeare's hero. The spectacular scene of the forbidden Blue Room in *Blue-Beard* might be regarded as a psychological symbolism relevant to our discussion; but, apart from any such interpretation, it will be clear that the mind-structure and emotional sympathies of the dramatist are close to those of the author of *Don Leon*. It may be significant that the persons who represent Colman's considered wisdom in two of his most important works, Steadfast in *The Heir-at-Law* and Peregrine in *John Bull*, are old bachelors.

But what, then, was Colman's purpose? Clearly, he cannot have expected Byron's authorship of *Don Leon* to be accepted; but he is equally clearly claiming to tell the truth of Byron's life. He might well have been, as, no doubt, were many others of Byron's friends, in a position to know the truth; *Julian and Maddalo* appears, as we have seen, to tell, or rather hint, the same facts; and we may suppose him, with all the abhorrence of hypocrisy so evident in his work, to have been deeply shocked by the burning of Byron's *Memoirs*. Moore is ironically warned:

> And, nor for filthy lucre, nor to dine
> At Holland House, erase one single line.
>
> (*Don Leon*, 51)

The poet fears

> Lest, under false pretences, thou should'st turn
> A faithless friend, and these confessions burn.
>
> (*Don Leon*, 1283)

That is being written by one who had known the *Memoirs* burned, and who, as have others, blamed Moore for allowing it. Moore's

123

Who Wrote Don Leon?

Life of Byron had appeared in 1830, with the assertion that the *Memoirs* cast no light on the separation. Was the author of *Don Leon* revealing the truth?

Whether he was working from his reminiscences of Byron's talk, or from letters or poems of Byron now lost, must remain uncertain. He diverges from Moore on the matter of Nicolo Giraud's parentage, and it would be interesting to know who is right. Certainly *Don Leon* must henceforth be faced as evidence. It is unlikely that a friend of Byron's, a kindred spirit whose sincerity rings in every couplet, was deliberately lying. The poems are honest. Had he wished them to be accepted as Byron's he would have avoided errors in date: the very first line of *Don Leon* is given a note, which seems to be the poet's, deliberately, and half-humorously, pointing to a discrepancy. What we have is really an imaginative reconstruction not unlike Shelley's *Julian and Maddalo*, only far more dramatically convincing, Byron's very accent being again and again captured with amazing skill. Nor is the author only out to interpret Byron's story; he is also using that story as a basis for a general challenge.

And the challenge is one of considerable power. On a literary judgement alone, I know nothing of the sort of so sustained a mastery outside Pope; throughout it is, as Byron said of Pope's, 'poetry without fault'. Handling in deadly earnest substances, both *risqué* and satiric, which can be felt behind the themes of Colman's humorous pieces, *Don Leon* blends indecency of reference with moral valuations of the noblest kind. Its refusal to pass by the injustice which 'hangs the pennyless and spares the lord' (929) is in direct line with both Colman's satiric outlook and Byron's horror of penal cruelty (*Lord Byron: Christian Virtues*, 200-2; and see 232, quoting Lady Blessington); the psychology, especially certain advice to parents, is profound; even the vigorous punning of the obscene passages, in the manner of Petruchio's wooing of Katharine (*The Taming of the Shrew*, II. i. 196-217), marks no relaxation of high seriousness. *Don Leon* ranks among the great satires of our literature, and its plea for those who, in every age, are driven to suicide by fear of society deserves respect:

> Britons! and will no penalty suffice
> Except the gibbet for a lecher's vice?
> To lose his country, to behold the chain
> That linked his best affections snapt in twain,

To find no refuge for his stricken head,
Where'er he goes to know his shame is spread,
And is not this enough, without he's cast
By judge and jury? Fiends would cry 'Avast!'
Blot out the crimson leaf! the glaive forbear!
Count o'er the wretched victims of despair,
The panic flight, the suicidal beam,
The knife, the bullet, do they trifles seem?
Thirst ye for blood? and will no punishment
But what Old Bailey metes, your hearts content?

(Don Leon, 988)

The attack is mainly against England, reminding us that 'that little spot which constitutes our isle' is not 'the world' (1387). Again:

God of the universe, whose laws shall last,
When Lords and Commons to their graves have past,
Are good and evil just as man opines,
And kens he thy inscrutable designs?

(Don Leon, 1401)

As in Pope's *Essay on Man*, we are reminded how one nation's heresy is another's creed.

It has not been possible to indicate the extent of the evidence supporting the view that *Don Leon* is the work of someone intimately acquainted with, and attuned to, Byron's life and opinions; nor the arguments against his authorship of the poem, as we have it, nor those which support that of Colman. Whatever be the truth, the poetry exists and challenges attention; it may be bold, but it is honest, and we today can surely appreciate its worth. There is, indeed, no satiric work in English of greater force:

My fears were just! Infatuated maid,
And have their arts your innocence betrayed?
How could'st thou go, *opinions* vile to beg,
And hang thy conscience on a lawyer's peg? –
Some lisping fool, with empty dictums big,
Proud of his LL.D. and periwig.
His mind was not the crucible to try
The deep arcana of love's alchemy . . .

(Leon to Annabella, 239)

Who Wrote Don Leon?

We are reminded of those 'big-wigged circuiteering judges' in our passage from *Two Parsons* and of the absurd and pompous Dr. Pangloss in *The Heir-at-Law*, Colman's most famous single creation, so proud of his status as 'LL.D., A double-S' (for *Artium Societatis Socius*).

The *Don Leon* poems are disturbing; some might call them dangerous; but they are great. Their poetry is all solid bronze, and their valuations just. In *Don Leon* a new planet swims into our ken.

CHAPTER III

Colman and *Don Leon*

———————————————

The Twentieth Century, CLIX. 952; June 1956.

IN MY ARTICLE 'Who wrote *Don Leon*?' in *The Twentieth Century* of July 1954 I gave reason to suppose that the two mysterious poems *Don Leon* and *Leon to Annabella*, which purport to tell the truth, involving both homosexuality and an illicit relationship with his wife, of Byron's main sexual tendencies, were the work of the well-known dramatist and poet, George Colman the Younger (1762-1836). It is my purpose here to drive home the argument for Colman's authorship.[1]

The *Don Leon* poems are in direct line with Colman's literary work. The general similarity in outlook, prepossession and characterizing technical tricks is in itself close enough to establish a case for his authorship. Colman is fond, like the author of the notes to *Don Leon*, of classical quotations, especially in his autobiography, *Random Records*; and his stage experience would have equipped him for the oriental descriptions. But there are also striking correspondences in detail.

Here are some, taken from the *Don Leon* poems in rough

---

[1] All Colman's light poetry, except for *The Rodiad* (see p. 129n. below), was collected and published in a single volume by Chatto & Windus in 1898. In quoting from *Vagaries Vindicated* I give *page* references to this volume. In my Colman quotations I follow mainly, but not always, the 1898 text, which reduces many of his original capitals. I would draw the attention of those interested in Colman to Jeremy Bagster-Collins' study (p. 122 above).

For the *Don Leon* poems I give line references, but have not done so for the other poems, since they are printed without them, and none of the pieces is long. The numerals of the 1866 edition of *Don Leon* go wrong at l. 1210; my references give the correct numbers.

sequence. *Don Leon* is throughout bitter against the spying of what we should call 'detectives':

> His secret haunts were hid from every soul,
> Till thou did'st send thy myrmidons to prowl . . .
>
> (*Don Leon*, 15)

These are 'the Bow Street gang' (66). Later we have 'Whilst at the scent unkennelled curs give tongue' (75), and

> some poor wight
> By Bow Street bloodhounds to their Jeffreys brought . . .
>
> (*Don Leon*, 859)

In *Two Parsons, or the Tale of a Shirt,* Colman writes of the 'Bow Street Officers' (see p. 121 above).

In *Vagaries Vindicated; or Hypocritic Hypercritics* (1814), an important poem composed in answer to reviewers, we have the 'low informers' of the literary world serving their 'mock judges'; that is, the reviewers (232: *page* reference; see note, p. 127).

The satire is often fierce. The word 'indignation' is accordingly apt. In *Vagaries Vindicated* (235) we find 'But how must indignation doubly boil', which can be compared with 'sheer indignation quickens into rhyme' in *Don Leon* (39). There, too, a hostile critic is compared to one of the Popes in point of sensuality:

> Pope of a prostituted press, who choose
> To thunder bulls against a trifling muse;
> A *half* tenth Leo – sensual as he,
> But no encourager of poetry.
>
> (*Vagaries Vindicated*, 224)

A note tells us: 'Leo the tenth was a very debauched Pope, but a great patron of the *Belles Lettres*'. This naturally points on to

> Look, how infected with this rank disease
> Were those who held St. Peter's holy keys . . .
>
> (*Don Leon*, 305)

The phrase '*heavy* gales of cant' (232) and clerical satire of *Vagaries Vindicated* are of similar satiric quality to

> Oh! England, with thy hypocritic cant,
> To hear the bench declaim, the pulpit rant . . .
>
> (*Don Leon*, 850)

Colman and Don Leon

In *Don Leon* (844-5) and the play *John Bull* (II. ii) we find a carriage in St. James's Street referred to with similar associations (p. 122 above). As already noted, in *Don Leon* we have the line 'Or could not pay a bedroom at the Key' (877), and Note 57 tells us that it was 'a celebrated brothel in Chandos Street'; and *Two Parsons, or the Tale of a Shirt* refers to 'the Key-keeper of Chandos Street'.

Colman is interested in the sexual associations of flogging. His satire *The Rodiad*,[1] which calls the rod 'Cupid's surest instrument', is specifically devoted to the subject:

> Mid folks of high degree the rod's astir
> At Eton, Harrow, Rugby, Westminster,
> Six days in seven making due sensation
> Among the best posteriors of the nation.

Now *Don Leon* also touches on what *The Rodiad* calls the 'Busby code', together with references to other famous headmasters:

> At college bred, and destined for the church,
> You turn a Busby, and you wield the birch.
> Think you there's no incentive in the sight
> Of sixth-form bottoms, naked, round, and white?
> Ask Drury, Butler, sleek-gilled Goodenough,
> How looks a kallipygic disk in buff?
> Ask him of Eton, who if fame speaks true,
> Made open boast he all his scholars knew
> By their posteriors better than their face,
> As most familiar with the nether place.
> Flog, lechers, flog, the measured strokes adjust:
> 'Tis well your cassocks hide your rising lust.
>
> (*Don Leon*, 910)

Later we have a reference to 'the pedagogue's lewd glance' (1202). 'Posteriors' occurred in our *Rodiad* passage. For 'buff' we might

---

[1] On *The Rodiad*, Dr. Joseph Wallfield (p. 139 below) points me to H. S. Ashbee ('Pisanus Fraxi'), *Centuria Librorum Absconditorum* (1879), 471-2. *The Rodiad* was apparently printed in 1871 as by 'George Coleman', misspelt, and dated 1810, though internal evidence indicates 1820 or after. Ashbee denies Colman's hand and claims to know, though he does not name, the author. See also Frederick T. Hibgame, *Notes and Queries*, 10th Series, I. 458-9; 4 June 1904. Hibgame accepts Colman's authorship, but Dr. Wallfield, who told me of the article, distrusts the accuracy of his dates and statements. I find it extremely difficult to believe that the poem's best lines (see my *Lord Byron's Marriage*, 165) are not by the author of *Don Leon*. Ashbee does not appear to have taken into account Colman's almost certain authorship of *Don Leon*. His statement on *The Rodiad* is quoted by J. O. Fuller, *Swinburne*, 1968; 68, note.

compare the Titian painting of a figure in 'luxurious buff' in *Two Parsons, or the Tale of a Shirt*, and reference to Lycurgus making his Spartan girls 'dance and sing in buff' in order to safeguard their boys' morality in *Vagaries Vindicated* (230). Our *Don Leon* couplet on 'cassocks' and 'rising lust', in the passage just quoted, repeats a thought in *Vagaries Vindicated* (235):

> Does history present to our research
> No Churchmen who were scandals to the Church?
> O'er nothing wanton can a cassock float?

We are not surprised to find among parish clerk Caleb Quotem's multifarious civic activities in *The Review, or the Wags of Windsor* the cutting of the 'rumps' of 'little school-boy Jackies' (II. i; the song is quoted in the 1898 volume, p. 127n. above, 401-3).

The 'blue beard Turks' of *Don Leon* (1066) remind us of the play *Blue-Beard, or Female Curiosity*, which is again recalled when Annabella gives way to temptation from curiosity:

> Who, that has seen a woman wavering lie
> Betwixt her shame and curiosity,
> Knowing her sex's failing, will not deem
> That in the balance shame would kick the beam?
>
> (*Don Leon*, 1259)

In *Blue-Beard* we have a mysterious Blue Room which is the only part of a paradisal palace that must not be entered. Before it Fatima and Irene speak, or sing, a duet:

> All is hush'd! No footstep falls!
> And silence reigns within the walls!
> The place invites; the door is near,
> The time is apt – The key is here.
> Say, shall we? Yes. Say, shall we? No!
> What is it makes us tremble so?
> Mischief is not our intent;
> Then wherefore fear we should repent?
> Say, shall we? Yes. The door is near.
> Say, shall we? Yes. The key is here.
>
> (II. iii)

There may well be a reference to illicit and abnormal sexual intercourse. The word 'key' – we may perhaps recall the brothel of that name noticed above – supports such a reading since, with

Colman, winding up a clock is a synonym for sexual intercourse. This we find in *Don Leon*, where women are compared to watches:

> Both are wound up at night – the watch behind;
> But where you place the key to womankind,
> Divulge it not, lest Lushington should know . . .
>
> (*Don Leon*, 1441)

This may be placed beside the account (noticed above) by Caleb Quotem in *The Review, or the Wags of Windsor*, singing of his various activities:

> At night by the fire, like a good jolly cock,
>   When my day's work is done and all over,
> I tipple, I smoke, and I wind up the clock,
>   With my sweet Mrs. Quotem, in clover.
>
> (II. i)

The thought is repeated a little further on with the phrase 'wind up clockery'. Here there is no necessary suggestion of abnormal intercourse, but the use of 'winding' is relevant to our purpose. Where the sinful adventure is in question, we find an interesting use of the word 'maidenhead' in *Don Leon*: 'The ingress smoothed to her new maidenhead' (1266). This neatly balances a similar use in *The Rodiad*, the satire on school flogging, where, though the point is not intercourse, but flogging, the same part of the body is involved:

> What! here's a virgin deaf and dumb with dread –
> Now he shall lose his schoolboy maidenhead . . .

Colman is fascinated by these secret parts, which he usually refers to as the 'tail' – a word which originally means 'hinder part', and does not necessarily bear the modern, specific, connotation. There is a clear pun on 'tale' in the sub-title of *Two Parsons, or the Tale of a Shirt*. In *Don Leon* we have

> Boys, tickled by the tail, in wisdom grow,
> And by their tails bashaws their honour show . . .
>
> (1425)

With which we can compare

> Grains of the grammar, which the flails
> Of Pedants thresh upon our tails

131

in the section 'A Reckoning with Time' of *Low Ambition*. The association of bashaws and tails also occurs elsewhere. Two or three horses' tails were carried before these Turkish dignitaries as a sign of honour, and the custom is referred to in *The Lady of the Wreck* (II. 21), where a cat is called 'only a one-tail'd bashaw'; and also, with emphasis, and a pun, in *Blue-Beard*:

> How prettily, now, he rails!
> But 'tisn't so easily done as said
> To smite a bashaw, and cut off the head,
> Of a man who has got three tails.
>
> (I. i)

The tails have another song (II. v). Colman welcomes any chance suggestion bearing on his favourite complex which is of almost cosmic importance to him:

> Look through the world! whatever mortals do,
> They still must keep their latter end in view –
> Not death; for that let bloated parsons quail:
> Our latter end – what is it, but our tail?
>
> (*Don Leon*, 1445)

'World' and 'end' occur in a passage of *Vagaries Vindicated* of exactly similar innuendo, in a reply to critics who have accused Colman of indecency:

> If I have sinn'd – while you my sins assail,
> Just as Dame Foresight lectures Mrs. Frail –
> Stand forth! – and own, my supercilious friend,
> That You, like Me, have *been at the World's End*.
>
> (225)

In both Colman's *Low Ambition* and *Don Leon* this particular spot is associated with 'honour' (see p. 122 above).

Perhaps it is worth noting that the word 'equipoise' occurs both in 'Things can no longer find their equipoise' at the end of *Don Leon* (1463) and in the line 'whose praise may equipois'd with censure seem' of *Vagaries Vindicated* (225). Also both *Don Leon* and *Vagaries Vindicated* use 'St. Stephen's' for the House of Commons. In the one we have:

> But whilst St. Stephen's candles still give light
> Let us resume our seats.
>
> (*Don Leon*, 1321)

Colman and Don Leon

In the other:

> When in the chapel of that Saint whose bones
> Were pelted, till he *fell asleep*, by stones;
> Where Britons now, although they do not kill,
> Unmercifully pelt each other still . . .   (248)

A note says: 'St. Stephen's Chapel, i.e. the House of Commons'. Another interesting correspondence is the unusual use of 'taper' as an adjective, meaning 'thin'. This occurs twice in *Don Leon* (656, 1160), and once in *Leon to Annabella* (167). Now in *Two Parsons, or The Tale of a Shirt* we have 'But finding guineas in the till run taper', and in Colman's autobiography *Random Records* we find 'but with legs much too taper to be efficient props of so grand a superstructure' (II. 118).

We pass to a rather more complex analysis. In the *Don Leon* poems the male sexual organ is felt as an independent, playful, entity or personality, as in 'The breechless vagrant has no settled spot' (*Leon to Annabella*, 297). Now 'urchin' is a word used for 'child' in *Don Leon* (1211), *Leon to Annabella* (223), and *Vagaries Vindicated* (236); and it can be used for both Cupid and the sexual organ. After being told of the absurdity of trying 'young Hymen's inoffensive sports' by law, we are told that 'the playful urchin meditates no sin' (*Leon to Annabella*, 281, 285). We have an interesting correspondence in *The Knight and the Friar* (Part I), where the poet addresses the 'God of Love' as 'urchin of spite and play', who often deserts 'saffron Hymen's quarters'. A directly sexual use of 'urchin' occurs in *Don Leon*:

> What! if the little urchin I pursue,
> As fancy guides, in either of the two . . .
> (*Don Leon*, 1413)

Sexual suggestion was also implied by the line we have just quoted:

> The playful urchin meditates no sin;
> Why sternly rein his wanton gamboling?
> (*Leon to Annabella*, 285)

Notice the words 'pursue' and 'rein'; it is either a sort of *chase*, or a question of *riding*. So the reluctant bride in Roman times

> Would pray her lord to spare a virgin's fear,
> And take his restive courser to the rear . . .
> (*Leon to Annabella*, 313)

Here the image is exact. And the country in *Don Leon* is *hilly*, as we make for 'that spot concealed by two o'er hanging hills' (1214).

Let us now turn to a complex passage in *Vagaries Vindicated*, which purports to be a defence of Colman's poetry against those who find it full of indecent innuendoes. It goes:

> 'Tis true, with little care, and far less skill,
> I pace a pony on the bifork'd hill,
> And when the bridle heedlessly is thrown
> Upon *his* neck, I think not of my *own*;
> Think not, when he curvets or makes a slip
> (And oft my minor Pegasus will trip),
> With what a headlong tumble I may go
> Into a *critical morass*, below;
> Forget the modern mud reviewers heap
> About the bottom of the ancient steep –
> Where dullness lurks, anonymous, in fog,
> To smother bards, in a Boeotian bog;
> Assisted in the despicable task
> By Scotch or English rancour, in a Mask.
>
> (227)

There are two levels of meaning. The surface asserts that his poetry incurs slander from the false morality of reviewers: 'bifork'd hill' indicates rhymed couplets; the horse is Pegasus, or poetry; and the poet's risk of his neck is merely part of the realism demanded by the metaphor; the 'morass', or 'bog', is the charge of indecency; and 'Boeotian' is used for legality, or a too-rigid, superficial morality. But, with the *Don Leon* poems in mind, we find another meaning: the 'pony' is the 'playful urchin' and 'courser' we have already met; 'bifork'd hill' recalls the 'two o'er hanging hills' recently noticed; the risking of the rider's neck is, in view of the prevailing penalty, exactly used; 'slip' points to 'that one slip of my poor silly tongue' in *Leon to Annabella* (264); and the suggestions of 'bottom', 'morass', 'mud', and 'bog' are only too clear. The use of 'Boeotian' may be compared with

> And live we then in some Boeotian land,
> That love and Themis should go hand in hand?

in *Leon to Annabella* (275). It is probably safe to say that the innuendoes of our passage from *Vagaries Vindicated* would not be perceived, at least by a modern reader, without some acquaintance with the *Don Leon* poems.

On this other level, Colman is maliciously once again committing the very offence of double-meanings about which he is defending himself against the reviewers. It may seem that he is giving his case away; but this is not so, since one of his main points in *Vagaries Vindicated* is that his double-meanings are meant to be amusing, and that is the reaction which he hopes for here, expecting to turn the laugh against the reviewers. He distinguishes humour from immorality:

> 'Tis not the laugh-exciting *equivoque*,
> The salt allusion, no, nor broader joke,
> That deeply injures innocence; the *droll*
> No *passion* moves, nor *penetrates the soul*.
> > (*Vagaries Vindicated*, 251)

So, too, after the accumulated punning at the close of *Don Leon*, we are told:

> Once these were epigrams to raise a laugh:
> The world is grown too scrupulous by half.
> > (*Don Leon*, 1460)

The viewpoints are identical. *Vagaries Vindicated* is both a reply to reviewers and an attack on cant:

> But is the world now grown so wondrous pure
> That all are modest who appear demure?
> > (*Vagaries Vindicated*, 224)

It starts from a realization that certain instincts exist, even in the clergy:

> Hence, let us learn, be callings what they may,
> Frailty and Crime *will* mix with mortal clay.
> > (*Vagaries Vindicated*, 236)

The facts of the human situation are *given*, and humour one, legitimate, approach. The poet is not to blame.

Though *Vagaries Vindicated* is about literature and *Don Leon* is about life itself, their ways of thought are the same. *Vagaries Vindicated* is a link between Colman's humorous poems and his final masterpiece. Both insist that the human tendencies in question should not be unnecessarily brought to light. *Don Leon* speaks of the 'sport obscene'

> Which none so brazened e'er presume to own,
> Which, left unheeded, would remain unknown . . .
>
> (*Don Leon*, 69)

Especially is this true of youth:

> In vice unhackneyed, in *Justine* unread,
> See schoolboys, by some inclination fed,
> Some void, that's hardly to themselves confest,
> Flying for solace to a comrade's breast.
>
> (*Don Leon*, 349)

Parents are warned of their responsibilities, and schoolmasters too, lest they make what they regard as bad far worse:

> Shut, shut your eyes, ye pedagogues, nor keep
> Too close a watch upon your pupils' sleep.
> For, though in boyish ignorance they may
> Stumble perchance on some illicit play,
> Which looks like lechery the most refined,
> In them 'tis not depravity of mind.
>
> (*Don Leon*, 377)

Now, if we turn back to *Vagaries Vindicated*, we find the same argument applied to the critical condemnation of obscene innuendoes, which, if left unexplained, would do no harm to the young, while amusing their elders. Here is a passage about the supposed dangers of such indecent writing to the characters of young girls:

> 'Tis then the stiff reviewer, seeming vex'd,
> Turns to the maid, and glosses on the text:
> Warns her of what its passages *may* mean:
> 'That is immoral! – this, downright obscene!'
> Till soon the curious fair, half-bursting, swells:
> 'Obscene! What's *that*?' she asks; and, then, he tells!
>
> (*Vagaries Vindicated*, 228)

Again, with a precise use of religious doctrine:

> Say ye! who, dozing and dogmatick, sit
> Starch drivellers over morals, science, wit;
> Whose page a mental brick-kiln walk supplies,
> To give young thoughts unwholesome exercise,

Do ye not, sage *old women* as ye are!
Stop frolick short, and go, yourselves, too far?
Deprave with preaching? and, corruptly nice,
Turn schools of virtue into schools for vice?
My slips, like underwoods, are scarce discern'd,
In the mind's Paradise of the unlearn'd;
Your Tree of Knowledge brings temptation in,
And all your tyros pluck the fruit of Sin.
(*Vagaries Vindicated*, 229)

For 'deprave' compare 'depravity of mind' in the *Don Leon* passage just quoted; 'slip' we have already discussed.

But indeed *Vagaries Vindicated* is throughout a preparation for *Don Leon*. It, too, contains aspersions on the law, if only by metaphor. Reviewers are self-appointed guardians of the law:

Proceed, mock Judges! Earn your vile support
Like low Informers, in the Muses' court;
Rake the fanatick's code for dormant law,
To prove the Poet's *licence* has a flaw . . .
(*Vagaries Vindicated*, 232)

We can see how this contains the germ of *Don Leon*, opening its attack, as it does, with 'Thou ermin'd judge, pull off that sable cap!' (1).

It is the same with the clergy. Here *Vagaries Vindicated* offers a number of remarkable passages too long for quotation. Colman had been criticized for treating the clergy lightly, and in return he emphasizes their failings. But this argues no essential disrespect:

But how must indignation doubly boil
When priests our reverence for their cloth would spoil;
If an impostor – worst of Satan's leaven! –
Clad in the worldly livery of Heaven,
Should drink, wench, gamble, bully, flatter, lie,
Commit all crimes – including Simony –
Must we not, then, to prove our zeal complete,
The more we love the *order*, loath the *cheat*?
(*Vagaries Vindicated*, 235)

We may recall the passage in *Don Leon*, accusing the House of Commons of all the crimes they punish, including 'sodomy' (1038-9); and it is likely that Colman chose the word 'simony' with reluctance, probably hoping that his readers would supply the deficiency. He continues:

> The cheat – and are there such? – Strange things, alas!
> Have among holy shepherds come to pass.
> Some, to the wolf abandoning their flocks,
> Have broke their necks by following the fox;
> Some have admired, as sundry folks opine,
> Their patron's *Tables*, Moses! more than thine . . .
>
> > (*Vagaries Vindicated*, 235)

The reference to fox-hunting recalls

> No parson of the quorum feels a blush
> To claim the honours of the stinking brush

in *Don Leon* (73). This apparently refers to the clergy hunting out the ugly sin. Whether there is a yet more direct innuendo in both poems appears uncertain; but, knowing Colman, we may suspect it.

Vagaries Vindicated, like *Don Leon*, is concerned too with statesmen, and has a passage (248-50) satirizing speeches in Parliament which recalls *Don Leon* (1002-31). But it is time to close, and the temptation to quote must be resisted. *Vagaries Vindicated* has many passages of fine poetry outside our immediate purpose, but these we must pass over. Its power of statement, precision of couplet-technique, and control of embodied language, approach the mastery of the later work.

We have quoted enough to establish our case. These similarities, drawn from what is only a small amount of poetry, are surely conclusive; the *Don Leon* poems are the work of George Colman. A study of *Vagaries Vindicated* helps us to understand how Colman, as licenser of plays, in later life could have exercised so strict a dramatic censorship as he did, whilst simultaneously composing *Don Leon*. Despite its indecencies, *Vagaries Vindicated* claims to be a moral poem. In his poetry Colman worked from the centre, using every resource of wit, pun, rhyme and humour to approach the heart of the human problem, as he saw it. He is particularly concerned about young people. In *The Rodiad*, *Vagaries Vindicated*, and *Don Leon* he is an educationalist, and fervent in the cause of what he took to be the best interests of youth. Whilst lustful flogging was a time-honoured practice, any amatory exchange of the boys themselves was considered a crime; the attack is rational. The poetry necessarily contains many indecencies; but Colman's plays, though impregnated with keen liberal satire, were always respectable enough. He was, by profession, a successful playwright and manager. Towards the close of his life we merely find both tendencies, the professional and the poetic, which existed simultaneously before, driven to an extreme. But he would have admitted no final inconsistency. In *Vagaries Vindicated* he can write well in some noble passages of the clergy at their best, not unlike Chaucer, whose problem was similar. He claimed to be a true supporter of both Church and Crown:

> Religious tenets, to my latest breath,
> Such as I have, I'll keep, and smile at death;
> March gaily down my slope of life, and sing
> 'God prosper long Old England's Church and King!'
> *(Vagaries Vindicated, 248)*

The key-word is 'gaily'. Colman's gospel and key, is, following Aristophanes, Chaucer and Rabelais, a gospel of humour; but the intention behind it is also serious; more, it is profound. It is probable that a true understanding of his life and work would show that his values were, on the whole, consistent and rationally ordered; but he never forgets, as his enemies did, that human nature is not rational, and that there are strange instincts, in himself and in others, which demand attention and sympathy.

ADDITIONAL NOTE: The conclusions reached in my two *Don Leon* articles were used in my book *Lord Byron's Marriage*, 1957. The press controversies in which I was subsequently engaged were summed up in the Appendix ('The Separation Controversy') to my *Byron and Shakespeare*, 1966.

My investigations have led to a valuable correspondence with Dr. Joseph Wallfield in New York, who plans an edition of the *Don Leon* poems with a full apparatus. This is not the place to record the findings of his brilliant scholarship, except perhaps to say that he adduces strong arguments indicating that the composition of *Leon to Annabella* must have preceded that of *Don Leon*. I have provisionally directed that in the event of my death his letters to me should be lodged with other of my Byron material in the Brotherton Collection in the University of Leeds.

Colman and Don Leon

On the central issue of homosexuality I quote part of my answer to a review of *Lord Byron's Marriage* in *Essays in Criticism* VIII. 4 (October 1958):

I should have thought that my evidence on homosexuality as an enduring *instinct* in Byron was reasonably strong, though throughout I was particularly careful (e.g. 212) not to assert anything too definite regarding continued practices. Mr. Rutherford conveniently ignores what I wrote (217-19) of the three agonized Missolonghi poems, independently related by both myself and Professor Leslie Marchand in his recent biography to Loukas Chalandritsanos.

Mr. Rutherford's review forces me, a little reluctantly, to release more evidence. Professor Marchand (I. 181n.) draws our attention to Byron's use of a code-phrase, 'Plen. and optabil. – Coit.', derived from Petronius' *'coitum plenum et optabilem'* in the *Satyricon* (para. 86, sec. 4). The context in Petronius leaves Byron's meaning clear. At Falmouth, waiting to embark in 1809, Byron uses the phrase in a message to C. S. Matthews, saying that they are 'surrounded by Hyacinths and other flowers', which he compares with those he expects to find in the Levant: 'one specimen I shall certainly carry off'. On which Professor Marchand comments: 'The facetious Matthews would easily understand the Latin abbreviations and the language of flowers' (Marchand, I. 181-2, and note). So *Don Leon* was perfectly correct in saying that Byron left England in expectation of such experiences.

On 23 August 1810 Byron wrote from Greece to Hobhouse: 'I have been employed the greater part of to-day in conjugating the verb "ἀσπάζω" . . . I assure you my progress is rapid, but like Caesar *"nil actum reputans dum quid superesset agendum"*, I must arrive at the pl & opte and then I will write to ——' (Marchand, I. 258n.). On 4 October he wrote: 'Tell M. that I have obtained above two hundred pl & optCs . . . You know the monastery of Mendele; it was there I made myself master of the first' (Marchand, I. 258n.). On 26 November we have: 'Mention to M. that I have found so many of his antiques on this classical soil, that I am tired of pl & optCs, the last thing I could be tired of' (Marchand, I. 263n.). Are these the letters of one merely, to use Mr. Rutherford's words, following 'the local fashion' in making 'some experiments in homosexuality' which may be regarded as part of 'a fairly normal man's development'?

Byron's letter of 4 October conflicts slightly with the statement in *Don Leon* (684-5) that Byron's first actual such engagement occurred in the monastery at Athens, referring instead to the 'monastery of Mendele'. 'Mendele' appears to be a variant spelling for 'Pendeli', a few miles from Athens, but it is again a monastery, and Colman was not far out.

140

Colman and Don Leon

Professor Marchand adduces evidence that the book found by Lady Byron, when she was searching, according to Hobhouse, for proof of 'that particular insanity' which formed so large a part of the separation troubles (J. C. Hobhouse, Lord Broughton, *Recollections of a Long Life*, II. 250; my 208), was de Sade's *Justine* (Marchand, II. 559n.); a work mentioned in a relevant, because homosexual, context in *Don Leon* (349).

Byronic studies are gradually being forced to admit what the *Don Leon* poems have been vociferously asserting for more than a century. That, alone, should solicit our respect for them. As Professor Marchand says, they are clearly written by 'someone who was no amateur and who knew many of the facts of Byron's life astonishingly well' (II. notes to Ch. XV. 586; notes 61).

It is unfortunately necessary to make these points in some detail, since Professor Marchand's valuable biography, though it contains some acute comments on Byron's homosexual and bisexual propensities (I. 90n.), is so arranged, as I have already elsewhere observed (*T.L.S.*, 21 March 1958), that only those with an eye for evidence are likely to see the point.

I have since noticed that the spelling 'Mendeli' occurs at *Childe Harold*, II. 87. E. Hartley Coleridge records that the MS. shows 'Pentele', erased (*Works, Poetry*, II. 157).

CHAPTER IV

Lawrence, Joyce and Powys

Essays in Criticism, XI. 4; October 1961.

THE RATIFICATION of *Lady Chatterley's Lover* (1928; first complete text in England, 1960) must not be allowed to obscure the book's sexual challenge. Lawrence is too often regarded as an apostle only of a revitalized normality; but his meanings are sometimes less simple, and after narrating a number of normal sexual encounters between Lady Chatterley and Mellors the story reaches its climax in an engagement of a different kind.[1]

Earlier engagements have been given the natural sexual associations of softness, peace and fluidity, of floods, waves and undulatory motion (X. 138-9, XII. 181; my page numerals refer to the 1960 Penguin edition). The new engagement has associations of earth, rock, the metallic, heavy ore, smelting, fire and savagery. The contrast is precise.

We have been carefully prepared for it by a repeated emphasis on the posterior locations which will appear to be involved (X. 130, XII. 180, 182, 184, XIV. 218, XV. 229), leading up to thought of the woman's buttocks during a dance as being 'offered in a kind of homage' to the man, followed by the man's caress of 'fire' on the two 'secret *entrances*' of and 'openings *to*' her body (my italics, XV. 230-3). Then the new consummation is attained (XVI.

---

[1] (1968) Two other writers came simultaneously to a conclusion similar to that advanced in this essay: Eliseo Vivas in *D. H. Lawrence: the failure and triumph of art* (U.S.A., 1960; London, November 1961); and John Sparrow in 'Regina v. Penguin Books Ltd.', *Encounter*, XVIII. 2 (February 1962), with 'Afterthoughts', XVIII. 6 (June 1962). Mr. Sparrow draws attention to a passing (but underdeveloped) reference to 'anal obsession' in *The Times Literary Supplement* of 4 August 1961 during a review of the Penguin account of the trial.

258-9). The experience is to be distinguished from 'love' and even 'voluptuousness' and associated instead with 'sensuality', 'fire', 'death', and – applied to the man – 'devil'. Through assaulting the 'oldest shames' in 'the most secret places' the man mines into the 'bed-rock' of the woman's physical being; and we are told that it is good so to 'burn out false shames and smelt out the heaviest ore of the body into purity'. There is a penetration into the 'very heart of the jungle' where exist the being's 'roots'; this, 'the core of the physical jungle' of herself, is also 'the last and deepest recess of organic shame'. That an entrance other than the normal is intended is suggested by the phrase 'this phallic hunting out'; and depth by saying that 'the phallos alone could explore it'. The 'sensuality' is 'awful', but cathartic: Lawrence once, on 12 February 1915, wrote in a letter to Bertrand Russell that the use of another's body for mere sensation led naturally to sodomy, and though the vein was there one of disapprobation, the theme is the same and similarly associated with 'rock' (Harry T. Moore, *The Intelligent Heart*, Penguin, 1960; III. 235, I. 83). This experience Lady Chatterley now realizes that she has always unconsciously desired 'at the bottom of her soul, fundamentally'; the words are exactly chosen. The writing has compression, density, and precision.

The integration of this episode within the story's structure shows a more studied and patterned artistry than is usual in Lawrence's major designs. It is carefully prepared for, and reverberates afterwards. Now that the meaning has been poetically established, it is driven home by Mrs. Bolton's letter on the rumours regarding Mellors' past actions of 'sensuality' with his now separated wife, which Lady Chatterley immediately relates to her own experience with him (XVII. 276). Even more explicit is her husband Clifford Chatterley's letter (XVII. 277-82) on these 'unspeakable things' which include 'unusual sexual postures' and using a wife, 'as Benvenuto Cellini says, "in the Italian way"'. Under the embarrassment of these scandalous rumours in which he appears to be regarded as a second 'Marquis de Sade' – the letter also associates him with Rabelais – Mellors, he says, now goes about like a dog with a tin can tied to his tail, and though he pretends unconcern must be inwardly repeating 'like Don Rodrigo in the Spanish ballad: "Ah, now it bites me where I most have sinned!"' 'Tail' is used in *Lady Chatterley's Lover* as a precise synonym for rump (XV. 232, also XVII. 277 and XVIII. 290). This quotation from the Spanish ballad (entitled 'The Penitence of Don Roderick' in J. G. Lockhart's *The Spanish Ballads*), together with the whole description of sensual encounter in Chapter XVI, was omitted from the expurgated edition.

At the conclusion of *A Propos of Lady Chatterley's Lover* Lawrence refers to conversations of his with Italians regarding the book's publication. One of them asks, 'What does it describe?' and when told, though what was told is not reported, wonders at Lawrence's anxiety, remarking, 'But we do it every day'. Another, more cautious, asks, 'You find it really necessary to *say* it?' In these conversations 'it' denotes a definite action.

An interesting passage in Clifford's letter sees humanity and its lusts as existing at 'the *bottom* of a deep ocean' (Lawrence's italics: the connotations are not those of the floods and waves noted above). Here we 'prey upon the ghastly subaqueous life of our fellow-men, in the submarine jungle of mankind'; but 'our immortal destiny is to escape' again 'into the bright ether' of our 'eternal nature'. The writing is not wholly unsympathetic; Clifford is perhaps the most objectively created person in the book; and it is arguable that his is a more complete survey than anyone's.

Clifford's image of subaqueous life might have been drawn from Middleton Murry's review of the earlier novel, *Women in Love*, in 1921; not 1931 as stated when reprinted in his *Reminiscences of D. H. Lawrence* (1933; IV. 218-27). This novel describes in imaginative terms certain sexual encounters of an abnormal kind, and Murry was violently antagonized. Lawrence's people, he wrote, 'grope in their own slime to some final consummation, in which they are utterly "negated" or utterly "fulfilled" '; his is a 'protozoic god' and he is 'passionately obscene in the exact sense of the word'; 'man and woman are indistinguishable as octopods in an aquarium tank'. Only Lawrence's 'passion', that is his prophetic fervour, can clear him of the charge of 'the crudest sexuality'; and yet 'not one person in a thousand' would decide that the actions in question 'were anything but the crudest kind of sexuality'. He admits that they may not be, but how, he does not know. Murry's apparent indecision is probably dictated by a reluctance to speak more openly. 'After all', he says, when defending his review against Mrs. Carswell's attack, 'I had known

Lawrence intimately'; his stature he recognized, and yet 'perhaps I knew what Lawrence *meant* by his writing far better than other men'. And:

Therefore I cried, with vehemence and passionate sincerity, over the debris of a broken friendship: '*Ecrasez l'infame*'.

(*Reminiscences*, IV. 239-40)

Murry discusses the end-chapters of *The Rainbow* (1915) and the important chapter 'Excurse' (XXIII) of *Women in Love*, in *Son of Woman* (1931; II. 88-92, 106-22). His acute commentary has assisted my understanding.

In 'Excurse' the woman, Ursula, denounces Birkin's sexual propensities in a passage associating his 'sex life' with 'death' and 'foulness' and calling it a mixture of 'spirituality' and 'dirt'. She calls him 'obscene', '*perverse*' and 'death-eating' (XXIII. 344-6; my page numerals refer to the Penguin edition of *Women in Love*). Birkin admits it, recognizing that he was 'perverse, so spiritual on the one hand, and in some strange way, degraded on the other'; 'he knew that his spirituality was concomitant of a process of depravity, a sort of pleasure in self-destruction' (XXIII. 347-8).

The theme of 'Excurse' has been prepared for earlier (XIII. 162-4, XIX. 282-3, 285-6, XXII. 330-1). Lawrence, says Murry, seems to be 'demanding a new kind of physical contact' accompanied by 'fear and terror' (*Son of Woman*, II. 111). Though fearful, for it is to involve 'the last physical facts, physical and unbearable' (XXII. 331), it is honoured above the 'mingling' (XIII. 164, XVI. 225) of normal union, 'this horrible fusion of two beings' which 'every woman and most men', despite its being so 'nauseous and horrible', insisted on (XXIII. 348). There is instead talk of fingers, loins, back, flanks, downward movement of the hand, electricity and darkness; and the word 'mystic' recurs. Frontal, phallic, sexuality is surpassed, and an otherness touched 'more wonderful than life itself' – a deathly otherness – 'the very stuff of being' at 'the darkest poles of the body' by the 'rounded' loins, 'the darkest, deepest, strangest life-source of the human body, at the back and base of the loins' (XXIII. 353-4, and see XIV. 203-4).

First the man, Birkin, is the active partner:

He had taken her at the roots of her darkness and shame – like a demon, laughing over the fountain of mystic corruption which was one of the sources of her being.... As for her, when would she so much go beyond herself as to accept him at the quick of death? (XXIII. 343)

Then we have the woman's tentative approach:

She had thought there was no source deeper than the phallic source. And now, behold, from the smitten rock of the man's body, from the strange marvellous flanks and thighs, deeper, further in mystery than the phallic source, came the floods of ineffable darkness and ineffable riches. (XXIII. 354)

'With perfect fine finger-tips of reality she would touch the reality in him' (XXIII. 360). 'Roots', 'shame', 'demon', 'rock', all point ahead to *Lady Chatterley*; and so, if we have regard to its one excremental reference and the later word 'foundations' (*Lady Chatterley's Lover*, XV. 232, XVI. 258), do 'the fountain of mystic corruption' as 'one of the sources of her being' and the man's 'marvellous fountains' (XXIII. 354). In *Women in Love* the implements are fingers; but, as again in *Lady Chatterley*, it is a matter less of love than of deliberate and 'impersonal' (XXIII. 343) 'sensual reality' (XXIII. 361, and see III. 48, VII. 87, XIX. 285-6), and is to this extent 'inhuman' (XIII. 162-3, XXIII. 361). It touches the inmost non-human being of the person 'mystically-physically' (XXIII. 354); as Murry observes (*Reminiscences*, IV. 222), 'it does not admit of individuality as we understand it'. In what Murry calls this 'ultra-phallic realm' (*Son of Woman*, II. 118) sexual distinctions are transcended 'beyond womanhood' in a dark 'otherness' at once 'masculine and feminine' (XXIII. 353, 361, and see XIII. 164, XIX. 282). The technique may be called 'ambisexual' in that either man or woman may be the active partner:

And he too waited in the magical steadfastness of suspense for her to take this knowledge of him as he had taken it of her. He knew her darkly, with the fullness of dark knowledge. Now she would know him, and he too would be liberated. (XXIII. 360)

Each, while remaining sexually inviolate, becomes semi-sexually empowered and integrated: 'They would give each other this star-equilibrium which alone is freedom' (XXIII. 360, and see XIII. 164, 168-70, XVI. 225, XIX. 287). Through touch of the impersonal roots, the centres of corruption and death, death itself being an 'inhuman otherness' (XV. 217), the true integration is accomplished. In his essay 'Pornography and Obscenity' (*Phoenix*, 1936; 176) Lawrence distinguishes between the sexual and excretory functions in terms of creation and dissolution, opposing their confusion as a mark of degradation. The terms ('dirt', 'flow', 'degraded') correspond with those used in *Women in Love*, though the concern is different. In his more imaginative and fictional 'Excurse' he is trying to blast through this degradation to a new health. Death and darkness – though darkness is used by Lawrence for more general purposes too – are natural associations, since the locations in question are those of expelled poisons and the non-human. So the deathly is found to be the source of some higher order of being; contact with a basic materiality liberates the person.

Murry correlates his discussion of *Women in Love* with three of Lawrence's poems: *New Heaven and Earth*, *Elysium* and *Manifesto*. In the first it is the man who puts his hand out 'further, a little further', touches the otherness, and is ignited. In the second the man is the passive partner:

> Ah, terribly
> Between the body of life and me
> Her hands slid in and set me free.

The true personality 'me' is liberated from the weight of the 'body of life', its material 'matrix' or life-basis, and the true self, which we must call in some sense a 'spirit-self' – in *Fantasia of the Unconscious* (Secker, New Adelphi edn. 1930; XI. 120) it is called 'soul' – is now born. *Manifesto* is yet clearer:

> I want her to touch me at last, ah, on the root and quick of my
>   darkness
> and perish on me, as I have perished on her. . . .
> When she has put her hand on my secret, darkest sources, the darkest
>   outgoings,
> when it has struck home to her, like a death, 'this is *him*!'
> she has no part in it, no part whatever,
> it is the terrible *other*,
> when she knows the fearful *other flesh*, ah, darkness unfathomable and
>   fearful, contiguous and concrete,
> when she is slain against me, and lies in a heap like one outside the
>   house,
> when she passes away as I have passed away,
> being pressed up against the *other*,

then I shall be glad, I shall not be confused with her,
I shall be cleared, distinct, single as if burnished in silver,
having no adherence, no adhesion anywhere,
one clear, burnished, isolated being, unique,
and she also, pure, isolated, complete,
two of us, unutterably distinguished, and in unutterable conjunction.
Then we shall be free, freer than angels, ah, perfect.

The italics are Lawrence's. Such is this strange achievement, neatly matched by the thoughts of W. B. Yeats's *Crazy Jane Talks with the Bishop*, where we are told that 'fair and foul are near of kin', that the one needs the other, and so

> . . . Love has pitched his mansion in
> The place of excrement;
> For nothing can be sole or whole
> That has not been rent.

The correspondence is close.

Murry did not like it; but he has suffered some injustice from admirers of Lawrence. Granted his knowledge, he was very reticent (e.g., on *Lady Chatterley* in *Son of Woman*, 365). There were reasons why he could not speak so clearly as we can today.

After *Women in Love* Lawrence passed on to the male interests of *Aaron's Rod* (1922), *Kangaroo* (1923), and *The Plumed Serpent* (1926), though sexually little is made of these. In *Lady Chatterley's Lover* he composed a final and comprehensive sexual statement. Such a man as Lawrence does not retreat; the abnormal claim staked out remains, with in *Lady Chatterley* a dual and lucid emphasis, corresponding to the diverse sexual engagements in *Women in Love* of Gerald and Birkin (for Gerald, XXIV. 388-90, XXIX. 451-2, XXX. 499-500), on (i) normal engagements and (ii) an abnormal penetration, the phallos replacing the fingers of *Women in Love*; that is the point of 'the phallos alone could explore it' (p. 143 above).

Whatever we may think of the implied teaching, Lawrence was certainly engaged on a deep problem. The easiest way to see its importance is to observe the part similar perversions play in James Joyce's *Ulysses*. My page numerals will refer to the John Lane edition of 1936, which has no chapter numerals.

The main human interest is divided between the middle-aged, placid and sensual Leopold Bloom of Jewish descent and the drifting and anxious young intellectual, Stephen Dedalus; 'water-lover' against 'hydrophobe' (632-3); and the story works up to the rescue of Stephen from the nightmarish brothel by Bloom, with the implied philosophy that the intellect needs support from the sensual.

Bloom's sensuality is almost entirely limited to the posterior locations, external and internal, which we have been discussing. When asked his opinion of H. G. Wells's comment in writing of *A Portrait of the Artist as a Young Man* that Joyce had a 'cloacal obsession', Joyce replied that Wells was a very appreciative critic of his work and that the only criticisms he objected to were those which suggested that he was not seriously involved. Once, hearing of a cannibal chief who chose his consort from the tribe's women by a simple inspection of their naked posteriors, Joyce 'without a ghost of a smile' remarked, 'I sincerely hope that when Bolshevism finally sweeps the world it will spare that enlightened potentate' (Frank Budgen, *James Joyce and the Making of Ulysses*, 1934, reprinted 1937; V. 108, IX. 194). We are reminded of the carefully described West African statuette in *Women in Love* (XIX. 285-6). Joyce's obscenities are both serious and central. Typical of Bloom's impulses are his interest in the back views of a servant girl and of a waiter (52, 266); in the fine lady mounting her equipage (66); and in how much posterior detail was actually included in the 'mesial groove' of the sculptured goddesses in the museum (189, also 165, 690). What he most likes in women is clear (290, 503, 512, 614). We observe the effect on him of Gerty MacDowell's leaning back to watch the rockets and his jealousy of the rock that she was sitting on; and his meditation on canine habits (349-50, 359, 358). We have Bloom's obscene postcards of 'illicit intercourse' and 'anal violation' (445, 682); Virag's words to him in the brothel, 'Lyum! Look. Her beam is broad', 'protuberances', 'potent rectum', 'leave nothing to be desired', and the rest (487); and Bloom's nauseating 'sins of the past' (509-10). Joyce can be variously revolting and amusing, but he has throughout a purpose. Bloom is a more important person than Dedalus and engaged more of Joyce's own interest: 'Stephen no longer interests me to the same extent' (Budgen, V. 107). As a cuckold he cuts a poor figure, but he treasures his wife's picture and is called, in a style of semi-humorous sympathy, 'that vigilant wanderer, soiled by the dust of travel and combat and stained by the mire of an indelible dishonour, but from whose steadfast and constant heart no lure or peril or threat or degradation could ever efface the image of that voluptuous loveliness which the inspired pencil of Lafayette has limned for ages yet to come' (399, and see 614). Bloom's Odyssey culminates in a well-defined solution:

In what final satisfaction did these antagonistic sentiments and reflections, reduced to their simplest forms, converge?   (695)

The answer is:

Satisfaction at the ubiquity in eastern and western terrestrial hemispheres . . . of adipose posterior female hemispheres, redolent of milk and honey and of excretory sanguine and seminal warmth, reminiscent of secular families of curves of amplitude, insusceptible of moods of impression or of contrarieties of expression, expressive of mute immutable mature animality.   (695)

'Animality' lends point to Lawrence's phrase 'this phallic hunting out' in *Lady Chatterley*. Joyce's concentration may be compared with the back view of a man's agonizingly beautiful body, 'rounded and soft', as almost 'too final a vision' to be bearable in *Women in Love* (XIV. 203-4, and see XIX. 285-6), and with the yet greater insistence on such thoughts, replacing vague terms such as 'loins' with a more precise terminology, throughout *Lady Chatterley's Lover* (VI. 68, X. 120, 130, XII. 180, 182, 184, XIV. 218, XV. 229-33, XVI. 243, XVII. 277, XVIII. 290). 'Adipose posterior female hemispheres', 'warmth', 'curves' and 'amplitude' correspond to Mellors' sense in 'frenzy' of Lady Chatterley's 'lovely, heavy posteriors', of the 'secret entrances' as 'folded in the secret warmth' between 'the curves and the globe-fullness'; and of the 'sloping bottom' such as 'a man loves in 'is guts' (*Lady Chatterley's Lover*, XV. 231-2); and it is this particular effect on him that more than anything registers pleasurably in Lady Chatterley's own mind (XVI. 243, XVII. 277, XVIII. 290). Joyce's concluding phrases correspond to Lawrence's emphasis throughout *Women in Love* on the desirability of an impersonal and inhuman contact with a physical being or 'thing' (XIX. 283) as distinguished from all individual impression, from the mind. Bloom is called 'dung-devourer' (503) and Birkin 'death-eating' (*Women in Love*, XXIII. 346). Though aspersions are now cast on Bloom's unsatisfying and uncreative marital sex-life as that of a decadent Oriental (391, and see also 513, 692-3, 696), he has had two children (322, 696) and his present perversions may to this extent be regarded less as symptoms of failure than as a development beyond the normal. His guiding star is his vision of the 'fairy boy', his lost son, Rudy (574); his rescue of the young Stephen is the book's crowning action, and his affectionate care for him genuine and selfless; he is conceived as a bi-sexual type (322, 635), and in the Brothel extravaganza undergoes a sexual change (e.g. 504-5).

Bloom's story ends, but the book itself moves to another and final climax on the same theme in his wife Marion's epilogue, turning over her memories of her various lovers and her husband's peculiar desires. It is packed with a sequence of staggering anal obscenities, on page after page. Of her husband she thinks:

> its a wonder Im not an old shrivelled hag before my time living with him so cold never embracing me except sometimes when hes asleep the wrong end of me not knowing I suppose who he has any man thatd kiss a womans bottom Id throw my hat at him after that hed kiss anything unnatural where we havent 1 atom of any kind of expression in us all of us the same 2 lumps of lard before ever I do that to a man pfooh the dirty brutes the mere thought is enough   (736)

Again, the thought of the unindividual, the material and impersonal. And so on rising to the violent and obscene climax of anal penetration, tongue[1] in Joyce in place of the fingers or phallos of Lawrence (732, 739-40), unquotable out of its context.

Marion Bloom accepts her husband's ways and her epilogue was called by Joyce 'the indispensable countersign to Bloom's passport to eternity' (Budgen, XII. 270). Her mind is a mixture of obscenities and earth-contacts; she loves flowers (740-1). She is an earth-symbol, 'Gea-Tellus' (697).

Both Lawrence and Joyce labour to interpret and redeem man in natural and human terms. Lawrence tries hard to keep his mysticism close-locked to physical creation. In *Fantasia of the Unconscious* (1923) he treads the border-line of the occult sciences, such as those of Rudolf Steiner and eastern philosophy; but he remains as close as may be to the physical as known by normal sense-perception. 'In talk', writes Frederick Carter, he would

---

[1] The word may at one point be being used as a synonym for penis, as apparently in *Leon to Annabella* (p. 117 above). Compare 'tongue' and 'tail' in *The Taming of the Shrew*, II. i. 217.

discuss the idea of nerve centres 'controlling or subduing a great power, [a] serpentine, dragon-like force' that lies within every human being (*D. H. Lawrence and the Body Mystical*, 1932; 24). This is presumably the Kundalini Serpent of Eastern mysticism coiled at the base of the spine, which when released towers up to unify the male and female principles in the mind and ignite the consciousness, though too ardent an ambition may plunge the aspirant into depravity: the process is described in Vera Stanley Alder's *The Finding of the 'Third Eye'* (1938; reprinted 1955, VI. 52-3; and see W. Y. Evans-Wentz, *The Tibetan Book of the Dead*, 3rd. edn., 1957; 216, 221, 224). However, despite his belief in spirit interpenetration and spirit survival (as at *Women in Love*, XV. 215-16) and his achievement of a sensitively manipulated spiritualism in the story *Glad Ghosts*, Lawrence's major art-forms offer us little of the specifically religious and the specifically occult, except in so far as we accept the dubiously satisfying theology of *The Plumed Serpent*. His great achievement lies in his quivering susceptibility to the electric contacts of physical being and his ability to transmit in words the dynamic of man or animal. He likes semi-scientific terms like 'electric', 'polarity', 'magnetism' and 'dynamic'; but there is a limit to what they can do, and when that limit is reached, he may be forced to speak paradoxically, as in *Women in Love*, of a living state 'more wonderful than life itself', associated with darkness, corruption and death, and of a person 'mindlessly smiling' from 'that other basic mind, the deepest physical mind' (XXIII. 353, 358). In *Fantasia of the Unconscious* he uses the word 'soul' (as at V, XI, XIII); he has here a vivid sense of the created universe as what others would call 'spiritualized'; but little more can be done without a more consistent recognition of some such intermediate reality as the 'etheric' or 'astral' dimension of esoteric teaching, conceived as interpenetrating the physical. The 'ether', we may recall, was handed over to Clifford in *Lady Chatterley's Lover* (p. 144 above).

Joyce's limits are more obviously objective and, according to our received phraseology, 'realistic', the Christian church and religion functioning as no more than questionable and sometimes comically satirized objects among other objects. Yet Joyce is nevertheless forced back on the miraculous; in the long Brothel extravaganza we have resurrections of the dead, of Stephen's mother and Bloom's parents and son, and other amazing happenings; but the extravaganza scarcely rises above the level of chaotic psychological symbolism and technical invention.[1] Neither Joyce nor Lawrence offers any coherent and grand-scale development of the supernatural, and still less can they be said to have placed their central problems within any such context. Each problem has to be solved in its own limited terms.

We turn now to John Cowper Powys's *A Glastonbury Romance*. His range is far greater. His psychological realism goes as deep as Joyce's and is more assured than Lawrence's; his use of myth and legend, indigenously rooted in his story's British locale, is more convincing than Lawrence's Quetzalcoatl or Joyce's use of the *Odyssey*; and with his sense of occult powers and the great First Cause itself as intertwisted in his drama we shall find little correspondence in either Lawrence or Joyce. It is all of a piece, a vast, organic, convincing whole, like a natural growth. Within it, and without straining, without anything of Lawrence's nervous insistencies or Joyce's top-heavy apparatus, a large number of themes of deepest importance are lucidly selected and developed. We shall concentrate on only one: on Sam Dekker's move beyond the sexual, corresponding to the move from normal to abnormal sexuality in both Lawrence and Joyce, to a different, yet again physical, consummation.

In his Preface to the 1955 (Macdonald) edition Powys regards Sam's Grail-quest as his book's central theme. Of the Grail he writes:

The Grail has its counterpart in the mythology of Greece and in the oldest heathen legends of Wales and Ireland. There are intimate correspondences between it and the traditions that reach us from both the extreme East and the extreme West. It changes its shape. It changes its contents. It changes its aura. It changes its atmosphere. But its essential nature remains unchanged; and even that nature is only the nature of a symbol. It refers us to things beyond itself and to things beyond words. Only those who have caught the secret which Rabelais more than anyone else reveals to us, the secret of the conjunction of the particular and extreme grossness of our excremental functions in connection with our sexual functions, are on the right track to encompass this receding horizon where the beyond-thought loses itself in the beyond-words. (Preface, xv)

[1] My remark here is countered by my commentary on pp. 50-1 above. There is more in Joyce's patterning than I had seen.

Powys comments on 'that incongruous and disgustingly humorous intermingling of the excremental with the sacramental of
which Rabelais makes so much' (xvi). The thought is extended
in his important study, *Rabelais*.

Powys's general world-view concentrates heavily, though not
exclusively, on the powers coming from below in man and on the
inanimate and the lower life-forms in nature, with a kind of
mystical sensuality blending Wordsworth, Joyce and Lawrence.
Now in the story of *A Glastonbury Romance* Sam, after an experience of passionate love, moves beyond the sexual to a state of
saintliness and service, and while on a river coal-barge has a
vision of the Holy Grail after a physical invasion by some transcendental power felt as a penetration of his 'guts' from '*below*' by
a 'gigantic spear' (1933, XXVIII. 981-3; 1955, 938-40). The
attendant phraseology has strong Lawrentian affinities: 'the hidden
darkness of his inmost organism', 'from abysses of the earth, far
deeper than the bottom of the Brue', 'from the quick of his being';
such phrases recalling the 'quick of my darkness' in Lawrence's
poem *Manifesto*, 'at the quick of death' and 'the very stuff of being'
in *Women in Love* (XXIII. 343, 353), and 'the very quick of her'
and 'the real bed-rock of her nature' in *Lady Chatterley's Lover*
(XII. 180, XVI. 258; 'dark' and 'quick' may also be used for a
normal engagement, XII. 181). For Sam the material universe splits
open to reveal the Grail, which appears as a transparent chalice,
and 'within it there was dark water streaked with blood, and
within the water was a shining fish'. Powys's interrelation, here
and elsewhere, of earth, water and water-life with the mystical
and the transcendent recalls, with a difference, Clifford's view of
mankind in *Lady Chatterley*. The spear is a successor to the
human implements of Lawrence and Joyce. It had been forecast
by the association of a spear – 'a craving that pierced him like the
actual thrust of a spear' – with the hero's semi-mystical love of
Christie in Powys's earlier *Wolf Solent*, where an important sexual
crisis is mastered (p. 157 below) by a towering 'will' like 'a
shining-scaled fish', corresponding to the Kundalini Serpent and
to the fish of Sam's vision (*Wolf Solent*, 1929; X. 233, 246, XX.
466, XXI. 510; 1961, 219, 231, 444, 486).

It will be clear that Sam's experience of physical penetration
conditioning vision serves to elucidate the interrelation of obscenities and spiritualities throughout my present book (listed

in Index B below). Note that the Grail itself contains blood.

In the course of his saintly life Sam is afterwards ministering to an old man suffering from piles:

Sam was not, it must be confessed, a born nurse; but he was a born naturalist and an unfastidious countryman. As he struggled with his task, bending over the old gentleman's rear, the tension of his spirit brought back with a rush the miraculous power of the vision he had seen. The two extremes of his experience, the anus of an aged man and the wavering shaft of an Absolute, piercing his own earthly body, mingled and fused together in his consciousness. Holy Sam felt, as he went on with the business, a strange second sight, an inkling, as to some incredible secret, whereby the whole massed weight of the world's tormented flesh was labouring towards some release.

(XXVIII. 991 or 948)

The repellent task corresponds to 'the last physical facts, physical and unbearable' which 'one accepts in full' of *Women in Love* (XXII. 331, XXIII. 358). A similar 'acceptance', together with a cluster of associations related to our discussion, characterizes a central mystic experience in *Wolf Solent* (1929; XIII. 292-4; 1961, 276-8). With Powys's 'massed weight', 'world' and 'release' we may compare 'world's end' in *Don Leon* (p. 132 above); Joyce's word-play on terrestrial and feminine 'hemispheres' to define Bloom's ultimate solution, and his wife as 'Gea-Tellus'; Mellors' praise of a 'bottom as could hold the world up' in *Lady Chatterley's Lover* (XV. 232); and 'Her hands slid in and set me free' in Lawrence's poem *Elysium*.

The new spiritual freedom described in *Wolf Solent* corresponds to that of Lawrence's *Manifesto*. Powys's prose unfurls with an unhurried and unperturbed ease that goes far to witness its authority; and on the strength of his revelatory passages the tormenting obsessions of Swift, the tragic lives of Byron and Wilde, the sex-agonies of Lawrence and obscenities of Joyce, may all receive, in retrospect, a new sympathy and justification.

CHAPTER V

Mysticism and Masturbation: An Introduction to the Lyrics of John Cowper Powys

Composed during 1968.

I

SOME OF POWYS'S most important lyrics cannot be properly understood without reference to his sadistic obsession. This we shall here discuss, and then pass, in my next essay, to the poems. Much of what I have to say has already been cursorily treated in my *Christ and Nietzsche* and *The Saturnian Quest*. I now present an expanded discussion.

In my essay 'Lawrence, Joyce and Powys' I drew attention to Powys's equation of the physically repellent with cosmic power. Rabelais was one of his great heroes (*The Saturnian Quest*, 85-7). Obscenities belong to the domain of comedy, and may not seem so very dangerous. But there is tragedy; close to tragedy lies sacrifice, and within both, the sadistic instinct. In his *Autobiography* (1934) Powys tells that his 'ruling passion' (Pope, *Moral Essays*, Epistle to Lord Cobham, 174-227), or central obsession, was sadism, and that since childhood he had indulged in sadistic fantasies. Sadistic action is a major theme in *A Glastonbury Romance* (1933), and recurs in many of his books. Commentators tend to discount Powys's personal confession in view of his known sweetness of temperament and universal kindliness: but this is to misunderstand.

Powys's own sadism was confined, almost entirely, to fantasy, and before discussing it we shall glance at fantasies of a similar, yet more innocent, tone in *Wolf Solent* (1929; 2nd edn., 1961) and *Porius* (1951).

Wolf has his private 'mythology'. It started, like Powys's sadistic fantasies, in his childhood, making him an 'infant magician'; it is a mystic vice (I. 15-16 or 7, XIX, 434 or 413). I quote from *The Saturnian Quest* (33):

This is a mystical-sensuous enjoyment given connotations of both moral conflict (XIX. 431 or 411) and viciousness, and described variously in imagery of submarine fish-life and vegetation in greenish depths (II. 35 or 27, XIX. 420 or 401, 434 or 414, XXI. 513-14 or 489, XXIII. 552 or 526). It is called 'Cimmerian' and may point towards some mystic soul-city (II. 29 or 20, VII. 168-9 or 157).

An impressionistic relation to much of Powys's favourite imaginative territory is clear; in such primal elemental terms good and evil mix. Wolf's 'secret practice' of 'sinking into his soul' and summoning from it a 'subconscious magnetic power' was accompanied by the 'arrogant' idea that he was taking part 'in some occult cosmic struggle' between 'what he liked to think of as "good" and what he liked to think of as "evil" in those remote depths' (I. 16 or 8). The 'mythology' depends on his 'inmost life-illusion – upon his taking the side of Good against Evil in the great occult struggle' (XIX. 431 or 411). He is aware of an 'extreme dualism' 'descending to the profoundest gulfs of being', in 'which every living thing was compelled to take part' (XIV. 302 or 286). He is presumably thinking of the way dark fantasies rise from our subconscious, perhaps sexual, being. The emphasis at first sight seems to be moral, but Wolf clearly *enjoys* the sensations. In our first quotation the phraseology indicates that it is Wolf's own, peculiar, 'good' that is meant, and the 'arrogance' exists perhaps in his daring to assume that the secret engagement *is* basically good. The experience is 'thrilling as a secret vice' (I. 16 or 7-8) and some kind of orgiastic, or even orgasmic, reference seems to be suggested: 'up, up it rose, like some great moonlight-coloured fish' (II. 35 or 27). Wolf fears that a sexual engagement with the girl Christie might kill his 'mythology', which is his inmost integrity, and when he is near submission his inmost 'will' interrupts: it 'rose upwards like a shining-scaled fish, electric, vibrant, taut, and leapt into the greenish-coloured vapour that filled the room!' (XX. 466 or 444). Finally he passes beyond his 'mythology' of opposites to some higher state in which 'body and soul' are fused (XXI. 513-14 or 489, XXIII. 552 or 526, XXV. 635-44 or 606-14).

In Wolf's 'mythology' the opposites in man appear to be searching for unification through some kind of sexual release, symbolized by the impressions of coolness, watery vegetation, and fish;[1] though the experience may also be related to a Wordsworthian blending with ordinary earth-nature (XIX. 434 or 414). In the preface to the 1961 edition Powys states that the book's key-thought is 'the necessity of opposites'. Man, we know, exists in a natural context which denies his sense of good; more, he has within himself instincts from that same nature which may be the extreme opposite of what he takes himself to be. In *Wolf Solent* the definition is imaginative. We are not told more. Wolf is not directly, so far as we know, involved in sadism. Here Powys appears to be making a generalized approach towards expression of sensations which were subsequently rendered explicit.

In the much later *Porius* (1951) we hear of the hero's 'secret' practice of 'cavoseniargizing' (V. 93), a term first coined by him as a 'little boy', for certain 'most private feelings':

He used the word as one of his precious sensation-symbols and to serve as a description of those recurrent moments in his life when the gulf between the animal consciousness of his body, the body of a youthful Hercules, and the consciousness of his restless soul was temporarily bridged; so that his soul found itself able to follow every curve and ripple of his bodily-sensations *and yet remain suspended above them.*   (V. 83)

Note that the 'soul' remains 'above', unaffected. The experience is once, rather obliquely, associated with moments when 'his erotic nerves were excited by something to which the rest of his nature refused to respond' (VI. 106). Cavoseniargizing is referred to throughout (V. 81, 93, IX. 146, X. 169, XIX. 396, 402-3). Through it Porius blends with the inanimate. The strange term, with its overtones of 'cave', 'energizing' and perhaps 'enlargement', denotes an empowering of the self through drawing on giant forces. The giants in *Porius* come from mountain caves (XX. 433, XXII. 519), and the word originated from some

---

[1] The fish was an important symbol in Christian tradition, and Powys uses the symbol powerfully in *Wolf Solent* and, in relation to the Grail, in *A Glastonbury Romance*. See *The Saturnian Quest*, 33, 37.

'chance occurrence' among 'the hills' (XIX. 402-3). We are being pointed to forces like those of 'the great Phallic Giant' of Cerne Abbas (*Autobiography*, IV. 132, 138).

The experiences in *Wolf Solent* and *Porius* are unions with nature, with the non-human; and so, in a yet more dangerous sense, is the experience of sadism, being a submission to the invasion of natural instincts hostile to man. Powys tells us that sadistic fantasies were for 'nearly half a century' his 'bosom-houris' and 'attendants at my pillow' (*Autobiography*, I. 8), and that such 'nightly orgies of sadistic imagination' (II. 69) left the ordinary world quite lustreless in comparison (I. 32-5). There was, however, no enjoyment of crude brutality: while 'the *idea* of sadism' could stir his erotic feelings to their depths, he could not tolerate 'savagery and blood' (IX. 397). It was a sadism more like that of a woman than of a man (IX. 426). It remained 'cerebral' (IX. 398), and on the rare occasions when he translated it into actions there was no enjoyment whatsoever, either during action or in recollection, though the originating thought had 'intoxicated' (V. 191). Such invasions render 'nothing else in the world important' (X. 467).

Imagination is the key factor. The fantasies were a kind of raw, unwritten, art, like Wolf's 'mythology'. Powys was an addict of sadistic French picture-books, which so excited him that his knees trembled (IX. 395-7; and see V. 191, X. 467, XII. 615). His sadistic thoughts were miniature narratives; he was always 'telling myself stories' of 'sadistic actions' (I. 10).

His own obsession was worked up into that fearful study of sadistic compulsion: Mr. Evans of *A Glastonbury Romance* (1933; 2nd edn., 1955). He, like Powys, is fascinated by sadistic books and pictures and tells himself stories: pictures and stories of a certain kind, or the 'performance' would not be a 'master one' (XVI. 518 or 500, XXIX. 1068 or 1020-1). The sexual activation and the 'melting sweetness' of it is described (XXIX. 1068 or 1020), and we are made to feel how the man is dominated. His desire is to see someone killed by a blunt instrument. He tries to exorcize his demon by acting the part of the crucified Christ in a passion-play, but the vice persists (XXV. 848 or 812). Hearing of a murder to be committed, he takes no steps of prevention, being impelled, and then deliberately planning, to witness it. His wife pits her mediocre sexual powers against his intention, with

F   159

partial success, so that he hastens to stop the murder, but is too late. He sees the deed for which he had craved, and is sick. The obsession then leaves him.

The evil has cosmic authority, coming direct from the First Cause:

In the nature of the First Cause there are two windows of manifestation corresponding most precisely to the eyes of such creatures as have no more than two eyes. From one of these slits into the Infinite pours forth good; from the other, evil. (XXIX, 1051 or 1004)

The evil eye is red, a 'little, round, red eye' (IX. 256 or 252).

At the moment when Mr. Evans is first deliberately committed to his criminal course, sex-prompting ceases. He is beyond enjoyment or excitement, the passion having been 'diffused' into the whole man, 'body, soul and spirit', and no longer sexually located (XXIX. 1051 or 1004).[1] There is now no pleasure:

What drove him on to it then? What drove him on to this pleasure-divested horror? The coiled snake-nerve of sex! And the strange thing is that the *insane will to the satisfaction* of this terrible sex-nerve does not demand pleasure. Pleasure? Little do the moralists know! . . .

Mr. Evans derives no pleasure from what he is set to do, or of 'satisfaction either – though it is the will to satisfaction that drives it forward' (XXIX. 1060 or 1012).

There was nevertheless the intensest pleasure conceivable in the originating fantasies; and it would seem that we should just let such fantasies remain *as* fantasies, and be contented. But Powys was not always so content. Not only was he at pains in his study of Mr. Evans not to transmit any tingle of infection such as he recognizes in Dante's *Inferno* (*Autobiography*, I. 9), but he also tells us that he has, at the age of fifty-two, stopped allowing him-

---

[1] Compare Byron, *Marino Faliero*, IV. ii. 93:

> It was ever thus
> With me; the hour of agitation came
> In the first glimmerings of a purpose, when
> Passion had too much room to sway; but in
> The hour of action I have stood as calm
> As were the dead who lay around me.

Mr. Evans's sexual activation seems to be of the same nature as more general experiences involving 'nerves' but without sexual sensation.

Compare also T. E. Lawrence's remark on persons so 'fulfilled' that he became unaware of their presence (p. 328 below).

self to indulge even in private for fear that his fantasies should build objective thought-forms that might affect others (*Autobiography*, I. 8-11, also IV. 121 and V. 191. For the objectivity of thought-forms see *A Glastonbury Romance*, XVI. 518 or 500). It is, however, doubtful whether this position was subsequently maintained: he knew that his 'devil' was not 'dead' (*Autobiography*, XII. 616).

I quote, with some adjustments, from my book *The Saturnian Quest* (119):

In *The Art of Happiness* (1935) we are advised 'to lower our spiritual buckets' cautiously into what is 'bad' in order to cope with life's battles through use of a 'diffused sadism' (V. 203-4). A helpful statement occurs in *In Spite Of* (1953). Whatever our insane perversities, he 'recommends, along with profound and absolute secrecy, a free indulgence for all the solitary ecstasies of the imagination', except only for 'the ecstasy of homicide'; this is a way to the unity of 'a new self-created self'; and though, as in nature-union, we through this 'indulgence' become temporarily one with the opposite of our self-engendered 'abortion', we all the time know that what is 'permanently ourselves' 'surrounds' and 'includes' both the good and the evil, and that we are merely 'playing at being saints and monsters'; that is, masochists and sadists (V. 129-30, 137-8). In *Morwyn* (1937) the Golden Age was found *below* Hell.

A simple trust is indicated, as though with a reliance on what Pope once called 'the God within the mind' (*Essay on Man*, II. 204);[1] which may perhaps be better supposed as some guardian angel, or spirit-guide.

My interpretation of 'saints' as corresponding to masochistic fantasy is probably sound: in letters to myself[2] of 11 December 1956 and 22 October 1957 Powys asserted an interrelation of the sadistic and the masochistic, though on 23 January 1957 he was less sure. They are compulsions of similar quality, even though

---

[1] Pope uses the term for man's instinctive ability to distinguish 'light' from 'darkness' in man's chaotic psyche. Here and elsewhere I perhaps expand it a little in regarding it as denoting an active power.

[2] These I have privately lodged in the Brotherton Library in the University of Leeds. I expect to lodge typed copies at Colgate University, Hamilton, U.S.A., and perhaps elsewhere. It is my wish that, if published, they should appear only as a complete and unexpurgated set (48 letters, 2 cards), together with the spirit-communication of 1963 (p. 164n., below) and my letter on Powys to the Nobel Committee of 15 January 1959.

one makes a criminal and the other a saint. Fantasies will vary with individuals, sadistic, masochistic, exhibitionist, obscene. These may intertwist and combine with various emphases. In *A Glastonbury Romance* we have a vivid description of a woman 'torturing herself' because she was a sadist (IV. 256-7 or 252-3).

Powys's ruling that the homicidal[1] alone must be excluded remains doubtfully satisfying: if the teaching is sound there should be no limits, provided that the little drama remain secret. The teaching in *The Art of Happiness* may help: for the 'diffused sadism' needed in life's normal affairs may well be, in the manner described by Pope in his *Essay on Man* (II. 175-94), a sublimated and respectable version of what in fantasy was horrible.

In *A Glastonbury Romance* and the *Autobiography*, sexual sensation is powerfully indicated; thought alone appears to be sufficient to prompt excitement with orgasm, as when 'the orgasm of ego-centric contemplation' in the First Cause is said to stir the responsive 'poison' in Mr. Evans (XXV. 848 or 812). Neither *A Glastonbury Romance* nor the *Autobiography* uses the term 'masturbation' but Powys used it freely in letters to myself during the year 1957.

On 6 January 1957 he wrote to me that since he had turned eighty he had lost all sexual impulse; that he had never known love as passion, but always known it, and still did, in romantic and idealized forms. His erotic sensations had always been sadistic,[2] ever since he had indulged in masturbation as a small boy. His mother had once told him that 'chastity' meant 'the opposite of what you do' (compare *Wolf Solent*, I. 15 or 7; also *Autobiography*, I. 32-3). He had always been a 'terrible masturbator' and would, if he had grandchildren, unhesitatingly advise them to masturbate. On 23 January he wrote that he had always been 'terrified' of sexual intercourse and regarded his begetting of a son as a 'miracle' (see *Autobiography*, VI. 207, VII. 275); his sex-life had been 'from start to finish' cerebral, a matter of 'life-long masturbation'; not even the fear of Hell could make him renounce his 'cerebral orgies of sadism', the vice being too strong.

I cannot recall what part my own letters had originally played

---

[1] For a valuable case-book of homicide, see Colin Wilson and Patricia Pitman, *Encyclopedia of Murder*, New York 1962.

[2] The word 'sadistic' was omitted, and in reply to my query asking if that was intended he wrote on 14 January: 'Sadism was the missing word'. There was, of course, in view of all the other references, no doubt as to his meaning.

in this correspondence, but I certainly replied sympathetically, recording similar, though not specifically sadistic, experiences. On 6 February he urged that were I to engage in lecture-tours 'as a new kind of Missionary' advocating masturbation which, he contended, does *good* and not *harm*, 'as a cure for all ills', I would bring help to thousands of young people, probably including 'young ladies' (see *Porius*, VI. 106). If a murderer had learned how to enjoy his crime 'in imagination' while 'he masturbated with the sensation of it' he would have remained innocent. This counsel Powys repeated, passionately. On 27 February he called 'cerebral' masturbation 'the greatest of all possible devices for keeping our vices to ourselves', and showed interest in my suggestion that some such technique may often have been advocated among monastic orders.

Two of the letters contained interesting transitions to thoughts on childhood and second childhood. His own sadistic fantasies started in childhood: 'from the age of three . . . this deadly vice transported and obsessed me' (*Autobiography*, I. 8). In the first of the two letters (6 February) children are called the wisest sort of people and the wisest books are said to be '*Grimm's Fairy Tales* and *Mother Goose*, tales including Blue-Beard in their scope'. The point seems to be that the instincts of childhood are to be learned from, and not thwarted. In the second letter (27 February) he wrote that now, in his 'second childhood', he has the greater insight into children; between them and the aged there is a 'magnetic' understanding. Later, on 12 October 1957, commenting on my review 'Cosmic Correspondences' in *The Times Literary Supplement* (p. 399 below), he wrote: 'Nobody but you has brought into an analysis of me as a writer the one essential thing – namely that I was born a sadist! Not until all *sex-urge ended for good* on my eightieth birthday or round about then, did sadism give place to the happiest of all the epochs of my life, the one I am enjoying now – which I know I am being absolutely correct in calling *second-childhood*'. It seems that now he could bring a dispassionate insight to bear on the instincts of youth and that he found it easier to write judicially on them after ceasing to be under their domination. From his letters it would appear that the claim in the *Autobiography* to have surmounted the vice in his fifties was, as he half-suspected (p. 161 above), only provisionally justified.

When I last saw Powys in 1963, a few months before his death, he did not talk, being very weak; but he gave me a book as a memento and at one point made vigorous signs, holding a finger of one hand in the other fist, perhaps urging me to deliver the teaching his letters had formulated.[1]

A few years after this 1957 correspondence Powys made his first public statement on masturbation, in *All or Nothing* (1960), his last published[2] work, using as a mouth-piece his well-loved Cerne Giant. The Cerne Giant is an ancient, white, chalk figure on a hill near Cerne Abbas in Dorsetshire. He is shown as sexually excited while wielding a heavy club, and accordingly symbolizes the sexually impelled violence that has throughout the centuries driven man in his huntings, murders and wars.

All or Nothing is composed as a children's story, with four adventurous children, or adolescents conceived very nearly as children, as its central characters. That Powys's most revolutionary, and many would say most dangerous, doctrine was delivered in a child's 'fairy-tale' will not, after the letters we have reviewed, seem strange, and the problems posed must be faced in a mood of child-innocence.

The Cerne Giant, the chief of Powys's many favoured giants, had appeared throughout his books. In *All or Nothing* he has become gentle and is a specifically *creative* power, a 'good giant' (XXVIII. 200; *The Saturnian Quest*, 117). He is found on the star Vindex, where he had been enslaved to a wicked giant Bog whom he had killed to prevent his devouring the children. Despite his cruelty, Bog was wise, having ears that heard all the various languages of the cosmos (XVIII. 131-4, XXVI. 185), which means that his wisdom was not limited to the biological valuations of any one planet, such as the Earth. He taught that there 'are other Dimensions' than those of our normal sense-perception, a 'parallel' world where everything has a different aspect (XXVII. 191-2). Our earthly reason, so often repudiated in Powys's lyrics, cannot be supposed the last word in wisdom. Somehow the worst dangers, the nihilisms, perhaps even the cruelties, have, provisionally, their place. So the 'good giant' learns from the wicked one.

[1] Of two psychic messages from Powys through Miss F. Horsfield, the first, thanking me for my support, was reported in *Psychic News*, 27 July 1963. The second was given by her to my brother, who relayed it to me on a postcard of 1 December 1963, saying 'Powys wants to give some evidential cross-reference: Miss Horsfield gets the word "sensualism", for you to explain'.

[2] I say 'last published'. Powys left some writings not as yet published.

Mysticism and Masturbation

'According to what Bog taught me', says the Cerne Giant, 'life is much more complicated' than we normally suppose:

In the matter of sex, Bog taught me that what in the English language is called masturbation – that is to say, the excited emission of semen by the use of our imagination – is a much more important and creative act than ordinary and natural fornication or the raping, if we are male, of our feminine opposite. (XXVII. 192)

The act is *creative*: just as normal sex-union makes a child, this union with instincts jetting from the greater cosmos makes a personality. This is, as *In Spite Of* told us (p. 161 above), the way to 'a new self-created self' whereby we are one with our 'opposite'. There appears to be a relation to the 'parthenogenesis' of *The Brazen Head* (1956; XIV. 211): 'I am not losing my maidenhead, and yet I am drawing from the inmost depths of myself a dew-drop of living creation'.

Whether Bog meant that the imagination in full wakefulness should initiate, as it can in sleep, orgasm and emission without tactile assistance is not clear; perhaps only for more imaginative types is that possible; from the letter of 6 February 1957 it seems that physical assistance would in general be expected (and see *Autobiography*, I. 32). It is nevertheless certain that for any creative result the imagination must be functioning as a main constituent. The attendant fantasy must probably involve thoughts which the normal self would repudiate (as in *Porius*, p. 158 above), since only a strong play of daring is likely to stimulate the excitement, in the manner noted in Pope's *Eloisa to Abelard*, 'How glowing guilt exalts the keen delight' (230). There the fantasy comes in sleep, but the process is similar: 'exalts' suggests physical erection and 'guilt' less perhaps an essential evil than a sense of breaking through some accepted taboo. Some opposite of our normal, social, self-respected selves functions as a sexual partner, and in unification with it we enjoy an enlargement; the creation from ourselves of a greater, non-social, self, drawing on the cosmic energies.

Fantasies will vary, and may well appear the exact opposite of the personality's appearance as shown to others and believed in by himself. The kindly man may be invaded by sadism, the cowardly by masochism, the proud by shame-fantasies, the prude by obscenities, the diffident by exhibitionism. These opposites will, to be effective (that is, sexually activating), probably come in shocking and perhaps ludicrous extremes. Types may intermix. In *Christ and Nietzsche* (III. 83) I noted three basic perversions: exhibitionism, sadism, and masochism. These may be regarded as extensions of elements within ordinary sexual intercourse. Each may also be subdivided into variations, and all intershade and intertwine. The subtleties are endless: though, as we shall see, Powys's lyric poetry is often exactly on the wavelength of Rupert Brooke's, Brooke knew a narcissistic self-enjoyment that is in violent contrast to Powys's statement that he is 'the extreme opposite' of a 'narcissist' or 'exhibitionist' (*Autobiography*, IX. 426). On 6 January 1957 he wrote to me: 'I've got a mania against *seeing* myself! I look hastily away if there's any risk of a glimpse of myself in any mirror'; and when I sent him a photograph of myself as Timon of Athens he said, on 11 December 1956, that he would not bare his shoulders like that even if the Queen commanded him. He might equally have been referring to Brooke's famous photograph (p. 307 below).[1]

Whatever the fantasies, the process is probably much the same; an assimilation of cosmic forces usually suppressed and a consequent release, enlargement and completion.

We often think of normal sex-impulse as psychologically central, but Colin Wilson was probably right in saying in *The Origin of the Sexual Impulse* (1963; IX. 223-4) that it is not so central as it seems, and that the true centre lies deeper; rather as when Powys in *In Spite Of* (IV. 116) tells us that the natural bride and natural bridegroom of every creature's soul is, not a human partner, but the 'outer world', as is clear enough from the paradisal experiences, celebrated by Wordsworth's famous ode on *Immortality*, of childhood. In his central statement in the 1814 Preface to *The Excursion* Wordsworth prophesies the 'creation', or self-creation, of greater personalities through a union of man's

---

[1] On 2 November 1948 Powys wrote to me saying that *Timon of Athens* was a play 'I hardly have read at all'. The late Nicholas Ross, a friend of Powys to whom I showed a copy of these letters from Powys, wrote saying on 23 March 1967 that 'he often quoted this play, and even added some of his favourite quotes from it in the Shakespeare Diary he made for me'. He also questioned Powys's statement to me on 9 September 1958 that he had 'never read' *Henry VIII* and did not even 'know it existed', since Powys had included favourite quotations from it, too (in 1940). Powys had included both plays in his lectures; see Langridge, *Record of Achievement* (p. 415 below), 22, 44 (and on Powys's memory, 184).

'mind' and the 'external world' (p. 44 above; discussed also in *The Saturnian Quest*, 19). In its submission of mental categories to non-mental, instinctive, powers from outside, Powys's masturbatory doctrine is really an extreme Wordsworthianism. We are not surprised when Powys tells us that his 'inner life' had been 'nourished' on Wordsworth's doctrine for 'sixty years' (*Obstinate Cymric*, 1947; X. 164). He expands Wordsworth. For him sex-promptings, whatever their nature, deliver messages not merely from earth-nature but from the outer cosmos. We remember the double-natured First Cause of *A Glastonbury Romance*. In *All or Nothing* we meet the Cerne Giant on the star Vindex; Bog's wisdom was drawn from what Powys regularly calls the 'multiverse'; and all the more extreme denials and abnegations in Powys's prose and poetry, all his strangenesses and aberrations, are the shadows cast by some great assertion only expressible in negative terms.

A question arises as to how the masturbatory experience relates to actions. In *The Art of Happiness* Powys recognized a relation between inward indulgence and the 'diffused sadism' needed to grapple with life's problems; as though the abnormal indulgence helped him to conquer his equally abnormal, unworldly kindliness and sensitivity; to strike, as it were, a balance. Pope tells us much the same, noting how various vices may have valuable, sublimated, expressions (pp. 170-1 below).

The simplest of all challenges to convention is that of bodily display. It may seem too simple to be deeply interesting, and yet it is extremely important: we may recall the part played by nakedness at the Fall in Genesis. Now, though exhibitionist fantasies may take extreme forms involving obscenities, absurdities and shame, and often must do so if they are to be sexually activating, yet their essence may be projected into action without much dilution or danger. We may fairly easily press through the good and the guilt alike, enjoying both, to a primal innocence and power; as when the strip-tease, the most basic of all art-forms, unveils the human figure in its true proportions; or when by the removal of civilization's trappings by sea or lake we receive the sun's burning kiss and enjoy elemental contact and a cosmic union. Here too, just as when Mr. Evans, once deliberately set on his fearful course, was no longer sexually excited, so in sun-bathing, acting, painting, modelling, action dissolves excitement which only existed as an impulse *from the one side*, and is part now of a total action, or creativity.

In exhibitionism, though ingrained taboo and even guilt may have to be countered, no violent challenge is involved and a sense of rectitude may be preserved. With Mr. Evans's sadism there is a deliberate surrender to what his normal self utterly repudiates: he has said, like Milton's Satan, 'evil, be thou my good' (*Paradise Lost*, IV. 110). But the process is the same, however dark the experience, quiescence accompanying action or the will to it: the psychology is independent of ethic. We may distinguish between the breaking of taboos through daring and a mastery of guilt but with no sense of *ultimate* wrong, and sheer evil, or at least what is considered so by the perpetrator, the reservation being necessary since it is impossible to know for certain what really is, in a final sense, evil. The first may under appropriate conditions be developed with little dilution from fantasy into some accepted artistic or otherwise creative *action*. The second must be confined to fantasy, and even there Powys at one point excludes homicide (p. 161), though in his letter of 6 February 1957 he did not; or it may be given some carefully sublimated expression. There is the possibility, and even value, of a 'diffused sadism' (pp. 161-2, 167), and clearly sadism may be rendered, with caution, into art, as in *A Glastonbury Romance*. Whether Mr. Evans's submission to crime was caused by too great an indulgence in fantasy or by not sufficiently following the doctrine of Powys's letters on secret indulgence, it is less easy to say. Indulgence succeeded for Powys.

We can now state five general ways of treating these taboo-challenging instincts: (i) total suppression, in thought and deed, leaving them to rankle, or assert themselves only in sleep and dream; (ii) full waking, but private, indulgence; (iii) a 'diffused' or sublimated expression in public; (iv) a considered acting of them, approved by the permanent self; (v) a deliberate surrender to an act which the permanent self rejects. We may also distinguish between the many obsessions that are reasonably harmless and the one which sticks out as uncompromisingly dangerous: sadism.

What is sadism? Thinking of Powys's 'double-natured First Cause' we can suggest that the natural order depends on the balance of voracity and propagation, destruction and creation, negative and positive. Animals and plants automatically conform;

168

but in man the two have become conscious and inflamed. Since they are both part of the natural scheme, man's creative, sexual, organism may become entwined with either or both; for, as Colin Wilson has observed, the 'imagination' can act as a 'detonator' of 'the sexual energies' (*Beyond the Outsider*, 1965; 181). Powys was sadistically fascinated at the age of three by a picture of an eagle seizing a lamb (*Autobiography*, I. 8). The sadist and masochist enjoy sexually the laws of nature. Extensions occur: pain, the concomitant of destruction, may be involved; also the destruction may be spiritual rather than physical, an infliction of indignity, to break down another's, or one's own, spiritual integrity. Sadism is power-craving, voracious and mastering; or it may be a vivisectional playing with another for a purpose, to increase one's knowledge.[1]

In so far as there is enjoyment we may draw a delicate and dangerous distinction: though the cruelty may be bad the enjoyment may be *in essence*, as is all joy, in itself a good; and perhaps that is why Wolf Solent's 'mythology' was simultaneously 'a secret vice' and on the side of 'good' as against 'evil', the *sensuous enjoyment* of it being there reflected into such liquid impressionisms as are throughout Powys, and in his lyrics especially, associated with blessings. When children enjoy tales of piracy and torture their enjoyment may be quite innocent. Nursery rhymes are notoriously grim. Powys has observed that though a dangerous fantasy may give pleasure the corresponding action gives none (pp. 159-60). If there were not some essential difference between the imaginative enjoyment of evils and the practice of them, most literature and much conversation would be poisoned at its source. In *Macbeth* we enjoy a magical power which has to be given a moral framing because that power has not as yet been satisfactorily placed in human evolution; but it is the power, not the morality, which we enjoy.

Even in actions the sadist is engaging in a kind of love-intercourse with his victim, and to that extent honours him: touch, love's medium, if too fierce becomes pain. According to Dante (*Inferno*, III. 6), Hell itself with all its torments is part of

---

[1] It is because he has realized the insistence of the sadistic instinct in man that Powys so detested vivisection. On the concern felt about animal experiments by other leading writers from Shakespeare and Dr. Johnson onwards (Hugo, Browning, Ruskin, Wagner etc.), see John Vyvyan's study *In Pity and in Anger*, 1969.

God's love. The subtleties are endless, and beyond all rational enquiry we have to face Taliessin's reference in Powys's *Morwyn*, that fearful sadists' *Inferno*, to 'a secret that bears upon the mystery of good and evil and upon the mystical light that sometimes shines out from the most noisome regions of evil' (III. 178). Taliessin, like Nietzsche and Powys, deliberately visits Hell for intellectual reasons (III. 145).

To return to our practical, day-to-day problem. The ethical intershadings are, beyond all possibility of clear study, complex: even the instinct for homicide may make a good commando and national hero. Generally we must reject *direct*, unsublimated sadistic behaviour. But in all periods and among all races bloodshed and torture have been assiduously practised and enjoyed. The God-implanted urges are there; they cannot be destroyed; they must be used, or, if not used, released. Or transmuted.

2

Powys's masturbatory doctrine crowns a long tradition of revolutionary challenge from the Renaissance down. Our two main Renaissance myths, the Faust myth and the Don Juan myth, challenge taboos theological and sexual respectively. The first, in its deliberate submission to the demonic, is in clear correspondence to Powys's doctrine; and even the hero's rejuvenation, as in some versions of the story, may be related to the influx of health and power which supporters of the doctrine would claim for it. Literature has many relevant figures: the various Satanic persons of Renaissance drama, Milton's Satan, the Gothic heroes in novel and drama, Emily Brontë's Heathcliff. Blake and Whitman were prophetic challengers. Central to our discussion are the vivid proclamations of Alexander Pope and Nietzsche.

Pope emphasizes the power in man of certain 'ruling' or 'master' passions and discusses the sublimated expressions of instincts themselves dangerous (*Moral Essays*, Epistle to Lord Cobham, 174-227; *Essay on Man* II. 175-248). He states the divine authority of instinct:

> . . . Reason raise o'er Instinct as you can,
> In this 'tis God directs, in that 'tis Man.
> (*Essay on Man*, III. 97)

Mysticism and Masturbation

'This' refers to 'instinct'. Instinct is necessary:

> The surest Virtues thus from Passions shoot,
> Wild Nature's vigor working at the root.
>
> (*Essay on Man*, II. 183)

The 'moving principle' is 'active', it 'prompts, impels, inspires'. Reason can exercise a check, but has no creative leverage (II. 67-81, 101-63). Ethic is safeguarded in that *actual* vice has only to be seen to be hated (II. 218); and yet virtue and vice are inextricably intertwisted, extremes combining 'to some mysterious use' in 'a thousand ways' (II. 206, 214). Beyond both instinct and reason there is a 'mightier Power', 'the God within the mind' (II. 165, 204), and to these we must trust. For practical purposes the central advice is that our reason should treat instincts as equals:

> 'Tis hers to rectify, not overthrow,
> And treat this passion more as friend than foe.
>
> (II. 163)

This is the way to collaborate with God:

> Th' Eternal Art, educing good from ill,
> Grafts on this Passion our best principle.   (II. 175)

That is, crisply, our key.

In all such writings we may feel a semi-sexual truth, or value, pressing for sanctification. Keats's *Ode to Psyche* is to be read not as an invitation to love-making but as a devotional piece to the Power behind, the erotic principle as developed into creative art (*The Starlit Dome*, 301-4; *Christ and Nietzsche*, IV 136-8). Keats's advice 'to let the mind be a thoroughfare for all thoughts' and not only for 'a select party' (letter-journal to George and Georgiana Keats, entry for 24 September 1819; *Letters*, ed. M. B. Forman, 1935; 426) may perhaps be extended beyond its context.

Our subtlest teaching on these difficult questions will be found in Nietzsche's *Thus Spake Zarathustra*. Physical instinct is regarded as authoritative. The body 'Saith not I but it doth I'; it is a 'great intelligence', the true 'self', ruling the 'I' and proving wiser than man's 'best wisdom'. Even the 'spirit' is, as in Powys (p. 160 above), regarded as its 'instrument' (I. 4).[1]

---

[1] My quotations are taken from the Everyman Translation (A. Tille and M. M. Bozman). In *Christ and Nietzsche*, I inadvisedly numbered the 'Introductory Discourse' as the first section of Part I; since then I have always regarded the introduction as separate.

The section 'The Pale Criminal' (I. 6) offers a striking diagnosis. In *Christ and Nietzsche* (V. 165) I wrote of it:

Nietzsche penetrates, after the manner of a Dostoievsky or a Powys, the cause of crime. We are shown the true motive, 'the bliss of the knife', rationalized into robbery even by the criminal himself through shame of his, to borrow a phrase from Coleridge's minor poetry, 'secret joy'; with a further insight into a simple, thwarted, and quite innocent craving behind even this – a similar diagnosis occurs in Pope's *Essay on Man* (IV. 41-4) – and a corresponding condemnation of the judge who, if he spoke his secretest thoughts, would cause all to cry, 'Away with this filth, this poisonous worm!'

Nietzsche's thought here may be applied to our international turmoils. Idealistic warring may be motivated by joy in battle-lust; if something of the kind were not there to be used, there could be no wars.

Nietzsche sees man as in 'pieces', as on a 'battlefield or a shambles', as a collection of unco-ordinated fragments; and his aim is to 'bring together' these fragments and make man whole (II. 20). To do this the basic instincts must be assimilated rather than rejected. Our normal state is one of self-deception: 'Good men never speak the truth' (III. 12). They dare not face their own prompting instincts and trust their 'bowels' or 'inward parts'; and 'He that believeth not himself is "ever a liar" ' (II. 15).

Truth, to be truth, must be dynamic, newly created, from the real, and total, self. To reach this may take many years and involve many fears:

All that the Good call wicked must flow together that a truth may be born: O my brethren, are ye wicked enough for *this* truth?

Rash daring, long mistrust, cruel nay-saying, disgust, a cutting to the quick – how rarely do *all these* come together! But from such seed truth is begotten!

Heretofore hath all *knowledge* grown up with an evil conscience! Break, break, ye Knowers, the ancient tables! (III. 12)

This is the heart of Nietzsche's teaching. Those of us who have taken this course will recognize how exact are Nietzsche's phrases.

Every word is important. Ethic, inhibition, taboos are active: Pope's 'God within the mind' (*Essay on Man*, II. 204) is clearly present, and the critical reason is awake. But so is courage; even rashness is a constituent and conscience no *final* guide. Just as, at the Fall, man's singleness was split into good and evil, here good and evil together must be recombined to achieve the reinstatement.

Nietzsche's Zarathustra is sometimes afraid. He is aware of some new and secret 'virtue', sweet but 'unutterable' (I. 5). Once, in 'The Stillest Hour' (II. 22), he admits that he knows, yet dare not utter, the secret truth. He is able, yet reluctant, to be utterly himself. He doubts his 'mountains', but is only too sure of his 'valleys'; and is, very naturally, reluctant to speak out while his first advances fail to gain a response. These once brought mockery on him, since when he has failed. He feels unworthy, lack's 'the lion's voice of command', is ashamed. He is told to become like a child 'without shame'; but he is still not 'ripe'. Elsewhere he fears lest 'swine and libertines break into my garden' (III. 10). Some personal secrecy is involved: at present he lacks the 'lion-insolence and wantonness' needed to call up the thought that he has always 'carried' in him and may yet deliver (III. 3). Meanwhile he advises his disciples, as does Powys (p. 161), to preserve secrecy, since the time has not yet come for understanding (IV. 13). He would rather die than confess his midnight fantasies (IV. 19).

The 'lion' and 'child' are important symbols. 'The womb of Being' (Powys's 'First Cause') speaks to man through his human, that is sexual, make-up (I. 3), and the Lion is the cosmic power in man. Only 'the lion in the spirit' (I. 1) can give the courage on which all human 'prehistory' has depended, since all advance has come through 'joy in the uncertain, the undared' (IV. 15). The Lion's 'I will' battles with the 'Dragon' of 'Thou shalt' (I. 1).

The Lion alone is not enough. He corresponds to the Old Testament of primal power, and we have to move on to the New Testament of beyond-good-and-evil innocence and new truth:

To create new values – even the Lion is not able to do this: but to create for himself freedom for new creation, for this the Lion's strength is sufficient. (I. 1)

Therefore the Lion must give way to, or become, a 'Child'. What is this 'Child'? We think of the New Testament, Blake, Wordsworth and Shelley (for Shelley, *The Starlit Dome*, 213-24). Nietzsche's definition goes:

The Child is innocence and oblivion, a new beginning, a play, a self-rolling wheel, a primal motion, an holy yea-saying. (I. 1)

173

That is an ordinary child. The Child-as-symbol is all that, but more. It is as far above the good-and-evil consciousness as the ordinary child is below it; in it the child-quality, the Tree of Life of Genesis, has been re-won. In 'The Stillest Hour' (II. 22) Zarathustra, an old man of youthful insight, is told that the 'pride of youth' is still holding him back among the inhibitions, and to 'become a child' he 'must surmount even his youth'. He is advancing steadily *backwards*. As Eliot in *Four Quartets* puts it, 'In my beginning is my end'; 'in my end is my beginning'; and when he arrives where he 'started' he will 'know the place for the first time' ('East Coker', I, V; 'Little Gidding', V). We may recall Powys's emphasis on his second childhood: 'I hope I'll get thro' my present Homeric studies quickly enough to write something in praise of *Second childhood* for if *theirs* is the kingdom of heaven what about doubling "theirs" with the dotage of a *second go* at that "something far more deeply interfused"?' (Letter of 14 January 1957).

The Child is needed to create the new values. Through daring, accepting, and so far as may be expressing, his own evil, man wins the innocence needed for the new valuation.

'*Evil*', or at least some 'guilt' or 'taboo', *must be present*, or there would be no advance. Man must, to gain a newer fullness and a higher virtue, *use powers hitherto rejected*. Humility is needed: 'Many a one can command himself, but falleth far short in obeying himself' (III. 12). That self is, or contains, the Lion. The Lion is more than crude instinct; he is a royal beast; and yet the instinct may well seem crude; perhaps the Lion symbolizes the true royalty within what we regard as crude instinct. 'The most evil thing in man is necessary to the best in him', and 'all that is most evil is his best power and hardest stone for the highest creator' (III. 13). Somehow this 'evil' is a vital constituent to the best. In this way man is to make of himself one 'god' out of his 'seven devils' (I. 17):

Once hadst thou passions and calledst them evil. Now hast thou only thy virtues: they grew out of thy passions.   (I. 5)

'Devils' become 'angels' (I. 5). Victory comes through gradual transformations:

Three metamorphoses of the spirit have I declared unto you: how the spirit becometh a Camel, the Camel a Lion, and the Lion at length a Child.   (I. 1)

Most of us remain Camels. The doctrine assumes a high degree of sensitivity and normal goodness as a preliminary. At one point Nietzsche says that solitude should by some be avoided as it would develop 'the brute within' (IV. 13; also 15). In the statement 'to the knower all instincts are hallowed' (I. 22), the reservation is important. It may all be very difficult, a life's arduous work, but only the power of the Lion and the 'holy yea-saying' of the Child can realize the God-implanted design already lodged within each of us: 'The thirst of the Ring is within you; for every ring striveth and turneth about that it may reach itself again' (II. 5). The conclusion is simple: 'Become that thou art' (IV. 1).

The correspondence with Powys is clear. The 'terrible Mistress' who visits Zarathustra in 'The Stillest Hour' (II. 22) may be compared with the nightly 'houris' of Powys's *Autobiography* (p. 159 above). Though Nietzsche's scalpel incisiveness and glittering thoughts are in a different style, one section, 'The Drunken Song' (IV. 19), is impressionistically Powysian.

It is midnight, with a moon, and silence. Zarathustra is with his companions, including the 'Ugliest Man', and has taught them to 'love the earth'. Powys's favoured seers are ugly and his earth-love is deep. Zarathustra, in half-trance, lays his 'finger' on his 'lip' – we shall find the same gesture in *The Ship* (p. 224 below) – and says 'Come!' Again, 'Let us be going! It is the hour: let us go into the night!' An old bell sounds from the deep, 'eerily', 'terribly'. Yeats's 'drunken soldiery' and 'gong' in 'Byzantium' may perhaps be related to Nietzsche's 'Drunken Song'. By night much may be heard 'that by day findeth no voice'. Midnight speaks 'intimately'. Zarathustra sinks into 'deep wells'. What is happening? Midnight fantasies awake:

Rather will I die, yea, die, than say to you what my midnight heart now thinketh!

These are the 'hot secrets of dreams that day cannot say' in Brooke's 'The Song of the Beasts' (p. 303 below). As before in 'The Stillest Hour', Zarathustra needs courage:

That hour wherein I shudder and freeze, that asketh and asketh and asketh: 'Who hath courage enough therefor? – Who shall be the lord of the earth? Who will say: "*Thus* shall ye flow, ye great and small streams!"' '

'This speech', we are told, 'is for subtle ears'. Some great truth is being shadowed: '*What saith deep Midnight, indeed?*' '*Thus* shall ye flow . . .' may, and probably must, refer to masturbation. 'Lord of the earth' may be compared with Ibsen's statement in *Emperor and Galilean* (*The Emperor Julian*, III. iv; my *Ibsen*, 42) that the great Third Empire will be inaugurated by the one who 'wills himself'.

When in a letter to me of 6 May 1949 Powys wrote of his 'frog-like soul on its hopping and croaking' the analogy was thoroughly characteristic (see *The Saturnian Quest*, 124), So, too, Zarathustra hears a 'drunken toad-song', coming 'from the ponds of love': it belongs to the blue-green depths of Wolf Solent's 'mythology'. As in so many of Powys's lyrics we are in a world 'deeper than ever day may deem'; as in those the day-time is rejected as unclean by the 'midnight-souls' that shall be 'lords of the earth'. Again Zarathustra calls himself 'a midnight-lyre, a bell-voiced toad that none understandeth'. The wind wakes. Midnight is a 'drunken poetess' who 'cheweth the cud of her woe in dreams'. This may mean that half-sleeping the mind enjoys grim fantasies in utter-most content. But 'joy', we are told, is deeper than 'woe': the experience is basically positive, because enjoyed, however negative it may seem; and so basically good and not bad.

'The Drunken Song' is repetitive, stammering, oblique. Finally a mystical rapture is reached, the self desiring only itself and accepting all, good and evil alike, eternally as it is. Opposites blend, the world is known as 'perfect', 'midnight' becomes 'noonday', which means that the dark fantasies are known as bright. As we shall find in Powys's *The Ship*, night becomes sun:

Pain also is delight, curse also is blessing, night also is a sun – hence then, lest ye learn that a wise man also is a fool.

Joy is acclaimed, joy that 'thirsteth for woe, for hell, for hatred, for shame, for the cripple, for the *world*, for this world. . . .' The words suggest analogies throughout Powys's *Autobiography* and poems. We touch the 'eternity of all things – *profound, profound* Eternity'.

We conclude with some lines on a world deeper than 'day', deep in its 'woe'; yet, 'deeper' still, is 'Joy' pressing into 'Eternity'.

Much of *Thus Spake Zarathustra* is more bright, celebrating a lonely, narcissistic self-love and self-completion, a 'more than marriage' (III. 10), accompanied by various erotic impressions and with dance, gaiety and sun. Its teaching is best described as winning through to 'the Golden Wonder, the boat of free will and its Master' (III. 14). The whole works up towards 'the great Noon' when Zarathustra is to announce his message to the world, and there it concludes. Powys's life-work shows a development from the macabre tones of his lyrics, *Wolf Solent* and *A Glastonbury Romance* to the colourful *Owen Glendower* and glittering *Atlantis*.

Both writers concentrate on self-making. What we are to do on life's stage is not stated: as in the New Testament, rules are avoided. The teaching is an inward counsel, on our self-making from within and the process of it. The more outward realization of Zarathustra's 'Great Noon' comes at the book's conclusion. What that is we do not know; only the process, if followed out, will show us. Religious feeling is active with, as deity, the Lady Eternity (III. 16).

Nietzsche looks for a superman of grace and gentleness, an all but seraphic being (II. 13; *Christ and Nietzsche*, V 170-6); but we cannot as yet define 'the Nameless One for whom the songs of the future will first find names' (III. 14). Meanwhile, there are as many ways as there are psychological obsessions: there are, in fact, 'a thousand paths' that 'none hath yet trod' and 'a thousand healths and hidden isles of life' to be discovered (I. 22). We must assume that God has already lodged within us our potential course; we are, as in Ibsen's *Peer Gynt*, a drama rich in relevant material, to realize in ourselves the God-implanted design (V. vii, ix. See my *Ibsen*, 28, 111); and what that is, or to what actions it will lead, we cannot know beforehand. In generalized terms, however, Nietzsche does once (III. 10) indicate, in the manner of Pope's *Essay on Man* (II. 175-94), how *voluptuousness, lust of power*, and *selfishness* may have diverse effects: the first may be 'sweet poison' to some, but a 'grand cordial' to the 'lion-willed'. The second may be a self-torment, grim, cruel, destructive; or may be a spiritual aspiration bearing love's glow; or may descend to win fame by humility, may be 'the virtue that giveth'; which last is said to be a possible name for the indefinable goal of human existence. As for selfishness, this may be 'the wholesome, healthy selfishness that floweth from a mighty soul' and perfect body, despising all negations.

Once Nietzsche brilliantly defined a move from insight to action:

If ever I laughed with the laughter of the creative lightning that is followed by the long thunder of the deed, growling but obedient . . .

(III. 16)

Mysticism and Masturbation

The intuition is called 'creative'. We may think of Christ's intuition of a spectacular sacrifice in 'I, if I be lifted up from the earth, will draw all men unto myself', the words signifying, we are told, 'by what manner of death he should die' (John, XII. 32-3); a thought perhaps conceived in joy but followed out, through humility to that joy's vision, in labour and agony. When the intuition is not 'creative' the process, as with Powys's Mr. Evans, may be the same. Sadistic fantasy in Powys himself was given creative pointing in *A Glastonbury Romance*, probaby the greatest study of evil that has ever been composed; in which, as Powys said of Dostoievsky, all is 'sublimated and purified by the power of the spirit' (*Autobiography*, I. 9). As Nietzsche puts it:

Thou goest thy way of greatness: now is that become thy final refuge which hath been hitherto thine extremest peril.

Thou goest thy way of greatness: thy highest courage must it be that there is no longer any way back! (III. 1)

After a certain point in submission there *is* no way back: this is true on all ethical levels, as true of Mr. Evans – until his wife's opposition – in *A Glastonbury Romance* as of Martin Luther's famous 'I can no other'. At such times one may feel simultaneously fearful and safe. The paradoxes are sharp; as also in 'extremest peril' and 'final refuge'.[1] 'Extremes' join in man to some 'mysterious use' (Pope, *Essay on Man*, II. 206). Only when the opposites touch and ignite, as they did at the end of *Wolf Solent*, have we the 'way of greatness'.

T. S. Eliot's poetry[2] is relevant to our present discussion. In his dramas the sadistic sexuality of *Sweeney Agonistes* and *The Family Reunion* is countered by the saintly masochism – to use for our purpose the crude term – of *Murder in the Cathedral* and *The Cocktail Party*. The criminal guilt, the abyss, of *Sweeney Agonistes* would have been well understood by Mr. Evans.

So would those words in 'Gerontion', 'After such knowledge, what forgiveness?' 'Gerontion' is packed with relevant, if uncoordinated, hints. Implanted evil makes life terrible. Spring, raising the voracious sex-vigour, is fierce:

---

[1] My own life, with all due reservations and no high claims, has pursued a similar course. I wish neither to parade my obsessions nor to appear to be suppressing them; but it is well to state that in these hazardous commentaries I write from some personal experience.

[2] The dates of Eliot's publications are given below, Ch. XIII.

Mysticism and Masturbation

In the juvescence of the year
Came Christ the tiger

In depraved May, dogwood and chestnut, flowering judas,
To be eaten, to be divided, to be drunk
Among whispers . . .

'Judas': nature's spring-flowering is 'depraved' and we have an inverted Communion Service or Mass. Therefore:

Think
Neither fear nor courage saves us. Unnatural vices
Are fathered by our heroism. Virtues
Are forced upon us by our impudent crimes.
These tears are shaken from the wrath-bearing tree.

The interrelation of good and evil is seen negatively, not, as in Pope and Nietzsche, positively; and man's plight is accordingly attributed to the Fall ('wrath-bearing tree'). While 'the tiger springs in the new year' normal sexuality is inhibited (see pp. 374-5 below).

'Gerontion' is expanded in *The Waste Land*. In the first section, 'April is the cruellest month' repeats 'Christ the tiger', and the mysterious 'corpse' expected to 'sprout' makes a similar paradox. Throughout, normal sexuality is presented as in some way gone wrong, nerve-racked or sordid. 'Death by water' (I, IV), the surrender to passion,[1] is an ultimate fear, but parched endurance through desert, rocks and fire the better alternative: 'O Lord Thou pluckest me out . . . burning' (III). What precisely the evils are, the obsessions, is not defined, but the general implications are recognizable:

Datta: what have we given?
My friend, blood shaking my heart
The awful daring of a moment's surrender
Which an age of prudence can never retract
By this, and this only, we have existed
Which is not to be found in our obituaries
Or in memories draped by the beneficent spider
Or under seals broken by the lean solicitor
In our empty rooms   (V)

[1] The equation is fairly general in poetry: see Colin Still's *Shakespeare's Mystery Play*, 1921. In the *Four Quartets* ('The Dry Salvages', I) Eliot tells us explicitly that 'the river is within you'.

The 'daring' of 'surrender' is exactly Nietzschean (p. 174). For 'blood' and 'heart' compare Powys (p. 159 above). We may recall how Pope's 'moving principle', the energic instinct,

> sees immediate good by present sense;
> Reason, the future and the consequence.
>
> (*Essay on Man*, II. 73)

Though Eliot's negative view shows it as ruinous to all 'prudence', that is to all normal, conventional valuation, yet he recognizes that *it is only through realizing the implanted instinct that one has truly existed*.[1] The secret remains blessedly veiled from biographer and solicitor.

It would at first seem that Eliot has left us with an ultimate confusion, admitting the insolubility of the human problem and only half-heartedly falling back on Church doctrine as a remedy. But this is not the whole truth. Rain from above finally comes, like 'the gentle rain from heaven' in Shakespeare (*The Merchant of Venice*, IV. i. 185), to relieve the parched sex-craving; the 'broken Coriolanus' is for a moment revived (V); and the boat, like that of Elizabeth and Leicester earlier (III), at the conclusion (V) responds, ruling the waters of passion, free now as the released ship in *The Ancient Mariner* or Nietzsche's golden boat of Freewill (p. 177); it is a soul-boat, and is too, or might have been, a love-boat. These are glimpses, 'fragments . . . shored against my ruins' (V). Apart from fire-salvation Eliot is searching within the water-realm of sex-energy for a solution in its own, or nearly its own, terms:

> I sat upon the shore
> Fishing, with the arid plain behind me.
>
> (V)

Within the passional element is a great good: we may remember the mystical significance of the Fish.

The Waste Land was followed by *The Hollow Men* which states a paradoxical ambivalence of relatedness and inconsequence

---

[1] After committing a fearful murder for revenge the sensitive young hero of John Marston's *Antonio's Revenge* cries:

> Methinks I am all air and feel no weight
> Of human dirt clog. (III. v)

He becomes 'all soul, all heart, all spirit' (V. v). The implications are terrible enough.

Mysticism and Masturbation

between instincts and actions, the same as that between fantasy and execution which we have already discussed in the case of Mr. Evans (p. 160 above). A crisp notation distinguishes, among others, conception and creation, desire and spasm. A fusing of the disparate elements in man is hinted twice by 'For Thine is the Kingdom' and once by 'Life is very long'; as though searching for solution to man's broken psyche either through Christianity or some evolutionary, Tennysonian or Nietzschean, philosophy. Though failure appears to be indicated, the suggestions, which remain generalized, are poignant.

In *Sweeney Agonistes* we gather that sex is lust and lust murder; every man must, at least 'once in his life', 'do a girl in'; and we end up awaiting execution. The theme recurs in *The Family Reunion* and is resolved. The murderous hero achieves his integration and the pursuing Furies, who are simultaneously evils and condemnation, become saving powers.[1] The Nietzschean teaching of 'extremest peril' becoming the 'final refuge' (p. 178 above) is exactly present:

> Now I know that all my life has been a flight
> And phantoms fed upon me while I fled. Now I know
> That the last apparent refuge, the safe shelter,
> That is where one meets them.　　　　　　(II. ii)

His business is now 'not to run away, but to pursue'; 'not to avoid being found, but to seek'. He would have preferred another way, but this 'is at once the hardest thing, and the only thing possible', as in Nietzsche's 'no way back'. With the formerly feared Furies, or Eumenides, leading him he will be 'safe'. Though now at last all but sane, he may well seem mad to others. Of the future, he is not certain:

> Why I have this election
> I do not understand. It must have been preparing always,
> And I see it was what I always wanted. Strength demanded
> That seems too much, is just strength enough given.
> I must follow the bright angels.　　　　　　(II. ii)

[1] Eliot uses the name 'Eumenides' which means the 'Kindly Ones'. Here, as in the original Greek, the term may be supposed to relate to their final beneficence, as at the conclusion to Aeschylus' *Oresteia*, where they are taken *beneath* the city and promised honour. They are powers that must be simultaneously *hidden* and *honoured*. Greek drama – Euripides' *Bacchae* is another – knows all about it.

Mysticism and Masturbation

We may remember Nietzsche's devils becoming angels (p. 174 above).

In *The Elder Statesman* the hero obtains spiritual release through facing a secret evil that has rankled throughout his life.[1]

In the *Four Quartets* Eliot balances his approaches. Subtle use of the natural elements and art-symbols link variously with metaphysics, Christian doctrine, Indian wisdom, and experiences of spirits and transcendental vision. The terrible stanzas on the world under 'Adam's Curse' as a 'hospital endowed by the ruined millionaire' ('East Coker', IV) constitute almost a satire on the Church's negative – or apparently negative – reading of the creative scheme. But in 'Little Gidding' we are to be restored by a 'refining fire' (II), in our burning torment 'redeemed from fire by fire', for Love is behind 'the intolerable shirt of flame' (IV), and finally spiritual quest and nature's sweetness are identified: 'the fire and the rose are one' (IV).

It will be clear from our pin-pointing of significant bits in what is anyway a fragmentary life-work that Eliot is engaged in a closely similar enquiry to our others. He differs in his peculiarly tentative, oblique, and fragmentary approach; as he once said, poetry may be a way of expressing oneself without giving oneself away (p. 25 above). But there is really more to it than that: it is the art of exact expression, which may involve half-statements or indirect ones. His very fragmentation adds somehow to the peculiar power with which the various hints jet up. More, Eliot has, despite the smallness of his output, taken a wider survey than the others in that he is always trying by association or contrast to relate the Nietzschean to the Christian system; as in *The Cocktail Party* he tries to fuse psychiatry and sainthood. These are the two ways of dealing with the enigma: the first accepts instinct and sublimates it; the second regards man as a fallen creature and looks to the Church for salvation. The Christian approach may be said to be covered in *A Glastonbury Romance* by Mr. Evans's attempt to save himself through crucifixion in the Passion Play; but the attempt is unavailing.

Eliot did not succeed in establishing a relation of the one approach to the other. We shall now attempt to do so.

[1] Eliot intended a relation, at the play's end, to Sophocles' *Oedipus Coloneus*. This relation may be the clearer from the reading of the Oedipus plays being prepared by P. H. Vellacott.

3

Among the confusing varieties we have discussed, one fact emerges: whereas most instincts may be, with due care, made our allies, one obtrudes as almost, because so dangerous, different from the others in kind: sadism. Even release through fantasy and masturbation is an admission of a split (because secretive) personality. Now the Bible and the Christian tradition has from the first faced this very difficulty by asserting a Fall. The Fall led on to a sense of good and evil, shame at nakedness, and death, this last a difficult thought which may best be interpreted as 'death-involvement'. Certainly it led on to murder and warring. Nature's destructive energies, themselves a necessary part of creation, become in man inflamed. In due course prophets arise, asserting goodness and love:

The wolf also shall dwell with the lamb, and the leopard shall lie down with the kid: and the calf and the young lion and the fatling together; and a little child shall lead them.   (Isaiah, XI. 6-7)

Hard though it be to follow, that is the message. After the prophets, Christ delivers a similar gospel of universal love, God caring for man and animal alike. He appears either unaware of, or to have seen through, the apparent horrors of the natural order, in the state described in Pope's first Epistle of the *Essay on Man*: 'All Nature is but Art, unknown to thee' (I. 289). But the negatives reassert themselves and his story culminates in the crucifixion, though that leads on to his own resurrection and to the entry of the great Spirit into history. The Crucifixion is the Church's central image, or symbol.

Christ's own recorded doctrine scarcely seems to face the horrors of earth-nature 'red in tooth and claw' (Tennyson, *In Memoriam*, LVI); but the Church certainly has faced them. From earliest times blood-sacrifice, of animals or human beings, has responded to the blood-toll apparently demanded by the Creator and lodged in our own psychological constitutions. Sacrifice has served to dispel poisons and liberate powers. The Church dismisses all sacrifices but one: that of Christ. If, asks the author of the Epistle to the Hebrews, the blood of animals has served in the past to sanctify, 'how much more shall the blood of Christ, who through the eternal Spirit offered himself without blemish unto

God, cleanse your conscience from dead works to serve the living God?' (Hebrews, IX. 14).[1] This sacrifice contains the old sadistic essence. As Nietzsche puts it, writing of man as 'the cruelest of beasts' in *Thus Spake Zarathustra* (III. 13):

In gazing on tragedies, bullfights, and crucifixions, hath he hitherto found his best happiness on earth: and when he invented hell for himself, lo, hell was his heaven upon earth.

There is however a difference: with the Crucifixion we are simultaneously aware of Christ's gospel of love; it is to be received within a total context, wherein opposites meet, to serve as a transition, or lever, from the hideous instinct to spiritual power.

Central to the Church's teaching stands the Crucifix with all its sadistic radiations and attractions. As Robinson Jeffers puts it in his *Meditation on Saviors*: '*This* people has not outgrown blood-sacrifice, one must writhe on the high cross to catch at their memories'. In his preface to *On the Rocks* ('Crosstianity') Bernard Shaw, after discussing Jesus' endurance of mockery and torment to entertain the soldiers and the crowd wrote:

All this was cruelty for its own sake, for the pleasure of it. And the fun did not stop there. Such was and is the attraction of these atrocities that the spectacle of them has been reproduced in pictures and waxworks and exhibited in churches ever since as an aid to piety. The chief instrument of torture is the subject of a special Adoration. Little models of it in gold and ivory are worn as personal ornaments; and big reproductions in wood and marble are set up in sacred places and on graves. Contrasting the case with that of Socrates, one is forced to the conclusion that if Jesus had been humanely exterminated his memory would have lost ninetynine percent of its attraction for posterity. Those who were specially susceptible to his [? this] morbid attraction were not satisfied with symbolic crosses which hurt nobody. They soon got busy with 'acts of faith' which consisted of great public shows at which Jews and Protestants or Catholics, and anyone else who could be caught out on a point of doctrine, were burnt alive. Cruelty is so infectious that the very compassion it rouses is infuriated to take revenge by still viler cruelties.

Shaw notes how exactly all this contradicts the teaching of Jesus himself. Such is the perversity of human nature that the very symbol which is meant to change cruelty to love may serve to

---

[1] My New Testament references follow the Revised Version.

change love to cruelty. Tennyson has left us a perfect commentary in *Queen Mary*. They are discussing the burning of heretics:

Mary: If we could burn out heresy, my Lord Paget,
            We reck not tho' we lost this crown of England –
            Ay! tho' it were ten Englands!
Gardiner: Right, your Grace.
            Paget, you are all for this poor life of ours,
            And care but little for the life to be.
Paget: I have some time, for curiousness, my Lord,
            Watch'd children playing at *their* life to be,
            And cruel at it, killing helpless flies;
            Such is our time – all times for aught I know.
Gardiner: We kill the heretics that sting the soul –
            They, with right reason, flies that prick the flesh.
Paget: They had not reach'd right reason; little children!
            They killed but for their pleasure and the power
            They felt in killing.
Gardiner: A spice of Satan, ha!
            Why, good! what then? granted! – we are fallen
                creatures;
            Look to your Bible, Paget! – we are fallen.

                                                              (III. iv)

Paget reminds his listeners of Christ's command that we should love one another; but, as always in such instances, the simple issue gets lost in an inconclusive argument.

We may compare the vivid treatment of religious sadism in Browning's *The Heretic's Tragedy*, high-lighted in Thomas Blackburn's *Robert Browning* (1967; 201-4).

The Church's emphasis on the Crucifix has not been, in itself, misguided, however it may have been perverted; rather it has been a supreme example, perhaps *the* supreme example, of psychological insight. The devotee is invited to entwine his own instincts, either sadistically or masochistically or both, with the supreme exhibitionism of this figure in naked torment; identifying himself with the cruelty, the suffering, and the shame; and also, in some strange way, the glory. The result has been, for centuries, an influx of spiritual power.

It started with St. Paul. To him the Cross was a great 'power' (1 Corinthians, I. 18). Though the doctrine of 'Christ crucified' was to many a 'stumbling block' and a 'foolishness', it was really part of 'Christ the power of God and the wisdom of God' (1 Corinthians, I. 23-4). Before his revelation and conversion Paul had been a peculiarly active persecutor, 'breathing threatening and slaughter' (Acts, IX. 1). Even after his conversion he continued to suffer from what seems to be some recurring, perhaps sadistic, obsession, described at 2 Corinthians, XII. 7-9:

And by reason of the exceeding greatness of the revelations – wherefore, that I should not be exalted overmuch, there was given to me a thorn in the flesh, a messenger of Satan to buffet me, that I should not be exalted overmuch. Concerning this thing I besought the Lord thrice, that it might depart from me. And he hath said unto me, My grace is sufficient for thee: for my power is made perfect in weakness. Most gladly therefore will I rather glory in my weaknesses, that the strength of Christ may rest upon me.

That is, we are to accept such invasions; and how true it is that such acceptances induce, even force, humility. Note St. Paul's proviso on God's 'grace', as though Satan's messenger is only harmless because God, or Christ – or some guardian spirit – is with us.

'Flesh', which translates Paul's word for lusts and passions, is a powerful concept in this Epistle. And yet, as Powys explains in *A Glastonbury Romance* (XII. 330 or 322), lust is not of the 'flesh' but of the 'nerves': the 'generative' sex-nerve communicates with the 'brain nerve', and it is all a matter of 'psychic' forces. Moreover the sadistic evil came from the 'red eye' of the First Cause itself (p. 160 above). Now St. Paul is well aware of this. It was not his 'flesh' but a 'thorn *in* the flesh' that troubled him. Again, when saying that his 'flesh' makes him do what he himself hates, so that it is 'no more I that do it, but sin which dwelleth in me', he refers to the 'sin which is in my members' (Romans, VII. 15-23). The 'sin' or 'evil' is in, or comes through, his 'members'. Elsewhere he says that his 'wrestling' is not against 'flesh and blood' but against 'the spiritual hosts of wickedness in the heavenly places' (Ephesians, VI. 12). In *A Glastonbury Romance* (XIX. 638 or 613) Powys relates this statement directly to Mr. Evans:

It was not, as St. Paul has put it so well – he the one among them all who would really have understood Mr. Evans – it was not with flesh and blood that he was contending, but with mysterious powers of evil upon levels revealed to few.

One can readily see why St. Paul was one of Powys's greatest heroes.

Powys's masturbatory teaching need not be limited to physical release. We may see it also as a means of turning horror into pleasure and using physical existence to dissolve a transcendental evil; rather as unrestful spirits can often be best helped by the 'rescue circles' of those on earth. Perhaps this is what human existence is for. (Compare my reading of *Macbeth* in *Shakespeare and Religion*, 192.)

Through the Cross of Christ St. Paul won liberation, seeing the natural order, hitherto in agony, now released: 'For we know that the whole creation groaneth and travaileth in pain together until now. And not only so, but ourselves also, which have the first fruits of the Spirit, even we ourselves groan within ourselves, waiting for our adoption, to wit, the redemption of our body' (Romans, VIII. 22-3). So St. Paul turned 'Christianity' into 'Crosstianity'; and though bright souls like Nietzsche and Shaw, whose own obsessions may have had little of the sadistic – tending in Nietzsche, on the evidence of *Thus Spake Zarathustra*, more towards a Shelleyan narcissism and masochism – may claim to be *above* the horror, St. Paul does not; nor does the Church; nor Powys. Instead we are to identify ourselves with it, even within limits enjoying it, and thereby win through to freedom with love.

If, indeed, we could suppose that God himself came down to earth in Jesus, not simply to 'die' for us, which for God would mean nothing at all, but to take on flesh and blood and nerves in order to endure excruciating torment for the dissolution or transmutation of evils on earth, and perhaps also in spheres beyond, then even today our twentieth-century emotions might respond. Herein is the meaning of salvation through Christ's 'blood'; the old phrases fall into place and dynamic pattern. Why, too, we may ask, is there so much emphasis throughout Christianity on the 'body'? 'This is my body which is given for you . . .' (Luke, XXII. 19). Today doctrines of vicarious sacrifice and payment drawn from St. Paul's metaphor 'Ye were bought with a price' (1 Corinthians, VI. 20) mean little;[1] but if we see the Cross offering itself as a lightning-conductor to receive the tingling electric of man's vicious nerves, then we may respond better to those noble

---

[1] I did once, however, offer a modern reading, in *The Christian Renaissance*, 2nd edn., 1962; 325.

words: 'Thou that takest away the sins of the world, grant us thy peace'.[1]

That comes from the Communion Service, which we might call the 'Identification Service'. It is, in fact, constructed in general correspondence to Powys's masturbatory doctrine. We are to feed on and enjoy the sacrificial body: 'Remember that Christ died for thee, and feed on him in thy heart with praise and thanksgiving'. We draw sustenance from the dismembered Body; and only after that comes the release, and the rising triumph with which the great Service concludes.

Whatever correspondences there may be to man's sexual nature have probably not been consciously recognized; nor, if they ever had been, could they have been openly admitted. A certain indirectness has been forced. Food and drink may often be felt as analogous to sex-fulfilment. It is significant that in the Gospel of St. John the presence of the Beloved Disciple 'reclining in Jesus' bosom' (John, XIII. 23) takes the place of the breaking of bread and giving of wine commemorated in the three Synoptic Gospels. In Eliot's *Sweeney Agonistes* cannibalism ('missionary stew') and love-lust are imaginatively identified, leading on to sex-murder. In 'Gerontion', a poem of sadistic innuendo, there appeared to be an enigmatic gesture towards the identification we are suggesting in the dividing and eating of the 'flowering judas', that is the evil fertility, the traitorous sex-sap, as though evil were having its own Communion Service – though this is really just what the true Communion Service is, in fact, doing. Eliot was glimpsing, and in his typical way half-phrasing, a great truth. Remember those perfect lines in the *Four Quartets* ('East Coker', IV):

> The dripping blood our only drink,
> The bloody flesh our only food:
> In spite of which we like to think
> That we are sound, substantial flesh and blood –
> Again, in spite of that, we call this Friday good.

We may be right to call it good, because there appears to be no alternative: we have to go through the horrors, and that may involve the enjoyment of them.

The Communion Service functions within a sacred and devotional context and with a full sense of Christ's life and gospel: it is

[1] I have written more fully on the Crucifixion in *Christ and Nietzsche*, III.

all done in terms of the knowledge of Christ under a supervening religious acceptance. St. Paul, we may remember, was reconciled to the 'thorn' troubling him by God's assurance that his 'grace' would protect him (p. 186 above). What we need is trust, or faith, in Pope's 'mightier Power' and 'God within the mind' (p. 171 above). This power is clearly active within Nietzsche's highly sensitive phrases, and in Powys too, not only in the terrible sense of evil throughout his account of Mr. Evans's crucifixion (*A Glastonbury Romance*, XIX, 'The Pageant'), but in his assurance of safety during evil encounters in *In Spite Of* (p. 161 above). In my *Laureate of Peace* (178) I stated that Pope's teaching leaves room for, and in fact needs, a religious support. Much of our teaching might be dangerous for those of no religious or spiritualistic sensibility at all. Perhaps much depends on upbringing: Pope grew up in a Catholic home, Nietzsche and Powys were sons of clergy-men. Powys's great hero, Rabelais, was himself a priest. When Powys says that during solitary indulgence we shall know that our true self is not really involved (pp. 158, 161), he speaks a half-truth, or more, of considerable importance. There must be some assurance that we are guarded by good spirits. Tennyson in *In Memoriam* (L. 1), anxious at the thought of our departed friends knowing our more reprehensible fantasies, not only concludes that they will understand, but asks that they be near.

And here a strange thought occurs: just as in the rituals of the ancient world (e.g. Homer's *Odyssey*, XI. 35-6) the blood of a sacrifice was supposed to facilitate the appearance of the spirits of the dead, may it be that the indulgence itself, as the orgy of obscenities in Joyce's *Ulysses* led up to the appearance of Rudy (p. 50 above), somehow opens out the way for the guardians? This would explain the great spiritual powers of a St. Paul and a Powys. It might also suggest that the recognition of Spiritualism is today being retarded by barriers which our doctrine removes (see p. 30 above).

Many of our most daring modern thought-adventures are implicit in the New Testament. *Thus Spake Zarathustra* is saturated with Biblical phraseology and unformulated reference. Nietzsche is no more daring than St. Paul. Christianity started as a breaking down of taboos and St. Paul claimed an advance beyond the Law which, without denying its necessity and goodness, he finds in his own experience so inextricably entwined with sin that it almost became a stimulant to sin (Romans, VII. 7-14); as, again, in Pope's 'How glowing guilt exalts the keen delight' (*Eloisa to Abelard*, 230). But we are now beyond all that, through Christ; the 'flesh', or passions, give way, if 'the spirit of Christ' is in you (Romans, VIII. 9-10). We are beyond good and evil as traditionally formulated; the Fall is countered. Indeed now 'all things are lawful for me', though, with a truly wonderful and important, and even amusing, reservation, 'not all things are expedient' (1 Corinthians, VI. 12, also X. 23).

4

Our Renaissance thinkers are really arguing for a new democratization of Christian doctrine in direct descent from the Protestant impulse. Today we need, on every level, to read Christ's story as symbolical of our own, humble, lives. Especially important is the symbolism of birth and resurrection: from a divine and not merely 'physical' beginning, through suffering and death, to survival in a form no less rich than earthly life; the mysteries of birth and survival being so presented as to counter our instinctive tendency to see the one as physical and the other as, in the enervate sense, 'spiritual'. The story is in part *our* story. Now this process of democratization was emphasized by Powys in his *Rabelais* (1948), where he explained that Jesus' personal claim was transferred by St. Paul to 'Christ in me' (e.g. Galatians, II. 20); and that the process was by Rabelais extended yet more generally to 'the deeper soul in us'; 'the inexhaustible creative energy in the depths of our own individual being'. When Powys goes on to write of 'that upward surge of seminal sap which is the vital impulse that forever creates and re-creates the world', 'the mounting world-sap', which is also 'the Christ-quality' in our own 'deeper' souls (*Rabelais*, 'The Wisdom of Blasphemy', 385-6, 395), the phraseology indicates a powerful sexuality.

This democratization is clear in our dramatic story. The Medieval Church allowed many concessions to human vices, as in the obscenities of The Feast of Fools and in its passion-plays with all the sadistic horrors of Christ's suffering, the flogging, mockery, shame, nakedness and Crucifixion, all worked up with evident appeal to a vicious pleasure. This I have elsewhere dis-

190

cussed (*The Golden Labyrinth*, 29-34). At the Renaissance, drama became secular and simultaneously more spiritualized: the physical sufferings of the semi-divine protagonist gave place to the more spiritual sufferings of numerous human protagonists corresponding to the varieties of human experience. The Faust myth and the Don Juan myth start their challenges, either as themselves or in tragic and comedic derivations, against theological and sexual taboos. Comedy has concentrated on normal sex interests, but the more tragic themes have rarely engaged in physical sadism. There seems to have been active a will to switch our interest away from the sadistic and other vices towards normal sexuality, the worst horrors being covered for us by our religion and its Crucifix; for that has been its specific task, to render all other sacrifices and sadisms unnecessary. But today we see an upsurge of the repressed substances. We have our 'theatre of cruelty', our removal of censorships, our acceptance of obscenities in literature and the visual arts. It may be questioned whether the more random and public indulgences of at least the more sadistic enjoyments are safe. In his writing Powys steered a subtle course: with an 'infinite care' (*Autobiography*, I. 9) and all the skill of a great novelist, perhaps the greatest of all novelists, one who at every moment *knows exactly what he is doing*, he avoids all risk of infection; and where masturbatory fantasy is to be indulged, he, knowing as few have known the fearful *depths* of evil, counsels an *absolute secrecy* (p. 161 above). Also, as we have already argued, the secret engagement must be indulged with the suffusing sense, not exactly of prayer, which might frighten away the demons we are welcoming, but of a child-like and prayerful state; so knowing oneself, in the depths, safe. One has to become 'as little children' (Matthew, XVIII. 3, 10); as Nietzsche puts it, 'like a child, without shame' (p. 173 above). We are often warned by the Spirit Guides, as by Powys too (p. 161 above), of the appalling powers of *thought*. We must however suppose that the evil fantasies we are discussing are not as dangerous as all that; perhaps because we are assuming, as we must, a religious background and life-way, and perhaps also for the very reason that *the sexual centres are involved*; for these are forces of health. It is not a matter of cold malignancy.

Though he does not refer to sex-activation, the great Indo-Persian mystic Meher Baba today gives a not dissimilar counsel to his disciples, as recorded in C. B. Purdom's *The God-Man* (1964; 286):

> For the purification of your heart leave your thoughts alone but maintain constant vigil over your actions. Let thoughts come and go without putting them into action.
>
> It is better to feel angry sometimes rather than merely to repress anger. Although your mind may be angry do not let your heart know it. Remain unaffected. If you never feel angry you will be like stone, in which form the mind is least developed.
>
> Let the thoughts of anger, lust and greed come and go freely without putting them into words and deeds. Then the related impressions in your mind begin to wear out and become less harmful.
>
> When you feel angry or have lustful thoughts, remember Baba at once. Let my name serve as a net around you.

For 'Baba', the Christian will put 'Christ'; others will think of some spirit-guide. It does not matter. For the rest, this extract is so relevant to our past arguments that little comment is needed, except perhaps to note the distinction between 'mind' and 'heart'. The sexual nerves and mind-nerves in reciprocity may be involved in dangerous fantasy while leaving the deeper self (pp. 158, 161 above) unaffected.[1]

One last thought. In so far as the masturbatory fantasies are allowed to dominate, one may be, though perhaps not necessarily, independent of a sexual partner; but the daylight imagination needs an ideal to balance the more repellent indulgences, and this from Plato, through the Boy Bishops of the Medieval Church (*The Golden Labyrinth*, 29-30), to the stream of youthful figures, boys or girls disguised as boys, in drama and poetry ever since, will function as what I call 'seraphic' persons. They are close to, and yet independent of, sexual instinct; they bisexually symbolize the fusion of all opposites; though human, they link us to the spirit-spheres.

In Powys's writings they are vivid. While denying homosexuality (*Autobiography*, IX. 426), he admitted to being 'spiritually' a homosexual (*Letters to Louis Wilkinson*, 17 August 1948; 252-3); and the evidence throughout the *Autobiography* amply bears out the statement (*The Saturnian Quest*, 59-60). In a letter to me of

---

[1] At one point (95) in Purdom's book we hear of an Indian seer showing his genital organs to Gandhi. It is likely that many supposedly 'perverted' actions or fantasies veil significances not easy to understand.

23 January 1957 he wrote of homosexuals that he 'tried very very hard to become one myself', but could not find in himself 'the faintest tendency in that direction'; which means, presumably, towards physical consummation, since the attraction was obviously there. The point is, it was more spiritual, or seraphic. Powys's statement here was clarified by the late Nicholas Ross who in the letter of 23 March 1967 already noticed (p. 166n. above) quoted as follows from one of Powys's letters to himself (the date not given). The stop after 'rarely' is my own insertion:

. . . of course I am attracted in some ways to boys and youths more than to girls. That's certain. But whether I ever feel sadistic towards boys and youths I am awfully doubtful. Perhaps very rarely. I feel I would get a lot more pleasure in kissing a boy – though *not* a youth – than in kissing a girl. I know one family of beautiful girls and *one* boy and 'tis the boy I'd like most to kiss. But on the other hand . . . no! I suppose it is hopelessly personal and individual. The odd thing is that in my old age I seem to turn to imagination even more than in my youth, but there! I was always strong for the imagination, and like Paracelsus creating Sylphs and Salamanders and Ondines and, and, and . . . well, what *are* boy-elementals called?

I myself, on good authority, use the words 'seraph' and 'seraphic'. Powys's imagination dwells on a bisexual figure corresponding to 'the dreams of all the great perverse artists'; of some 'Saturnian' sex unknown on earth except by approximations (*Rodmoor*, I. 18; *Autobiography*, VI. 207). The one extended love-romance described in the *Autobiography* (IX. 405-14) concerns Powys's association in Italy with the 'ambiguous beauty' of a lady who dressed as a boy, whom he calls a 'boy-girl'. His narratives rely on a succession of physically repellent seers and dangerous giants, but against these are his seraphic boys or youths: the youths in *Rodmoor* (1916) and *Ducdame* (1925). In *Rodmoor* Baptiste is as 'a young god' of 'an unearthly beauty' and 'supernatural power' (XXVI. 433). In *Ducdame* the troubled hero sees his future son as a youth comforting him with a smile 'the penetrating sweetness of which diffused itself through every fibre' of his body; his face possessing 'a beauty and power in it beyond anything' he had previously conceived (XIX. 310). Then there are the boys in *Wolf Solent* whose 'classic nakedness' when swimming in Lenty Pond turn the psychological ailments of villain and poet into redeeming and beatific ecstasies (XIV. 300-2 or 284-6), and the schoolboy who comforted the schoolmaster hero with 'a smile of such sheer, innate sweetness and goodness' that he 'was staggered' (XXIV. 589 or 561-2); the attractive Larry Zed in *Weymouth Sands* (*Jobber Skald*); the extended study of Elphin the Herald – heralds and angels are close – in *Owen Glendower*; and the young heroes enjoying the graces of Powys's final period in *Atlantis*, *The Brazen Head*, *The Mountains of the Moon* and *All or Nothing*.

Such figures stand against sadistic and other obsessions. They are the corresponding 'good' to the sadistic 'evil'.

But, evil though it be, the obsession must be faced and handled; and Powys has indicated a way. I believe that his masturbatory doctrine stands central to our evolving culture. He was surely right when he wrote in *Maiden Castle* (1937, IX. 422; 1966, 433-4) that 'no religion that doesn't deal with sex-longing in *some* kind of way is much use to us'. What in the Medieval Mystery Plays, the Communion Service (or Mass) and the use of the Crucifix was centred on Christ is to be allowed a free but secret flowering – Eliot's 'flowering judas' – in attunement to the varieties of human obsession. In *The Saturnian Quest* (125-6) I wrote:

Powys is precise: he meets Lawrence's recognition, stated at the conclusion to 'The Real Thing', that regeneration 'is not a question of knowing something but of doing something' (*Phoenix*, 1936; 203, and see 'The Reality of Peace'). How much good counsel of apparent profundity is in effect no more than a mental influence? But Powys works on the one pivot of man's earthly, psychic-physical, being. The 'doing' advocated, which Lawrence too, urging acceptance of the 'sickening' thing within, the 'serpent of secret and shameful desire' in the psyche, all but stated in 'The Reality of Peace' (*Phoenix*, 675-80), is the free and waking use of the giant enginery of sex-located instinct, *whatever the nature of its fantasies, which vary with each of us*, for what is, in effect, a creative end.

Though Lawrence in 'Pornography and Obscenity' (also in the collection *Phoenix*) writes denigratorily of masturbation in contrast to his gospel of normal sex-activity, his intensity of concern witnesses his involvement, as though he were attacking himself and urging a doctrine which he could not, himself, live (see p. 219 below). Anyway, all that we have said will apply not only to those deep in sexual divagation, but those also who live normal sexual lives and yet have an over-plus of energy otherwise directed; and of these there are surely many, since humankind shows every sign since Eden of having been in a state of sexual and psychological constipation.

It is easy to see what all our dangerous ethical thinkers such as Pope, Blake, Nietzsche – and many another – really *meant*. When Blake wrote in *The Marriage of Heaven and Hell*: 'Sooner murder an infant in its cradle than nurse unacted desires' he was not counselling crime. The thought is expanded by Lord Henry in Wilde's *The Picture of Dorian Gray* (II):

> But the bravest man amongst us is afraid of himself. The mutilation of the savage has its tragic survival in the self-denial that mars our lives. We are punished for our refusals. Every impulse that we strive to strangle broods in the mind, and poisons us. The body sins once, and has done with its sin, for action is a mode of purification. Nothing remains then but the recollection of a pleasure, or the luxury of a regret. The only way to get rid of a temptation is to yield to it. Resist it, and your soul grows sick with longing for the things it has forbidden to itself, with desire for what its monstrous laws have made monstrous and unlawful. It has been said that the great events of the world take place in the brain. It is in the brain, and the brain only, that the great sins of the world take place also.

To what extent Lord Henry is being approved need not concern us; but his argument does. Wilde here concentrates less on actions than on the mind. Lord Henry tells Dorian Gray: 'You have had passions that have made you afraid, thoughts that have filled you with terror, day-dreams and sleeping dreams whose mere memory might stain your cheek with shame . . .'. Lord Henry's arguments are faultless and yet his counsel, as stated, is too dangerous. That is our paradox. Powys resolves it. There is no other way.

The doctrine makes of us each our own criminal, scape-goat, sacrifice and deity; forces us, as it must, to fearful humility in knowledge of our uglier selves; by breaking down ethical obstructions (Nietzsche's 'Thus shall ye flow', p. 175 above) it temporarily reconciles us to the horrors, which are also the harmonies, of nature; attunes us to the serenities of art; and, it may be (p. 189 above), to the presence of beneficent spirits whose presence must, anyway, be expected. We may even be allowing our sexual selves to be used on earth in order to drain away or transmute some transcendental evil (cp. *Shakespeare and Religion*, 192). Accepting the good and the bad, we become greater than ourselves. For our normal selves are, as the Gospel of John (X. x) tells us, only pigmies compared with what we might be: 'I came that they may have life, and may have it abundantly'.

We are now in a position to discuss Powys's lyric poetry; especially his great poem, *The Ship*.

CHAPTER VI

The Ship of Cruelty:
on the Lyrical Poems of
John Cowper Powys

━━━━◦◦◦◦◦◦◦◦◦◦◦◦◦◦◦━━━━

Composed during 1968.

I

POWYS'S POETRY HAS a haunted, elfin quality with earth contacts dissolving into the elements of air and water, often a moon-
struck world challenging on every front the accepted mind-
structures of normality. Like his prose it searches back to some
lost, Saturnian age. Its dominating impressions are 'liquid, cool,
and infinite' ('Saturn', p. 204 below). It has much in common with
Wolf Solent's 'mythology' (p. 157 above). Ethical terms are
ambiguous and death a positive value.

A substantial compilation has been made by Kenneth Hopkins
in *John Cowper Powys: a Selection from his Poems*, London, 1964.
From this volume I shall quote, using its page-numerals. The
original publications were as follows, my bracketed numerals
referring to the pages in Mr. Hopkins's collection: *Odes and Other
Poems*, 1896 (19-31); *Poems*, 1899 (32-58); *Wolf's Bane*, 1916 (59-
120); *Mandragora*, 1917 (121-82); *Samphire*, 1922 (183-211).

Natural impressions are easily grouped. Typical are 'rain-wet
ferns' (166), reeds (152), moss (166), mists and marshes (120, 153,
182), 'cold wet dawn' (107), 'the sea's edge windy and lone'
(97). The Sun may be disliked and feared, but the Moon, recurring
throughout, and certain planets or stars, are honoured. Coolness
is preferred to warmth; wetness and darkness to solidity and heat.

The vast sea and its horizon is as a liberation. Dawn and twilight are preferred to day. Darkness may be excellent, especially, as in Rupert Brooke too, in woods by night, 'where the old world's shadow lies' (96). Above dead lovers lying beneath 'grey and ghostly cypresses', trees utter an 'evil whisper' (168). But such evil is for Powys really one with the favoured magic of 'wood-gods' (167), and these are old, as in 'The Wood' (166):

> In every plant and in every sod,
> The old earth-wisdom here is furled . . .

'Whispers' arouse memories from the 'caverns of sleep', bringing strange meanings and intimations from the 'magic wood' and a dimension beyond ethic where sins do not matter.

Life-forms are chosen for their elemental yet semi-human relevances. The curlew's 'wailing' (83) is as a ghostly spirit-cry; a plover's 'scream' sounds 'the world's release', 'like a human voice' (90-1). In 'The Old Pier-Post' (188) 'a tress of shining hair' from parted lovers blends with a 'shining feather' from mated sea-gulls 'wrenched' apart by fate, the feather covered with 'sea-scum' and scales of the 'mackerel bright', symbolizing a brief joy, which together they had caught.

The Feather (as also on 131, 143) is an interesting Powys symbol, to be associated with water-birds. It seems more important than any actual bird, symbolizing some spirit-property relevant to man, and so 'The Old Pier-Post' knots its impressions into a significant unit:

> A shining tress, a feather, a thought –
> With these I create a soul . . .

A heron's Feather is important in *Wolf Solent*, and so are the exquisitely personalized White and Black Feathers of the Dove and Raven from the Flood in *The Mountains of the Moon* (*The Saturnian Quest*, 110; p. 406 below).

Though he can write of lovers, Powys's own life-way by-passes love's normality. In 'The Old Story' (93), he is agonized at not having seized an erotic opportunity; but the title itself indicates that the inhibition was firmly planted. He is apart. 'Affinity' states the main contrast crisply (83): Circe made from a 'burning sun' – the Sun in these lyrics may be hostile – cannot mingle with one made from 'marsh-lands old' where the curlew wails, 'wind' and 'ghouls' converse, and the Moon is 'drowned in the pools'. We shall presently find coldness to love emphatic in two key-poems, 'The Saturnian' (148) and 'Saturn' (153). The trouble is, his life's wavelength, its vibrations, are pitched wrongly. In 'The Tune' he plays 'a crazy tune' to river-reeds and moon. His love draws nigh:

> But I played a note too high
> Or I played a note too low . . .
>
> (152)

So he remains alone with the elements.

Life may be felt as negated and death welcome. He escapes from human love to 'an ancient haunted lawn' and a death-dance (183); 'airs of the dead' drive away love (191). More generally, in 'The Voice of the Worm' (94), the worm, associated with Satan, Demogorgon and Lucifer, opposes the false optimism of Prophets and Saints. We are invited, in this sorry world of illusion where the Morning's Son was fated to fall and Christ was entombed – for Christ is counted among the rebels – to reject Faith, Courage and that last illusion, the Will to Live.

At home with Death, he is fascinated by drowned bones, 'tossed and tangled', that wish for warm life despite its pains (61). In 'Mortmain' a Marvellian wit plays on the thought of lovers' bodies mingling in their graves (168). Once, with a brilliant use of a concrete and vital analogy posing a vast metaphysical paradox, he meditates on a skull whose former thoughts 'like mice have scuttled back into the air' (85).

Death is sweet. In 'The Escape' he would leave 'the dreadful city's roar' for a garden that 'touches a burying-ground', his bones mingling with 'honest earth-mould' (106). In 'Finis' burial is blended with dawn mist, white clouds and cowslips, to make a perfected end (107). In 'The Wood' 'dead trunks' catch the light more beautifully than living vegetation, for death is 'strange' and 'magical' (167). Through death some strange positive is felt, but it is left undefined. Powys likes best to compose *on the borderline of life and death*, favouring the half-way stages of dawn and twilight, or of solid and fluid, matter and spirit. Once, among his loved mists and marshes, the territory so powerfully developed in *Porius*, he asks: 'Did ever life come so near to death?' (153). He does not say much of another world and spirits but prefers graves-as-powers, or nature blending solidity and moisture,

G* 199

placid and cool. In an enigmatic lyric 'The Visitor', a 'feather' and a 'leaf' symbolize the return of one who has died (143). The dead may be thought of as personalities: in 'Worship', by the 'sea's edge' their 'moan' joins with that of the living as they cry for what is eternally 'refused', and the Sun rises in its cruel splendour 'heedless of our doomed race', ironically making children play and lovers worship (97). Sometimes we are aware of a blessed face, a human countenance that is also a death, or in death. In 'Sleep' the sleepers of a city first turn unrestfully and are then still 'like corpses in their shrouds' (98). In 'Duality' sleep is like death, and death is divine:

> I never pass a sleeper's head
>   But another head I see;
> And Christ – or Christ's own Mother – dead
>   Lies there in front of me.

(101)

On the Downs' has a 'peewit's cry' sounding like 'a human voice', with intimations of 'release'; a 'lost face' appears and the poem ends: 'I can die' (91). 'Prayer' (101) cries out for 'air', 'space' and 'death'.

Powys's favourite borderline of mists and clouds naturally shows an emphasis on whiteness. The colour is as emphatic here as in Rupert Brooke's poetry, with similar mystical connotations. As in Brooke a Face may appear, associated with whiteness.

'White clouds' pass over a grave, contributing to its peace (107). Honour is accorded 'silver bright' Lucifer and the 'white dawn' (154-5), like the white dawn in *Jobber Skald*, *Weymouth Sands* (XIV. 538 or 516). White is a spirit-colour in the 'ghost-moths whitely winging' (183), as in the mystical conclusion, through sea to white death, in *Rodmoor* (XXVII. 456-8; and see XXI. 326).

Whiteness is happily charged, as in Brooke, though one poem, 'The Face', which we shall discuss later, introduces us to a dangerous face with 'white lips', which is contrasted with happy love called a 'white bird' (194-5): the two whitenesses are used for two compelling powers, fearful and sweet. A face occurs elsewhere, as in the pathetic 'white face' of 'The New Magdalene' (96). In the moonlit scene of 'On the Downs' impressions of 'cold' seaweed, 'night-winds', 'parsley white' lead on to a 'lost face' and contented death (90-1).

'Dilemma' sees human existence as a fitfully illuminated transience where milestones 'glimmer white' for travellers who pass and are lost in darkness (103). But there is a quest in the travel. The 'moonlight' and 'sea-margin' of 'Obsession' are as the 'haunting eyes' and 'hand' of some lost loved one always wavering and gleaming ahead on life's 'long white roads' (176). In 'Euthanasia' he drifts in a 'trance' that is a kind of 'death', while a 'white wraith-figure', with white arms, hands and breast, is beside him, fulfilling old intimations now realized (172-3). The ghostly quest is associated with coolness, whiteness, silver and moon; as, we may say, against warmth, colour, gold and sun. 'Piety' celebrates 'white arms' and a 'siren's song' by the silver of moonlight casting a spell, so that he plants a 'red rose' on his *human* love's 'tomb' before giving himself to the *other* 'tide' (170). In 'The Last Worshipper' 'the golden censers' are broken, while in their stead a 'face' lit by 'candles of paradise' 'gleams like a silver cup'. Gold, like the Sun, is not really wanted here, whereas silver is 'of paradise' (86).

The implications are defined in the poem 'Whiteness' (178):

> A whiteness glimmers on my days,
> A whiteness hovers o'er my nights.

Dews, new moons, dawns, 'flickering feet', 'gleaming' hands, dancing 'limbs', each is in turn called 'white':

> O child, O maiden-acolyte,
> Whose censer breathes such silvery breath,
> Pour wine white as the flesh of Christ
> Upon the altar of white death!

In contrast 'all red things', 'flame', 'roses' and 'blood', shall fade while we 'voyage' over the 'white sea' of God's 'tears'. 'God' is on the side of the silvery powers, as against blood; and he is weeping.

Death, whiteness, and sea are interrelated. In 'On the Downs' (90) the poet is happy with the ocean, and

> Its drift of shells and shingle far from land,
> Far out to sea, where the great steamers go.

'I', he writes (188), 'am the seaward-looking one'. He thinks in terms of horizons, of the twilight sinking over 'the world's mysterious rim' (104); or of 'the cool clear air' of 'the other side of the moon' in the lyric of that name (69; for the Moon's 'other side' see *The Saturnian Quest*, 112). 'The Horizon' describes 'pale' trees, mist, valleys, a pier and lake, a road, wild-fowl, a heron's 'melancholy cry', an 'ancient wood'; all making a 'solitude', half solid and half fluid, and with a refrain beating 'But what is beyond?' leading up to 'Beyond, till we cross the world's last hill' (140-1). 'The Cry' (162) tells of a female voice crying 'out and away and beyond'. Is it the grasses sighing to the pond-lilies? The wind wailing? The wild swans flying west? It is these, and more; but the reality is 'away and beyond', 'beyond and afar', 'out and away and beyond', the sound rising and falling like the music in *Maiden Castle* (IV. 146-54 or 158-65, VI. 243-5 or 255-7) and *Owen Glendower* (V. 131). The poet knows that he would be mad were he not to recognize and follow this all-demanding, God-sent, sound. 'Noon' (174-5) shows him with a friend 'that can be no more than a friend' and intimations of 'old dethroned gods'; there is a breath 'falling' and 'rising', and an 'immortal presence'. Here 'our help comes from beyond the hills' and 'the horizon has no end'. The gods that separate such friends may indeed be 'wise', but there is nevertheless 'some old forgotten god', 'dethroned' and 'unsceptred', who ratifies union. In 'Candle Light', while winds call and logs smell, 'two lovers' are carried over sea to 'the unknown islands' and a 'great host' of the dead outside 'time' and 'space' and 'the world'; and are lost in one 'vast procession of lovers' souls' (206-7). Again and again the wind is as a voice, a spirit-voice made of air. In 'Wayfarers' (124) there is, as in the nipping air of the ghost-scene in *Hamlet* (I. iv. 1-2), a cold wind, and though the 'heart' shivers, the 'soul' cries 'Follow the wind'. They visit the City of Dis, the 'great Babylon' of desire, but the call is repeated; the City of God, and the command still sounds; and the City of Dreams, where all possible imaginations would seem to be fulfilled, but still the Soul cries 'Follow the wind'. In 'The Rider' (185) he rides exulting on 'the horses of desire' to whatever may be his doom; and in 'Piety' (170), drawn by a siren's song, he cries: 'I come! I come!'

In 'The Flute-Player' the poet knows he belongs to a dream-city of flute-music, denied reality by reason but real to the 'heart' (122-3). Wherever we go there are 'strange omens'; we are always treading 'the brink of more than mortal mysteries' (146). 'Duality'

(100) tells us that every 'human house' has its etheric counterpart, 'made of air'. It is the same with roads, floods and churches:

> I never cross a lonely road
> But another road I see. . . .

A world of 'phantoms' interpenetrates or reflects or balances normal existences. The human face in sleep is as a dead Christ. When will these baffling and tormenting confusions be resolved? When will spirit and matter be one? And life, like sleep, be 'divine'?

Powys looks back to a lost golden age, the age of Saturn, the 'dethroned' god who ratified the union of friends in 'Noon' (174-5). The use of the term 'Saturn' or 'Saturnian' may be applied, as the *Autobiography* makes clear (VI. 206-7), to the rejection of normal sexual love for some more esoteric, seraphic or spiritual, sometimes bisexual, dream-figure, demanding through the ages poetic allegiance (*Rodmoor*, I. 18; p. 193 above). We have seen how, in 'The Tune' (152), Powys was on the wrong wavelength for a normal love-encounter. 'The Saturnian' (148-9) is explicit:

> Ah, I must follow it high and low,
> Tho' it leave me cold to your human touch!
> Some starry sorcery made me so;
> And from my birth have I been such.

He 'follows' a 'tender-muffled crying', the rustling of 'dawn-wind' on 'river-reeds', 'wild', 'sad' and 'sweet'; a 'lonely horn' from the place where 'all streams meet' (the image is used by Eliot too in 'Marina': 'Under sleep, where all the waters meet'); and where 'horizons disappear'. Other ships may come home to their 'moonlit wharf', but 'beyond every coast' where it might 'anchor', his thought goes; the call is like a 'reef-bell' in ocean, another image used by Eliot ('The Dry Salvages', I). Though to find the 'beauty' he quests for were to 'die', he is drawn on, over every hill, by his 'longing'. Once when 'burning noon' poured down on moss and stone, he had seen 'the great blue flower that God made for the Son of God'; and now that he has breathed its scent, all ordinary beauty leaves him cold. At this high moment the sun-heat is accepted, marking triumphant attainment; and there is colour too, though significantly the spirit-colour blue rather than the blood-colour red.

The Ship of Cruelty

The Sun is, however, terrible enough in 'Saturn' (153-7). Lucifer, the rebel hero of Powys's narrative poem *Lucifer*, is here the 'silver' dawn-star of the half-light, and associated with Saturn, dethroned but to return. It is to be contrasted with the red of life, and daylight. We have already found the Sun's cruel power contrasted with our suffering and the claims of the Dead, in 'Worship' (97).

In 'Saturn' many favourite impressions cluster. The night is 'liquid, cool, and infinite', lit by star-lamps of the 'old gods', a 'flowing sleep', 'water-meadows', 'shadowy reeds', 'mists and marshes'; it is 'no human dream'. The winds are quiet, listening and waiting. At the moment just before dawn, 'life' all but touches 'death': a blessed balance, almost an identity, is established. The silver Star appears

> In his old immortal guise,
>   Looking down on the reeds,
> Luminous, lovely, silver bright,
>   Heaven's antagonist, bearer of light. . . .

'Silver': the contrast is that of the silver and gold in 'The Last Worshipper' (86; p. 201 above). Vegetation voices from earth's 'primal gendering', from every 'child of ancient mystery', from the forests sweetly 'cold' as a humming sea-shell, tell us that Saturn will 'come again'. Men thought him mad and buried him; but 'faces tender and sad and cool' assert his return to 'bring back the old and tender things' where 'twilight is lovelier than day' and the 'white dawn' remains, like the wonderful white dawn (p. 200 above) near the conclusion of *Weymouth Sands* (*Jobber Skald*). The planet 'silver-scornful', guardian of the softer values, rides the 'ether', for a while, 'alone'.

But now Lucifer pales. The sweetnesses shrink back to their 'primal springs'. Terrible wheels are rolling up the sky:

> Out of the east with a stream of blood,
>   With music no man has understood,
> With splendour, with power, with terrible joy,
>   With strength to create and strength to destroy;
> Kissing all life with a careless kiss,
>   Creating pain, creating bliss;
> The dead, the dead only, free from him,
>   Red with blood from rim to rim,
> Over the conquered throat of the world
>   The chariot of the sun is hurled!

204

The Sun's might is terrible. The oracles have 'lied'; Saturn will not come. The poem ends with a cry, grouping associations already found in 'The Voice of the Worm', for Saturn, Lucifer, Christ, and Love. Against these the Sun is our appalling antagonist. We can readily see why in *A Glastonbury Romance* the Sun recognizes his enemy in 'the stalwart priest of Christ' (XII. 328 or 320; for the Sun, see also I. 1-3 or 21-3, XIII. 368 or 358).

2

Our knowledge of Powys's sadistic obsessions illuminates his poetry. Much of it is on a mystical, other-worldly quest rejecting the horrors of earth-life, as we know it. Man himself is split. As the Church has always told us, he is ill. 'The Voice of Demogorgon' (78) calls our world, as it is called in Eliot's 'East Coker' (IV), a hospital:

> Palsied and fevered and blind,
>   Driven by madnesses strange,
> Aching and loathing it all,
> In our planetary hospital,
>   Day and night we cry for a change.

In this 'hospital of the world' our 'mad-house' humanity curses God (as in Jason's lyric 'The slow worm of Lenty curses God' in *Wolf Solent*, XII. 268-71 or 252-5). But a breath from beyond the torturing opposites, neither human nor divine, of life or of death, comes as a 'weird voice from the deep' telling us that we are 'dreams' and shall one day 'wake'.

Meanwhile, we are pretty nearly mad. There is more in these lyrics than a simple Wordsworthianism – if Wordsworth, who also had his mad emphases, is simple. There is more too than an ascetic rejection of sexual partnership. What we have is a considered rejection of cosmic cruelty, symbolized by the Sun; and therefore, of all daylight normality and reason. Man's soul rejects its earthly context: it demands something better, and less cruel. It prefers death to life, madness to sanity.

In 'Saturn' the old god was buried because regarded as 'mad' (155). In 'Exiles' (177) man is on an 'alien earth' getting 'memorial glimpses' of his 'true home', 'near, yet far'; a home 'wilder, lovelier, madder' than ours, where are 'the lost gods'. 'Mad' recurs. The lines of 'The Tune' (152)

> I played a crazy tune
> To the river-weeds

cover a large part of this poetry. It is more than a poetic gesture; it is a considered philosophy. In 'The Epiphany of the Mad' (99) he writes:

> I am the voice of the outcast things,
> The refuse and the drift. . . .

As in Nietzsche's 'Drunken Song' (p. 176 above), 'sewers' 'abortions', 'mad-house', 'hearse', all are honoured, all negations and repellences saluted, by this 'mad Moon-madrigal'. Powys likes the Moon, as the obvious guardian of lunacies, believing it to belong to 'some earlier stellar system' (*A Glastonbury Romance*, X. 284-5 or 278-80). He likes certain stars as well, or sometimes better:

> But all my thoughts as I sing this tune
> Are about a little star
> That soon or late, that late or soon,
> The evilest things beneath the moon
> Approach and cleansèd are.

The evil things, as in masturbatory fancy, 'approach', are welcomed, and cleansed. The 'little star' is important. Stars are in Powys magical, as in the 'starry sorcery' of 'The Saturnian' (148). The Morning Star we have met as 'Lucifer'; as 'Venus' it is exquisitely described in *A Glastonbury Romance*, a power bringing 'comfort' which, whether as 'Morning Star' or 'Evening Star', has had 'the worship of the generations' (XVII. 559 or 538-9, V. 123 or 135). In *All or Nothing* the Cerne Giant was found by the children on the star Vindex.

Powys's acceptance of filth and all normal repellences is in a reputable saintly tradition, and groups naturally with tenderness. It may be extended to what is called the 'obscene'.

'The Classic Touch' (88) shows us the poet in a city, in agony. Its 'raw hideousness' and the 'unending lines' of people, such as those of Eliot's London in *The Waste Land,* and the noises – it all makes a kind of Hell. His eye lights on 'a patch of ancient wall':

> And there an indecent sketch
> Limned by some laughing boy –
> O lovely and obscene wretch! –
> Swept from me all annoy.

The 'hideous iron place' of 'crowds' and 'cars' is dissolved in the greater universe, 'whirled into outer space and diffused among the stars'. His 'soul' is again 'gay', reading 'Rabelais':

> And the old great shades returned
> And the large sweet thoughts flowed free. . . .

The 'laughing boy', recalls the seraphic smiles of the school-boy in *Wolf Solent* (pp. 193-4 above). Here what I call the 'seraphic' is interestingly associated with the 'obscene'.

The enjoyment of obscenity may be liberating. But what of the sadisms? Of the Sun?

We often find obscenities grouped with sadistic and other perversions, and they may in various ways accompany each other. But Powys throughout his life tends to group obscenities both with humour and with the softer, more 'Christian', valuations, as his study *Rabelais* indicates. He is, as this study shows, our first, perhaps our only, authority on the meaning and challenge of great humour. But he is also, as his study of Mr. Evans in *A Glastonbury Romance* shows, probably the greatest authority on human evil that our world has had. It is by no fortunate chance merely that he should be both. Both handle the breaking of taboos, corresponding respectively to comedy and tragedy and to the two great myths of Renaissance Europe, the Don Juan myth and the Faust myth. The health-giving nature of the one we can accept; but what of the other? One may form part of Powys's spiritual questing; can the other?

We may now bring to bear on certain difficult poems what we have learned concerning Powys's masturbatory fantasies. When in 'The New Magdalene' (96) a satyr worships the suffering 'wanton', bringing 'heathen litanies' and 'ancient balm' to heal her from men's 'burning eyes', we are on comparatively safe ground, in the world perhaps of Ernest Dowson; but, knowing Powys's addiction to sadistic books bought in France (*Autobiography,* see p. 159 above), and Mr. Evans's fearful reading, we shall be inclined to feel worse dangers adumbrated in 'The Book' (170), wherein a love-presence from death is summoned by 'the moonlit spell' of a 'dark heathen book' to make him 'a monk for evermore'; that is, his sexual energies are devoted to the inward obsession instead of to a normal partner. The title 'The Malice-Dance' (183) may have sexual-sadistic overtones; the poem celebrates a 'drugged' rejection of 'reason' in favour of ghostly 'malice dances full of treason'. When in 'The Wood' (166) a deep 'wisdom' comes from 'caverns of sleep' we are in a world of *secrecy*, beyond ethic:

> Is it life, is it life, that all these years
> We've been living, tasting, and calling good?
> Ah! Your eyes are full of tears!
> The wood has caught you, the magic wood.
>
> Something breaks down where the wood begins;
> Something breaks down in this hidden spot!
> What are our virtues? What are our sins?
> It matters not! It matters not!

It is all 'strange' and 'magical'; some indirect relation at least may be supposed to lonely, sex-prompted, fantasies.

'The Castle of Gathore' (190) is yet more revealing. It takes us to a place which 'none knows but I', of 'mystery' and 'dead things' leading on to 'the Immensities'. Death is emphatic. 'Black morgues of leafy doom' made of centuries of past forests lead up to the 'terrible steps' of the Castle. It towers as

> A Nightmare image, a thing of fear,
> Revealed to me alone!

Here he has at last found his real 'home', whence came all 'those airs of the dead' which drove one 'true love' from his 'bed' and the other from his 'side'; heterosexual and homosexual love being apparently intended. So

> This is what divides me from him and her
> And the blessed light of the sun;
> Till the eyes of Algol and of Altair
> Are my only benison!

The star 'Algol' we shall meet again, and we may remember the 'little star' of 'The Epiphany of the Mad'. He knows what makes people shun him; they sense it in his eyes. He lives a 'phantom' existence, 'alone with the Immensities'.

Both 'The Wood' and 'The Castle of Gathore' are written by one who has dared the recesses of enjoyed evil, like Taliessin visiting Hell (p. 212 below), for a salutory purpose. The stars 'Algol' and 'Altair' are important as symbols of evil and good (p. 222n. below). Note the references to *secrecy* in the 'hidden spot' when ethical distinctions cease, in the one poem; and the 'Nightmare', the revelation 'to me alone', and the 'home'-coming, in the other.

There is, too, that strange lyric, 'The Face' (194), wherein whiteness, Powys's mystical colour, comes in as both positive peace or love and fearful danger. The Face is a danger, 'the ultimate Fear', 'throned in the dark'. The poet goes 'whistling' to his love, called a 'white bird', symbolizing normal happiness and sex-love. But the 'wreckage of the whole damned race' is in that other, silent, Face, symbolizing or addressing man's fallen, ruthless, sadistic state. The Moon shines on it: a 'terrible face for the sweet moonlight to shine upon'. Provided only that it remain *silent*, there is safety. It *too is white*:

> Oh white, white lips that hang so mute,
> As I go whistling to my Love,
> That ultimate Fear would be absolute
> If you should move!

The two whites denote a similarity in difference; just as in Eliot's *Waste Land* water may be associated with either lust or grace (pp. 179-80 above). Notice the stress – we shall meet it again – on *silence*, as in the 'secrecy' of *In Spite Of* (p. 161 above), the 'hidden spot' of 'The Wood', the aloneness of 'The Castle of Gathore'.

The suffusing impressions are dark and deathly; the horror is a 'Nightmare'. We are in the world of Powys's relaxed mysticism and rejection of life's colours, though behind this mysticism we may suppose a play of abnormal sexual, or semi-sexual, sensation. The ambivalence, which is that of Wolf Solent's 'mythology' (p. 157 above), is stated in 'The Face', where white is, as in Melville's discussion (p. 216 below), ambivalently sweet or fearful.

But the poetry is not confined to relaxation. The dark

experience, as we have just seen, opens out 'Immensities', just as
did the boy's obscene drawing in 'The Classic Touch'. More, we
remember the quests already noticed, the opening of horizons.
These quests may be water-quests. Liquidity is emphatic in
Powys's poetic impressions; marshes and sea are frequent. Now
water is in poetry a normal sexual correlative: voyages may often
be voyages through sexual turmoil. In Coleridge's *The Ancient
Mariner* the motiveless, and to that extent sadistic, murderer of
the Albatross has to *love the water-snakes* before his becalmed ship
can move; in Yeats's 'Byzantium' human spirits ride their
dolphins, their biological existences, through a passionate ocean
of mire and blood, to a new dimension; Eliot's *Waste Land* works
through sex-troubles and water-fears to the soul-boat's, which
may be the love-boat's, freedom and control (p. 180 above), and
in his 'Marina' a mystical attainment is expressed in terms of
ship and voyage. In Eliot's *Four Quartets* we are told that 'the
river is within us' ('The Dry Salvages', I).

That we are right to read into many of Powys's poems a sexual
reference may be argued from his favourite use of a water-voyage.
In 'Euthanasia' (172) he 'drifts' and 'floats' on a 'barge' down a
'river' to the great 'sea'. More purposive and energic is 'A Question' (169) where, confronted by a normal love, he replies, 'Not
to that harbour steers my mind'. In 'The *Disaster*' (210) the brig
Disaster, which is his 'soul', drifts rudderless in the 'madness of
the gale'; 'sea-slime', 'sea-weed' and 'sea-crust' cover its 'ghostly
keel', the soul tainted with lust. 'Phantom-white' sea-gulls scream
from the mast-spars, as the 'derelict' drives on. From an earthly
view its case is hopeless, but to 'the drowned men' deep in ocean,
that is from the dimension of death, it is a different story. To them,
'The brig *Disaster* goes merrily'. The soul lets itself be driven on
without 'captain' or 'mate', 'sails' or 'compass', submitting to the
winds and waters. Somehow it is proud of its very submission:
'lost – exultant, desolate!'

There is no conscious battling or guidance, no attempt at a
moral conquest of the dangerous powers, but rather a submission,
with an enjoyment and a pride in the desolation. Something is
being purposively played out.

The relation of water-voyages to sexual feeling is clear in 'The
Ultimate' (184), wherein psychological agonies turn, as the poem
develops, into a voyage. It is man's fate that 'rats' and 'weasels'

Eat at our hearts with teeth of bane,
And tug at the sick white roots of pain
Where every man's alone,
And scrape a tune on the deep nerve-string
That is love and life and everything,
And gnaw our flesh to the bone.

The teeth of wicked fantasies are lodged in us, unavoidable as
Zeus's vultures in the myth of Prometheus. We experience them
'*alone*'; more, they make a rough *music*, suggested by 'scrape' and
'tune' (in 'The Tune', p. 199 above, the word 'tune' is used in
close association with sex-contact), on the sex-nerve ('nerve' is
regularly used by Powys for the sex-organ's excitement in *A
Glastonbury Romance* and elsewhere). This 'nerve-string' is said to
be basic to love, life and creation: we cannot deny it, however
agonizing its 'gnaw'. It is called 'deep', sinking, or seeming to
sink, to the depths of reality.

And yet this is not 'the ultimate'; it is by itself 'nothing', as
In Spite Of told us (p. 161 above). True, '*some* human dramas' stop
here: that is, presumably, remain in torment, or put lusts into
action. What is wanted, however, is to keep the co-presence of
opposites in 'play' within the 'mind' or 'soul':

But the play that the high gods love
In their Theatre of Space
Has the mind, the mind for the stage thereof
And the soul for its dancing place!
Oh shapes of terror and fear,
Oh shapes of loathing and lust,
That gibber and jibe at us *here*
Ye break earth's shallow crust.
Far back that stage recedes –
Who knows where that stairway goes?
Who knows where that passage leads?
And that door? Who knows? Who knows?

Note that it is the dark powers themselves that 'break earth's
shallow crust'; they force us into the profundities. 'At this
point', we are told – at the point of the dance, which suggests
sex-play – the rats stop gnawing at 'each rib and joint' of the
'vessel'. The earlier flesh and bone have now become a 'vessel',
which the rats now leave, fleeing from it as it 'steers for the open

sea', 'the prow of its bleeding lip' pointed towards 'eternity'. There is movement and purpose.

The ship signifies a voyage, a quest, central to which is the masturbatory, if we remember 'tune', experience. Within us goes on an interplay of good and evil, like that behind Wolf Solent's 'mythology' (p. 157 above), but passively experienced from the positive angle, and more 'play' and 'dancing' than conflict; that is, the rights and presumably enjoyments of the evil are being allowed. Only so will the rats leave their worrying and the ship turn its 'bleeding' prow to the open sea. To quote again from 'The Epiphany of the Mad':

> But all my thoughts as I sing this tune
>   Are about a little star
> That soon or late, that late or soon,
> The evilest things beneath the moon
>   Approach and cleansèd are.

Again, the evils *'approach'* of their own accord, and by our embrace are 'cleansed': we are cathartic agents.

3

In *Morwyn* (1937), that Inferno of inquisitional and vivisectional sadism, location of Powys's worst horrors and fears, his well-loved poet Taliessin, who alone among bright spirits deliberately visits Hell, claimed that his poetry touched

the deepest secret of all in our ancient religion; a secret that bears upon the mystery of good and evil and upon the mystical light that sometimes shines out from the most noisome regions of evil.   (III. 178)

In *Morwyn* the Golden Age is found *below* Hell; one has to descend through the horrors to find it. After *Morwyn* Powys's writing grew steadily brighter; more light, more youthful, more trustful of life and sun. The paradox is uncompromising, though not new: it is really all in Euripides' *Bacchae*, where through failing to honour Dionysus, the god of semi-sadistic orgy – for so in this play he is – Pentheus is the victim of a terrible revenge, being murdered by his own mother in a state of dementia. We have to honour the greater powers if we are to preserve our freedom. The New Testament

'Resist not Evil' may be given a wide, psychological, meaning.

The lyrics we have discussed have seemed obviously tragic and mystical. Were it not for the assertion of a quest, they might appear too much dominated by negations. When the central, which we assume to be the sadistic, horror is welcomed and mastered, it is only done within an atmosphere of agony, nightmare, and death. Even when the half-light of dawn or evening or the moon, or the half-way stages of marsh and mist, are saluted as comforts, we may, noting the many references to death, feel that the sadistic torment, which is at the extreme a death-force, is in the background, being turned to a masochistic and mystical purpose. We may sense its presence, forcing Powys into this half-darkened world. Exactitude is impossible. All we can so far say for certain is that the psychic territory is one of a half-way, life-death, impressionism, and that within that area is both a welcoming of horror, a liking for death, and a sense of questing and infinity. But meanwhile two things have been uncompromisingly rejected: normal sexuality and the Sun. We shall now examine these two rejections.

What keeps our life-trust alive is the romantic vision. It is so for Powys. His most strongly idealized poems are, as his total work makes abundantly clear, seraphic figures of what he calls some 'Saturnian' sex, either as boys or, more rarely, girls-as-boys (p. 193 above; *The Saturnian Quest*, Index C, Seraphic Intuitions). The poetry has something, but not much, to show. Normal love is in the main rejected, and boys appear attractively. We can point to the desired union with a friend 'that can be no more than a friend', disallowed by society but ratified by an old 'dethroned' god (i.e. Saturn), in the poem 'Noon' (174-5). In 'The Castle of Gathore' we found a reasonably clear hint of the homosexual. 'The Old Song' (85) invokes a transient love-opportunity in 'Kiss the boy who kneels with you', and concludes with 'God have mercy on all lovers'. In 'Knowledge' (120) 'the witch-girl pressed the rook-boy's lips until they bled'. In 'The Writer' (121)

> I wrote of Adonis the lovely boy,
> And of winged Psyche's virgin joy
> As she clung to Eros' lips.

In these last the boy is the loved-one. We may add the 'laughing boy' whose obscenities bring health and freedom in 'The Classic Touch' (p. 207 above); the word 'classic' recalling the 'classic nakedness' as a health-giving power of the boys in *Wolf Solent* (p. 193 above).

The poems offer nothing so vivid as Baptiste in *Rodmoor*, the 'angel' of the hero's Nirvana (VI. 85, XXI. 323, 326; see p. 193 above), or Rook's vision in *Ducdame* of his son now grown to a youth speaking lovingly with a smile 'the penetrating sweetness of which diffused itself through every fibre of the man's body'; the face possessing 'a beauty and power in it beyond anything he had ever approached' (XIX. 310, and see XIX. 307-11, XX. 328, XXII. 359, XXV. 433-4). We have just enough in the poetry to keep the seraphic intuition before us; it is not, as in the prose, fully explicit, but the link is there, though we should probably not notice it without our reading of the prose.

So is it, too, with the sadistic obsession; without what we know from other sources we should probably be confused by 'The Wood', 'The Face', 'The Castle of Gathore' and 'The Ultimate'. The poems speak obliquely, they veil as much as they reveal; it is as though, in respect to both the homosexual and the sadistic, these lyrics are cautiously avoiding too vivid a revelation. We remain in twilight.

The Sun is rejected: in 'Saturn' (157) it is 'red with blood' riding careless over 'the conquered throat of the world'. Red is also the colour of normal love-romance, put aside to make way for the silver and white in 'Piety' (170). Red stands for creation in all its full-blooded richness and cruelty. But surely we cannot remain content with such a wholesale imaginative rejection? The Sun, or perhaps rather its *light*, is in his prose one of Powys's major glories: 'sunlight and water' are 'the nearest revelation of Ultimate Being' that man can attain (*Jobber Skald, Weymouth Sands*, XI. 406 or 392); 'sun upon water' opens out 'Nirvana' (*Autobiography*, IV. 145). The images may denote a blend of light and sexual instinct. It is less Sun than light that is revered, as again in *The Art of Happiness*, where anything touched by early or late sunlight is an 'enchantment' (V. 188). Now twice in the lyrics sun-power accompanies a fully achieved experience, but in terms not of 'sun' but of 'noon', so avoiding any sense of the Sun as a semi-personalized being. It was in 'Noon' (174), under 'the noon-tide heat', that he writes of 'the friend that can be no more than a friend'; and in 'The Saturnian' (148) his lonely quest is given a triumphant expression:

The Ship of Cruelty

Ah! Once when the burning noon was poured
    On moss and stone and dreaming sod,
I saw the great blue flower that God
    Made for the Son of God.

And do you think I can go content,
    With the beauty we meet with everywhere,
When I have breathed that flower's scent
    And seen it melt into the air?

Oh, I must follow it high and low,
    Though it leave me cold to your human touch,
Some starry sorcery made me so;
    And from my birth have I been such.

The quest is 'low' as well as 'high': it may involve what is, or
seems, bad. The 'cold' of his 'starry' quest, going back as did his
sadistic obsessions to childhood ('birth'), is *really part of, or leading
to, this 'great blue flower' of Christ*. It is in the cause of something
not less but more burningly suffused than our sun, more richly
coloured than nature's flowers, that we suffer all our moonlit
madnesses, our twilights and pallors. As in spiritualistic descriptions of Elysian or etheric planes, we here receive the sense of
solar quality without a *personal* sun; that is why the word 'noon'
is used. In the light is the 'blue flower'. Blue is the spiritual, as
red the earthly colour (*Wolf Solent*, XXV. 632 or 603; *A Glastonbury Romance*, XXIV. 788 or 755; *Jobber Skald, Weymouth Sands*, X.
363 or 352); as in Eliot's 'In blue of larkspur, blue of Mary's
colour' in *Ash-Wednesday* (IV).

We return now to the sadistic obsession. If that really is, as
Powys has claimed, the key to his life; and if, as his letters (p. 163
above) stated, the sensation of it was accepted as a health-bringing
positive, do not our poems suffer a certain limitation in so rele-
gating it to dark impressions and talk of evil? And to moon and
star rather than sun? True, Powys's own fantasies were nocturnal;
but the Sun has been regarded as a sadistic force; and one would
expect it to play a more central part.

We may suppose that the mystical passivity and the sensuous
sweetness involved in Powys's love of twilight and marshes bear
some relation to sexual sensation: water is in poetry a correlative
to sexual passion, and Powys's poetry returns again and again
to water and the sea. But the sadistic seems clearly to be grouped

with the Sun, deity simultaneously of hideous blood-slaughter and miraculous creation; and with colours, especially red (pp. 201, 204 above). Opposites finally coalesce in the golden conclusion to *Wolf Solent*. Coalescence we must have, or strive for: we cannot for long remain content with mysticism and whiteness; we may remember the attack on whiteness in Herman Melville's chapter 'On the Whiteness of the Whale' in *Moby Dick*. We cannot remain finally satisfied with madness, death, the Moon and stars. We should expect the Sun, in some indirect way, as in the 'burning noon' of 'The Saturnian', to be shown including both health and horror. If only we could say that the horror *is*, after all, the great Blue Flower; or if not the horror, at least the imagination's sex-activating enjoyment of it. Is this what 'The Saturnian' hints? Or even says?

The matter is of appalling, and central, importance, and vast issues are involved. In *Rodmoor* and *Ducdame* fearful books were being composed – we remember the sadistic picture-books that so enthralled Powys and Mr. Evans (p. 159 above) – on destruction as the key to existence in the one, and on the secret of some 'anti-vital energy' in the other (*The Saturnian Quest*, 24, 27; *Ducdame*, X. 144). In those we have the sadistic raised to cosmic proportions. Powys returned to the theme with the disintegrating powers of Morsimmon Esty's 'devolutionary cosmic ray' in *The Inmates* (XV. 279). *Up and Out* and *All or Nothing* play upon thoughts of cosmic destruction or not-being. Today the human race is flirting with such activities not in secret masturbation but on the world-stage: we see it in our ever-multiplying vivisectional horrors, our crime records, our warrings, our hydrogen bombs. The disease must be attacked *at its source in man*; and that means in man's sexual being. 'No religion that doesn't deal with sex-longing in *some* kind of way', said the hero of *Maiden Castle*, 'is much use to us' (IX. 422 or 433-4).

What we want is a fusion of the Blue Flower, or some equivalent, with the sadistic horrors; corresponding to the perfection of sun-on-water. There is help for us in *Porius* (1951). The hero's encounter with the two Giants, man and daughter, is a high point in Powys's work. The atmospheric setting is of both *yellow mist* and *sunlight*. The daughter is a young, 'goddess-like', yellow-haired creature who matches Porius' 'secretest broodings' (XXII. 517-18). Formerly ill-at-ease he now at last, on seeing her, achieves self-realization. Body and mind are no longer opposed: now his mind *uses* his body (XXII. 512). The reading of a man-of-action state as that of one in whom the body is rather servant than partner corresponds to what we find in T. E. Lawrence (pp. 327, 341; p. 466n., on Francis Berry). Porius becomes a bold lover, fighting to win the goddess from her cannibal father, who was carrying the half-devoured corpse of a 'beautiful' youth (XXII. 510).

During the fight the daughter is accidentally killed and the Giant plunges with her into 'sun-illumined depths of emerald-green water' (XXII. 523). The dead giants lived on in Porius' memory as an ultimate vision: the 'clear green water' and the 'two pairs of eyes staring up at him through clotted blood and drowned hair' opened a 'chasm' giving him entrance into 'an ecstasy of life-worship indescribable in words'; it was an entrance into 'another' world (XXIII. 538). Pure blue would be here inapposite, but green is already a mixture of blue and yellow, and the co-presence first of yellow mist and sun and then of sun and green water, the eyes, the yellow hair and the blood, together with the union in death of cannibal giant and goddess-daughter, all this constitutes a perfected blending suited to Porius' new-found domination of his own cumbrous body by his mind. The whole heroic action is before us; and its bloody yet idyllic result lived on within Porius as a magical power. Evil has been assimilated, as in epic: 'What theme had Homer but original sin?' (W. B. Yeats, 'Vacillation').

There is more help for us in Peter Peregrinus, the Anti-Christ of *The Brazen Head* (1956), and his demonic 'Little Pretty', a seven-inch pinkish-grey phallic lodestone or magnet, which, when pressed near his genitals and aimed, can be used to fearful effect; as when it is used to assure the future agony of Edward II (XIX. 281-2, XX. 295-6). Peregrinus and his 'Little Pretty' – the name reflects a titillating sensuality – are satanically dangerous; and the dangers, being sexually impregnated, are more energic than Friar Bacon's 'Brazen Head'. The one indeed appears to condition the other (*The Saturnian Quest*, 106). They are twin magical devices, sexual and cerebral, the balance corresponding to our recurring balance of obscenity and spirituality, sadistic and seraphic. At the book's conclusion, Peregrinus and his love-partner Lilith turn the magnet first on the Hell-castle Lost Towers, evil slaying evil, and then *on themselves* (cp. p. 163). They become one 'fiery ball' of 'dazzling' brilliance; they then destroy the Brazen Head, which has at last begun to speak, and vanish (XXII. 347-8). Their powers dominate and are finally bright. Though the Brazen Head was magically impregnated by contact with the virgin Ghosta's sexual parts (VII. 92, 97, XIII. 207, XIV. 210-11), it remains, comparatively, passive. Peregrinus is Powys's sadistic contribution to the medieval legend. It seems that he and his lodestone half-belong to, and finally enter, some new dimension. Remember 'the great blue flower' of 'The Saturnian'. Lost Towers becomes a star vanishing upwards into 'the blue depths of the empyrean' (XXII. 347); and Peregrinus and Lilith, after they have become a fire-ball or 'meteor', shine with the blaze of a 'sapphire'. We have the fusion at which 'The Saturnian' hinted.

We might well complain that all these intershifting impressions and good-and-evil ambiguities leave us confused. Twice only, it appears, has Powys left us a firm statement on the central issue: once in the letters which we have quoted, followed by the related passage in *All or Nothing* (pp. 162-5 above); and once in a poem called *The Ship*. Though the letters may help us to understand it, the poem is direct. It does what the letters cannot. For this reason: masturbation – the word is itself ugly – cannot be described without falsifying the experience, since the wickedness or absurdity of the accompanying thoughts bear no rational relation to the thrilled sensation of the experience. That is why, as Lawrence in 'Pornography and Obscenity' (*Phoenix*, 178) observed, masturbation is 'the one thoroughly secret act of the human being'. In *In Spite Of* (p. 161 above) Powys counselled secrecy and in 'The Face' (194) he was, as we have seen, fearful lest the *silent* Face were to speak. For all such masturbatory, or other, secrecies the only way to expression is through the use of objective impressions which correspond to what is positive in the subjective sensation; and that means poetry. It may be very difficult. We see why Eliot was so anxious about *words*, as in the sadistic *Sweeney Agonistes* ('I gotta use words when I talk to you') and in the *Four Quartets* ('East Coker', II, V; 'Little Gidding', V). Neither sadism nor masturbation need, of course, be the involvement; but for when it is, Powys's poem probably succeeds as has no poem on record. Or rather it is the only such poem we have, unless we regard Keats's *Ode to Psyche* as a forerunner.

Before turning to the poem it may be as well to establish the revolutionary nature of Powys's doctrine by quoting the time-honoured and still conventional view of masturbation as expressed by D. H. Lawrence in 'Pornography and Obscenity' (*Phoenix*, 178-9). After saying that, since sex 'must' go somewhere, some educationalists have been known to advise masturbation, he continues:

Is masturbation so harmless, though? Is it even comparatively pure and harmless? Not to my thinking. In the young, a certain amount of masturbation is inevitable, but not therefore natural. I think there is no boy or girl who masturbates without feeling a sense of shame, anger, and futility. Following the excitement comes the shame, anger, humiliation, and the sense of futility. This sense of futility and humiliation deepens as the years go on, into a suppressed rage, because of the impossibility of escape. The one thing that it seems impossible to escape from, once the habit is formed, is masturbation. It goes on and on, on into old age, in spite of marriage or love affairs or anything else. And it always carries this secret feeling of futility and humiliation, futility and humiliation. And this is, perhaps, the deepest and most dangerous cancer of our civilization. Instead of being a comparatively pure and harmless vice, masturbation is certainly the most dangerous sexual vice that a society can be afflicted with, in the long run. Comparatively pure it may be – purity being what it is. But harmless!!!
The great danger of masturbation lies in its merely exhaustive nature. In sexual intercourse, there is a give and take. A new stimulus enters as the native stimulus departs. Something quite new is added as the old surcharge is removed. And this is so in all sexual intercourse where two creatures are concerned, even in the homosexual intercourse. But in masturbation there is nothing but loss. There is no reciprocity. There is merely the spending away of a certain force, and no return. The body remains, in a sense, a corpse, after the act of self-abuse. There is no change, only deadening. There is what we call dead loss. And this is not the case in any act of sexual intercourse between two people. Two people may destroy one another in sex. But they cannot just produce the null effect of masturbation.

Lawrence's 'corpse' may bear some relation to Powys's corpse-like seer Uryen in *Maiden Castle*, the deathly odours in *Porius* and indeed the emphasis throughout his prose and poetry on death. Powys honours the corpse-god of ancient Welsh mythology (*A Glastonbury Romance*, XXIV. 788 or 755). He would replace Wordsworth's 'the pleasure which there is in life itself' by 'the pleasure which there is in life and death' (*The Art of Happiness*, I. 42-4, 47). However, despite his self-directed sexuality and many ailments, Powys lived a gigantically creative life to his ninety-first year.

Lawrence is probably envisaging a day-time practice of direct physical action; Powys's 'houris' were nocturnal visitants and his emphasis is on the 'imagination' (p. 165 above). Powys is not just out to facilitate physical release; he is using physical release to heal spiritual disorder. Like St. Paul he is engaging in battle with cosmic evil. The young, he said (p. 163 above), should be deliberately *taught* to indulge their more dangerous instincts through imagination accompanied by a self-directed sexual activity; so turning evil into sex-play, tragedy into comedy, demons into angels.

Such complexities are not Lawrence's concern. He is thinking in terms of a simple contrast of normal sex-intercourse and masturbatory action. It is true that without some motivating or collaborating fantasy the result might be as he says; there would, as he says, be no partner. But for Powys there *is* a partner, which he calls one's own 'opposite' (p. 161 above), leading to an imaginative *influx* accompanied by physical *release*. The result is creative and self-creative (pp. 165, 161); either, we may suppose, through the unifying of a previously divided self, or perhaps through the self or soul's submission, playing Psyche to Eros, to some external powers, as when Mr. Evans is sexually partnered and stimulated by an orgasm from the First Cause (p. 162 above). Indeed, we may suggest that what we call 'imagination' may sometimes be the approaches of a spirit-entity.

Lawrence's sexual gospel, if that is the word, was however, as we have seen (pp. 142-8 above), itself in many ways abnormal, and always unrestful; and in mid-career he was driven on to a concern with 'dark gods', blood-sacrifice, and narratives of barbaric tone. At the end he returned, in *Lady Chatterley's Lover*, to celebration of a man-woman relationship *incorporating the savage powers of his recent work* (p. 148 above); and also, in *Last Poems*, to death, spiritually, and even *spiritualistically*, conceived.[1] Much of

[1] In the poem 'The Ship of Death' there is a voyage into 'oblivion', but oblivion is not the end. The body finally 'emerges strange and lovely' and the 'frail soul steps out'. It is for us, in our earth-life, to 'build' our own 'ship' for the death-voyage. See George A. Panichas's fine handling of the poem in *Adventure in Consciousness*:

the story is sympathetically reviewed by Middleton Murry in *Love, Freedom and Society* (1957). Murry pays respect to the demonic energies and aberrations of Lawrence, though remaining critical. He admires *Lady Chatterley's Lover* while appearing not too concerned with the savagery written into it. He has his own position, asserting the centrality and prime need of a marriage relationship combining physical sex and spiritual love. This is scarcely a comprehensive solution, however desirable. The demons are too insistent, and Lawrence probably did well to incorporate a demonic element into his final reading of man-woman sexuality in *Lady Chatterley's Lover*. He underlines, as surely as do Powys and Eliot, and Joyce too in the Brothel extravaganza of *Ulysses*, the appalling pressures of the sadistic.

In turning from his attempt to imagine a new Aztec religion in *The Plumed Serpent* to *Lady Chatterley's Lover*, Lawrence might be said to have returned from Dionysus to Aphrodite; but it was an Aphrodite who now included Dionysus. Or we may think of Eros as deity behind both. If we suppose the existence of some external and invading entity, the myth of Eros and Psyche is certainly relevant. The soul, Psyche, is supposedly female, and Eros male; but we should not think too closely in terms of sexual differences since we are concerned with the transcending of opposites, and in such transcendings each is always ready to turn into the other. We do best to plant our trust in the term 'bisexual'; and even in terms of a life-death unity. In Powys's *Atlantis* the prophet Enorches tells us that Eros, 'the secret behind life' and Dionysus, 'the secret behind death', are really identical; the orthodox Olympian theology he despises; he supports the culture of Atlantis with its bisexual innovations; 'the young Eros of the Mysteries' could love, and be loved by, 'both sexes'. Only now, he says, 'do Eros and Dionysus appear in their true light' (V. 143, VIII. 259-60, V. 157, 137). In the myth of Eros and Psyche we appear to have a valuable relation of the masturbatory imagination to the seraphic.

Whatever our views we must admit that Powys, for himself,

The Meaning of D. H. Lawrence's Religious Quest, The Hague, also London, 1964; 197-207. Prof. Panichas discusses the poem's relation to ancient Etruscan beliefs, and also, elsewhere, to Greek philosophy: see his 'D. H. Lawrence and the Ancient Greeks', *English Miscellany* 16, ed. Mario Praz, Rome 1965.

succeeded. The success is recorded in his poem *The Ship*, which bears to our other lyrics a relation like that of the Golden Journey to Samarkand in Flecker's *Hassan* to the enervate sensuousness of the main action. It is strong, vibrant, and explicit. It is the clearest statement we have of Powys's life-doctrine; his life, properly known, *was* his doctine. *The Ship* corresponds to Wolf Solent's attainment, beyond his 'mythology', to a complete harmony within the 'Saturnian' gold (*The Saturnian Quest*, 35); or again to Powys's development from the mystical depths of *Wolf Solent* and *A Glastonbury Romance*, through the rocks, sea and dawn of *Weymouth Sands*, to the clear-cut colours and golden strength of *Owen Glendower* and the glittering Mediterranean mythology of *Atlantis*; to *The Mountains of the Moon* and *All or Nothing*.

We have already discussed some of Powys's poetic sea-quests. But his claims demand expression in a more triumphant voyage than those, corresponding to Nietzsche's 'the Golden Wonder, the boat of freewill and its Master' (*Thus Spake Zarathustra*, III. 14), or to the spirit-voyages through sea-turmoils to the Golden Birds of Yeats's Byzantium. 'Golden' establishes a great value; throughout the Bible and later literature jewels and rich metals are correspondent to transcendent attainments and realities. Powys has used 'silver' often; in *The Ship* silver is still used but is accompanied by a figure-head of 'chalcedony', one of the dazzling stones used for the New Jerusalem in The Book of Revelation (XXI. 19).

In 'The Rider' (185), the poet rides to his doom on 'the lions of exultation'. That golden beast is felt at our ship's prow pressing through typical wraithly impressions of wailing gulls and 'phantom-moon' over waters 'purple and green', the colours respectively of *A Glastonbury Romance* and *Wolf Solent*. The figure-head and lion-prow may be compared with the ambivalent figure-head of the ship in that other symbolical voyage of *Atlantis* (*The Saturnian Quest*, 99). We have, inevitably, a star, here Algol, called 'the Eye of the Demon', a dark star corresponding to the 'red eye' of evil in the Double-natured First Cause (p. 160 above); we have met it before with Altair, in 'The Castle of Gathore', the two serving there as guiding stars, evil and good.[1] We are to use both

[1] Algol, in the constellation Perseus, is a varying star of light and dark, tradition-ally considered evil: the name probably derives from the Arabic *al-ghul*, 'the ghoul'. Altair is a very *bright* star in the constellation Aquila.

the good and the evil, symbolized in the Ship's two masts, silver and black. The higher reality transcending opposites may be reflected into a mastery of sex-opposition, as in Eliot's Tiresias central to *The Waste Land*, an ideal found most often in youthful, boy-girl form. This is Powys's love-ideal, countering his grim themes. In *The Ship*, boy and girl combine to make one bisexual god, called 'Love'. There is an emphasis on child-innocence. We have not only Nietzsche's Lion; we have his Child too (pp. 173-5 above).

The voyage is undertaken in loneliness and secrecy, and yet the seraphic being is present. The loneliness is a loneliness apart from men, with a divine companion.

As the voyage goes on the Sun and Moon change places, which means that the moon, guardian of witchery and madness, becomes sun-wisdom; just as the Sun, earlier feared, becomes beneficial in *Weymouth Sands* and *Owen Glendower*; and as Helia, daughter of the Sun, appears from the Moon's other side to meet the young hero of *The Mountains of the Moon*. After our earlier discussions we see readily why they must *change places* in this victorious poem. As in 'The Ultimate', where the rats leave the ship, we find as the voyage advances that the demonic gives place to the seraphic; while the 'curious' Ship, at first called 'Cruelty', is now said to be 'without a name'; as in 'The Ultimate' (p. 211 above), it all turns out to be a 'game'. The evil as 'evil' has just gone, as in Masefield's *The Hounds of Hell* and Francis Berry's *Murdock* (pp. 289, 460 below). As often elsewhere in poetry the ship-voyage is to be regarded as a voyage through sex-sensation; and we must, of course, especially where cruelty is involved, *have our guardian angel*, St. Paul's Christ or Pope's 'God within the mind' (p. 161n. above). Here the Ship has its 'god' who is also the seraphic partner, bisexual and beyond or including opposites in the child-consciousness of an Eros-figure, called 'Love'. The lines are addressed to a 'Prince', signifying the young royalty of future man, like the young heroes of Powys's last books, for whom the doctrine is being offered.

I apologize for this list, but it is necessary to indicate how exactly the poem sums and solves our difficulties. As in *The Art of Happiness* (p. 161 above) we are safe, with ivory bulwarks. The ship sailing heavenwards as silver flame on purple sea matches the end of *The Brazen Head*. Nothing is omitted.

The Ship of Cruelty

The poem stands, probably, alone in the world's literature in exact description of man's one available technique for using the giant enginery of sex to transmute cosmic evil to the service of love. We today often hear of a new 'Aquarian' age ahead to succeed our present dispensation in 'Pisces'. Powys uses these terms throughout 'Pair Dadeni' (*Obstinate Cymric*, VII; and see *Rabelais*, VIII. 374). The Aquarian Age lies ahead of us. *The Ship* is its testament.

THE SHIP

I made a ship of my cruelty,
    A wonderful, terrible ship,
With masts of silver and ebony,
    And bulwarks of carven ivory,
And a figure-head of chalcedony,
    And a prow like a lion's lip.

And I sat in the stern of my ship,
    Alone, be it said and known,
You are always alone in that kind of ship,
    Put your finger upon your lip!
Christ's mother, how deep alone!

And in my ship I sailed;
    And the waters were purple and green;
And all day long the sea-gulls wailed
    And the sun went down and the waters paled
And a phantom-moon was seen.

And under the moon I still sailed on;
    But not only the moon was there!
Algol, the Demon's Eye, looked down—
    Algol, the Eye of the Demon, shone,
Thro' the chill and frozen air.

Oh ship, my ship, called Cruelty!
    Is it forgotten then of thee
How we came in the hour of dawn
    To a land where silence covered the sea,
To a harbour of virginal mystery
    And a little pier forlorn?

The Ship of Cruelty

For the people fled away
  When they saw my terrible ship,
Livid, phantom-like and grey,
  Led by Algol, at break of day,
Into that harbour slip!

But one fled not. One stood
  On the edge of the little pier,
A boy – a boy in his solitude!
  A girl – a girl in her fear!

No boy – no girl; a god, a god!
  And I hoisted the sails of my ship;
And Cruelty, with Love on board,
  – Your finger on your lip!
Went sailing, sailing over the sea
  Till the sun grew like the moon;
Till the moon – oh, mother of mystery!
  Till the moon grew like the sun.

And Algol, the Demon's Eye, looked down
  Upon that curious ship;
Algol, the Eye of the Demon, shone –
  Your finger on your lip!
But Love and I played a deeper game
  Than any Demons know,
And my ship, my ship without a name,
  On the purple sea a silver flame,
From Earth to Heaven did go.

O Prince! make of your cruelty
  A ship and not a sword.
Give it masts of silver and ebony!
  Give it bulwarks of carven ivory,
And a figure-head of chalcedony;
  And take on board a god!

ADDITIONAL NOTE: After completing my present collection of essays I happened to read Richard Cavendish's *The Black Arts* (Routledge, 1967; Pan Books, 1969; my page numerals apply to the latter). I was interested to note the part played by masturbation in magical practice:

To know the angel and have intercourse with the demon, which are the attendant spirits of Abramelin the Mage, means to summon up and

liberate the forces of the magician's unconscious. The performance of
the ritual is accompanied by masturbation and the mounting frenzy
with which the barbarous names of power are chanted is paralleled by
rising sexual excitement, ending in a climax which is both physical and
psychological and in which the magician's innermost powers are unleashed. (III. iv. 161)

I have already, in discussing Powys's doctrine, suggested that
more than release may be supposed to be involved (p. 220 above).
So is it in the magical tradition:

But the *Liber Samekh* is much more than a method of taking the libido
out for a run. It is a ceremony in which the magician asserts his divine
power and his mastery of the universe. The sexual force of the male
is the human parallel to the creative power of God. In fact, raised to
its highest pitch and directed by the will, the male generative force *is*
divine creative power. (III. iv. 161)

In this way the 'angel-demon' which is the magician's 'inner self'
is awakened to command lesser spirits.

Of 'The Hermit' in the Tarot pack we hear:

Isolated and withdrawn from the world, he is yet a light and a beacon
to others. *Yod* is the letter of the phallus, creative power, and in terms
of sexual symbolism the Hermit means masturbation – the true self
has reached puberty, as it were, the magician has found the Master in
himself. Complete in himself, solitary and virgin, the Hermit's plants
all have white flowers, emblems of purity, uninvolvement. He is a
symbol of the fertility of absolute self-reliance. (III. ii. 128)

Union with Christ or Guardian Angel may be the imagined concern. Relevant references appear at I. iv. 44, III. i. 102, 105, 111-12
('animal driving forces'); and VI. ii. 279, 288.

The book's title is misleading since its subject is not all 'black'.
It is a survey of magic, as such, existing as a rival to religion and
repudiating limitations of ethic and convention. It has much in
common with modern psychology. Magic aims at the inclusion
and use of opposites, light and dark, good and evil, in correspondence to the created order and the constitution of man:
'Each man', we are told, 'has attached to him a guardian angel
and a malevolent demon' (III. iv. 156). Evil spirits are to be
mastered and used; but they are not worshipped. Magic resembles
drama, but is, unlike drama, concerned with direct action. Its
quest is control, power, and the realization of god-hood in

one's self. Words and names may, as in poetry, exert force. Body-concentration is strong, with an employment variously of elaborate robes and nakedness. Sexual or homosexual activity, asceticism, blood-sacrifice, sadisms and obscenities are used to generate power and call up spirits. We may compare the cauldron scene in *Macbeth* and the 'magic' chapter of Joyce's *Ulysses* (pp. 50-1 above).

Much of all this appears extravagant, some of it ludicrous and some dangerous; but much also, concerned as it is with the whole, good-and-evil, Nietzschean complex, seems like an expansion of elements contained in our poetic, and especially our dramatic, traditions. Again and again I am aware of correspondences to my own interpretations. Magic is closer to literature than to modern Spiritualism, which preserves and develops only the unwavering *light* of the New Testament, or Christ. The Christian Church, with its Crucifix, Mass and other rituals, may be regarded as a fusion of (i) magic and drama with (ii) the Christ, or Spiritualism (for the Mass as magic, see Cavendish, VII. iii. 363).

Apart from the more general descriptions of ritual and practice, Cavendish's volume includes detailed accounts of astrology, alchemy and the symbolism of the Tarot pack. The book certainly helps us to see why Wolf Solent's childhood 'mythology' caused his father to regard him as an 'infant magician' (p. 157 above).

PART THREE

Spiritualities

CHAPTER VII

The Scholar Gipsy

The Review of English Studies, New series, VI. 21; January 1955.

MUCH OF THE poetry which we think we know best stands in need, today, of reinterpretation. By taking a wider view than has been customary, we can often expose a new vein of meaning in a well-known work which has hitherto eluded observation. Especially must we be prepared to follow Sherlock Holmes's advice by giving particular attention to any elements which appear to be intrusions, or irrelevancies, since these can often point us to a final understanding.

So advised, we may find ourselves drawn to ask whether the long simile with which Matthew Arnold ends *The Scholar Gipsy* is organic, or merely an over-elaborated device to give us a smooth conclusion. The extended description of the Oxus at the end of *Sohrab and Rustum* carries overtones as a symbolism of life, from youthful impetuosity to complexity and tragedy, and so out to the sea of death, which are relevant to the preceding narrative. Can we say the same of the conclusion to *The Scholar Gipsy*?[1]

The simile of the Tyrian trader has been prepared for by an earlier, shorter, simile of the same kind. Arnold's Scholar, we may remember, is contrasted with the thought and society of the nineteenth century, which he is urged to avoid:

---

[1] The question has, naturally, been asked before, and the propriety of the simile supported, on general impressionistic grounds, by E. K. Brown in *Revue Anglo-Américaine*, xii, February 1935; 224-5 (quoted C. B. Tinker and H. F. Lowry, *The Poetry of Matthew Arnold*, 1940; 212-13). See also Louis Bonnerot in *Matthew Arnold: Poète*, Paris 1947; 473-4.

The Scholar Gipsy

> Still fly, plunge deeper in the bowering wood!
>   Averse, as Dido did with gesture stern
>   From her false friend's approach in Hades turn,
> Wave us away, and keep thy solitude.

(207)

Dido, Queen of Carthage, a colony of Tyre, is a figure of feminine appeal and oriental glamour who failed to distract Aeneas from fulfilling his destiny as the founder, through Rome, of western efficiency and organization. She, like the Scholar, is a wraithly personality, and, like him, has slight respect for the values to which Aeneas, and his descendants in Arnold's day, were dedicated. This simile touches the ascendancy of Rome; and our main, concluding, simile, pushing back yet farther into the origins of our western tradition, the ascendancy of Greece. Both involve Tyre, and both are used with exact reference to the Scholar.

Here are our two final stanzas, with certain important words italicized:

> Then fly our greetings, fly our speech and smiles!
>   – As some *grave* Tyrian trader, from the sea,
>   Descried at sunrise an emerging prow
>   Lifting the cool-hair'd creepers *stealthily*,
>   The fringes of a southward-facing brow
>   Among the Aegean isles;
>   And saw the *merry* Grecian coaster come,
>   Freighted with amber grapes, and Chian wine,
>   Green bursting figs, and tunnies steep'd in brine;
>   And knew *the intruders on his ancient home*,
>
> The young *light-hearted* Masters of the waves;
>   And snatch'd his rudder, and shook out more sail,
>   And day and night held on *indignantly*
>   O'er the blue Midland waters with the gale,
>   Betwixt the Syrtes and soft Sicily,
>   To where the Atlantic raves
>   Outside the Western Straits, and unbent sails
>   There, where down cloudy cliffs, through sheets of foam,
>   *Shy* traffickers, the dark Iberians come;
>   And on the beach undid *his corded bales*.

(231)

On these stanzas there is much to say.

The Scholar Gipsy

In driving the Tyrian traders before them the Greeks established their mastery of the Mediterranean: it was the first step in a story whose sequels were the defence of Greece against the Persians, culminating in Salamis; the conquests of Alexander; and the unsuccessful challenge of Carthage, originally a Tyrian colony, against Rome. It was, therefore, the first step in establishing the western, or European, tradition, as we know it.

But there are other, more ancient, traditions, and these the Tyrians represent. The words 'grave', 'intruders on his ancient home' and 'indignantly' suggest a spiritual authority recalling Shakespeare's 'We do it wrong, being so majestical . . .' (*Hamlet*, I. i. 143). In contrast, the Greek moves 'stealthily'; he is tricky. He is also, in this period, at the birth of our European story, called 'merry' (237), 'young' and 'light-hearted' (241); that is, care-free, with suggestions of youthful bravery and, perhaps, irresponsibility.

As the Tyrian flies the Greek, so the Scholar is told to fly the society of nineteenth-century Europe existing within the tradition inaugurated by Greece and Rome. As he fled to the Gipsies, so the Tyrian flies to the Iberians. They are called 'shy' (249), a word elsewhere associated with the Scholar (70, 79). The undoing of the 'corded bales' makes a firm conclusion, leaving us with a fine sense of secret goods, well protected, weighty, and of value. You see the dark-eyed traffickers eagerly awaiting the disclosure.

Either this is all an irrelevant decoration or we must suppose that the poem which it is there to elucidate possesses a corresponding weight and depth. But in *The Common Pursuit* (1952; 29-31) F. R. Leavis argues that *The Scholar Gipsy*, though a 'charming' poem, throughout pretends to be very much more than it is; that the Scholar's 'one aim, one business, one desire' (152) is insufficiently defined; and that the poem has little to offer regarding the serious engagements of our existence. On the premises of contemporary criticism, that may be a natural conclusion. Nevertheless, those of us who are moved by Arnold's poem will not readily subscribe to it; and if we return to the text with the concluding simile in mind, we should be able to demonstrate its inadequacy.

We must accordingly search within the main body of the poem for qualities roughly corresponding to the oriental powers symbolized by the Tyrian trader. The Scholar is a young man of originality and brilliance (34), who, in a mood of dissatisfaction with the prospects offered him, leaves Oxford in comparative immaturity to join the Gipsies. His state is one of youth, 'fresh, undiverted to the world without' (162). Official studies he has repudiated, and gone off 'roaming the countryside, a truant boy' (198). He lives with something more than the immortality of a literary creation, 'living as thou liv'st on Glanvil's page' (159), enjoying an 'immortal lot' and 'exempt from age' (157-8) precisely because he has left the world with 'powers' (161) untainted. We may call him the 'eternal undergraduate'.

He moves ghost-like about the Oxford countryside. He has 'dark vague eyes and soft abstracted air' (99), and is called 'pensive', 'in a pensive dream' (54, 77). He is elusive, averse from social contact, preferring 'shy retreats' and 'shy fields' (70, 79), 'retired ground' (71) and 'solitude' (210). But there is nothing weak about him: he is 'rapt' (119), that is dedicated, almost as in a trance, to an expectance defined as the 'spark from Heaven' (120), for which he is always waiting. Nor is his life easy. While his former companions live *below* in warmth, at least part of what Dr. Leavis calls his 'eternal week-end' is an arduous enough existence, a spiritual battling, on the snow-driven hills:

> And once, in winter, on the causeway chill
>   Where home through flooded fields foot-travellers go,
>   Have I not pass'd thee on the wooden bridge
>   Wrapt in thy cloak and battling with the snow,
>   Thy face towards Hinksey and its wintry ridge?
>   And thou hast climb'd the hill
>   And gain'd the white brow of the Cumner range,
>   Turn'd once to watch, while thick the snowflakes fall,
>   The line of festal light in Christ-Church hall –
>   Then sought thy straw in some sequester'd grange.

(121)

Sometimes we need to read poetry with what might be called a 'stage' eye; to produce it, as it were, for our own advantage; to allow it all the visual and spatial significance that it can carry, and to read that significance in depth. If we accord this stanza such a reading, we shall begin to understand that the Scholar is more than a renegade from the established tradition. He is that certainly; but he is also a sentinel on the heights, an outpost of learning; more, we may even begin to see him as the presiding genius, the over-watching and guardian spirit, of Oxford, of the university.

It is right that such a guardian deity should be, not a don, but one of 'glad perennial youth' (229); one who is eternally immature. The don has knowledge; he is a pillar of the established tradition; he probably holds academic honours. It is possible to have, and be, all this, and lack wisdom; more, it is extremely hard to have all this, and preserve wisdom; for you cannot buy wisdom with less than wonder. But in the undergraduate you have, or should have, the essence of true learning; the opening of the mind, the wonder, the intuition of fields unexplored. That is why the presiding deity of a great university may be felt as the eternal undergraduate.

But what of the Gipsies? Gipsies are supposed to possess occult abilities. The word 'gipsy' derives from 'Egyptian'; gipsies are, in fact, of Hindu origin; and on both counts they may be associated with the mysterious arts and wisdom of the East. In *The Scholar Gipsy* we are told that they have 'arts' of a strange sort able to rule 'the workings of men's brains'; and the Scholar means, when he has mastered the secret of this magic, to offer it to mankind, presumably in terms that our western culture would understand (44-50). The secret of these 'strange arts' (135) is clearly supposed to be a great good: the Scholar expects to play the part of a benefactor.[1]

What, more exactly, is intended? We may relate the conception to that of Wordsworth's *Recluse* fragment (printed in the preface to *The Excursion*), with its emphasis on 'the mind of Man' as the 'haunt' and 'main region' of his 'song'. 'Mind' and 'thought' are important and power-bearing concepts in both Byron (e.g. the 'eternal spirit of the chainless mind' in the Sonnet on Chillon) and Shelley.[2] They must be regarded less as registering faculties than as active powers. As Hamlet tells us, 'There is nothing either good or bad but thinking makes it so'; and in Shelley's *Prometheus Unbound* man's liberated state is one where evil and suffering, though still present, are mysteriously changed, like wild beasts tamed, so that 'none knew how gentle they could be' (IV. iv.

[1] The comparatively crude magic of Glanvil's narrative was suppressed by Arnold and expanded, through preliminary thoughts of 'the Wandering Mesmerist', into qualities of more philosophic import; see Tinker and Lowry, 207.

[2] See respectively my *Lord Byron: Christian Virtues*, Index A, vii; and *The Starlit Dome*, discussing *Hellas*, 245-51.

404-5). Certainly the liberation of dormant faculties able to modify or control our mental experience might go far to solve the human enigma.

Such possibilities have, throughout the ages, been the concern of the esoteric schools originating from the East, though certain famous Europeans, such as Swedenborg, Goethe, Blake, Rudolf Steiner, Gurdjieff, and today John Cowper Powys, have enjoyed direct experience of them. Traces of such a wisdom may be discovered, on the level of symbolism, within a great deal of our western poetry. The wisdom in question is, however, less easily mastered than the traditional learning of the West, since it aspires to be an active, and directly affective, power, and its exercise may involve arduous training and discipline. Or again, it may appear to function at choice moments without these, as though by the grace of God; and that is why the Scholar says that 'it needs heaven-sent moments for this skill' (50).

The Scholar who is to personify the striving for such a wisdom is presented as one of 'glad perennial youth' (229); and much of what he symbolizes is probably best understood by us in youth, before the 'clouds of glory' have dissolved, before education has fitted on us its strait-jacket, and conditioned us for all those 'exacting' demands which Dr. Leavis complains that our Scholar, as indeed he does, repudiates. Among those likely to see the Scholar there is accordingly a high proportion of youthful persons. He gives flowers, but without speaking, to the maidens who have been engaging in May dances (81-90); and we have elsewhere 'boys' (64) and 'children' (105). He is also seen by such simple people as shepherds (57), the 'smock-frock'd boors' (59), and the 'housewife' of a 'lone homestead' (101), and by the blackbird (116). He may be glimpsed, too, by others enjoying active contact with nature, such as the 'riders blithe' (72) and the bathers (95). On the most important occasion of all, it is the poet himself who sees him battling with the snow, and looking down on the Oxford lights (121-9).

To men he remains elusive: his whole being is set on the 'spark' (120, 171, 188). The word 'spark' is interesting. It and 'brains' (46) are our only two *verbal* keys to the central mystery.

'Spark' is a word of some authority. Byron was fond of it. *The Curse of Minerva* (165) contains a caustic comment on a man 'without one spark of intellectual fire'; in *Manfred*, the 'mind', 'spirit', or 'Promethean spark' in man can challenge the elements (I. i. 154); in *Don Juan* the 'mind' is 'a fiery particle' (XI. 60); and revolutionary ardour is a 'spark' (*Journal*, 9 January 1821; *LJ*, V. 163). Related examples are given in my *Lord Byron: Christian Virtues* (170, 177, 241, 243-5) and in *Byron and Shakespeare* (272-8). In Byron the word is a nucleus for a cluster of valuable associations which can be regarded as summed up in Browning's 'finish'd and finite clods, untroubled by a spark', in 'Rabbi Ben Ezra'. The word has esoteric authority as the divine spark in man, the Sanskrit *atman*. It is a faculty, or power, lodged within and awaiting development, to be fanned into a blaze of total illumination. Arnold's use of 'fall' in 'waiting for the spark from Heaven to fall' (120) may, I think, be criticized: he appears to have forced together conceptions deriving respectively from the *atman* and Christian orthodoxy. The Scholar is surely waiting for the spark to be awakened rather than to fall. But we must not call the word 'spark' itself a vague or ill-defined image, since it has an honourable pedigree. It is just because it has precise traditional connotations that we are aware of a discrepancy in 'fall'. There may even be a point in the discrepancy, since it serves as a symptom, or symbol, of the poem's total meaning, which strives, as its title *The Scholar Gipsy* as good as tells us, towards a fusion of two traditions, western and eastern.[1]

The main emphasis is on this very striving. Both the Scholar himself and the culture with which the poet contrasts him are shown as *awaiting* the revelation. But there is a distinction. He is contrasted with those

> Whose insight never has borne fruit in deeds,
> Whose vague resolves never have been fulfill'd. . . .
>
> (174)

This stanza suggests throughout a state of not-being, false starts, and continual disappointment, in a retrogressive and retrospective existence without purpose, recalling Macbeth's 'all our yesterdays. . .'. As a type and an exemplar of this existence we are shown one occupying our 'intellectual throne' who can do no better than recount for our dubious benefit 'all his store of sad experience', his 'wretched days', 'misery's birth', and 'how the

---

[1] Since writing this I have been told by Mr. Simon Caradoc Evans that mystics do sometimes refer to a falling light.

dying spark of hope was fed' (181-90). In him the essentially backward, devitalized, 'realistic', thinking of the contemporary intellect is personified. The state indicated is unhealthy, nerveless, and guilty of self-pity.

In contrast, the Scholar is forward-searching: his very being is creatively pointed. We, it is said, 'wait like thee, but not, like thee, in hope' (170); and again, 'none has hope like thine' (196). He is 'nursing' his 'project in unclouded joy', with no doubts (199). In religious phraseology, he has faith. But his faith is less intellectual than instinctive, an 'impulse', and this impulse is freedom, and pushes forward:

> Still nursing the unconquerable hope,
> Still clutching the inviolable shade,
>   With a *free onward impulse* brushing through,
> By night, the silver'd branches of the glade. . . .
>
> (211)

Because he possesses uncontaminated this expectance, his very being is orientated forward. This is the difference between his waiting and ours.

Such is the challenge which our poem levels against the intellectual and spiritual confusions of the 'light half-believers' and 'casual creeds' (172) of Arnold's day. The challenge is precise enough, since there clearly exist areas of wisdom and faculties of the mind neither tapped nor respected by the western tradition.

That tradition is symbolized by the Shepherds with whom the poem opens. These, though to be grouped with the 'smock-frock'd boors' (59) among those who see the Scholar, are also to be understood as an adverse party – we may recall that the Scholar is repelled by the 'drink and clatter' (61) of the inn – within the strict forms of the pastoral, and originally Greek, convention. Pastoral can carry a number of meanings, personal, poetic, academic, and religious. In *Lycidas* pastoral phrases ('drove a field', 'battening our flocks') apply to Milton and King studying at Cambridge; in 'the hungry sheep look up and are not fed' the implications are religious; and the river Camus and St. Peter appear together. When in *The Scholar Gipsy* the Shepherd is told not to 'leave thy wistful flock unfed' (3) we think inevitably of Milton, but the reference is here rather academic than religious.[1]

---

[1] The identification of this Shepherd with Clough (Tinker and Lowry, 209) need not conflict with my reading.

The Scholar Gipsy

Our first two stanzas acknowledge the rights of the established tradition *by day*, but *at nightfall*, when the 'fields are still', and men and dogs 'gone to rest' (6-7), we as 'shepherds' are to renew the other, more mystic and mysterious, quest (10). The distinction is important and applies throughout. The shepherds are creatures of day and nature cultivated; the Scholar, though in the past associated with 'the sparkling Thames' (202), is now mainly a creature of night, and of wild nature.

The quest (i.e. to find the Scholar) is to be undertaken by night, when the 'green' is 'moon-blanch'd' (9). The Scholar himself is seen 'on summer nights' crossing the Thames (73); his eyes rest 'on the moonlit stream' (80); he roams through 'the darkening fields' (84); and looks down on 'the line of festal light' in Christ Church (129). Children see him gazing on the flocks by day, and going off 'when the stars come out' (109); he is one to 'brush' through, 'by night, the silver'd branches of the glade' (214) and listen in woodland depths to the nightingales (220). The association is carried on into the corresponding figures of our similes; he is urged to 'plunge deeper in the bowering wood' like Dido among the shades of Hades (207-10); the Tyrian ship holds on its course by day 'and night' (243); and the 'dark Iberians' come down from 'cloudy cliffs' (248). The Scholar's eyes were 'dark' (99). When light and the Scholar draw close, it is at an 'abandon'd' spot 'where black-wing'd swallows haunt the glittering Thames' (94).[1]

On the other side we have the weighty harvest, noon, and sun impressions of our first stanzas; and, since the poem is mainly about the Scholar, there is nothing more to record until the Greek ship's 'emerging prow' seen at 'sunrise' (233). Nature is here civilized. We open with 'distant cries of reapers in the corn' (19), and, though there are wild flowers in the third stanza, they are 'scarlet poppies' that 'peep' through the 'thick corn', convolvulus creeping 'round green roots and yellowing stalks', and 'lindens' that '*bower*' the poet comfortably from the sun (23-9). Nature is either directly cultivated, or, in its general effect, civilized, humanized. The flocks are part of man's civilization, as are the 'feeding kine' later (108). The Grecian coaster of the concluding simile emerges from '*cool*-hair'd creepers' (234) that recall the

---

1 'Haunt': migrating swallows seeking 'spring' are compared by Dryden with the soul 'packing up' at death (*The Conquest of Granada*, 2; iv. ii); and see *The Starlit Dome*, 301, on Keats's *Ode to Autumn*.

'tendrils' and shady 'air-swept lindens' earlier (25-6), and is freighted with grapes, wine, figs, and tunnies (238-9). Here, as in our pastoral opening, there is material abundance; but it is never quite satisfying. There is something enervate and oppressive about the heat, 'scent', and 'perfum'd showers' (27) of our early stanzas. We have noise in 'nor let thy bawling fellows rack their throats' (4), the bleating of sheep and cries of reapers (18-19), a noisy and tiring activity like the 'drink and clatter' of the inn (61), and the 'sick hurry' of our contemporary civilization so emphatic later (204); or, in gentler phrase, 'all the live murmur of a summer's day' (20). The noon sun is a burning weight (29). So the poet craves relaxation, and takes up, for relief, the Scholar's story (32).

The pastoral poetry and the Greeks, with sun and cultivated nature, fall on one side; and on the other, we have the Scholar, the Gipsies, Dido, and the Tyrian trader, at home with the shadows of night-time or the under-world, and with nature wild and untrimmed.

The Gipsies are themselves called a 'wild brotherhood' (38). The Scholar himself haunts the 'green-muffled Cumner hills' (69), pointing on to the dark Iberians descending from their 'cloudy cliffs' (248); he gathers wild woodland flowers (78, 86-9); is seen at a waste spot, near 'breezy grass', sitting on an 'o'er-grown' bank (93, 97); is so much part of the forest that the feeding blackbird is not disturbed by his passing (116); battles with the snow on the heights (124); was perhaps buried under flowering nettles (139); plunges deep in the woods, and brushes through them by night (207, 213-14). He is a creature of solitude (210), withdrawn from, but *watching*, the doings of man. He is said to 'watch' (i) the 'threshers' and 'feeding kine' (103-8), and (ii) 'the line of festal light in Christ-Church hall' (128-9); and these twin interests help further to establish the identity of pastoral and education. He watches like a presiding, perhaps even a guardian, spirit.

Our images of wild nature attain their climax in the Tyrian trader fleeing across the 'blue', and safe, Mediterranean, past 'soft' Sicily, out to 'where the Atlantic raves'[1] (244-6). Nature's darkness, cold, or violence hold no terrors for Scholar or Tyrian. The Grecian ship, we may remember, was called a 'coaster' (237); it remains close to the safe boundaries of earth. But the Tyrian is at home on the deeps and with the infinite. Both Scholar and

---

[1] The relevance of this image is appreciated by Louis Bonnerot (473).

The Scholar Gipsy

Tyrian may, however, be afraid, or 'shy' (70, 79), of human contacts, except with those who deeply want, and have some right to possess, what they have to offer, as when the Scholar gives the maidens of Maytime piety his flowers (82-90), or the Tyrian finds a market for his wares among the 'shy' (249) Iberians. The Scholar himself may be supposed to fear especially the shepherds, whom he occasionally meets (57), but avoids, and who are always trying to catch him:

> And I myself seem half to know thy looks,
>   And put the shepherds, Wanderer, on thy trace.
>
>   (62)

He is that for which our schools of learning are always searching; which, indeed, they exist, precisely, to discover; to which the poet, who is himself 'half' – but only 'half' – in the Scholar's world, would direct them; but which has always found, though perhaps it need not continue to find, its chief enemy in the established schools.

Arnold's poem confronts our western tradition with suggestions of a wisdom, lore, or magic of oriental affinities or origin. The intellectual legacy of ancient Greece has clamped down with too exclusive a domination, too burning a weight of consciousness, or intellect; and the practical genius of Rome has reinforced it in the field of public affairs. Our consciousness has become, to use Nietzsche's terms, too purely 'Apollonian', too heated, and needs fertilization again from the cool depths of the 'Dionysian', the more darkly feminine, and eastern, powers. Both *The Scholar Gipsy* and *The Birth of Tragedy* see our contemporary culture as too purely academic, a new Alexandrianism; materially fecund, but spiritually static, infertile, and dead. Such a criticism is not new. The mind-structure of Europe has had need, again and again, of fertilization from the older, and deeper, wisdom. So the Olympian hierarchy was challenged by the cult of Dionysus; so the developing stream of classical culture was saved, modified, and reinforced by Christianity; so Medieval religion was challenged by Faust and by Renaissance poetry which, though it owes much to Greece, contains deep-bedded in it a mass of wisdom from the esoteric cults, and the East. But this is a process we are still within, and of which *The Scholar Gipsy* itself is part.

The wisdom is old, and nature-rooted; and yet it is the young rather than the old who understand it. True, the Greeks were 'the young, light-hearted Masters of the waves' (241); but here 'young' drives home rather their function as the youth of a long story, with youthful confidence, and over-confidence; and we all know what has become of its maturity. The Scholar's youth is different: based on an age-old wisdom, it is yet a 'perennial youth' (229), knowing nothing of maturity. Such is the spirit of wonder and devotion nurturing the divine spark, or *atman*, which shall eventually kindle the mind of man into powers beyond our imagining. Therefore, though a 'truant' from learning, he is that learning's sole justification and final hope, as indeed the questing shepherds realize; since, in so far as academic studies become blind to the central powers, they are dead. That is why the Scholar, who rejects Oxford, becomes, through that very act of dissatisfaction and further seeking, its guardian deity.

The Scholar Gipsy is a perfect example of the way in which such elusive truths as it handles should be projected through a poetic organization. They may, indeed, be truths beyond the personal thinking of the poet himself, and I leave it to others to discuss their relation to the rest of Arnold's work.[1] But all such investigations would be no more than ancillary: the poem is what it is, and says what it says, independently of external corroboration. Its true nature and meaning can only be apprehended by attention to its various effects in mutual, and spatial, interaction; and from such an approach we gain insight into the poetry's, which is not necessarily the poet's, wisdom.

[1] Materials for such a discussion may be found in the studies already cited, together with Lionel Trilling's *Matthew Arnold* (London and New York, 1939). See also J. G. Curgenven, '*The Scholar Gipsy* etc.', *Litera* (Istanbul), III. 1956; 1-13 (he has other articles on Arnold in Vols. II, IV and V); also V. S. Seturaman, '*The Scholar Gipsy* and Oriental Wisdom', R.E.S. New Series, IX. 36; November 1958.

CHAPTER VIII

Poetry and the Arts:
Tennyson, Browning, O'Shaughnessy, Yeats

Essays and Studies, The English Association, 1969.

LITERARY ART, SAID Joseph Conrad in his preface to *The Nigger of the Narcissus*, 'must strenuously aspire to the plasticity of sculpture, to the colour of painting, and to the magic suggestions of music'. In epic, drama, and novel, human affairs and energies are given design and rhythm; in lyric, personal emotions are expressed by song, melody and rhyme. Sometimes poetry of weight deliberately takes the other arts as its subject, often in contrast with nature, and in so doing makes valuable commentaries on them, on itself, and on the meanings of existence. Whether in literature or in life it will be found that the separation of the spatial and the temporal, of sight and sound, is provisional only, and often dangerous, whereas the aim must always be a fusion. Life exists in space-time, and space-time may be equated with eternity (p. 41 above). Symbols of eternity must have conviction and weight; but if too heavily used, or too rigidly demarked from organic life, they lose authority.

In writing of Milton's style in my recent *Poets of Action* (in an essay originally published in *The Burning Oracle*), I showed how his attempt to impose eternal significances on his material by too heavy a stress on solidifications, too insistent a reliance on design and artefact, could, except when a supreme event was being treated, become constricting. In my *Laureate of Peace* the exquisitely handled spatial arts of Pope's *Temple of Fame* were contrasted with the more directly human concern of his other poetry. *The Starlit Dome* explored the pervasive use throughout the Romantics of domes and other architectural, usually sacred, structures in balance with nature; it found 'Kubla Khan' to be a key-poem and Keats's peculiar excellence to be a perfect fusion, moment by moment, of the fluid and the solid, of nature and art.[1] In Wordsworth's later poetry the use of architecture is excessive; and indeed the dome-symbol itself may, if used with too recurring a facility, constitute a temptation and a danger.[2]

Both Tennyson and Browning have left us interesting critiques of what Nietzsche called the 'Apollonian' arts of spatial design. In them they suspect, as he did, the will to tidy up and control the disconcerting mysteries and energies of existence; and certainly, when poetry relies on them, the eternity symbolized may be too easily depicted; may be, as it were, claimed without having been properly recreated. Such symbols lure the poet from the far more arduous task of creating *structure* and *form* from the complications and turmoils of human existence, while offering instead a too-easy insight parasitic on another art.

This is the theme of Tennyson's 'The Palace of Art' (1832; later amplified). The poet makes for himself 'a lordly pleasure-house' set high on rock, with wonderful lawns and artefacts of all sorts; active fountains, cloisters 'branch'd like mighty woods', windows that burned with 'slow-flaming crimson fires', each room carefully devised 'from living Nature'. There are numerous pictures on tapestry showing various actions: the hunter with 'puff'd cheek' blowing his horn, a roaring sea which you can almost hear, reapers at their labour, a smiling Virgin with her Child, St. Cecily in sleep over-watched by an angel, Houris awaiting 'the dying Islamite', Arthur asleep in Avalon,

> Or hollowing one hand against his ear,
>   To list a foot-fall, ere he saw
> The wood-nymph, stay'd the Ausonian king to hear
>   Of wisdom and of law.

---

[1] For a valuable recent discussion of Keats's peculiar excellences see also John Jones, *John Keats's Dream of Truth*, 1969.

[2] Byron's use of the spatial arts is entangled in his prevailing humanism and sense of energies. See my *Byron and Shakespeare*, 48-50; and my discussion throughout of *Don Juan* in *Poets of Action*.

There is music too, great bells which 'moved of themselves, with silver sound', and portraits of great poets, Milton, Shakespeare, Dante, Homer. The floor is a mosaic illustrating 'cycles of the human tale'. The arches 'lift' up the ceiling – it is all, as in Pope's *The Temple of Fame, living* – and it seems that angels rise and descend from on high, bringing and taking gifts. Outside there is statuary:

> And high on every peak a statue seem'd
> To hang on tip-toe, tossing up
> A cloud of incense of all odour steam'd
> From out a golden cup.

In this elevated retreat the poet's soul sings, accompanied by the great and wise of all ages and enjoying a god-like isolation.

Though our description emphasizes at every point the living and moving qualities of the designs, yet the retreat is parasitic on the visual arts or antecedent works of great poetry. It represents an Apollonian contemplation and contentment with no engagement of the Dionysian, the basic energies, nor any relation to society. We are next shown how this severance from human-kind, regarded by the supercilious poet as beasts, cannot for long satisfy 'the abysmal deeps of Personality'. Ghosts, nightmares, uttermost melancholia and neurosis assail and torment him; and we are made by a succession of poignant stanzas to feel that such a retreat is suicidal. This recognized, the solution is simple: to descend again to mankind, and will to lift them to the palace.

The poem is important not only as a key to Tennyson's later work, but as marking a necessary choice, a diverging of the ways, to be faced by all poets; indeed by all men. Not only poetry, but life itself, can be discussed in these terms.

In his *Allegory of Love* (1936; VII. iii) C. S. Lewis contrasted Spenser's Bower of Bliss with his Garden of Adonis; the one a place of enervate sensuousness and metal artistry, the other of movement, dance, and creation. Such are the dangers of relaxation; at its worst, the sluggard self-enjoyment of Tennyson's Lotus Eaters; at its best, what Nietzsche calls the 'pure' or 'will-less' contemplation of Apollonian pictures (*The Birth of Tragedy*, V, XXII); art-for-art's sake; idolatry. Above all, there is the danger of failing to live, or write, from the vital, human, centres; the denial of nature's, which are, as Pope tells us, the divine, energies.

No one believed in those energies more firmly than Browning, who ranks high among our poetic humanists. No poet had more right than he to name a volume *Men and Women*. He offers exactly what the Romantics, apart from Byron, lacked, while lacking what they offer. Browning gives us humanity with comparatively little emphasis on either nature, except for fire and the heavenly bodies,[1] or on the transcendent, except in so far as it can be felt to flower from human instincts, passions and purposes. His human projection is nevertheless one of abundant resource and interest. The emphasis is equally physical and spiritual, specifically concentrating on a just balance, as when in 'Rabbi Ben Ezra' (1864) he sees man in his temporal existence as a 'cup' being moulded by the Potter's artistry into a 'whole' of which age is as important a constituent as the physical 'rose-mesh' of youth. Life in time is creating an entity, a completed solid, made for use in another dimension:

> Look not thou down but up!
> To uses of a cup,
> The festal board, lamp's flash and trumpet's peal,
> The new wine's foaming flow,
> The Master's lips a-glow!
> Thou, Heaven's consummate cup, what need'st thou
> with earth's wheel?

Perhaps in no other poem do we see more clearly how well the super-temporal may be approached in terms of plastic art, provided always that distinctions are not too rigid and vitality be preserved. The 'clay' here is bodily life; the Potter's wheel 'spins fast', impressing a still circularity on temporal motion; the whole cup, from birth to death, is made; then, and only then, is its purpose realized, in festal splendour.

Two of Browning's dramatic monologues concerning painters are peculiarly revealing. In 'Andrea del Sarto' (1855) we have a painter of assured technique who nevertheless knows that he has never properly expressed that urgent inner life that is the 'soul'. His work is perfected, but static, and lesser artists have more of the real thing:

> There burns a truer light of God in them,
> In their vexed beating stuffed and stopped-up brain,
> Heart, or whate'er else, than goes on to prompt
> This low-pulsed forthright craftsman's hand of mine . . .

[1] See C. Willard Smith, *Browning's Star-Imagery*, Princeton U.S.A., 1941.

246

His art, as art, may be higher than theirs; but, by reason of its very perfection, because his 'reach' does not exceed his 'grasp', he, as a man, is not orientated towards the reality of 'heaven'. In our other monologue 'Fra Lippo Lippi' (1855), we meet an artist who, urged to paint pictures that incite men to devotion rather than any interest in the human form, defends the rights of the body while insisting that the spiritual will be only of value if flowering from the physical. We can feel Browning fighting for physical reality and vitality as against a premature spiritualizing of the human. The two monologues make a single emphasis.

Browning emphasizes the value of effort, of striving, of the indomitable will to accomplish more than is possible. From the vital centres alone, as Pope too insists, can any real virtue, in art or life, blossom. 'The Statue and the Bust' (1855) is accordingly a central poem.

The Great-Duke Ferdinand loves a lady prisoned in a palace at Florence and married to a stern man; and she returns his love. Both plan to elope, but, Hamlet-like, they put off the action day by day:

> But next day passed, and next day yet,
> With still fresh cause to wait one day more
> Ere each leaped over the parapet . . .

Originally the Duke had planned to win his 'cup of bliss', whatever its cost 'to body or soul'; but worldly wisdom intrudes, for, after all, 'the world and its ways have a certain worth'. Day by day the Duke rides through the square and sees his lady at the window; and she returns his glance; and that is all. But at last the lovers begin to age, and so the lady asks her attendants to summon a skilful sculptor

> Who fashions the clay no love will change,
> And fixes a beauty never to fade.

She has her bust set in the window to perpetuate her love 'waiting as ever, mute the while'. After death, it will, ironically, prove a solace, since

> I did no more while my heart was warm
> Than does that image, my pale-faced friend.

Similarly, the Duke has his statue placed in the square, done on horseback to the life, 'as the crafty sculptor can', 'brave in bronze'.

Their romance is thus perpetuated; and in their remaining content with such a perpetuation lies their condemnation.

Life has passed them by. True, the proposed act was a sin, but the poet explicitly asserts that his statement exists below, or above, moral distinctions:

> I hear you reproach, 'But delay was best,
> For their end was a crime' – Oh, a crime will do
> As well, I reply, to serve for a test.

The doctrine is a doctrine of perpetual striving:

> Let a man contend to the uttermost
> For his life's set prize, be it what it will!

If virtue be the argument, what virtue *is* virtue without such striving, such inner energy, as the prerequisite? Such was the virtue of the 'soldier-saints' who 'burn upward each to his point of bliss'; and such virtue the parable negatively defines. It is interesting to observe how the rejection of life and its opportunities is here related to the extreme Apollonianism – in Nietzsche's terms – of sculpture. We may recall the different reference of Hamlet's not dissimilar problem to the more dynamic art of acting: 'Is it not monstrous that this player here . . .' (*Hamlet*, II. ii. 585).

Browning knows well enough the excellences of painting, and in *Pippa Passes* (1841) he has given us a remarkable passage on the way a sculptor fashions his various materials, bringing out their dormant potentialities:

> To see, throughout all nature, varied stuff
> For better nature's birth by means of art.

(II)

But he can nevertheless emphasize the inadequacy not only of any art, but of all the arts together.

The thought is developed in 'Cleon' (1855), an epistle from the poet and artist, Cleon, to a king, Protus. Cleon is a practitioner in various arts and a connoisseur of them all: poetry, song, sculpture, painting, music and philosophy. He is one in whom all the best of Hellenic paganism appears to be consummated. Rationally, he has reason for pride. He claims for himself no supreme excellence, but,

great as were the supreme artists of the past individually, there is,
he argues, no point in emulating them, in doing again what they
have done. What one can do is to possess the whole, to *be* the man
for which all art exists, the perfect recipient:

> I have not chanted verse like Homer, no –
> Nor swept string like Terpander, no – nor carved
> And painted men like Phidias and his friend:
> I am not great as they are, point by point.
> But I have entered into sympathy
> With these four, running these into one soul.
> Who, separate, ignored each other's art.
> Say, is it nothing that I know them all?

He is a man of superb Apollonian accomplishment; he is more
than a temporal king, since his mind surveys and possesses all
things, rather like Tennyson's poet in 'The Palace of Art'. Besides,
his own practice in the various arts has attained considerable
success. If there is any supreme purpose or meaning in art, he
ought, certainly, to be a high type of being, one who has built *all*
the arts into himself and so reached 'the very crown and proper
end of life'. And yet, what of death? The King to whom Cleon is
writing will, it is true, have nothing better than a 'brazen statue'
to commemorate him. But can the artist claim more? What is art
in a context of death? These constant references to sculpture
underline the far-reaching implications of the statue-coming-to-
life in *The Winter's Tale*: 'What fine chisel could ever yet cut
breath?' (V. iii. 78).

Cleon feels himself utterly ineffectual. He has imitated life,
understood life, but not lived it; and even if his works persist,
that gives him as a man no immortality. Art is not *being*:

> Because in my great epos I display
> How divers men young, strong, fair, wise, can act –
> Is this as though I acted? if I paint,
> Carve the young Phoebus, am I therefore young?

Though growing old, yet every day his 'sense of joy' becomes
'more acute'; his soul is 'intensified by power and insight', 'more
enlarged' and 'keen'; and yet he is failing in body. Has God no
more to offer? No word from above regarding *another stage* of
being?

I dare at times imagine to my need
Some future state revealed to us by Zeus,
Unlimited in capability
For joy, as this is in desire for joy,
– To seek which, the joy-hunger forces us:
That, stung by straitness of our life, made strait
On purpose to make prized the life at large –
Freed by the throbbing impulse we call death,
We burst there as the worm into the fly,
Who, while a worm still, wants his wings. But no!
Zeus has not yet revealed it; and alas,
He must have done so, were it possible!

Cleon concludes his epistle by replying to a request by Protus that
he should forward a letter to one 'Paulus'. Cleon admits having
heard of him and his preaching concerning 'Christus'. But surely
no wisdom can be expected from a 'barbarian Jew'. He has heard
accounts of Paulus' followers:

And (as I gathered from a bystander)
Their doctrine could be held by no sane man.

The ironic conclusion is exquisite, and pregnant. It might be
related to the advent of Spiritualism in our own century.

We must notice: (i) the valuable thought of *all* the arts, with
their corresponding senses and perceptions, together accomplish-
ing what none alone or in separation could do; (ii) the implied
inadequacy of artistic enjoyment or practice to meet the human
problem; (iii) the demand of the soul to live beyond old age; and
(iv) the impinging of Christianity on the ineffectuality of Hellenic
paganism, coming as, in Nietzsche's terms, an influx of the
Dionysian on an effete Apollonian culture. We may remember
Arnold's attribution of action to Hebraism and thought to
Hellenism, in *Culture and Anarchy*. We may suppose that the real
incarnation of art in its totality would indeed give us a superman;
would somehow correspond to the resurrection from the statue
in *The Winter's Tale*. We should note, too, that what we hear
through trance-mediumship of conditions on higher planes
beyond death suggests that we shall there enjoy a totality of
sense-perception unlimited to the body's separate inlets, which are
at death broken to make possible a greater, sense-summing,
experience; no longer, as Marvell has it in his 'Dialogue between

the Soul and the Body', 'blinded with an eye' and 'deaf with the drumming of an ear'. But intimations of any such richer stages of being can only mature from a deeper, more Hebraic or Dionysian, experience than Cleon has achieved. With Nietzsche the Dionysian, conceived as the *alpha* and *omega* of creation, is equated with music; and it is significant that the only art that Browning unconditionally honours as the voice of the eternal, the resolver of antinomies and healer of mortality, is the music of 'Abt Vogler'; and even so, it seems that one must live, be identified with, the music, both compose and perform it *ex tempore*; not merely listen, or write it down. One must *be* the music. We turn next to this central poem.

There is a recurring poetic association of music with sacred or numinous architectures. On its most obvious level we have Milton's 'Il Penseroso':

> But let my due feet never fail
> To walk the studious cloister's pale,
> And love the high embowed roof,
> With antique pillars massy proof,
> And storied windows richly dight,
> Casting a dim religious light.
> There let the pealing organ blow
> To the full voic'd choir below,
> In service high and anthems clear,
> As may with sweetness, through mine ear,
> Dissolve me into ecstasies,
> And bring all Heaven before mine eyes.

That is simple enough. But more often the music is the creative, Dionysian, source, aspiring to structure, and therefore, at the limit, as we find in Eliot's *Four Quartets* ('Burnt Norton', V), to stillness, or silence. We may recall the palace built by organ music in *Paradise Lost* (I. 705-32); the music-built palace of *Lamia*; and the dome which the poet wishes to build 'in air' by the aid of 'music loud and long' recaptured from the Abyssinian maid's song-symphony, in 'Kubla Khan'. We may assert a poetic equivalence between sacred, or otherwise mystical, or numinous, architectures and music; both distend intellect beyond its capacities, or to their limit, as in Byron's stanzas on St. Peter's, 'all musical in its immensities' (*Childe Harold*, IV. 156). Byron was fascinated by Schelling's description of architecture as 'frozen music' (*Journal*, 17 November 1813; *LJ*, II. 326).

So much may be said in introduction to Browning's 'Abt Vogler' (1864), wherein for once an art is allowed by the poet to measure up to and even to out-distance those eternally valid and indomitable energies that to him are the inmost stuff of human nature.

Abt Vogler is an organist who describes his art as a palace-building art recalling the magic powers of Solomon to enlist both 'angels' *and* 'demons' to 'pile him a palace straight' for his loved one. So, too, is his own 'beautiful building' made of music:

Would it might tarry like his, the beautiful building of mine,
    This which my keys in a crowd pressed and importuned to raise!
Ah, one and all, how they helped, would dispart now and now
    combine,
    Zealous to hasten the work, heighten their master his praise!
And one would bury his brow with a blind plunge down to hell,
    Burrow a while and build, broad on the roots of things,
Then up again swim into sight, having based me my palace well,
    Founded it, fearless of flame, flat on the nether springs.

And another would mount and march, like the excellent minion he
    was,
    Ay, another and yet another, one crowd but with many a crest,
Raising my rampired walls of gold as transparent as glass,
    Eager to do and die, yield each his place to the rest:
For higher still and higher (as a runner tips with fire,
    When a great illumination surprises a festal night –
Outlining round and round Rome's dome from space to spire)
    Up, the pinnacled glory reached, and the pride of my soul was in
    sight.

The conception makes of music a concrete reality that directly meets Rudolf Steiner's concept of sound as carving out etheric solids. We are, in so far as we take the metaphor seriously – and all good metaphors should be taken seriously (p. 285 below) – beyond all rational categories and plunged into possibilities outspacing normal perceptions. Music is regarded, as it was by Schopenhauer and Nietzsche, as the creative origin. It is here more than an art; it is a living act of the soul, since Abt Vogler is not merely composing, but simultaneously performing, and therefore in a unique sense *living*, the music. The transcendence is realized 'all through music and me'; the inmost 'I' of the creator is, as with Pope's Pindar in *The Temple of Fame*, who is shown as *melting* into his music, engaged; there is an identification, corresponding to Eliot's 'you are the music, while the music lasts' (*Four Quartets*, 'The Dry Salvages', V).

As for painting, it is, says Abt Vogler, static, a thing, as Nietzsche tells us, of calm Apollonian contemplation merely; it just stands – though logic would demand that Abt Vogler should sound also into the painter's experience in composition, which may have been as vivid as his own – to be looked at. All he observes is that its 'process', presumably when completed, is not so 'wonder-worth'; not, that is, part of the wonder. As for poetry, where there certainly *is* a process, yet you can apply reason to it and understand its laws. Music is beyond all that:

> But here is the finger of God, a flash of the will that can,
> Existent behind all laws . . .

'The will' is here used as Nietzsche and Schopenhauer use it to denote the central divine, or cosmic, purpose. Even though the palace *seems* to dissolve, the faith is next transferred to God as the source and therefore presumably the ratifier of the experience. The music-palace has revealed, or created, the eternal stuff which somehow knows no transience and assures us that 'there shall never be one lost good'. What is incomplete here is with God completed:

> On the earth the broken arcs; in the heaven, a perfect round.

Every good longing is there found existing 'not its semblance, but itself', eternity affirming 'the conception of an hour'. Especially, all the failings, the impossibilities, the *thwarted* things, the tragedies of life, are 'music sent up to God'; so

> Enough that he heard it once: we shall hear it by and by.

Failure is earnest of triumph; the paradox within all tragedy is, as with Nietzsche, resolved in terms of music:

> The rest may reason and welcome: 'tis we musicians know.[1]

---

[1] Beside the views of music expressed by Nietzsche and Browning, we may set a passage from *The Testament of Beauty* (II. 825-39), where it is observed that animals can respond to music, but not to pictures, or to their own reflections. The visual arts depend on mental development. See p. 60 above, on Sherlock Holmes.

The eternity-symbols of 'Abt Vogler' should be compared with the remarkable passage in 'An Epistle containing the strange medical experience of Karshish, the Arab physician' (1855), wherein Lazarus is imagined, after the experience of the richer existence beyond death, as suffering from his forced return to the 'thread' of earthly life, of time,

> Which runs across some vast distracting orb
> Of glory on either side that meagre thread,
> Which, conscious of, he must not enter yet. . . .

All normal valuations, based as they are on considerations of time, are now to Lazarus meaningless. To him 'right and wrong' exist 'across, and not along', that is, at right angles to, 'this black thread through the blaze'. Such intuitions form the living core of Browning's work.[1]

In discussion of these clustering symbolisms we are near the heart of poetry. Alone of the arts poetry sums all the rest; in it sound and image, thought and sight, are fused. Rhythm and music project it, with all its weighty substances, into activity, according to the scheme defined in Nietzsche's *Birth of Tragedy*. We may feel, at choice moments, that all human and other creations are as architecture, musically, and so spiritually based, as in that gem of Tennyson's 'Tithonus' (1833):

> Like that strange song I heard Apollo sing,
> While Ilion like a mist rose into towers.

It is not surprising that a minor poet such as Arthur O'Shaughnessy should, in handling such symbols, have been raised above his normal level. In lines entitled 'Ode' (1874) he is writing of poets:

> We are the music-makers,
>   And we are the dreamers of dreams,
> Wandering by lone sea-breakers,
>   And sitting by desolate streams;
> World-losers and world-forsakers,
>   On whom the pale moon gleams:
> Yet we are the movers and shakers
>   Of the world for ever, it seems.

---

[1] I have been concentrating on symbolic projections. For Browning's more general thoughts on mysticism and immortality, see F. R. G. Duckworth, *Browning: background and conflict*, 1931; also Dallas Kenmare, *Ever a Fighter*, 1952.

With wonderful deathless ditties
We build up the world's great cities,
    And out of a fabulous story
    We fashion an empire's glory:
One man with a dream, at pleasure,
    Shall go forth and conquer a crown;
And three with a new song's measure
    Can trample a kingdom down.

We, in the ages lying
    In the buried past of the earth,
Built Nineveh with our sighing,
    And Babel itself in our mirth;
And o'erthrew them with prophesying
    To the old of the new world's worth;
For each age is a dream that is dying,
    Or one that is coming to birth.

These three stanzas, sometimes printed as here, alone, make a compact unit. The poet's expanded version, which runs to a number of stanzas, seems weaker. There appears to be both danger and safety in such basic symbolisms: it is when O'Shaughnessy leaves them that authenticity sags.

So it was, too, in my opinion, with his more famous compatriot, W. B. Yeats, whose two outstanding poems, 'Sailing to Byzantium' (1928) and 'Byzantium' (1933), are both compacted, as his other work is not, of strong symbolisms forcing on us the opposition of art and nature, the static and the dynamic, in significant interplay.[1] Both poems are weighty and colourful creations. Byzantium brings its famous historic and sacred associations to act on us as did Samarkand in Flecker's *Hassan*; or, rather differently, Kubla Khan in Coleridge's poem. In each a sharply located historic magnificence lends definition and detonation to a poetic universal. Byzantium and Samarkand are the more poetically valuable in that as sacred cities both, and Byzantium especially, suggest a blend of the secular and the sacred.

'Sailing to Byzantium' presents its terms in stark opposition.

---

[1] My present interpretations expand the brief accounts given at the conclusion to *The Starlit Dome* in 1941. I follow my usual method of direct interpretation without regard to sources. For these see A. Norman Jeffares, *W. B. Yeats, Man and Poet*, 1949, Index, 'Byzantium'.

The poet, like Browning's Cleon, is growing old, and like him he endures a painful discrepancy between ageing body and lively soul. Like Browning's Rabbi Ben Ezra, he demands that the soul should rejoice as the body wanes, and accordingly plants his hopes in 'monuments of unageing intellect', monuments of its, the soul's, 'own magnificence'; that is, works of art, intellectually and, if only by metaphor, plastically conceived. So he prays to the

> ... sages standing in God's holy fire
> As in the gold mosaic of a wall

to be his masters and rescue him from the natural order; from the young 'in one another's arms', the 'dying generations' of birds, and the teeming fishes of river and sea, 'fish, flesh or fowl', 'whatever is begotten, born and dies'. The 'sensual music' of physical life – music, by an interesting transposition, here accompanying the biological – is set in contrast to a metallic symbolism:

> Once out of nature I shall never take
> My bodily form from any natural thing,
> But such a form as Grecian goldsmiths make
> Of hammered gold and gold enamelling
> To keep a drowsy Emperor awake;
> Or set upon a golden bough to sing
> To lords and ladies of Byzantium
> Of what is past, or passing, or to come.

The metal bird both corresponds to the soul-body, in some eastern cults called the 'diamond' body, of the spirit after death, and symbolizes an all-seeing eternity. The bird itself is a sheer artefact, but then Byzantium is here chosen to symbolize the soul's refuge precisely because of the metallic, stiff, other-worldly, yet rich, qualities of its especially sacred art: 'gold mosaic' is a typifying phrase. In contrast, we have summer, 'all summer long', sensuality and almost violent biological fecundity. The opposition is stark. The heart, 'fastened to a dying animal', and yet, like Cleon, 'sick with desire', can only cry to be gathered 'into the artifice of eternity'. 'Artifice' is a deliberately cold word, balancing the insult of 'animal'.

The second, and more complex, poem, 'Byzantium', presents a similar contrast, though with a more satisfying fusion. We are in the Emperor's palace. The 'unpurged images of day' give place to the purity of darkness; the 'drunken soldiery', now 'abed,' establish a contrast of riotous life and sequent quietude. We pass through the singing of 'night-walkers'and the numinous summons of the 'great cathedral gong' to

> A starlit or a moonlit dome disdains
> All that man is,
> All mere complexities,
> The fury and the mire of human veins.

Through night and eternity-symbols we pass next to intuition of an 'image', human yet a 'shade'; more 'shade', that is spiritual, 'than man', and yet fully concrete and so 'more image than a shade'. We are in the world of death, unwinding the 'mummy-cloth' which is also the unwinding of the 'winding' maze-path into 'Hades'.[1]

This being's 'mouth', having neither 'moisture' nor 'breath', can 'summon' the 'breathless mouths' of the dead to itself. The poet is aware of some more than human, but not inhuman, presence:

> I hail the superhuman;
> I call it death-in-life and life-in-death.

The poem has moved from an earthly Emperor's palace by night to a sense of a life in, or beyond, death.

We are again introduced to a golden bird, now felt as neither 'bird' nor 'handiwork', but as a 'miracle'; on a 'star-lit golden bough', compared to the 'cocks of Hades', and angry at the moon with its changes, and reminders perhaps of the sun, preferring its own supernal nature; in its 'glory of changeless metal' spurning the lower nature and 'all complexities of mire or blood'. It seems more *alive* than before. Again, we return to the Emperor's hall, now a place beyond nature where 'flit' flames independent of the natural order, 'flames begotten of flame'; and to them come the 'blood-begotten spirits', the phrase underlining what might seem the paradox of the natural, biological, order as the begetting source of a spiritual after-life.[2] There is a death-agony, but it is a

---

[1] The ancient symbol of the 'maze' or 'labyrinth' used with respect to the passage from this life to the next is discussed throughout my brother's *Cumaean Gates*, reissued in *Vergil: Epic and Anthropology*, 1967, Index II. For the 'Golden Bough', which occurs in both Byzantium poems, as a passport to the other world, see 156 and Index II. Compare also Yeats's 'Vacillation', II.

[2] Compare I Corinthians, XV. 44-9.

move beyond 'complexities' and 'fury'; at once a 'dying into a dance', and a dying into 'an agony of trance', an entry into a supernatural but unhurting flame which cannot 'singe'.

Our conclusion asserts a victory. Multitudinous spirits are seen riding on 'the dolphin's mire and blood'; that is, man riding his own physical life in violent motion. Next, the Emperor's 'golden smithies' are said to 'break the flood', annihilate the sensual and biological, and all violent action in time, while 'marbles of the dancing floor' – a neat fusion of smooth solidity and harmonious motion – vanquish the 'bitter furies of complexity'.

We have the gong, sacred architecture, rich metals, marble, and flames, all balanced against: 'the fury and the mire of human veins'; violent motion; the dolphin, animal of watery and so passional, to use Colin Still's term (*Shakespeare's Mystery Play*, 1921), life; and 'the flood'. The poem ends with

> Those images that yet
> Fresh images beget,
> That dolphin-torn, that gong-tormented sea.

'Dolphin-torn' suggests the violent motion of things in the order of time, nature and passion; the 'gong-tormented sea' is the biological order ruthlessly dominated by the transcendent. But what are the 'images'? Earlier, 'image' was used for a spirit-body beyond nature in contrast to the 'unpurged images' of daytime perception; a form between 'man' and 'shade', like the 'image' of Attis in the poem 'Vacillation'; spirit 'flames' were 'begotten of flame', not of other, plural, flames; and yet the spirit of man was, strangely, 'blood-begotten'. Our conclusion seems to blend the two sorts of begetting, answering the earlier paradox by adumbration of the truth that spirit has been functioning from the start, its 'image', perhaps with a reference to God making men in His own 'image' in Genesis, first at work in ceaseless human propagation and then making man, as spirit, ride his 'dolphin', or physical body, through a nature both 'torn' by man's own violent course and 'tormented' by the gong summoning from the flames and gold.

The fusion here is more satisfying than in 'Sailing to Byzantium'; the impressions of the 'superhuman', of 'miracle', of living spirit-flames, and above all of the 'dance', together with the sense we get of assured, purposeful, and living activity on the part of the more metallic and supernal entities, leave us with a resultant harmony. The two poems most admirably serve to define our main opposites, in contrast and creative interplay. They, and especially the second, provide fascinating exemplars of the way great poetry chooses to base its more visionary structures on a tangible foundation. Logic is discounted. We move from historic Byzantium through night and sleep to a transformation whereby the Emperor has suddenly become God and his palace paradise; much the same happened in Coleridge's 'Kubla Khan'. The Byzantium poems will surely be more and more clearly recognized as Yeats's greatest work. They stand out proudly from his more personal records and more ascetic manner; as also from the more *attenuated* spiritualism of his dramas (discussed in *The Golden Labyrinth*). Their outstanding importance derives from the nature of the symbols used, enlisting all our resources of known reality and sense-perception to make us enjoy a more than sensory recognition.

CHAPTER IX

Masefield and Spiritualism

Mansions of the Spirit, edited by George A. Panichas: New York 1967.

'The dead don't die. They look on and help.' D. H. Lawrence in a letter to J. Middleton Murry (2 February 1923)

In this essay I append the original date of English publication as given in Geoffrey Handley-Taylor's indispensable bibliography *John Masefield, O.M.* (London 1960), at a book's first mention and again at a main entry. For the prose I give chapter numerals when available.

I

THE POET LAUREATE'S [1] sixty years of creative writing has certain qualities of epic and spiritual significance elsewhere unmatched. His style, preferring direct narrative to 'discussion of states of mind and soul' (*So Long to Learn*, 1952; 103), is lucid: what cannot be said simply will not be said at all. Even in literary criticism, his *William Shakespeare* (1911; new version, 1954) and *Chaucer* (1931),[2] he illustrates Arthur Quiller-Couch's ideal of the concrete noun and the active verb. Though his life's survey covers the most awful problems of human destiny, he has written little that cannot be followed by a boy.

[1] John Masefield was Poet Laureate from 1930 until his death in 1967. He has been succeeded by Cecil Day-Lewis. A handsome bibliography of the works of our new Laureate has been compiled by Geoffrey Handley-Taylor and Timothy d'Arch Smith (St. James Press, Chicago and London, 1968).

[2] For a valuable consideration of Chaucer as Masefield's poetic 'master' see Professor Francis Berry's 1967 Inaugural Lecture, *John Masefield: the Narrative Poet*, University of Sheffield, 1968.

Masefield and Spiritualism

Though his early *Multitude and Solitude* (1909; VI. 139, VII. 170) asserted the importance of a moral purpose, Masefield's social novels lack fire. *The Hawbucks* (1929) is an indecisive study of country gentlefolk, perhaps saved only by a hunt and a blizzard. *Eggs and Baker* (1936) is a strong indictment of social injustice, rising to an exciting murder trial in which two men are convicted, one unjustly. In *The Square Peg* (1937) an armaments manufacturer who loathes the cruelties and crudities of a fox-hunting society creates a garden city and an art-centre. Of these the second has its claims: no one else has written more strongly on the horrors of the death penalty; but the colouring of all three is dull. It seems that the novel of moral engagement proved for Masefield a blind alley.

His strength is in action. Games and sports, honoured by classical epic, and today – in their bridging of combat and their friendliness – perhaps our best hope on the international scene, are given their poetry: hunting in *Reynard the Fox* (1919), racing in *Right Royal* (1920), cricket in 'Eighty-Five to Win' (*The Bluebells and Other Verse*, 1961), and boxing in *The Everlasting Mercy* (1911) and 'A Tale of Country Things' (*On the Hill*, 1949). In *Multitude and Solitude* (VI. 139, VII. 170) literature is contrasted with action; and so in *Dauber* (1913) is painting. Art is best when it is itself action, as in the combination of artistry and athletics in the circus (*King Cole*, 1921, and *The Country Scene*, 1937); in ballet (*The Square Peg* and *Tribute to Ballet*, 1938); in spoken verse (*With the Living Voice*, 1925, and *So Long to Learn*, 195-217); and in drama, especially, as in *A Macbeth Production* (1945), if home-made. Art must honour its basis: 'All art comes from the power that does rough work, and the pride and joy of doing that rough work well' (*The Square Peg*, 52). Masefield asks for a new totality of 'supreme art' (*So Long to Learn*, 183) both communal and inclusive, 'exquisite to hear' and 'beautiful to watch' (*I Want! I Want!*, 1944; 18).

His outlook is youthful. In the visionary 'Ossian', III (*The Bluebells and Other Verse*), supernal experience is set in 'the land of youth'. From the small boy Kay Harker in the child-fantasies *The Midnight Folk* (1927) and *The Box of Delights* (1935) to the youths of the adventure stories, his heroes are young. In *A Book of Discoveries* (1910) a man of active experience initiates two boys into the wonders of woodlore and the skills of scoutcraft. Boys should learn to enter 'other lives than their own . . . they should know what the red thing in the pond eats, how the weasel hunts, how the partridge calls at twilight. There is no greater delight on earth than to enter another brain by an act of the imagination'. Life, 'always miraculous', is 'the only lesson worth learning' (206). Again, all 'wisdom' and 'progress' come from 'looking so closely at a thing' that one sees 'its meaning as well as its appearance' (311).

Nature is to be both learned and fought. In narrative after narrative we are shown the terrifying antagonists of ocean and jungle and how to master them; by skill and with the help of spirits. Masefield's keen sense of spirit-powers is one with his poetic ability to realize *action* in animal and man, for action and spirit-powers are close. In his world, spirits intervene, like the deities in Homer and Vergil.

To Homer, Masefield was devoted (*So Long to Learn*, 213), and in his own narratives of contest and exploration he is Homeric. He has Homer's admiration of beautiful and efficient crafts, as when he sees 'strength and beauty' in a reef-knot (*Jim Davis*, 1911; IV. 48), or writes at length of his experiences in a carpet factory in *In the Mill* (1941). He has also Homer's acceptance of terrible deeds, as uninhibited as those of the children in *The Box of Delights* (III. 82) playing at pirates: 'And you'll be captured and tortured, and then you'll have to walk the plank'. In his accounts of sixteenth- and seventeenth-century buccaneering in *On the Spanish Main* (1906) he records massacres and tortures with an unruffled calm. In *Lost Endeavour* (1910; I. X. 84) we have:

'A lad of tender heart,' said one of the Spaniards.
'Bueno', said the others, when my remarks had been translated to ·hem. 'Bueno joven.' They looked at me as if I were some rare bird, as if goodness were stuck about me like feathers.

We must not look for sensitivity where it does not exist. Brave men, however rough, win respect.

Spanish America holds for Masefield a fascination which gives *On the Spanish Main* and his poetic drama *Philip the King* (1914) a lustre not quite enjoyed by his other historical books: *Sea Life in Nelson's Time* (1905), grimly detailing the horrors of naval service; *The Tragedy of Pompey the Great* (1910); the novel *Badon Parchments* (1947), on Arthurian Britain; the Byzantine stories *Basilissa* (1940) and *Conquer* (1941); and *Martin Hyde* (1910), notable for its description of the Battle of Sedgemoor, on Monmouth's rebellion. Masefield's knowledge of the logistics and technicalities of ancient and modern warfare appears inexhaustible.

Writing on the two World Wars (*Gallipoli*, 1916; *The Old Front Line*, 1917; *The Battle of the Somme*, 1919; and *The Nine Days Wonder*, 1941), Masefield makes heroism burn from a straight description of what was done and of the techniques and courage that did it. Even in propaganda lectures for America, while attributing the war to the evils of an autocracy, he is characteristically reluctant to 'abuse our present enemies' ('The War and the Future', in *St. George and the Dragon*, 1919; 65-9). His instincts tend toward the dramatic impersonality of Sherriff's *Journey's End*.

His views on fox-hunting are significantly ambivalent. *Reynard the Fox* is written from an exact identification with the activating instincts of fox, hounds, and huntsmen in turn and without favouritism. The fox, gracious in movement 'above all English animals' (*Martin Hyde*, XXIII. 283), he loves; and yet he can in his essay 'Fox-Hunting' (*Recent Prose*, 1924; 160) regard a hunt as 'the most beautiful and the most stirring sight to be seen in England', the thrill of horn and hounds in cry 'ringing into' the 'soul' and awaking racial and animal memories 'of when one hunted with the pack, or was hunted'. But again, the whole novel *The Square Peg* turns on a withering indictment of the brutality and stupidity of hunting. These uncanny balances recall the balance of sensitivity and admiration in Byron's descriptions of a bullfight and the Battle of Waterloo in *Childe Harold* (I, III). When in *Eggs and Baker* two boys engage a bull for fun, they felt that 'for the first time, they were really living' (60).

Masefield writes from the heart of human and animal creation. Knowing man's animal instincts and stern destiny, he can forgive much, as in this from *Live and Kicking Ned* (1939; 81): 'Mind, he was a cruel, terrible savage who had murdered two men, one of them in cold blood. I didn't care about that. I know that I would have given my life to save him. There was something about that fearful creature that I could love and pity'. In *The Midnight Folk* (1927; illus. edn., 1931, 135) we hear that 'courageous energy is always valued' and criminals accordingly remembered. A corresponding sympathy is accorded all victims of the 'unjust cruelty' of 'criminal law' (*Martin Hyde*, XXI. 263). Where, however, evil is undiluted and sophisticated, the answer is immediate. In *Sard Harker* (1924; 318) a declared apostle of evil who scorns rough seamen as brainless slaves is told: 'Their religion is to risk their lives and mortify their flesh in order to bring bread to their fellows. . . . In doing that, they make iron swim and dead-weight skim and the dead thing to be beautiful. Show me a finer religion, you who are already carrion for the want of one'. Masefield has left little social propaganda, and he prefers insight to morals. Nevertheless, his admiration for the bravery of simple men and his identification with their lot do them honours unknown to propaganda.

His central valuations are imaginative. From *Salt Water Ballads* (1902) onward he is fascinated by ships and navigation. He has written of actual ships in *The Conway from her foundation to the present day* (1933) and *New Chum* (1944) – both on the *Conway* – and in *The Wanderer of Liverpool* (1930). Of these he lists, knows, and loves every detail. Ships, often regarded as living creatures, have the grace and beauty men usually attribute to women (*The Bird of Dawning*, 1933; 23), whose place they fill in Masefield's narratives, where his feminine characterizations are slight, the boy-girl Aurelia in *Martin Hyde* being perhaps his best; but in drama his women are strong.

Ships take us to Central and South America, where nature is terrifying, but where there is colour, gold to be won, and an atmosphere, as in *Lost Endeavour*, wherein ancient spirit-wisdom survives. The treasure may, as in *On the Spanish Main* (XII. 161, XIV. 198) and *The Midnight Folk* (as above, illustrated, 6, 274-5), be ecclesiastical treasure. More widely, all gold-quests reflect that gold written into the lyrics 'The Golden City of St. Mary' (1902) and 'The Seekers' (1903?), with its quest for a 'Holy City' beyond the horizon. So the Frenchman of 'El Dorado', in *A Tarpaulin Muster* (1907), risking his life for Inca gold, is 'a pilgrim, a poet, a person to reverence'.

Though seldom a moralist, Masefield has what might be called a 'super-morality' and a 'super-sociology' concerned with what is basic, elemental, and universal. His evil is the chaos to be mastered by man on every level of craft and art. His wisdom-bearers are outsider types: the anarchic hero of *The Everlasting Mercy*, the half-mad Gaffer of *The Tragedy of Nan* (1909), and the Madman of *Good Friday* (1916), as well as King Cole in *King Cole*. These

challenge no particular society; their 'wild souls', as the Madman
has it, exist as a challenge to society in general, even to life itself.

There is for Masefield 'some soul of goodness', to adopt
Shakespeare's phrase, in things wild. In the poem 'Fire' in *On the
Hill* a young Hunter rejects marriage for the powers of nature's
vastness:

> I shall ask no more of the world, for the world is here,
> A power so great, it is past man's power to speak;
> Beauty and truth more bright and keen than a spear,
> Joy for the sorrowing man and strength for the weak.
> I fear no horror that death and the world may wreak,
> I am a thing the Fire that burned me bought,
> I am the Fire's now and Fire I seek,
> I have been aware of the wilds and living is nought.

There is much of Shakespeare's Timon in Masefield: the elements,
whether as comrades or contestants, are his soulmates. Nevertheless, like Shakespeare, he respects society, for he believes in
civilization and order; but somewhere in what is *wild* lie a beauty
and a truth which they lack. This he knows because he is an artist
and because he is aware of spirits. The concepts 'Beauty' and
'Truth', or 'Wisdom', recur almost as a theology, but not 'Goodness', for ethical terms are soiled. His hope is rather to draw men
'to thoughts like planets and to acts like flowers' (*King Cole*).

2

The artist-hero of *Dauber* (1913) qualifies painfully as a seaman,
battling mast-high in a storm of 'devilish' malice (VI). Later he
has a fatal accident and dies with the words: 'It will go on'. So it
does, for the great ship comes safe to port: 'onwards she thun-
dered, on', 'the new-come beauty stately from the sea', moving
'like a queen' (VII). The implications are pure Masefield. The
word 'devilish' is important. Man's conflict with the elements on
the material plane of skill and science is part of a wider elemental
conflict of demonic and angelic powers. At moments of crisis
those greater powers may be sensed.

Two of the best prose narratives, *The Bird of Dawning* (1933)
and *Victorious Troy: or The Hurrying Angel* (1935), make contact

with these powers. In the first a ship engaged in the homeward race of the China traders meets disaster and sinks; and we are with sixteen men in a small boat commanded by the young second mate, Cyril Trewsbury. We follow their fears, angers, hunger, thirst, and thwarted hopes, all demanding of the hero every resource of leadership. The situation is new: 'In all his previous sea-service the wrestle had been with the wind, to use it and master it'; now it is only the 'appalling water so close at hand' (93). The ocean assumes an evil quality: its waters are 'devils', a great wave crests 'like the Judgement Day', sharks draw near, foreshadowing death (93-4, 128, 179-80). Against these antagonists stands man's will (122).

In half-sleep the men are 'haunted' by evil 'shapes' (172-3); but to Trewsbury on his waking the stars promise a greater power, and he has a conviction of 'someone much greater than a human being' who is 'trying to convince him that all would be well', a guardian 'spirit of blessing', maternal, saintly, and loving (173-4). Then they find the newly deserted *Bird of Dawning*, man her, and win the race home. The relation of the two parts is loose, but in Masefield's world meaningful: disaster, endurance in a small boat, spirit-help, and the winning through to victory. The elemental antagonist is regarded as evil.

Yet more powerful is *Victorious Troy*. The ship *Hurrying Angel* is commanded by an experienced but tyrannical captain given to drink who runs improper risks to make better time. A cyclone approaches. Through the mind of our eighteen-year-old apprentice hero, Dick Pomfret, we have a succession of sickly atmospheric experiences leading to associations of 'the Enemy', 'hell', and devils (49). The ship seems to be 'suffering' and 'crying' for help (48). Impressions of horror accumulate. The water is 'malevolent' (133) and the air devilish (193). There is a fiendish quality about it all: 'like a revolution or a war, it had drawn into its madness all the sanity near it' (203). There is no sensation of 'majesty' or 'power', no 'big, determined evil, but limitless hordes of selfish evils . . . determined each to rend his neighbour, even if it rent himself' (209). We are told that men have been known to go mad 'from the sight of a cyclone sea' (211).

The descriptions attain amazing feats of startling, fantastic, lurid light and colour: 'a flash of bluish, searing fire' leaps down the mast into the sea, burning, as it seems, 'a hole' in it:

266

Instead of collapsing, the mizen-mast shone out conspicuously with balls or fuzzes of luminousness, which crowned the snapped cap, went down the lifts to the yard-arms, and stuck like globes there. . . . One greenish globe flopped across the poop close to Dick: it was like a fish that he had caught in a night of phosphorescence.

(204)

Pressure and suspense are maintained by a descriptive colouring the more cogent for its entanglement with every relevant detail of ship and navigation and the psychology of men in peril. When a vast wave threatens destruction, one is not 'scared' but just 'interested' (83).

The cyclone is a living entity: 'it *is* dogs; nothing else could make that noise' (80); or 'guns' (46, 192). Its appalling abnormality is driven home: 'This noise could not be wind. This was some new, untested, unknown force coming into the world for the first time' (96). It is alive and it is evil. Its intended victim, the ship, is also alive, 'like an animal cruelly hurt, kicking in death' (193).

As in *The Bird of Dawning*, there is help from beyond. The hero, Dick, late from college, has to assume control and, when exhausted, dreams that he is being questioned by an ironically contemptuous Examiner as to the correct procedures to be followed in such a crisis (184-9). Dick answers as best he may. During the interrogation the Examiner gives advice which is eventually followed. It is more than a dream: 'Dick was in a state between sleep and stupor. In that state the figure of the Examiner seemed present just in front of him' (189). The spirit-powers use Dick's college memories to get a message through.

The ship loses two of her three masts; she is a hopeless derelict, foundering. The officers are overboard or out of action. Dick finds the captain, grievously hurt. Hitherto he has been unreasonable and brutal, but he is a fine sailor and a man of authority. He at first curses Dick, but later softens and ratifies his position in command. The first sign of his softening comes at the moment when, the cyclone's centre being cleared, the danger is passing. The elemental drama is for an instant reflected into the human soul. The stars as 'Sons of God', now again clear, herald salvation (207). The *Hurrying Angel* is saved, the hero acclaimed, and his professional future assured. Never was a happy ending more convincingly won.

In these two narratives elemental evil is mastered by human

will, courage and efficiency, with the aid of spirit-powers greater
than the antagonist. Calamity is not always so averted: the title
Victorious Troy refers to the book's sonnet epilogue on the contrasted sufferings of ancient Troy.

The elemental antagonist may be either sea or land. *Sard Harker*
(1924) and *Odtaa* (1926) are adventure stories set in tropical
America within a surrounding action of imaginary politics, but our
main interest is again in man's contest with nature, with evil
through nature, and in spirits of help.

The sailor Sard, guided by a recurring dream, gets into trouble
on land preventing his return to his ship, the *Pathfinder*. Nature
is horrible. Once he has to fight through vegetation 'sickly with
the forms and the smell of death', 'evil' in its 'over-abundant
life'; among poisonous plants and swarming insects; and through
a sucking bog which 'chuckles' in triumph (119, 121, 127). Later,
after escaping from a prison, Sard comes on a house among foot-
hills which radiates goodness. Good people must once have lived
there. He calls but gets no answer, and yet 'he felt quite certain
that the thicket was full of people looking at him' (204). He finds
a ruined chapel with faded painted heads in fresco. For Masefield
childhood is a strong power; and in his sleep Sard hears and sees
a boy friend, who had died eleven years before, calling as from a
vast 'distance'. Above the altar stand blessed figures and a
trumpeter, pointing and urging him to be gone:

'What is it, Peter? What is it, you great spirits?'
But the women faded from him, Peter faded from him into the
wall, but he could still see the shining trumpet and notes like flakes
of fire falling all around him. The trumpet dwindled slowly and
resolved itself into the blossoming branch that had grown through a
crack in the wall (207-8).

As he wakes, the figures are again the old frescoes. A smell of
burning mingles with his memory of the command to be gone.
Warned in time, he escapes a bush fire.

Later, lost among mountains, he sees in 'dream or fever' a
female figure like the 'spirit' of his ship, the *Pathfinder*, 'fierce,
hard and of great beauty'. It says: 'I am the *Pathfinder*. I can find
a path for you'. He is directed to safety. Afterward 'it was in
his mind all blurred, like the events of a fever, sometimes it
seemed the only reality among things dreamed' (243-4). In such

events Masefield works on the borderline of sleep and waking.

In *Odtaa* the eighteen-year-old hero, Highworth Ridden, is plunged into a succession of appalling jungle experiences, again in South America. Alone with his horse he comes up against a horrible bog and a pool of reddened water like 'stagnant blood', with hundreds of dead trees standing in it (XII. 203). He is starving, blistered, nearly blind (XIV. 233).

Once earlier he had awakened by night in mid-jungle: an impulse 'from the heart of things was calling him to rise'. His horse is staring at something he himself cannot see, and 'a wave of fear' passes from animal to man. Whether the enemy is beast or ghost he cannot tell. The tension lessens, and the horse's eyes follow the enemy as it moves slowly round. It again returns: 'When it deliberated, its will hardened against them, the horse knew it, and Hi knew it from the horse' (XII. 198-9). There is in or behind nature a more than natural evil, compared with which nature's normal evils are a relief:

Then the night, which for some minutes had seemed to hold her breath, began again to speak with her myriad voices out of the darkness of her cruelty. The whisper and the droning of the forest sharpened into the rustlings of snakes, the wails of victims, the cry of the bats after the moths, and the moan of the million insects seeking blood (XII. 199-200).

Dawn brings the brighter energies of daylight nature. Meanwhile, Hi 'had never understood what night was, now he knew' (XII. 201; for another account of a ghostly night, see 'Ryemeadows' in *Old Raiger and Other Verse*, 1964).

There are good spirit-powers also. Hi hears voices advising him, as from a flock of invisible birds (XIV. 228-9). He wins through to comparative safety. In a hut with a stranger, Anselmo, he senses the spirit of a former occupant, Dudley Wigmore (XV. 244-5, 249, 257) and in the 'fiery mist' (XV. 250) of sleep is aware of its distress. Later in a dream and also *after waking* Hi sees him 'distinctly', and, as he fades, sees the wall too, through him (XVI. 263). Wigmore, who had been murdered by Anselmo, urges Hi to escape. Words come unmediated without sound: 'a sentence floated into his mind as clearly as though a voice had spoken in his ear' (XVI. 263-4). On the way to his escape, Hi sees Dudley Wigmore clearly, by day, and under his direction eludes Anselmo (XVI. 269, 276-7).

Masefield and Spiritualism

Afterward, again in dire straits, Hi is visited in sleep by a figure known in his *childhood* dreams: 'all peace, courage, goodness and happiness were in her face' and 'hope so bright' that danger pales. As on certain other occasions, but even more powerfully, the spirit-reality is not confined to sleep. She helps him to rise, leads and accompanies him, gives him medicaments, and empowers him with a song. 'What happened to him in these hours he never knew, save that he was miraculously helped'; 'they were among the intensest hours of his life' (XVII. 287-90).

Other novels show similar tendencies. In *The Hawbucks* (256-7, 261) the hero, battling by night against snow, senses, as in *Odtaa*, his horse's fear and then hears a cry which later turns out to have come *either* from a girl then dying at a distance *or* from an intuition of that death received by a woman within call; and in *Eggs and Baker* and *The Square Peg* tragedy is averted by conclusions of spiritualistic tone. In *Martin Hyde* the boy-hero is encouraged by a sense of the presence of his dead father, who had believed in the rightness of Monmouth's cause (XVIII. 228, XXIV. 293). In *Conquer* an inspiration from some 'spirit' (117) enables Origen to save Byzantium.

In our four adventure narratives we have watched heroes faced by hostile nature, together with an evil coming from or from behind nature, and the advent of help from spirit-powers. The conditions of their breaking through are in Masefield's valuations the hero's will and hope; he does not use the word 'faith'. In the sonnet epilogue to *Victorious Troy* we read of 'Hope the living Key unlocking prison'; and 'Helpers' are grouped with 'Hopes' in the Epilogue to *Grace before Ploughing* (1966).

That such powers attend human adventure is witnessed by Homer, Vergil, and the Old Testament. There are other and recent evidences. In *My Early Life* (1930 and reprints, XXI) Winston Churchill tells us how, when at a loss during his escape from a prison camp in South Africa, he was 'led' by an 'unconscious or sub-conscious' power, which recalled the power he had known when writing with a 'Planchette pencil', to an Englishman's house, and safety.[1] Another interesting experience is recorded in

[1] Churchill appears to have received similar help twice during the Second World War; see Jack Fishman's biography of Lady Churchill, *My Darling Clementine*, 1963; 132-3, 134-5. For a simultaneous recognition of spirit-helpers by two temporarily entombed miners, see *Psychic News*, 6 March 1965.

Masefield and Spiritualism

Charles Lindbergh's account (p. 54 above) of his Atlantic flight in *The Spirit of St. Louis* (1953; VI, Twenty-Second Hour, 389-90). Troubled by drowsiness and uncertain of his navigation, he became aware of spirits around him – just like the spirits in *Odtaa* – speaking with human voices, 'conversing and advising on my flight, discussing problems of my navigation, reassuring me, giving me messages of importance unattainable in ordinary life' (389). He was 'on the border-line of life and a greater realm beyond', and death was known as an entry to a greater freedom (390). In Harold Owen's *Journey from Obscurity* (1965) there is a comparable account of ancestral spirits functioning as saviours from an 'incalculable distance' (as in *Sard Harker*) during the author's nightmare experience when alone on an evil-impregnated hulk in the South Seas. Since then he has been convinced of a reality transcending 'all earthly happenings' (Vol. III, 1. 9-10, 11. 28-33, 37). Even more impressive is his account of how, on entering his cabin in South Africa, he learned of Wilfred Owen's death, finding his poet brother seated there with soft eyes 'trying to make me understand' (XIV. 198-201): in *Goodbye to All That* (XIV) Robert Graves reports a similar experience. In a note to *The Waste Land* (V. 360) T. S. Eliot wrote: 'The following lines were stimulated by the account of one of the Antarctic expeditions (I forget which, but I think one of Shackleton's): it was related that the party of explorers, at the extremity of their strength, had the constant delusion that there was *one more member* than could actually be counted'.

Masefield had himself had a major experience of the paranormal. In *So Long to Learn* (1952; 185-7) he describes how, years before, when his work was not progressing, he heard a male voice say, 'The spring is beginning'. Soon after, *while crossing a fence separating a wood from open ground*, the spirit-helpers apparently using that action for their purpose, he knew that he was to write 'a poem about a blackguard who becomes converted'; the poem appeared 'in its complete form, with every detail distinct', and he started writing it down *at once*. That night, alone in a country house, he continued hour after hour until the door of his room 'flung itself noisily wide open'. He took the warning and went to bed. *The Everlasting Mercy* (1911) proved the turning point of his literary career.

Such help is perhaps most usually, and certainly most strikingly, experienced by men of action who risk death. Will, courage, hope, and perhaps loneliness and the dark, appear to be favourable conditions. It may happen to a whole community in war-time. When in *St. George and the Dragon* (5, 17) Masefield writes of 'the dead' creating a nation's 'great soul', able to guide it in 'trouble' and 'calamity', or calls the victory at the Marne a 'miracle', the phrases are more than decoration. In *The Nine Days Wonder* (54), on the sea rescue at Dunkerque, after observing the 'will to help from the whole marine population of these islands', he continues:

It is hard to think of those dark formations on the sand, waiting in the rain of death, without the knowledge that Hope and Help are stronger things than death. Hope and Help came together in their power into the minds of thousands of simple men, who went out in the Operation Dynamo and plucked them from ruin.

On a national scale the event was of similar quality to those which we have been discussing. The belief in the Angels of Mons arose from a similar recognition.

3

In treating of these events of spiritualistic perception, Masefield handles, with a precision probably finer and more enlightened than that of any of his predecessors, truths that have saturated imaginative literature from the Bible and Homer to Blake, Byron, Ibsen, and the spiritualistic dramas, studied in my book *The Golden Labyrinth*, of the last hundred years. Among our leading contemporary poets, Yeats, Eliot, D. H. Lawrence ('The Ship of Death'; see G. A. Panichas, *Adventure in Consciousness*, pp. 220n., 221n. above), Auden ('The Cave of Making', in *About the House*), and Francis Berry (*Ghosts of Greenland*, pp. 471-2 below) make poetry from spirit-survival and spirit-communion; and on all occult matters John Cowper Powys writes as an adept.

His uncanny genius for experienced fact unclouded by theory empowers Masefield's uninhibited treatment of the supernormal. As a boy he came to the *Conway* with a store of ghost stories (*New Chum*, 28-9, 109-10, 117). The short pieces of *A Tarpaulin Muster* (1907) are rich in hauntings and fairy lore ('The Pirates of Santa Anna', 'Ghosts', etc.); and water spirits are vivid in 'Sea Superstition', in *A Mainsail Haul* (1905; enlarged edn., 1913). In *Sea Life in Nelson's Time* (Epilogue, 216-18) the spirits of long-dead sailors are imagined as watching the good which their sufferings have won for later generations. *In the Mill* (118) recalls an experience by Masefield himself, in a dream, of precognition.[1] Many late poems handle events of an uncanny nature. In the volume *On the Hill* (1949) we are in 'Jouncer's Tump' fascinated – 'it staggers me' – by an old man's unaccountably knowing the contents of an ancient tomb; in 'Cry-Baby Cottage' by the weepings of a murdered child leading to the discovery of its bones; and in 'Blown Hilcote Manor' by an old house filled with 'happy folk' from its past. In *The Bluebells and Other Verse* (1961) 'John Grimaldi' tells of the well-established yet brief return of a lost sailor which seems to have been caused by his longing for home when he was dying at sea. The narrative poem *Old Raiger* (1964) turns on an act of purposeful soul-projection. In the poem of childhood reminiscences, *Wonderings* (1943), Masefield tells us how as a child he saw 'three immense floating giants . . . linked as one'. It is presumably these who are recalled in *Grace before Ploughing* (1966; XI, 'The Angel') as two linked figures like and yet unlike an angel, of 'enormous power'.

A too exclusive concentration on spirit-reality, or on mysticism or religious dogma, will no more make great literature than will an exclusive reliance on an earth-plane realism. Imaginative literature arises from the impact of the one category on the other; its central aim is to involve us in the entanglement and interaction. Nor is it enough to state this, however exquisitely, as Eliot states it in his *Four Quartets*: men and spirits are dynamic beings, and only through the literature of action in narrative or drama can their *inter*-action be effectively established.

Masefield's balance of animal and spiritual powers may be illustrated by a comparison of *Reynard the Fox* (1919) and *Right Royal* (1920). In the first, emphasis falls on human and animal instinct: the huntsmen's excitement, the 'hot gulps' of scent giving the hounds 'agonies of joy', and the fox's strength failing as he hears 'the thud in the blood of his body deeper'. The poet is inside each in turn; but this power of 'being inside' is itself an agile telepathy beyond sense-perception; like the fox's own

[1] See also Mary E. Monteith, *A Book of True Dreams*, 1929; 26 and 206 (on Masefield).

alertness in sleep coming from 'the self who needs neither eyes
nor ears'.

In *Right Royal* the emphasis falls on spirit. The very 'Force' of
the horse Right Royal is capitalized as almost a spirit-being; we
are told that 'a Spirit gives some' of his 'Power'; and at a crisis
his 'soul' 'thrilled up through each hand' of his rider. The
thoughts and desires of people watching the race are like 'floatings
of fire' affecting the contestants for good or ill. The spirit 'Helpers'
of those concerned may, like the assisting deities in Homer and
Vergil, be invoked. They are powerless to aid the 'despairing', but
otherwise able from their 'glittering' world to assist, when things
are difficult, by cunning, indirect, telepathic ways:

> As the white, gleaming gannet eyes fish in the sea,
> So the Thought sought a mortal to bring this to be.

This 'thought from the Helper' duly fixes in the mind of a friendly
racer who, during the race, hands it on to the rider of Right Royal,
and confidence returns not only to the rider but to the horse also:

> All his blood was in glory, all his soul was blown bare,
> They were one, blood and purpose, they strode through the air.

'Blood' and spirit-realities, animal and man, are intermixed. The
action is tangled in recognition of a 'world beyond sense', where
'man' and 'beast', 'spirit' and 'soul' are in direct communion: 'the
World as it Is', whence come 'Beauty' and 'Wisdom', countering
the 'Fate' which normally rules existence. Given the psychological
conditions, Fate's barrier may be broken and the Helpers act.

The prose narratives already discussed have shown spirit-
realities breaking into human existence. Two earlier stories,
Multitude and Solitude (1909) and *Lost Endeavour* (1910), were written
more wholly around this relationship. Masefield established his
main axes of reference early.

In the first story a writer, after the death of his idealized love,
Ottalie, is led by a series of coincidences to believe that she is
impressing him, 'using the torn page, the magazine, and the naval
officer, as her messengers' (VI. 123), to a scientific exploration in
Africa to find a cure for sleeping sickness. In Africa the hero and
a companion come on a kraal of natives dying from the disease
near ancient ruins left by Phoenician gold-traders. They are
deserted by their servants and fall ill themselves. A fearful storm,
in Masefield's magnificent style, unlooses its terrors; and by night,

in this community of dead and dying, his companion unconscious, the lonely hero, himself sick almost to death, endures a sense, as did our other heroes, of a supernatural evil, here associated with the pagan ruins (XI. 266-8). Ottalie's 'presence' is felt, and he calls for help in his experiment: it was 'as though an older, unearthly sister walked with him, half friend, half guide' (XI. 271, 274). Now at last his experiment succeeds, and the two men are saved, though on their return they learn that their discovery has been forestalled.

The medical matters are handled in scientific detail. To science, nature is an enemy: 'we are out to fight her wherever we can find her' (X. 237). Against nature stand man's courage and will, wresting victory, inspired and aided by the dead. The key thought is: 'Perhaps the dead look on the living souls as notes in a music, and play upon them, making harmony or discord, according to the power of their wills and the quality of their nature' (II. 31).

Within a surrounding action of seventeenth-century slavery and buccaneering in Central America, *Lost Endeavour* concentrates on the finding of a community living near the ruins of an ancient civilization, preserving its traditions and faith and expecting the advent of a young leader and the return of the old gods. This community practices a magic such as would be condemned by the Christian Church (2. X. 205-8). There is a temple with hieroglyphs in Egyptian style and walls ablaze with colour.

Masefield's historical imagination is fascinated by ancient ruins: at home, the hill camp and fortifications of *A Book of Discoveries*; in Africa, the Phoenician ruins of *Multitude and Solitude* and the mysterious white civilization in *Live and Kicking Ned* (1939); in the East, the carved memorials of a golden age in the poem 'Pavilastukay' (*Natalie Maisie and Pavilastukay*, 1942). In America there is the chapel of *Sard Harker* and an ancient Sun Temple in *Odtaa* (XVI). In *Lost Endeavour* the theme is exploited in direct relation to Masefield's spiritualistic insights, which are here given their philosophy. There is a higher wisdom and magic than that of the Indian community, 'preserved at a college of priests' on an adjacent island (2. X. 210) and to be related to that 'immortal nature' of which our world of colour and odour is a mere shadow and which itself is 'shadow' of a yet 'higher spirit' (2. XI. 211).

One of our two heroes fights towards this island college through a 'nightmare' jungle of 'pulpy' vegetation, poison-weeds and spikes like 'skeleton fingers', where 'a low kind of life festered and wallowed'. The question is 'which should win' – it, or man with his wits and machete (2. XI. 220-2). There is a smell 'as of death', such as is always found 'where nature is left alone to her luxury and waste'. When the man is near exhaustion, the forest is full of 'fiendish glee'; but he recovers. A strange sound turns out to be a 'war-whistle' made from a stream filling an artificial receptacle perforated with holes (2. XII. 224, 228, XIII, 233).

He climbs to a sea view, with now 'a salt clean tang' in the air (2. XIII. 236). From this height at sunset the woods below, no longer hideous, flame out scarlet, crimson, and gold. His 'guardian spirit' offers him shelter in an ancient cave cell with an altar and mosaics, wherein are remains of a long-dead priestess 'of some higher race than the Indians' (2. XIV. 238). Here he has a dream:

My dream was not like common dreaming, in which the dream dominates the personality; but wonderful and kingly, my own self, awake and strong, directing my own actions. When I say that I dreamed I express myself badly. I should say that I woke up into a new and vivid life, more splendid than this, a life of intenser colour and finer ecstasy, in a world conducted by another intelligence and governed by other laws. It was, as I suppose, the real world, of which this world is nothing but the passing shadow. I woke up, then, in the cave where I had fallen asleep, but I woke up into its reality. The walls of hewn stone were changed to opal in which fire burned. The fire on the hearth was like visible music. I cannot describe the beauty of the flame in any other way. The trees outside stood like an array of knights in mail. Their fruits were like lamps, their leaves like jewels (2. XV. 243).

Old plaques take on colour and life. Two great serpents hiss and sway to a sound of drums. He is somehow 'aloft', looking down on his own body. There is music:

Then, in the middle of the music, the inner wall parted with a crash, and I was within, touching the altar, which glowed red like a great pulsing ember. It was like a heart, contracting and expanding. It was an ecstasy to touch it; for it was no longer a slab of rock for sacrifice. It was the very heart of the goddess which received the sacrifice (2. XV. 244).

The 'withered' remains of the long-dead priestess become alive: 'The figure rose slowly, full of life and power; glowing with life that was like an internal fire, visible and tangible to me' (2. XV. 245). Throughout, sensory perception is strong. Senses ('visible music') mix, dissolved into a direct perception including all senses but dependent on none.

Suddenly he is standing outside the cave cell, on a hill, seeing the island as a map and the Temple of Wisdom. Then he is back in the cave. Relics and dust are as before. The grand snakes are mosaics; the priestess is a shrivelled figure beneath a cloth. He finds the Temple, massively loaded with 'golden carvings', 'the worth of a kingdom' (2. XVI. 254), but for the rest, there are only skeletons. The inhabitants had died from a pestilence, unknown to the Indians on the mainland.

The story is saturated with spirit-properties. Again and again the mind receives 'something like a word spoken inside my brain', which some would call 'an intuition or some other absurd name, such as the English delight to make for things which they do not understand' (2. X. 198). 'The Occult Way' is said to be 'for the enlargement of Human Knowledge, which must ever be the aim of a Rational Man' (2. VII. 183). The book's crammed sensory effects are one with the occult significances: 'I felt that those lands and islands, where the moon is glorious and the air is heavy with spice as though incense was always being crushed, were full of all manner of presences' (2. VII. 187). The natives are attuned to what lies beyond: 'It needs the Indian life to make it all that – fireflies, and the moon coming, and the incense smouldering on the copper; but if I had an Indian drum here, and could beat long enough, as the Indians beat, I would take you out of your personal lives into the life into which all life ebbs at death' (2. XII. 229). Masefield's imaginative obsession with tropical America in all its natural threat and golden promise is explained. Gold may be either treasure to loot or a spiritual symbol; in *Lost Endeavour* the Temple's gold is finally looted by unprincipled men, to the distress of the two heroes, who try to prevent the sacrilege.

Multitude and Solitude and *Lost Endeavour* are patterned on man's will to control nature by, in the one, a spirit-guided science and, in the other, magic. Magic, as in Shakespeare's *The Tempest*, has a poetic authority not readily present in theology or metaphysics; it is more dramatic, and it is dramatic because it concerns human activity within an environment to be mastered. In both books there are helping powers, though they cannot assure a complete success.

Masefield and Spiritualism

Lost Endeavour turns on 'some secret, long forgotten by the white races', which is able to establish direct 'communion' with supernal powers: 'And why, in that great strange land, overgrown with forests in which mysterious peoples had built and vanished, should there not be a record of wisdom, wilder and stranger than any wisdom preserved by us?' 'Wilder': this is, as in *Fire* (p. 265 above), a key thought (3. XIV. 352). Here, as in 'Pavilastukay', Masefield's emphasis corresponds to John Cowper Powys's intuitions, studied in my book *The Saturnian Quest*, of a lost, golden life-way hard to recover.

We today probably find magic easier to accept when mediated through childhood fantasy. *The Midnight Folk* (1927) and *The Box of Delights* (1935) handle lightly and often with a delightful humour substances elsewhere within Masefield's serious concern: woodlore and animals, hunting, piratical adventures. Many of the more amazing events, such as the adventures into a mythological or historical past, have imaginative validity. The philosophic and the absurd join forces. In *The Box of Delights* the metaphysics of Time make brilliant fun in Arnold of Todi's song (X), and the melodramatic villain Abner's argument on the good done by his multifarious villainies offers a fascinating insight into the moral paradoxes of life and letters (XI). When in *The Midnight Folk* (illus. edn., 1931; 157, 275, 279) the image of 'the lovely golden lad', St. George, is missing from the salvaged ecclesiastical treasure, being still with the Mermaids, we have a symbolic gem inviting exact interpretation.

Magical paradises of sea depths or woodland have visionary impact. The boy-hero's many flights in sleep are of the kind known as 'astral projection' and may be related to a remarkable passage on crashing death followed by release and thoughts of ascending flight in *A Book of Discoveries* (155-6). On one of these flights, in *The Midnight Folk* (200), he enjoys clairvoyant perception of the townspeople as they sleep: 'There they all were, and floating about them as they slept were the loveliest people Kay had ever seen; they were like people made of light and of rainbows, and with exquisite faces and hands'. Both stories work on the interplay of sleep and waking life in such a way as to jostle the spiritualistic and the normal. When halfway through *The Midnight Folk* the dream events unexpectedly become part of daylight reality, the shock is purposeful: it happened like that in

Lost Endeavour and *Odtaa*. Similarly, when pictures come alive
we are reminded of *Lost Endeavour*, *Sard Harker*, *Melloney Holtspur*
(1922), and *The Dream* (1922). Masefield's two child-fantasies
may be read as introductions to his world.

Cole Haulings, in *The Box of Delights*, the Punch and Judy
wizard at home in all ages of history, is a relative, or more, of the
central figure of what is probably Masefield's most important
poetic narrative, *King Cole* (1921). A disgruntled travelling circus
in bad luck and ill humour is confronted by King Cole, who
since death has returned as 'an old, poor, wandering man, with
glittering eyes' to help those in distress. His dialogue with the
Showman is a fine example of unforced stichomythia:

Showman: What trade are you?
King Cole: I am a wandering man.
Showman: You mean, a tramp who flutes for bread and pence?
King Cole: I come, and flute, and then I wander thence.
Showman: Quicksilver Tom who couldn't keep his place.
King Cole: My race being run, I love to watch the race.
Showman: You ought to seek your rest.
King Cole: My rest is this,
      The world of men, wherever trouble is.

Fluting, he leads the mud-bedraggled circus through the town.
As his 'soul' enters his fluting, 'the spirits that inhabit dream'
gather round him. The circus takes on glory: 'they shone like
embers as they trod the road'. Then:

> And round the tired horses came the Powers
> That stir men's spirits, waking or asleep,
> To thoughts like planets and to acts like flowers,
> Out of the inner wisdom's beauty deep:
> These led the horses, and, as marshalled sheep
> Fronting a dog, in line, the people stared
> At those bright wagons led by the bright-haired.
>
> And, as they marched, the spirits sang, and all
> The horses crested to the tune and stept
> Like centaurs to a passionate festival
> With shining throats that mantling criniers swept
> And all the hearts of all the watchers leapt
> To see those horses passing and to hear
> That song that came like blessing to the ear.

> And, to the crowd the circus artists seemed
> Splendid, because the while that singing quired
> Each artist was the part that he had dreamed
> And glittered with the Power he desired,
> Women and men, no longer wet or tired
> From long despair, now shone like queens and kings,
> There they were crowned with their imaginings.

King Cole's spirit-magic is bedded in human psychology; the glorified circus is an externalization of a 'Power' already humanly conceived, and so existent. It is also embedded in earth-nature. Masefield's favourite country animals are present: foxes, hares, rabbits, stoats, mice; birds who 'bring delight and understanding' to man; and flowers. The glorified circus reminds the Prince, who is visiting the town, of his childhood:

> Once in my childhood, in my seventh year,
> I saw them come, and now they have returned,
> Those strangers, riding upon cars that burned,
> Or seemed to burn, with gold, while music thrilled . . .

The circus artists bring 'Beauty and Wisdom'. They are later called 'the Bringers Down of Beauty from the stars'. They are honoured both for their athletic 'skill' and also for 'wisdom'. Their circus rises beyond the daily 'coil' of existence; its art is 'lived' within 'eternity' beyond worldly miseries, in 'speed', 'colour', and 'beauty'. It is an ordinary circus, no more. Its glory as it entered the town was simply the artists and their art seen as by a spiritual X-ray, like Kay Harker's clairvoyance.

The performance is successful. The tent is struck, the circus gone, King Cole alone as night falls, piping of man's troubled life, until he fades. What he has revealed is what all of us, at times, may know:

> But where the juggler trudged beside his love
> Each felt a touching from beyond our ken,
> From that bright kingdom where the souls who strove
> Live now for ever, helping living men.
> And as they kissed each other, even then
> Their brows seemed blessed, as though a hand unseen
> Had crowned their loves with never-withering green.

Love, art, and spirit-communion, all are as one, from the one 'kingdom'.

The poem is warmly realized. Its Berkshire terrain is exactly located, and King Cole a legendary figure known in carols. It is beautifully patterned on the inter-shifting planes of sordid exterior and inward glory.

The natural medium for occult projection is drama, and Masefield's dramatic achievements are powerful. In *Philip the King* (1914), a poetic drama recalling Aeschylus' *Persae*, Philip awaits news of the Armada. His imperial pride is countered by avenging spirit-voices from those whom he or his nation has wronged, at home and abroad. Receiving news of the outcome from ghosts of his lost sailors and a messenger, he accepts disaster with a noble, and religious, equanimity. His imperialism is one with his religious faith, and there is no dramatic condemnation, except, following *The Persae*, against his pride. Fate rules:

> We are pieces played,
> Not moving as we will, but as we are made.

Chastened, he plans another Armada. Throughout, historic insight combines with numinous perception.

The Tragedy of Nan (prod. 1908; pub. 1909)[1] and *Melloney Holtspur* (1922) are major works. In the first the emphasis is on the earth-plane, and in the second on spirit-life; but both dramatize the interplay. Both have powerful, wronged, heroines.

Nan, a drama, in the Gloucestershire dialect, of rustic life and sordid deeds by the Severn, is close to earth and country ways, to farm life and woodland and the great river whose flood dominates the conclusion. From these flower its glory. The girl Nan is probably Masefield's best feminine creation. Her father had been unjustly hanged for stealing, and she is herself further wronged on all sides by human baseness. She murders her unworthy lover and, inspired by broken phrases from the wandering yet half-purposeful mind of the old Gaffer, goes garlanded for death to drown herself in the flood, our sense of tragic exaltation being echoed by the Gaffer's cry accompanying, in morality's despite, Nan's crime: 'O Love, you be a King. A King' (III).

The driving force, as in Shakespeare's *Timon of Athens*, is that great Love which for Nan has been desecrated and for which she dies. The drama raises tragedy to glory, but the glory is

---

[1] I have written more fully on *Nan* in *New Hyperion*, ed. Geoffrey Handley-Taylor, 1950; see also *The Golden Labyrinth*, 332-4.

earth-based and redolent of earthly experience, including Nan's ghastly, yet applauded, deed.

Symbols flower from actual events. The horn of a coach becomes in the Gaffer's mind a horn calling Nan, hoof-beats correspond to heartbeats: 'The horn. The horn. Cold hoofs beating on the road. They beat like the ticking of a 'eart. Soon. Very soon. The golden trump'. A Gold Rider assumes presence, slaying ghosts, slaying death-as-death: 'Angels. Gold Angels. The devil walks the dark at twelve. Ghosts. Ghosts. Behind the white 'eadstones. Smite 'em, Gold Rider. Smite 'em with thy bright sharp spear' (III). 'Gold Angels' both suggest the St. George-figured coins paid to Nan by the Government in recompense for her father's unjust execution and blend into the Gold Rider, a St. George figure whose horse's hoof-beats are also those of the coach in which the Government officials are to return. The Severn Bore is a natural event, but is here also a summoning as from a dimension beyond death. The interlockings awake intimations that what on one level are chance events may on another shadow meanings and purposes unguessed. As Pope tells us in his *Essay on Man* (I. 57-60):

> So Man, who here seems principal alone,
> Perhaps acts second to some sphere unknown,
> Touches some wheel, or verges to some goal;
> 'Tis but a part we see, and not a whole.

In *Multitude and Solitude* the hero was led to his destiny by a series of spirit-impelled 'chances'.

In *Melloney Holtspur* Melloney has been deeply wronged by her artist lover, Lonny Copshrews, and after the death of both impresses a person on earth to reveal his deeds to the mother of his daughter's lover in order to obstruct the girl's marriage. The action, involving two generations and two types of existence, is complicated for the reader but would be clear in performance. Lonny wants the 'old stain washed away' (II) by the new generation, but Melloney and the Man in Armour, a figure in the old house serving as the voice of cosmic law, demand his suffering.

There are three orders of dramatic conflict: that on earth; that of Melloney and Lonny as earth-bound spirits in mutual opposition; and that of the one drama with the other. The influence of spirits on human beings is accepted as normal: 'This life is a mysterious game, and we only play half our game ourselves' (I). There are three children of brilliantly characterized talk, one of whom enjoys a direct sight of Melloney's spirit such as the other two cannot because 'they have not the power' (III).

Dramas of spirit-vengeance and evil descending from one generation to the next date back to the Greeks; and when Lonny denounces the law refusing to let evil dissolve, we are in the world of Aeschylus' *Oresteia*. *Melloney Holtspur* brings to the Aeschylean and Shakespearian tradition insights learned from the spiritual-istic advances of our century. Never was the hell of self-recogni-tion and self-judgement, adumbrated by the tragic heroes of Shakespeare and by Byron's Manfred and asserted by Spiritualism, more fearfully convincing than in Lonny Copshrews' agony as he watches his past actions maturing through the revengeful Melloney to hurt his daughter. Melloney is no angel. She is in her own hell of earthbound vengeance. The only ultimate authority here is the Man in Armour, who insists on 'atonement' (IV). What exactly that means and how it eventually comes is not quite clear, but come it does: Melloney forgives, she and Lonny are freed from their torment, and the young are made happy.

The agonizing results of wrong-doing are before us, but we also hear that Lonny, being a great artist, had, whatever his sins, 'greatness of soul' (III). Masefield's own valuations are regularly more aesthetic than ethical. What he here dramatizes is less a judgement than the inevitable sequence, which Spiritualism teaches, of cause and effect: 'You set the wheel of the law moving. It has to go on to fulfilment' (IV). This is probably the most authoritative spiritualistic drama yet composed. Asked what is Reality, the Man in Armour, blending the creeds of Nietzsche and of Spiritualism, answers: 'The godhead of man. The brotherhood of man. The communion of spirits' (II).

4

We have considered works entangling the spiritualistic and the earthly. Christianity, dramatizing the Incarnation, is our supreme imaginative expression of this entanglement. We often do well to regard the Christian myth as symbolic of general truths. All men are spirits mysteriously incarnated into earthly life; all are poten-tially sons of God; and all pass through suffering and death to a

Masefield and Spiritualism

new state, or resurrection, of a plenitude no less than physical. Were the Christian dogmas not widely relevant, humanity would not have responded. So also the Christian's belief in Christ's presence is as a universalization of the experience of all ages and races, culminating in modern Spiritualism, that those who have died exist as powers. It follows that a poet by nature or experience spiritualistically attuned will be the better qualified to handle the Christian myth. I use the term 'myth' advisedly, since I am regarding the Christian story, including all its miracles and marvels, in terms rather of imaginative authenticity than of ecclesiastical command.

If indeed his Helpers guided Masefield when in literary difficulties to compose, as he tells us (p. 271 above), a narrative poem on the theme of Christian conversion, they chose wisely: for nothing could hold better promise of both poetic power and popular response.

The Everlasting Mercy (1911) presents an anarchic young man – poacher, fighter, and drinker – whose violences culminate in a denunciation of society and his charging by night through the town naked, ringing the fire bell, banging on doors, and shouting that hell is let loose. Like Shakespeare's Timon, Saul Kane denounces society as a 'sanctimonious crowd' of petty vices, and condemns the Parson and his Church as time-serving descendants of Cataphas helping to crush the poor while supporting privilege in the name of God. The Parson has his defence. The existing order has come about through centuries of laborious growth, and it does, in fact, work, however imperfectly:

> We're neither saints nor Philip Sidneys
> But mortal men with mortal kidneys.

The balance is held. Even so, this couplet acts as a reminder of superlative human excellences, in church and state; and the poem's power is lodged not in the Parson but in the hero who, though an unbeliever, claims kinship with those 'sons of light' preferred by Jesus to the 'trained' minds that merely 'talk' of light while remaining sceptical of any genuine experience.

Christian feeling, intermittent throughout, rises to a climax at the hero's conversion:

> And in my heart the drink unpriced,
> The burning cataracts of Christ.

284

The crashing power of this needs no advertisement, but its exact nature may be missed. Official Christianity is respected, but what the poem's *action* offers is at once more Pauline and more Nietzschean. Saul Kane's violences, like Paul's (or Saul's) first 'threatenings and slaughters' (Acts, IX. 1), rise from a directionless power subsequently directed, from negative to positive; but it is all one power. As Pope tells us in his *Essay on Man* (II. 183-4):

> The surest Virtues thus from Passions shoot,
> Wild Nature's vigor working at the root.

The names 'Kane' and 'Saul' define the transition.

It is possible over a number of years to recognize this and to recognize the compacted force of the 'cataracts' couplet, without recognizing that the two recognitions are the same. 'All convincing imagery', wrote John Davidson, 'is scientific truth' (*The Triumph of Mammon*, 1907; Epilogue, 160). The couplet could be suggesting a new, more fiery 'drink' for the 'heart', in place of Kane's former intoxicants; but there is more to it than that. During his period of intransigency he had compared himself to the 'sons of light', and his conversion is now given the line 'O glory of the lighted mind'. The 'burning cataracts', soft syllables supervening on harsh, are *the powers of Niagara transmuted to electricity, torrential water to light, passion to spirit*. In pursuance of his habitual insights into the elemental powers, Masefield has composed a couplet that rings supreme in the poetry of conversion. Thereafter in the poem the word 'Christ', so often feared, is daringly reiterated. The poet has won this freedom.

Good Friday (1916) stands supreme among British dramas of Christ. The Trial and Crucifixion are approached through an exact respect to historical detail. Jesus himself does not appear, but his presence is felt, and the nature of his challenge is defined by the aged Madman, personifying martyrdom; once rich, but now, for having seen 'truth like a perfect crystal, life its flaw', blinded and a beggar. His central speech is synchronized with, and enacts for us, the Crucifixion.

Wild birds have their flight, but whenever the 'wild souls of men' – men with the wildness and vision of Saul Kane and the Hunter of *Fire* – step beyond their companions' blindness to 'where the skies unclose', they are met by 'the spitting mob' like a 'bull gone mad': Masefield's poem of reminiscences, *Wonderings*

(1943), records what terror a bull could be to him in childhood.

Like those earlier visionaries, Jesus is now himself suffering. He is regarded not as unique, but as one of many:

> Beauty and peace have made
> No peace, no still retreat,
> No solace, none.
> Only the unafraid
> Before life's roaring street
> Touch Beauty's feet,
> Know Truth, do as God bade,
> Become God's son.

Only he with the courage for it becomes, like Jesus, 'God's son'; but the way is open to all. There is a pause. Then, with yet another emphasis on courage:

> Darkness, come down, cover a brave man's pain,
> Let the bright soul go back to God again.
> Cover that tortured flesh, it only serves
> To hold that thing which other power nerves.
> Darkness, come down, let it be midnight here,
> In the dark night the untroubled soul sings clear.

> [*It darkens*]

> I have been scourged, blinded and crucified,
> My blood burns on the stones of every street
> In every town; wherever people meet
> I have been hounded down, in anguish died.

> [*It darkens*]

> The creaking door of flesh rolls slowly back;
> Nerve by red nerve the links of living crack,
> Loosing the soul to tread another track.

The voice should pause on 'soul' and again on 'tread', and its tone change for 'another track'.[1]

After the agony comes release, and to the understanding of it we must bring full knowledge of Masefield's spiritualistic insights:

---

[1] I was fortunate to have the opportunity of playing the Madman in a production by A. A. Dams at Stowe, in 1942.

Beyond the pain, beyond the broken clay,
A glimmering country lies
Where life is being wise,
All of the beauty seen by truthful eyes
Are lilies there, growing beside the way.
Those golden ones will loose the torted hands,
Smooth the scarred brow, gather the breaking soul,
Whose earthly moments drop like falling sands
To leave the spirit whole.
Now darkness is upon the face of the earth.

The lines are to be read as widely applicable for all such men of suffering and courage. The 'Golden Ones' are spirit guardians waiting to welcome the new arrival, as when in *A Play of St. George* (1948) Spirits guide the martyred hero beyond death, asking him to listen for the music, saying, 'That is the language here'.

The Madman's central speech is in itself a compacted drama. Masefield has a Shakespearian power of rising to a supreme occasion, though Shakespeare never handled such an occasion as this. The Crucifixion lines have a dramatic force scarcely equalled, certainly never surpassed, in English; and the conclusion holds a spirit-gospel whose every phrase demands an exact reading.

Good Friday is not doctrinally governed; it handles the living facts on which doctrine was subsequently based. Masefield himself moves cautiously in that direction. The less vivid prose-drama, *The Trial of Jesus* (1925), develops more fully Jesus' Messianic claim to divine Sonship. In *The Coming of Christ* (1928) various Spirits discuss with Anima Christi, 'the Soul of Christ', his coming Incarnation; and though he is called the 'Divine One', there is also fear of the Incarnation inspiring some future 'creed' for 'the apathy about Man's brutal heart'. When one of the Shepherds bases his belief in God on certain saving experiences he has known like those recurring in Masefield's prose stories, we have an interesting link. *Easter* (1929) dramatizes not the physical resurrection of a man but the appearance from the tomb of the 'Anima Christi' which Mary Magdalene, thinking of the man, calls 'His quickened spirit'.

In these later, small dramas Masefield is trying so far as may be to develop his visionary Christianity, as the life of Jesus was

K   287

developed by the Church, to include the philosophical and the doctrinal. He does not so much follow doctrine as identify himself with the process of its making. He is still writing from his own imaginative centre.

Masefield's beliefs never range far from the humanistic and the spiritualistic. The creed of *Melloney Holtspur* includes 'the godhead of man', and any man brave enough may, in the Madman's words, become 'God's son'. In 'Pavilastukay' the hero finds ruins of a golden age:

> Slowly, still marvelling, he crossed the grass
> Towards the Palace, thinking 'This was wrought
> By men who never let Life's minute pass
> But stretched their eager hands to it, and caught,
> And pressed this glory from it, strength and thought
> Working as one, to this undying thing
> In praise of Man, Earth's only god and king'.

That, though not to be read as a final or inclusive statement, is part of Masefield's poetic world, in alliance with other apprehensions.

5

Masefield's strength is one with the sternness of his outlook. His *Collected Poems* (1923) opens with 'A Consecration', promising to write of the abandoned and unhonoured; and from buccaneer to prophet, he has done so. Fearful, mostly unjust, hangings, as in *The Camden Wonder* (1909), *Nan*, *The Widow in the Bye Street* (1912), *Eggs and Baker*, *Dead Ned* (1938), and presumably *The Condemned Cell* (1927?, not published), are an obsession. Never were Christ's physical sufferings more unflinchingly described than in *The Trial of Jesus*. *Sea Life in Nelson's Time* is a cold and cauterizing account of how our 'naval glory' was built by the agonies of 'barbarously maltreated men' (123). Modern war is presented in stark, factual outline. Nowhere in literature is elemental nature more fearful.

In 'Pavilastukay' – on the lost golden age – we are told that contemporary man 'gives his brief gasp to cut his brother's throat'; that, though nature is pitiless, 'Man is not Nature but a something gained', gained at 'great cost' and now in peril. Splendour once existed:

> Pray not to any god for it, but plan,
> Imagine, work, determine, struggle still
> That out of modern man there may come MAN.

Despite

> any devilry devised
> By things called soldiers serving things called states,

the thought of Pavilastukay remains a 'star'. What has been, can be, though 'man's paces as a spirit are not swift' (*The Wanderer of Liverpool*, 80).

The seventy pieces, most of them sonnets, of *Lollingdon Downs* (1917) probe the co-presence in man of physical brittleness and spiritual power; nothing of scepticism is shirked, nor its countering by deathless intimations. In 'The Night of Kings' (*The Bluebells and Other Verse*) a balance of spirit evidence and scepticism is subtly related to the birth of Christ. 'A Creed' (1910?, in *Ballads and Poems*) is a memorable statement on reincarnation. Such poems go as far as static enquiry can, but Masefield's greater contribution is in the dynamics of narrative and drama, since beauty only 'lives in the attempt to make it ours' (*The Wanderer of Liverpool*).

We are not alone. However dark the hour, there is always some 'muttering from beyond the veils of Death' ('August, 1914'). In *King Cole* we learn that 'up on the bitter iron there is peace' and that 'there is a help that the abandoned know'. In *Grace before Ploughing* ('Early Reading') Masefield records his early certainty of pre-existence, survival, and 'spiritual powers' ready to help 'bright human endeavour'. His life has been given to the defining of this help. It depends on man; it is born of his hope, awakes his courage, and makes him godlike. The heroic, though seldom coloured except through the actions concerned, is once finely enphrased when the troops at Gallipoli are seen as 'bronze'-bodied 'gods' more 'grand' in their 'half-nakedness' than 'clad men' (*Gallipoli*, 165). Courage is spirit-prompted. In 'The Hounds of Hell' (*Enslaved and Other Poems*, 1920) St. Withiel twice fails in courage before a pack of devil-hounds ravaging the land. The third time he is encouraged by carolling bird-spirits whose task it is, we are told, to reveal to man *his own* resources, which he cannot know 'unless we give the clue'. Then, brave, he faces the pack, and the horror shrivels.

Birds may be spirits, and so, with their 'steeple'-pointing masts (*Sard Harker*, 25), driven by the upper airs to plunge through ocean, may ships. The names *Bird of Dawning, Hurrying Angel* (in *Victorious Troy*), and *Pathfinder* (in *Sard Harker*) are significant: the *Pathfinder* actually appears as a spirit. The experience can touch ecstasy, as in this passage from 'Being Ashore', in *A Tarpaulin Muster* (1907), on voyaging off the River Plate:

We were tearing along across a splendour of sea that made you sing. Far as one could see there was the water shining and shaking. Blue it was, and green it was, and of a dazzling brilliance in the sun. It rose up in hills and in ridges. It smashed into foam and roared. It towered up again and toppled. It mounted and shook in a rhythm, in a tune, in a music. One could have flung one's body to it as a sacrifice. One longed to be in it, to be a part of it, to be beaten and banged by it. It was a wonder and a glory and a terror. It was a triumph, it was royal, to see that beauty.

And later, after a day of it, as we sat below, we felt our mad ship taking yet wilder leaps, bounding over yet more boisterous hollows, and shivering and exulting in every inch of her. She seemed filled with a fiery, unquiet life. She seemed inhuman, glorious, spiritual. One forgot that she was man's work. We forgot that we were men. She was alive, immortal, furious. We were her minions and servants. We were the star-dust whirled in the train of the comet. We banged our plates with the joy we had in her. We sang and shouted, and called her the glory of the seas.

Against 'the base ones of the spiritual world', for there are bad spirits enough, a fine ship is 'guarded by a presence, erect, winged, fiery' from 'the intellectual kingdom', strong and 'mailed' ('Ghosts', in *A Tarpaulin Muster*).

But it is only because Masefield knows and loves every fact and artefact of their constitution, every spar, bolt, and rope and the exact stresses on each at any moment of good or evil fortune, and what to do about it, that he has the right, of a kind perhaps which no comparable writer has ever had, to know ships as spiritual entities. There is no sentimentalizing. Ships are life itself, in its danger, its suffering, and its perfection. Within a ship there may be 'a hell': 'men mutinous, officers overdriven, boys in misery, the captain drunk'; yet from without she is an 'image of wonder', and 'one should not question beauty' (*Captain Margaret*, 1908; 274).

The Wanderer of Liverpool (1930) is an account in prose and poetry, with name-lists, dates, statistics, technical descriptions, and pictures, of the various voyages of Masefield's favourite, ill-fated ship. It is a love relationship and has a notable farewell entitled 'Wanderer and Wonderer':

> We two were subtlier linkt than most
> By thrilling atoms of the ghost
>
> And shall perhaps be, still, anon,
> In wondering and wandering on,
>
> From whence none knows, to where none knows,
> Save from the gas-whirl to the rose,
>
> And from the rose to man, and thence
> To spirit that has beaten sense.
>
> To that that can annihilate,
> To Heat, all Death, to Light, all Fate,
>
> And is all spirit, spark and spur,
> Magnificence and minister,
> To Wonderer and Wanderer.

So he parts, for a while, from his 'sea-wandering bird' (119).

We today study and use physical creation without recognition of the spirit-powers lending it life, form, and grace. Our art is consequently chaotic, ugly, and inert. In place of intellectual obscurity and psychological disease Masefield offers lucidity and health; in place of inertia, action. This he can do because he knows both the worst terrors of terrestrial existence and the sources of help.

In his *Shakespeare and Spiritual Life* (1924), on Shakespeare's entangling of supernatural phenomena with human drama, he has left us a valuable comment on *The Tempest*: 'The attainment of intellectual power, being a life-work in itself, takes the man who should be the ruler from his government: he is thereupon deposed by the knavish and the greedy, and cast out among the brutish:

unless he can bend spirits to his aid, this world will be no safe place for his daughter'. The word 'bend', correctly following the action of Shakespeare's play, should not mislead us. Elsewhere, in accord with the teachings and experiences of modern Spiritualism, Masefield knows that no such 'bending' is in question. The Helpers are waiting, and it is for us, by Hope, to make possible their entry.

CHAPTER X

Rupert Brooke

Promise of Greatness: the War of 1914-1918, edited by George A. Panichas, 1968.

ON THE MENTION of Brooke's name we think first either of his five war sonnets or of the famous bare-shouldered photograph by S. Schell, used for the 1915 collection of his *Poems* and the original of the plaque in Rugby Chapel by Havard Thomas, whose version is in the National Portrait Gallery, where copies are sold. I shall indicate a relation between Brooke's poetry and this portrait, called by Christopher Hassall in his biography *Rupert Brooke* (London, 1964) 'A visual image that met the needs of a nation at a time of crisis' (390).[1]

Brooke was not obviously fitted for the role of patriot. He had, it is true, certain social advantages. He struck a figure at Rugby and Cambridge, his poetic powers rapidly won attention, and he mixed with leading personalities in literature and politics. He had brilliance and wit. But the general tone of his conversation and writing was iconoclastic and unorthodox; he was a Socialist in politics and a pagan if not atheist in religion. His poetry was often of a kind to shock. He links the aestheticism of the nineties to the realism of postwar writing; he has affinities with both Wilde and Eliot.

Like Byron and Wilde, he had a strong personal impact. His appearance was striking; men such as Henry James, Walter de la

---

[1] I quote Brooke's letters from Hassall's biography. I have not used the fine recent volume of Brooke's letters, edited by Sir Geoffrey Keynes, for fear of expanding my essay. For those using the New York edition of Hassall, it may help to say that the fourteen chapters start on pp. 17, 34, 64, 96, 146, 186, 247, 293, 320, 359, 396, 448, 490, 514.

Mare, and Sir Ian Hamilton were conquered by it. The many records are extraordinary: 'astounding apparition' with eyes 'like the sky' (221); 'so beautiful that he's scarcely human' (258); 'a young man more beautiful than he I had never seen' (399); one who summed 'the youth of all the world' (441). But the accounts vary. Though he had the 'rosy' skin of a 'girl' (240), of 'girlish' smoothness (442), his appearance was all male, 'there was nothing effeminate' (441), and we hear also of a deeply tanned face and sturdy form, large feet and hands, and clumsy movements (241-2). It seems that he could appear variously male and female, clumsy and ethereal, according to mood. His complexion was rich, as though the blood 'was near the surface' (242). An inward power radiated out through the blood to the complexion, the eyes, and red-gold waves of hair, and it was some inner, spiritual, reality that gave him a 'shining impression' as of one 'from another planet' (524), so that he entered a room 'like a prince' (527). According to Henry James, much of Brooke's importance as both poet and person could not be conveyed to posterity, since it depended on 'the simple act of presence and communication' (523).

He was an *embodiment* of poetry: 'There are only three good things', he once said, 'in the world. One is to read poetry, another is to write poetry, and the best of all is to *live* poetry'; it 'kept one young' (143). Siegfried Sassoon felt poetry in his presence, as of a 'being singled out for some transplendent performance, some enshrined achievement' (451). He had the baffling bisexuality of such persons. Though he could oppose bisexual doctrines, he also admitted that 'the soul of persons who write verse is said to be hermaphroditic' (442, 446, and see 440). He was aware of his endowments: 'I looked at myself, drying, in the glass, and I thought my body was very beautiful and strong, and that I was keeping it and making it splendid for you' (304). 'For you': but also, perhaps more, for himself, since there was in him an element of Whitmanesque narcissism. He was bodily conscious: 'While the Samoans', he once wrote, 'are not so foolish as to "think", their intelligence is incredibly lively and subtle'; even a European living among them 'soon learns to *be* his body (and so his true mind) instead of using it as a stupid convenience for his personality, a moment's umbrella against the world' (460).

He preserved a child's bodily self-interest and a child's integrity;

as 'both man and boy' he was 'the child he must have grown from' (231); he was 'a symbol of youth for all time', doing up his shoes with 'the absorbed seriousness of a child' (277). Brooke remembered as a child often touching a 'higher level' of existence and recognizing that we are normally 'asleep', and the experience could be repeated in maturity, when he could say 'I more than exist' (257). In the South Seas he came near to a full recapture of this childhood magic (421).

He was obsessed with nakedness, usually in relation to bathing, at Grantchester, the South Seas, or by a Canadian lake, 'lying quite naked on a beach of golden sand' (409). In the South Seas he wrote of himself 'in a loin-cloth, brown and wild' by a 'sun-saturated sea', among 'naked people of incredible loveliness' (419). Here men were strong and beautiful in their unclothed bodies, and with finer sensibilities than Europeans (427-8), so that 'one's European literary soul begins to be haunted by strange doubts' (421). When war came, Brooke expected to 'find incredible beauty in the washing place, with rows of naked, superb men', either by sun or moon (463). If the many revulsions in his poetry point on to Eliot, his body obsession points to Lawrence. It is less likely that this obsession (other relevant references occur in Hassall's biography at 208, 255, 265, 266, 280, 282, 390, 410, 413, 418, 421, 424, 427, 429, 443, 523, 526) came from knowledge of his own beauty than that that beauty flowered from the inward obsession. He was, in fact, an integrated, or near-integrated, man.

His sex life was difficult. Living within the presexual or super-sexual, Nietzschean and lonely, integration at an age of physical maturity may be hard. His experience in the South Seas was not, he said, that of a love paradise; it was the opposite to alcohol according to the Porter's definition in *Macbeth*, 'for it promotes performance but takes away desire' (422). That is, presumably, sex functioned without a partner.[1] Brooke had known intense love in England, but it had failed. He had had a severe breakdown. He had contemplated suicide, feared madness and was reluctant to have children (355). Hassall refers to 'some obscure emotional

---

[1] The words might be read differently: compare Michael Hastings, *The Handsomest Young Man in England*, 1967; quoting (165) a reported statement by Brooke that in Tahiti he found that sexual relations tended to precede instead of following love. Here, as in all my studies, I prefer to avoid precise statements on sexual actions. Reports or confessions are rarely to be trusted, either way, and objective evidence is unavailable. See *Othello*, III. iii. 398-406.

distemper' (521), but leaves the 'root of his unsureness' undefined (445). Here is a late self-diagnosis:

Oh, I've loved you a long time, child: but not in the complete way of love. I mean, there was something rooted out of my heart by things that went before. I thought I couldn't love wholly, again. I couldn't worship – I could see intellectually that some women were worshipful, perhaps. But I couldn't find the flame of worship in me. I was unhappy. Oh, God, I *knew* how glorious and noble your heart was. But I couldn't burn to it. I mean, I loved you with all there was of me. But I was a cripple, incomplete (462).

In some moods he was an antifeminist (445), rating friendship above love (425). But he does not appear to have experienced male romantic friendships; imagination was turned inward, narcissistically, on himself.

We pass now to the poetry. It strongly attacks romantic love. The two sonnets 'Menelaus and Helen' show knightly romance giving place to blear-eyed impotence and nagging. 'The Beginning', 'Sonnet Reversed', 'Beauty and Beauty' tell the same story. In 'Kindliness' youth's infinite hunger has to make terms with a 'second-best'. In 'Mutability' our 'melting flesh' aims at impossible absolutes. 'Jealousy' contrasts young love with the slobbering age which follows, and in 'A Channel Passage' there is little difference between 'a sea-sick body or a you-sick soul'. In 'Dead Men's Love' love is reduced to 'dust and a filthy smell'. There appears to be some achievement in 'Lust', but the only real gleams are, as we shall see, in some new dimension beyond earth.

Brooke's sense of physical perfection led to a corresponding reaction. Man's body could so easily be repellent: in 'Wagner' and 'Dawn' physical nausea is emphatic. Brooke questions the human form itself: in 'Heaven' the fishes must see God as a great fish, and 'On the Death of Smet-Smet' shows savages worshipping a hippopotamus goddess. Our human valuations are arbitrary. 'Thoughts on the Shape of the Human Body' is a critique of sexual intercourse:

> . . . We love, and gape,
> Fantastic shape to mazed fantastic shape,
> Straggling, irregular, perplexed, embossed,
> Grotesquely twined, extravagantly lost
> By crescive paths and strange protuberant ways
> From sanity and from wholeness and from grace.

What is wanted is a more harmonious love 'disentangled from humanity', 'whole', a 'simplicity' like a 'perfect sphere', loving 'moon to moon'; the kind of love so often found in Platonic-homosexual engagements, though there seems to be nothing of primary importance recorded of Brooke. The moon's radiance is white, and whiteness is Brooke's colour, as it was Powys's, for beyond-earthly intimations.

Brooke was thrown back on himself. In 'Success' his loved one's 'white godhead', 'holy and far', is entangled with 'foul you', 'shame' and a 'black word', leaving the poet 'alone'. In 'I said I splendidly loved you' he admits the lie, conscious that he has been following 'phantoms' or 'his own face'. 'Waikiki' shows him correspondingly 'perplexed'. In 'The Voice' a love assignation horribly interrupts his lonely meditations in the night-darkened woods: 'By God! I wish – I wish that you were dead!' Elsewhere, in the dark woods of 'Flight', he has left daytime loves for the night's scents, weeping and stroking his own face. 'Paralysis' shows him in his 'white neat bed' laughing in his 'great loneliness'. In 'Town and Country' two lovers may be 'drunk with solitude' in the city, but in the woods by night love dissolves into a vaster, cosmic, loneliness. 'The Chilterns' tells us that:

> . . . a better friend than love have they,
> For none to mar or mend,
> That have themselves to friend.

He will have freedom enjoying the roads and winds and hedge-rows. He is with Wordsworth and John Cowper Powys, for whom the natural partner of the human soul is, not a sexual partner, but the objective universe (*In Spite Of*, IV. 116; in my study of Powys, *The Saturnian Quest*, 90). 'The Great Lover' is a key poem, listing a fine assortment of loves ranging through all the senses from wet roofs, the smell of burning wood, 'the rough male kiss of blankets' and 'furs to touch', to the miracles of earth nature. This Powysian mystique is expanded in a remarkable letter to Ben Keeling, quoted in Hassall's biography (236-9).

Perfection is attainable in young beauty or in sense enjoyment of external objects. But what of the future? In 'The Great Lover' he knows that life beyond death must be very different. He is ready to distinguish body from soul or spirit. In sleep the 'soul' leaves the body like a 'dress' laid by, and yet why then can the countenance appear troubled? Or smile? Surely, too, the sensuous is itself spirit-born, as in the mysterious sleep of 'Doubts':

> And if the spirit be not there,
> Why is fragrance in the hair?

This was Powys's concern. On its bodiless excursions the soul still, even at a great distance, uses the senses of the body it has left behind (*In Spite Of*, IV. 109, VII. 215; *The Saturnian Quest*, 88, and see 75).

This thought-teasing paradox of soul and body is brilliantly handled in a poem from Fiji, on the old cannibal practice of letting the victim see parts of himself eaten. Will this be his own fate? In comic if almost unreadable couplets, composed as for a past lover, he traces the horrors:

> Of the two eyes that were your ruin,
> One now observes the other stewing.

> (Hassall, 426)

The verses are simultaneously a critique of physical glamour and an assertion of the mind's, or soul's, independence. Perhaps nowhere else, apart from Byron, are crucial metaphysics so lightly handled.

Brooke was as strongly obsessed with the spiritual as with the physical. Though love fails on earth, there is hope for it beyond. 'The Goddess in the Wood' sets, in mythological terms, a type. In 'The Call' lovers may be 'one' *above* the 'Night', and in 'Victory' 'beyond all love or hate', 'perfect from the ultimate height of living', they challenge 'supernal' hosts. Wounded on earth, love may win success at the 'eventual limit of our light', in 'The Wayfarers'. 'Choriambics II', balances solitude in dark woods and some 'face of my dreams', gleaming down through the forest 'in vision white'. White is for Brooke, as for Powys (*The Saturnian Quest*, 24, 26, 48), a mystical colour. In 'Blue Evening', after 'agony' and 'hatred' the poet's love is felt within the moon's 'white ways of glamour', blessing him with 'white brows'. 'Finding' shows him after love's failure 'lone and frightened' in the 'white' moonlight's 'silver way', with around him trees 'mysteriously crying', 'dead voices' and 'dead soft fingers', and 'little gods' whispering, and he sees his love radiant beyond 'the tides of darkness', so that nothing was true

> But the white fire of moonlight
> And a white dream of you.

Such love is not sexually limited. 'Sleeping Out: Full Moon' shows him alone under the lonely Moon-Queen, and he feels the whole world pressing toward 'the white one flame' of a 'heatless fire' and 'flameless ecstasy'; 'earth fades'; 'radiant bands' and 'friendly' presences help the stumbler to the 'infinite height' and *maternal* eyes. We remember Brooke's desire for a perfect, un-entangled, love, loving 'moon to moon' in 'Thoughts on the Shape of the Human Body'. The visions are beyond sexuality in line with the contrast, in 'Success', of 'white godhead' with 'that foul you' – a contrast, in some vital way, of spirit with personality. We are all, already, part of some other, spiritual dimension. 'In Examination' develops a vision of ordinary life transfigured, revealing the 'scribbling fools' as with flaming hair, God-like, 'white-robed' in the 'white undying Fire' among archangels and angels; as beings in a dimension of which our normal seeing refracts only a miserable simulacrum. 'Desertion', on the death of a loved friend, asks pathetically *why* he has gone? Had he known something that made him distrust earth's 'splendid dream'? Is perhaps earth's seeming splendour – and often to Brooke it seemed sordid enough – a mere nothing in comparison?

Such intuitions touch Spiritualism. Though 'The True Beatitude' asserts 'an earthly garden hidden from any cleric' Brooke's poetry can be intensely spiritualistic, as when in 'Oh, Death will find me. . . .' he imagines his love's arrival in Hades tossing her hair 'among the ancient Dead'. 'Dust' vividly exploits the freedoms of an after-life. Though the 'white flame' of love's earthly visions has gone and we 'stiffen' in darkness, yet, in the manner of Byron's *Childe Harold* (III. 74):

> Not dead, not undesirous yet,
>   Still sentient, still unsatisfied,
> We'll ride the air, and shine, and flit,
>   Around the places where we died . . .

Beyond 'thinking' and 'out of view' (i.e. in an existence impossible to define):

> One mote of all the dust that's I
> Shall meet one atom that was you.

The old love reflames in the 'garden'; all senses are mixed – is it 'fire', 'dew', of 'earth' or the 'height', 'singing, or flame, or scent, or hue'? All that can be said is that it is 'light' passing on to 'light'.

Brooke had extrasensory experience. 'Home' recounts how, returning by night to his room, he was aware of

> The form of one I did not know
> Sitting in my chair.

Then it goes. All night he 'could not sleep'.

He wonders variously about the after-life. 'The Life Beyond' imagines it as hideous. 'Mutability' asks if indeed there is 'a high windless world and strange' beyond time? 'Our melting flesh' fixes Beauty there and 'imperishable Love', but all we actually know is earth experience, where kisses do not last. The poem 'Clouds' ponders the belief that 'the Dead' remain close to those on earth, but suggests rather that they pass above like clouds, reflecting 'the white moon's' beauty, and 'break and wave and flow' like a silent sea. But shall we remember the past? 'Hauntings' imagines a 'poor ghost' 'haunted' by vague recollections of earth-life – as earth beings are 'haunted' by spirit-life – which are unintelligible:

> And light on waving grass, he knows not when,
> And feet that ran, but where, he cannot tell.

Official Spiritualism is given the 'Sonnet (Suggested by some of the Proceedings of the Society for Psychical Research)'. After death we shall

> Spend in pure converse our eternal day;
>   Think each in each, immediately wise;
> Learn all we lacked before; hear, know, and say
>   What this tumultuous body now denies;
> And feel, who have laid our groping hands away;
>   And see, no longer blinded by our eyes.

The lines report what Spiritualism tells us: speech by telepathic immediacy, halls of learning and progress; the earth body as a limiting factor which narrows and constricts, so that we feel more keenly and see more clearly without it, as in Andrew Marvell's 'Dialogue between the Soul and the Body'. The next plane, where sound and colour are one, is richer, not poorer, in sense experience; depending not on a mentalized summation derived from separate sense-inlets, we shall respond directly to the totality of which these allow parts only to trickle through and which we can on earth only approach by attempts at some total dramatic art blending intellectual awareness with sound and colour.[1]

Brooke came near such a total experience in the South Sea Islands. 'Tiare Tahiti', rejecting the 'broken things' of earth, introduces us to a world of Platonic archetypes, to 'the Face, whose ghosts we are' and to 'Dance' without 'the limbs that move', all lovely things meeting in 'Loveliness'. All colours, white especially, but also coral, pearl, green, gold, red, are there; all earth beauty recaptured and eternalized. And yet – must 'feet' become 'Ambulation', and what of kisses? Meanwhile, let us enjoy the 'flowered way' and 'whiteness of the sand', 'well this side of Paradise'. We may be nearer the spirit reality at choice, sense-summing moments of earthly life than with *mental* accounts, however accurate, of that reality, which is all, and more, of what we experience on earth. Such is the truth flowering from this cleverly balanced poem.

Brooke lived and wrote on the border between earth and paradise, life and death. The transition, as with Powys, involves what may be called the 'elemental'. In nature Brooke loved night woods and the moon, and also his own, and others', nakedness, swimming and water. These are as transition mediums between modes of existence.

Herein lies the importance of the poem 'The Old Vicarage, Grantchester'. It contrasts the regulated officialdom of Berlin, where the lines were composed, with the luxuriant freedoms and 'unofficial rose' of Grantchester; more widely, civilized constrictions with elemental freedom. At Grantchester one runs on 'bare feet' to the river 'deep as death':

> In Grantchester their skins are white;
> They bathe by day, they bathe by night. . . .

Spirits are here: 'His ghostly Lordship swims his pool', and among the trees flits 'the sly shade of a Rural Dean'. It is a place of 'lithe children lovelier than a dream' and 'youth', where suicide is preferable to 'feeling old'.

The phrase 'deep as death' is important. In the Hades of Byron's

[1] See my discussion on Spiritualism and Poetry appended to *The Starlit Dome*, 1959, 318-20; and to *The Christian Renaissance*, 1962, 328-9.

Cain and in Ibsen's *Lady from the Sea* and *Little Eyolf* water naturally blends with the dimension of death. Brooke once, in imaginative vein, described his Grantchester night bathing:

I stood naked at the edge of the black water in a perfect silence. I plunged. The water stunned me as it came upwards with its cold, life-giving embrace. . . . (Hassall, 208)

Then a figure appeared, some 'local deity' or 'naiad of the stream', who urged him, as Powys often urged us, not to search beyond present existence. But with the elements, especially by night, we are already on the border-line, living life-and-death. Diving into blue-green waters at Fiji was perhaps better than poetry (Hassall, 421). Water is death and life. The dead of 'Clouds' 'break and wave and flow' like a silent sea. The visionary figure of 'Blue Evening' comes 'rippling' down the moon's 'glamour'. 'Day That I Have Loved' imagines the day as a dead loved one, gone out to sea, and darkness. 'Finding' tells of 'the words of night' and 'dead' spirit-voices and 'the dark, beyond the ocean'. Brooke's lines in 'Seaside':

> In the deep heart of me
> The sullen waters swell towards the moon,
> And all my tides set seaward

correspond exactly to the conclusion to Powys's *Rodmoor*. In both Powys and Brooke we meet a mystique of water, darkness, and a great *white* peace (*The Saturnian Quest*, 26). In 'The Jolly Company' the stars are a 'white companionship' of 'lonely light'.

Sea life is as a new dimension. 'The Fish' blends life and death:

> The strange soft-handed depth subdues
> Drowned colour there, but black to hues,
> As death to living, decomposes –
> Red darkness of the heart of roses,
> Blue brilliant from dead starless skies,
> And gold that lies behind the eyes,
> The unknown unnameable sightless white
> That is the essential flame of night. . . .

As elsewhere, *darkness* is one with the *white* vision. 'Behind the eyes' corresponds to Eliot's 'more distant than stars and nearer than the eye' in 'Marina'. A fish's life contrasts with love's unrest; it is a lonely self-enjoyment of the blood rhythms. In Powysian vein, for these cool, atavistic depths are exactly Powysian, 'His bliss is older than the sun'.

Brooke's progress through love-agony and love-failure to a lonely delight in his solitary, narcissistic, childlike, integrated self, body and soul, to a superb culmination of swimming naked among the glorious nakedness of the South Sea Islanders, was not all easy and innocent. It had its violent, non-moral aspect: 'I had to have a bath and dance many obscene dances, in lonely naked-ness, up and down my room, to get sober' (Hassall, 443). In the early 'Song of the Beasts' the 'sober' and 'dull' consciousness of 'common day' is contrasted with 'shameful night' when 'God is asleep':

> Have you not felt the quick fires that creep
> Through the hungry flesh, and the lust of delight,
> And hot secrets of dreams that day cannot say?

The night 'calls' and we leave the house, going

> Down the dim stairs, through the creaking door,
> Naked, crawling on hands and feet. . . .

We are 'Beast and God', serving 'blind desire', past 'evil faces' and 'mad whispers', out of the 'city', 'beyond lust', to level moon-lit waters, and the 'calling sea'. An embarrassment, half-shame, half-pride, is written into 'Mary and Gabriel', wherein Mary feels both 'her limbs' sweet treachery' and her 'high estate', to be used for some high purpose. She feels 'alone', her 'womb' – or Brooke's own beauty – not exactly hers, and yet, we are told, it *will* be; some half-glimpsed purpose will be fulfilled and known.

Death is, and yet is not, the end. In the early (1908) 'Second Best' the poet is 'alone with the enduring Earth, and Night'. Death, he thinks, is the end. If so:

> Proud, then, clear-eyed and laughing, go to greet
> Death as a friend!

The poem advances to a sense of death as containing all that was life:

> Exile of immortality, strongly wise,
> Strain through the dark with undesirous eyes
> To what may lie beyond it. Sets your star,
> O heart, for ever! Yet, behind the night,
> Waits for the great unborn, somewhere afar,
> Some white tremendous daybreak. And the light,

Returning, shall give back the golden hours,
Ocean a windless level, Earth a lawn
Spacious and full of sunlit dancing-places,
And laughter, and music, and, among the flowers,
The gay child-hearts of men, and the child-faces,
O heart, in the great dawn!

Brooke's earthly poetry is mostly a night-time poetry. Brightness, the sun, the white dawn – like that in the penultimate chapter of Powys's *Weymouth Sands* (*The Saturnian Quest*, 48) – all seem to lie, apart from his experiences in the South Seas, beyond.

'The Little Dog's Day' (1907) is an early forecast of his death. After these supreme experiences in the South Seas, he had had his day: on his chosen line, there was little more. He had realized himself on the border where supreme self-enjoyment touches a new dimension, and he knew himself ripe for death. There was, he said, 'point in my not getting shot', but 'also there's point in my getting shot'; 'life might be great fun' and 'death might be an admirable solution' (Hassall, 491). The famous war sonnets are less like patriotic trumpetings than paeans in praise of death. As in R. C. Sherriff's *Journey's End*, war is simply an elemental power, or death force: the sonnets could be applied, *mutatis mutandis*, to a young German.

The first, 'Peace', contrasts the inadequacies of poetry and love with 'swimmers into cleanness leaping' and a consequent 'release'. Only the body will be broken, and Death is both 'enemy' and 'friend'.

In the second, 'Safety', war, or death, 'knows no power'. One will be 'safe' whatever happens: 'And if these poor limbs die, safest of all'. 'Poor' registers both Brooke's emotional self-involvement and a recognition of the body's inadequacy.

'The Dead' celebrates 'honour', but remains typical in 'the rich Dead' who 'poured out the red sweet wine of youth'. Youth's sacrifice is more than patriotism. Called 'holiness', it is a thing in itself, youth's perfect hour.

The fourth, also called 'The Dead', remembers how they, as in 'The Great Lover', had known the varied sense-impressions of earth. 'All this is ended.' Instead, the glittering wavelets are now frosted to

a white
Unbroken glory, a gathered radiance,
A width, a shining peace, under the night.

Moonlight is assumed, or stars.

In 'The Soldier' Brooke concentrates on his body, made by England, after dying in a foreign land, where there shall be 'in that rich earth a richer dust concealed'. The 'heart' (i.e. mind or spirit) will preserve the sounds and scents of its earthly experience. The impressions are both physical and eternal.

These sonnets necessarily avoid extended statements on spirit-life. The problem of war sacrifice is one mainly of *body* sacrifice, as in Masefield's remarkable quatrain, printed in *The Times*, 16 September 1938, on the occasion of Neville Chamberlain's meeting with Hitler:

As Priam to Achilles for his Son,
So you, into the night, divinely led,
To ask that young men's bodies, not yet dead,
Be given from the battle not begun.

Those lines and Brooke's five sonnets preserve necessary limits.

We now return to the Schell portrait. The mockery it at first received at Cambridge as 'obscene' or as 'your favourite actress' (Hassall, 390) signals the nature of its importance. It was used as a frontispiece to the 1915 collection of his poems and copied for the Rugby Chapel plaque. It became symbolic: 'bare-shouldered, long-haired, Greek god-like, mystic, wonderful', it was 'on the retina of the public eye, the soldier poet, the nation's sacrifice' (Richard Usborne, 'The Lost Heroes', *Sunday Times Magazine*, pictorial supplement, 29 January 1967).

What is its secret? The head rising from bare shoulders suggests a totality unconstricted by the mufflings of civilization. The profile of lips and nose, the waves of hair, the upward tilt of the head and eager eyes, are riveting. Its deliberated pose may have seemed 'a travesty' of one whose attractions were normally 'unconscious', lacking the 'candour' of glance his friends knew (Hassall, 390-1); but though critics thought the Rugby plaque 'sentimentalized', his mother saw it as the living image of the youth she had loved, and liked its appearance of 'pressing forward' (Hassall, 525).

The upward challenge of its meaning corresponds to Brooke's desire in the early 'Second Best' to 'greet Death as a friend', 'clear-eyed and laughing', and to the use of 'lifts' in the 1913 poem 'The Night Journey', wherein a rushing train symbolizes human destiny:

> Hands and lit faces eddy to a line;
>   The dazed last minutes click; the clamour dies.
> Beyond the great-swung arc o' the roof, divine,
>   Night, smoky-scarv'd, with thousand coloured eyes
>
> Glares the imperious mystery of the way.
>   Thirsty for dark, you feel the long-limbed train
> Throb, stretch, thrill motion, slide, pull out and sway,
>   Strain for the far, pause, draw to strength again. . . .
>
> As a man, caught by some great hour, will rise,
>   Slow-limbed, to meet the light or find his love;
> And, breathing long, with staring sightless eyes,
>   Hands out, head back, agape and silent, move
>
> Sure as a flood, smooth as a vast wind blowing;
>   And, gathering power and purpose as he goes,
> Unstumbling, unreluctant, strong, unknowing,
>   Borne by a will not his, that lifts, that grows,
>
> Sweep out to darkness, triumphing in his goal,
>   Out of the fire, out of the little room . . . .
> – There is an end appointed, O my soul!
>   Crimson and green the signals burn; the gloom
>
> Is hung with steam's far-blowing livid streamers.
>   Lost into God, as lights in light, we fly,
> Grown one with will, end-drunken huddled dreamers.
>   The white lights roar. The sounds of the world die.
>
> And lips and laughter are forgotten things.
>   Speed sharpens; grows. Into the night, and on,
> The strength and splendour of our purpose swings.
>   The lamps fade; and the stars. We are alone.

Compulsion that 'lifts'; the darkness; the white lights roaring, sound and sight one in the new dimension; the intoxicating purpose and the conclusion on 'alone' – here is Brooke's total metaphysic, nobly stated.[1]

[1] The 1946 edition (imp. of 1963) prints: lights in lights. The 1912 edition (imp. of 1923) has: lights in light.

Rupert Brooke

The Schell portrait is, in its quiet way, a statement of this empowered message. It shows, necessarily, nothing of the blood radiance or red-gold hair which Brooke's friends knew. The definition is faint, a shadow kills the head's outline at the nape, and the far shoulder is lost in light (the definition is stronger in Havard Thomas's plaque). The dominating effect is of whiteness, as of a spirit body,[1] its nakedness that of the 'naked seraph' of Shelley's additional lines to 'Epipsychidion' or the 'immortal nakedness' of the young Caponsacchi's ecstatic sacrifice in Browning's *The Ring and the Book* (VI. 971). Some lines of Brooke's 1908 'Choriambics II' were prophetic. They address a dream-figure who

> Somewhere lay, as a child sleeping, a child suddenly reft from mirth,
> White and wonderful yet, white in your youth, stretched upon foreign earth,
> God, immortal and dead!

The child, or youth, may seem to sleep, but the seraph awakes, eager, as in the portrait. 'Immortal' yet 'dead': death in youth, and youth in death.

The bare-shouldered portrait was Brooke's own idea.[2] Michael Hastings (p. 295n. above) writes (48): 'When Brooke posed for Sherril Schell, the photographer claimed it was Brooke's idea to have, out of the twelve frames, a picture of himself naked from the waist up.' This was the basis of the famous portrait, of which Brooke wrote:

> Nothing's happened: except that my American photographer has sent me a photograph of me – very shadowy and ethereal and poetic, of me in profile, and naked-shouldered. Eddie says it's very good. I think it's rather silly. But anyhow, I don't look like an amateur popular preacher – as in those others.
> And no one will ever be able to put it into an interview, with the words 'We want great serious drama' underneath (Hassall, 390).

---

[1] Once having by an error received from a photographer a picture of a woman instead of himself, Brooke wrote: 'Modern photographers seem to an old-fashioned person like me, to retouch almost *too* much. Or perhaps you only take the soul? The soul of persons who write verse is said to be hermaphroditic, but not I protest, *so* feminine' (quoted by Timothy Rogers, 'Rupert Brooke: Man and Monument', *English*, XVII. 99; Autumn, 1968; and see Hassall, 446).

[2] See S. Schell, 'The Story of a Photograph', *The Bookman* (New York), LXIII. 6, August 1926; 688-90.

His self-exploitation might, he knew, incur mockery, but at least it distinguished him from conventional religion and the literary intelligentsia.

Brooke's death was in attunement with his life and thought. It came as an inevitable, half-willed, instinctive flowering. This does not detract from the sacrifice but rather raises it to artistic and universal status. It was not by chance but rather, to quote *Coriolanus*, by a certain 'sovereignty of nature' that his dying became, like Byron's, symbolic. His memorial at Skyros (Hassall, 528) was well devised by the sculptor Tombros as a nude statue not so much of Brooke himself as of 'a young man symbolizing Youth'.

CHAPTER XI

T. E. Lawrence

Composed during 1968.

He looks as man was made; with face erect,
That scorns his brittle corpse, and seems ashamed
He's not all spirit.

(John Dryden, *Don Sebastian*, I. i)

I HAVE USED chiefly Lawrence's *Seven Pillars of Wisdom* (privately printed 1926; Jonathan Cape, 1935; Penguin Books, 1962), giving chapter numerals and Penguin page-numerals; Lawrence's *The Mint* (London, 1955); *The Letters of T. E. Lawrence*, ed. David Garnett (London, 1938); *T. E. Lawrence by his Friends*, designated below as *Friends*, reminiscences collected and edited by A. W. Lawrence (London, 1937); all published by Jonathan Cape. Also four articles on Lawrence by Colin Simpson and Phillip Knightley, *The Sunday Times*, Weekly Review section, 9, 16, 23 and 30 June 1968; now expanded, and with the authors' names reversed, as *The Secret Lives of Lawrence of Arabia* (London, 1969).

Other works referred to are: *With Lawrence in Arabia*, Lowell Thomas (London, 1924); *Lawrence and the Arabs*, Robert Graves (London, 1927); *T. E. Lawrence: In Arabia and After*, by B. H. Liddell Hart (London, 1934); *Lawrence of Arabia: The Man and the Motive*, Anthony Nutting (London, 1961); *T. E. Lawrence, or The Search for the Absolute*, Jean Beraud Villars, trans. P. Dawnay (London, 1958).

Important recent source-books are: *Letters to T. E. Lawrence*, ed. A. W. Lawrence (London, 1962) and *T. E. Lawrence to his Biographers*, ed. Robert Graves and Liddell Hart (London, 1963).

T. E. Lawrence

LIKE BYRON, AND for the same reasons, Lawrence has become a legendary and controversial figure. It is my purpose here to define the nature of his impact. If he was as faulty as his detractors claim, then that impact is only the more amazing, even magical; and it is just this, the magic, that I aim to discuss.

Most of the attacks were levelled long ago, by himself. In later life he tended to discount his military contribution (p. 350 below); and he was forthright in confessing both his craving for popularity and his scorn of that craving (CIII. 580)[1]: he makes all the relevant apologies. In his 1926 preface to the *Seven Pillars of Wisdom* he states that it 'does not pretend to be impartial' and must be read as a 'personal' record. No critic of the book as literature could be more stern, even cruel, than he was (see Letters numbered 161, 225, 266, 270, 363). In it he wrote of his own personality:

My brain was sudden and silent as a wild cat, my senses like mud clogging its feet, and my self (conscious always of itself and its shyness) telling the beast it was bad form to spring and vulgar to feed upon the kill. So meshed in nerves and hesitation, it could not be a thing to be afraid of; yet it was a real beast, and this book its mangy skin, dried, stuffed and set up squarely for men to stare at.

(CIII. 581)

The implied criticism of all writing is Byronic. Lawrence perhaps expressed himself more easily in his admirable letters than in his more formal writing; many have thought that of Byron, too. Lawrence admired Byron's letters (Letter 347; to William Rothenstein, 14 April 1928. For Byron, see also Letter 360; to David Garnett, 14 June 1928).

Lawrence cannot be better introduced than by noting his many resemblances to Byron.[2] Both had aristocratic fathers and were brought up by their mothers. Both were regularly called impish or Puckish, loving practical jokes, and yet the anger of both could be terrifying (for Byron, *Lord Byron: Christian Virtues*, 276-7). Both enjoyed penetrating humbug and falsities. Though

---

[1] My references in this style apply to *Seven Pillars of Wisdom*.

[2] Support for the statements that follow will be found: for Byron, in my two books, which contain subject indexes, *Lord Byron: Christian Virtues* and *Byron and Shakespeare*; and for Lawrence, throughout this essay, especially Section 6, on the reminiscences of his friends.

not exactly studious types, they had vast stores of general, and especially historical, knowledge, drawn from wide reading and perfected memorizing, with an especial regard for the Old Testament (*Friends*, 413). Each showed a strong though unformulated religious sensibility (*Friends*, 594; see also 245, 306-7, 408). Both believed in God but not in dogma. Each has an unusual capacity, throughout, for self-judgement. Lawrence was as ready as Byron 'to exaggerate the less worthy elements' in himself (B. H. Liddell Hart, *Friends*, 185).

They were both by temperament generous (*Friends*, 299, 594-5), like Shakespeare's Timon and Oscar Wilde. Lawrence's refusal to profit financially from his writing balances Byron's similar refusals during his early career; and his readiness to advance the literary work of others while scorning his own is exactly Byronic (E. M. Forster, *Friends*, 283, and for Byron, *Lord Byron: Christian Virtues*, II). They both enjoyed anonymous giving.

Their habits were similar. Both liked to work by night and sleep by day (*Friends*, 249; and see 326). Both all but starved themselves, for reasons clearly envisaged, mastering physical compulsions and clarifying their minds. They seemed more *mental* than was natural for a man. William Parry's words on Byron might have been written of Lawrence: 'He was more a mental being, if I may use this phrase, than any man I ever saw. He lived on thought more than on food' (*The Last Days of Lord Byron*, 1825; V. 107; *Byron and Shakespeare*, 289). And yet they exerted strong physical charm and beauty, their blue eyes and auburn hair being noted, the eyes especially; and there are many portraits or sculptures of both. But again, there were physical limitations; Byron was slightly lame from a childhood accident and Lawrence, after breaking a leg when saving a boy from a bullying at school (*Friends*, 26), never grew to full stature. These physical disabilities had their psychological results. His lameness worried Byron acutely, and Lawrence's diminutive stature acted on him almost as a 'neurosis' (*Friends*, 295). Byron often feared madness: his Manfred prayed for it as a blessed relief (*Manfred*, II. ii. 133-4). Lawrence once wrote:

This sort of thing must be madness, and sometimes I wonder how far mad I am, and if a madhouse would not be my next (and merciful) stage.

(Letter 207; to Lionel Curtis, 14 May 1923)

Lt.-Col. Ralph H. Isham refers to Lawrence's contact with atavistic powers 'too strong for suppression', and making him 'doubt his sanity', all being part of 'the fermentation of contradictory elements that boiled within him' (*Friends*, 296-7). The phrases might have been composed for Byron.

In personal relationships we find a similar liking for male youth. Byron had heterosexual affairs, but they were often half-reluctant, generally tormenting and happiest when tending towards companionship or the sisterly, or the maternal. Peter Quennell once suggested that he would really have been better placed in an age of monasteries. Lawrence's tendencies are regularly called 'monastic', by himself and others. He avoided women, but eventually derived strength from his friendship with Mrs. Shaw (Simpson and Knightley, *The Sunday Times*, Weekly Review, 30 June 1968; 45-6; *Secret Lives*, Index). If, as Anthony Nutting tells us, Lawrence's inhibitions were derived from a school experience 'which produced in him a horror of physical contact' (Nutting, 241), we can compare this with Byron's early experience with Lord Grey de Ruthyn, said to have had so great an influence on his subsequent sex-life (*Lord Byron's Marriage*, 202-3).

Both men had strong homosexual tendencies. A. W. Lawrence's 'His friendships were comparable in intensity to sexual love' (*Friends*, 591) corresponds with Byron's 'My school friendships were with me *passions*' ('Detached Thoughts', *Letters and Journals*, V. 455), the loves of Byron corresponding to Lawrence's devotion to Dahoum, who was at about the age of Byron's boy-loves when Lawrence first met him at Carchemish. In both, devotion to a youth of a race suffering under Turkish oppression, Nicolo Giraud and Loukas for Byron and Dahoum for Lawrence, may be felt as empowering their militant activities in the cause of that race's freedom (p. 330 below).

Both are simultaneously sensitive poetic types and men of action. They are magnetic leaders receiving devotion from wild and rough warriors as to a natural superior in mind and courage. Their personal bodyguards or retinues, Byron's Suliote mountaineers at Missolonghi and Lawrence's young Arabs, were deliberately chosen from ferocious types: 'They were blood enemies of thirty tribes, and only for my hand over them would have murdered in the ranks each day' (LXXXIII. 476). Byron had to do much the same sort of controlling at Missolonghi. Lawrence,

T. E. Lawrence

like Byron, set himself to master physical weakness, living on simple fare and dominating illness, as Byron did at Missolonghi, by power of mind. In both, courage was a mental, fully conscious self-mastery. Both were expert marksmen with pistol or revolver (*Friends*, 407; and see 92). In the arts, both loved music (*Friends*, 515) and responded to – Lawrence practised it – sculpture (*Friends*, 29, 89, 276, 285, 368, 589; for Byron, *Byron and Shakespeare*, 47-50). Lawrence learned to shed blood freely. From this Byron was saved; whether he could have done it we do not know.

The two stories show similar curves of a rise to fame followed by a plunge to a lower stratum, with a willed preference for association with the lowly to accepting equality with the high. Each was avid of greatness, but preferred degradation to the falsities of fame and insincerities of society. Both positively enjoyed showing disrespect to the great, while showing consideration to the humble (*Friends*, 547-8). Neither would pay the price of social or political advancement:

I could not tame my nature down; for he
Must serve who fain would sway; and soothe, and sue,
And watch all time, and pry into all place,
And be a living lie, who would become
A mighty thing amongst the mean – and such
The mass are.

(*Manfred*, III. i. 116)

That is how Lawrence, too, felt. He, like Byron, would – in some moods – be '*aut Caesar aut Nihil*' (Journal, November 1813; *Letters and Journals*, II. 339; *Lord Byron: Christian Virtues*, 236). Each was only administratively at ease as a leader; Byron at Missolonghi, Lawrence among his Arabs.

Strangers could be amazed. Expecting a man of terrifying power they found a quiet, demure, boyish figure, happily responsive; though both could be angered by people coming merely to observe.

The co-presence in both of fun and agony, child and superman, has proved baffling. They emitted psychic rays that were disturbing, alternating anger with seraphic charm. They were almost as beings from another sphere – Byron's 'something unearthly' (*Childe Harold*, IV. 137) – and have accordingly awakened the myth-making faculty in others, becoming legendary not only in

Greece and Arabia, but across the world. Like Byron in *Don Juan*, if Lawrence showed any signs of sentiment, he would at once turn them to ridicule (*Friends*, 92). Each had rich comedic interludes when he could regard his best accomplishments as farcical; and yet they were also proud. Naturally enough, both have been accused of posing; they sometimes themselves delighted in contributing to the mystery, as though enjoying the performance. Each could be as baffled as everyone else by his own personality.

As we watch Lawrence wrestling with his own demonic powers, repudiating his great achievement, and steadily attuning himself to a less spectacular self-making and creative purpose, we remember not only Byron's steady development from turmoil to serenity, but Nietzsche's definition of self-transcendence:

> His deed is itself the shadow that lieth upon him; the hand obscureth him that handleth. Not yet hath he surmounted his own deed.
>
> Truly I love in him the steer's neck: but I would also see the angel's eye.
>
> He must yet unlearn his hero will: he shall yet be one that is lifted high, and not merely an eminent man: the ether itself shall lift him without will of his!
>
> He hath subdued monsters, he hath solved riddles: but he must yet resolve his monsters and his riddles, he must change them to heavenly children.
>
> (Thus Spake Zarathustra, II. 13)

'Ether' suggests a spirit-being. The physical images fit Lawrence's strong jaw and radiant eyes. Eric Kennington writes: 'Though not broad, he was weighty from shoulders to neck, which jutted, giving a forward placing to the head, and a thrust to the heavy chin'; but the eyes were 'maternal'. He was 'puzzled how the head could be at once so strong, and so sensitive' (*Friends*, 264-5). It is my purpose to show that, in his own context of nation, time, opportunity and psychology, Lawrence came close to the realization, in full scope, of Nietzsche's prophecy.

2

During his Arab campaign Lawrence was collaborating with men of primitive yet proud values, with 'heights and depths beyond our reach', realizing absolutes of 'good and evil' (CVII. 607). They had a ferocious sense of honour: in them the Homeric and epic qualities showed naked, as though the desert's naked terrain had its psychological correlative. Instincts being uninhibited, they were easily whole, and therefore graceful in poise and bearing (LXXV. 424).

In gearing his own Western sensibilities to the affairs of this fiery people, Lawrence personifies and acts a fusion of Christianity and epic. The paradox was well put by Yeats in his *Vacillation*: 'What theme had Homer but original sin?' Lawrence was destined for such a role: from youth he had studied war, specializing in medieval castles in Europe and the Near East, and also on old Churches, in England and France. He was by instinct medieval, pre-Raphaelite: he once named William Morris as his favourite author (Graves, 437). But his was the 'real medievalism' of Malory and the Crusades (Graves, 159). He carried the *Morte D'Arthur* with him in Arabia (LXXXVII. 495). He aspired to that chivalric unity which was split by the Renaissance into Church and State, so that soul and nation were henceforth opposed and man tugged between Christ and politics in a world of warring. Lawrence is central to our present confusions: that is why he fascinates.

As man of action he was accordingly complex, a Hamlet and Fortinbras in one. He did not wish to be a leader, but was forced to it by events. He 'hated responsibility', was more at home with 'objects' than with 'persons', and with 'ideas' than with 'objects'; and he 'hated soldiering' (XVII. 117). This self-diagnosis is only true for the Hamlet in him; and there was more than that. Unlike Byron's, Lawrence's destiny involved him in actual bloodshed, and though both show a balance of sensibility and soldiership, Lawrence was certainly the more attuned to warring. His reservations are nevertheless interesting. The nature of his campaign was peculiar and his considered strategy one of avoiding bloodshed. In contrast to the massing of force and carnage on the Western front, his plans were for mobility, speed, and the use of empty spaces; and also for mental or spiritual deployments, with assessments of morale, and propaganda (XXXIII. 197-202; discussed by Liddell Hart, 160-78).[1] His high-strung and mentalized

---

[1] Lawrence's technique of avoiding direct engagement (XXXIII. 200) has a fascinating analogy in certain aspects of Cassius Clay's (Muhammad Ali's) technique in boxing. See p. 79 above. Liddell Hart defended Lawrence's methods in a letter to *The Times Literary Supplement*, 3 November 1961.

being was projected into a psychic warring prophetic of the
Second World War and of the Cold War that has followed with
its balancing of risks and imponderables; and both these wars are
in their turn prophetic of that ultimate fusion of war-values and
the Sermon on the Mount for which Byron laboured at Missolonghi.

Lawrence knew the guilt of bloodshed. Of the battle of Tafileh,
where he had light-heartedly accepted the Turks' challenge to a
conventional engagement, he wrote:

This was villainous, for with arithmetic and geography for allies we
might have spared the suffering factor of humanity; and to make a
conscious joke of victory was wanton.   (LXXXV. 485)

He accuses himself of buying self-advertisement with unnecessary
slaughter, for 'the destruction of this thousand poor Turks would
not affect the issue of the war'; there was no 'glory' in it
(LXXXVI. 491). But when there was need he could himself, on
one grim, and grimly described, occasion, execute a man (XXXI.
186-7); and towards the end of the campaign, embittered by their
recent atrocities, he and his Arabs summarily shot down a body
of captured Turks (CXVII. 654). Anthony Nutting says that
towards the end of the campaign he became a 'killer' (Nutting,
245). There were, naturally, many less-deliberated slaughterings
in battle; and many trains were blown up. At the time, he wrote
of it with a mixture of romantic fervour and ironic disclaimer:

You want apparently some vivid colouring of an Arab costume, or of
a flying Turk, and we have it all, for that is part of the *mise-en-scène* of
the successful raider, and hitherto I am that. My bodyguard of fifty
Arab tribesmen, picked riders from the young men of the deserts, are
more splendid than a tulip garden, and we ride like lunatics and with
our Bedouins pounce on unsuspecting Turks and destroy them in
heaps: and it is all very gory and nasty after we close grips. I love the
preparation, and the journey, and loathe the physical fighting. Disguises, and prices on one's head, and fancy exploits are all part of the
pose: how to reconcile it with the Oxford pose I know not. Were we
flamboyant there?

(Letter 103; to V. W. Richards, 15 July 1918)

Lawrence is always trying to understand the paradox of heroic
warring. He is aware of every issue. He knew that in war the

instinct to fight takes over; war is made of 'crises of intense effort', leaving one exhausted from the expense of 'nervous' energy (XCII. 523). It is not, for most of us, quite natural. Or again, in its context, it may be: 'What now looks wanton or sadic seemed in the field inevitable, or just unimportant routine' (I. 29).

The problem was the more excruciating in that he knew that Britain's promises to the Arabs were unreliable. He had accordingly divergent allegiances, to his own country and to the Arabs.[1] He was conscious of *using* the Arabs' peculiar idealism as a 'godless fraud inspiring an alien nationality' (XCIV. 564). His insight into the psychology of the Arabs is witnessed by his notes for handling them (Liddell Hart, 142-7).

Beyond that, he knew that human instinct, whatever the race, will accept any fervency believed in by a group – though to man's reasons all wars, national or religious, are cheats, human life being so 'private' that nothing can justify violence (XCIX. 565). Nevertheless, he helped to give the fiery but directionless Arabs, by nature 'pilgrims' – Lawrence is remembering Flecker's *Hassan* – 'intent always to go the little farther' (XCII. 522), a definite purpose, a 'finite image', though the reality remained one of 'unending effort towards unattainable imagined light' (XCIX. 565). This is really a comment on *all* warring, of which Arab psychology helps us to see the naked truth, unveiled. In heroic war the impulse is good but the actuality worthless. Knowing all this, 'it was a hard task for me to straddle feeling and action'; 'the epic mode was alien to me, as to my generation' (XCIX. 565).

So, 'thought-riddled' (C. 568), he went through the campaign as Hamlet-Fortinbras:

There seemed no straight walking for us leaders in this crooked lane of conduct, ring within ring of unknown, shamefaced motives cancelling or double-charging their precedents. . . . (C. 569)

How exactly he became involved and successful, he cannot say; but since the first few adventures he 'bitterly repented' his 'entanglement' (C. 569), though carrying on. Sometimes the Arab

---

[1] His reasons for anxiety are the clearer from the new political facts revealed by Simpson and Knightley in *The Sunday Times* and *Secret Lives*; and see Suleiman Mousa, *T. E. Lawrence*, 1966. But see also the important correspondence in *The Times* of 31 July and 2 and 4 August 1969.

war 'seemed as great a folly as my sham leadership a crime' (LXVIII. 387).

Here we may place Lawrence's acceptance of a slap in the face from a British officer who, coming on him in his oriental costume after the capture of Damascus, thought that Lawrence, who had been labouring hard at relief work, was himself responsible for the state of a Turkish hospital:

He glared at me, muttering 'Bloody brute'. I hooted out again, and he smacked me over the face and stalked off, leaving me more ashamed than angry, for in my heart I felt he was right, and that anyone who pushed through to success a rebellion of the weak against their masters must come out of it so stained in estimation that afterward nothing in the world would make him feel clean. (CXXII. 682)

Lawrence may have been thinking of his own recent and ruthless actions during the advance. Byron once, with an analogous recognition, though with perhaps less reason for it, refused to defend himself on the grounds that he was, in the depths, more guilty than any accusers knew: 'Prosecute? Oh no. I am a great friend of the liberty of the press, even at the expense of myself. Besides, do I not deserve all this? and am I not in reality much worse than they make me?' (To Lady Melbourne, March 1814; *Correspondence*, ed. John Murray, I. 247).

Despite his doubts, Lawrence played his part strenuously as leader, counsellor, often in effect general, almost king. He had his bodyguard, with camels chosen for 'speed and power', all in colours, though he himself wore white silk with a 'gold and crimson Meccan head-rope' and gold dagger; but he refused to be thought of as 'a King' (LXXXIII. 474-5, XCIX. 563). He could, had he wished, probably have made himself an emperor, just as Byron could have been king of Greece (Graves, 50, and see 57; Nutting, 199. For Byron, see Leslie A. Marchand, *Byron: a Biography*, 1957; 1099 and note; William Parry, *The Last Days of Lord Byron*, 1825; VIII. 179-81n.; *Byron and Shakespeare*, 327).

His guard liked serving him. There was a strange transcending of 'the personal', and of all normal, common-sense valuations, in service to an 'ideal' that was itself 'transient'; to some principle of 'Activity', 'external to our atomic structure', from a realm beyond sense-phenomena, which was then translated into 'unrest of mind and soul and body, beyond holding point' (LXXXIII. 476). The aim was indefinable, and 'always the ideality of the ideal vanished, leaving its worshippers exhausted: holding for false what they had once pursued' (LXXXIII. 476). Lawrence's own deepest instinct too was for service. He once said that he did not really believe in any course deeply enough to initiate, or create, but merely laboured to perfect. He wished to serve: 'Allenby came nearest to my longings for a master'; though he feared disillusion (CIII. 582). Again:

All of them, through incapacity or timidity or liking, allowed me too free a hand; as if they could not see that voluntary slavery was the deep pride of a morbid spirit, and vicarious pain its gladdest decoration.

(CIII. 582)

This is scarcely the whole truth, and we must always remember that the *Seven Pillars* was written in retrospect. What is wholly true is that nothing he did satisfied him. What was in his 'reach' he 'no longer wanted', his whole enjoyment being in the 'desire', content to know that it had been within his 'strength' (CIII. 583). Always we return to the same thought: the drive for a satisfaction beyond human attainment.

This drive turns him inward on himself and the concept of 'sacrifice'. In his *Meditation on Saviors* Robinson Jeffers writes of Christ as driven by some inner, 'incestuous' obsession, 'frightfully uplifted for having turned inward to love the people'. Some secret enjoyment – 'that root was so sweet Oh, dreadful agonist?' – forces him on. Jeffers's poem (discussed in *Christ and Nietzsche*, III. 100) is closely relevant to Lawrence's story. Lawrence's thoughts on war harmonize naturally with the metaphysic of sacrifice: on this profound level, War and Christ, State and Church, are one. When 'sacrifice' is in his mind, his phrases are redolent of the Christian story: Anthony Nutting thinks that he, at one period, saw himself as a new Christ (Nutting, 243).[1] The 'Synopsis' to Chapter C in the 1935 edition of the *Seven Pillars* includes the words 'Atonement' and 'Redemption'. In the revolt and its

---

[1] On the old terrain, too. Is there some peculiar magic in the Near East, from Greece to the Caspian? Our culture was born there. It is an area of fusions, and so of poetic action, as in the Crusades and with Byron. Flecker of 'The Golden Journey' wrote, and Brooke died, there. Masefield's best war book was on Gallipoli and Yeats's best poem on Byzantium.

'endurance' of suffering there was an expectation of a 'redemption', 'perhaps for all [? of] a race'. There was an 'enlargement' in taking on another's 'pain' and getting away from 'our sultry selves' (C. 567). In sacrifice the victim derives pleasure from 'choosing voluntarily another's evil to perfect the self'; and there was accordingly 'a hidden selfishness in it, as in all perfections' (C. 568). Here, too, Lawrence's probing analysis reveals a falsity:

His purer part, for the mediator, might have been to stand among the crowd, to watch another win the cleanness of a redeemer's name. By the one road lay self-perfection, by the other self-immolation, and a making perfect of the neighbour. . . .   (C. 568)

He knew that 'there was nothing loftier than a cross from which to contemplate the world'; 'the pride and exhilaration of it were beyond conceit'; but it left others in a secondary position (C. 568). Lawrence is clearly thinking of Church doctrine.[1] If done in a 'child-minded' way, 'redemption' might be 'honest'; but if 'the expiator was conscious of the under-motives and the after-glory of his act, both were wasted on him' (C. 568). The expression, as often, is tangled, but the general sense of (to quote Eliot's *Murder in the Cathedral*) doing 'the right deed for the wrong reason' is clear. We shall see later that Lawrence did, in fact, attune himself to his own astringent teaching.

This interweaving of thoughts on redemptive sacrifice with close analyses of war is, for Lawrence, natural. His probing psychology, or metaphysic, works at a depth from whence both stem out, strange though that be. He is at the heart of that unity we crave, of Church and State, Christ and War, and the unifying medium is death: 'the whole business of the movement seemed to be expressible only in terms of death and life' (C. 567). That the central concentration of the *Seven Pillars of Wisdom* is nearer metaphysics than epic is advertised by its title.

For Lawrence, war was a tragic pursuit; a pursuit, that is, of mystical import, not necessarily susceptible of rationalization on a horizontal, sociological, level. Once when their warriors were reluctant, Lawrence and Ali ibn el Hussein devised an extraordinary oration or argument (LXXIV. 421-2) on the facts of

---

[1] For a caustic reading of Jesus' sacrifice as a surrender to the Devil's cunning see W. Somerset Maugham, *The Razor's Edge*, 1944 (Penguin, 1963; 209-10).

human destiny. Life, especially in the desert, was an endless striving 'with an enemy who was not of the world, nor life, nor anything, but hope itself; and failure seemed God's freedom to mankind' (for the emphasis on 'hope' compare Masefield, pp. 289, 292). So 'Death would seem best of all our works, the last free loyalty within our grasp'. The aim must be 'to bring forth immaterial things, things creative, partaking of spirit, not of flesh', denying 'physical demands':

There could be no honour in a sure success, but much might be wrested from a sure defeat. Omnipotence and the Infinite were our two worthiest foemen, indeed the only ones for a full man to meet, they being monsters of his own spirit's making; and the stoutest enemies were always of the household. In fighting Omnipotence, honour was proudly to throw away the poor resources that we had, and dare Him empty-handed; to be beaten, not merely by more mind, but by its advantage of better tools. To the clear-sighted, failure was the only goal. We must believe, through and through, that there was no victory, except to go down into death fighting and crying for failure itself, calling in excess of despair to Omnipotence to strike harder, that by His very striking He might temper our tortured selves into the weapon of His own ruin. (LXXIV. 422)

This strange 'Crispin' speech was aimed at the Arab mind, and appears to have succeeded. For Lawrence himself it was sincere. The arguments were probably of his own devising, and the text, as quoted, is his. He felt and lived a philosophy of beyond-life striving, of spirit dominating flesh. Death he liked, even wooed: 'A man's own death was his last free will, a saving grace and measure of intolerable pain' (XCIX. 565). Of Turkish corpses stripped by their foe after battle, he wrote:

The dead men looked wonderfully beautiful. The night was shining gently down, softening them into new ivory. Turks were white-skinned on their clothed parts, much whiter than the Arabs; and these soldiers had been very young. (LIV. 315)

He arranged them, one by one, more comfortably, 'longing to be of these quiet ones' rather than among their wrangling and boasting victors (LIV. 315). Of another occasion he writes: 'I was bitter that these perfected dead had again robbed my poverty' (XCIII. 529). Lawrence often half-wanted to die in action (XCIX. 561). His own death-craving was the secret of his amazing and successful courage, for, as Byron puts it in *The Deformed Transformed* (I. i. 353):

> You lately saw me
> Master of my own life, and quick to quit it;
> And he who is so is the master of
> Whatever dreads to die.

Both Byron and Lawrence had that mastery.

Lawrence as a man of action was pre-eminently a man of spirit: and the term 'spirit', as used in his oration, is exact. For him 'war' is to be equated with 'spirit', and both with service and sacrifice; not for any demonstrable end, but in the manner of Hamlet's admiration of Fortinbras as a warrior who 'makes mouths at the invisible event' (i.e. embraces risks boldly) for a mere nothing (*Hamlet*, IV. iv. 50).

3

We have found Lawrence's emphasis on service merging into spiritual categories. We shall now discuss these matters in more concrete terms: these will concern (i) masochism, and (ii) spirit-reality.

The 'adolescents full of carnal passion' who made Lawrence's bodyguard, impelled by their 'Eastern' obsession 'with the antithesis between flesh and spirit', took pleasure, we are told, 'in subordination', deliberately 'degrading the body' to assert 'freedom in equality of mind.' So they accepted 'the sword of justice' and 'the steward's whip' printing 'red rivers of pain about their sides'; but their contract was 'voluntary' and their 'spirits' their masters' 'equal'. 'Love for a cause – or for a person' discounted the pain. It was a kind of love-affair (LXXXIII. 475-6). Whether or not this was a correct diagnosis of these young Arabs, it certainly holds a general truth in relation to Lawrence himself. He was obsessed with such punishments. There are many references to whippings in his book. The mischievous boys Farraj and Daud, so important in the story, were first brought to Lawrence's notice when Farraj was in trouble and to be beaten; through Lawrence's influence Daud was allowed to divide the punishment (XL. 244). Once when their jokes had become dangerous, Lawrence had them caned, and strokes were added by others (XLVII. 277-8).

For another of their pranks they were caned by Yusuf, Governor of Akaba, and imprisoned; Lawrence got them out for a necessary expedition by promising 'another dose of his treatment for them when their skins were fit'; but for a while they had to walk, calling their saddle-soreness 'Yusufiyeh' (LXXI. 401-2). On another occasion, for an act of rashness, they were made by the Arab authorities to sit 'on scorching rocks' till they apologized (LIV. 318). It was difficult to know what to do with them since, if sheer cruelty was to be avoided, 'the surface pain seemed only to irritate their muscles into activities wilder than those for which they had been condemned'; and yet to hurt them 'mercilessly', so that 'their self-control melted and their manhood was lost under the animal distress of their bodies, seemed to me degrading'; it was as an 'impiety' towards their happy youth (LIV. 318). Notice the opposition here of body and spirit ('manhood'). Up to a point punishment was stimulating; after that, degrading. The subtleties are exactly handled.

Then there was the whipping of Awad and the fierce camel-boy Mahmas for drawing daggers, Mahmas's tears incurring disgrace (LXXXVII. 495). Naturally, much was forced by circumstances:

With the sorrow of living so great, the sorrow of punishment had to be pitiless. We lived for the day and died for it. When there was reason and desire to punish we wrote our lesson with gun or whip immediately in the sullen flesh of the sufferer, and the case was beyond appeal. The desert did not afford the refined slow penalties of courts and gaols.

(I. 29)

Lawrence himself was continually reducing the punishments, which were often too fierce. But he was certainly, like his young followers, 'fascinated' (LXXXIII. 475) by such punishments, as his vivid reporting shows. As a climax we have his own fearful experience at Deraa, where, after being captured on a spying expedition, he was ordered by the Governor to be flogged for refusing his sexual advances. What exactly happened is not clear; but it would seem that he eventually gave way either to the Governor or his underlings, or to all of them. 'That night', he tells us, 'the citadel of my integrity had been irrevocably lost' (LXXX. 456). At one point the suffering gave way to a warm pleasure: 'I remembered smiling idly at him, for a delicious warmth, probably sexual, was swelling through me' (LXXX. 454).

The incident (helpfully discussed by Anthony Nutting, 112-16, 244-5) is generally regarded as a determining pivot in Lawrence's later story, though it may be more true to regard it rather as a central dramatization of his life's whole direction, from youth onwards: 'pain' was 'a solvent, a cathartic, almost a decoration, to be fairly worn' (LXXXIII. 476).

Accordingly, when Simpson and Knightley adduce new evidence that Lawrence in later life arranged to have himself regularly birched by a young friend,[1] always 'round about' the anniversary of the Deraa incident (*The Sunday Times*, Weekly Review, 23 June 1968; 46), we cannot see this simply as a self-punishment for having lost, on that occasion, his sexual integrity. Anthony Nutting, who writes well on Lawrence's masochism, though he notes that Lawrence had, before Deraa, been 'in the habit of scourging himself' in expectation of some later test of his endurance (244), suggests that his giving way at Deraa under torment after having considered himself a Messiah, together with the new knowledge, through the 'probably sexual' warmth he experienced (p. 323 above), that he was a sexually-attuned masochist, made him realize that his regular endurance of pain 'disclosed a perversion of the flesh rather than a triumph of the spirit'. That, says Nutting (244), is why he submitted to the Turks' sexual approaches. Nutting next quotes from the first 'Oxford' (privately distributed, 1926) edition of the *Seven Pillars*. For this I follow Simpson and Knightley's *Secret Lives* (213), which seems the better text:

It could not have been the defilement for no one ever held the body in less honour than I did myself. Probably it had been the breaking of the spirit by that frenzied nerve-shattering pain which had degraded me to beast level when it made me grovel to it, and which had journeyed with me since, a fascination and terror and morbid desire, lascivious and vicious, perhaps, but like the striving of a moth towards its flame.

(Nutting, 244)

The passage is crucial. It describes a submission of 'spirit' to physical 'pain', leading on to 'lascivious' desire.

We must not forget that *all* our quotations from *Seven Pillars*

[1] John Bruce. In a letter to *The Times* of 22 November 1969 Prof. A. W. Lawrence doubts the trustworthiness of his recollections; but he does not dispute the facts we are discussing.

were written in retrospect, and that their colouring is subsequent
to the experience here recorded. All that Lawrence says of sacrifice
and self-mastery, as well as his passages on willed degradation,
pain and punishment, are to be read as part of this one masochistic
complex, or obsession, involving both spirit and body; it is a kind
of sexual union between body and soul, like that, on another level,
recorded in Wordsworth's *Tintern Abbey* and Keats's famous
journal-letter about 'the body overpowering the mind' and the
'heart' as the 'mind's Bible', from which the intelligence 'sucks its
identity' (to George and Georgiana Keats, 14 February – 3 May
1819; Letters, ed. M. Buxton Forman, 1935; 315, 336; discussed
by J. Middleton Murry, *Keats and Shakespeare*, 137. See *Christ and
Nietzsche*, IV. 130-3). When at the conclusion of Powys's *Wolf
Solent* the hero's conflicts are resolved by a union of body and
soul, so that he feels through a body that is yet more than that,
he realizes that 'it's my body that has saved me' (XXV. 635, 642;
new edition, 606, 613). Nor must we necessarily suppose that our
greatest exemplars of martyrdom and sacrifice have acted independently of such impulses; and there is probably no final distinction between noble sacrifice and what is known as 'sexual
perversion'. This Lawrence may have recognized, his image of the
moth and flame corresponding to Browning's use of it for
Caponsacchi's nobly *desired* self-immolation, in *The Ring and the
Book*: 'the very immolation made the bliss'; it was 'as if the intense
centre of the flame' should turn out to be a 'heaven' to the 'fly'
who seeks it; the 'ecstasy' has a 'thrill' that can 'out-throb pain'
(VI. 953-73).

Lawrence writes his *Seven Pillars* from this total recognition,
which is also behind his deliberate guiding of his own life into
ways of humility and degradation accompanied by the birchings
less perhaps for remorse than for celebration – or for both
entwined – near the anniversary of Deraa.

He accepted himself, and could write freely, rationally, of the
result:

I liked the things underneath me and took my pleasures and adventures
downward. There seemed a certainty in degradation, a final safety.
Man could rise to any height, but there was an animal level beneath
which he could not fall. It was a satisfaction on which to rest. The force
of things, years and an artificial dignity, denied it me more and more;
but there endured the after-taste of liberty from one youthful sub-

merged fortnight in Port Said, coaling steamers by day with other out-
casts of three continents and curling up by night to sleep on the
breakwater by De Lesseps, where the sea surged past.　　(CIII. 581)

This must have been before the war; the white overseers at Port
Said encouraged their coolies with a whip.[1]

We have faced the bodily aspect of masochism; but spirit is
involved too, and it, with all its usual, more respectable, values,
forms part of the total complex. Directly after Lawrence's
pleasurable sensation from the flogging at Deraa, his smiles were
greeted by a brutal blow by one of his tormentors into his 'groin':

A roaring, and my eyes went black: while within me the core of life
seemed to heave slowly up through the rending nerves, expelled from
its body by this last indescribable pang.　　(LXXX. 454)

We may compare Masefield's lines on the soul freed from its
agony in *Good Friday* (p. 286 above). The spirit, or soul, is felt by
both Masefield and Lawrence as an *objective* reality; and it may be
the more clearly seen when silhouetted against pain. Pain defines,
objectifies, releases, it. War is a matter of intense crises drawing
on a 'nervous' 'eagerness' or energy which, at an extreme, tears
apart 'flesh and spirit' (XCII. 523).

Lawrence at one point disclaims the antithesis of body and
spirit accepted by the Arabs. He held instead

that mental and physical were inseparably one: that our bodies, the
universe, our thoughts and tactilities were conceived in and of the
molecular sludge of matter, the universal element through which form
drifted as clots and patterns of varying density. It seemed to me un-
thinkable that assemblages of atoms should cogitate except in atomic
terms.　　(LXXXIII. 477)

A spiritualist might well agree; the sense here of intermerging
planes, with etheric realities less dense than the physical, and yet
still concrete, is spiritualistic. Even so, Lawrence calls his monism
'perverse'. As we have seen, he could write of a punishment which
reduced the spirit to a bodily subservience (p. 323 above). Normally he realizes the distinction sharply. He writes of his activity
on behalf of the Arabs as follows:

His body plodded on mechanically, while his reasonable mind left him,
and from without looked down critically on him, wondering what that

[1] This I recall myself, going East on a troopship in 1917.

futile lumber did and why. Sometimes these selves would converse in
the void. . . . (I. 30)

His amazing feats of endurance are described in spiritualistic
terms:

While we rode we were disbodied, unconscious of flesh or feeling: and
when at an interval this excitement faded and we did see our bodies, it
was with some hostility, with a contemptuous sense that they reached
their highest purpose, not as vehicles of the spirit, but when, dissolved,
their elements served to manure a field. (LXXXIII. 477)

Once, nearly exhausted and 'approaching the insensibility' usually
beyond his 'reach', since he was 'one born so slug-tissued that
nothing this side fainting would let his spirit free', he had a
vivid experience:

Now I found myself dividing into parts. There was one which went on
riding wisely, sparing or helping every pace of the wearied camel.
Another hovering above and to the right bent down curiously, and
asked what the flesh was doing. The flesh gave no answer, for, indeed,
it was conscious only of a ruling impulse to keep on and on; but a third
garrulous one talked and wondered, critical of the body's self-inflicted
labour, and contemptuous of the reason for effort.
(LXXXI. 461)

These 'divided selves' were all, he says, part of his true self: at the
extreme of exhaustion one would see one's 'thoughts', 'acts' and
'feelings' as 'separate creatures', 'eyeing, like vultures, the passing
in their midst of the common thing which gave them life' (LXXXI.
461). They are all part of the one, personal, life.[1]

Normally Lawrence despises the body. In his general activity
he says that all was 'Will' and that 'there was no flesh' (CIII. 581);
and certainly his almost miraculous feats of endurance, even when
suffering from illnesses, bear out such statements. Apart from that,
he tells us that he was not at ease among men of physical existence:

They talked of food and illness, games and pleasures, with me, who
felt that to recognize our possession of bodies was degradation enough,
without enlarging upon their failings and attributes. I would feel shame
for myself at seeing them wallow in the physical which could be only a

---

[1] We might compare T. S. Eliot's note on the third figure in *The Waste Land*; see
p. 271 above.

glorification of man's cross. Indeed, the truth was I did not like the 'myself' I could see and hear. (CIII. 584)

We may adduce some lines of Byron:

> For if the beings, of whom I was one –
> Hating to be so – crossed me in my path,
> I felt myself degraded back to them,
> And was all clay again.
>
> (*Manfred*, II. ii. 76)

Like Manfred, Lawrence was already, or at least so felt himself, in some spirit-sphere beyond earth; he was a man whose 'brain was sudden and silent as a wild cat' and whose 'senses' were 'like mud clogging its feet' (CIII. 581). This is typical:

Especially for me was it hard, because though my sight was sharp, I never saw men's features: always I peered beyond, imagining for my-self a spirit-reality of this or that: and today each man owned his desire so utterly that he was fulfilled in it, and became meaningless.

(LV. 322)

This perhaps is why, as he complained, his book lacks colour (p. 337 below). To Byron, too, people became 'transparent' (*Byron and Shakespeare*, 121; pp. 339, 342 below). Like Byron, Lawrence could sense the presence of spirit-powers, as when he writes of the ghostly sounds and haunting presences of Azrak and Rum, saying '*Numen inest*' and 'Both were magically haunted'. At Azrak there were 'ghostly guardians', who could be heard (LXXV. 423, LXXIX. 447-8; for Byron, *Byron and Shakespeare*, 43-6).

4

Contact with humanity was for Lawrence hard:

I was not modest, but ashamed of my awkwardness, of my physical envelope, and of my solitary unlikeness which made me no companion, but an acquaintance, complete, angular, uncomfortable, as a crystal.

(CIII. 579)

He had a horror of being touched: this was 'an atomic repulsion, like the intact course of a snowflake' (CIII. 580-1). He was thus coldly 'complete' and 'intact'. He had never really been a soldier, never deeply involved: all he did was 'conscious', 'with my detached self always eyeing the performance from the wings of criticism' (CIII. 580). In this he was truly Byronic. In the best, perhaps the only helpful, passage of *Astarte* (1921; I. 12), Lord Lovelace wrote:

When he took a part in the low comedy of bad company, his immutable self, unknown to such bystanders, was watching in tragic contemplation of the ribald nightmare, judging and condemning the transient self with the surrounding crew.

That applies widely to both Byron and Lawrence.

Lawrence was not really so inhumanly cold as he may seem. Indeed he had so great a 'craving to be liked' that he could not 'open' himself for terror of 'failure'; and for him all intimacy was 'shameful' without a perfect attunement. Though so 'complete' and 'intact' he could also see himself as the exact opposite, wishing he were as 'superficial' and 'perfected' as ordinary lovers: they being, on their own level, more at peace than he on his. But, he says, 'my jailer held me back'. He could not 'surrender' to 'the supremacy of the material'; try as he might, his mind remained 'bitterly awake' (CIII. 580-1). His masochistic and flagellatory excesses were as a relief and rebound from this untouchable obsession; his will to degradation a rebound from his excessive spirituality. Such a combination of spirituality with sexual perversion is not unusual; and the love-ideal of such men will often be a male youth, combining human existence with seraphic intimations. So it was with Lawrence.

Early in his oriental adventures at Carchemish in 1911, he became devoted to the boy Sheikh Ahmed, also known as Dahoum.[1] He used him as a model for a nude sculpture, which he set on a roof; and the relationship aroused criticism (Sir Leonard Woolley, *Friends*, 89). This, he said later, was the best time of his life (119), as Byron said of his early days in Greece, thinking probably of Nicolo Giraud (*Byron and Shakespeare*, 32). He once took the boy home, to Oxford. The *Seven Pillars* has a dedicatory poem, addressed to 'S.A.'. This was revised for publication by Robert Graves, but the original text has now been printed by Simpson and Knightley in *The Sunday Times*, Weekly Review

[1] On Dahoum see David Garnett, *The Letters of T. E. Lawrence*, 103-4; also J. B. Villars, 40-1. His name now appears to have been Salim Ahmed (*Secret Lives*, 163).

T. E. *Lawrence*

(16 June 1968; 49); also in *Secret Lives* (158) with a variant (earnings):

> I loved you, so I drew these tides of men into my hands
> and wrote my will across the sky in stars
> To gain you Freedom, the seven-pillared worthy house,
> that your eyes might be shining for me
> > When I came.

Lawrence's whole Arabian endeavour is here attributed to his love for Dahoum. But Dahoum died before the victory, and so the poem continues:

> Death was my servant on the road, till we were near and saw you waiting:
> When you smiled, and in sorrowful envy he outran me and took you apart:
> > Into his quietness.

> So our love's earning was your cast-off body to be held one moment
> Before earth's soft hands would explore your face and the blind worms transmute
> > Your failing substance.

> Men prayed me to set my work, the inviolate house, in memory of you.
> But for fit monument I shattered it, unfinished: and now
> The little things creep out to patch themselves hovels in the marred shadow
> > Of your gift.

Lawrence's love for 'S.A.' is balanced against the communal cause as Byron's last three poems balance his love for Loukas against the cause of Greece (*Lord Byron's Marriage*, 217-20). The dedication is well discussed by Simpson and Knightley, and the evidence for the identification of 'S.A.' deployed. There appears to be little doubt of it.

Dahoum was Lawrence's companion in the East before the war, and they engaged in adventures together. An expedition to Sinai was reported in a letter (Letter 69) of 28 February 1914, 'To a Friend':

The night just under the hill-top was bitterly cold, with a huge wind and blinding squalls of rain. We curled up in a knot under a not-sufficiently-overhanging-rock and packed our sheepskin cloaks under and over and round us, and still were as cold and cross as bears. Not thirsty though, at all.

On such an occasion that would be natural enough. But the last words are significant, and the description chimes with the famous passage in the *Seven Pillars*:

The public women of the rare settlements we encountered in our months of wandering would have been nothing to our numbers, even had their raddled meat been palatable to a man of healthy parts. In horror of such sordid commerce our youths began indifferently to slake one another's few needs in their own clean bodies – a cold convenience that, by comparison, seemed sexless and even pure. Later, some began to justify this sterile process, and swore that friends quivering together in the yielding sand with intimate hot limbs in supreme embrace, found there hidden in the darkness a sensual coefficient of the mental passion which was welding our souls and spirits in one flaming effort. Several, thirsting to punish appetites they could not wholly prevent, took a savage pride in degrading the body, and offered themselves fiercely in any habit which promised physical pain or filth.   (I. 28)

As so often, the slightly off-centre phraseology of 'habit' is ambiguous, but the general statement of homosexuality blending into masochism is clear. Note that, as in Lawrence's own story, the love of war-comrades is one with the communal effort; as it was, too, in the valuations of ancient Greece. 'Thirsting' balances the 'thirsty' of our Sinai passage: both are used as metaphors for general desire (compare 'slaked', p. 332 below). The sex-thrill of union seems to be identified with the other thrill of punishment for that first thrill; an interesting passage, compact of meaning; as though all sex-instinct is masochistic, a willing self-abasement before cosmic power.

Of Lawrence's private actions we cannot speak, any more than of Shakespeare's; nor do we wish to. It is however important that we admit that some physical element is in play; it is in part through their bodily appearance that such youths appeal. There are many possible variations between non-sensuous, mental, companionship and complete intercourse.

The *Seven Pillars* is rich in impressions of young Arabs, called 'lithe' (LXXI. 401), and liked for their very litheness, like boy-Ariels; but they were physical too, with bodily instincts. We hear of Awad the rough camel-boy, promoted to the bodyguard, 'a ragged, brown-skinned lad of perhaps eighteen, splendidly built, with the muscles and sinews of an athlete, active as a cat', coming before Lawrence, confused and self-conscious, 'talking to me of his animal joys in jerky phrases with averted face' (LXXII. 404-405); 'little Mahmas', 'tight-lipped' and ferocious, who quarrelled with Awad (LXXXVII. 495); Turki, aged seventeen, 'an old love of Ali ibn el Hussein', for 'the animal in each called to the other, and they wandered about inseparably, taking pleasure in a touch and silence' (LXXIII. 415); Ali himself, whose 'beauty was a conscious weapon', proud and dignified except when he laughed unawares, and then 'the youth, boyish or girlish, of him, the fire and deviltry would break through his night like a sunrise' (LXXIX. 446-7); and young Metaab, 'stripped to his skimp riding-drawers for hard work, with his black love-curls awry, his face stained and haggard' (LXXXVI. 488).

Such vignettes of boy-girl, seraphic youth, lithe yet vigorous, blending grace and power, are of a usual kind. Here alone Lawrence's human apprehensions are warm and happy. From this soil flowers his book's most poignantly realized theme, the love-story of Farraj and Daud:

They were an instance of the eastern boy and boy affection which the segregation of women made inevitable. Such friendships often led to manly loves of a depth and force beyond our flesh-steeped conceit. When innocent they were hot and unashamed. If sexuality entered, they passed into a give and take, unspiritual relation, like marriage.

(XL. 244)

Note the contrast implied by 'flesh-steeped' and 'unspiritual'. We are reminded that in the East a woman, having been denied equality, becomes merely 'a machine for muscular exercise', that is for physical intercourse; while 'man's psychic side could be slaked only amongst his peers'; and so 'arose' those 'partnerships of man and man, to supply human nature with more than the contact of flesh with flesh' (XCII. 521).

These two gave Lawrence 'great satisfaction'. He liked their bravery and cheerfulness and joint friendship against the world (XLI. 250), going 'barefooted, delicate as thoroughbreds' (XLIV. 260); 'two imps, whose spirits not all the privations of our road had quelled for a moment' (XLVII. 276). They were, as we have seen, always in trouble for mischief and continually being punished. Their story is aptly introduced by their delight at Lawrence's intercession in arranging that they should divide the strokes that had been allotted to one of them (p. 322 above). Their jokes could certainly be amusing, as when they painted the Governor of Akaba's camel red and indigo and as a result of their canings so suffered from 'Yusufiyeh' – we should say 'Yusufitis' – that they had to walk instead of ride (p. 323 above). Lawrence, in whom there was a similar strain of Puckish mischief, regularly saved them from the worst, as when their superiors forced them to sit on the burningly hot rocks, which seemed wicked: 'Their sins were elvish gaiety, the thoughtlessness of unbalanced youth, the being happy when we were not'; and to so degrade them through agony into submission seemed 'almost an impiety towards two sunlit beings, on whom the shadow of the world had not yet fallen – the most gallant, the most enviable, I knew' (LIV. 318).

'Elvish': so too Byron in 1810 called Nicolo Giraud and the other boys at Athens 'sylphs' (to J. C. Hobhouse, 23 August 1810; *Correspondence*, ed. John Murray, I. 14). Such sunlit youth is seraphic, almost divine, and to desecrate it is 'impiety'.

They were also elemental, at home in water: 'pearl-diving in the gulf had made them like fishes in the water' (LXXIV. 419). Once Daud hurled Farraj into a rock-pool and was terrified when he did not reappear, and dived in, to find him hiding under a ledge. They fought, and returned and came out all muddied and 'more like the devils of a whirlwind than their usual suave delicate presences' (LXXIV. 419).

After Daud's death, Farraj became silent:

These two had been friends from childhood, in eternal gaiety: working together, sleeping together, sharing every scrape and profit with the openness and honesty of perfect love. So I was not astonished to see Farraj look dark and hard of face, leaden-eyed and old, when he came to tell me that his fellow was dead; and from that day till his service ended he made no more laughter for us. (XCII. 520)

Farraj invited death by a suicidal advance on the enemy. Wounded, he was happy to die. Lawrence found that they could not carry him and they dared not leave him to be tortured by the Turks:

I knelt down beside him, holding my pistol near the ground by his head, so that he should not see my purpose; but he must have guessed it, for he opened his eyes, and clutched me with his harsh, scaly hand, the tiny hand of these unripe Nejd fellows. I waited a moment, and he said, 'Daud will be angry with you', the old smile coming back so strangely to this grey shrinking face. I replied, 'Salute him from me'. He returned the formal answer, 'God will give you peace', and at last wearily closed his eyes. (XCIII. 529)

Lawrence prefers not to report his action more directly than by saying that with a 'second bullet' he shot Farraj's camel.

5

Lawrence's subsequent rejection of society will be readily understood. He had seen too deep into his own self, and others. He enlisted in the Royal Air Force in 1922; was against his wish discharged in 1923, and entered the Tank Corps; but succeeded in returning to the Air Force in 1925, where he remained till 1935.

Living among rankers of the Tank Corps he was disgusted at the 'carnality' of their talk; sex sickened him, and yet 'we are all guilty'; all 'flesh' is made of it; these men are the naked 'reality' and idealists like himself are the false 'wrappings' (Letter 206; to Lionel Curtis, 27 March 1923). It was worse here than in the Air Force:

The R.A.F. was foul-mouthed, and the cleanest little mob of fellows. These are foul-mouthed and behind their mouths is a pervading animality of spirit, whose unmixed bestiality frightens me and hurts me. There is no criticism, indeed it's taken for granted as natural, that you should job a woman's body, or hire out yourself, or abuse yourself in any way. I cried out against it, partly in self-pity because I've condemned myself to grow like them, and partly in premonition of failure, for my masochism remains and will remain, only moral. Physically I can't do it: indeed I get in denial the gratification they get in indulgence. I react against their example into an abstention even more rigorous than of old. Everything bodily is now hateful to me. . . .
(Letter 207; to Lionel Curtis, 14 May 1923)

In the 'animal reek' of the Hut he lies awake 'with horror' at the 'truth' of 'mankind' (Letter 212; to D. G. Hogarth, 13 June 1923).

In the Air Force he had been as 'contented' as could be; there the men were utterly different in mind and talk; and the sight of a 'blue uniform' makes him 'homesick' (Letter 212, as above). The contrast is imaginative; the heavy, lumbering tanks against the ethereal aeroplanes; in terms of colour, mud-khaki as against sky-blue.

It was, in truth, Lawrence's spirit-cravings that made him love and enter the Royal Air Force, which was to him both symbolic and prophetic. He once rejected the implication of a 'supernatural background' to his thinking, though he allowed the terms 'un-wordly' or 'unearthly', claiming to suffer from an 'excess of reason' (Letter 285; to E. M. Forster, 26 April 1926). He was impelled to live out his high cravings and psychic apprehension in what practical ways were available; and that meant the Air Force.

In *The Mint* he set down an account of his first impressions while training in the Air Force, where 'the distinction between armies and soldiers' was 'dinned' into them (1. XXII. 77):

We are vowed to this enterprise . . . to win the freehold of the upper element in as full measure as man's licence on land, or a sailor's liberty at sea.   (1. XXII. 78)

Again:

The R.A.F. for me is now myself: a vocation absolute and inevitable beyond any question under the sky: and so marvellous that I grow hot to make it perfect.   (2. XXII. 161)

He is angry that 'inept handling' should damage its 'virginal recruits'. A bad N.C.O. 'sins against the Air' (2. XXII. 161). He could defend his 'faith':

By our handling of this, the one big new thing, will our time be judged. Incidentally, for the near-sighted or political, it has a national side: upon the start we give our successors in the arts of air will depend their redressing our eighteenth-century army and silly ships.
                                                                                          (3. VIII. 181)

It is all 'something bigger than ourselves' which in humble service 'we translate' into 'talk of nuts and bolts' (3. VIII. 182).

He hoped to write a 'real book' on the Air Force, dealing with 'Life in a Flying Flight' (*The Mint*, 3, 'An Explanation', 165). This was 'the biggest subject I have ever seen' (Letter 364; to E. M. Forster, 6 August 1928). On 9 December 1933 he told Mrs. Shaw that he meant to devote himself to a comprehensive work on the Air; for this was, after all, the main 'purpose of my generation' (Simpson and Knightley, *The Sunday Times*, Weekly Review, 30 June 1968; 46; *Secret Lives*, 264-5). It was to be called 'Confession of Faith', the title used for his lines printed among the *Letters* as 367A (1929):

> Not the conquest of the air, but our entry thither.
> We come.
> Our soiled overalls were the livery of that sunrise. The soilings of our bodies in its service were prismatic with its light. Moody or broody. From ground to air. First we are not earthbound.
>
> In speed we hurl ourselves beyond the body.
> Our bodies cannot scale the heavens except in a fume of petrol.
> The concentration of our bodies in entering a loop. Bones, blood, flesh all pressed inward together.
> Not the conquest of the air. Be plain, guts.
> In speed we hurl ourselves beyond the body.
>
> We enter it. We come.
> Our bodies cannot scale heaven except in a fume of burnt petrol.
> As lords that are expected. Yet there is a silent joy in our arrival.
> Years and years.
> Long arpeggios of chafing wires.
> The concentration of one's body in entering a loop.

The thoughts drive earthly experience beyond itself into spiritualistic adventure. Every phrase should be studied in depth, and compared with the air poetry of C. Day-Lewis and Michael Ayrton's *The Testament of Daedalus* (pp. 64-5, 69-73). Lawrence was a prophet both of the advance of science and of the spiritual implications of that advance. As far back as his Arabian campaign he had associated the air with death. Once travelling on a rickety aeroplane he had expected a crash, 'almost hoping it', since 'death in the air would be a clean escape':

> Instinct said 'Die', but reason said that was only to cut the mind's tether, and loose it into freedom.   (XCIX. 561)

The 'tether' is the 'silver cord' of occult science (e.g. at Ecclesiastes, XII. 6; see, on Powys, *The Saturnian Quest*, 83, 88).

'In speed we hurl ourselves beyond the body'; here he must be thinking of his other obsession, of speed. He was not himself an air-pilot, but an ordinary mechanic: his own beyond-the-body

T. E. Lawrence

cravings were met by his motor-cycle, or succession of motor-cycles, named 'Boanerges'.

When my mood gets too hot and I find myself wandering beyond control I pull out my motor-bike and hurl it top-speed through these unfit roads for hour after hour. My nerves are jaded and gone near dead, so that nothing less than hours of voluntary danger will prick them into life.

(Letter 207; to Lionel Curtis, 14 May 1923)

Boanerges was to him as a personal love, like the ship *Wanderer* to Masefield. It was as a living creature: he writes in *The Mint* of 'Boanerges' first glad roar at being alive again'. Again: 'It was a miracle that all this docile strength waits behind one tiny lever for the pleasure of my hand' (3. XVI. 199). He describes his speeding with exultation, the scream of wind, the 'flying' over a road 'dip', 'the weighty machine launching itself like a projectile with a whirr of wheels into the air at the take-off of each rise'; the sudden wobble caused by ruts, so that it 'swayed dizzily, wagging its tail' till its 'head' could be straightened; and finally 'I stabled the steel magnificence of strength and speed. . . .' During the ride his 'flight' was 'birdlike'; he claims to have raced, and beaten, a friendly aeroplane, touching above ninety miles an hour (3. XVI. 199-201).[1] It was all deeply meaningful to him:

A skittish motor-bike with a touch of blood in it is better than all the riding animals on earth, because of its logical extension of our faculties, and the hint, the provocation, to excess conferred by its honeyed un-tiring smoothness. Because Boa loves me, he gives me five more miles of speed than a stranger would get from him. (3. XVI. 202)

One of Lawrence's latest tasks before leaving the Air Force was the designing and trying out of speed-boats for rescuing airmen.

Speed beats through his story. As we have seen, his Arabian strategy depended regularly on speed, and he himself performed striking feats of speed on his various journeys. He was by instinct attuned to speed and the swift vibrations of the spirit. The *Seven Pillars* is written throughout from a sense of psychic realities: he himself attacked it (p. 328 above) for lacking colour (Letters 225

[1] Compare my independent yet similar descriptions, drawn from my experiences as a despatch-rider in North Persia, in *Atlantic Crossing*, VI. 170; amplified – with a correspondence to Lawrence's 'wobble' – in *Road to Kasvin*, an extended account of my war-years as yet unpublished.

and 266; to Sydney Cockerell, 22 October 1923; to Edward Garnett, 13 June 1925). 'My head', he wrote, 'was aiming to create intangible things' (Letter 559; to Robert Graves, 4 February 1935).

6

The student of Lawrence must recognize the many authoritative statements collected by A. W. Lawrence in *T. E. Lawrence by his Friends* (1937; abridged 1954; my references are to the original edition). Men of highest repute, military, political and artistic, speak with nearly a single voice. From this collection I shall now quote, giving page numerals; with actual names for the longer quotations only, or where there seems to be some special reason for doing so.

On the Arabian campaign he had been, in 'camel riding and shooting, in endurance and in courage', the Arabs' 'master' (166); he 'could outride, outwalk, outshoot and outlast the best of them' (97; Lowell Thomas reports that the chieftain Auda, hero of numberless battles, after praising Lawrence's capacity for work and skill as a camel-rider, added: 'By the beard of the Prophet, he seems more than a man!'; *With Lawrence in Arabia*, 292). From a British viewpoint, Lt.-Col. W. F. Stirling says that he was 'immeasurably our superior', breaking all records for speed and endurance (154). His mental powers corresponded: Liddell Hart says that his ambition was to be 'supreme' both in action and in thought, enjoying a 'knowledge, in its width and depth', such as no man of action has perhaps equalled (183). His knowledge of every subject, technical or otherwise, astounded (546).

He was normally quiet, speaking clearly with a soft voice (227, 405, 444, 453, 549). His movements were unobtrusive: 'mouse'-like (259), opening a door 'silently', a 'shape gliding in' (268); while still present, he could fade out like the Cheshire Cat of *Alice in Wonderland*, becoming insignificant (425). He had a way of 'noiselessly vanishing and reappearing' (178). He was also swift, rising 'in one movement like a steel spring unbending' and then walking 'as on silent wheels, perfectly smoothly, without any perceptible jolt'; he made 'no noise at all' (551-2). In general, he was 'bird-quick' (453). His faculties were 'like lightning, zig-zag and instantaneous' (64):

T. E. Lawrence

I never heard him raise his voice, and never saw him move suddenly or quickly yet he had all the signs of speed, and must have been like lightning, in a fight.   (Eric Kennington, 270)

And yet he was not impulsive. 'He moved little, using bodily presence just sufficiently to make brain contact. I had never seen so little employment or wastage of physical energy' (264). Again, 'we could not imagine his performing the most insignificant action thoughtlessly or without a sufficient reason' (551). He was an adept at all small, practical matters, 'scrubbing a barrack-room table' as it had never been scrubbed before (371); or in his cottage, where a guest was 'the astonished witness of his capacity for speed in movement'; 'I have seen no movement in ballet more magical' (121). Even his stillness was impressive: 'he stands as if he were floating – like a fish' (265).

Such comments suggest a being of some highly spiritualized order. His 'awareness amounted at times to clairvoyance' (296). He could be embarrassed by his powers. Once, having mysteriously stated the exact dimensions of a distant object, he pretended to have measured it 'last night' (435). Mrs. Kennington has a good statement:

He might be gay or remote, then there was a sudden blaze of blue from his eyes and a most startling sensation of power, and one realized he could know at will all there was to know about one; that he could make one what he willed, if he willed. It was like mesmeric power not being used at the moment, latent and terrific. This stopped my shyness because I saw it was no use, he knew all about one and that was just that.   (311)

So too people were 'transparent' to Byron (*Byron and Shakespeare*, 121). Mrs. Kennington had had a miscarriage and was in extreme depression, wanting to die. Lawrence talked to her, clarifying, with a feminine intuition, all her private anxieties and shames 'from the woman's point of view', while 'warmth' and 'power' streamed in. She says he saved her life (312-13). Eric Kennington says that Lawrence's visit was the turning point (271). In the Tank Corps he treated a tall soldier with a weak ankle with success (361-2).

He had an 'uncanny' power to 'probe behind' people's 'minds' and 'uncover the well-springs of their actions' (185); he 'seemed to read the minds of the people he was with, so that speech became almost unnecessary' (332). He ranged over time: 'To my ignorance, he seemed to have all past life in his mind' (266). He foresaw the future. Though no soldier, he had had no doubts about his success in Arabia: 'True. But I felt it as something already *done* and therefore unavoidable. I felt on sure ground' (297). Again:

He foresaw, possibly within certain definite limits, future events and occurrences in a manner that was perfectly normal to himself, but which in our ignorance we might term psychic.

(Flight-Lieut. R. G. Sims, 552)

From England he could 'consciously' influence a portrait-painter working in Arabia (268). His spirit was so unconstricted that his physical presence was not necessary for the enjoyment of his companionship (281). He 'seemed to be a phantasm of the living as now he is of the dead'; he will have gladly answered the 'call', and be welcomed on 'the other side' (181). 'Phantasm' recalls John Galt's reference to 'the incomprehensible phantasma which hovered about Lord Byron' and was 'more or less felt by all who ever approached him' (*Byron and Shakespeare*, 315). Lawrence is called 'ghostlike' (265), a man 'essentially apart from material life' (334):

One felt that he was good in a sense larger than the merely ethical, that he was completely aloof, half removed from earth, that power surrounded him.

(G. W. M. Dunn, 444)

Again:

Those light blue eyes of his and his light hair and his light springing step all helped to express the feeling of mountain tops, of withdrawn-ness, of seeing through anything at all, that one felt with him.

(Hilda Chaundy, 332)

Despite, or perhaps because of, these psychic qualities one of his central characteristics was his keenness on, and expertise with, material objects: mechanical inventions, nuts and bolts, gadgets of all kinds. He rated as high as did Masefield the skills of a craftsman.

What then of his ruthless opposition to the physical, so often stressed? He is called 'a one-man monastery' achieving mastery of the body 'by methods advocated by the saints whose lives he had read' (A. W. Lawrence, 592). But the physical was not really being slighted. Our quotations bear witness to the uncanny 'poise' (353) and grace of his physical being:

> I never met a man whose body was kept in such perfect discipline, transmitting naturally each movement of a steady flow of spirit.
>
> (E. H. R. Altounyan, 118-19)

The physical transmitted spirit. His 'superlative mind' was kept 'in absolute control of his body' (260). Major Yeats-Brown thinks that he unwisely rejected Yoga exercises because he 'hated his body', which he would master only by his 'will'; and yet he exercised 'a latent psychic superiority over me and mankind in general'; and the result of it was 'a radiant physical awareness' and 'a power of giving happiness such as I have never known another man to possess' (425-6). The physical radiated spirit. His brother, Prof. A. W. Lawrence, quotes an opinion that he had

> achieved a balance between spirit, intellect and body to a degree few even imagine, and that in spite of an extremely high evolution of the spirit, as a result of which the balance was so unusual as to appear to most people unbalanced. (592)

That is as good a solution as we can expect.

Physically, he had charm. His 'gentian-blue eyes' (177) and red-brown hair struck people, the eyes especially, as vividly beautiful. His eyes were strange:

> The eyes roamed round, above, and might rest on mine or rather travel through mine, but never shared my thoughts, though noting them all. He stayed higher on another plane of life. It was easy to become his slave. These crystal eyes were almost animal, yet with a complete human understanding. And at moments of thought, when he would ignore the presence of others, retiring into himself, they would diverge slightly. Then, he was alone, and as inscrutable as a lion or a snake.
>
> (Eric Kennington, 264)

The eyes could be dull, and then flash out. They could glint 'with roguish impudence' (168), or in anger they 'set hard, tempered like knives' (444). He is continually referred to as 'impish': he was often joking, and was as ready as Byron to deflate any sort of pretension (e.g. 81, 137, 185, 252, 269, 553; for Byron's similar penetrations, see my *Lord Byron: Christian Virtues*, 268-9, and *Byron and Shakespeare*, 121-2). Sir Hubert Young calls him 'a little monkey' and 'mischievous little imp' (125). Lady Byron after the separation said that Byron 'was always half-mad, mischievous as a monkey, wild as a tiger, but with many good feelings' (*The Amberley Papers*, II. 284). Both seemed to enjoy a permanent youthfulness (303, 372). Again and again Lawrence is called, as was Byron (*Byron and Shakespeare*, 120-1), 'boyish', the term coming more naturally because of his 'slight boyish figure' (166), 'a small shy youth' (287). His voice is once called 'girlish' (168). Lt.-Col. Ralph H. Isham lists various characteristics which he regards as those not of a mature man, but of a boy, together with an amazing intuition amounting to 'clairvoyance' (296). It is natural to equate him with the many idealized youths of poetry and drama, which I have regularly termed 'seraphic'; though Eric Kennington, at a first meeting, was surprised to see 'a small grinning, hatless kid' quite unlike the 'screen-seraph' of Lowell Thomas's film (262). But there are seraphic descriptions also: 'of eternal youth' and beauty, and of 'a slight upright blue-clad figure' standing 'high up in the bows of a boat, with one electric light turning his hair into gold' (552, 558).

Like Byron, he not only *was* youthful, but also liked and understood young people, including children. Again and again we hear of his easy contacts with children (e.g., 84, 270, 298, 449, 537 – 'He could talk to me in child's language' – 559, 566, 585).

And yet 'here was a power who seemed to command one's very soul' (169); he was compared by E. M. Forster, writing of Lawrence's sense of literary inferiority together with his Byronic pleasure at others' achievements, to 'a god who envies mankind' (283). He, who had been regarded by the Arabs almost as a 'deity' (409), made new sense of the statement that 'God created man in his own image' (544).

He could control people, mysteriously. Eric Kennington says that in anger his size seemed to be doubled (270). When he thought of introducing him to a man of similar psychic qualities, Lawrence telepathically read his intention: 'I was aware of a tautness, almost as if I were being paralysed. . . . He had, by a psychic power, entered my mind and was in charge of it. Then he deliberately giggled'. He told Kennington: 'I am not going to see your old teacher. He . . . might upset me' (271).

Major Yeats-Brown once came on Lawrence dressed in a bathing slip, and in a temper. Two taller, clothed, aircraftmen were with him shrinking 'under the spell, as I was, of some atmosphere of menace'; the sun gleamed on 'his wet red hair' and 'small brown body'. Yeats-Brown was afraid. What would he do to him? He felt paralysed, wishing 'to avoid this cosmic force', yet remaining 'rooted to the spot'. It turned out that Lawrence was only annoyed after two hours' work, much of it under water, at a faulty dynamo in a speed-boat. Yeats-Brown knew he had seen 'the power' that Lawrence had exercised in Arabia; 'he had terrific, indeed terrible, energies pent in his small body' (426-9).

Again, Flight-Lieut. Sims came on him reading a document, and was taken for a reporter. The paper

was slowly lowered, and a pair of the bluest, most flashing eyes I had ever seen blazed forth, whilst a vast forehead, equal in size to the terrific chin beneath, simply radiated scorn and hate at me. (550)

Yet Sims was not afraid:

I was full of admiration and joy at the sheer beauty of his face. It was that of a very small boy, angelically fair, from whom another boy has just pinched an apple. (550)

Finding it was no reporter, Lawrence changed; the glare vanished; from a small boy he now suddenly looked his real age. The changes are various and kaleidoscopic.

How closely all our descriptions recall Byron as described by the Countess Albrizzi. His eyes were of 'varied expression', and like Lawrence's of 'azure':

His face appeared tranquil like the ocean on a fine spring morning; but, like it, in an instant became changed into the tempestuous and terrible, if a passion (a passion did I say?), a thought, a word, occurred to disturb his mind. His eyes then lost all their sweetness, and sparkled so that it became difficult to look on them.

(Byron, *Letters and Journals*, IV, App. ii. 441-2)

In such descriptions eyes are regarded as powers, as though projecting rays, sweet or fearful.

Lawrence had a gift for making people happy (375, 426). Henry Williamson was one:

Never before and never since have I felt so free from myself, so without body: happiness beyond the consciousness of happiness. . . . I felt an immense easy power within myself; as though one could, and would, live forever. (453)

He gave one 'a sense of elation comparable to that which music can give' (307).

Churchill calls him 'one of nature's greatest princes', and says that he looked it (195):

His pride and many of his virtues were superhuman. He was one of those beings whose pace of life was faster and more intense than what is normal. Just as an aeroplane only flies by its speed and pressure against the air, so he could only fly in a hurricane. (200)

After the war there was accordingly nothing for him but the course he took: in a religious age he would have entered a 'monastery' (201): the thought occurs throughout, suggested by many, including Lawrence himself. Peter Quennell once said precisely the same of Byron. Churchill continues:

Solitary, austere, inexorable, he moved upon a plane apart from and above our common lot. Existence was no more than a duty, yet a duty faithfully to be discharged. (201)

'I deem him', says Churchill, 'one of the greatest beings alive in our time' (202).

It is not surprising that Lawrence was himself baffled, perhaps terrified. He was in possession of unusual powers he could use or not at will: he could 'switch off the great current of force that was in him' and his face was then a blank (295). Again:

I have seen a crowd of men become silent as soon as he lifted a finger or opened his lips. In those rare moments he seemed detached, fey, greater than his body, a power which flowed out, irresistibly, from that very quiet little figure. With an effort he had switched himself on. I believe it exhausted him. He had given himself away when his great desire was to be whole and intact.

(G. W. M. Dunn, 449)

Col. S. F. Newcombe saw him as

a hero shaken by his vision, not of past accomplishment, but of incredible possibilities which unless he was very careful would become, were becoming, actualities leading to regions where he instinctively felt it would be terribly dangerous to remain. (116-17)

This corresponds to Byron's terror at thought of his own, more-than-Napoleonic being (Augusta Leigh to Lady Byron, 22 January 1816; see my *Byron and Shakespeare*, 101-2). 'They've offered me Egypt', Lawrence once remarked, but he had refused, knowing that it 'would make me vicious' (376).

His powers exceeded that of a normal man of action; they were more 'psychic', nearer Nietzsche's 'superman' than men of ordinary greatness. That is why he is compared to a 'saint' (227, 450) or 'mystic' (431). There is the inevitable comparison with Christ (191, 398). He had early planned a study of Christ's historical background (A. W. Lawrence, 585-7). Eric Kennington suggests that in Arabia he had experienced 'the third temptation of the exceeding high mountain', partly yielded, and later did penance for it (272). In *Lawrence of Arabia* Anthony Nutting develops the thought, saying that when Kennington composed a design showing a deity looking down on the Arab campaign, Lawrence was amazed at its exact reproduction of how he had himself felt at the time (Nutting, 243-4).

Like Byron, Nietzsche, and Shaw, he believed in the necessity of man transcending his present state. I am thinking of Byron's ruminations in his 1814 Journal (9 and 19 April; *Letters and Journals*, II. 409-11; discussed in *Poets of Action*, 286-8) on Napoleon's ignominious fall, in which, for Byron, the whole race was involved; and of Shaw's *Caesar and Cleopatra*, admired by Lawrence (Letter 184; to Bernard Shaw, 7 December 1922). The first act of *Heartbreak House* Lawrence called 'metallic, inhuman, super-natural: the most blazing bit of genius in English literature' (Letter 347; to William Rothenstein, 14 April 1928); Lawrence always liked metals and machines, for their 'extension' of human faculties (p. 337 above); and Shotover's *magnetic* powers were as an extension of his own. It has been suggested that Shaw was thinking of Lawrence when he created the heroine of *Saint Joan*; certainly he did a stage portrait of him in Meek[1] in *Too True to be Good*, which Lawrence saw and enjoyed (Letter 462; to Walter Hudd, 3 September 1932). But in searching for a superman Lawrence was not thinking mainly of himself: instead, he passionately wanted someone to idealize, as he tried to idealize Allenby (p. 319 above), and later admired Air Marshal Trenchard.

[1] I had once the good fortune to play this part, in a production by the Staff Dramatic Society of the University of Leeds.

Lawrence once wrote that literature had not given him satisfaction. Poetry was a collection of sweets only, of 'bonbons':

> Failing poetry I chased my fancied meal through prose, and found everywhere good little stuff, and only a few men who had honestly tried to be greater than mankind: and only their strainings and wrestlings really fill my stomach.
>
> (Letter 171; to Edward Garnett, 23 October 1922)

Discussing politics with Ernest Thurtle he said that he would always have scorned (like Byron) the scramble and place-seeking needed for 'democratic leadership', and concluded:

> What is wanted is a new master species – birth control for us, to end the human race in fifty years – and then a clear field for some cleaner mammal. I suppose it must be a mammal.
>
> (*Friends*, Ernest Thurtle, 355)

This is Byron's loathing of the 'human species' at Napoleon's fall (*Journal*, as above, p. 345); or Tennyson's 'Strike dead the whole weak race of venomous worms' (p. 422 below).

7

Lawrence's later actions cannot be understood without a full recognition of his difficulties. Pride was probably a severe temptation.[1] Some, like J. B. Villars (*T. E. Lawrence*, 345-6), regard his claims as, on occasion, unwarranted and egotistic. Major Yeats-Brown suggests that he had 'a desire to astound the world' (*Friends*, 424). No doubt he could, as Stendhal said of Byron, at times 'pretend to everything' (Byron, *Letters and Journals*, III. App. viii. 444). He himself admits it in his *Seven Pillars*:

> There was a craving to be famous; and a horror of being known to like being known. Contempt for my passion for distinction made me refuse every offered honour.
>
> (CIII. 580)

This 'contempt' was itself a pride, like that of Shakespeare's Coriolanus, who was also ill-at-ease with honours (*Coriolanus*, I. ix. 13-53; commented on in *The Imperial Theme*, 169). But it was also the result of recognizing falsities both in society and in himself. He knew that 'at bottom we are carnal', rationalizing

---

[1] In Jane Sherwood's *Post-Mortem Journal* (1964), a book of spirit-communications as from T. E. Lawrence, we hear that in the after-life he has aimed to make amends for his apartness and 'defensive egoism' (81) on earth.

'beast-qualities' into 'hopes and ideals' (Letter 241; to Harley Granville-Barker, 7 February 1924). He had probably from early youth known sex-activated compulsions to degradation, including flagellation, first in masturbatory fantasies and later in action. This may well have been part cause of his hatred of his own 'physical envelope' (p. 328 above). But this was all the inevitable consequence and obverse of his spirituality. The keyed-up and ascetic pace of a superman forces relief.

Shakespeare puts it well in Sonnet 118 (discussed in *The Mutual Flame*, 124-6; with reference to Byron, *Byron and Shakespeare*, 62-3), where the sustained and 'ne'er-cloying' perfection of his apprehension makes him so 'sick of welfare' that he has to descend for a 'purge' to 'bitter sauces'; 'rank of goodness', he would 'by ill be cured'. The same experience is stated in 'The Night Song' of Nietzsche's *Thus Spake Zarathustra* (II. 9; discussed in *Christ and Nietzsche*, V. 178):

Oh, unblessedness of them that give! Oh, eclipse of my sun! Oh, desire for desire! Oh, raging hunger in the midst of satiety!

Men 'take' from him, but he makes no contact with their 'soul', and accordingly hungers 'for wickedness', to make some contact, his very 'virtue' wearying of its own 'abundance'.

Somewhere within this area we shall place Lawrence's impulses to self-humiliation, including what seems to have been an early experience as a coolie at Port Said (p. 326 above). There are analogies in the Gospels, especially the Gospel of St. John, where Christ at the Last Supper washes his disciples' feet. There are analogies in all of us whenever the charade of civilization demands relief in disreputable fantasy. Apollo surrenders to Dionysus. Dark horrors may be involved, or obscenities, either tragedy or comedy, or both.

In such seemingly reprehensible surrenders (discussed more fully on pp. 195, 220) there is an invasion of sexual and cosmic powers from beyond ethic. We may call them 'elemental'; and Lawrence, in Timon mood, grew to love, like Brooke before and Lindbergh after him, the elements. Lt.-Col. Ralph H. Isham tells us (296):

He loved speeding through the air or plunging deep in water because, he said, it gave him the illusion of becoming actually part of those elements.

When he tried 'deep sea diving' he took to it as though he had done it for years (434). He loved the open Dorset moors (373), and 'the solitude and stillness of the long nights' (415). *The Mint* concludes with a richly Powysian experience of sun-bathing while on duty in the Air Force, watching the sky for a balloon:

We were too utterly content to speak, drugged with an absorption fathoms deeper than physical contentment. Just we lay there spread-eagled in a mesh of bodies, pillowed on one another and sighing in happy excess of relaxation. The sunlight poured from the sky and melted into our tissues. From the turf below our moist backs there came up a sister-heat which joined us to it. Our bones dissolved to become a part of this underlying indulgent earth, whose mysterious pulse throbbed in every tremor of our bodies. The scents of the thousand-acre drome mixed with the familiar oil-breath of our hangar, nature with art: while the pale sea of the grass bobbed in little waves before the wind raising a green surf which hissed and flowed by the slats of our heat-lidded eyes. (3. XVIII. 205)

So 'the mail and plate of our personality' is resolved back into the 'carbohydrate elements of being' (206). Here is a relaxation, a warmth and colour of apprehension vastly different from the keyed-up, highly spiritualized, vibrations of the *Seven Pillars*. Air Force training brought a simple elemental happiness, whatever the season: in winter 'rain and wind chivy us, till soon we are wind and rain'. And there is water, the 'translucent swimming pool', diving into 'the elastic water which fits our bodies closely as a skin' (3. XVIII. 206).

Were then Lawrence's later actions so strange? What had high office or decorations to give him in comparison? But we could still charge him with a retreat from responsibility; the responsibility of using his powers for his country and for mankind. The charge can be answered.

Why was Lawrence so *urgently* obsessed by the Air Force? Why did he so hate being relegated to the Tank Corps, and have no rest until he was reinstated as an air-mechanic? As with an uncanny prescience, while the world around him was wondering why he did not accept the Governorship of Egypt or some similar appointment, he elected instead to place himself *in precisely the most important spot, nationally speaking, that was open to him*. He did not think, or live, in terms of normal valuation: the scrubbing of a table, at least while he was doing it, was as important as the winning of a campaign. To both his superself and his underself high place meant nothing; to the one it was trivial, to the other undeserved. He was happy working from below, *his secret impulse to degradation coming openly and creatively into play*. In the ranks of the Air Force he established a union between his two selves, body and soul coming together as at the close of Powys's *Wolf Solent* (p. 158 above), the masochistic obsession becoming one with noblest service. As Nietzsche says in *Thus Spake Zarathustra* ('The Wanderer', III. 1):

Thou goest thy way of greatness: now is that become thy final refuge which hath been hitherto thine extremest peril.

Thou goest thy way of greatness: thy highest courage must it be that there is no longer any way back!

So, putting all his human and military insights, all his expertise as a craftsman, and all his perversions, at the service of the Air Force, Lawrence found his 'way of greatness'. He himself called it 'inevitable' (p. 335 above).

Nor was it a spectacular way. He knew (p. 320 above) 'the pride and exhilaration' of a cross leading to 'self-perfection'; but better still was 'self-immolation' and the 'making perfect of the neighbour'; and it was precisely this which with an almost incredible selflessness he undertook, choosing his ground with care. Nothing could be less spectacular, and yet nothing, from his view, more important.

He was not posing as a modern messiah, nor even as a religious man; and yet Liddell Hart may have been right in suggesting that he had the requisite qualities for such a role: 'Free from pettiness, freed from ambition, immeasurable in understanding, his individualism springs from the wisdom of the ages' (Liddell Hart, 448). A modern messiah must certainly cover state as well as church; action as well as spirituality; war as well as peace. Like Byron, Lawrence shows this inclusiveness. He graduated through war to mysticism and thence to humility; and all three contributed to his last years of service; where, by a happy paradox, his main concern was the designing of speed-boats for the preservation of life.

The Royal Air Force was new. It needed every possible support; above all it must be efficient. Lawrence was 'hot to make it perfect' (p. 335 above). 'At Farnborough' he once wrote, 'I grew suddenly on fire with the glory that the air should be, and set to work full steam to make others vibrate to it like myself' (quoted by Lionel Curtis, *Friends*, 261).

Writing to Robert Graves (Letter 559; 4 February 1935) about an obituary of himself that Graves had been asked to prepare, Lawrence did not wish his Arabian campaign high-lighted; nor even what he regarded as more important, his subsequent help, with Churchill, to make a Middle-East settlement. Instead, he thinks of the Air Force; he regards the conquest of the air as the main task of his generation, and he believes that progress is made 'not by the single genius, but by the common effort':

Wherefore I stayed in the ranks and served to the best of my ability, much influencing my fellow airmen towards a pride in themselves and their inarticulate duty. I tried to make them see – with some success.

The letter gives an extended account of what he accomplished against opposition, especially in the designing of the speed-boats. Though witnessing in detail to his technical expertise, this letter contains no trace of self-glorification: on the contrary, he is at pains to insist that it was a *collaborative* task.

As an exemplar and an influence, it is impossible to assess the extent of the contribution he may have made. Liddell Hart said that 'he was a greater spiritual force than the whole board of Chaplains in raising the standard of decency, fair play and unselfish comradeship' (Nutting, 235).

More widely, Lawrence's choice was symbolic. Not only was he implemental in procuring a number of important reforms within the Air Force; his presence had propaganda value which, though the authorities did what they could to suppress it, must have worked to their advantage. The new Force needed help; it needed propaganda: and we were all soon to have reason to be grateful for its efficiency. Soon the nation's life was to depend upon the air. In putting aside all obvious temptation to present fame and glamour Lawrence was, in fact, quietly, and in his own unique and prescient way, devoting himself to victory in the Battle of Britain.

One other thought. His instinct was to work either from below or among the peaks, to say, like Byron, '*aut Caesar aut Nihil*' (p. 313 above). When, after his retirement to Clouds Hill, Henry Williamson suggested, in the year 1935, that he should

T. E. *Lawrence*

meet Hitler, he responded with alacrity: here was something within his natural range. 'You alone', Williamson had written, 'are capable of negotiating with Hitler' (Nutting, 235). Lawrence rode off at once to arrange, by telegram, a preliminary discussion. On his return, swerving to avoid two boys, he crashed and was killed. There is a report of a mysterious black car that may have caused the accident, though the boys saw nothing (*Letters*, note by A. W. Lawrence, 872-3). It seems to have been an ordinary accident. Had Lawrence met Hitler, power measured against power, world events might have been deflected.

ADDITIONAL NOTE: Since writing this I have read John E. Mack's 'The Inner Conflict of T. E. Lawrence' in *The Times*, Saturday Review, 8 February 1969). He relates Lawrence's flagellatory obsession to punishments administered by his mother in boyhood. He also lays a strong emphasis on Lawrence's suffering from knowledge of his idealized mother's unmarried state and his own illegitimacy. I doubt if the flagellatory obsession can be more than obliquely related to any specific event, and Professor Mack is rightly cautious. After all, it is a well-known obsession.

Tribute is paid to the heroism of Lawrence's final abnegations. He is seen as a type or personification of conscience within our changing attitude to public affairs and military glory.

CHAPTER XII

J. Middleton Murry

Of Books and Humankind: Essays and Poems presented to Bonamy Dobrée, ed. John Butt, 1964.

WHEN AFTER LEAVING Oxford I was groping for a way to express what I had to say about Shakespeare, Middleton Murry's articles in the monthly *Adelphi* magazine acted on me like an avatar; and to his writings of this period my debt remains. Here was someone who without reservations was proclaiming the religious importance of literature in a voice of authority.

After the death of Katherine Mansfield, Murry had had a mystical experience which he describes in *To the Unknown God* (1924; 42-4) and *God* (1929; 35-6). Here is his description, written soon after the experience:

Then in the dark, in the dead, still house, I sat at the table facing the fire. I sat there motionless for hours, while I tried to face the truth that I was alone. As I had wanted to turn back, so now I longed to turn away. There was in me something that simply would not look, and, again and again, as it turned its eyes away, I took its head in my two hands and held its face towards what I had to see. Slowly and with an effort I made myself conscious that I was physically alone. Prompted by some instinct, I tried to force this consciousness into every part of my body. Slowly I succeeded. At last I had the sensation that I *was* in my hands and feet, that where they ended I also ended, as at a frontier of my being, and beyond that frontier stretched out the vast immensities, of space, of the universe, of the illimitable, something that was other than I. Where I ended, it began – other, strange, terrible, menacing. It did not know me, would never acknowledge me, denied me utterly. Yet out upon this, from the fragile rampart of my own body, I found the courage to peer, to glance, at last to gaze steadily. And I became aware of myself as a little island against whose slender shores

352

a cold, dark, boundless ocean lapped devouring. Somehow, in that moment, I knew I had reached a pinnacle of personal being. I was I, as I had never been before – and never should be again.

It is strange that I should have known that. But then I did know it, and it was not strange.

What happened then? If I could tell you that I should tell you a secret indeed. But a moment came when the darkness of that ocean changed to light, the cold to warmth; when it swept in one great wave over the shores and frontiers of my self; when it bathed me and I was renewed; when the room was filled with a presence, and I knew I was not alone – that I never could be alone any more, that the universe beyond held no menace, for I was part of it, that in some way for which I had sought in vain so many years, I *belonged*, and because I belonged, I was no longer I, but something different, which could never be afraid in the old ways, or cowardly with the old cowardice. And the love I had lost was still mine, but now more durable, being knit into the very substance of the universe I had feared. And the friends whose words had been so meaningless were bound to me, and I to them, for ever. And if it should prove that I had a work to do, or a part to play, I should no longer draw back at the last.

This experience had subsequently fused in his mind with his interests as a literary critic and in the *Adelphi* he was delivering a gospel based on that experience as corroborated by literature. His views at this period are covered by the volumes *To the Unknown God* (1924) and *Things to Come* (1928), most of which appeared originally in the *Adelphi*. These volumes I designate 'UG' and 'TC'.

The teaching is a teaching of soul-discovery through tragic experience and the final aim a 'change of consciousness' (*UG*, 184, 191, 296). Through suffering and tragedy the soul is realized and such a realization conditions and empowers both the teaching of Jesus and the greatest literature. The interior and exterior worlds of human knowledge (*UG*, 220) are transcended: the more harmony there is in oneself the more harmony is discovered in the external order (*Adelphi*, IV. 1; July 1926; 5). Jesus, says Murry, taught that there is a faculty attainable by which man can see beyond the apparent good and evil outside and within (*TC*, 170). Mind and heart may be unified to create this soul-sight:

The soul is simply the condition of the complete man. And to this completeness in the man, which is his soul, there corresponds a completeness and harmony of the world of his experience.

(*TC*, 171)

J. Middleton Murry

That world now 'becomes God'; and the knowing of it is simultaneously a supernal love.

This state is achieved through loyalty to one's own experience (*UG*, 9, 60). Great writers are authoritative only because the soul recognizes their authority. Truth is immediate and is recognized by the momentarily integrated man when

> through his whole being there comes a flash of sudden awareness of unity within him, and from some place that he scarcely knew leaps up a sense of knowledge and a sense of oneness in that which knows; when his deepest, unfamiliar self rises and takes possession of all that he is, body and mind and soul, and declares: *This is true* . . .
>
> (*UG*, 75)

But what is experienced cannot be easily defined. Intellect 'is the servant, not the master, of life' (*Adelphi*, IV. 1; July 1926; 5); it cannot harmonize or create, but only elucidate (*TC*, 227). Again:

> To make artistic creation possible your knowledge *must* give way; you must resign yourself to the deep unconscious purpose that is in you, and 'let that which is creative create itself'. Purpose will declare itself in despite of all your philosophies, as it does in Hardy and Tchehov. But if you will not, or you cannot, do this, if you will *know* and know all the time, then there is an end. The books you write are dead, and you have slain the art you loved; and slain it when it would have saved you. For by its own operation the art of literature has power to recreate the sense of purpose in the soul.
>
> (*Adelphi*, IV. 3; September 1926; 144-5)

This 'purpose' is 'prior to all its symbolisms, literature itself included' and 'religion depends upon it, not it upon religion' (*Adelphi*, IV. 3; September 1926; 145). Murry tends to avoid any detailed commitments. Great literature is a revelation of a harmony that *cannot be interpreted*:

> Art holds the place it does in our secret loyalties – so it seems to me – because it does reveal what cannot be uttered. That, and no other, is the test of its authenticity. (*UG*, 265)

Murry's attitude to 'God' is similar. He uses the term, but will not commit himself to a 'personal' God:

> The only record of the nature of God is history – the things that were and are. The inscrutable process of the universe, this is He; and man, in whom the great process knows itself for a moment, can know it is

not in vain. Little enough indeed, yet enough, and more than enough. To know that there is a purpose, yet not to know the purpose – that is blessedness indeed. To see but a tiny inch into the million miles of the unknown future – this is not forlorn and despairing, as orthodoxy would persuade us, but an authentic *sursum* to the soul. To know the future – what utter weariness! (*TC*, 227)

In which there is a psychological truth to which we may respond.

Murry's position involved a conflict with religious orthodoxy. Christ is his supreme hero, but a hero as a man whose unrivalled perfection drove him to a tragic death. Official Christian dogma and doctrine are no longer acceptable (*UG*, 135-7, 190-1, 193-203). Just as Murry rejects the 'intellectually premeditated' technique of James Joyce as a distortion of the creative impulse (*Adelphi*, IV. 3; September 1926; 140), so he distrusts dogma as a pandering to intellect. During this period he was engaged in a controversy with T. S. Eliot as a romantic against classicism (*UG*, 134). Murry aligns Catholicism with classicism (*UG*, 136). His central tenet is this:

When literature becomes a parlour-game and religion a church-mummery, they are alike only in their deadness. But between the literature that is real and the religion that is real the bond is close and unbreakable. (*UG*, 164)

For Murry orthodoxy was no longer 'real'. The Renaissance was the beginning of a new individualism, and it is useless to look back and 'sigh after a unity of religiousness that can never be ours' (*Adelphi*, IV. 4; October 1926; 205-6). In discussing the Abbé Bremond's *Prière et Poésie* he will not allow that poetry aspires to the condition of prayer, putting it the other way round (*TC*, 217), and insisting on Eckhart's mysticism of descent, of a return to the actual, which is the concern of literature. Many today 'know that they are religious' and yet that 'the religion of today has no *meaning* for them'; while 'the words that have meaning for them are the words of the poets' (*TC*, 218).

Difficulties present themselves. Despite Murry's trust in poetry and his acute discussions of metaphor in *The Problem of Style* (1925), he rejects a personal God, saying that 'such metaphors', necessary in the past, are now dangerous (*TC*, 226). That may be, but it seems dangerous for an apostle of poetry to regard metaphor as in itself a limitation. Elsewhere he justly regards the doctrine

J. Middleton Murry

of the Incarnation, which he personally rejects, as an example of the poetic process (*TC*, 209). We are really faced less with any rejection of dogma in the name of poetry than with the simple rejection of certain types of poetry in favour of others. He is thinking as a critic. He has every right to do this, but we must be aware of what he is doing.

In 1926 and 1927 Murry published in *The Adelphi* two items of mine, one on Wordsworth's *Immortality Ode* (p. 28 above), and another, which won a competition on a point of interpretation, on *Julius Caesar*. The association was at first happy. Murry invited me to meet him in London, and another Shakespeare essay was printed in the *Adelphi's* quarterly successor the *New Adelphi*; but after a while Murry's reactions became less favourable. Simultaneously, my own Shakespearian investigations were becoming surprisingly successful. I found myself doing what I had expected Murry himself to do. New significances were seen unrolling in the tragedies and the plays of Shakespeare's final period. These insights were conditioned by the surmounting of the critical faculties and an acceptance of what was there, in detail and major outline alike. I looked at images and symbols as entities speaking in their own right, almost, one might say, out of context; and thrilled to the coming-alive of Hermione's statue as keenly as I responded to the death of Lear. My results countered what was generally supposed; but, in tune with Murry's own gospel, I refused to let the intellect interfere. And when I wrote *The Christian Renaissance* (1933), though I was myself as ill-at-ease with orthodoxy as Murry himself, I engaged in the same acceptance, and applied the same method, to the New Testament and Christian dogma.[1] To these discoveries I gave the name 'interpretation'.

Murry had himself regarded Shakespeare's last plays, except for their idyllic young persons and Prospero's 'cloud-capp'd towers', in terms of weariness and an 'idle weaving of words' (*UG*, 184; and see 287); and when my *Myth and Miracle* appeared in 1929 he reviewed it in *The Times Literary Supplement* unfavourably. His *Adelphi* review of *The Wheel of Fire* was also unfavourable. He was still friendly in correspondence but regarded me – he said so in one of his letters – as an 'intellectual'. Though I was at the time,

---

[1] I see now that my handling of the parables in the Gospels in *The Christian Renaissance* must have been influenced and aided by Murry's 'The Parables of Jesus' in *Things to Come*.

356

and for some years after, surprised, thinking that I had been dropped just when I had found my direction, yet nowadays on rereading his letters[1] I am struck by his kindness and regularity in correspondence with a younger man. His rejection was consistent. Interpretation in my sense he had never, except perhaps in his *Dostoevsky* (1916), of which I reminded him, aimed at; and when he replied that Dostoievsky was different, the statement was in line with his earlier remark on him as 'the ultimate outpost of the attempt at an *intellectual* discovery of life' (my italics; *UG*, 128). As for *Keats and Shakespeare*, that was an interpretation of Keats's life and letters, not of the poetry.

Even so, he was nearer to my interpretations, or so I thought, than the opposing, 'classical', camp; and yet support was to come through the generosity of T. S. Eliot, who recommended *The Wheel of Fire* for publication and wrote for it an invaluable Introduction; and one of my most understanding reviews was written by Bonamy Dobrée in the *Criterion*.

While Murry was writing me off as an 'intellectual', I was becoming aware that he himself put too firm a reliance on the academic scholarship then current. In reviewing *Myth and Miracle* he regarded my emphasis on the Vision in *Cymbeline* as evidence of a lack in Shakespearian sensitivity. During my years in Canada I formulated certain criticisms of Murry's work, writing of his *God* in the *Canadian Journal of Religious Thought* (November-December 1931; 364-9) that his system lacked 'the picture-language of imagination and the mystery of symbol', and that, while the dogmas of 'the early imagination of Christendom' were cast in 'the three-dimensional forms of figurative thought', like poetry, Murry's system, though seeming true, was only true on the lesser, intellectual, level. In the *Canadian Forum* I reviewed his collection of the less mystical, literary-academic, essays of *Countries of the Mind* (1931), saying:

He can be either rational, and, if we grant his critical premises, impersonal, or profound and personal; but not both at once. He refuses to formulate the deeper emotions with precision, probably because he is too much afraid of not telling the truth. But truth may be composed of a myriad of falsehoods, and the bold writer turns out one profound lie after another unashamedly.

[1] I expect to lodge these letters in the Brotherton Collection at the University of Leeds.

J. Middleton Murry

I agreed with Murry's fears of intellect when autonomous, but claimed nevertheless that it could be

> a glass through which we may focus reality; or as a prism to split the unsearchable golden fire into blending tints.

Murry renounced sharp and detonating statements in the name of truth. My conclusion was:

> Intellect, like the devil himself, is a dangerous master but an invaluable servant. Mr. Murry will not make terms with the intellectual Mammon of unrighteousness. It therefore, in different ways, still dominates, instead of serving his vision.
>
> *(Canadian Forum, December 1931; 107-8)*

Observe that each had now charged the other with intellectualism. In reviewing Murry's *Shakespeare* (1936) in *Saturday Night* (Toronto) I attributed its delayed appearance to an 'inward uncertainty' of which signs were now also evident in the result. I concluded:

> The section on the final plays, though genuine profundities are scattered here and there, cannot be said to do more than flirt with the vast issues involved. *(25 April 1936)*

Which brings us to the heart of the disagreement.

As prophet, Murry concentrated (i) on the tragic and (ii) on ineffable recognition in and through the tragic. What he refused was (iii) any attempt to formulate that recognition. Shakespeare's system of values, apparently so 'divorced from any faith in immortality', cannot be analysed: 'The order is there, but it is the inscrutable order of organic life' (*TC*, 200-1). An analysis which revealed in Shakespeare intimations of immortality was for him suspect. Even had he been convinced, he would have been repelled, as he was by Church dogma, fearing to be forced beyond his own experience.

He could himself write of 'a hidden universe' and 'a glimpse of what is beyond this mortal world', but such gleams could only be known through a man's 'deepest, unfamiliar self', through 'a new principle of authority in and through the deeper knowledge of the self' (*UG*, 61, 240; 75, 182). Man's own experience is the one court of appeal; 'It lies in the very dignity of man to stand or fall by his own knowledge' (*UG*, 197). Those who accept religious dogmas only do it by achieving 'some sort of willing suspension of disbelief' (*UG*, 196). But what of Murry's own insistence that 'your knowledge must give way' (p. 354 above)? And is not this willing suspension of disbelief the characteristic of what the Romantics meant by 'imagination'? My divergence from Murry, as a writer, was this: he wrote from his own spiritual experience, I from the imagination. My reading of Shakespeare's last plays originated from an acceptance of what others, and sometimes my own instinct, regarded as impossible. Imagination is precisely the faculty for apprehending and accepting what is *not* covered by one's own experience. It might be said to offer substitutes for the mystical experience, and such substitutes Murry would not accept. Shaw's *Saint Joan* aroused his admiration, but he rejected the Epilogue (*UG*, 242-3), that wonderful composite of spirit-life and astral travelling, as irrelevant. Christ's tragic suffering was to him authoritative (e.g. *Adelphi*, IV. 10; April 1927; 593-4), but the resurrection, at least as stated, impossible (*TC*, 95). Nor, anyway, was it *needed*; Murry received all he wanted from tragedy as tragedy. And yet Sophocles has his *Oedipus Coloneus*, and all great dramatists push beyond tragedy. If tragedy becomes an end in itself, it ceases to be greatly tragic. Its majesty, the dark majesty of death, is the shadow cast on our minds by a presence that is not dark.

Writing of the contemplation of Christ's death, Murry is himself forced into a symbolism beyond tragedy:

And then, suddenly, strangely, out of the chaos, the despair, the agony of this contemplation, rises a voice like the singing of a solitary bird after the terror of the storm. Some mysterious song of triumph rises and swells within our darkened souls . . .

(*Adelphi*, IV. 10; April 1927; 594)

But this can only come, he says, through an absolute acceptance of death as death: 'Life, spelled with a capital, is life *and* death'; and that 'Life', says Murry, 'goes on' and it is for us to 'serve' it through 'acceptance' of 'death' (*Adelphi*, IV. 4; October 1926; 209). Neither 'life' nor 'death' is complete; they are 'partial manifestations of one hidden, living and eternal reality' (*UG*, 63). We must not 'strive to overcome death, by striving to believe in personal immortality', for 'this is not to overcome death' but simply to 'falsify' it by trying to 'change death into life' (*UG*, 298).

J. Middleton Murry

Those who believe in 'personal immortality' make death 'the plaything of life', so wronging its 'majesty'. The 'magnificent opposition' of life and death '*must* be a formulation of that which is beyond them, and is one' (*UG*, 299; and see *TC*, 119-20).[1] Theosophy, Rudolf Steiner, Gurdjieff and Madam Blavatsky are scornfully dismissed (*UG*, 279-80). There is worse:

The prying spiritualism, the muck-raking of eternity, into which even men of science have lately fallen in [is?] a degradation of human dignity; and the instinctive nobility of the human soul turns away from it in pity and disgust. In our hearts we know better than that; we know how to choose between these sordid affronts to the majesty of an event that fills us with awe and wonder . . .   (*UG*, 299)

The venom, so unusual for Murry, is a symptom of unease, and perhaps fear.

One must, he again argues, at all costs preserve intact the 'glory' of death's 'substantial mystery' (*UG*, 300); and of that 'greater thing' which encloses both life and death 'we can *say* nothing', though we can be 'aware of' and even 'know' it (*UG*, 300-1). Death is central in Murry's argument: the opposition of life and death, he says, includes all other oppositions (*UG*, 302-3). The mystery of death is not, however, likely to be quite so easily dissolved as he fears. Nor is it only scientists who have involved themselves in this 'degradation of human dignity'. A study of the relation of literary genius to Spiritualism during the last hundred years would involve a dazzling list of names. But at any point when the relation becomes assertive, Murry would be likely to condemn it, as he condemned the Epilogue to *Saint Joan*.

His uncompromising denial of personal immortality elicited an interesting rejoinder from William Archer, who was dying. Archer pointed out the evidence of Spiritualism:

If there is one thing I am certain of in this world, it is that there is *something* which we do not begin to understand behind the phenomena which we loosely describe as spiritualistic.   (*TC*, 66)

This, he said, is something 'which science must, so to speak, fathom and assimilate, on pain of wilfully living in an incomplete

---

[1] Murry's emphasis on the acceptance of *life-and-death* corresponds exactly with that of Powys in *The Art of Happiness*. His agnostic mysticism has much in common with Powys.

360

universe' (*TC*, 67); and he proceeded to give as good a summary as I know of regarding what Spiritualism demonstrates, and what interpretations are open to us. He wrote from actual experience.

In answer Murry assured him that though he rejected '*personal* immortality', he yet believed that 'something survives' and 'most emphatically' did not believe in 'annihilation' (*TC*, 69). Archer died. Murry composed a fictional dialogue (*TC*, 70-7) such as, in his opinion, there might have been between him and Archer, in which he describes the birth of a 'spark' which 'knows, and is your self and is something quite other than yourself'; this is the 'soul'. At which the fictional Archer shakes his head, saying that it means nothing to him. Murry explains that if the soul 'exists out of time and space and belongs to another order of reality' it would be 'wrong', 'vulgar' and 'belittling' to speak of 'personal survival'; the soul 'eternally is', 'in another mode of being, which neither our senses nor our mind but our soul alone can comprehend'. To 'reimpose personality upon the soul which is the triumph over personality' would be 'strange'. But if the soul is not born during life, then, says Murry, it may be born in death, and at death perhaps 'we do indeed put on this incorruptible', everyone, 'saint or sinner, wise man or fool'; and this would explain Archer's spiritualistic convictions.

Murry is here in retreat so far as the central beliefs of Spiritualism are concerned, but he still argues that we should win our souls through death-conquest and avoid communication. The dead 'live indeed, but not with our life'; one must not 'seek to compel' them – the usual error, drawn from the Faust tradition, of those who have no first-hand knowledge of Spiritualism – to return. Asked if he condemns communication, he now says 'I condemn nothing'. But he insists that we should attain a condition which realizes that real communication is impossible. When Archer insists in reply that he has himself had an obviously genuine communication, Murry – not to be outdone – replies: 'So have I, though I did not seek it'. It told him, too, that there was 'something there'. He concludes well:

The knowledge that 'something is there' may come to a man by many ways; but to know the something that is there – to that, I believe, there is but a single way. (*TC*, 77)

He has admitted Archer's contention, while denying its value.

J. Middleton Murry

His phraseology has been dangerously confusing. The denial of personal immortality turns out to be, pretty nearly, its opposite. In an essay 'Personality and Immortality' he attempts a clarification:

The immortality of this personality is a contradiction in terms: the mere fact of immortality would make this personality quite unrecognizable. (*TC*, 82)

If by 'personality' we mean 'that which does not survive', it is true that its survival will be inconceivable; but the statement merely wastes ink.

Murry replaces the word 'personality' by the word 'soul': 'a man has a self that is beyond and hidden from his self of everyday' and this 'hidden and higher self' is the 'soul' (*TC*, 80-1). His earlier phraseology had said as much: the soul was the 'highest' and 'unawakened' part of us, whose language is great poetry (*TC* 29); and he had used the phrase *'non omnis moriar'* (*UG*, 155). He is not being inconsistent; he is merely being unfair to the reader. Our 'reality', we are told, lies deeper than the phenomenal 'I', and 'personality' is a 'veil' only (*TC*, 83). This reality he neatly relates to the children's angels beholding God in the New Testament (*TC*, 264-5). But if this soul-reality is after all immortal, then much of our previous heart-searching has been in vain; for achieving one's soul makes one, in Murry's system, 'in the truest and highest sense, an individual' (*TC*, 31); the soul 'is ourselves in a new wholeness, without division' (*TC*, 173); and if this 'wholeness' is what survives, that is surely enough to satisfy the most demanding of us.

So when Murry is attacked by a theologian for offering mankind an immortality 'less than personal' he rightly replies that what he is offering is not less but 'more' than personal (*TC*, 87). On the conflicting accounts of the resurrection in the New Testament and on the Church's dogma of the resurrection of the body he registers some telling hits. He is nevertheless willing to believe that Jesus' followers had an *experience* of his existence after dying, and that soul may make contact with soul across the barrier, as did St. Paul (*TC*, 95-6). The theologian makes a good point too:

The poet's vision, no doubt, is untranslatable into argument, but so is a pain in one's finger. Theologians attempt to explain one kind of experience, physiologists another. The best of their theories or 'dogmas' may be no more than shadows; but, as long as men are afflicted with rationality, so long will such theories continue to appear.

(TC, 91)

That is a statement I would myself apply to poetic interpretation.

Our confusions can only be resolved by some such intermediate link as the etheric or astral body known to esoteric tradition from ancient times and announced today by spirit-communications. This was the line taken by St. Paul when he defined the resurrected body as a 'spiritual' body (1 Corinthians, XV. 42-9). Spiritualist accounts give doctrines such as Murry's concerning a supernal reality their proper place, while explaining that it cannot be achieved in one leap by so simple a process as dying: there are intermediate planes.

These accounts, the accounts I mean delivered by high Spirit personalities through trance mediumship or the direct voice, have, moreover, certain advantages to be distinguished from the mystic experience. Some of us have never had such an experience, and those who have may pass through moods when they distrust it. Objective evidence appealing to the prosaic consciousness is surely not to be despised. Similarly my poetic interpretations depend not at all on any spiritual experiences of my own, but are valid only in so far as the patterns exposed are there for all to see. Murry put sole faith in his own mystical experience. That was his final authority, and if great literature, or interpretations of it, or spiritualist communications, countered, or even added to, his central intuition, he tended to oppose them. The tendency aligned itself naturally with his profession as literary critic, for whereas such esoteric matters are regularly the concern of creative writers, they are with equal regularity ignored by the academic scholar and the literary critic. The school of criticism which, as it were, took over from Murry's *Adelphi*, replacing prophecy by its own astringent doctrine, was that of *Scrutiny*; and the writers of *Scrutiny* shirked occult categories. To this extent criticism and works of genius remain always divided. When they are no longer divided, criticism as we know it will have ceased to exist (p. 104 above).

Murry, mainly interested in his religious experience, and finding himself now cut off by his own rejections, and perhaps also by my own interpretations, from his moorings in literature, proceeded to apply his insights on a variety of fronts, writing in favour of communism, pacifism, democracy, British patriotism and finally of the necessity for a war of prevention against Russia. He came near to taking orders. Each book in turn is strongly reasoned. His story is told in F. A. Lea's excellent biography. We may be tempted to smile at these shifting allegiances, but there was a single conviction running through them, and in the process he shed light on each in turn. His community farm had been adumbrated as early as 1924 when he had dreamed of a community 'shaping some small fragment' of the external world 'into harmony with the world within' (*UG*, 222). There is pattern in Murry's story. His life and writings form a unique commentary on the thought-confusions of his generation.

He was a man of brilliant critical intellect who had had, and tried frantically to remain true to, a mystical experience; and the interaction of mysticism and intellect produced many apparent contradictions and seeming insincerities. He had, however, few of the characteristics usually associated with literary genius in the Renaissance era. Of these, I here emphasize two: the first, involvement, as though by instinct, with the Faustian and spiritualistic fields; the second, sexual abnormality, sometimes pushed, perhaps with humour, to obscenity. Murry reacted against both: all his prophetic writing remained well within the conventions of twentieth-century respectability. His 'pity and scorn' for spiritualistic investigators we have already noticed. In the sexual field he was brought up against D. H. Lawrence, whom he denounced for a perverted sexuality. Murry was, as I have shown in my essay 'Lawrence, Joyce and Powys' (pp. 142-8 above), right; and those who have tried to build up Lawrence as in any normal sense a moral counsellor in sexual affairs while criticizing Murry for his attacks in *Son of Woman* (1931) and *Reminiscences of D. H. Lawrence* (1933), falsify the facts. Murry's subsequent soft-pedalling of Lawrence's sexual abnormalities may perhaps be attributed to consideration for his widow. Murry comes out of it well.

In his relations with Lawrence, Murry acted as a man of sound British normality and common-sense; but he was not acting as an interpreter of genius, nor even being true to the loneliness of genius, so excellently handled in his treatment of Jesus (*UG*, 199). His *Adam and Eve* (1944), one of his best later books, is a study of sex-relations from a normal viewpoint.

The problem was raised again by his admirable *Jonathan Swift*, published in 1954. In my review of it for the *Yorkshire Post* on 26 May 1954, high praise was countered by a reservation:

While honestly trying to face the challenge of genius, he has always been reluctant to depart too far from traditional valuations in either religion or the psychology of sex; and that is not so easy.

Murry recognized Swift's genius but was antagonized by his neurotic disgusts. My answer, referring to men of genius, was:

Had these men been sexually normal, would they have composed their greatest works? And should we still be writing books about them? What, then, is the secret of their enduring appeal – of this strange *malaise* which proves more vital than health?

After praising the book highly I concluded my review with the suggestion that 'it will be for others, should they choose, to delve deeper'.

I sent Murry the review. I had, I think, written to him only twice since 1929, and had on each occasion received kind replies. I now received, in his old exquisitely neat handwriting, this answer, dated 31 May 1954, from Thelnetham:

Dear Wilson Knight,

Thank you very much for sending me the *Y.P.* review. I had seen it, and *had* wondered what you meant by yr. last sentence.

I have lately been reading some of your Shakespeare books which had escaped me – nearly 12 years' farming puts one well behind; but now, being practically retired, I have begun to pick up the threads again. I was particularly concerned with yr. *Crown of Life*, because of its argument for the entire authenticity of *Henry VIII*, in which I have never been able to believe.

I am afraid you did not convince me. But you must put that down to the excessive 'normality' of my mind. Though I had not realized that my mind was a very normal one, I think it is probably true. I am abnormally normal, so to speak: at least that seems a fair description of a man whose literary criticism ends up by putting him in charge of a co-operative farm. (I mean this literally: my farming is the direct consequence of my effort in literary criticism.)

Or, to put it differently, my mysticism is a mysticism of descent. Yours isn't. And I get lost in your high speculations as applied to Shakespeare. I was acutely conscious of this divergence as long ago as *Myth and Miracle*, though it came out at a time when I was distracted with domestic anxiety and was unable to set out the reasons of my disagreement with the fullness that initial essay of yours deserved.

However, I am in a very small minority – not perhaps a minority of one as I used to think, but very near it. My normality is therefore (as I said) peculiar.

On the particular question of Swift, you may well be right in thinking that the appalling power of Gulliver IV derives from Swift's 'unhealthy and unreasoned disgust'. But that does not justify you in generalising that supreme literary power is, in general, derivative from sexual abnormality. Indeed, I should say that the specific literary genius is utterly independent of sexual constitution, though that will certainly play an important part in the particular *manifestation* of literary genius. And, again, literary genius at the highest is not exempt from moral judgement; – though the moral judgement to which it is amenable is not the facile judgement of moral convention, but one based on the deepest philosophy (or religion) of which the critic is capable.

Yours sincerely,

J. Middleton Murry

That is a fair statement, though I would lay no personal claim to 'mysticism'; and what there is in my writing is, surely, 'a mysticism of descent', in that I have preferred the multi-coloured qualities of literature to the one soul-centre on which Murry concentrated. I have been more drawn to Shakespeare, Pope and Byron than to Donne and Blake.

More important is it to note Murry's conclusion. At the limit he writes not as an interpreter of genius but as a critic; the final court of appeal in his own judgement. But, it may be said, so is everyone's; and it would then be merely a question as to where to draw the line. Should not I myself be antagonized by a work deliberately counselling sadistic cruelties? My reply would be this: in so far as the imagination has ratified a work of literature, the critical intellect must be silenced. Sadistic horrors, if extreme and approved, would not have been ratified by the imagination, within which certain moral valuations appear to be contained. But the imagination has, in myself and others, already ratified the life-work of Swift. We sense in him a supreme importance: and therefore the approach must be interpretative. However far we may be, in normal life, from approving it all, there yet may be *something which our normal thinking has left out of account.* That is why an imaginative interpretation may be needed.

366

J. Middleton Murry

Murry's life-work may be defined as a continuous attempt to remain true to his one great experience. This experience he tried desperately to align with his love of literature and for a while, and within limits, succeeded magnificently. When a divergence was forced he followed the law of his own greater 'self', or 'soul', going his own wandering way. The choice was honourable.

ADDITIONAL NOTE: My *Yorkshire Post* review of Murry's *Jonathan Swift* is printed in *Poets of Action*.

Mrs. Mary Middleton Murry reminds me that my essay does not take due account of Murry's final treatment of Lawrence in *Love, Freedom and Society* (1957). 'Here' wrote F. A. Lea in his indispensable biography, *The Life of John Middleton Murry* (1959; 349), 'all the defects of *Son of Woman* – the over-emphasis on one side of Lawrence's message, the under-estimate of his later works, the stark oppositions – are made good. *Son of Woman* is not denied, but transcended'. With that judgement I would now agree (see p. 221 above).

In her beautiful memoir, *To Keep Faith* (1959; 183), Mrs. Murry quotes an entry from her husband's diary which shows that he was 'particularly impressed' by Lawrence's 'After All Saints' Day' (in *Last Poems*), on 'the little slender soul' a-voyage beyond death, and aided by love from earth.

After he had been twice widowed, Murry's third marriage was boundlessly happy, and towards the end he wrote of the after-life in the lucid terms of a Spiritualist. I quote again from his diary (*To Keep Faith*, 185):

Maybe the condition of Love, complete, fulfilled, utterly reciprocal, abounding in absolute trust, rich in the sense of simple incessant miracle, is in itself an assurance that Death must be the gate of Life, of some equally simple but unimaginable kind.

The key-word here is 'simple'. Mrs. Murry records (190) what appears to have been a valid, and valuable, telepathic message from him, after death.

CHAPTER XIII

T. S. Eliot

I. T. S. ELIOT AND MODERN POETRY

Appended as a note to *The Christian Renaissance* in 1933. Originally composed for the radio, and delivered through the Canadian Broadcasting Corporation in February 1932.

THE BEST MODERN poetry is often difficult. To say in its defence that this is true of all great work is to shirk the issue, since recent poetry is clearly difficult in a new way. Taking T. S. Eliot's work as representative of the best that is being done today, I shall try to make clear its direction and the kind of thing we should expect.

Poetry is always a mixture of thinking and feeling. It is not purely logical. Yet hitherto poets have, on the whole, tried to give their imaginations some logical form, in plot, in sentence-structure, in punctuation. Even so, the most important things in poetry were never only, or primarily, these, but rather consisted of colour, suggestion, association and verbal magic. This we are today beginning to understand, and so the modern poet sometimes tends to cut out the starting-point of logic and plunges straight into the world of imagination. On the roof-top of vision, he carelessly kicks away the ladder, and so makes it a little difficult for others to join him. And yet something is gained: we are in less danger of mistaking the surface for the essence. Modern poetry often has no surface. In T. S. Eliot's work I shall therefore notice shortly his imaginative shades and colours rather than any explicit philosophy: and this is what we should always first do in interpreting metaphysically a poet's work.

368

T. S. Eliot

His earlier poems are pessimistic. Often we find some form of present-day sordidness put beside bright images of legend or history. Drabness is set against vivid colour. Here is an example from 'A Cooking Egg' (1920), where 'eagles' and 'trumpets' are used to suggest the heroic and romantic:

> The red-eyed scavengers are creeping
>   From Kentish Town and Golder's Green;
>
> Where are the eagles and the trumpets?
>
>   Buried beneath some snow-deep Alps.
> Over buttered scones and crumpets
>   Weeping, weeping multitudes
> Droop in a hundred A.B.C.'s.

The contrast is the more powerful left just like that. So often in Eliot's work it is as though a scarecrow were set to droop its rain-soaked rags beside a Greek statue. And this poetic act is very interesting. The world's history is bright with romantic splendour. Heroes of myth stride colossal and divine across the ancestry of our race, and Christianity is the culmination of a necessary and universal instinct. It would be rash to call such stories false. They keep alive our romantic faith, when romance is, at first sight, hard to discover in the present; yet it must be there too.

> Where are the eagles and the trumpets?

The answer is that they are to be found somewhere very close to the 'buttered scones and crumpets'. To know this is easy, to feel it is often, but not always, impossible.

Eliot's poetry has deep meanings. It is metaphysical rather than narrative and nearer to Dante and Shakespeare than Homer or Chaucer. His longest single work is entitled *The Waste Land* (1922). It is a difficult poem, but again the essence is a starkly cruel association of past romance with present reality. We wonder whether it is we who today are blind or whether the racial memory has false-painted history with a harlot's art. And one with this jostling of the centuries is the poet's frequent use of time-honoured literary quotations left to sprout and flame exotically in their grim contexts. At one moment we have

> I think we are in rats' alley
> Where the dead men lost their bones.

And, soon after, a line from *The Tempest*:

Those are pearls that were his eyes . . .

(II)

The Waste Land is chaotic. But the gaps in its logic may be said to serve a purpose since to fill them in would show a sequence and relation where the poem emphasizes rather the absence of any relation.[1] In *Macbeth* we also have a chaotic and illogical world but there it is easier to approach, because inwoven with a simple story. The sharp juxtaposition of different periods in history is not peculiar to recent poetry: we have it in *A Midsummer Night's Dream* and Goethe's *Faust*. But probably no earlier poet has so emphasized as has Eliot the illogical chaos of things temporal. At the extreme of negation we necessarily find all history unreal:

> What is that sound high in the air
> Murmur of maternal lamentation
> Who are those hooded hordes swarming
> Over endless plains, stumbling in cracked earth
> Ringed by the flat horizon only
> What is the city over the mountains
> Cracks and reforms and bursts in the violet air
> Falling towers
> Jerusalem Athens Alexandria
> Vienna London
> Unreal

(V)

Notice how the celestial Paradise, the City of God, towers over the desert pilgrimage of time, dissolving, reforming, bursting – and the fallen pieces are as the broken pieces of the cities of this world.

This is, therefore, poetry of essential death, and Eliot's sombre work is finely consummated in the 'death' vision of 'The Hollow Men' (1925). Here we have a choking darkness, blindness, strangling impressions of light, sight, stars, which dimly penetrate the murk:

---

[1] My reservation in 'may be said' left the question open. When a little later, about 1934, I remarked to Eliot that students found the poem difficult, he replied that they were looking for what was 'not there'. Presumably he meant that there was no supervening plan.

This is the dead land
This is cactus land
Here the stone images
Are raised, here they receive
The supplication of a dead man's hand
Under the twinkle of a fading star.   (III)

*   *   *

The eyes are not here
There are no eyes here
In this valley of dying stars
In this hollow valley
This broken jaw of our lost kingdoms   (IV)

The poem concludes with a struggle between the cynical and distorting intellect with its dark army of abstractions and the breaking light of a Christian dawn. But cynicism wins.

Yet its victory is not final. Eliot's later poems advance with varying assurance toward visions of light and life. These are mostly sought in terms of Christianity. This new style gives us *Ash-Wednesday* (1930), a sequence of religious monologues reflecting our present religious incertitudes in a subtle poetic technique made up of delicate assonances, alliteration, internal rhyme, a delightful texture of inwoven sound and meaning:

Where shall the word be found, where will the word
Resound? Not here, there is not enough silence
Not on the sea or on the islands, not
On the mainland, in the desert or the rain land,
For those who walk in darkness
Both in the day time and in the night time
The right time and the right place are not here . . .   (V)

This may seem insubstantial beside the reverberations of *The Waste Land*. That is not surprising. The positive themes of life and light are more difficult to crystallize into the solid phraseology of poetry than are the corresponding negatives. It is far easier to write powerfully about Hell than about Heaven. Eliot's latest work marks an advance in vision, and, after the death-valleys of *The Waste Land* and 'The Hollow Men', we find images of life and hope: the 'children at the gate', the 'veiled sister' (V). We have the brilliant immortality line:

While jewelled unicorns draw by the gilded hearse.
          (IV)

And in 'Animula' (1929) we find a study of childhood reminiscent of Wordsworth's great Ode.

Perhaps the finest of Eliot's recent (in 1932) poems is 'Marina' (1930), closely related to Shakespeare's *Pericles*. Two themes are blended: a wearied ship piercing through the fog toward the bird music of some magic island; and the death of death, as the wanderer wakes into some new mode of life and recognition, and love. Here all who indicate death

> Are become unsubstantial, reduced by a wind,
> A breath of pine, and the woodsong fog
> By this grace dissolved in place
>
> What is this face, less clear and clearer
> The pulse in the arm, less strong and stronger—
> Given or lent? more distant than stars and nearer than the eye
>
> Whispers and small laughter between leaves and hurrying feet
> Under sleep, where all the waters meet.

The poem ends on a note of breathless expectancy:

> What seas what shores what granite islands towards my timbers
> And woodthrush calling through the fog
> My daughter.

Again we have children – the 'small laughter' and 'hurrying feet'; and the suggestion of childhood in 'my daughter'. This blending of 'child' symbolism, the ship, the sea, and a magic shore, reminds us variously of *The Tempest* and Wordsworth's 'Ode'. The whole poem is, as it were, breathless with adoration and expectancy, on the brink of an impossible awakening, an undreamed joy.

Eliot's work is typical of our generation. Typical of its despair, and of its sense of futility. But typical too of the stirring which today heralds a revival to dispel our consciousness of death. That Eliot's more positive poetic statements should be presented in terms of Christian Orthodoxy is extremely significant. It is equally significant that his most recent, and perhaps his most exquisite, happier poem should be directly related to one of Shakespeare's supreme acts of paradisal vision.

It is seldom wise to descend from objective and interpretative analysis to the personal prejudices that make class-lists of poets, arranging them in order of merit, grouping them as 'classic' and 'romantic', and so on. But this much may be said, perhaps, even of a contemporary. Eliot's work has all the characteristics of enduring literature. His most powerful imaginative effects are not esoteric and personal, but rather repeat the traditional symbolisms of the Bible, Dante, Shakespeare, Goethe, Shelley, Tennyson. We must attend always in studying poetry to these, the symbols, the impressions of 'life' and 'death', the riches of imaginative statement; not to superficial differences of techniques between poet and poet. Then all poetry will become more easy, and far more important. Moreover, if we regard Eliot's work as a whole, we find a small but intense poetic world of the same quality as Shakespeare's and Dante's. It has its visions of darkness, its progress towards paradisal radiance. Starting from the Old Testament of cynicism and death, it is moving now towards the New Testament of victorious life.

ADDITIONAL NOTE, 1933: Since writing this I have been shown an essay by Prince D. S. Mirsky, which draws attention to Eliot's use of water and fire in *The Waste Land*; which recalls my interpretation of Goethe's *Faust*. Eliot's poem is full of these and other such naturalistic and fertility symbolisms. On such, all good poetry must to a large extent depend; and probably *The Waste Land* – its title is significant – is far closer to such a work as *Faust* than is usually supposed. All poetry celebrates a divine creation by marriage of humanity and nature.

ADDITIONAL NOTE, 1968: It was Eliot himself who showed me Prince Mirsky's essay. In *The Christian Renaissance* I grouped together sections on Dante, Shakespeare and Goethe. In 'T. S. Eliot as a Critic' (*T. S. Eliot: the Man and his Work*, p. 382 below), Mario Praz, after observing that Eliot grouped these three together in his 1955 Hamburg lecture 'Goethe the Sage', notes that Wellek relates his change of opinion in regard to Goethe's poetic status to Ernst Lehrs' *Man or Matter*. Perhaps *The Christian Renaissance*, about which Eliot wrote to me when I submitted it to Faber & Faber in 1932, may also have had some influence.

T. S. Eliot

An expansion of a commentary, mainly on Four Quartets, written about 1953.

T. S. Eliot's 'La Figlia che Piange' (1917) dramatizes a moment of poised intensity involving, it would seem, some pivotal choice, some bifurcation of the ways, some rejection, it may be, of love; leading to a half-life of self-masking, of 'gesture' and 'pose'.

The poem opens:

> Stand on the highest pavement of the stair –
> Lean on a garden urn –
> Weave, weave the sunlight in your hair –
> Clasp your flowers to you with a pained surprise –
> Fling them to the ground and turn
> With a fugitive resentment in your eyes:
> But weave, weave the sunlight in your hair.

Action is so clasped within the two 'weave, weave' lines that it becomes static; we have an eternal, evenly poised, moment, in full sculptural embodiment and dramatic force, of what seems neither action nor inaction, neither motion nor stillness. Temporality is for an instant split open and we are left, as *The Waste Land* has it, 'looking into the heart of light, the silence'. I am thinking of the passage:

> 'You gave me hyacinths first a year ago;
> They called me the hyacinth girl.'
> – Yet when we came back, late, from the Hyacinth garden,
> Your arms full, and your hair wet, I could not
> Speak, and my eyes failed, I was neither
> Living nor dead, and I knew nothing,
> Looking into the heart of light, the silence.

(The Waste Land, I)

The two passages appear to be related.

The memory twists and gleams as a silver thread through Eliot's poetry. In 'Gerontion' (1920) knowledge of some sexual negation (pp. 179, 391-2) prevents a simple response and forces introspection:

374

T. S. Eliot

I that was near your heart was removed therefrom
To lose beauty in terror, terror in inquisition.
I have lost my passion: why should I need to keep it
Since what is kept must be adulterated?
I have lost my sight, smell, hearing, taste and touch:
How should I use them for your closer contact?

In *The Waste Land* (V) 'the awful daring of a moment's surrender'
may be one's only claim to true existence, and we pass to the
hypothetical assurance of

> The boat responded
> Gaily, to the hand expert with sail and oar
> The sea was calm, your heart would have responded
> Gaily, when invited, beating obedient
> To controlling hands.

In 'The Hollow Men' the poet fears to see in dreams those who
have passed with 'direct eyes' to the Kingdom of death. In 'death's
dream kingdom' he would still wear his 'deliberate disguises'
and avoid a final meeting (like that, perhaps, of Aeneas with Dido
in the *Aeneid*). Meanwhile, religion is an alternative, a second-
best: 'Lips that would kiss', we are told, 'form prayers' to 'broken
stone'; that is, to an outworn faith. Nevertheless, that faith exerts
its own force, between 'idea' and 'reality', 'motion' and 'act',
'desire' and 'spasm'. At this point in man's evolution a perfected
integration is inhibited; but 'life is very long'. The concluding
'whimper' need not here concern us.

We feel the lost vision within the regrets of *Ash-Wednesday*:

> Because I do not hope to know again
> The infirm glory of the positive hour
> Because I do not think
> Because I know I shall not know
> The one veritable transitory power . . .

(I)

It may be indirectly present within the 'maytime' garden-figure
'in blue and green':

> Blown hair is sweet, brown hair over the mouth blown,
> Lilac and brown hair.

(III)

It is behind the poem's wavering choices and hesitant advance, 'wavering between the profit and the loss'. The pilgrim watches 'the white sails still fly seaward, seaward flying' with 'unbroken wings', and pines for the 'lost lilac':

> And the weak spirit quickens to rebel
> For the bent golden-rod and the lost sea smell . . .
>
> (VI)

The 'positive hour' may have gone, and yet there is new hope, hope in garden imagery and the poem's sacred ladies, in 'blue of larkspur, blue of Mary's colour' (IV), and still more perhaps in

> Redeem
> The unread vision in the higher dream
> While jewelled unicorns draw by the gilded hearse.
>
> (IV)

Here an esoteric symbolism covers, for a moment, both sides of the opposition, human and devotional; in strict relevance more-over to immortality.

These ambivalences are deployed throughout the more settled meditations of the *Four Quartets* (1935-42). 'Burnt Norton' harks back to the parting of the ways:

> Down the passage which we did not take
> Towards the door we never opened
> Into the rose-garden.

If choice was wrong, it may matter less than one thought, since

> What might have been and what has been
> Point to one end, which is always present.
>
> (I)

There seems still hope of recapturing what was missed; the bird-spirits invite and the leaves are 'full of children' laughing. There is even the 'heart of light' again (I). It is as though one were to find intact what one had rejected. The fault was forgivable, for 'human kind cannot bear very much reality' (I).

Since further 'speculation' on 'what might have been' is rightly regarded as a profitless 'abstraction' (I), the poet's thinking proceeds to the metaphysics of time and timelessness, of spatial patterns, of sound and silence. These are at least provisionally definable. But perhaps silence says more than any words: in *The Waste Land* 'the heart of light' was grouped with 'silence'. We may remember the importance of silence in Keats's *Ode on a Grecian Urn*. In 'Burnt Norton' silence is contrasted with words, with poetry:

> Words move, music moves
> Only in time; but that which is only living
> Can only die. Words, after speech, reach
> Into the silence. Only by the form, the pattern,
> Can words or music reach
> The stillness, as a Chinese jar still
> Moves perpetually in its stillness.
> Not the stillness of the violin, while the note lasts,
> Not that only, but the co-existence,
> Or say that the end precedes the beginning,
> And the end and the beginning were always there
> Before the beginning and after the end.
> And all is always now. Words strain,
> Crack and sometimes break, under the burden,
> Under the tension, slip, slide, perish,
> Decay with imprecision, will not stay in place,
> Will not stay still.
>
> (V)

Beside this we may place the 'music heard so deeply that it is not heard at all' of 'The Dry Salvages' (V). The end of the temporal arts, music and language, is stated to be a 'silence' analogous to the silence of the Chinese jar, which nevertheless has its own mysterious motion. The poet is trying to hint that which all art aims to express, but which remains inexpressible by art. The statement of art is, to use the convenient and not unprofitable word, 'eternity'; no more, nor less. But since the word explains nothing, the aim of art is to define, provisionally, the dimension beyond our grasp, in which 'all is always now' ('Burnt Norton', V). The most complete, because so non-committal, language often appears to be music; either that, or the 'silence'. Nietzsche, writing of Greek lyrics, has an apposite phrase to balance Eliot's lines on the impotence of words: 'Language is strained to its utmost to imitate music' (*The Birth of Tragedy*, VI).

Our passage from 'Burnt Norton' is followed by a movement

which recalls the all-inclusive, eternity-possessing, virginity of
Keats's lover:

> The detail of the pattern is movement,
> As in the figure of the ten stairs.
> Desire itself is movement
> Not in itself desirable;
> Love is itself unmoving,
> Only the cause and end of movement,
> Timeless, and undesiring
> Except in the aspect of time
> Caught in the form of limitation
> Between un-being and being.
> Sudden in a shaft of sunlight
> Even while the dust moves
> There rises the hidden laughter
> Of children in the foliage
> Quick now, here, now, always –
> Ridiculous the waste sad time
> Stretching before and after.
>
> ('Burnt Norton', V)

The 'dust', mentioned earlier, moves; the old memory *becomes
alive*.

'Children': how often, in poet after poet, seer after seer, are
children associated with supreme insight, or experience.

We have here an interesting contrast with Keats, whose lover
was clearly presented in 'desire', 'in the aspect of time', and so
'caught in the form of limitation'; but, in that his pose was
rendered enduring, the temporal desire itself was felt *sub specie
aeternitatis* and the very state 'between un-being and being'
became a symbol of love 'unmoving' and the eternal 'now'.

There is a distinction to be made between Eliot's poetic philosophy and the doctrine of the eternal energies offered by Browning
and Nietzsche; but the distinction is more tenuous than it might
seem. Though in this last passage the 'love' is said to be 'unmoving', the central stillness is distinguished from 'fixity':

> At the still point of the turning world. Neither flesh nor
>   fleshless;
> Neither from nor towards; at the still point, there the dance is,
> But neither arrest nor movement. And do not call it fixity,

Where past and future are gathered. Neither movement from nor
  towards,
Neither ascent nor decline. Except for the point, the still point,
There would be no dance, and there is only the dance.

('Burnt Norton', II)

A neat use of circular motion in the manner of Dante's *Paradiso*
points us to a coalescence of stillness and motion similar to that
from which Keats derived his insight into the identity of beauty
and truth. 'Neither flesh nor fleshless' looks back to the earlier
poem 'Marina', and recalls Yeats's mysterious figure, at once
'man', 'shade' and 'image' in 'Byzantium'; while pointing also to
the 'etheric' body of Spiritualist doctrine. The negation of all
categories of distance may be compared with the paradox 'more
distant than stars and nearer than the eye' in 'Marina'; and with
Browning's 'there was no more near nor far' in 'Abt Vogler'. The
ultimate reality is not static. Instead, we are told that there is 'only
the dance', just as in Nietzsche's scheme there is the drama, the
eternal interaction of Dionysian and Apollonian. Eliot's metaphysic feels the perfected existence, as does Yeats also, in
'Byzantium' and elsewhere, as dance. We find it again in 'So the
darkness shall be the light, and the stillness the dancing' ('East
Coker', III), and 'Where you must move in measure, like a dancer'
('Little Gidding', II). In Nietzsche's *Birth of Tragedy* we have a
main emphasis on drama, the highest genius aspiring to the condition where he is 'at once subject and object, at once poet, actor,
and spectator' (V); and so, 'It is only as an aesthetic phenomenon
that existence and the world appear justified' (XXIV). In both
dance and drama there lies the will to interpret the deepest
mysteries of existence in the paradox-resolving terms of art.
When acting one is not exactly living, nor not living, the part, but
on the knife-edge between impulse and control; a state which is
neither yet both; both within and outside.

  Though the smooth symbolisms of the *Four Quartets* are rather
Dantesque or romantic than 'metaphysical', there is no surface
lustre, no eternalizing, in the language, nor any consistent reliance
on metrical discipline. For long passages the poems follow the
metaphysical tradition of deliberate philosophic probing in a
colloquial idiom. Such passages are primarily concerned with
time and its corollary, eternity.

There are three approaches. We have (i) ordinary time, as usually understood; (ii) timeless moments, which are nevertheless experienced in time; and (iii) a new time made of, or rather glimpsed through, those timeless moments. For (i), we have the world moving 'in appetency, on its metalled ways of time past and time future' ('Burnt Norton', III). Such time is associated with the weakness of our present existence. It protects men from 'heaven and damnation', 'time past and time future' allowing 'but a little' of that 'consciousness' which can be fitfully experienced at (ii) certain moments of timeless intuition, that are nevertheless only to be remembered 'in time' ('Burnt Norton', II). Such is 'the intense moment isolated, with no before and after' of 'East Coker' (V) or the 'sudden illumination' of 'The Dry Salvages' (II). These moments will be the more exactly understood from reading Browning's record of moments of high insight in 'Bishop Blougram's Apology'. But we also hear of (iii) 'the tolling bell' from the waters measuring 'time not our time', a time 'older than the time of chronometers', 'unhurried', in another dimension, ringing its 'perpetual angelus' ('The Dry Salvages' I; IV). This recalls Keats's Urn as the 'foster-child of silence and slow time', where 'slow time' incloses atmospherically the Urn's figures. The two are, presumably, akin, and belong to the same world as the sudden illuminations, since both the timeless intuition and endless time may serve as approximations to eternity. Our difficulties are elucidated by a passage in 'Little Gidding':

> A people without history
> Is not redeemed from time, for history is a pattern
> Of timeless moments. So, while the light fails
> On a winter's afternoon, in a secluded chapel
> History is now and England.
>
> (V)

History depends on the significant, and so timeless, moment, or event; and since significance involves freedom, we have Byron saying that, if liberty of speech goes, 'there is an end of history' (to J. Hunt, 8 January 1823; *LJ*, VI. 160). Such significance is somehow ever-present, and so the greater time is 'now', what we may call an eternal, persisting, 'I am'. The lesser, unreal, time is 'time past and time future'; and the bridge between them is the timeless moment.

T. S. Eliot

To possess and live real time – Bergson's *durée* – is beyond most of us:

> Men's curiosity searches past and future
> And clings to that dimension. But to apprehend
> The point of intersection of the timeless
> With time, is an occupation for the saint . . .
>
> ('The Dry Salvages', V)

Such an occupation would be 'a lifetime burning in every moment' ('East Coker', V). Most of us have to remain content with the sudden illumination of occasional, unrelated, intuitions, the 'moment in and out of time'; or, with a thought recalling 'Abt Vogler':

> music heard so deeply
> That it is not heard at all, but you are the music
> While the music lasts.
>
> ('The Dry Salvages', V)

The music does not last. We lag behind, get out of step; but could we live the music, we should know ourselves part of a living Now, the 'all is always now' and the 'quick, now, here, now, always', of 'Burnt Norton' (V); a kind of *dramatic*, vertical, time, which has nevertheless extension, and is in some sense moving horizontally too. As with Malcolm's mother in *Macbeth* who 'died every day she lived' (*Macbeth*, IV. iii. 111), every moment, we are told, is a 'death', a moment whose quality is all-important, and within this eternal, persisting Now, we are to 'fare forward'. Such is the way to a conquest of 'past and future', meaning both true 'freedom' and 'right action' as contrasted with mere movement driven on by 'daemonic' or 'chthonic' powers ('The Dry Salvages', III, V).[1] Conceptually, this is the heart of the matter; but the explanation is not conceptually clear. Too much depends on the space-metaphor 'forward'. We are being – as one always is – forced into spatial symbol.

It is not my aim to offer a general interpretation of Eliot's poetic metaphysics, but merely to abstract, for my own purposes, certain important intuitions regarding time and eternity. From 'Prufrock' on, Eliot's work concentrates on that knife-edge between action

---

[1] Compare Bergson's: 'The more we succeed in making ourselves conscious of our progress in pure duration, the more we feel the different parts of our being enter into each other, and our whole personality concentrate itself in a point, or rather a sharp edge, pressed against the future and cutting into it unceasingly' (*Creative Evolution*, trans. A. Mitchell, 1928; III. 212).

and inaction which on the conceptual plane becomes variously the jagged paradoxes of 'Gerontion' and the feather-light balances of *Ash-Wednesday*; it is all so delicately *poised*, with an attendant and anxious dissatisfaction at the impotence of words, starting with 'It is impossible to say just what I mean' in 'Prufrock' and culminating in the more amplified dissatisfactions of 'Burnt Norton' (V) and 'East Coker' (II and V) and the beautifully defined will to verbal mastery in 'Little Gidding' (V). The *Four Quartets*, often nearer 'interpretation' than 'poetry', serve to distil volumes of poetic and philosophic argument, concentrating throughout on the fusion of opposites, including 'the moment which is not of action or inaction' ('The Dry Salvages', III). Complete success can only come through symbols of space-time, or eternity.

To return to our 'silver thread', our love-thread. 'Burnt Norton' remembers 'the moment in the rose-garden' (II), but in 'Little Gidding' (III) we touch the 'expanding of love beyond desire'. The experience is glimpsed by Celia in *The Cocktail Party* (1950):

> For what happened is remembered like a dream
> In which one is exalted by intensity of loving
> In the spirit, a vibration of delight
> Without desire, for desire is fulfilled
> In the delight of loving.   (II)

The opposites of 'motion' and 'act' in 'The Hollow Men' have joined. Celia knows that the 'vision' was real, but learns that she has been seeking for it 'in the wrong place'. It is to be regarded less as a human than as a religious or mystical experience, one of those timeless intuitions of the *Four Quartets*: 'We had the experience but missed the meaning' ('The Dry Salvages', II). 'Burnt Norton' is, however, rich with the presence of garden, flowers, birds and children; and 'Little Gidding' concludes with an identification of fire and rose; that is, of spiritual advance and romantic joy.

3. LITERARY IMPRESSIONS

T. S. Eliot: the Man and his Work, ed. Allen Tate, 1967; a collection first published in *The Sewanee Review*, LXXIV. 1; Winter 1966.

During the years following the First World War London's more advanced literary thinking was dominated by John Middleton

Murry and T. S. Eliot, editors of the *Adelphi* and the *Criterion*. Murry's approach was personal and emotional, Eliot's more objective and intellectual: they engaged once in a controversy regarding the respective rights of 'intuition' and 'intelligence'. Murry appeared to me the apostle of a new age; my own first articles were published in the *Adelphi*; and yet as my work developed, his approval was withdrawn. This was a disappointment since I had supposed our approaches to be similar.

Meanwhile Eliot's *The Sacred Wood* (1920) and *For Lancelot Andrewes* (1928) had contained essays very different from Murry's. Cool and urbane in manner, they appeared to be objectifying, even distancing, the literatures discussed. I found his adverse judgements disturbing. I saw Eliot as primarily a 'critic', and Murry as an 'interpreter', of literary genius. The prophetic element in literature, all-important to Murry, seemed to be scanted by Eliot. This was my impression, and there was little doubt in my mind to which camp I belonged.[1]

I had however an article on *Hamlet* submitted to *The Criterion* (which appeared in *The Wheel of Fire* before it could be published in the magazine), and when I called at Eliot's office he told me that he found its emphasis on death more illuminating than previous commentaries. I found him a man of a strangely urbane and yet disarming authority, very different from the withdrawn intensity of Murry. He invited me to dinner, to meet his wife, but owing to her ill-health the invitation was replaced by a lunch at his club. He was very kind.

Now, when my own investigations were beginning, as in my essay 'The Poet and Immortality' in *The Shakespeare Review* of October 1928, to assert the mystical properties of Shakespeare's last plays, I found Murry, who had himself had a powerful

---

[1] [1968] I say 'my impression'. In his early essay 'The Perfect Critic' Eliot's position was theoretically close to mine. He tells us that 'in matters of great importance the critic must not coerce, and he must not make judgements of worse and better. He must simply elucidate: the reader will form the correct judgement for himself'. We are warned against the 'tendency to legislate'; 'the free intelligence is that which is wholly devoted to enquiry'; and the true critic's aim is 'the return to the work of art with improved perception and intensified, because more conscious, enjoyment'. I doubt if Eliot's practice maintained this position. Nor can I see how 'judgement' can well be opposed to 'critic': 'criticism' *means* 'judgement'. In introducing *The Wheel of Fire*, Eliot admitted a previous prejudice against 'interpretation'. But perhaps his deepest instincts lay in that direction. The entangling of thought with symbols in the *Four Quartets* is emphatically interpretative.

mystical experience which he was anxious to relate to poetry, unable to accept my formulations, while Eliot, whose critical writings had been, or at least to me appeared, in opposition to mystical interpretations, was strangely sympathetic. He received my 1929 brochure *Myth and Miracle: on the Mystic Symbolism of Shakespeare* with a degree of approval, and offered to recommend, and even himself personally take, my other Shakespearian essays, which had been appearing in various religious periodicals, to the Oxford University Press, where they were published as *The Wheel of Fire*. On looking back I have two main impressions. One is of the extraordinary power Eliot had even then; for though I had earlier received a dubious reply from the Press regarding the prospect of their doing such a book, a word from Eliot and all went smoothly. Second, I am struck by his generosity in so putting himself out to forward a line of research diverging from his own critical tenets. When I told him that I had written a preliminary essay distinguishing between 'criticism' and 'interpretation', he replied, as though newly impressed by the thought: 'Ah. A necessary distinction'. On the publishers' suggestion he agreed to write an introduction. It was not written from the standpoint of the essays themselves; it engaged in complications which I, rightly or wrongly, do not feel to be necessary; but the status which it gave, and still gives, my life's work has been invaluable.

That Eliot's response to *Myth and Miracle* had been more than courtesy was witnessed during this same year, 1930, when he sent me his 'Marina', inscribed 'for' me as 'with, I hope, some appropriateness'. He had mentioned my 'papers' on Shakespeare's last plays in his introduction to *The Wheel of Fire*, referring perhaps mainly to the typescript of my 1928 (unpublished) book on them, *Thaisa*, which, since it had been submitted to Faber & Faber, he is likely to have read. This script Murry never saw. I had however solicited the interest of John Masefield, visiting him on Boar's Hill at Oxford, but though he generously devoted time to it and wrote an opinion for me, he remained dubious of so philosophical an interpretation.[1] How strange it all was. I have always regarded

[1] The inscribed copy of 'Marina', the typescript of *Thaisa*, and John Masefield's letter are together lodged among my other papers in the Reference Library at Birmingham. The poem's 'one June' and 'another September' presumably refer respectively to *Myth and Miracle* and 'Marina': the dates fit (see Appendix). *Myth and Miracle* is included in my volume, *The Crown of Life*.

Masefield's 1924 Romanes Lecture *Shakespeare and Spiritual Life* as a main influence behind my interpretations; and his own prose and poetry are saturated in spiritualistic apprehension. But neither Masefield nor Murry, who reviewed *Myth and Miracle* adversely in *The Times Literary Supplement*, was now responsive; and it was Eliot who, despite his own critical caution stopping short, as he once (at the conclusion to 'Tradition and the Individual Talent') put it, 'at the frontier of metaphysics or mysticism', as a poet had seen so exactly what I was doing that he had composed, in 'Marina', a perfect poetical commentary on those Shakespearian meanings which I had unveiled. His full critical acceptance was witnessed further by his reference to them in his 1932 essay on John Ford, and again in his 1961 lecture 'To Criticize the Critic'; and also, on imagery, in 'The Music of Poetry' (1942).[1]

Soon after the publication of 'Marina' Eliot asked to see my commentary on *Coriolanus*, then in preparation, because, he said, he was engaged on a poem inspired by Beethoven's *Coriolan*. I must have first sent him some notes because on 30 December 1930, he wrote, after receiving my finished essay:

You had already, so far as I am concerned, put the gist of it into the notes you sent me. That does not mean at all that you have not done quite right to expand it. What the complete essay adds for me is chiefly the detailed and convincing analysis of the type of imagery. That does increase my understanding and appreciation.

The allusion probably refers to my treatment of 'stone', 'metal', and 'city' imagery in Shakespeare's play, since 'stone', 'steel', and 'paving' occur in 'Triumphal March' (1931). Beyond that, my reading of *Coriolanus* as a dramatized balance of warrior values and love, rising to a powerful climax at love's victory, is reflected in, and perhaps lends point to, the repeated Shakespearian reminiscence of 'Mother' and 'O mother' in the second 'Coriolan' poem, 'Difficulties of a Statesman' (1931).

Shakespeare had dramatized a conflict of clearly separated values. Eliot was aiming at more than that, at a fusion of heroism and love, and six marvellous lines in 'Triumphal March' glimpse the achievement within a figure of heroic repose, in close accord

---

[1] The relation is discussed by Philip L. Marcus in *Criticism* (U.S.A.), IX. I; Winter 1967. See also Appendix, below; for Colin Still, Preface, above.

with the description of Nietzsche's 'super-hero' in *Thus Spake Zarathustra* (II. 13):

> There is no interrogation in those eyes
> Or in the hands, quiet over the horse's neck,
> And the eyes watchful, waiting, perceiving, indifferent.
> O hidden under the dove's wing, hidden in the turtle's breast,
> Under the palmtree at noon, under the running water
> At the still point of the turning world. O hidden.

It is a vision of poetry incarnate, according to Keats's definition of poetry as 'might half slumb'ring on its own right arm', in 'Sleep and Poetry'.

The vision could only be glimpsed in static and imagistic terms. The super-hero envisaged may be beyond need of 'interrogation', but the secret of how war can be assimilated to the softer values remains 'hidden' within the resolving spirit, 'under the dove's wing'. In the second poem, 'Difficulties of a Statesman', the elements draw apart, divergent as they are in Shakespeare's play. The difficulty of blending the Renaissance and the Christian ways, or war with love, is shown in these two poems as the harder for the multiplying logistics and committees attending state affairs as we today know them. Eliot is here at the very heart of our Renaissance conflict. That he should have attempted in two such brief pieces the task to which Byron's whole life was devoted and which forced Ibsen into the twin dramas of *Emperor and Galilean* was characteristic of his genius; and that he should have left the intended 'Coriolan' sequence uncompleted is also characteristic. Nor did he engage this task again. *Murder in the Cathedral* (1935) shows little concern for any such balance of church and state as Tennyson gave us in *Becket*.

In 'Marina' and 'Triumphal March' Eliot was searching within a humanistic, or Renaissance, field for a positive direction to follow *The Waste Land* and 'The Hollow Men'. Christian orthodoxy had already been formally accepted, but as 'Journey of the Magi' (1927) and *Ash-Wednesday* had shown, it was no easy acceptance. *Ash-Wednesday* opens by renouncing 'the infirm glory of the positive hour' called, by a brilliant paradox apt to Shakespeare's Sonnets and *Troilus and Cressida* (both of which, one directly and one implicitly, are recalled on the first page, lines 4 and 18), 'the one veritable transitory power'; orthodoxy is being regarded, with a striking poetic honesty, as a *second-best* to the 'blessed face' of some more immediately authoritative experience. If the first-best is recorded in the early 'La Figlia che Piange', we can relate the 'pose' of that poem to much of the later Eliot. He was renouncing a human wholeness through recognition of human inadequacy. This wholeness was momentarily recaptured in the lines on the 'hyacinth girl' in *The Waste Land*. It is present, in mystical terms and with the help of Shakespeare's poetry under a modern interpretation, in 'Marina', Eliot's one uncompromisingly direct, happy, and assured statement (for the shock conclusion on 'granite' and 'timbers' is nearer elation than fear); and in the six marvellous lines of 'Triumphal March'. But the alignment (the 'hope' and 'new ships' of 'Marina') was not to be prolonged, and the Renaissance positive, though 'veritable', proved 'transitory'. The 'Coriolan' sequence got only as far as its second part and was then dropped: heroism and love, state and church, remained apart. The world of *action* had proved intransigent.

Eliot's most whole-hearted devotion at this period was given to Dante, who both in his political thinking and in the *Paradiso*, so rich in the romantic essence, asserted the alignment at which he himself was aiming. When in 1930 or 1931 I was at King's College, London, giving a lecture to the Shakespeare Association on Shakespeare's tempest-symbolism (later published in *The Symposium*, New York, and afterwards expanded into *The Shakespearian Tempest*), I suggested to Eliot, who was there and had, if I recall aright, arranged the lecture, that he should crown his poetry with a new *Paradiso*. His reply was characteristically diffident; but this was, as the colourings of *Ash-Wednesday* suggest, his instinctive aim.

Such an aim was also reflected in the year 1933 in my book *The Christian Renaissance*, which was written from the romantic imagination in an attempt to harmonize Christian mythology and dogma with Renaissance poetry; and I added as an appendix (p. 368 above) a brief commentary on Eliot, drawing particular attention to 'Marina', his poetry at this brief Renaissance period being obviously relevant to my purpose. When I next saw him he showed pleasure at my essay, wherein I had compared his poetry to Dante's and Shakespeare's. For many reasons I scarcely expected him to like the main book, though in an official, publisher's, letter he said that he regarded it as important, and expressed no adverse

opinion. It was not a devotional work. In it I had no more committed myself to orthodoxy in a devotional sense than Eliot had
been committed to Renaissance vision in 'Marina' and 'Triumphal
March'. Neither would at any time have denied the authenticity
of the statements made, but an imaginative adventure is not a
personal commitment. It touches apprehensions beyond one's
personal limitations and decisions.

My subsequent writings did not expect a continuance of Eliot's
personal support. Nevertheless, our family was not destined to
break the contact, for, while my own association with him was
now less close – though he liked my *Chariot of Wrath* in 1942 – that
of my brother, W. F. Jackson Knight, became strong, and
probably stronger than mine had ever been, since the affinities
went deep. He had (in 1938) contributed a review to *The Criterion*
and had also written three books on Vergil, when in 1942 I
suggested that he should show his recently completed *Roman
Vergil* to Eliot with a view to publication by Faber & Faber. It
was accepted, was published early in 1944, and won a considerable
success.

My brother's literary temperament had much in common with
Eliot's. The religious sympathies of both were Anglo-Catholic;
both were cautious and self-critical, with a strong moral sense not
only in life, which is natural, but in literary disquisition too, which
is another matter. Both honoured the classics and set a primary
value on the past, on tradition. 'Tradition' was a key-concept for
Eliot, and my brother's view of great poetry, and in particular
Vergil's poetry, saw its greatness as the re-working, re-harmoni-
zing, and culmination of vast stores from the mythology, folklore,
and literature of the past. This was also Eliot's method. Both, too,
were instinctively drawn to the Continent. Eliot's *Criterion* and
much of his thought were continental in reach, and my brother's
scholarly contacts and correspondence ranged widely among the
French, German, Italian, Spanish, and Portuguese, as well as in
England and North and South America. The Cumaean Sibyl of
Aeneid VI, germane to my brother's *Cumaean Gates*, had appeared
in the epigraph to *The Waste Land*.[1]

---

[1] An interrelation between *Cumaean Gates* and Eliot's *The Waste Land* was noted
by Grover Smith of Yale in 'T. S. Eliot's Lady of the Rocks', *Notes and Queries*,
19 March 1949, notes 6 and 8.

Cumaean Gates and the earlier *Vergil's Troy* are now included in one volume
entitled *Vergil: Epic and Anthropology*, ed. John D. Christie, 1967.

The cultural complex thus shared might be called 'Vergilian'. The word covers much of what we mean by such terms as 'classical', 'the European tradition', 'Western culture', and even Christianity too, since Vergil has for centuries been accepted by orthodox Christians as one of themselves, *'anima naturaliter Christiana'*. When at the foundation, on the initiative of Father Bruno Scott James, of the London Virgil Society at a dinner on 12 January 1943, my brother was offered the presidency, he accepted with the proviso that T. S. Eliot should be invited first. Eliot became president and he himself secretary, and they were in mutual correspondence on matters of policy. In 1945 he showed Eliot a book-script on Homer, composed before *Roman Vergil*, which Eliot greatly liked, but wanted amplified; and though the reading for the amplification went on year after year, Eliot's interest in the projected volume remained firm. On 12 August 1949 he answered a letter of mine, written in view of my brother's acute anxiety about the delay, assuring us of his understanding; on 23 November 1953 he sent my brother his 'blessings and good wishes for a masterpiece'; and on 28 February 1963 his secretary wrote to him: 'Mr. Eliot said that he has never quite given up hope for his book on Homer'.[1]

My brother's mental powers were nearer Eliot's than mine could ever have been. His natural insight and sympathy are evident in the essay 'T. S. Eliot as a Classical Scholar', which he contributed to Neville Braybrooke's *Symposium* for Eliot's seventieth birthday in 1958. His brilliant, darting, and comprehensive mind was at home with the complexities of modern poetry; he enjoyed all kinds of complexity; his conversation tended to be indirect and allusive, making the hearer's mind leap; and, above all, he liked complexities drawn from stores of racial history, as in Vergil, Eliot, or David Jones's *The Anathemata*, which he reviewed in the *Listener*. His own researches, in *Cumaean Gates* and elsewhere, had been largely concerned with anthropology and ritual; and with other origins within the subconscious, the link being Jung's concept of racial memory; and with the way centuries of twilight experience were caught up into the sophisticated poetry of a Homer or a Vergil, to be stamped with authority for subsequent ages.

[1] My brother died in 1964. His Homer papers were published in 1968 as *Many-Minded Homer*, ed. John D. Christie.

While he was searching back into origins and bringing the story up to Vergil, I myself was on a different task: starting with the Renaissance, my field has been a later poetry, and this I have treated with scant regard to origins, but rather, inspecting its form and present contents, searched it for a future and prophetic pointing. The two lines of research were complementary. We were both exploring the mysterious reality behind and within poetry, he in terms of the past, I of the future, but both equally sensing its present otherness, its eternity, of which past and future are aspects. 'What is Poetry?' Byron once asked himself, and answered, 'The feeling of a Former world and Future' (*Diary*, 28 January 1821; *LJ*, V. 189); where, as so often in Byron's prose, an offhand simplicity conjures up vistas.

Eliot was as a writer more at ease with legend in *The Waste Land* and the ancestral places of the *Four Quartets*, and also with the psychological diagnoses of human causes in *The Family Reunion* and *The Cocktail Party*, than in attempts at teaching and prophecy, the best of which are to be found in the choruses of *The Rock* and certain passages in the *Four Quarters*, and the weakest in parts of his prose and the semi-prose of his last three dramas. Of symbolic statement he was a master; in his more direct thinking he was more moralist than prophet, drawing on, rather than reacting from, established authority. Therein lay from the start his divergence from Murry, on whom the prophetic mantle sat easily.

In the appendix to *The Christian Renaissance* I wrote that Eliot's was 'a small but intense poetic world of the same quality as Shakespeare's and Dante's'; and I was honoured when I next saw him by his evident pleasure at this brief essay by so unrenowned an expositor. I believe that, again like my brother, Eliot was in some deep way wanting in self-trust. When in 1948 or thereabouts he told me that he had deleted long passages from *The Waste Land* in deference to Ezra Pound's blue-pencilling, in particular an extended piece of sea-poetry near or in the section 'Death by Water',[1] I was shocked. It was now clear why *The Waste Land* was so *fragmentary*.[2] That it is inartistically so may be seen from the

---

[1] In *The Waste Land* 'Death by Water' signifies an ultimate, static, sensual disaster to be contrasted with fertilizing rain and mastery of water in moving craft; and with fire, signifying purgation and spiritual advance. See p. 395 below.

[2] Since I wrote this the original MS. has come to light. Our understanding of the poem is likely to be affected.

relegation to a note of an organically needed statement regarding the function of the bisexual Tiresias as 'the most important personage in the poem, uniting all the rest'. 'What Tiresias *sees*', we are told, 'is the substance of the poem'. Without retracting my comparison of Eliot's poetry, at its best, with Dante and Shakespeare in point of 'quality', I should now say that his seems scarcely a *single* 'poetic world', being too fragmentary. 'These fragments I have shored against my ruins' (*The Waste Land*, V) applies widely to his work: *Sweeney Agonistes* (1932) was published as 'Fragments of an Aristophanic Melodrama', though I have heard that more exists and was used at a memorial performance in London; the 'Coriolan' sequence was never finished; certain of his essays were deliberately – he seems to have *enjoyed* the emphasis – designated as part of an uncompleted book. Eliot's poetic world is not unified: Christian pieces are juxtaposed to those which are humanistic, and a relation is not – at least until 'Little Gidding' in 1942, and then only in meditative terms – established; his occasional use of successive noun-groups starting with 'the' is a symptom, on the level of syntax, of unrelatedness, of addition in place of multiplication. Pieces appear, big or little, in their own right, static and unrelated. There are good, if not finally satisfying, reasons for all this. The cause appears to be in what may be called 'diffidence': sometimes a fear of speaking out, of active commitment; perhaps more especially a fear of letting any poetry stand that fails of perfection, of the most perfect fusion; a desire for the purest verbal or imagistic gems, and those alone; together with a praiseworthy fear of pretending to a relation which has not been found.

Eliot did, however, perhaps relying on the achieved harmony of 'Little Gidding', attempt a more general relatedness in his last plays, though with doubtful success. What he could state in a poem was less easily realizable under the test of action. We shall do well to regard his critical writings on dramatic language as masking the real problems of his dramatic involvement. He had concentrated on the Jacobean dramatists in the nineteen-twenties. He was deeply aware of the sexual horrors lurking within human instinct[1], and the Jacobeans presented these horrors raw. *The Waste Land* shows sexual revulsion; in *Sweeney Agonistes*, a key-statement, romance is equated with lust and lust with murder;

[1] This strain in Eliot's poetry I have discussed more fully in *Christ and Nietzsche*, 1948; 92-3, and in *The Golden Labyrinth*, 1962; 362-6. See also p. 179 above.

and this sexual horror is submitted to the mechanics of psycho-logical diagnosis in *The Family Reunion* (1939). It is characteristic of Eliot that *The Rock* (1934) and *Murder in the Cathedral* (1935) were interposed, offering Christian solutions in morals and martyrdom. In 1948 or thereabouts Eliot told me that he rated higher his modern dramas than a costume-piece like *Murder in the Cathedral*; implying perhaps that they came nearer to facing the central sexual problem. *The Cocktail Party* (1950) handles both the marriage sex-problem and the other consummation of martyrdom, thus covering in one design all earlier dramas, though with a loss in dramatic power. Eliot's early dramatic writing, in which I include *The Waste Land*, had jets of impressive force; but these were in the easier field of revulsion and horror which was to become so poetically powerful in *The Family Reunion*; and a vigorous *action* was never at any time engaged. *The Cocktail Party* has skill, teaching, and diagnosis but, despite its title, too little of blood or fire for the task in hand.

The complaint may be precisely formulated. The drama labours to fuse modern science with Christian sanctity by the creation of a psychiatrist who is also, in effect, a priest. The attempt to graft Church doctrine on to humanistic science is clear; and the attempt to twist what people today believe into a higher belief is praise-worthy. But though we have an ingenious mental pattern, it scarcely succeeds as drama. Sir Henry Harcourt-Reilly, and there-fore the whole work of which he is the human pivot, is made from a factitious joining of scientific and religious externals. For the desired fusion a stronger element of the Dionysian, of spirit-blood, of that which is the basis equally of life and death, and therefore of science and religion, was needed. The arbitrary wine-libations, on the stage, do little: there is no soil for them, no atmosphere, to grow from. From ancient times until today drama of weight has been saturated in Dionysian properties; in what lies beyond the threshold of reason and daylight knowledge, beyond what is easy to accept; in ecstasy, in the occult, in ghosts, in spirit-lore of all kinds.[1] We find them in the Jacobeans and the Gothic plays of the Romantic period. The Faust tradition is made of them. The rise of modern Spiritualism has given them vigour and

---

[1] My reasons for attributing such wide powers to Dionysus are given in *The Golden Labyrinth*, 1962, I. See now also John Pollard, quoting Heraclitus, in *Seers, Shrines and Sirens*, 1965; 86, 89.

T. S. Eliot

impetus. Occultism is active in Shaw, in Masefield's *Melloney Holtspur*, in the dramas of W. B. Yeats. This story I have traced in *The Golden Labyrinth* and have added to it in *Encounter* (XXI. 6; December 1963), enlisting, among others, *Huis Clos*, *Death of a Salesman*, *Waiting for Godot*, and the plays of Eugène Ionesco (see pp. 74-5 above). Dionysus is part of the fabric of drama because he is part of the fabric of life and death, and the relation of the one to the other.

The Waste Land has its 'famous clairvoyante' (I), but more important is its mysterious 'third' presence, 'gliding' and sexually ambivalent (V; see p. 271 above). In 'The Hollow Men' death's 'Kingdom' is darkly but powerfully realized and its 'perpetual star' and 'multifoliate rose' a visionary hope – though there said to be believed in only by 'empty men'. The Eumenides of *The Family Reunion* (called 'ghosts', II. iii), were superbly realized in poetry, but their stage realization was arbitrary and static; they failed to interlock with action and acting.

The Cocktail Party has its passing references to 'guardians'. The gesture is to this extent made, but how many of the audience know that they are what Spiritualists call 'spirit-guides' – like Masefield's King Cole? Dramatically they scarcely register. As for Sir Henry Harcourt-Reilly, on whom so much depends, there is no suggestion that he possesses occult powers until the last act. They form no part of his stage personality. He remains a puppet made of the will to force together science and sanctity.

And yet – how much more illuminating is Eliot's failure than the successes of lesser poets. For though they are not dramatically realized the needed spiritualistic elements are, verbally, present; and Eliot has here forced us to enquire whether, quite apart from drama, our two modern cultures, scientific and religious, can be harmonized, and action engaged, without such deeper contacts. More, we find ourselves asking whether the madhouse of incompatible disciplines that make of a modern university – to quote from Pope's *Essay on Criticism* – 'one glaring chaos and wild heap of wit' will ever become inter-communicative until each and all admit their spiritualistic basis. In 'Tradition and the Individual Talent' Eliot wrote of the poet's mind as a 'finely perfected medium' in which various experiences 'enter into new combinations', and continued with his famous analogy of the catalyst.

Well, Dionysus, god of nature, wine-fire, and the occult, of drama and of all deep poetry, is the supreme catalyst.

Both my brother, though he remained within the Anglican Communion, and myself, he influenced by that fine Vergilian, Professor T. J. Haarhoff, and I by him, became Spiritualists. Spiritualistic acceptance was for us natural. My brother's researches in ancient folklore and death-ritual and my own in the more occult symbolisms of Renaissance poetry were by these new experiences ratified.

In more personal, meditative terms Eliot had, however, already achieved, or come near to achieving, success. The plays themselves if read as meditative patternings have their value, distinct from drama, in his progress. But only in the *Four Quartets* (1935-42) was the end properly attained. Here, in short space, though the state issues of 'Coriolan' are not engaged, a universe is nevertheless subsumed. Elements of air, water, earth, and fire; paradisal gleams; purgatorial suffering; death; wisdom, Sanskrit and Christian; historic tradition and the metaphysics of space and time in mutual and living pattern – all cohere in a loose yet convincing organization, as Eliot reviews his own poetic world and brings it, as near as may be, toward peace.

It would be dangerous to read these as Christian poems; they are quite as near, or nearer, the undoctrinal meditations of *Thus Spake Zarathustra*. Eliot has never, apart from *The Rock* and *Murder in the Cathedral*, been a whole-heartedly Christian poet in the sense that the seventeenth-century poets, or Hopkins, or Francis Thompson were Christian. His early balancing of Hippopotamus and True Church in 'The Hippopotamus' (1920) sends little echoes reverberating down his subsequent reservations. His most assured religious lines, those on Light in *The Rock*, are fruits of a general religious apprehension, independent of dogma; and much of the rest, as we have seen, views conversion as nearer agony than peace. Prayers are lifted to emblematic ladies, exquisitely pictured, in *Ash-Wednesday*, but there (V) the poet knows what it is to 'affirm before the world and deny between the rocks'; and our one memorable reference to Christ comes in the significantly explosive 'Christ the tiger' of 'Gerontion'.

The paradisal intimations of 'Burnt Norton', recalling 'La Figlia che Piange', the hyacinth girl in *The Waste Land*, *Ash-Wednesday*, and 'Marina', are expressed through images of flowers, bird-song, and children without doctrinal implications; and the wonderful lyric in 'East Coker' (IV) starting 'The wounded surgeon plies the steel', surely the grimmest statement on the Christian world-view ever penned by a devotee, offers a universe so riddled with negations and agonies that we must go to the anti-Christian polemics of Nietzsche – which its cutting phraseology recalls – for an analogy. 'East Coker' opens out, at its conclusion, to 'the vast waters of the petrel and the porpoise', recalling the elemental sea-freedoms opening out in 'Prufrock', 'Gerontion', *Ash-Wednesday* (VI) and *The Waste Land* (V). In these there is release, to be expanded in the nature poetry of the river as 'a strong brown god' and the sea-descriptions of 'The Dry Salvages' (I), where there is nevertheless also a Lady-prayer of orthodox devotion (IV), recalling *Ash-Wednesday*.

In the *Four Quartets* rival world-views, all honest and all tenable, are still left in the main mutually unrelated, except that they are all presented in autobiographical relation to the poet, and there is a recurring drive for sainthood, or something like it, and moments recording 'the impossible union of spheres of existence' ('The Dry Salvages', V). There is comparatively little 'pure poetry' – in my judgement – that can compare with the pieces already praised in this essay; to which I should add 'The Hollow Men', my earliest delight. If we receive, as I think we do, a sense of final harmony, the credit for it goes mainly to the concluding piece, 'Little Gidding', Eliot's culminating achievement, which ends, convincingly, with an imagined weaving of spirit-flames into a 'crowned knot of fire', so that 'the fire and the rose are one'. The fire is that of agony and spiritual advance, as in 'O Lord Thou pluckest me out . . . burning' in *The Waste Land* and 'the intolerable shirt of flame' woven by Love earlier in 'Little Gidding' (IV); and the rose covers all romantic flower-intimations from 'La Figlia che Piange' to 'Burnt Norton'. The longed-for union, already hinted in *Ash-Wednesday*, of Eros and Christ, though Christ is not named, is convincingly stated.

If 'Little Gidding' does indeed achieve this integration, it does so only through obedience to the principle we have already defined. For so ambitious an integration there must be present the catalyst, Dionysus, as god simultaneously of nature and the occult. The authority of the *Four Quartets* derives from the numinous atmosphere generated and pervading, helped by the suggestion of music in both structure and reference. Bird or spirit voices and unseen presences, like those in Masefield's 'The Hounds of Hell', de la Mare's 'The Listeners', and 'Marina' are awake in 'Burnt Norton'. In 'East Coker', we meet ghosts of forgotten dancers, and death weighs as a dark portal to garden laughter. Converse with 'spirits' is grouped with other occult practices, and 'daemonic' and 'chthonic' powers are touched on, not without respect, in 'The Dry Salvages'. In 'Little Gidding' the ancestral powers dominate:

> And what the dead had no speech for, when living,
> They can tell you, being dead: the communication
> Of the dead is tongued with fire beyond the language of the living.
>
> (I)

Than this there is surely no more potent spiritualistic statement in our literature. In 'Little Gidding' 'We are born with the dead'; 'they return, and bring us with them' (V). But this is not all. The only dramatic personality in the *Quartets* is the 'familiar compound ghost' of 'some dead master', recalling the 'affable familiar ghost' of the passage on spirit-writing in Shakespeare's Sonnet 86, and probably to be identified with, among others, W. B. Yeats, who speaks a long passage of authoritative counsel, ruling the poem (II). Our final authority is thus a figure combining (i) poet and (ii) spirit-being. The ghost is spiritualistically conceived as living 'between two worlds become much like each other'; meaning, presumably, that he has found the planes less different than he expected. The delineation owes nothing to orthodoxy. 'Death' exists 'between two lives' (III), and the poet is writing from direct spiritualistic acceptance, like W. B. Yeats and John Masefield. The acceptance is common to a tradition of experience descending from the ancient world, active throughout the poetry of all times and all places, though today enjoying a more precise understanding and formulation than hitherto; and only through such an acceptance of the 'occult', meaning the 'hidden', which recalls the 'hidden' of 'Triumphal March', and the 'hidden laughter' of 'Burnt Norton' (V), may harmony be attained.

Eliot's contribution has been unique. Refusing easier expedients, he has concentrated on what in our time can make poetry of a high order; and in so doing has used poetry as a test for what is, and is not, valid. The complete canon, poetry and prose, may show a lack of harmony, of interlocking; neither state affairs nor dramatic action was artistically mastered. But Eliot's juxtapositions of disparate mind-adventures have had a clarity and a detonation that premature attempts at interrelation – the danger is clear in the last plays – might have reduced; the impacts would have been softened, and unity bought, as it was perhaps in *The Cocktail Party,* at too dear a cost. No poet has been more deeply honest. The results are simultaneously personal in substance and impersonal in technique. I write of Eliot as a poet, of his poetic self; and this self, I have argued, cannot be regarded as wholly, or even mainly, Christian: he has left no visionary statement so happily assured as 'Marina'. As a man he was, we know, a Christian; his conversion existed in the order of decision and life-action, not of art. The two orders are distinct.

ADDITIONAL NOTE: My reaction to *The Cocktail Party* corresponds exactly to that of W. R. G. Branford in *Lingua,* University of Cape Town (I. 7; March 1951), 'The God in the Machine'. I have heard, and can well believe, that the play is cogent on sound radio. In a recent notice (*The Times,* 7 November 1968), Irving Wardle observed 'the growing significance of the "guardians" from the moment Edward first stumbles on the word'. The delay may have point. I have not witnessed Sir Alec Guinness's performance.

Sir Henry Harcourt-Reilly's clairvoyance in Act III is spiritual-istic:

> When I first met Miss Coplestone, in this room,
> I saw the image, standing behind her chair,
> Of a Celia Coplestone whose face showed the astonishment
> Of the first five minutes after a violent death.

The thought corresponds to that in Eliot's 'For the Indian Soldiers who Died in Africa' (*Of Books and Humankind, Essays and Poems presented to Bonamy Dobrée,* ed. John Butt, 1964):

> action
> None the less fruitful if neither you nor I
> Know, until the moment after death,
> What is the fruit of action.

This is the spiritualistic teaching, in contrast to doctrines of resurrection or assimilation into a world-soul: one is the same person, in full consciousness, the moment after death as one was the moment before. An earlier version (*Collected Poems*, 1963) had 'we' for 'I' and 'judgement' for 'moment'.

Sir Henry Harcourt-Reilly starts comically, becomes psychiatrist and priest, and ends as a spiritualist. The sequence is carefully planned to entice the audience on from what is normal to what is new. The meanings are artificially imposed rather than dramatically generated, but where so significant a plan is being deployed it would seem that commentary must shift its ground.

Other discussions of Eliot's poetry appear on pp. 178-82 above; and see Appendix.

CHAPTER XIV

John Cowper Powys

A review essay on the appearance of *Up and Out* in *The Times Literary Supplement*, 11 October 1957.

OF HIS TWO new stories *Up and Out* and *The Mountains of the Moon* (published together in 1957 under the title of the first) John Cowper Powys writes:

The feeling, for it is more than a doctrine or an idea, underlying both these stories, is that there is nothing in the universe devoid of some mysterious element of consciousness, however small, queer, ridiculous, or whether animal, vegetable or mineral, such a thing may be.[1]

This feeling pervades all Powys's writings; and it is perhaps this that has held up the understanding of them. He has been writing now for more than forty years and during the past twenty-five his output has been prodigious; and yet, though authentic voices have never been wanting to assert his genius, the prevailing critical mood of the past two generations has been strangely lethargic in response.

Many subsidiary reasons could be given. The difficulties of James Joyce, serious as they are, are just such as appeal to the twentieth-century literary mind, which loves nothing so much as a puzzle; and as for D. H. Lawrence, though his more esoteric intuitions are not always easy to assimilate, yet his approach, the kinetic descriptions, the nervous, fiery impressionism, the hammering repetitions, the speed, the social attack, all are on the wavelength of our 'age of anxiety'.

[1] This was, if I recall correctly, a note on the jacket. It is not in the book.

John Cowper Powys

Powys is never obscure; and his large works, with their long and classically modulated periods, their wealth of vocabulary and allusion, their strange assurance and utter independence of what most of us would say that he ought to be writing, pursue us with the unhurrying and unperturbed pace of Francis Thompson's God in 'The Hound of Heaven'. Escape has proved impossible, and we are today watching the steady rise to full recognition of one of the outstanding writers of our century. But that recognition must in part depend, too, on an understanding of the more deeply seated reason for the reluctance which some readers have felt in face of even such obviously great novels as *A Glastonbury Romance* (1933) and *Jobber Skald* (1935; as *Weymouth Sands*, 1963). This deeper reason will hardly be elucidated by any study of the history of the novel; it is far closer to the histories of mythology and poetry. Little enough divides Powys's rich deployment of Biblical and Greek mythology in his recently published poetic narrative *Lucifer* (1956; composed 1906) from the prose descriptions of his novels.

The myths and legends of all races, with their fauns, dryads and nymphs, their trolls and fairies, have from earliest times asserted the spiritual properties of natural phenomena; and in our own literature we can watch a reliance on such 'personifications' gradually giving way to the more explicit doctrines of a Blake or a Wordsworth, and the deliberate dramatization of Earth's awakening in response to Man's liberation in Shelley's *Prometheus Unbound*. But, except for Carlyle's *Sartor Resartus* and John Davidson's prophetic asseverations in both prose and poetry in the early years of this century, there has been little more, in England, of power and authenticity until Lawrence and Powys; and of these two, whereas Lawrence's non-human vitalism concentrated mainly, and with a success matched in our literature by Byron alone, on the higher, dynamic animals, Powys's favourite concentration falls on the lower orders: on the reptilian kinds, and insects; on plant-life, trees and earth; and on minerals. To him the humblest variety of unnoticed vegetation is an actor in his drama, and from his first novel *Wood and Stone* (U.S.A., 1915) onwards stone is impregnated, continually, with a spiritual significance.

Such intuitions are not new. The total wisdom, the cosmic consciousness, expressed, in which you begin to feel that the vibrations of man's little story are responsive to, and may in turn

John Cowper Powys

affect, not only the earth itself but the farthest star, has been embedded in occult teaching for centuries; astrology is merely one symptom of it, just as mythology is another. Both Lawrence and Powys search back to the ancient world: Lawrence to the Etruscans and the mythological traditions of the Aztecs, Powys to the Greeks and the Celtic records of *The Mabinogion*. It is a wisdom often lost, and always hard to capture in direct consciousness. It is not necessarily un-Christian: it may be said to be implied by Hooker's doctrine of immanence in the *Ecclesiastical Polity*, and it is certainly true that nature is being regarded *sacramentally*. The magical, animistic understanding has been alive, beneath the academic surface, in many periods, and nearly always in poetry; as today in the work of Edith Sitwell. At present its main supporters, outside the various schools of admittedly occult tradition, are our imaginative writers, and whenever from time to time a work of more explicit and scientific formulation, such as Sir Francis Younghusband's *The Living Universe*, appears, it is quickly forgotten, there being no official guardianship for such studies.

A considerable responsibility falls accordingly on our literary consciousness. The critical temper of our time has been countered by Middleton Murry's life-long, if indecisive, attempt, from his own mystical experience – as recounted in his book *God* – onwards, to relate the mystical fact to poetic truth; and we have recently read of Aldous Huxley's enjoyment of a newly vital and colourful perception of objects under the influence of mescalin, his adventure closely repeating the many examples reported by William James as the results of mystical experience in his *Varieties of Religious Experience*. But what Murry received through a single, shattering insight which did not prove permanent and Huxley has known through drugs, Powys in his fascinating book *In Spite Of* (1953) regards as achievable by all of us through a deliberate, psychic technique constituting the first step of an evolutionary advance in human consciousness. The statement corresponds closely to that of Wordsworth's well-known *Recluse* fragment, as published in the Preface to *The Excursion*.

This perception lies at the heart of *A Glastonbury Romance*; and since this book is also the heart of Powys's work, a retrospective comment may prove helpful. Its opening, which includes a discussion of certain correspondences between solar activity and a human consciousness, has been regarded as a stumbling-block to the pusillanimous reader; and yet this is a deeply considered and necessary introduction. It is precisely Powys's ever-present contact with the vital, or spiritual, principles within the universe which enables him to explore with so uncanny a penetration the deeper problems of that comparatively small section of the universe – or, as he would say, multiverse – which constitutes man; and this is how his human delineation comes to register an advance on that of previous novelists, and even dramatists. *A Glastonbury Romance* is rooted firmly in its cosmic setting and more especially in the soil and vegetation of Somerset. Within this setting, and one with it, are the people. These are many, and the minor persons are drawn with as much sympathy as the greater: the gardener Weatherwax, Mad Bet, the boy Elphin Cantle, are as convincing as any such in Hardy or Shakespeare. But our, if not the author's, main interest falls inevitably on those in the centre; and here the range and depth of experience depicted is enormous. But again, it is only because Powys has as deep a sympathy for, and insight into, his ferns and funguses, his Mad Bets and Elphin Cantles, as in his sun or Grail or the First Cause itself, that he can handle the greater – if they are greater – mysteries with such consummate ease.

Such an awareness of the magical, corresponding to what John Davidson in his introduction to *The Theatrocrat* (1905; 25) regarded as the *bisexual* electricity within phenomena, is likely to be peculiarly authoritative in the expression of sexual instincts. The chapter of *A Glastonbury Romance* headed 'Consummation' offers us probably as profound an insight into the willed submission of feminine love as we shall anywhere find; and here Powys may be contrasted with Lawrence, whose women appear so often to love with a male complexity which appears more characteristic of the author than of the female sex. No experienced reader of Powys will lack confidence in his human exploitations, however strange the adventures; and in *A Glastonbury Romance* we meet one of the strangest and most terrifying studies in fiction – the sadistic Mr. Evans.

Mr. Evans is a lovable, academically minded man with a fondness for old Welsh manuscripts but tormented by a recurring sadistic obsession utterly at variance with his better nature. It is not – apart from one suggestion of a pre-natal incident (XXIX, 1068 or 1020) – handled as a 'perversion', attributable to some fault in upbringing or character; rather is Mr. Evans's sexual mechanism shown as directly reflecting and responding to that side of the creative process, or great 'First Cause', which is responsible for the manifest cruelties of the cosmic scheme.

On the human plane, we must search for ways to escape; and two ways are suggested. First, Mr. Evans tries to conquer the evil by acting the part of the crucified Christ in a Passion Play, with the inevitably suggested corollary that it is this particular instinct, as a universal problem in man and in nature, which lies behind both the necessity and the power of Christian symbolism. Second, Mr. Evans's pathetically plain wife pits the dubious, and yet partly successful, charms of her own body against her husband's evil possession.

Beside the evil we have the good. Growing naturally from Powys's spiritual, or magical, apprehensions, Glastonbury is shown to us as a spot uniquely open to what T. S. Eliot has called the 'intersection of the timeless with time'. Those poignant intimations of the *Four Quartets* are here found massively and realistically expanded for us in direct descent from the main mythological traditions of our island: there is little arbitrary, or personal, in the treatment, which feels myth as objectively and potently active as any beast or tree; as part, indeed, of nature itself. Two persons in the book attain a semi-transcendental stature: the miracle-working and ghost-exorcizing Mr. Geard, and the saintly Sam. These studies are the more convincing in that they are done without any touch of idealism. Mr. Geard's religious phraseology is that of a peculiarly crude revivalist. As for Sam, his vision of the Grail comes directly before he has to minister – and we are spared no physical detail – to an old man suffering from piles. In line with the great traditions of Christian sanctity, we are forced to buy our visions at the price of what is humanly repellent. Nor must we forget that there is throughout a Rabelaisian humour. But this in no sense lowers the theme. Rabelais, of whom he has published a notable study, is one of Powys's own most persistent influences; and his most searching analyses are habitually given with ironic detachment and a play of humour.

A Glastonbury Romance was a great act of courage; and Powys's *Autobiography* (1934), in which he claims to recognize the presence of the sadistic instinct within himself, was an even greater. The power of *A Glastonbury Romance* matures from its controlled survey of good and evil as balanced and artistically accepted principles within the universe and within man. This acknowledged, we may next suggest that Powys's genius, his extraordinarily wide and deep comprehension of human instincts and potentialities, derives from his own intimate experience of a terrible evil; through accepting without surrendering to it he has gained an inclusiveness known to few in immediate contact with the origins, beyond good and evil, of creation. And surely, it is this very acceptance, as an intimate and personal experience, of the deepest and most fearful cleavage and antagonism of opposing principles within and yet intrinsic to the cosmic scheme, which enables him so uncannily to focus the secret life of sticks and stones, recognizing in them what theologians would call the immanence of the Deity.

This dispassionate balancing of good and evil, and in particular the evils of cruelty, could scarcely be, on all occasions, maintained. When an evil is too pressingly known, there is also the compulsion on the artist to descend into the arena, to fight; and for many years Powys has engaged himself strenuously against his main horror, vivisection. This campaign found its most satisfying projection in *Morwyn* (1937), a richly compacted 'Inferno' where, among others, the majestic figures of Taliessin and Merlin appear as powers of good.

The novels of Welsh history, *Owen Glendower* (1942) and *Porius* (1951), completed Powys's weightier works. Since those appeared we have been aware of an easier, more buoyant manner in the Homeric *Atlantis* (1954) and medieval *The Brazen Head* (1956). These later books take us directly to a world of myth and enchantment which allows a new freedom in the handling of the animistic properties of nature, as in the delightfully argumentative Fly and Moth of *Atlantis* and the parts played, in both narratives, by certain peculiarly wise trees. The importance of these lively creations was well emphasized recently by Mr. Roland Mathias in a valuable broadcast. And here we are brought to the threshold of the two new stories published under the title *Up and Out*.

We have Powys's own authority for regarding the animistic insight as their key; but this is not necessarily a happy insight. It is just because he makes no distinction between the sensitivities of animals and men that his horror of vivisection is so great. The first story opens with an attack on this recurring horror, in comparison with which the subsequent brief and unsensational announcement that the world has just been destroyed by atomic warfare comes, with a typical stroke of Powysian idiosyncrasy, as an anti-climax. Four survivors voyage on a fragment of Earth into space. The fantastic adventure shows us the slaying of Time, conceived as an amorphous slug, and its swallowing by Eternity, an even more repellent creature which next swallows itself. The stars, through Aldebaran as representative, elect to commit general suicide. Representatives of Oriental, Greek, and Welsh mythology and religion accompany these remarkable events by argument and comment. Finally the four survivors meet God and Satan in friendly colloquy, after the manner of Goethe's *Faust*, and hear God's personal account of the creation which has proved so disastrous and his plan for a new attempt without either animal slaughter or free-will. The book's hero suggests instead that they all – God, Satan and the four survivors from Earth – attempt a plunge 'up and out' into the new 'dimension' sometimes discussed by philosophers. The attempt is made, but it leads only to extinction for all concerned.

The story constitutes an attack not only on vivisection and the lust for scientific knowledge, but also on all avenues of escape offered by such abstract concepts as 'eternity', 'dimension' and 'the Absolute', or any fixed theology. And yet the apparent pessimism is countered by so irrepressibly buoyant a style and so lively a play of humour that it can scarcely be regarded as final. The characterization of God is particularly attractive and entertaining. Never was there a more well-intentioned deity: simple-minded, unpretentious, courteous, kindly, indeed wholly lovable, and, like the God of Connelly's *Green Pastures*, surprisingly convincing. It almost seems as though Powys is nowadays at his happiest when speaking through the voice either of God himself or of some insect or inanimate object.

The two narratives are published, and may have been conceived, as complementary; certainly they should be read together, like the 'Everlasting No' and 'Everlasting Yea' of *Sartor Resartus*. The second is by far the happier. This fantasy takes us to the Moon, and is filled by heterogeneous persons and events moving with a dreamlike inconsequence which yet holds together as a pleasing unit. Among its constituent elements are some exciting meditations on the mystery of life, a stick in telepathic communication with a club, and a Moon-giant who possesses a collection of 'Milestones of Terrestrial History', including a fragment of the Ten Commandments, Achilles' heel, Nero's fiddle-string, a white feather from the Dove of the Ark, a piece of one of King Alfred's burnt cakes, the half-bitten apple-core from Eden. Among the Moon-dwellers we find an academically minded and clairvoyant spinster and her friend, a professional, but baffled, philosopher; and from Earth we have a Welsh lady whose soul visits the Moon's soul in sleep. A romantic conclusion shows us the young hero, successor to the young heroes of *Atlantis* and *The Brazen Head*, climbing 'up and up and up' to find union with the daughter of the Moon and Sun on the ridge of the Moon's mountains which divides its known from its unknown face.

The fantasy, carried in a style of purity and charm, is wholly pleasing. The mysteries of 'space' and 'infinity' are metaphysical positives coming under no such condemnation as did 'time', 'eternity', and 'the Absolute' in the previous tale: indeed, the contrast is stated. Most vivid of all is the dance of the Terrestrial Milestones and the characterization of the Dove's White Feather as she finds union with her long-lost love, a Raven's Black Feather from the Raven which did not, according to the account in Genesis, return to the Ark. No person of fiction was ever created with more masterly a touch, nor more warmly convincing in life and speech, than this fascinating White Feather. A few pages only, but the miracle is performed. Again, a line or two and a few scattered phrases endue a piece of quartz dancing 'ecstatically' down a slope with a lovable, semi-human vivacity surely new to our literature.

Here rather than in Powys's denials lies his true genius, and its meaning for us today. Rationally, he has always maintained a certain agnosticism; and yet each book in turn is saturated in a sense of the occult, of magic, of some hinterland to the phenomenal world of prodigious strangeness and importance. In his latest work this divergence appears to be widening. The uncompromising repudiation of immortality throughout *In Spite Of* stands in firm contrast to the range of possibility beyond death surveyed in his earlier book *Mortal Strife* (1942). Again and again he now urges us, just as did Wordsworth in the *Recluse* fragment and John Davidson in many an impassioned paragraph, to transfer finally our more numinous speculations from the altar to the earth, to the observable universe and all its children. And yet the more uncompromising his religious scepticism becomes, the more his narratives are charged with a sense of the miraculous. Perhaps he would say that when once we have touched the living magic of creation, then all the rest, our immortalities and eternities and dimensions and theologies, will be handed back to us, if we still want them; but not till then. In *The Mountains of the Moon* the hero, Rorlt, told by his faithful club, Blob, to 'listen', hears the still, sad music, not merely of man, but of the whole creation, understanding

that there was some mysterious harmony in the souls of us all, in the souls of animals, vegetables and minerals, in the souls of water, air, earth, and fire, only, as Shakespeare says 'whilst this muddy vesture of decay doth grossly close it in we cannot hear it' – yes, that weird procession he had just heard and seen, of forms that were indistinguishable from the shapes created in the mind by tragic music when it transcends all particular sorrow and goes beyond all personal grief and is full of a strange sadness that all nature feels . . .   (208)

But now this tragic music, the central theme of so many of Powys's philosophical discussions, must itself be surpassed:

It struck him as a revelation of something, but of something that it was essential for him to pass by, pass over, to shake off, to leave behind.

So the young Rorlt goes on to his union with Helia, while his trusty club, symbol of what we call the 'inanimate', slithers back, on *this* side of the ridge. Presumably this 'shaking off' includes the surmounting of all the cruelties and voracities of nature and perhaps even the vivisections, sadisms and atomic warring of men; and perhaps it is not fantastic to see in the poignant love-intercourse of our White and Black Feathers some delicate intimation, some feather-light whisper, hinting an answer. If so, it is an answer which Powys has not as yet explicitly formulated. His latest fantasy moves in advance of the main body of his teaching.[1]

---

[1] The answer may be supposed to have come in the masturbatory doctrine of *All or Nothing*: see pp. 164-5 above; also p. 223, for 'black' and 'white', the masts in *The Ship* corresponding to the Feathers here.

John Cowper Powys

2. ENIGMATIC DEITY

A review of *Homer and the Aether* (1959) in *The Times Literary Supplement*, 1 May 1959.

Homer and the Aether is an unusual study. Superficially it might seem simple, but appearances are deceptive. The greater part of it is an enjoyable paraphrase of the *Iliad*, abbreviated for the purpose and accompanied by a commentary on the warring of Greeks and Trojans from a modern viewpoint; what we might call a series of 'personal impressions', mainly interesting for the pleasure of having the well-known story transposed with new highlights and emphases into the form of a Powys narrative. That alone would justify it; but there is more to be said.

We have first an introduction on the nature of the Homeric art, followed by a chapter 'The Aether Speaks' introducing us to a deity who claims to have acted as Homer's inspirational assistant; and then our main narrative, interspersed with comments by the Aether, whose function appears to be complex, variously seeing into Homer's mind, injecting into it particular thoughts and insights, or just discussing in general terms the mental processes of the people and the implications of the action. The interpretative value of this original and engaging method will be assessed differently by different readers; but far more important is the nature of the attempt; and perhaps even more important still, the choice by Powys, at this crowning period of his literary life, of 'the divine Aether' (191-2) for this particular office.

Powys admires Homer for two main reasons: for his peculiarly vivid realization of inanimate objects, whereby they become more significant than our normal apprehension supposes; and for his honest facing of existence in its unsystematic and haphazard quality, well symbolized by the unruly actions of his Olympian deities disputing with one another and confusedly taking part in the human action; dominated, it is true, by Zeus, but presented with slight sense of reverence and much of humour. Now both these are primary trends in Powys's own philosophy: his feeling for the indwelling spirit of the inanimate is as strong as, and more widely ranging than, Wordsworth's; and he is a consistent repudiator of the concept 'universe', preferring the word 'multiverse', to leave room for chance, for the unconditioned and the unknowable. To all tidy theological systems he responds with the same kind of provisional and half-humorous acceptance as Homer gave to his Olympians.

And yet, as has been pointed out in these columns in a previous review (p. 399 above), no living writer, and perhaps no former seer in our literature, is more saturated with a sense of occult powers active within the living universe; and this sense is closely involved with his lifelong use of great writers as a guide to living; and, among these, Homer has always been his first choice. The Homeric inspiration may therefore be closely equated with Powys's most fundamental beliefs. His new book not only repeats but dramatizes his philosophy; and since dramatization involves personification, we find the repudiator of monistic systems inevitably drawn into acceptance of a deity corresponding to his central trust and impregnated with a far higher degree of poetic belief than the mythical Olympians: the divine Aether, 'the Immortal One, beyond all gods and men' (28). The Aether functions rather like the lady Eternity within the supposedly godless *Thus Spake Zarathustra* (III. 16), or Lilith at the end of Shaw's *Back to Methuselah*, as a central and supernal, though not necessarily all-powerful or omniscient, principle.

The Greek $\alpha i \theta \eta \rho$ is defined by Liddell and Scott as 'ether, the upper, purer air, as opposed to the lower air or atmosphere'; it signifies 'the clear sky, heaven, as the abode of the gods'. It corresponds accordingly less to theology than to some abode or basis of the divine; it is more ultimate than theology. Ether is defined in the *Oxford English Dictionary* as originally signifying 'a purer form of fire or of air' which came to be regarded as a fifth element. Physics until recently postulated the 'ether' as a continuum within which to place its findings, and without some such postulate these findings are scarcely definable in any but algebraic terms. Modern Spiritualism has its 'astral' or 'etheric' body, or dimension, corresponding to the 'spiritual body' of St. Paul (1 Corinthians, XV. 44-6). 'Ether' is a key-concept in what might be called the astral adventures of Byron's *Cain* (II. i. 29, 99; II. ii. 183). Our poetic tradition abounds in such uses. George Darley has a 'bird of Paradise' living 'on ether' (*Thomas à Becket*, IV. v). That unjustly neglected poet-prophet John Davidson placed his trust in the 'ether' as the basis of all things.[1] And now Powys, our supreme exponent of the twentieth-century poetic consciousness at its finest point of what might be called, by paradox, 'visionary scepticism', chooses 'the everlasting Aether' (248) to function as the personified agent of human inspiration. The Aether contrasts itself, or herself, with both the Greek οὐρανός, the upper sky, and earth's lower atmosphere, ἀήρ, which in comparison seems 'a sort of mist, or fog' (268). It is not all-inclusive, but to man it is the necessary prerequisite for the enlargement of consciousness. Somewhere, we may suppose, within the area covered by this multi-radial and undying concept lies the spring which might throw the various and mutually exclusive specialities of modern learning into new harmony.

The Aether's authoritative pronouncement in the second chapter tells us how, while allowing Homer his intellectually gathered knowledge and his traditional poetic technique, it adds to these an insight into the thoughts of men and gods otherwise unattainable, together with an insight into the consciousness enjoyed by inanimate objects. Here Powys advances beyond his previous statements. Such objects, says the Aether, enjoy a semi-consciousness drawn from the human beings who have known them. In this there is an undeniable truth, as the modern practice of 'psychometry' proves and as has been half-recognized throughout the ages, a good classical example being Cassandra's reading of past events from the palace at Argos in Aeschylus' *Agamemnon*; and similar examples are described in the present narrative (172, 178). Powys's Aether is the 'ether' of physics with 'the power of passing through every form and shape which matter, consciously or unconsciously, has taken'. But it is also the 'shining Aether', conceived as a power of 'gleaming and penetrating light' which induces in the poet a 'special kind of ecstatic trance' through a use of air and water transfigured by its own suffusing radiance (23-5). It exists at the point where physics and poetry together dissolve into clairvoyance.

And here we come up against the problem of Powys's recent scepticism – though his earlier pronouncements were less definite – regarding human survival: 'O, and how lucky you terrestrial

---

[1] See John Davidson's Introduction to *The Theatrocrat* (1905). This, and also his prose Epilogue to *The Triumph of Mammon*, deserve a reawakened attention. For his dramas, see *The Golden Labyrinth*, 312-17.

creatures are', says the Aether, 'that when the end comes you can lie down and go to sleep and never wake up again!' (29). But, as Powys's rejection of monistic systems is countered by his artistic use of this central deity, so his rejection of human immortality is not allowed the last word. This is only another instance of that literary phenomenon whereby his own genius impels an author to state artistically what he, as a person, might deny. So we next hear, in an exquisite concluding passage, that those who are 'afraid of annihilation' are given sweet dreams of 'some blest Elysian Field' where there are reunions – like those in Shakespeare's last plays – and forgetfulness of anguish. That is the Aether's final word, in its context so beautifully placed and phrased that it holds an authenticity and a finality beyond the contained logic. It is as though, in invoking the divine Aether, a conception drawn very obviously from his own inspirational experience, Powys has himself come more powerfully than ever under its control; and it is perhaps this enigmatic deity, rather than Powys, who speaks.

It is fascinating to watch so fine a creative intelligence at work on the problems posed variously by his own scepticism and his own inspiration.

3. HOMAGE TO POWYS

The Yorkshire Post, 6 October 1962.

Prophets are often not appreciated during their own life, but even so it remains difficult to understand why the works of John Cowper Powys should have been so curiously neglected by the literary critics of our time.

He had, you would suppose, every preliminary advantage. He was the eldest of a family that contained at least two other writers of distinction, Theodore and Llewelyn; and each gained in esteem from association with the others.

When, well past middle-age, he devoted himself wholly to writing he had already gained a reputation throughout the United States as a lecturer of phenomenal power, and had had a number of books published in America and some in Britain. After the appearance in rapid succession of *Wolf Solent*, *A Glastonbury Romance*, the *Autobiography*, *Jobber Skald* (reissued as *Weymouth*

Sands) and *Maiden Castle*, he was recognized by creative writers both here and in America as a genius of the first order.

Nevertheless Powys is still not nearly so well known as he should be. He has a strong but limited following, perhaps more intense abroad than at home; but those kinds of critical publicity that do most to introduce a writer to his potential public have remained silent.

His appeal may have suffered through his having followed his most obviously great works of the 1930s by two difficult yet equally great, and some might say greater, novels of Welsh history, *Owen Glendower* and *Porius*, which make rather heavy demands on a hasty and over-confident generation. Since the 1930s Powys has settled in North Wales; he traces his descent to Welsh forbears and to the family of the poet Cowper. He writes often as the literary voice of Wales. But the historical learning incorporated into the Welsh narratives should, one would have thought, have gathered round them a swarm at least of academically minded researchers; but this has not happened. No. The real trouble lies elsewhere.

Powys writes from a vast comprehension of human and beyond-human powers which exists as a challenge to the contemporary intellect. He accordingly alienates those influential middle-men of contemporary literature, the professional or semi-professional critics. Never perhaps has academic criticism been so dangerously powerful as it is today in deflecting the tastes of those who are to constitute our reading public; and it has done hardly anything to support our foremost man of letters.

What has been done has been done, or rather said, not by critics but by creative writers on both sides of the Atlantic. No study of Powys's achievement has appeared in England since the necessarily brief treatment in Richard Heron Ward's *The Powys Brothers* in 1935. He has received only two academic honours: the Plaque for 1957 of the Free Academy of Arts in Hamburg; and, this year, the degree of Doctor of Letters from the University of Wales.

The case for Powys's greatness is almost ludicrously easy to establish. The combination of antiquarian learning, historical atmosphere and human characterization in *Owen Glendower* and *Porius* has surely established him as the finest historical novelist in English literature; and he is equally surely our greatest nature-writer. Extended passages throughout his works penetrate the secret life of vegetation, attune us to the hidden powers of rock and stone, feeling into the Wordsworthian livingness of the 'inanimate', of earth and sea; delineate the subtlest changes in cloud, mist and light; and respond to psychic radiations from moon and sun. All is described with the exactitude of a trained naturalist and in close human and psychological reference. It is also done with the insight of a seer. To read Powys is to explore creation.

His human drama is set within a context both of nature and of the past, sensing the presence of the dead and a wide hinterland of legend and mythology. As his work progresses the mythological and magical elements grow stronger, passing through the Welsh histories – *Porius* might be read as a text-book on comparative religion – to *Atlantis*, *The Brazen Head*, *Homer and the Aether* and the fairytale fabrics of *Up and Out* and his last published work, *All or Nothing*.

Throughout, a realistic and contemporary engagement is maintained. Powys is always writing for us, today; but he is seeing himself and us in a historical and cosmic, sometimes a magical, context.

His people accordingly flower from a soil; they have roots and sap; and they are treated, as he treats himself in the *Autobiography*, with a compelling honesty. He is aware of the terrible strain of the sadistic entwisted in man's sexual being. Evil, as in *A Glastonbury Romance*, can be appalling; and it is because he knows the nature of this sadistic instinct and the cunning with which it veils itself from its possessors, that he cries out, again and again, and pre-eminently in his 'Inferno', *Morwyn*, against what he regards as the root crime of our civilization: vivisection.

And yet, despite his probings of human evils, Powys creates no fully delineated evil persons. He is kindly to his people and never degrades them, treating their criminal instincts with understanding and their foibles with whimsicality. He is a subtle humorist; an undertone of humour may be found in the most unlikely places. Rabelais ranks high among his literary heroes and in his study, *Rabelais* (1948), we have our one adequate discussion of the nature and meaning of broad, obscene and liberating humour – the humour of Aristophanes, Chaucer, Rabelais, and Falstaff. Powys is both our most profound authority on the semi-sexual origins of evil and our only authority on great humour.

John Cowper Powys

That his *Autobiography* is among the few most important autobiographies in our language is generally admitted; but surely it is *the* most important. For who else has so honestly confessed to the secrets of his own sexual psychology? Among letter-writers, how many can compare, for humour, vivacity and day-by-day courage in face of adversities, with that remarkable collection of letters to Louis Wilkinson, published in 1958? He is an unremitting and generous correspondent. One wonders how there has been time for it. There are other examples of prodigious output in the literatures of our own and other lands, but few if any can have drawn level with this staggering record from *Wolf Solent* onwards.

Apart from the long novels – and yet *is* 'novels' the right term? – there runs parallel the sequence of more purely philosophical works. For years Powys has suffered gravely in health; his diet is, perforce, of the most meagre, consisting of tea, milk and bread; he has lost the sight of one eye. Yet to meet him is to draw strength from a spiritual giant, overflowing with well-being, benevolence and power.

Of bitterness, of personal hostility, of dogmatism, of literary, sociological or spiritual snobbishness or implications of superiority, there is in him – and of how many of his famous contemporaries could this be said? – nothing.

Drawing on as wide a vocabulary as any of his predecessors or contemporaries in English literature, he indulges in no tricks of style, offering instead his own grand modulation of phrase and syntax interspersed with the homeliest of touches, which never, because the grandeur is never a false, never a 'literary' grandeur, seem out of place. Powys writes with simplicity, kindliness and humour; and with humility; and courtesy. Despite his almost unprecedented imaginative equipment, he appears to regard his every least reader as his equal.

Perhaps his greatest accomplishment of all is that, despite the profundity of his insights, he never claims to have all the answers. He never lets us forget that there are sufferings so awful that no theological system nor his own techniques, explained in his philosophical books, can wholly reconcile us to them.

After reading one of his major volumes, we have been immeasurably enriched; we have ourselves registered a creative achievement, for to read him adequately, and that means slowly –

for to read him fast is not to read him at all – is to stretch our own creative powers to the limit. But we are not drawn to complacency; the mystery of our existence remains a mystery; and we are never invited to claim more than mortal destiny allows.

On Monday John Cowper Powys registers his 90th birthday.

ADDITIONAL NOTE, 1968: A general survey of Powys's prose works is given in my book *The Saturnian Quest* (1964). Derek Langridge's *John Cowper Powys: a record of achievement* (1966), a bibliography with much additional material, is a necessity for all students. H. P. Collins's *John Cowper Powys: Old Earth-Man* (1966) is an astute critical study, and Kenneth Hopkins's *The Powys Brothers* (1967) an excellent guide. The issue of *A Review of English Literature* devoted to Powys (IV. i; January 1963) contains important essays, including tributes by A. Norman Jeffares, Henry Miller, J. B. Priestley and Angus Wilson. See also Bernard Jones in *Dorset Worthies* No. 3 (Dorchester 1962).

In *The Saturnian Quest* my note on the word 'cavoseniargizing' in *Porius* was written without the passage on the word's invention, which occurs on page 83 of Chapter V, in mind. This passage I had half-remembered, but could not trace. What I said about the word's *imaginative* connotations remains unaffected.

One of my sentences on *Atlantis* might be seriously misunderstood. In line 3 of page 102 of *The Saturnian Quest* the words 'into science' should be inserted after 'astray'. I intended no suggestion that the 'bisexual penetrations' were, as such, bad.

My attention has been drawn by Mr. Michael Greenwald to *The Complex Vision*, a work of general philosophy published by Powys in New York in 1920. With neither the subjective emphases nor the profundities of his subsequent books, it has a basic and impersonal quality of different value. Working from first principles, it probably constructs a system clearer, more comprehensive and more objectively convincing, than any comparable work, in English, of our century. We must hope for a reissue.

PART FOUR

Totalities

CHAPTER XV

Excalibur: an essay on Tennyson

The Times Literary Supplement, 10 October 1942; reprinted in *Hiroshima,* 1946. My text and references follow the Macmillan 'complete' edition of 1932 (originally 1894).

ANTHOLOGIES ARE ALWAYS as likely to damage as to enhance a poet's reputation, and those who think of Tennyson primarily as the author of 'The Brook', 'The Lady of Shalott', the songs from *The Princess* and – to name a more important poem – 'The Lotos-Eaters', might remember that such popular favourites have been selected not by the author but by the anthologists. In the mass of Tennyson's work the delicate and rich craftsmanship of these lyrics is of slight comparative importance. Nor is it enough to concentrate on those gems of gossamer apprehension, capturing nature's miracles in a lightning focus of phrase and image, such as the poet himself has described in unconscious self-definition in his address to Vergil. Technical appreciation in itself is always as likely to fog as to elucidate our understanding. A comprehensive judgement must be based rather on an unwavering search for the major outlines, the dominant symbolisms and massed colourings of a poet's total achievement, until from the dissolving clouds the living structure appears.

To such an understanding Tennyson is revealed as a great national poet. His early 'Palace of Art' describes his rejection of a limited romanticism and a corresponding will to raise the inert mass of communal evil to his own, poetic, level; rather as Prospero draws the evils of society into the charmed circle of his magic island.

Risks there may be. Tennyson's adulatory and military excursions appear on occasion no more than competent laureate hackwork; but these are short and unimportant. More characteristic is the smouldering anger of his early sonnets on Napoleon and the partition of Poland and the grim ferocity, near the end of his life, of his general condemnation in 'The Dawn' (1892):

> Red of the Dawn!
> Screams of a babe in the red-hot palms of a Moloch of Tyre,
>   Man with his brotherless dinner on man in the tropical wood,
> Priests in the name of the Lord passing souls through fire to the fire,
>   Head-hunters and boats of Dahomey that float upon human blood!
>
> Red of the Dawn!
> Godless fury of peoples, and Christless frolic of kings,
>   And the bolt of war dashing down upon cities and blazing farms,
>   For Babylon was a child new-born, and Rome was a babe in arms,
> And London and Paris and all the rest are as yet but in leading-strings.

Amid such sinks of iniquity it is not strange that

> . . . the press of a thousand cities is prized for it smells of the beast,
> Or easily violates virgin Truth for a coin or a cheque.

The attack, powerful in the first, attains to violence in the second 'Locksley Hall' (1886):

> From the golden alms of Blessing man had coin'd himself a curse:
> Rome of Caesar, Rome of Peter, which was crueller? which was worse?

Man's inhumanity not only to man but to the beasts also is, in the manner of John Cowper Powys today, emphasized:

> Are we devils? Are we men?
> Sweet St. Francis of Assisi, would that he were here again,
>
> He that in his Catholic wholeness used to call the very flowers
> Sisters, brothers – and the beasts – whose pains are hardly less than ours!

Such realism forbids any easy faith in reform: the 'present' must be held 'fatal daughter of the past' and those who think otherwise are cauterizingly handled:

> Tumble Nature heel o'er head, and, yelling with the yelling street,
> Set the feet above the brain and swear the brain is in the feet.

Bring the old dark ages back without the faith, without the hope,
Break the State, the Church, the Throne, and roll their ruins down
the slope.

The attack is the more merciless for its preservation of sanity.

Tennyson's satiric fury never becomes suicidal, as does Swift's,
though it can compass a gloom comparable with Hardy's, as in
this, from *In Memoriam* (1833-50):

> 'The stars,' she whispers, 'blindly run;
> A web is wov'n across the sky;
> From out waste places comes a cry,
> And murmurs from the dying sun.'

(III)

The resigned solemnity and falling rhythms of *In Memoriam* are
deeply characteristic: how often in Tennyson, as in the western
voyage of 'Ulysses' and the dwindling barge of 'The Passing of
Arthur' (1869; expanded from 'Morte D'Arthur', 1842), the tragic
intuition clothes itself in some sunset image of a great good falling
below man's horizon; like 'great Orion sloping slowly to the West'
in 'Locksley Hall' (1842). And yet the cosmic pessimism is not
final. Man 'who roll'd the psalm to wintry skies' (*In Memoriam*,
LVI) cannot be destined to futility, and there is a recurring tendency, clearly formulated in two slight pieces 'By an Evolutionist'
(1889) and 'The Making of Man' (1892), to place his agonies and
crimes within the greater context of religious hope and vast time-
periods of evolution. 'What will our children be', Tennyson asks
in 'The Dawn', 'the men of a hundred thousand, a million summers
away?' We are as yet 'far from the noon of man'. His imagination
wanders continually among those justifying mysteries of the infinite which to Tolstoy also, as William James records, proved a
redeeming thought at the climax of his spiritual suffering. So
Tennyson ranges across not centuries, but aeons, searching for
that far-off splendour 'to which the whole creation moves' (*In
Memoriam*, CXXXI). Such is the stage-setting, infinite in depth
and vista, for his 'imperialism'.[1]

Maud (1855) is the heart of his life's work; it is, as he aptly

[1] Tennyson's hopes were not limited to evolution on earth. He had strong
spiritualistic insights. *In Memoriam* contains some of the best writing on spirit-
communion in our literature. See XLI, XLIII-XLVII, LI, LXXXII, LXXXV,
XCII-XCIV (stanzas of the last used for the Spiritualists' National Union Hymn
Book, 80).

named it, his *Hamlet*. The hero suffers the usual Tennysonian
inroads of social revulsion from the supposed 'blessings of
Peace', now rendered a 'curse' by man's greed and lusts, filmed
over with shallow talk of human 'advance':

> Is it peace or war? Civil war, as I think, and that of a kind
> The viler, as underhand, not openly bearing the sword.

(I. i. 7)

The social oppression of his own century when 'chalk and alum
and plaster are sold to the poor for bread' (I. i. 10), is seen as
directly in line with ancient pagan cruelties, and war is invoked as,
at least, a grim relief:

> Is it peace or war? better, war! loud war by land and by sea,
> War with a thousand battles, and shaking a hundred thrones.

(I. i.12)

On this barren tract of reviling and self-reviling rises the dawn of
young love, peopling the desert with colour, rising to the flower-
chorus in the garden. But, as the tragic situation matures, a new,
Timon-like intensity replaces both melodramatic horror and
sentimental idealism:

> Arise, my God, and strike, for we hold Thee just,
> Strike dead the whole weak race of venomous worms,
> That sting each other here in the dust;
> We are not worthy to live.

(II. i. 2)

So the poem tunnels the underworld of madness to re-emerge
after its many and varied modulations into the stately periods
of a selfless, national, devotion, pitted against an 'iron tyranny'
and 'giant liar', with a faith in a land 'that has lost for a little her
lust of gold', and in the heroism of its sons (III. vi. [i]. 2, 4).

Tennyson's imperial beliefs follow the tradition of Cranmer's
prophecy in Shakespeare's *Henry VIII*, Milton, Pope's 'Windsor
Forest' (with the satires as a necessary complement), Burke and
Wordsworth. The democratic principle is felt as balanced, indeed
preserved, by the Crown, as with 'freedom in her regal seat of
England' (*In Memoriam*, CIX). To this greater royalty of our
'crown'd republic' the Queen herself, called 'loyal to the royal
in thyself', must subscribe ('To the Queen', following *Idylls of the
King*, 1869); empire existing not to repress but to 'make the bounds

of freedom wider yet' ('To the Queen', 1851). For Britain is high priest and missionary of Freedom, addressed in some early lines in 'Of old sat Freedom on the Heights' (1833) as:

> Grave mother of majestic works,
>   From her isle-altar gazing down,
> Who, God-like, grasps the triple forks,
>   And, King-like, wears the crown.

Her favour is not won by the removal of checks; rather, as in his poem 'Freedom' (1885), Tennyson envisages a slow, laborious process, the hard-won provinces of liberation only with great difficulty captured. In such a process Great Britain is seen in 'England and America in 1782' (1833) as central:

> Whatever harmonies of law
>   The growing world assume,
> Thy work is thine – The single note
> From that deep chord which Hampden smote
>   Will vibrate to the doom.

This strong belief is summed best in certain lines from the 'Ode on the Death of the Duke of Wellington' (1854):

> O Statesmen, guard us, guard the eye, the soul
> Of Europe, keep our noble England whole,
> And save the one true seed of freedom sown
> Betwixt a people and their ancient throne. . . .
> For, saving that, ye help to save mankind
> Till public wrong be crumbled into dust,
> And drill the raw world for the march of mind,
> Till crowds at length be sane and crowns be just.

'Crowds' and 'crowns': the balance so carefully worked out in Britain's history is exactly preserved by her greatest poets. In Tennyson the complexities of the immediate are justly handled, and the vast future always remembered in terms of which man as at present constituted remains a 'raw' recruit.

In 'Locksley Hall' (1842), freedom widens through conflict to world-order:

> For I dipt into the future, far as human eye could see,
> Saw the Vision of the world, and all the wonder that would be;
>
> Saw the heavens fill with commerce, argosies of magic sails,
> Pilots of the purple twilight, dropping down with costly bales;

Heard the heavens fill with shouting, and there rain'd a ghastly dew,
From the nations' airy navies grappling in the central blue;

Far along the world-wide whisper of the south-wind rushing warm,
With the standards of the peoples plunging thro' the thunderstorm;

Till the war-drum throbb'd no longer, and the battle-flags were furl'd
In the Parliament of Man, the Federation of the World.

Tennyson believes that this great process pivots on the integrity of Britain.

Naturally enough he was impelled to express his acute sense of historical Britain in dramatic form; passing, rather like his hero in *Maud*, from personal revulsion to the discipline of historical research and free air of impersonal drama. His main plays, *Harold* (1876), *Queen Mary* (1875) and *Becket* (comp. 1879), investigate key-moments in our history untouched by Shakespeare, to whose work they constitute an invaluable though neglected addition. It is to be questioned whether those who dismiss Tennyson with a snap judgement have ever read these plays: it is almost certain that they cannot have acted in them.[1] The blank verse, unlike Hardy's, is as dramatically varied and forceful as Shakespeare's, and to be rigidly distinguished from the simple falling rhythms of his narrative manner. Here the language often holds the lightning transitions of high dramatic psychology. It can compass a noble dignity, as in William of Normandy's concluding speech in *Harold*, with weighty pauses conveying quietude after battle and a sense of Britain's futurity descending on her almost dazed conqueror:

> Wrap them together in a purple cloak
> And lay them both upon the waste sea-shore
> At Hastings, there to guard the land for which
> He did forswear himself. . . . Since I knew battle,
> And that was from my boyhood, never yet –
> No, by the splendour of God – have I fought men
> Like Harold and his brethren, and his guard
> Of English. Every man about his king
> Fell where he stood. They loved him: and, pray God

---

[1] My own experience was gained in dramatic recitals, like those I did of Shakespeare, during the last war.

> My Normans may but move as true with me
> To the door of death. Of one self-stock at first,
> Make them again one people – Norman, English;
> And English, Norman; we should have a hand
> To grasp the world with, and a foot to stamp it
> Flat. Praise the Saints. It is over. No more blood!
> I am king of England, so they thwart me not,
> And I will rule according to their laws.
>
> (V. ii)

The linear or phrasal rhythms normally lift upwards, as dramatic speech should, ready to rise in *Becket* to a towering Shakespearian conception of awakened tragic passion:

> Back, I say!
> Go on with the office. Shall not Heaven be served
> Though earth's last earthquake clash'd the minster-bells,
> And the great deeps were broken up again,
> And hiss'd against the sun?
>
> (V. iii)

The last act of *Becket* stands surely among the chief glories of our stage. An equal dramatic mastery characterizes the pointed reserve of the description of Cranmer's end, in *Queen Mary*.[1]

All three plays are seriously concerned with (1) the conflict of Church and State and (2) Britain's relation to the continent of Europe. They are, moreover, deeply though unobtrusively imbued with feeling for England's peculiar toughness and integrity, as in Harold's boast of the innate honesty of his subjects, or Becket's care, beyond all other allegiances, for what he calls 'the mother church of England, my Canterbury' (V. ii), and his dying prayer to its 'tutelar' saints; or in so strikingly significant a touch in *Queen Mary* as Howard's question concerning Cranmer:

> Peters, you know me Catholic, but English.
> Did he die bravely? Tell me that, or leave
> All else untold.
>
> (VI. iii)

The central conflicts are given dramatic, never explicit, resolution; but one with the dramatic wholeness is this dominant tone-quality hinting England's greatness. This higher resolving unity

---

[1] Quoted in *The Golden Labyrinth*, where Tennyson's dramas are more fully discussed. *Becket* was composed in 1879 and Henry Irving's version produced in 1893. I have a stage copy of this Lyceum version, well printed and bound, dated 1893.

receives more explicit projection in the two main Arthurian poems, in which Arthur as a mythical hero contains both terms of the opposition in *Becket* – the secular but conscientious wisdom and justice of the king and the religious single-mindedness of the archbishop. Arthur typifies mystic heroism and his sword Excalibur, 'cross-hilted' and presented by the Lady of the Lake, is both a water-symbol and a symbol of Christian empire among mankind always ready to 'reel back into the beast'. On it is written both 'Take me' and 'Cast me away' ('The Coming of Arthur', 1869). Through the legendary hero Tennyson projects his sense of Britain's imperial responsibility, the oncoming of great tumult and the passing of an old order. 'This last, dim, weird battle of the west' ('The Passing of Arthur'), with its 'death-white mist' and blind self-destruction, forecasts the great wars and cloudy incertitudes of our own time.[1] But the uncertainty whether Arthur actually dies or is to return, or whether he really goes to Avilion (for on all this his own mind 'is clouded with a doubt'), reflects Tennyson's own uncertainty in 'To the Queen' (1869) concerning the 'one isle'

> That knows not her own greatness: if she knows
> And dreads it we are fall'n.

It may be for us, in our time, to answer his doubts.

Such a reading of the Arthurian poems aligns them variously with Tennyson's other works, with the well-known vision of world-federation ushered in by aerial commerce and combat in in the first 'Locksley Hall'; with the poignant cry for social and religious regeneration read from the New Year bells in *In Memoriam*; and the quest of the wearied Ulysses deserting an outworn civilization for some nameless world beyond the mysteries of sunset. But perhaps nowhere throughout Tennyson lies a profounder reading, not of any one war but of War itself, its necessity and end, than in those lines from 'Love thou thy Land' (1833):

---

[1] We have Tennyson's own statement: 'The storm will break. I shall not live to see it, but you will . . . I have no doubt the old order will yield place to new, and we shall yet find higher gods than Mammon and materialism. But the storm will come, the battle of Modred in the West will yet be fought' (H. D. Rawnsley, *Memories of the Tennysons*, Glasgow, 1900; 104).

Excalibur: an essay on Tennyson

Even now we hear with inward strife
  A motion toiling in the gloom –
  The Spirit of the years to come
Yearning to mix himself with Life.

A slow-developed strength awaits
  Completion in a painful school;
  Phantoms of other forms of rule,
New Majesties of mighty States –

The warders of the growing hour,
  But vague in vapour, hard to mark;
  And round them sea and air are dark
With great contrivances of Power.

*   *   *

Oh yet, if Nature's evil star
  Drive men in manhood, as in youth,
  To follow flying steps of Truth
Across the brazen bridge of war –

If New and Old, disastrous feud,
  Must ever shock, like armed foes,
  And this be true, till Time shall close,
That Principles are rained in blood;

Not yet the wise of heart would cease
  To hold his hope through shame and guilt,
  But, with his hand against the hilt,
Would pace the troubled land, like Peace;

Not less, though dogs of Faction bay,
  Would serve his kind in deed and word,
  Certain, if knowledge bring the sword,
That knowledge takes the sword away –

Would love the gleams of good that broke
  From either side, nor veil his eyes:
  And if some fearful need should rise
Would strike, and firmly, and one stroke.

*   *   *

Notice that peace is to be won by armed control in association
with a 'love' for what is good in our adversaries, in strong contrast

to the more usual alignment of pacifism linked to hatred. It is an early poem with a vast reach.

Tennyson's imperialism, though firmly held, is based less on what is than what should and must be; and the shadows of futurity falling across his page hold never a merely national reference, nor are even limited to establishment of world-order. They are, rather, cosmic, with glimmering sight, even in the second 'Locksley Hall' through the driven sleet of the scudding rhythms that race and whine like a thousand furies above the desolations of history, of some yet mightier Man or superman under creation with the 'slow-develop'd strength', to borrow a phrase from the New Year bells (*In Memoriam*, CVI), of 'the Christ that is to be'.

ADDITIONAL NOTE, 1968: Since it may be unknown to many readers I append an interesting poem which was printed in the *Twentieth Century* of January 1955 (CLVII. 935). It had been discovered among the papers of the late James Knowles, founder of the *Nineteenth Century*. He left a note saying that in 1870 he and Tennyson had been discussing the conscription for military service of the man who took the part of Christ in the Oberammergau Passion Play; they had also been discussing the Vatican Council's recent promulgation – which was accompanied by a thunderstorm – on Papal infallibility. The note continues: 'Then, quite impromptu, as he lay upon his bed, he made and chanted in a great voice the following lines'. Here is the poem:

THE CHRIST OF AMMERGAU

They made the old Pope God –
  Which God, if He will, may pardon –
And Christ stepped down from the cross,
  Christ came out of the garden.

They made the old Pope God
  While God was rolling his thunder,
And Christ came out from Ammergau
  To massacre, burn, and plunder.

Christ came out from the Play –
  Children, love one another! –
In bitter earnest out he came
  To mash the skull of his brother.

Went to slay and be slain,
  Arm'd with his gun and his sabre,
To show the world he loved himself
  No better than his neighbour.

'Lebe der König!' 'Vive la guerre!'
  Let the brother mangle his brother,
For, O little children, we see by this
  What love ye bear one another.

When in 1954 Miss Eirene Skilbeck, then editor of the *Twentieth Century*, showed me the poem and asked me for an opinion, I at once supported, on general grounds, its authenticity. It has been included, with textual notes indicating what improvements (now in our text) had been made by Tennyson on his first impromptu version, in Professor Christopher Ricks's important new edition (1969) of Tennyson's poems.

CHAPTER XVI

Owen Glendower: Powys

A Review of English Literature, IV. 1; January 1963.

SURELY NO WORK in English shows a more amazing artistry than John Cowper Powys's *Owen Glendower* (U.S.A., 1940; London, 1942); and it is unlikely that we shall find anywhere a work in which so close a regard to historical exactitude is accompanied by so profound a metaphysic.

In the early fifteenth century an old culture was giving way to new trends in art and thought. Innovations in dress, hair-style, interior decoration, furniture, architecture, chimneys, latrines – all are noted in meticulous detail within this storehouse of antiquarian scholarship. These externals contribute to a close realization of the period's mental atmosphere. In Wales we find medieval Christianity cohabiting uneasily with native mythology and superstition; scholasticism is throughout Britain being attacked by Lollardry; there are two Popes – at Rome and at Avignon. In this seething cauldron of clashing cultures and new ways struggling for birth is set the revolt of Wales under Glendower against the King of England starting in the year 1401. Every relevant twist of ecclesiastical and political history is before us: the ways of churchmen and the ways of statesmen, and the psychologies of men varying with the Welsh, or Norman, or Saxon strains that work through them. The Welsh tongue jostles ecclesiastical Latin. Bards and prophets claim to foretell the future; and overbrooding all is a sense of ancient, pre-Brythonic, peoples and their stone records among the mountains.

This massive creation is rich in the sensory life of smell and colour. We scent the perfumes of the chamber, the tang of smoke, the odours of vegetation. Colours are everywhere: the greens, yellows, scarlets, black, silver and gold costumes and accoutrements and the varied colourings of flowers, vegetation, and sky. Red and gold dominate in emblazonry, in people's hair, in the flames of torches reddening or yellowing the passages of castle or fortress, and in the great sun. And there is blood, and the agony of wounds. Over the action loom the twin threats of burning at the stake and the blood-ritual of the scaffold. As dawn's crimson gives way to gold, gold, at high moments, dominates. Owen himself is often described as a golden figure: the dragon-emblems of his standard may be either gold or red (XII. 396, 406, 430, XVIII. 696; and see IX. 289).

Within this variously lurid and splendid world we are aware of human souls. The language of the 'soul' is the eye (722). People in *Owen Glendower* are characterized by their eyes: eyes blue, green, grey, black, hazel, even – for a dragon – red; eyes 'shining' or 'flashing', 'starry' or 'staring', 'carefree' or 'inquisitorial', 'restless' or 'lustrous', or 'frantic' under torment; and the eye of death. We hear of Rhisiart's eyes 'screwed up into burning, glittering points, out of which the soul of the lad rather than his intelligence gleamed' (XI. 383); Father Pascentius' eyes seem to suck up 'the sacredest quintessence' of the 'human souls' into which they thrust (XI. 371), and are said to plunge, like 'ferrets' into a 'rabbit-burrow', into Rhisiart's 'soul' (XVII. 626). With their eyes people search 'each other's souls' (XX. 836); they 'cling' together with them; 'eye-glances' collide like jousters in the lists (X. 333, XI. 347, VI. 160). In contrast words may be no more than 'broken speech' (X. 333).

Though the most awful evil *instincts* abound, Powys's generous humanism has comparatively slight sense of evil *personalities*. Our nearest to that is the background figure of the woman Lowri, who exerts an evil fascination. She is, however, the mother of the exquisite Tegolin for whom she can show genuine feeling and whose visionary excellence affects her (XVIII. 691); and she ends in slave-like devotion to a man whom she loves (XXI. 903). Similarly the brutal David Gam becomes a faithful and dog-like servant. The one-eyed prophet of Derfel, Crach Ffinnant, may be allowed, with reservations, his subversive place. Our worst condemnation here is accorded the company of women, Lowri included, as they desecrate the corpses after the battle of Bryn

Glas; and the vivisectional experiment on a dog, attended by both Lowri and Crach Ffinnant, of the repellent but scarcely delineated Gilles de Pirogue.

Apart from Lowri and Tegolin and the lovable dwarf Sibli, the women are not outstandingly drawn; they exist mainly in terms of the men's thoughts and desires. The gallery of men is varied and rich.

Father Pascentius, the authority on Thomas Aquinas, has for eyes what seem 'a pair of shiny blacknesses peering out with indestructible vivacity from a thatched porch' (XIII. 445). They seem 'to feel, and smell, and hear' (XIII. 466). Symbolizing medieval scholasticism, they are simultaneously all-devouring and all-penetrating; and so beyond all ordinary 'human feeling' (XIII. 444). But he is not unlikable. His embracing Catholicism, in a passage of deep humour, readily finds a theological defence for the uncompromising Lollard, Master Brut (VII. 232-6); he is a shocked opposer of de Pirogue; and there is warmth in his love of rare herbs. In contrast the blue-eyed Brut is a forecast of Protestantism; a forthright and indomitable person organizing games for the young with high-pressure *bonhomie*, utterly convinced of Jesus' living presence at his elbow, extremely practical, irrepressibly optimistic and sometimes a bore; and when faced with burning, heroic almost beyond belief. There is no favouritism: each is drawn with a whimsically critical insight that includes admiration.

Some of our people we already know in Shakespeare: Hal, first presented as a pale long-faced boy; Hotspur, a kindly man less instinctively attuned, despite his reputation, to fighting than to diplomacy (XI. 355); the Lollard Sir John Oldcastle, a blend of grand gentleman and Shakespeare's Falstaff (XII. 399, XIII. 465, XIX. 776-82, XX. 835, 838); and King Henry IV, a terrifying study of sleepless guilt (XX. 845-55). Shakespearian reminiscence is frequent in phraseology and suggestion.

Much of the action is seen from the viewpoint of the young Rhisiart-ap-Owen who becomes Glendower's secretary. He is a studious youth legally trained and aspiring to statesmanship. With women, though he avoids sexual intercourse (XVIII. 715), he is subject to dangerous lusts and loveless magnetism; he itches to fondle beautiful boys, he is capable of an idyllic romance with Owen's daughter Catherine, and he has in him a vein of sheer sadism (II. 35, IV. 91). Through all runs his association with Tegolin to whom he looks for comfort, regards as 'part' of himself (XVIII. 699), and eventually marries. He is not heroic: he can certainly fight, but on two occasions (II. 45, XII. 386, XVII. 627) courage only comes through a possession beyond his control; and he is willing that Tegolin should save him from the scaffold at the cost of her honour (XX. 835-8). His main life-impulses are: to compass a sexual love with domination (XVIII. 717); and, yet stronger, to sacrifice himself for Glendower (X. 335-6, XI. 349-50, XI. 366, XII. 387-8, XVIII. 716-17). During the story the 'geir-falcon gaze' (XVII. 661) of his eyes forecasts the judge he is to become under Henry V. Rhisiart's development from an adventuring youth to a sedate judge is so well handled that it appears in retrospect inevitable.

Owen Glendower himself, the shifting colour of whose eyes varies from grey-blue to sea-green (V. 120, XVII. 767), may seem to be less a person than a presence as he moves through the narrative 'like an abstracted armorial ghost' (XVIII. 714-15). His personality is hard to capture, and yet his appearance, thoughts and actions are meticulously described; what blurs him is the magnitude and depth of Powys's conception.

Glendower is a great gentleman and a fine warrior. He studies astrology and has the reputation of a magician. He is as closely attuned to Welsh mythology as to Christian belief, and is influenced by the semi-pagan cult of Saint Derfel (VII. 242, IX. 290, 300, XII. 392, 400, 405, XV. 538, XVII. 665). He is genuinely angered by English tyranny (XIII. 464), but why he leads the revolt, and what is to come of it, remains mostly vague (XII. 419-420, 432-3, XV. 541, XVII. 626).

Before his coronation as 'Prince of Wales' he deliberately breaks his crystal to avoid 'meddling with the future', and prays that the universal 'purpose' should remain dark (XII. 393). He is henceforth transformed into a 'medium' for the 'high invisible Powers', acting through an 'appalling passivity' at whatever cost in others' suffering (XVI. 561-2). Internally this means trusting the irrational, even demoniac, powers within himself (XVII. 647, XX. 810-11); he, too, has a strain of the sadistic, and on one grim occasion gives it rein (XIII. 438-40). And yet he wears a penitential 'mail shirt' (XII. 393, XVI. 573) and is – unlike Rhisiart – at his best when pain or failure enable him to test 'the resources of his spirit'

(XIX. 758). He is tragically (VII. 257) conceived and empowered, and in this endurance is a personification of Wales (XIX. 781, XXI. 885-6, 889-90, 914).

He attributes his revolt's failure to his having allowed himself, despite his earlier renunciation, to be influenced by the prophet Hopkin: 'one-eyed' men like Crach Ffinnant the prophet of Derfel are his danger; and he should have made terms with the King of England (XX. 812-13).

He certainly has about him 'something unearthly' (XVIII. 696) – the phrase another liberator, Byron, applied to himself (*Childe Harold*, IV. 137) – and it is generally supposed that spirits are at his command (e.g. XIX. 728). But his magic exists really in one faculty called by Powys the 'exteriorizing of his soul' (XII. 427), leaving his eyes, its expression, inanimate (V. 120-1) in such a way as to view all immediate concerns, himself included, with impersonal objectivity (e.g. XIX. 729). His culminating achievement comes at the end when as an outlaw in hiding he succeeds, by what is nowadays termed 'astral projection', in creating a vision of himself, accompanied by a blast of *cold air*, to recipients at a distance (XXI. 904-6, 913-14). His powers are in accord with the findings of our own psychic science. When, while fondling a cat his dead brother had loved, he becomes aware of and talks to that brother, we have a neat blend of modern psychometry through the 'mediumship' (XIX. 752) of the cat with old beliefs regarding familiar spirits in feline guise. Powys shows uncanny skill in disentangling the genuine from the superstitious. Owen himself moves stealthily like 'a great golden cat' (XVII. 655). Gold is his colour: beard, armour, accoutrements, robes, circlet, all are golden. In his 'fantastically gorgeous attire' he appears like a 'golden image' (XIV. 511). He responds, brilliantly, to the sun (XIX. 769).

The darker mysteries of mortal existence and the lusts and other powers that invade it are throughout juxtaposed to three figures of ideal beauty or goodness: the page Elphin, the itinerant Franciscan, Mad Huw, and Tegolin. All are bisexually conceived.

Male youth is idealized. Owen's son Meredith is a young man of grave, ironic and in part effeminate charm, with a sweet, spiritualized smile (III. 48-9, V. 137, XXI. 937). Rhisiart is in danger from beautiful pages (VII. 197-200, 209-10, VIII. 269, XVI. 604) and sees a fearful example of society's revenge on a homosexual's comparatively innocent love-approaches (VII. 253); and yet on one occasion the young Rawlff's proximity raises him *above* the 'worser' fascination of Lowri (VIII. 269). The horrors of war are related, as in Vergil and Shakespeare, to slaughtered youth: Rhisiart's baptism of blood at Bryn Glas is the ghastly driving of his sword into the mouth of a 'freckled' boy with whom he had recently exchanged smiles; and the pathetically ambitious Rawlff is knighted by Owen, on the field, before death (XV. 550, 558, XV. 553-4).

Our most important youth is the page 'Elphin', a name already used in *A Glastonbury Romance*. He is presented first as a shy, dark-eyed boy of exquisite, half-feminine delicacy in face and limb, 'girlish' and 'slender' (VII. 197, XVI. 604); growing to 'a grave and comely youth' (XVII. 653), he is made a herald (XVIII. 689-90); and he develops a gift for painting, concentrating on visionary unicorns with human expressions (XIX. 745-6). Sexual activity repels him (XIX. 733, XX. 806); a seraphic equivalent to esoteric symbolism, he is virginal as his unicorns; he would like to envisage human affairs through the artistry of heraldic beasts (XX. 794). His beauty is such that once he looks 'more like a Herald of Saint Gabriel than of any earthly prince' (XIX. 748). He is not however sentimentalized. He can be terrified, is no warrior and cannot watch the sacking of a village (XIII. 475-7, XX. 801, 814). His companion, the tough boy Iago, contrasts with him as 'cynicism' in contrast to 'idealism' (XIX. 746).

Elphin is a realistic study in sweetness of temperament. When we last see him he has developed from the virginal bisexuality of the youth 'Elphin' to the asexual maturity of the 'gentle-hearted' (XXI. 871) priest, 'Father Sulien'. As tutor to Owen's grandson he shows a parental care, suiting his office; and he has the sensibility of a woman (XXI. 875). At Owen's dying words he alone hears them as coming not from Owen's physical presence but outside it (XXI. 925-6). Such seraphic persons are traditional but perhaps nowhere else shall we find so subtle and realistic a delineation.

Our story remembers the ill-fated Edward II who suffered hideously for love of Gaveston (VII. 199, XIV. 494); and Richard II, of similar propensities (VII. 199); and yet, despite these tragic examples, we remain impressed by the perceptions

symbolized by Elphin and his unicorns. Moreover, Richard II
lives for us through the Franciscan friar, Mad Huw, our next
wholly lovable person, whose obsession it is that Richard, 'God's
wounded rose', 'sweet passion-flower' and 'sacrifice' of 'love', is
alive yet, a 'sacrifice for us all', who will save Wales by his 'blood'
and who, knowing the 'secret' of love more potent than war, will
prevail over all oppressors. He is, for Mad Huw, 'my hero, my
saint, my rose of Britain' (II. 32, IV. 100, 109, 111, 119, XIII. 470).
He is all but another Christ. 'Saint Francis is here with me,'
Richard tells Huw, 'and Saint Francis says, "To love is better
than to think"' (XVIII. 709-10). Mad Huw is bisexually conceived, having 'beautiful womanish eyes' and refusing to regard
a woman's wearing male dress as sinful (XVIII. 685, 687). His
story comes to a climax when, confronted by the King, Henry IV,
he denounces him in 'scoriac' words (XX. 853).

Our third 'bisexual' person is Tegolin, illegitimate daughter of
a priest and the evil Lowri; her hair is 'blood-red' and 'flaming'
(V. 142, XI. 343). She appears first in page's dress as Mad Huw's
devoted guardian, and we are as continually reminded of her
'boyish', as of Elphin's 'girlish', appearance (e.g. X. 316, XIV.
484, 487): Mad Huw forgets that she is a woman (III. 59). When
soon after their meeting she and Rhisiart sleep together in a barn,
sexual activity is not engaged and his feelings, despite his instincts
for domination, are in this bisexual experience only 'amorous'
with 'a tender, sweet, diffused sensation' (VII. 250). Thenceforward she is his counsellor as well as Mad Huw's protector and
'mother' (XIV. 519); she becomes part of Rhisiart's 'natural background', like the 'earth' (XIV. 502, 511). Her feelings for him are
'protective'; when in anguish for another love he falls at her feet
in tears, as at a mother's, for 'comfort' (XVII. 647, XIV. 520,
XVIII. 685, 689, XX. 831). She is 'part' of him (XVIII. 699).

From a 'delicate' figure in page's dress she grows into a 'lovely
girl' in a woman's (IV. 118, XVII. 647); and then she changes
again when Owen, influenced by Hopkin's prophecy, decides that
this 'Maid of Edeyrnion' should lead his army in armour, like a
precursor of Saint Joan; and at this moment her 'white-and-gold
form with its burning hair' becomes as an 'apotheosis' to be gazed
on with 'awe', beyond all imagination (XVIII. 691-5). When
after the expedition has failed she visits Rhisiart, now her husband,
in prison, and finds him ready to accept for his own sake her

sexual sacrifice to another, her forgiveness is not even recorded (XX. 838); we know it.

Like Elphin she graduates from bisexual youth to the parental; but the maternal element, and strength, was with her throughout. She is stronger than Rhisiart (XX. 837), perhaps stronger than anyone. She dominates, often unobtrusively, as a 'fiery flower' (XIV. 495), a spiritual yet intensely human and saving force. It is she who saves Master Brut from the stake.

The historical novelist enjoys a god-like view of temporal sequences and on them *Owen Glendower* plays some fascinating variations.

The people see their own time much as we see ours. 'Don't be silly', someone says, 'we're in the fifteenth century, not the fifth' (XVIII. 681). In poetry Owen's preference of past grandeurs to the stylistic trickery of a new realism has analogies in the age of Euripides and today (XII. 389-90, XIII. 473-4, XXI. 917). Often our knowledge of the future adds significance to what is said. A later sociology is embryonic in Master Sparrow's reiterated expectance of a people's uprising independent of nations (XII. 423-6, XV. 542, 553, XVI. 560, 581, XVII. 626, XVIII. 692, XX. 788). Rhisiart's over-confident assertion that Brut's protestantism can never touch more than a 'few', since the 'philosophy of religion' can arouse no response in 'simple brains', is a brilliant stroke (XI. 342). The highly cultured Owen recalls having seen 'a fragment in the Tuscan vernacular about Paradise', but cannot recall the author (XIX. 722).

Especially neat is Powys's handling of prophecy. The seer Hopkin predicts the crowning of a Welsh prince in London, the anointing of a king by a girl in armour, and a suicidal war in which mankind will perish. The first two events Owen, to his cost, relates to himself; and yet in these Hopkin was genuinely touching future history, and may have been right in the third. At the signing of the Tripartite Pact by which Britain was to be divided up, Glendower invites Hopkin to attend, and he does so, to the reader's amusement, in full professional style, wearing a dress covered by zodiacal designs and with brazier, divining rod, and cinnamon sticks. Yet Rhisiart, while sensing the smell of the old prophet's perspiration and chemicals (XVII. 663), becomes aware of an extraordinary 'Presence', which he knows is about to make a certain objection regarding boundaries; he then sees

Hotspur's sword pointing at the map, though Hotspur, who is present on this occasion in Shakespeare, was already dead; and he hears in Hotspur's voice the Shakespearian lines

See how this river comes me cranking in . . .

Though Hotspur was dead, it seemed like 'a ghost out of the future' (XVII. 661). All Rhisiart knows is that he heard Hotspur's voice like a 'great and gallant ghost' from 'beyond space and time' speaking these 'wanton', 'whimsical' and 'careless' lines (XVII. 663). The metaphysic of it is discussed: it was a 'timeless' and 'psychic' experience of some 'inner reality' such as great poetry reveals (XVII. 659-60); the lines seemed to tell 'the truth of the present out of the future' (XVII. 661). Rhisiart had touched some super-temporal Shakespearian dimension. Meanwhile, despite his superstitious paraphernalia, the powers of Hopkin, who appears to have functioned without knowing it as medium, have again been illustrated. Though he may have little personal understanding of them he is rightly called 'inspired' (XVIII. 674).

Equally powerful is our mystique of the past. Ancient objects are venerated: Rhisiart's 'antique' Crusader's sword (XV. 538, I. 10), the sacred sword of Eliseg (VIII. 270), Owen's ancestral 'golden-hilted sword' and 'antique' lance (XII. 397, XX. 815). We are aware of the older pre-Brythonic race of which Owen has in him a strain (XIX. 760, XXI. 889), and of giant figures of mythology and legend. 'The past' says Owen, 'is the eternal', and opens 'into another dimension' (XII. 415). We have glimpses, as though through 'a crack in the visible' (XXI. 925; and see XVII. 651, XXI. 937), of some such 'over-dimension' (II. 45, XVI. 592, 611, XX. 861) 'outside space' (XIX. 722, XXI. 917). And what of death? For some the problem is beyond human discussion (XIX. 775-7); and yet Owen can sense 'the souls of the dead' (XII. 417) and half-expects and craves conscious survival (XII. 393, XIX. 753). A corpse is irrelevant to the 'indestructible spirit' which we have loved; and true lovers are together in life or death (XX. 865-6).

And yet we are not in a world ruled by abstractions. Indeed, our strongest advocate of death as the supreme good – by which he means loss of personal identity (XIX. 775) – is the 'neolithic giant' (XIV. 495) Broch-o'-Meifod, all but a creature of pre-history believing in the deathly other-life and enduring power of rocks and stones, and claiming this to be the next revelation for man (XIII. 456, 472, XIV. 519, XV. 538). He is ancient Wales incarnate – its mists and mountains, its rocks and grey slate – who 'in his strange yearning for the impersonal, for the non-human' is one with the landscape 'along which the majestical spirits of the past might move in tremendous procession towards the far-off mountain-peaks' (XXI. 887). He seems to grow from the earth and from forgotten peoples whose magical secrets are housed in magical names (XII. 413, XV. 538), and whose wisdom was good, the remains of their altars showing no receptacles for blood (XII. 419, XXI. 911). Broch easily terrifies the vivisector, de Pirogue (XVII. 634-5). Though he is in battle a stalwart supporter of Owen, he with his wife exist as a standard of judgement, like the hills themselves, in comparison with which politics are dwarfed or condemned. His wife, regarding Owen as a Brythonic newcomer, curses him with 'the oldest curse in the world', 'the curse of the water and the wind' (XII. 433). Even so Owen, as protagonist in action, has a different honour, and at his best moments draws strength from the 'blazing orb' (XV. 549), the sun.

Natural descriptions are exactly integrated into the story. Its fierce events are reflected in references to such predatory or ominous birds as the eagle, falcon, hawk, owl and raven. Twice a golden sun gives place to a weird and fearful, *female*, moonlight: when the 'golden haze' and autumnal bracken of the journey to Mathrafal are followed by the moon-lit curses of Broch's wife (XII. 432-3); and again when the great dawn before Bryn Glas is followed by the women's hideous desecration of corpses beneath a 'ghoulish half-moon' (XV. 457, 555). The human fecundity and tangled instincts of our story are reflected in the dripping vegetation and tangled undergrowth of the Forests of Tywyn (XVI. 581-92). Happier is the castle of Harlech, by a magical sea where 'the golden sun-path upon the in-rolling tide' (XVII. 623) accompanies the narrative's highest crest of imaginative splendour before tragedy ensues. Harlech presents a *blending of sun and sea*, which means a blending of the principles of upstanding action and elemental endurance, of Owen and Broch, the union twice compacted in our sight of Broch as a creature of *gleaming* sea-shells and gulls' feathers and with limbs dripping from the waters the while his bald head is 'aureoled by sun-sparkles' (XVII. 633, XIX. 774).

Owen Glendower: *Powys*

Powys is the greatest master of natural description in our literature, but what is so marvellous about *Owen Glendower* is the way each description is exactly and variously integrated into the multifarious twistings and turnings of the story.

There is more in this book of nearly a thousand large pages, as meticulous in antiquarian exactitude and all the ramifications and cross-currents of narrative detail as it is in the deepest plumbings of human and cosmic speculation, than we have the right to demand of human composition. For we have said nothing of the horses; of the mare with her vision, at a key-moment, of the Mother-Mare of creation (XVIII. 701-2), or of Rhisiart's faithful piebald pageant-trained Griffin of heraldic name – 'a horse', as the grave judge recalls later, 'of wonderful colours, a grand, tall, *old* horse, a law-abiding, obedient horse' (XXI. 901). Horses are naturally vivid in such a story. The chivalric note was fiercer at the start when Owen Glendower's bard, at first small beside his great harp, became 'a towering, formless, shapeless personality' as he shook from it an elemental music and a vibrant and heroic song, in rhythms ancient as the hills (VI. 154-7). At the 'wild Pendragon chant' accompanying Tegolin's instatement, the 'bardic mystery' embraces the Christian, as though pointing to some distant synthesis (XVIII. 693, 713).

In *Owen Glendower* we have, as Dryden once said of Chaucer, 'God's plenty'.

ADDITIONAL NOTE: It is a pleasure to point to John A. Brebner's important article '*Owen Glendower*: The Pursuit of the Fourth Dimension', *The Anglo-Welsh Review*, Pembroke Dock, XVIII. 42; February 1970.

CHAPTER XVII

Francis Berry

SECTION I AND parts of Section 2 of the following essay appeared first as an article in *The Poetry Review*, XXXII, May-June 1941, which was reprinted in my *Hiroshima* in 1946. A brief appreciation of Berry's poem 'Spain, 1939: from Devon' appeared in *The Wind and the Rain*, I. 4; Spring 1942.

Berry's poetry has been published in *Gospel of Fire*, preface by G. Wilson Knight (Elkin Mathews & Marrot), 1933; *Snake in the Moon; Poems* (Williams & Norgate), 1936; *The Iron Christ* (Williams & Norgate), 1938; *Fall of a Tower and Other Poems* (The Fortune Press), 1943; *Murdock and Other Poems* (Andrew Dakers), 1947. The main contents of these volumes, with the exception of *Gospel of Fire* from which a small selection only was preserved, are collected in *The Galloping Centaur, Poems 1933-1951* (Methuen), 1952; new edition, 1970. Recent volumes are: *Morant Bay and Other Poems* (Routledge & Kegan Paul), 1961; and *Ghosts of Greenland: Poems* (Routledge & Kegan Paul), 1966. Many of the poems have been broadcast.

Francis Berry's most important literary studies are: *Poets' Grammar*, 1958; *Poetry and the Physical Voice*, 1962; and *The Shakespeare Inset*, 1965.

I

Great literature could be defined as the union of realism and mystery. Yet work catering for either extreme alone will always more easily find a following, since every such union, though itself the justification of literature and secret of its eternal appeal, is at first

baffling, if not repellent, to the age of its creation. The work of
Francis Berry is in this more comprehensive tradition.

The Romantics laboured to reveal life and personality in the
natural universe. Wordsworth's mountains are live presences and
Shelley's *Prometheus Unbound* dramatizes the awakening of Earth.
Poetry in our day has concentrated on city-life and sordid detail.
Now whereas this strain in Eliot, though I do not suggest that his
poetry was ever limited to such effects, may be balanced against
his move in *Ash-Wednesday* to religious dogma, Francis Berry
advances to realization of the dormant magic within city streets
themselves. In *Gospel of Fire* his first lyric 'Duae Voces' significantly rates a barrel-organ above a cathedral, and is followed by a
remarkable characterization in 'The Lamp-Post' of 'King Lamp-
post', head and shoulders, 'like Saul', above men; feeling into its
personal existence and starry imaginations, its dislike of summer
and enjoyment of extended life through long winter nights. 'The
Beggar's Soul' contrasts the outer appearance and street music of
a one-legged organ-grinder with a romantic soul-energy which
arches up in victor-music towards spectacular and ecstatic chariot-
mastery and triumphal speed in ancient Rome; to fall suddenly
back, in the last line, to the limping, grinding melody in which
those splendours are *implicit*. In *Snake in the Moon*, 'The Sky
Rocket' pursues a similar course from a dirty bottle through
cosmic and 'cross-spangling' brilliance to a cabbage-patch. Such
arching triumph is a characteristic of Berry's poetry.

Our next lyrics are, unless otherwise designated, from the
volume *Snake in the Moon*.

Today we hear much of 'mechanization'. But whereas so much
of recent poetry falsely, and no doubt quite unintentionally,
subdues human vitality to dead mechanical analogies, we find here
the reverse process, the mechanical being given its due rights of
electric and explosive and often most beautiful vitality, as in 'A
Ride in a Sports Car':

> Streamlined aluminium chastity –
> O Artemis of the Great West road,
> Shifting silver secrets as she flies.
> Her tonneaux like the breasts of foam-born
> Cytherean, furnaced in the factory.
> Wheel-wings Juno-wristed: O miracle
>   Of man-made majesty.

A childlike sense of wonder, perhaps the greatest of all poetic qualities, is maintained. Now clearly so powerful a vitalization of mechanic energy may also – my former objection negated – act *in service to* human life. In 'Adam and Eve' a richly varied and semi-humorous approach compares Eve to 'a piece of the moon', her eyes to 'unsounded lunar craters', with black hair falling 'like a Congo cascade'; and, next, her veins are 'runnels' through a 'marble desert' littered with relics of dark paganism ('tipped-up Dagons, tripped and tumbled-over Magogs'), or – skipping the centuries and narrowing the emphasis to our own place and time – like

> Quicksilver injected into limestone
> Swerving and sizzling with a droning fury,
> Like that stinging insect called mosquito
> Singing, winging, ringing in the aural orifice.
> Or like the road-drill spurting sperm through concrete,
> Screeching elixir through a grinding surface –
> Such were Eve's veins.
> Magnetic wires twisted by turbines,
> Lacing and lashing her flesh in livid ecstasies.

In contrast, sun against moon, we have Adam a 'red man', his blood sun-fired, savage and with 'blazing eyes':

> This Adam must have been a hairy-chested man,
> Making the woodland bracken wobble on its weedy stalks
> To feel him breaking through in vehement venery,
> With spear in knuckling grasp – until he foamed
> At the flat sight of an inland lake,
> Befooled, with dragonflies and heather round him.

Moon and sun preside mischievously over the sexual encounter of which they are themselves cosmic archetypes:

> Sniggering and errant moon! putting out her tongue
> To smoothe her chapped lips, deceitfully:
> 'You're in the know! – stainer of honours.'

So Moon addresses Sun. Remembering Milton we might regard the poem as iconoclastic. But the end holds a compacted

romantic pregnancy at once continuous with and interpretative
of the rest:

> Then Eve received Adam unto her
> Whilst the mist walked round like a wraith,
> And the birds sang,
> And the rose closed with a final puff of perfume.

The compressed vigour is never purely mental, and never orna-
mental, but nature-rooted and organic, like the thick heart of a
cabbage or a tightly-folded rose-bud.

Francis Berry's poetry is rooted in the darkest centres of the
human psyche. It twines deep into physical promptings, deeper
than Lawrence, to a level where of living writers John Cowper
Powys alone provides an analogy; as in 'The Dark Inhabitant' (in
Gospel of Fire) and the title-poem 'Snake in the Moon' – the latter
especially rich in hot sensuous magic. Such Astarte-wisdom
attains full contemporary impact and daylight projection in the
complex fusion of 'Photograph'. Here marvels of man's inventive
genius serve a naïve sensuousness in a cheap advertisement
photo shot through by cosmic mystery. The poem pierces conventional thought-trappings of vulgarity and money-business to
the naked simplicity of the picture's immediate effect. Compression
of phrase and easy cohabitation of usually disparate realms are not
self-consciously forced but well from a depth allowing expression
of superb ease:

> How the camera's enchanted eye
> Can capture heaven with a violet wink!

And

> The camera with his artist chivalry
> Gives me his piercing flash of focus rapture,
> Though you adorn an opening sheet
> Of an illustrated social weekly
> Advertising underwear –
> However mean the purpose of that poise
> Now I admire the camera's darting fire
> That shook the hot heart of the universe
> And gave its bodied beauty
> In a bare instant.

The picture makes us forgive the 'greasy palm' and 'staly craft'
of 'counters', 'cashiers', 'cheques and bills':

Francis Berry

And if I meet that rotund business-man,
I'll say, You surely advertise
Not corset-wear, but Paradise!

The subject might be called trivial, the instincts involved are those usually termed 'baser'. But the poem ends in a vivid self-interpretation, with the swiftness of a camera's action capturing and revealing the immensities such catch-words disguise:

With a mere click
The camera conceiving you
Was as a giant in seizure
Who turning to the ground beneath his feet
Beheld another hemisphere of stars.

The poetry of Francis Berry itself acts, precisely, as such a camera.

His range is remarkable, with no personal taboos. In 'Virgin under the Moon',[1] addressed by a devotee to Artemis, chastity is celebrated with equal fervency. His mythological resource, instinctive as Keats's, is rich and varied, passing beyond the Hellenic to oriental paganisms and Norse myth. We find a strong use of Old Testament themes in 'The Book of the Prophet' and 'Moses and the Curate': Berry's poetic interests are simultaneously sensuous and religious.

2

So inclusive an imagination and so direct a response to *energies* makes a poetry peculiarly able to master and interpret the dominant issues of world-affairs today. Francis Berry's *The Iron Christ* is the most deeply relevant war-poem of our time. Its subject is the referring of a dispute between the Argentine and Chile to the British throne for arbitration, and a consequent making from guns of a Christ-figure to be grounded on a mountain frontier separating the disputants. The imaginative setting is vast, especially in mountain-description of a rugged grandeur kin to the giant conceptions of Robinson Jeffers. It is characterized through a series of violent images in all its jagged and inhuman, yet also living, threatening, volcanic power. The Andes are as one great,

---

[1] A short poem, headed with a reference to W. F. Jackson Knight's *Vergil's Troy*. It is not in *The Galloping Centaur*.

tormented, beast, at once nature's rugged formation and prone statue of some giant but subhuman life:

> Stone-transformed, fixed backbone of the beast
> Which heaved its forelegs flat across a continent,
> Expiring hunched, and huge, and harpy-hideous.
> Sharp-dagger thrusts from vertebrae that wrestling with
> Its thighs have torn the piercing passion from its loins,
> Frenzy inculcated by the penal verdict,
> Unreprieved by bearded God, the violent twister
> Of clanging subterranean chains.
> Condemned until the final rending of the world,
> Straddling, till the fork-joint, cracking, splits in twain,
> Life's genitals are spun into the vacuum
> While the broken fragments hiss in flaming currents
> Of roaring tides of hollow winds.

(I)

Ancient myths of giants prisoned beneath volcanoes are constituent; but we feel a grim crucifixion at work; and also a giant thing in bodily dislocation; a self-conflict and disruption *within the physical organism*. Damnation is expressed in an uncouth stone-formation related to primeval nature, beasts, and gigantic, sub-human, tormented life. It is as though our human pain were part of some great cosmic endurance.

The cause of the two nations' dispute is Tierra del Fuego, Land of Fire. The opportunity is seized, and we have some magnificent and apt lines on Prometheus suffering on Caucasus for his theft of fire:

> In fire Man wrestles with his thighs, to sky
> The airy regions to the clanging bars
> And furnaced courts of Jesus and the Virgin . . .

(II)

Man's self-torment is part of a creative, ascending quest, and lusts for sex, power or possession are necessary constituents to some great purpose. Meanwhile, the conflict of nations is as the splitting of a vast brain 'tangled in that territory' and 'split in cranial wrangling'; a 'maddening headache'. Strong physical impressions are throughout preserved, as though the human race were one body, one organism, in physical, self-conflicting agony. Varying claims for land-possession are felt as inevitably controlling

A nation as an individual,
Until the earth itself shall catapult
Its humming weight against a rival order.   (II)

So:

The steady hammer of eternity
Nails a crisis to the present hour.   (II)

The scene is set.
  There follow lines in a more relaxed, softer mode:

Wombs are wonderful, the one that wrought
Young Jesus, those that wrought the first white whales . . .
                                                             (III)

A vast range of human and animal procreation is suggested in
these and the succeeding lines. But there are other 'mechanical'
wombs of man's inventive genius, producing 'siege engines',
compared to dinosaurs 'gluttonous for life', emerging from fur-
nace-factories where 'tired spades push phallically the broken
coals'.
  The people are maddened by war-propaganda and thirst for
blood. There follows a vivid poetic capturing, through a rich
marshalling of pause and repetition, internal assonance and jingle,
of national war-awakening:

People turn like tides to speeches, move
More quickly, blood in tension, hope of change
To purpose, promise of heroic blush.
Masses pool town-squares in swirls, relief
Translates a sacred wish to words: To kill,
Assert the fist – to kill – to crown our race
With virile name, we'll kill, embrace the iron
Of gun or helmet, rejoice in pounding loins
Of squat-mast battleship. We'll kill, we'll kill
To pride the kinship, ancient breed, our blood and soil.
Man-march to kill, the ranks and tanks and flanks,
The cheers, big stance of warrior, recoil and rear
Of rifle-gear, artillery, the bursting fear
Observes race-pride, man-might. Assert and kill,
Hear ancient songs, the brass bands' patriot thrill,
Blood and soil. We'll kill.

The Andes stare down, standing in the cold still.   (III)

Francis Berry

And here is our diagnosis:

> Agony, frustrations, lonely hours,
> Drowned hope, the many omens shouting Yield,
> Withered understandings, throat-sob at night,
> Unforgiving tortures, need resolve.
> So wars come.
> No other way than this? With lighted eyes
> Be dishonest, be the virile child,
> Drug disappointment with a warrior poise . . .   (IV)

Poetic realization and psychological penetration are inter-affective.

There is a sermon (III), again rich with physical images, by Archbishop Benvenuto, urging the people to 'crucify yourselves in a model of Christ' and search out Chilean spouses rather than 'cold graves'. One of the great mountains of the Cordillera de los Andes, Illimani, responds, rumbling with internal pains, growing to 'louder coughings' from the 'intestine'; there is choking and stench, a violent sickness, hot substances demand exit till the agony displaces a 'cold cap of snow', 'fire' proclaiming a 'triumph over ice' (III). Observe that mountain-fire is *at once* the torment *and* the release; just as the Christ is to be made *from*, not merely *instead of*, the guns. Throughout, lust for war is balanced against physical fruition in love; the sexual centres, through a careful deploy of imagery, are kept before us; we watch, as it were, a bending over of a single impulse from one direction to another. Physical impressions are violent.

The Christ-making from guns is subtly manipulated to express regeneration with power, the agony-content of the process serving to preclude any facile play on surface-deep Christian associations. It is no easy, idyllic making: the process is almost horrible. The 'gaping guns', like living things, 'await their execution' while furnaces clamour for their 'victim'. The Christ is made from the guns; the Dionysian energies are to be incorporated. So the workmen are at it feverishly: 'sinews python-toss and writhe in naked backs' (V). What is it all for?

> To make, remake;
> In take
> The old life
> To clamp and rive
> Together someone new instead.

Ears hammered on the head,
Shoulders level glowing
While the pulley slewing
Round, hitches brigand arm.
Thighs lifted from the mass,
Horny torso set in place
Dripping with its natal grease
Bit by bit emerges It,
Gun, Iron, Man, Christ.   (V)

It is a laborious, difficult, painful, yet finally triumphant fabrication. The whole poem, with striking consistency, works in terms of the physical organism, whether in violent biological action – or construction – or in firm, man-made poise and power.

The Christ is made; he has to be placed. Every stage of the journey is vividly presented; trolley, mountain train, mules. The Christ 'moves on'. But he is not, at first, beauteous:

Moves on. And in the smoulderings of his eyes,
Thick nostrils, grime of cheekbones, there is stamped
Crucible embroilings, memories still
Of agony in wet froth; and those lips,
Dense in misery, bear still the thought
Of crawling scum along the copper sides,
Sighing in metallic heat, so unendurably black.
Oils torture now his brow, break and lather
Temples, throbbing from the hammer-hits. . . .   (V)

Nevertheless, still and helpless though the lumbering effigy may seem, there is victory within. Within his very 'stillness' there yet 'lurks a typhoon power' resembling 'Frankenstein's incipient robot stalk'; in him all the horrors of human mechanism are present though now transmuted. For his power is also the power of a martyr 'trussed to stake', 'helpless' yet himself housing, in his very helplessness, a 'gunpowder force' (V). The railway mountain-climb is a slow, midnight, laborious Calvary through jungle. The journey's difficulties, the screaming, skidding engines, the enlisting of a second engine, and last the slipping, sliding, mountain mules, are given with a wealth of vivid detail to realize the ascent, the more descriptively powerful for the midnight setting, as when

sparks
Illumining the Image, random flamings
Feather his jaw and father angry jest.   (VI)

Francis Berry

By an exact stroke of poetic organization all Nature – wild-cat, jaguar, vultures – appears to be angered by, to threaten, this strange, unnatural, intruder:

> A wild-cat spits,
> Eyes focus, green fury, glaze; screech from red throat;
> It vanishes.
>
> (VI)

This snapshot realization of animal vitality, a dramatic miniature relevant to our earlier discussions, keeps the irrational fury of nature's substratum before us as context for the human drama and the making and ascent of the more than natural perfection, the Christ.

The Figure climbs to twenty thousand feet, to a desert plateau where it lies 'glinting blue in steel regard of stars'. Around, all is 'corpse silence'. Soldiers place it on the mule-truck; at last, the summit reached, men of both sides haul with a 'body strain', hands 'of Argentine and Chile mingled', heaving to lift the giant effigy till

> Horizontal to perpendicular
> It marches, notching travelling constellations,
> Grazing Leo, Aquarius, groaning Wain,
> Ratcheting against the Dragon, shaves
> Capricornus; Orion, girdled, threatens,
> Then rocks upon his feet.
>
> (VI)

The visual trickery by which earthly inches may appear to contain infinities of stellar distance is cleverly used to give the Christ a universal dominion. The human meaning of the vertical stance is infused with cosmic triumph as, despite Orion's threats, the Christ 'rocks upon his feet', is gradually *balanced*, every notch of its rise across the stars marked by the 'growl-salute' of guns. They howl again, roar, the Southern Cross shining on 'the dome-bust of the Iron Christ'. Andes acknowledge his dominion, the 'mouth-bleeding' guns – all have *animal* life – recoiling to 'their heavy haunch'. And now

> The Iron Christ stands upon his straddled toes,
> Perilously casts his bulk this side and that,
> Then swaying to attention.
>
> (VI)

We have a 'perilous' reaching for balance, for steadiness, as though the beyond-war state must first be a difficult poise, till at last Christ is 'fixed' and 'firmly positioned'. The mountains are to crumble to dust before 'our Nations will forget this Man'.

War-power is throughout incorporated, and past violences of imagery exactly condition the final, sun-impregnated stature. Dawn is described in a prose passage of great pregnancy, interweaving impressions of kingship, light, music and precious metal to make a setting for the interchange of Sun and Prince of Peace:

And then over the clear horizon came the rising sun, shaping itself bigger and clearer and fresher in the air. Expanding in yellow radiance, he asserted morning-glory, so majestically he moved up. Kingly joy. He marshalled like mellow cadences his beams on the snow, directing wild light in a rich deploy which startled condors (who had already had a bad night) into the air. The long, pale, but warming, rays struck a Lapland brilliance, a casket glitter, on that weary snow world, so high, high up, so that the ice began to gleam, and the men of Argentine and the men of Chile embraced each other, the light in their eyes. In ever-swelling Andean pride the sun rose, and focussed on the Christ. The beams embroidered on his massive dark mouldings, playing caresses on his thighs, flooded his chest, burnished: and last the sun looked into the Iron Christ's eyes, and on the balls fixed a mild blaze.

(VI)

The whole poem works to this final picture; the sun, the burnished chest, the eyes. Even so, to prevent any too-simple trust in the finality of social progress, we conclude with sight of the rock-implanted Man of Iron eternally fronting sun and stars amid mountain solitudes that distantly promise, not a world, but a 'universe without wars'; as though the earthly problem were all but insoluble and man's troubled destiny involved, inexorably, in some greater order.

That this great poem, for a great poem it surely is, should have remained almost completely ignored by our contemporary literary consciousness, suggests how far removed our consciousness remains from intuition of those basic energies of which it treats. The strain and effort, the slow agony of the Christ's making from guns, reflects the will to forge from the Dionysian energies themselves, the volcanic and giant forces in nature and in man, some yet greater and victorious, Apollonian peace.[1] Throughout the substances are living *bodies*; the great mountains, the guns, the animals, the human beings, the effigy; and through this keen sense of biological and body-housed energy the war-impulse is diagnosed, transmuted, balanced and surmounted. The narrative is based on the laws of statuary involving a trinity of conflict, purpose and poise. In this sense too the effigy is to be regarded less as a memorial than as a living Christ.

Much fine poetry is written in a minor key, subjectively motivated by cerebral pressures and dominated by provisional doctrines, social, philosophic or credal; and it would be foolish to deny to such a poetry a limited value. But there is a greater poetry. Berry writes primarily of the objective world, of things and of events; and he shows at every turn an extraordinary resource of verbal play and rhythmic modulation in the fitting of manner to matter. In thought, his sole commitment is to the spirit of life. He is from the start an adept at revealing the miracles of existence – barrel-organ or lamp-post – however trite or despised. He is concerned less with his own 'burning atoms of inextinguishable thought', as Shelley has it, than with those cosmic energies prisoned within the most seemingly trivial and atomic object or experience; not so much generating as releasing power and wonder wherever his muse wanders, like Keats's moon in 'Sleep and Poetry' 'with silver lip kissing dead things to life'. His main subjective interests lie in those cosmic sexual promptings, objective to the mental ego, which are so powerful in 'The Dark Inhabitant' and 'Snake in the Moon'. And these have two directions, slaughterous and sweet: both are present in *The Iron Christ*.

Such is Berry's equipment; and such an equipment alone, touching at every point the universal heart, can properly handle the greater issues and relate the actions of nations to the destinies of mankind.

3

Francis Berry has been deeply involved in the great events of our time. In the autumn of 1939 he wrote 'Spain, 1939: from Devon'

[1] The thought corresponds to Milton's phrase 'the campaign of peace'. In his *Second Defence of the People of England*, after pithily remarking that 'War has made many great whom peace makes small', he urges his countrymen to subdue their vices: 'Let these be the first enemies whom you subdue; this constitutes the campaign of peace' (from Milton's Latin, Bohn edition; Yale edition, Vol. IV, 680-1).

(first published in *The Wind and the Rain*, Spring 1942, and subsequently included in *Fall of a Tower*). Commenting on the Spanish civil war, he treats it less as a struggle between Fascism and Communism than as a symptom of the greater conflict already developing between militarism and civilization. Europe's leaders, Mussolini and Hitler, are cleverly pictured:

> There the bronze-lipped and astounding boast
> Of bum-jawed Fascist, and the bounding step
> Of Führer, resound upon an alien coast. . . .

There is, however, no superficial satire. Berry knows all about the more violent instincts; he in part admires them; his Iron Christ itself was made from guns. That is precisely why he is so helpful. But the metallic must be surpassed. He contrasts Iron with 'the soft-fleshed Jesus, joyous as a musicked June': the final aim is a human sweetness.

The poem was composed as a public address:

> Consider
> In you lives a Fascist and a Christ.
> Flares up the Fascist when you thrill at midnight
> Rumble of artillery, or at harangue
> Conjuring pagan shouts in glimmering bannerdom –
> But the proud step paces to the morgue
> And the full crow limps across the warred-on field
> And drops a tired saliva to an aching sun.

The associations of Spain, home of the Don Juan myth, make easy an identification, such as we had in the Archbishop's sermon of *The Iron Christ*, of sex-love with the sweeter powers:

> In you both Christ and Fascist and a Spain:
> Sex-song that chants from kiss full warm and prodigal
> Or sex inflamed by blood, a shrill red madrigal.

Red is a favourite colour, powerfully used. 'Murderous Meseta' we are told, is only too ready to 'mount' in all of us. The choice of directions is ours:

> Which shall rejoice,
> Hurrah the ultimate gay holiday,
> The Fascist, or the Human, voice?

The contrast, however, seems more simple than it is.

The alignment of sexual energies with Christianity is a challenge to tradition; and may it not be that sex-impulses have been traditionally suspect precisely because they so easily, as Berry's lines have indicated, become violent? Some disentangling is needed, and another and longer period piece, *Fall of a Tower*, is so engaged. It was started before 'Spain, 1939', in 1938, completed in 1940, and published in 1943.

In it the instinctive, and in some regards Fascist or Germanic, powers are levelled against Church tradition. There is a huge Church with a Tower and clanging bell, dominating a town; the Sea near-by; and a Hill.

The Church is called 'this gorgon bully of the Town' (I. i). It represents a repressive, inhuman, dominance, and is so described 'darkening and dooming all' (I. i). Its high square Tower signifies its unnatural, and dangerous, claims, like the Tower of Babel in the Old Testament. Its transcendence lacks both rondure and health. It is not only, despite its lift, 'ponderous'; it is 'a square and pus-filled paw', a threatening disease (I. iii). Its bells have 'all the tons and chimes of iron' (I. i), a 'battery of iron-lipped creatures' dispatching 'battalions of resounding clangs in big globes or heavily bouncing bubbles over the Town' (II. vii). This is the 'great cathedral gong' of Yeats's 'Byzantium', seen – or felt – differently.

The Sea (I. ii) is ambiguous. It is in a state of continual unrest, by turns roaring and wailing, and is given unpleasant associations: 'shark-miseried', 'flotsam', 'bled', 'gangrene sweat', 'stenches'. It swears 'watery oaths'. On its bed are armless statues and skulls; a legless figurehead meets another and the two 'procreate'. Since the Sea naturally corresponds to sexual instinct, these disjointed pieces may denote a psychological disruption. Ocean has buried wealth,

> chests
> Of treasure-loot whose foreign rubies wink
> At the green flit of fishes . . .

(I. ii)

Chains jangle 'red-rust tunes'. Slaughter goes on there, and whales 'boil and wallop in grey lust'. We do well to look for psychological, especially sexual, correspondences: a magic once strong but now gone is in the sunken 'lost cities', Atlantis and Lyonesse; and thought of these leads on to the skeletons of 'lost lovers', seaweed-tangled, their bones locked together until 'with sigh' a wave parts them, 'their surfeit to allay'. In the Sea with all its 'stenches' we have correspondences to modern man's broken, ugly, death-dominated condition, his splendours lost. Nevertheless 'this monster Ocean', whether it 'croons' or 'snores', is 'tremendous in its power'.

Then there is the Hill. Unlike the Tower it is 'rounded', and its 'lonely crown' is honoured. It is called 'palaeolithic', and is 'a stoic' in endurance, silently containing, in an alien age, its burden of 'anger' (I. iii). On it are mounds above 'the remains of heroes' (II. i): it is waiting for a heroic deed.

Our hero is a pale and neurotic youth, Edmund. His sexual instincts, repressed by the Church's tyranny, induce in him a general loathing of physical existence. From the Sea come words suggesting some Fascist or Hitlerian challenge:

> Blood or Iron
> The Sun the Soil . . .
>
> (I. v)

They are reiterated, with variations. Edmund climbs the Hill, and swears a vow.

That night he suffers nightmare and claustrophobic fears relieved by sex-fantasy and orgasm. Next day, in the town, his muttered 'Blood and Iron' awakes a response from a member of a secret society (the conception was based on the I.R.A.), who directs him to an address where he is given explosives, while street players are making 'strange red music' (II. v). We regard the Church, more than ever ugly, its hideous gargoyles and bell-ropes like intestines, its tortured martyrs and its 'presence of Death' (II. vii). Edmund's course is fixed.

He is serving the Sun:

> Lord Sun, Glory Sun: Sir, all radiant now
> Shalt thou be summoned to thy throne by those
> Subject too long to Shadow of the Tower. . . .
>
> (III. i)

Urged on 'by Sea-voices' and 'Sun-heroes old' from the Hill, who once 'loved their Prince', he detonates the charge, fire and powder meeting in 'Death-coition'. The Tower's bells are lashed into a last 'alarm'; the building collapses, burying Edmund in its ruins.

Variations have been played on 'Blood', 'Iron', 'Sun' and 'Soil'. The aim is to disentangle the good from the bad, and now 'Iron' drops out:

> Now praise to thee Blood-Prince, O Glory Sir,
> And gorgeous life to thee on thy return.

(III. ii)

Our last section is a long 'Hallelujah' paean, remarkably sustained:

> So Hallelujah, Hallelujah to the coming Sun
> With lightning trumpets gleaming down the dawn;
> > Lift banners brave
> > Gleam-trumpets blow
> Cruise through the violet fairways of the sky
> Your strong notes to the East's crowned Sun.

(IV. i)

The Sun is to be praised by 'exquisite and glowing Jesus, come from the Dead':

> O powerful and loving Jesus, released from the Tomb:
> > Praise him and magnify him for ever.
> O handsome and golden Jesus, at Easter alive:
> > Praise him and magnify him for ever.

(IV. i)

Praises are scattered in a shower of glory: 'Blood-Prince', 'Full Prince', 'Gold', 'risen Sun', 'Jesus-Sun', 'Golden Sir'. As the glory expands, all creation is enclosed within a Magnificat of splendid power ranging from stars in their courses to earth in its different zones, and beasts of air, sea and jungle, concluding:

> O ye Children of Men, bless ye the Sun. Ye handsome Youths, ye lovely Girls so brown on beach, bless ye the Sun (and O ye Girls, make ye your Bathing Costumes brief, or better naked be, for He the Sun is brave, a handsome Lover, his kisses sweet, so show forth your breasts to the Sun): praise and magnify the Lord for ever.
> O ye Blondes, and ye Brunettes, dance to the Sun, kiss those that love him!
> O ye Heroes of the Sun, bless ye your Lord:
> O ye Spirits of the Brave, Beautiful, Gentle and Generous,
> O ye Compassionate and Understanding, bless ye the Sun:
> O bless you, glowing and gentle Jesus, Bless You, the Sun:

Glory be to the Sun, and to the Sun, and still to the Sun.

O Sun, Compassionate and Wise, Powerful and kind, now you
arise all sun-less organized wars will cease. Glory be to the Sun, as
it was in the beginning, was lost, and is returned, O Jesus-Sun,
Christ without End. Amen.

(V. i)

'Jesus' blends with 'Sun' to make 'Christ'. Traditional theology
is used and expanded to define the new alignments being celebrated.

As epilogue we have the raising, as of a 'new Heliopolis', of a
Sun-Temple in flashing modernistic, 'aluminium' style with 'a
Dome of patterned glass'. The sky has already been called an
'enormous Dome' (IV. i), and the temple's dome corresponds,
its rondure contrasting with the Church's *square* Tower. It is
built, in time-honoured poetic fashion,[1] to the music of violins
and flutes. It is a place for love, including sex-love:

> Boys and girls their love-bliss will profess
> And kiss beneath this Dome of rich Christnéss.

(V. ii)

The awkwardly accented final word jerks us into sense of a new
Christianity, not too easy to conceive and hold, whereby the
Christ-*quality* percolates human existence.

The contrasts in *Fall of a Tower* are today easy to follow, and
also to relate to our evolving culture – to Church tradition, to
Hitlerian revolt, to sex-freedoms, to a newly Christian, un-
Hitlerian, humanism; and to the youth-rebellions of our own time.
As in *The Iron Christ*, it is as though *iron* were being changed to
what Browning in 'Rabbi Ben Ezra' called the 'rose-mesh' of
physical sweetness: the emphasis is on flesh and blood irradiated.

A more universal and less historically defined opposition is
established in *Murdock* (1947). Written in Malta during the war, it
grows from home memories. The English village has affinities to
Hardy and, still more, John Cowper Powys's *A Glastonbury
Romance*; and the tight and lucid verse-rhythms occasionally recall
Masefield. The prevailing atmosphere is one of folklore and superstition. As Berry's work develops there is an increasing emphasis
on our culture's mythological hinterland within what Shakespeare

---

[1] For 'musical buildings' see p. 251 above; also my *Poets of Action*, 63, on Milton
and *Laureate of Peace* (or *The Poetry of Pope*), 86-90.

in *The Tempest* (I. ii. 50) calls 'the dark backward and abysm of
time'; emphasis on atavistic fears and impulses active within the
human psyche, 'images' and 'shapes' – as Byron tells us – 'still
unimpaired, though old, in the soul's haunted cell' (*Childe Harold*,
III. 5). So, using a country legend of two ghostly Brothers
haunting a wood in murderous conflict, Berry gives us a condensed
narrative-commentary on the human predicament. The Wood is
in all of us; in our benighted lower selves of violence and murder;
and we are terrified.

The villagers in their fear are exactly characterized and the
Wood grippingly realized. Never was a literary work more soaked
in unmediated perception:

> And who among our neighbour Villagers,
> Hearing the Brothers scuffling in the Dark,
> Pulls not all Blankets over Ears?
> Or holds his Wife more near? Or mutters Prayers?
> Or lights his Candle with a thumping Haste?
> Or gropes his Way and bolts his Door most fast?
> Though Reverend Evans scoffs upon our Dread
> Yet he has heard and sweats upon his Bed –
> For Murdock Wood is known through all the Shire.
>
> Last night Ted Wilks was riding Home his Mare,
> And late from courting took the Murdock Road,
> He reached the Gate that led into the Wood
> When reared the Mare, and right up straight she stood,
> She yelled her Horror from an upright Head,
> With Nostrils wide and Eyes that filled up red.
> Next Day she cast her Foal. It came out dead.

                                                                    (I)

'Red' we have met it before – is Berry's colour for violence and
threat.

The Wood itself is thick

> With Boughs like Hooks that hide their Clutch;
> Holes in Oaks that wink and watch;
> And Weeds like Thongs that bide to catch. . . .

                                                                    (I)

It is simultaneously a real wood and our own dark underworld.
There are Weeds, Nightshade, a Toadstool as a sweating monster;
nature is a nightmare. 'Days are ill, but worse are Nights'. We

are waked, like Eliot's Sweeney at the conclusion of *Sweeney Agonistes*, in terror at 'Hell's drop':

> And it is dark, and it is steep,
> Hoof and Horn and Mistletoe,
> Toad and Stool and Who-knows-what?
> Old Nan she laughs upon her Cot
> And she is bald, her Wits are fled,
> And she is mad, and Who is not
> Hearing Brothers from a Bed?
> Nightly in the Wood they go –
> Hoof and Horn and Mistletoe.
>
> (I)

The village compresses mankind in its terror and inward evils, only too vividly externalized in the terrors of the natural order. All are in the Brothers in their slaughterous internecine conflict. Evils multiply in the village, to animal and man. All are under a curse, and madness spreads.

The Devil Himself, we are told, long past begot these Brothers on a woman, and wherever their blood spills falls a curse. Their Sin is older than the Flood; older, we may suppose, than Cain. It is, like the fantasies in Nietzsche, Brooke, and Powys (pp. 161, 173, 175, 209, 303), veiled by *silence*. It is something 'no one has heard' (II), and yet everyone in Murdock is tainted with it.

The folk dread – it is the exact dread of Powys's poem 'The Face' (p. 209 above) – that the Brothers will emerge from the wood; but they do not. And yet they are within us: 'always the Brothers moan inside her Head' (III). They are a living death: 'The Live are Dead, the Dead Alive' (III). They come on us by night, in our solitude:

> We have to face these Things alone,
> (What Woman gave Them Blood and Bone?)
> And Them we dread when every Day is done.
>
> (III)

Above all, we fear lest they *come out of the wood*.

We are told that this they cannot do. But if they did, what then?

> To know the Worst is still a sharp Delight –
> There's Mastery in that but none in Doubt.
>
> (IV)

They are now imagined as *coming out*. In conceptual terms this means that we are to envisage the true essence of the horror prisoned within man's psyche. It is found related to (i) strength, (ii) ascent, and (iii) insight.

The Brothers are pictured ranging in fight above seas and lands, across Europe, moving from sodden England to brighter skies. They become gigantic, scaling mountain heights. Their battling *ascent* resembles the mountain fight of Porius and the Giant in Powys's *Porius*:

> first One pursues, then flies,
> As crashing upward They increase in Size.
>
> (IV)

The icy peaks attained at the hour before Dawn so loved of Powys, they stand in their might, quiescent. Then, their age-old feud mastered:

> In Snow They stand like Flame,
> Haughty yet calm, and their quiescent Eyes –
> Like Martyrs' – shine from mastered Mysteries.
>
> (IV,

In the 'white' radiance of the Moon they sing, with 'shining Tears' a song that loosens

> All fears, from bleeding Womb to bloodied Hearse,
> Endured by Man or by the Universe.
>
> (IV)

As in *The Iron Christ*, there is thought not of earth alone but of the 'universe'. 'Flame' and 'snow' are again associated, recalling the unsingeing flames of Yeats's 'Byzantium':

> And still They sing, in Snow They sing like Flame –
> For Murdock's Brothers are the World's new Fame,
> Its high, unborn and glistering Renown,
> Its present Dread resplendent in its future Crown.
>
> (IV)

'Unborn': the resolution may be stated, but cannot be further defined.

The mastery of fears with resultant triumph resembles that of Masefield's 'The Hounds of Hell'; the need to face the secret horrors – and no writing more vividly faces horrors than Berry's –

corresponds to Powys's doctrine. The conclusion has analogies in the final act of Shelley's *Prometheus Unbound*, where the change of tone from drama to paean is of similar significance; in the 'sunny pleasure-dome with caves of ice' of Coleridge's 'Kubla Khan'; and in the icy peaks and sun-splendours of *Thus Spake Zarathustra* (e.g. *Thus Spake Zarathustra*, III. 6; *Christ and Nietzsche*, 186). From earth-bound evil flowers supernal insight, strength, and victory.

While in Malta, Berry became a Catholic. This was no sharp reversal: his early lyrics on Jesus, 'Lama Sabachthani?' in *Gospel of Fire* and 'The Devil' in *Fall of a Tower etc.* witness to a natural Christian attunement. Though his resolutions, reversing horror to splendour, are Nietzschean, the poetry shows no contrapuntal jostling between the Christian and the Nietzschean as one feels there is in Eliot; nor any change of direction or tone, or any particular moment of conversion. He still writes freely, and except when he is on a specifically Christian theme his religious allegiance never obtrudes; unless his prevailing charity of understanding and acceptance be called Christian. It is as though he has found within Catholicism a catholicism not always found in Catholics.

4

By making patterns of powers and directions, poetic literature serves to attune man to his destiny. Unlike conceptual studies it reflects what is dynamic in art-forms themselves dynamic, either narrative or drama. Drama tends towards the theological, relating human action to powers above or below; it gives a horizontal story vertically pointed, the vertical dominating, as in the symbol of the cross. Nietzsche in *The Birth of Tragedy* saw drama as primarily 'Dionysian' and epic as 'Apollonian', the one involved in the mysteries, the other acting along the surface, of human existence. But all great epic is dramatic and all drama tells a story; it is a question of emphasis.

Berry is a narrative poet writing from strong Dionysian impulse. Western epic, from Homer through Vergil to Milton, has steadily and increasingly laboured to assimilate human energies to humane values, the Christian religion being part of the process and beginning to dominate in Spenser, Milton and Tennyson. Berry has vertical allegiances both to the Dionysian forces of jungle instinct and atavistic compulsion and, looking up, to Christian and divine authority. He has moved beyond his predecessors not only in so richly impregnating narrative by insights more usually found in drama, but has gone farther than any in the yet more difficult task, within the area of the dramatic, of handling with an equal sympathy its two poles of instinct and sensibility, of Dionysus and Christ. Since these criss-crossing relations are hard to capture and hold, his narratives are, like dramas, short; narrative is compressed and perceptions forced into the vertical, like an explosion.

He remains, however, primarily a narrative poet – one who tries, so far as may be, to maintain a rational and convincing sequence and to study in horizontal terms how and why events occur. The danger to avoid is the abstraction and isolation of persons and causes: we too readily think of Cromwell, Napoleon, Hitler, Churchill, as persons responsible for this or that; or of events such as Britain's recent action at Suez or America's Vietnam engagement as simple issues liable to moral approval or condemnation. We nevertheless know well enough that every happening flowers from an infinitude of contingencies exhausting analysis. This is why in a Shakespearian play the protagonist's doings are poetically related to the community, earth-nature, the cosmos and the yet greater powers beyond or within.

In 1957 Berry visited Jamaica and subsequently wrote the narrative *Morant Bay* (1961) on the negro rising of 1865. In *The Iron Christ*, *Fall of a Tower* and *Murdock* the concern was to relate the mysteries, high or low, to a new though not exclusive humanism. *Morant Bay* is more specifically concerned with the horizontal forces of geography, economics, definable psychology and politics. It is to this extent the more attuned to contemporary interests and practice, and the style is correspondingly modernistic in its freedoms of accentual verse, colloquial parenthesis and analytic comment.

Actions grow from history and exist in a context. We are shown a flash-back of Jamaica's past, its slave-trade and economy based on sugar and rum with a consequent amassing of wealth. The terrain is before us, its mountains and coffee-plantations, and its people. Old horrors are recalled: the whippings and other savageries of white masters rising to the 'sadistic fury' of roasting rebellious slaves 'over a slow fire' in process of what was genuinely

regarded as the maintenance of a 'necessary subjugation' (II). All
is described without rancour. Nevertheless sympathy with the
negroes goes deeper than comment: it is present in the sharp
realization of negro talk and the brilliant mastery of detail in the
description of an Ashanti witch-doctor at his 'Obeah' rituals (II).

Our attention is narrowed down to the 1865 Rising some years
after the emancipation which had created new problems and an
uneasy situation, economically the worse from shortage of rain
and the American Civil War. Though we are warned not to 'take
sides', remembering that our own leisured judgements are of a
kind that were 'not open' to those 'caught' in the immediate confrontation, the event to be narrated is grim enough. It ought, we
are told, to have been a matter for some children's story-book, or
if not that, for historical study only, not for present happening (I):
an interesting distinction between the *legitimate*, even salutary,
pleasure of both children and grown-ups in fictional or even
recorded horrors and the terrors of actuality (cp. pp. 163, 169 and
262 above).

The primary *immediate* cause of what happened is traced to racial
animosity. We are urged to transcend sensory antagonism:
instances of racial sex-mingling have already, in our introductory
passages, been vividly glimpsed. Repulsion and attraction act in
close conjunction, almost a reciprocity, and we have in all such
reactions a choice:

> The one way
> Is to recoil in disgust, the other way
> Is to accept as with love the smell and the sordor
> Till it becomes as sweet as the sweat of a beloved, or
> Entering the humanness of this flesh and its excrement
> Enlarge to a possession of Africa, possessing as a glory
> Its dust and its dirt, the drone of its suns,
> Here transplanted, and now the darker, more complicated
> So transplanted.
>
> (IV)

Our main agents are three:

> It was *a* White, *a* Coloured, *a* Negro
> Who reacting – chemically, physically, physiologically –
> Created this Outbreak.
>
> (III)

Each is exactly defined for us in behaviour, talk and outlook: E. J. Eyre, the Governor; W. C. Gordon, the subtle, legalistic schemer; and the massive Paul Bogle in his fantasies 'resurrecting the red glow of an African Kingdom' (III). These three 'created' or 'released' the rising which was born of their peculiar qualities and interaction. Had they been other, their violences might have been controlled and all resolved 'in the chilly progress of a lean rational fabianism' (III). The conflict itself is, in its way, creative, because true to the inward realities, and so at least more to be honoured, and perhaps in the long run more helpful, than an attenuated solution. That is why such works of literature, especially those with strong dramatic oppositions, exist; and why we like them, however terrible.

Eyre's dinner-talk is beautifully characterized in its superior European tone. He is far from realizing

> That a nude negro is aesthetically more valuable
> Far than an ill-developed, pink and white Englishman
> Sitting round-shouldered on the sands.
>
> (IV)

We are however, with a typical honesty, reminded that Eyre had earlier won respect in Australia as 'Protector of the Aboriginals' (IV). We learn moreover that his career as a man of action had been motivated by inferiority resulting from a school birching at Sedbergh. Motives are not simple.

W. C. Gordon is a half-caste member of the Jamaican Baptists

> who married the rhythmic salvations of Africa
> To the Christian faith.
> (IV)

He is cunning. He uses his legal equipment with set purpose to fluster Eyre and make him feel inferior, so raising his hatred in return. Though now elected to the House of Assembly, Gordon has not the gifts or personality to match his political ambitions.

Paul Bogle has, in every way, a greater stature, simple though he be. He is Deacon of a Baptist Chapel in the Blue Mountains. A long passage in vivid negro talk brings preacher and congregation to life.

> Aah hear Deacon when he talk,
> When he preach how he work
> Us people up!

How
His face glisten, and his two eyes
Dey roll all roun'. . . .   (IV)

Bogle has an innate grandeur:

This Bogle was a magnificent creature of God,
Or of nature, or of his parents, or of all, for superb
In his massive black build, and in the African dome
Of his chest, he conceives of a home
Inarticulate yet magnificent,
Of a kingdom, a residence,
Splendid beyond the designs of Gordon, or the thoughts of Eyre. . . .
                                            (IV)

He nourishes dreams 'of a renewed Africa'.

These three are called each 'incomplete' in their peculiar excellences, yet within their conflict they become 'perfect'. Their fault is only that they do not each recognize their limitations; a warning is stated for us all (IV).

The rioters confront a small body of Europeans in the Court House at Morant Bay under the magistrate, a German, von Ketelhodt. The deep-down 'forces' of Africa-in-Jamaica are as 'a dark lake of passion' which 'condenses' into the crowd's 'single pulsating heart'; as though one enormous visage were there 'shouting', 'red-throated' and 'saliva-flecked', craving, in a sharply revealing phrase, 'an orgasm more purgative than union'. The Europeans are terrified, and their terror is physiologically described:

                and the adrenalin
Expands the square, expands those in the square, and the gland
Decants its substance into the blood, its transforming
Agent, but still there was time. Not yet the sudden
Break or loosening, when the floor of the basement of being
Collapses. . . .   (V)

Throughout the poem we sense the biological, psychological, political and spiritual all interweaving, and the persons acting and reacting on themselves and each other until the event is forced. On this soil of physical fear is poised the *mental* decision of Ketelhodt.

When we talk of 'men of action' we mostly mean 'men of

decision'; and the decision must often be immediate.[1] Games like cricket and football depend more on this than on physical strength; even a golf-swing is a matter of exact timing, of the application of force at the moment of impact. At the crisis Ketelhodt failed. There was still, we are told, time before fears and furies usurp control:

> But what with the terror, and the glands
> Working, discharging their scents, and the sounds
> Of shells blown – cranular boom – and the thump
> – Goatskin on wooden frames – of the drums, what with the wee-wee
> Shrill of the pipes, and the susurrating wail
> Of the approach, Ketelhodt and his Meeting
> Were unable to provide the word. (V)

Ketelhodt from the Piazza spread 'his pudgy hands' and 'cried out the wrong thing':

> and if it had been anyone else
> In the Vestry who had come out and cried what Ketelhodt cried
> It might have been the right thing. 'Peace, peace', he cried
> And the heart of what had meant to be a demonstration only
> Valvular jerked and cried out 'War'. (V)

There is no obvious error: Ketelhodt just lacked the instinct to meet the immediate situation with the action exactly appropriate, at this particular moment, to his own personality. A certain genius, such as T. E. Lawrence had pre-eminently, is needed at such a crisis. Perhaps Ketelhodt too obviously showed fear; perhaps from *him* a better line would have been anger, even bluster.

The crowd becomes a vast power rooted in history, the crucial moment part of a vast context:

> and the tusks of Africa
> Elephantine, ancestral, waved
> Branches, and the branches weaved
> Into the texture of air
> Certitude of history, and the broad nostrils
> Flattened as the mouths opened
> War. (V)

[1] Compare the emphasis on mental control by himself and others, in T. E. Lawrence; and also Powys's statement on his hero in *Porius* (XXII. 512), who only becomes a man of action after his mind and body are unified under the control of the former.

The terror of the Europeans accelerates:

> And those in the Court House
> Suffered chemical changes: the pulps, sacs, polyps, glands,
> Bellows of the lungs, responding to the message of the hearing
> Transmitted by the white slim worms of the cortex, reacted and
>   shot
> Juices into circulating seas, and the faces
> Of the Vestrymen altered . . .   (V)

And yet it is all a mistake: Bogle had brought out his followers not for bloodshed, but simply for a 'clamouring'.

A bottle is thrown, rifles fire, the Court House is burned and the Europeans are massacred. Then the outbreak dies. Mass executions follow. Eyre has his revenge on Gordon, who was not present but whom he includes, on poor evidence, as the prime instigator. The conclusion is:

> Neither weep, nor condemn
> Nor waste energy with those that mourn.
>   If we condemn
> We become a member of those we condemn,
> Condemning a part of our own body.
>   Rather,
> Remember we are all subject to an obeah
> Whose magic undergoes all manner of transfer,
> But cannot be cast out.   (VI)

Perhaps not; but we have been shown, in vast survey and intricate detail, how such events occur.

The story moves swiftly, especially at the close.[1] Narrative aiming at so total an inclusiveness has to be brief and move fast so that we can hold it all, vast history and present event, and all the various interactions and causations, in simultaneity. We live the only true, because whole, actuality, and attain to comprehension.

5

Much of the complexity of modern poetry arises from our consciousness of diverse specialities, religious, scientific and

---

[1] The swift close was carefully planned. Originally there had been an extended description of the brutal repressions and executions, but this was rejected. The description was subsequently published in *Ghosts of Greenland: Poems*, 1966.

Francis Berry

psychological; and any attempt at a satisfactory statement is likely to be packed and dense. Berry's *The Iron Christ* and *Morant Bay* incorporate such tendencies into a new kind of narrative poetry, making various avenues of knowledge converge on a central event. But here a distinction is needed: whereas so much contemporary writing is paradoxical and inconclusive, Berry's narratives are simple and the contributory elements convergent, not divergent. We are brought, on the most important issues, to insight.

Though so earth-rooted and even weighted with exact and various knowledge, the material is mastered in narratives of urgency and speed; all is easily carried and seen, as it were, from above, because understood. Rhythmic language, as in Homer, gives as prose could not a sense of urgency, touching the magical moment-by-moment sequences of existence, a time more subtle than clocks, like Bergson's '*durée*'. Drama, being weighted with internal conflicts, however fierce and rapid its vertical oscillation, moves more slowly along the line of sequential events. The narrative poet will not concentrate on self-conflict. Berry's agents are shown, for the most part, as units; the conflict is that of one agent, or power, with another, deployed before us. The objectivity is nevertheless countered by a dramatized psychology of idiomatic speech and by astute interpretative comment. We have a newly captured balancing of literary modes.

Homer and Chaucer are often praised for their poetic simplicities; they can make objects or events marvellous in themselves, without metaphysics. So can Tolstoy. The relevant philosophy is given by Powys's Taliessin in *Porius* (XIX. 418; *The Saturnian Quest*, 78):

> The centre of all things, yet all on the surface,
> The secret of Nature, yet Nature goes blabbing it
> With all of her voices from earth, fire, air, water!

In such apprehensions the split between mind and object is healed. Time is 'freed at last from its ghostly accuser' and the supernatural becomes irrelevant; the magic is in the obvious and the ultimate is revealed. We cannot however, as I argued in *The Christian Renaissance* (1962 ed., III. 38-40), live always on that level, and in literature we need to supplement Homer with Aeschylus, Chaucer with Shakespeare, Tolstoy with Dostoievsky – these

468

others involving us in metaphysics and including a greater sense of the numinous.

Berry's central contribution is his ability to see and feel the marvels of existence; things or beings of *any* sort. In my preface to his first volume I wrote of his early poems:

> Above all, they seem to me to reveal continually a fiery life pulsing within the outwardly sordid, dead, and unromantic: and primarily on this, which I take to be the essential activity of all true poetry, I base my conviction of their importance.

The same insight empowers his narratives. They are rich in details glowing with life and relevant to their locale and period. More widely, the events recorded are themselves objectively presented and, so far as may be, allowed to speak for themselves.

There is nevertheless, even in the short poems, more than a magically effective presentation. The object before us, from 'The Lamp-Post' on, is, even when inanimate, realized with an inward perception into, as it were, the very 'I' of the thing before us – so that we not only recognize but subjectively experience the mystery and the marvel. In so well making us simultaneously outside and within the object or the story, Berry is exercising a power not evident in English poetry outside Shakespeare. This is, indeed, as I have argued at length in 'The Shakespearian Integrity' (*The Sovereign Flower*, 1958; included in the World's Classics volume *Shakespeare Criticism*, *1935-60*), the key to Shakespeare's greatness; and here Berry is, precisely, Shakespearian. In the longer narratives the inwardness can only be realized through use of atmosphere and a sense of the numinous, through nature or from beyond; and here we come up against an interesting problem.

In any full deployment of human affairs a poet is likely to rely on spirit-agencies of one kind or another: Homer and Vergil have their various gods taking part in the action. Today such agencies will generally come within what is denoted by the word 'Spiritualism'. In Yeats's 'Byzantium' poems and his dramas, throughout Masefield's prose and poetry, in Eliot's 'Little Gidding', the emphasis is explicit. What of Berry?

He had from the start, quite apart from *The Iron Christ*, a keen Christian sensibility, as in those two lyrics on the sufferings of Christ, as gripping as any in our literature, 'Lama Sabachthani?'

and 'The Devil'; and after becoming a Catholic he has written, from time to time, on Christian themes. As for Spiritualism, there is one delightfully comic spiritualistic poem in negroid dialect called 'Back an' Beyon'' (*Morant Bay etc.*), where Lizzie and Scipio keep advancing to higher planes in the etheric and Lizzie's lover Nelson is always a stage below. Elsewhere the apprehensions may be more 'ghostly', as when a horse in *The Iron Christ* (VI) is imaged as

> shying at spot
> Where the hanged man returns to grope at four.

'Ancestral Tomb' (*Morant Bay etc.*) treats briefly of death, life and love in enigmatic co-presence. 'Poem for November' (*Morant Bay etc.*) is an extended meditation on the 'dead people' clustering round in need of human companionship and warmth. This is the time of Guy Fawkes and fireworks, but the poem's content flowers from a more primitive seasonal superstition. The vast numbers of the dead and of the unborn are considered; all 'converge to a point' which is 'us'. The mystery appals. The poem's tone is however less 'spiritualistic' than, as always with Berry, sensory. His amazing skill in realizing immediate experience in words, as when in treating of Squibs he refers to 'their phizz and their phutt' – a shorthand of human existence! – is also present in treating of spirits:

> For the dead are thick about us in wind or fog,
> and they cry. . . .

Note the word 'thick': the poetry insists on a sensory basis, and it is *the way of great poetry to do this*.

What we call 'spirits' and the 'spirit-world' are normally deductions from experience; they are not, when known from mediumistic evidence or books, immediately experienced except to the mediums themselves who are anyway often in trance. 'Spirit' and 'spirits' as matters of psychic study are abstractions from a greater whole of life and death and that which subsumes both. In the spirit-world it may well be that what we call the sensory is preserved and even expanded with perceptions the richer for the removal of the separate sense-inlets (see Index B, 'sensory etc.'). But we are not yet there, except perhaps sometimes in sleep; the spirit-world can very rarely have been a fully assured daylight experience to earth-dwellers. So the poet, *qua* poet, tends to search within folklore, superstition and mythology, where he can find death-apprehensions already made, as it were, homely, and saturated in centuries of human experience. In such or other earthly or semi-earthly terms we may come nearer to realizing what may be experiences awaiting us beyond death than in reading or hearing far more correct reports of such experiences. This is why the numinous perceptions of such poets as Vergil and Shakespeare are saturated in legend, folklore and mythology.

Berry's use of ancient lore is strong in the autumn section of 'Mediterranean Year' (*Murdock etc.*), celebrating the ritual death of a Priest-King. It is a poem of long-vowelled rhymes: surrounds, mounds, moans, horns, urns; dunes, moons. Its theme is Death, ending:

> The King is dead on borders; under tarnished moons
> The horsemen beaked are spying; with crooked mops
> and mows
> The river hums from narrows to the bearded dunes
> With death at end of long wrong stream –
> O, my darling, dream.

It is a poem of haunting tones.[1]

One expanded, semi-dramatic poem is dominated by spirit-life: 'Illnesses and Ghosts at the West Settlement' in *Ghosts of Greenland* (1966), written after a visit to Greenland. The poem, though treating of saga material, purports to come from the poet's direct contact with the long-dead heroine:

Gudrid herself stung into me her experience; and 'stung' means a piercing of the dialectal curtain: she spoke in English, I heard in an Old Norse which had already slanted into a Greenlandic dialect, or *vice versa*.

(I take *'vice versa'* as applying to 'English' and 'Old Norse'.)

Gudrid and Eiric the Red re-live their story, 'doing it again and again', though 'dead'. The conception resembles that of the Noh-plays of Japan or the verse dramas of W. B. Yeats and

---

[1] The ritual evocations of this autumnal section of 'Mediterranean Year' appealed strongly to my brother, W. F. Jackson Knight.

Gordon Bottomley. The drama, which was composed for radio, concludes:

Gudrid: . . . But I in Greenland now
      Hover not only with my body, and I stung
      These words into a man when he came into Greenland.
      These are my words said into him, and he then wrote them
      And now a woman says them and, if not happy, I AM.
Eiric: And I not so far off, and in this death
      Would catch you, as I could not, underneath.
Gudrid: You can have me now.

What might be called the 'spiritualistic' framing is preserved.

It is not only preserved; it is of the essence. Berry's poetry is throughout characterized, if not dictated, by sensory perception; and it is to be noticed that the spirit-apprehensions here are *one with the geographical setting*. The association, and even scientific relation, of psychic phenomena to cold air is well-known. Temperature has been observed to fall at a séance and the cold can be felt. Cold and sometimes wind are reported, as with the wind at Pentecost. The Sumerian epic *Gilgamish* tells of a wind at a moment of spirit-raising (W. F. Jackson Knight, *Elysion*, 1970; 152-3). There is the biting cold air in the ghost scene of *Hamlet*, and the cold and wind in the penultimate scene of Flecker's *Hassan*:

Fountain Ghost: It is the wind. I must go down into the earth.
Ghost of Pervaneh: Ah, I am cold – I am cold – beloved!
Ghost of Rafi: Cold . . . cold.

These impressions contrast with the vigour of life-as-we-know-it in the Golden Journey that follows. Greenland is naturally fitted for ghostly apprehensions.

The poem-drama opens with a speech by Greenland itself, personified, including such phrases as 'swinge of sea', 'whine of wind', 'clang of cold', 'ice-berg' and 'ice-pack'. Thenceforward the tale treats of witchery, death, disease and lust. There is a Witch, contrasted with Christianity, and through her help and the appropriate 'Spirit Songs' spirits manifest and prophecies are made. Such are our emphases; but the human passion is simultaneously realized, and all the sufferings and pathos of distant people brought close. The tone of the Sagas is captured and the verse, often alliterative, pounds with stresses of Old English.[1]

In a wide survey one is inclined to say that no earlier English poet has come anywhere near Berry's powers of attunement to places and races ancient or modern. He is our first to respond fully to the global consciousness of our time. He is as much at home with the 'coffee eyes' of Chilean admirals in *The Iron Christ*, the racial minglings of modern Jamaica and the Icelandic adventurers of ancient Greenland as with the rustics of *Murdock*. He is now writing a poem on the Mogul emperor Shah Jehan. Hot and cold, all zones are honoured, dialect is vivid on every social or racial level; and as for poetic technique, every known resource of both traditional and modern artistry is by turns employed without critical taboos; as always, inclusive rather than exclusive. Animals are sympathetically and inwardly presented: as in 'Lumping It' (*Morant Bay etc.*) on a boa-constrictor, and 'Predicament' (*Ghosts of Greenland etc.*) on a bat prisoned in a tree. Superstition, folklore and mythology find their voice. Above all we sense, often *smell*, the people and the places, our minds distend to more than mental largeness so that in silent reading we gain experiences that usually have to await *performance*, as when written thoughts become gigantic through an enriched vocalization, or a play's text assumes depth and magic unguessed until produced.

If we think of Britain's heritage in letters we find a fairly clear tradition of national emphasis. Now 'Empire' has changed to 'Commonwealth', and the Commonwealth is scarcely a unit of power. Britain and the world change year by year, power is continually being redistributed and realigned. But in this changing world Britain has its place, and culturally this is still – if only through her language and the works of Shakespeare – a central place. Today a major poet who speaks for England must speak not for Britain as a nation, nor for an empire, but for the world, hoping for that world 'parliament' and 'federation' for which Tennyson looked in 'Locksley Hall'. Berry with his range of racial and geographical insights writes accordingly of England, or Britain, in her new role. If this 'role' be denied we may regard it as, at least, a potentiality, and Berry as, if not its conscious prophet, a prophetic symptom; for I doubt if any other language

[1] In *The Sheffield Morning Telegraph* of 14 May 1966 Philip Hobsbaum, in the course of a notable appreciation, writes of 'Illnesses and Ghosts at the West Settlement' as 'What I firmly believe is the greatest poem of one of the two great poets writing in this country today'.

can show a contemporary poet of such racial inclusiveness.

It is right then that, among his poetic interests, London should not be neglected: he has written a substantial poem 'In Honour of London Town', published first in *Furioso* (Northfield, Minn., U.S.A., VII. 1; Winter 1952), and included in *The Galloping Centaur*. It originated from a dream-vision of London experienced as by astral travel ('body's exile', II) during the war, in Malta.

We have a close 'geography': Walbrook, Ludgate, Aldgate, Southwark, Stepney, Putney, Wandsworth. London's past is remembered, legendary Dick Whittington and John Stow, the city's Elizabethan historian, Dickens and Sherlock Holmes, with a survey of London's officials, Lord Mayor and Aldermen. London is present in past mythology and contemporary actuality. The ancient sea-god, Lud, dominates, and he has two 'horns' which are variously sexual organs, horns that sound, searchlights, and a victory 'V-sign'. The poem is difficult. The compression is perhaps too dense, making it opaque as a London fog, though at one point we have a joyous lyric as light and tripping as the rest is heavy. Obscenities abound: London is a whorish old woman, yet unconquerable and lovable.

At the first publication in *Furioso* some helpful notes were appended (these appear, revised, in the 1970 *Galloping Centaur*). The 'V-sign' was taken from 'some mural paintings in the love-making rooms of villas at Pompeii, showing nude men who are doubly endowed by nature'. We are told that the Malta experience described in Part II preceded the composition of the poem by eight years, and also that the vision of Lud's horns, described originally as bronze (II), was later corroborated 'when fragments of a pair of bronze horns of Celtic workmanship were uncovered by an explosion in the City'.

In the vision, wherein sight and sound came together, there was a strange 'humming' that chimed with 'Lud's dun' and 'London' (II), older than African drums:

> A hum not of Masai or Dinka woman with her thighs of rondure,
> Formidable posteriors, opening to absorb with a humming,
> But an older hum from under London's cones
> (Two captured waxy trussed-down morbid moons)
> From those two trounced hills, with saucy and abominable cleft,
> Ever calling for some superlative colossal masculine shaft,
> Your ramps – your rumps – Old Lady crone. . . .   (II)

Francis Berry

London with its two low hills is called both 'whore' and 'virgin' (I), and her mate is the sea-god, Lud, who penetrates – the reference is to the now submerged Walbrook – between the rump-like hills. Lud's two horns are the 'erecting V-sign' (I) for victory in the World War:

> I saw and heard them at a time
> When London was a red London, reddening
> In the red blaze from incendiaries. . . .
>
> (IV)

The horns sound a warning. But even if London is later destroyed by a hydrogen bomb, Lud's 'double horns' will still be 'erect'; and on the Judgement Day too, in comparison with which the Bomb is 'a paltry bump or mere lover's pinch'.

> Then Lud – having blown – presents his Twin Horns
> In cockolorum V-Salute.
>
> (IV)

The poet presses through the present actuality to the supernal with a final prayer to the Old Woman, London, to plead before Mary her part in the human tradition.

Whatever we make of the original psychic experience it is typical of Berry that it should have included both sound and sight; that the horns should also become sexual symbols; and finally that the massive and often obscene sensory impressions which make 'London' should be caught up into a Judgement Day where all its inhabitants rise – with a lively preservation of earth-existence – in 'their period costumes' (IV). The poem illustrates – more, it *lives* – Berry's way of using all the senses in order to establish the super-sensuous: he is less out for what is called 'extra-sensory perception' than for a totality of sense-perception, such as we may suppose, following Andrew Marvell, Rupert Brooke (pp. 250-1, 300-1) and modern psychic evidence, will characterize existence in higher spheres.

Perhaps Berry's greatest contribution is his relation of the terrors of human instinct to his own Christian sensibility: somehow the two must be related. At this task great poetry, for centuries, has been labouring, and Berry has probably gone further and come nearer to success than any: as I wrote, in *Poets of Action* (1967; xiv), 'he has brought insight into atavistic and sexual impulsions and yearnings' to an understanding of human 'violence', and accordingly has been able to relate 'the psychology of action to a Christian sensibility'. This can only be done through a total, preliminary acceptance. London was told at one point not to worry over damnation. What we need is *a sympathy with both sides, as themselves*; and this sympathy is evident in every phase of Berry's poetry. Dispassionately, therefore, in 'Poor Old Hudders' ('New Poems', *The Galloping Centaur*) he describes the hanging of a pathetically ugly criminal in Anglo-Saxon times, every detail of what happens horribly before us; among the attendants one is sympathetic, but most quite care-free and some cruel or amused. A baby boy watches, a youth assists and finally, around the hanging corpse, 'winsome boys wheel'. The juxtaposition of human cruelty with such youthful and therefore seraphic touches makes an almost unbearable confrontation. All is done without comment, except that the narration is interspersed with prayers to a 'sad Christ' to 'save our dun flesh'.

Berry writes of peoples and places as they are today and as they were in distant ages, and often the ages are co-present. All the main themes of my present volume are contained. Through this totality of apprehension he is not only able, but by instinct is forced, to handle the key problems of our generation: of war, of youth-revolt, of racial antagonism, of sadistic instinct. By religion he is a Catholic, in poetry a humanist; but it is hard to distinguish because his Catholicism is so richly human, and his humanism is so Catholic that it becomes, in itself, religion.

I believe that Francis Berry ranks high among the great poets of our national tradition, and that he is the greatest of all who have written within the present century.

ADDITIONAL NOTE, 1968: I append a poetic self-analysis composed by Francis Berry. A typescript in my possession bears a note by my brother, W. F. Jackson Knight, which runs: 'Composed at my request, dictated, and given to me Tuesday 3 June 1947 by Francis Berry'. On 31 August 1968 Berry wrote: 'I think he had asked me how I created a metaphor and whether the process or sensation was different from that of making a simile'. The poem discussed is 'Photograph' from *Snake in the Moon* (p. 444 above).

Francis Berry

Poetic Vision by Francis Berry – an Experience

It is best to give a remembered example.

> Wind in the telephone wires that leap across a mad moor
> Beneath a whining moon – such a sounding terror
> Emerges from the gipsy balance of your breasts.

1. Ever since I can remember I have been much moved by the sound of wind among telegraph wires and poles. The kind of feeling is most accurately given in the word 'awe'.

2. While writing a poem about a photograph advertising lingerie I had – in the midst of the flow of the poem – a vision of telegraph wires and poles 'leaping' across a 'mad moor'. By vision I mean that I seemed to see them at a range sufficient to show the horizon over which the wires fell out of sight. I – the see-er – was not so much *on* the moor, but floating above it by a distance of ten feet. All this came quickly and unexpectedly, since my conscious attention was on the photograph. Now the moor began to roll like a wide-decked ship; the 'leaping' was no doubt a memory of the apparent behaviour of telegraph poles seen from the window of a fast-moving train. The hearing was as distinct as the seeing, but it was the moon that was 'whining' (the sound has filled me with awe since childhood) and not the wires beneath it.

3. This vision was instantaneous, and then the thing happened that is now customary with those visions which cause, or are included in, a poem. There was a rapid close-up, almost as in a film where a distant object on the screen is quickly magnified as it rushes to the foreground. But here there is more than close-up; the vision continued to race forward beyond the limit of the screen – so to speak – into the auditorium, and up to, and then into, myself. The moor, poles, wires and cloud-tossed moon all ran into my body, took possession of me, while yet leaving a miniature, undynamic and uninteresting replica outside, and occupying the place whence the real ensemble came before it inhabited me.

4. Inside me the ensemble was active and tumultuous. Since the moor was leaping (in contrast the miniature external replica was immobile) I containing it also seemed rocking, and felt I could scarcely hold it, distend sufficiently that is, since the whole ensemble seemed to enlarge.

5. Then came the solution, the relief, almost emptying of this occupation into the last line quoted above – 'Emerges from the gipsy balance of your breasts'. The subject of the poem was still the advertisement photo, which never lapsed during the sudden vision and its invasion. Here the rocking of the moor, as a ship on its keel or a

pendulum on its pin, or a pair of scales or a knife-edge, became one with the oscillating balance of the model's breasts in the photograph.

6. So solved, the miniature, external replica promptly faded. and the express theme of the poem was the only concern until the next vision a few lines later.

7. I take it that some such procedure as this occurs whenever a metaphor arises in composition. I think I would further venture to say that a simile only occurs where a vision arises without a consequent close-up and merger with myself.

Finally, after the merger, the internal possession of the ensemble and the commotion it caused seem much more important at the time than the photograph-like replica it left in the place it first occupied. After the merger *I was* the moor with its wires, poles and moon above them. The seeing was inseparably combined with hearing and all other sense impressions.

Within this identification the external objects remain dominating and unmodified. In her recent study *The Central Self* (1968) Patricia M. Ball discusses (7-8) Coleridge's distinction between Shakespeare and Milton as poets who respectively (i) enter into objective forms and persons and (ii) assimilate such forms and persons to the self. In this opposition Berry would be on the Shakespearian, and Eliot on the Miltonic, side. Each mode has its specific value. The general issues are well raised and handled throughout Dr. Ball's important book.

PART FIVE

Epilogue

CHAPTER XVIII

Herbert Read and Byron

The Malahat Review, University of Victoria, IX; January 1969.

IN THE BRITISH COUNCIL booklet on Sir Herbert Read, Francis Berry, discussing the *Collected Essays in Literary Criticism*, observes that, despite the range and value of its commentary on pre-Romantic writers, 'these are not substantial contributions in the way that his studies of Wordsworth, Coleridge, Shelley and Keats (and even Byron) are'.

That bracket poses a problem central to both Byron and Read. Roughly, both may be called 'romantic'. Byron's romanticism is, however, only part of his contribution, since his literary valuations and much of his practice, first in heroic diction and later in dramatic form, are Augustan. He bestrides two periods as did Milton and Shakespeare before him. This is what Read did also, in his own way, within the context of twentieth-century letters.

He reverses the Byronic divisions. His literary and social philosophies support 'organic' rather than established forms and 'personality' in place of 'character'. But he was one of Eliot's circle, and a life-long friend. In literary practice his peculiarly reserved and unpretentious tone, or wavelength, corresponds, and may accordingly be called 'classic'.

In his British Council booklet on Byron, Read follows certain conventional views with which we can now part company; in calling Byron an 'atheist' he is wrong (see *Lord Byron: Christian Virtues*, Index A, XVI, Religion). And yet the brief essay abounds in original comments that strike home. He accords the right priority to, and quotes in full, Byron's 'On This Day I Complete my Thirty-Sixth Year'; he finds Byron's to be 'the wildest poetic energy in the whole range of post-Shakespearian poetry'; and he believes that Byron was 'in some sense beyond good and evil, one of Nietzsche's "free spirits".' When in the preface to my *Poets of Action* I referred to Read as 'that fine Byronist', he wrote in reply, on 10 December 1967, that it was 'a compliment I would like to deserve'.

I had known him for some years. We met first in 1947 at the Present Question Conference at Birmingham where I gave a lecture bearing the Nietzschean title 'The Avenging Mind' (included in *Shakespeare and Religion*, 1967). He was generous in approval; as again, when I subsequently sent him my book *Christ and Nietzsche*. Later in London in 1950 I showed him some photographs of dramatic poses, and he sent me a book by M. Feldenkrais, *Body and Mature Behaviour* (1949), which I used for the commentary on the pictures of my *Symbol of Man*, as yet unpublished. After that, in 1951, I sent him, as a director of Routledge & Kegan Paul, my *Lord Byron: Christian Virtues* which was proving difficult to publish. It quickly won his, and the firm's, support. Read invited me to his club in London. He greatly liked my *Lord Byron's Marriage*, and on the publication of *Byron and Shakespeare* he sent me a reprint of his *Byron* booklet inscribed to me, with a generosity of phrasing, as 'Byron's greatest interpreter'.

That is the record of what Read did, not only in support of a contemporary but, what is more important, for Byron. His actions were impelled by a creative, Byronic, generosity; and without him my three Byron volumes might not have appeared.

His interest in Byron was reflected in two recent publications. In *High Noon and Darkest Night* (Monday Evening Papers, 3; Center for Advanced Studies, Wesleyan University, U.S.A.), an answer to José Ortega y Gasset's strictures on modernistic art, he quoted for his purpose various passages from Byron: 'Perhaps it is Byron who gives the best expression to this romantic ideal of essential Night'.

In 1953 there was a broadcast of Read's dialogue *Lord Byron at the Opera* (published by Philip Ward, 28 Parkfield Crescent, North Harrow, 1963). The main persons are Byron and Stendhal, and the setting a box at the opera in Milan, in 1816. The dialogue shows a delicate skill, with scholarship. In a preface defending dialogue as a medium, Read notes: 'There is hardly a sentiment or even an expression in this dialogue for which chapter and verse could not be quoted'.

The formal, even stilted, manner may be a true capturing of aristocratic, period, conversation; but it is rather strange that Read, so receptive to the tumultuous in Byron, could have so resisted all temptation to let the Byronic fire ignite.

True, this is a dialogue, not a drama. But when during the fifties Read sent me a typescript of a drama, *The Parliament of Women*, to comment on,[1] I was aware of a similar limitation. The play is nevertheless fascinating. It dramatizes a French occupation of Greece in the thirteenth century, and the historical reading and creation of 'atmosphere' are compelling. Against a background of imperial warring and political duplicity, flowers a simple love-interest asserting the rights of the heart against convention. In 1960 the play was published, exquisitely produced and illustrated, in a limited edition of one hundred copies, by the Vine Press (Hemingford Grey, Huntingdon). I was honoured to receive a copy of it.

The Parliament of Women bears an interesting title. In the dramatic heritage of the West, women, from Ancient Greece to Shaw and O'Casey, regularly present a challenge to male warring and politics; and in this play, where women are left for a while in political control, Read had a theme which touched some of his most cherished tenets. The requisite sexual balance is established and the points firmly made; sentences are finely chiselled and thought is keen; and there are opportunities for sensitive production in grouping and stately movement to delight the eye. But there is less excitement than one expects; the whole is statically conceived with little Dionysian thrust from the female party, and no strong dramatic conflict emerges.

Nor was that aimed at. Read contributes a preface on poetic drama, which includes a tribute to Byron's *The Two Foscari*. In his dramas Byron aimed at classic form and a lowering of dramatic tempo: 'What I seek to show in *The Foscaris* is the *suppressed* passion, rather than the rant of the present day' (to John Murray, 20 September 1821). Read was following Byron. The play has

[1] My letter on the play is lodged in the McPherson Library of the University of Victoria. See *The Malahat Review*, as above, 221; the issue now published by Methuen & Co. (*Herbert Read: a Memorial Symposium,* ed. Robin Skelton, 1969).

exquisite verse interludes, one a messenger-speech and others of
choric tone; in these the drama quietly takes wing into a more
rarefied, clarified, often philosophic mode; but passions are not
unleashed.

In rejecting what he regarded as the Shakespearian extravagance
Byron was only in part successful; there was so much dramatic
power in him that his theories did little or no dramatic harm; but
with Read one feels that control came perhaps too easily. Drama
was less instinctive to him than to Byron. Much of his life was
given to the Apollonian arts of sculpture, painting, and ceramics;
though here too, as in literature, he was responsive to the darker
energies and a strong supporter of modern innovations. All
this he could see and know and, as a critic, experience; but
it was not quite natural to his own, more gentle, Apollonian
personality.

His was, the more one thinks of it, a baffling personality. A
distinguished soldier, and decorated for his service, he became a
pacifist; an anarchist by political tendency, he accepted, and did
well to accept, in all humility, a knighthood.

To understand either a work of art or a personality one must
search for the point where its contained opposites are blended;
perhaps, if we are fortunate, found, if only for an instant, identical.
The opposites in Read are (i) his natural respect to instinct, and
(ii) his serene, perhaps 'classic', manner. Similar oppositions are
in Byron and Nietzsche too, but for them instincts were more
unrestful, the struggle for serenity harder, and their life-works in
consequence the more richly varied. Even so, in Byron the originating core or impulse was, as I showed, following Thomas Moore,
in my *Byron and Shakespeare* (194-5), a softness, a thwarted love;
and probably it was so for Nietzsche too. Both these in their later
works, in *Sardanapalus*, *Cain*, and *Thus Spake Zarathustra*, registered a victory in full attunement to the softer powers; for we must
remember that in Byron's *Cain* our first and archetypal murder
is shown as motivated by horror of cruelty to animals. The ethical
problem is not simple: original sin may be easier for us to place
and handle than original virtue.

Now Read, a man, if ever there was one, of original virtue, was
by temperament peculiarly able to focus and express this very
problem. Here, in *The Parliament of Women*, the opposites come
together, are identified:

Herbert Read and Byron

Geoffrey: There are some things, that concern a man's heart, that he
    does not share with even his nearest friends.

William: There I do not follow you. Guilt is the only feeling we do
    not willingly share.

Geoffrey: No; there are innocent feelings that are shy of the light.

(III. ii)

That goes very deep into our human state. Our most terrible evils
arouse a warm and congenial response; we are at home with them,
and never more so than when we indulge in field-days of moral
criticism. But what if such evils are all, in the manner of Cain's
murder, reactions from some unconfessed and feared good,
which, if recognized, would strike greater terror than evil? As
Nietzsche has it:

So alien to your soul is the great that the Superman would seem to
you *terrible* in his goodness.

(Thus Spake Zarathustra, II. 21)

Some new assessment of the good-and-evil within us may be
needed. Advance might be arduous, bringing not only dread but
also, and perhaps worse, embarrassment; for we might have to
admit many an 'innocent' feeling that avoids 'the light'.

Appendix and Indexes

T. S. Eliot and *Pericles*

(see p. 384n. above)

WHEN IN A LETTER from Cheltenham of 26 June 1929 I was writing to my brother of some telephone conversations with T. S. Eliot, I reported on his favourable reaction to my monograph *Myth and Miracle* (subsequently included in *The Crown of Life*), which I had recently sent to him. He probably responded chiefly to my especial high-lighting of *Pericles*. His considered views were set out in an important, but unpublished, lecture in two parts, 'Shakespeare as Poet and Dramatist', which was delivered at Edinburgh University in 1937, and at Bristol University in 1941, and was subsequently adapted for delivery in Germany in 1949. By the generosity of Mrs. Valerie Eliot, who has given me these details, I am allowed to quote freely from this address.

Developing and clarifying the thoughts of his 1930 Introduction to *The Wheel of Fire*, Eliot discusses, in relation to what he courteously designates my own 'important contribution', the 'musical' and 'ultra-dramatic' patterns which interpenetrate Shakespearian drama. After *Hamlet*, here brilliantly treated as a pivot to the general movement, these qualities are seen to grow steadily more insistent, giving us the abnormal protagonists of the great tragedies and culminating in the visionary humanism of the final period:

> The personages of *Cymbeline, The Winter's Tale, The Tempest* and *Pericles* are the work of a writer who has finally seen *through* the dramatic action of men into a spiritual action which transcends it . . .
> Mr. Wilson Knight has done a useful service in pointing out the importance of recurring symbolism in all the plays from Shakespeare's maturity, and especially in the late plays. This analysis helps the mind to understand what is being done and why, but we must

remember that the *appreciation* of these plays is not a matter of conscious enjoyment of each passage as it comes, but of a cumulative effect like a great piece of music. The term 'musical pattern' which I first used, may now be seen to be inadequate; because in a play of Shakespeare this is a pattern in which all the senses are used to convey something beyond sense—not only the sense of ear and eye, because, in reading *Pericles*, I have a sense of a pervading smell of seaweed throughout. Similarly, we do not arrive at an understanding of the play through the characters, but of the characters through the play. To compare Perdita or Miranda or Imogen or Marina with, for instance, Juliet, to call them by comparison insipid or unreal, is to use a wholly irrelevant standard. They belong in a world from which some emotions have been purified away, so that others, ordinarily invisible, may be made apparent. To my mind the finest of all the 'recognition scenes' is Act V, sc. i of that very great play *Pericles*. It is a perfect example of the 'ultra-dramatic', a dramatic action of beings who are more than human. Shakespeare's consummate dramatic skill is as bright as ever; his verse is as much *speech* as ever: only, it is the speech of creatures who are more than human, or rather, seen in a light more than that of day.

Pericles calls for 'fresh garments' and 'robes':

The scene becomes a ritual; the poetic drama developed to its highest point turns back towards liturgy: and the scene could end in no other way than by the vision of Diana.

Here Eliot's two primary devotions, religion and literature, coalesce. The lecture is accordingly the most comprehensive prose discussion he has left us; just as *Marina* is his most compelling poetic statement.

He did not publish it, though a version has been printed in German under the title 'Shakespeares Verskunst' (*Der Monat*, II. 20; May 1950). He was perhaps in prose not quite at home with, or perhaps even always sure about, the experience that lay behind the creation of *Marina* made, as the poem records, 'between one June and another September' (September 1930 was the date of publication). A certain diffidence is reflected in the line

Made this unknowing, half conscious, unknown, my own.

But, though the 'rigging' may be 'weak' and the 'canvas' 'rotten', what was seen will yet live 'in a world of time beyond me', speaking from a period of spiritual imperceptivity as a seed for the 'awakened' humanity to be, the 'new ships'.

INDEXES
by
Iain Stewart

Index A
Names and Titles

Indexes

Indexes

Indexes

Indexes

Indexes

Index B
Selected Themes and Impressions